MUNBY
MAN OF TWO WORLDS

MUNBY
MAN OF TWO WORLDS

❋

The Life and Diaries of
Arthur J. Munby
1828-1910

DEREK HUDSON

GAMBIT

And did he marry her? Oh yes!
   And did it answer? Well—
Those only, who have heart to bless
   A working wench, can tell.

For she is still a working wench,
   And sits with hands still bare,
O' Sundays, on the poor folk's bench:
   But he is with her there.

A. J. Munby: 'L'Envoy' from 'De Haut
en Bas', *Vulgar Verses*, 1891

. . . 'Ah', my darling added, as she sat talking thus, in the easy
chair, still in her working dress, but her face and her bare arms
now rosy and clean, 'Ah, ours is a story that, a hundred years
hence, no one would believe!' Not so: perchance they shall
both know and believe it; and, if they honour her as she
deserves, it is enough for me.

A. J. Munby: Diary, 7 May, 1874

CONTENTS

ILLUSTRATIONS

Illustrations

* *These illustrations and all of the line drawings, which are by A. J. Munby, and appear in the text, are from the Munby Papers and are reproduced by kind permission of The Master and Fellows of Trinity College, Cambridge.*

† *In the possession of Dr. A. N. L. Munby and reproduced by his kind permission.*

INTRODUCTION

I first became aware of A. J. Munby in the autumn of 1968. I was looking through *The Oxford Companion to English Literature* and came to the heading: MUNBY, ARTHUR JOSEPH (1828–1910). After mentioning various books of his verse, the brief entry concluded: 'Munby was secretly and happily married to his servant, who refused to quit her station. The fact explains some of the allusions in his poems.'

I found this information so intriguing that, on my next visit to a reference library, I made a point of reading the notice on Munby in *The Dictionary of National Biography*. The article by Austin Dobson increased my interest; for it stressed that the dominant note of Munby's poetry was 'the glorification of the working woman', and added that Munby had bequeathed to the British Museum deed-boxes 'containing photographs, MSS., diaries, &c., on condition that they were not to be opened or examined before 1 Jan. 1950'. It also mentioned his friendship with R. D. Blackmore.

Having ascertained that nothing had yet been published about Munby, I wrote to the British Museum to ask whether they had, in fact, obtained the boxes and whether they had been opened. The reply proved disappointing; the Museum had never had the boxes, and the *D.N.B.* was apparently mistaken. Here my quest for Munby might have ended, if I had not remembered that I possessed a copy of a biography of Blackmore by Waldo Hilary Dunn, which I had reviewed on its publication in 1956. Re-reading it, I found a number of references to Munby in the text, and in the preface a note of the author's gratitude to Dr. A. N. L. Munby, Librarian of King's College, Cambridge.

One further effort now seemed worth while, and I addressed a letter of enquiry to Dr. Munby. He replied by return of post. He explained that the deed-boxes were at Trinity College, Cambridge, and that they had been opened but nothing had been done about their contents. Dr. Munby added that 'a very fascinating & strange book could be written about my great-uncle Arthur. I much hope you will undertake it & I will give you any help I can.'

As soon as possible I travelled up to Trinity College, Cambridge, where I was cordially received by Dr. Philip Gaskell, the Librarian, and allowed to explore the three deed-boxes. The material was not only more voluminous but more important than I had anticipated. There was a complete run of A. J. Munby's annual diaries from 1859 to 1898; and for the first fifteen of these years they were particularly full and detailed. Dipping into them at random, I found intimate references to people like Ruskin, Rossetti and Swinburne, which I had not expected at all. Many volumes had been indexed by the diarist, whose handwriting was easy to read. Moreover, it soon became clear that the story of A. J. Munby's secret marriage, as revealed in his diaries—and also in the letters and reminiscences of his wife Hannah (an unforeseen bonus)—constituted a record as compelling as it was unique.

The overriding preoccupation in the diaries, nevertheless, remained Munby's concern for working women in general, and especially for manual workers of the roughest kind, such as collierywomen, fisherwomen, farm-workers, milkwomen and acrobats: his interviews with these women, in the manner of Henry Mayhew, occupied many pages. So, too, did Munby's vivid descriptions of public events in the mid-Victorian years, a period in which diarists of his quality were rare. The deed-boxes also contained dozens of photographs of women, many of them commissioned and sometimes posed by himself; and a series of Munby's sketchbooks revealing him as an amateur artist of talent.

I made my way back to London, somewhat overwhelmed, but determined to try to do justice to this remarkable Victorian. A major difficulty disappeared when the Master and Fellows of Trinity College, Cambridge, obligingly agreed to the temporary transfer of the papers to the London Library; and I thereupon began the task of reading, extracting and transcribing which has occupied me for the past two years. As the words of the Munby papers are numbered in millions rather than thousands, I found that I had to be highly selective.

Agreeing with Dr. Gaskell that it would be valuable to preserve the period authenticity of the original diaries, notes and letters, I have endeavoured to present the extracts exactly as they were written, and in general to follow the spelling and paragraphing, as well as Munby's practice of running together certain words that, a century later, would either take the hyphen or be separated. It is hoped this will present no difficulty to the reader, who should also be warned of Munby's occasional trick of diving into the third person: a device which may have originated in an instinctive desire for self-protection.

I could not work so closely on the diary text without learning to appreciate Munby's innate goodness, his scholarship, his love of beauty, his humour, his gifts as a writer. At the same time, I became increasingly aware of the extraordinary strength of the obsession which was the driving force of his life. Munby's compassionate feeling for working women was comparable to his contemporary Lewis Carroll's intense concern for little girls; Munby's inner compulsion culminated in his secret marriage no less surely than Carroll's crystallised in the *Alice* books.

I have considered the psychological implications of Munby's case later in these pages. At best, they can provide only a partial explanation of the behaviour of an extremely talented eccentric. It is equally necessary to understand how the choking conventions of upper-class Victorian society could twist a discriminating, idealistic mind into strange fantastic shapes verging on the macabre.

Fantasy is necessarily present, though often unrecognised, in any age. Lewis Carroll and Edward Lear provided unexpected magic for the early and mid-Victorians; so too, a shade more conventionally, did Dickens. Yet these public fantasies were exceptions (not universally appreciated by contemporaries) to the mid-Victorian assumptions of scientific progress, industrial prosperity and class distinction. The fantastic aspects of the Crystal Palace were not generally revealed to the men of the Fifties and Sixties. But the more we consider these mid-Victorians— and the scrutiny still brings surprises—the more we realise how many, including some of the most sensitively intelligent, were forced by the pressures of a materialist age to live out a world of fantasy in their daily lives.

Among them A. J. Munby, minor poet, respectable civil servant, barrister, teacher, and amateur artist, takes his place. Even his name sounds like an invention by Max Beerbohm; and because the poet and man have been forgotten, Munby—'an Englishman of the period', as he saw himself —has to be re-created before he can be appreciated. To satisfy the reader's curiosity, I have added a selection of his poems in an appendix; others appear in the text.

Munby was able completely to accept the eccentric genius of his friend Rossetti because it was revealed in poetry and painting that accorded, more or less, with his own mediaeval taste and philosophy of life. Rossetti's protégé Swinburne proved a more awkward proposition for him; and when Ruskin, another friend, overturned established ideas of political economy, Munby was shocked by his impetuosity—and by the 'airy' way in which he delivered his conscience. Yet Munby too was aware as a practising Christian that things were wrong—badly wrong—between the classes and the sexes in Victorian society. He himself did what he could to break down barriers—his one-man mission, like Gladstone's, being more of a crusade than an indulgence.

It was essentially as a gentleman, 'a verray parfit gentil knight', that Munby operated. He was as self-conscious a gentleman as the White Rabbit with his kid-gloves ('O my fur and whiskers!'); but being also a compassionate poet, Munby had his own steadfast vision of brotherhood and sisterhood. Lacking a powerful creative talent, born before Freud and Jung, he was compelled to work out his romantic philosophical ideas in painful privacy.

It is a strange double life, then, that is revealed in Munby's copious diary. The successful writers, artists and professional men who enjoyed the intelligent company of this conscientious civil servant and man-about-town may, in some cases, have been aware of his idiosyncrasies, but would have been amazed to learn the extent of his hidden life among 'inferior' women. For Munby, who taught Latin to the working class, his secret marriage with a maid-of-all-work was only the logical climax of an abiding dream.

Like many outstanding diarists, but more than most, Munby is a bundle of contradictions—he is a Kilvert in emotional naïvety; a Mayhew among the poor; a Clough in his better poetry, and a Tupper in his worst; sometimes a Pooter in endearing absurdity. By turns compassionate and snobbish, tragic and comic, patriot and reformer, Munby—White Knight or White Rabbit, antiquarian or gossip—worries his way observantly through the heart of the Victorian age. Living in the long hey-day of the English middle-class, Munby displays the leading men of the time, especially the Pre-Raphaelites, in a fresh descriptive light. No other Victorian diarist can show such a range of experience.

With it all, Munby in his obstinate idealism had something individual to offer. His love for Hannah redeemed him while it condemned him. It is this special contribution that makes his picture of the age unforgettable. In Hannah, the most thoroughly documented housemaid in Victorian history, he found a companion as irrepressible as himself, with a refreshing personality and philosophy of her own. This is her book as much as his; but it was Munby who was determined to make it so.

*   *   *

I could not possibly have prepared this book without the co-operation of Dr. A. N. L. Munby, whose name stands first on my list of benefactors. Not only has he contributed many details from his own research into the life of his great-uncle, and also photographs and MSS., but he has given me an unfailing sustained encouragement which I have appreciated greatly. Next, my thanks are due to Dr. Philip Gaskell, Librarian of Trinity College, Cambridge, whose good wishes and practical help have been no less spontaneous and heartening; and I am especially indebted to the Master and Fellows of Trinity for permission to use the Munby material at my discretion. I must also sincerely thank the Librarian and Deputy Librarian (Mr. Douglas Matthews) of the London Library for much courtesy and assistance.

For his advice on Munby's psychological situation, I am deeply indebted to Dr. Robin McInnes; and for some personal exploration in Shropshire, I am grateful to my friend, Mr. Richard Brain. Others whose help on various points I acknowledge with gratitude are Mr. P. G. Croft, of St. Peter's School, York; Mr. O. S. Tomlinson, City Librarian, York; Mr. W. W. S. Breem, Librarian, Inner Temple; Miss M. Surry, Librarian, Fawcett Society; Sheila Lady Birkenhead; Mrs. Thea Holme; Mr. D. T. Richnell, Goldsmiths' Librarian, University of London Library; Mr. R. J. Dobell; Mrs. N. K. M. Gurney, Archivist, Borthwick Institute of Historical Research, University of York; Mr. Harry Carter; Mr. Graham Reynolds; Mr. Graham Norton; Mrs. Helen Ware; Mr. Philip Unwin; Mrs. P. H. Shaw; the Rev. J. Roberts, Vicar of St. James's, Clerkenwell; the Records Officer, Church Commissioners; Mr. G. C. Nutley, Clerk of Shifnal Rural District Council; the Secretary of the Parish of Wisley with Pyrford; and the obliging staff of the Inner Temple Treasurer's office.

Those who have exerted themselves to send me letters written by or to Munby, and Munby MSS., include: Mr. D. E. Muspratt, Archivist of the Working Men's College, who also helped me in other ways; Mr. Christopher Dobson; Mr. Kenneth Dobson; Dr. James M. Osborn, of Yale, and the Associate Curator of the Osborn Collection, Dr. S. R. Parks; Mr. Donald Gallup, Curator, Collection of American Literature, and Mr. Robert Balay, Head, Reference Department, Yale University Library; the Librarian, University of Chicago Library; and Mr. N. F. Nash, University of Illinois Library, Urbana. I am grateful for permission to publish some of these letters in whole or in part. I also thank Mr. Philip Kelley, President of the New York Browning Society, for informing me about Browning's letters to Munby, and Messrs. Maggs for enabling me to check texts published in one of their catalogues. My thanks are due to the *Spectator* for identifying two anonymous reviewers of Munby's poems.

I am obliged to Major P. I. C. Payne, Curator, Royal Shakespeare

Introduction

Theatre, Stratford-upon-Avon, and to the National Portrait Gallery, for permission to reproduce a portrait of Helen Faucit and a self-portrait of Mary Severn, respectively. I am more than ordinarily thankful to my neighbour Margery Long-Fox for typing my manuscript so accurately. I have been fortunate to have had the enthusiastic support of my old friend Jock Murray in the whole project, and his advice has been invaluable. I hope I may be excused for having omitted the names of others who have helped me; I should like to apologise in advance, and to thank them all in-discriminately.

D.H.

Hindhead, May, 1971

1

A YOUNG MUNBY

1828–58

The name of Munby, with the variants Munbee and Mumby, has long been known in Yorkshire. In 1109 Alan de Munbi witnessed a charter of the Abbey of St. Mary, York; still earlier references have been conjectured. A. J. Munby discovered from the registers of Sutton St. James in Holderness that the family of Munby had lived in that parish since the reign of James I. His grandfather Joseph Munby was articled to the town clerk of Kingston upon Hull, and admitted a solicitor in 1794.

After moving to York, he became Under-Sheriff of Yorkshire. He was something of a versifier, for his grandson described 'a clever and interesting MS. poem of our Grandfather's . . . full of proofs of his good taste and culture' (Diary, 27 August, 1879). This Joseph Munby married Jane Pearson and died in 1816, leaving five children, of whom the eldest, again Joseph and again a solicitor, became the father of the poet and diarist.

The last-named Joseph Munby, born in 1804, was married in 1827 to Caroline Eleanor Forth, daughter and heiress of the Rev. John Forth, sometime Rector of West Heslerton and Fellow of Jesus College, Cambridge. Through her mother, Elizabeth Woodhouse, the bride—a charming but delicate woman—was a great-niece of James Woodhouse, three times Lord Mayor of York. It was a love match, yet one incidentally qualified to advance Joseph Munby's claims in York society. He succeeded, however, on his own merits, as an admirable hardworking Christian gentleman.

The couple began their marriage at a house in The Terrace, a group of three houses in Clifton, a village on the north-west outskirts of York. There the first child, Arthur Joseph, was born on 19 August, 1828; and he was baptised on 2 September at St. Olave's. Thus he was born a countryman, a fact significant of a lifelong preference. They did not stay at Clifton long, but soon moved into York, to an interesting old house next to St. Martin's Church, Coney Street, where the second and third sons, John Forth and George Frederick Woodhouse, were baptised in 1831 and 1833. In 1838 the family went to 3 Blake Street, the former home of Mrs. Forth; the house had been built by her uncle James Woodhouse, the Lord Mayor, and was in close proximity to the office of the family firm at No. 4, which still survives as Munby and Scott.

Joseph Munby lived an exceptionally busy life. His professional standing was recognised by his appointment as clerk to the York magistrates in 1836, but he was equally active as amateur musician and philanthropist. For fifteen years he played the organ at St. Martin's, Coney Street; he was chairman of the York Choral Society and a talented violinist. He held the offices of secretary of York County Hospital for 36 years, and of the York-shire School for the Blind for 43 years. As a father he set an exacting standard for his sons, especially the eldest of the seven children.[1]

Arthur was placed in the charge of Hannah Carter, whose tombstone in York cemetery records that she was 'for 28 years a faithful and Respected Nurse in the family of Joseph Munby Esqre'. She died in 1879, having spent her last years in Dame Middleton's Hospital, York. That she inspired Munby's lasting interest in working women is clearly a pos-sibility, but it cannot be proved, though he faithfully visited her in retire-ment. At the least, she may have predisposed him to favour the name Hannah.

Little survives of Munby's infancy, except a charming silhouette of him holding a whip (Plate 2). The first official news is that he entered St. Peter's School, York, at the Christmas term, 1842, aged 14. The school in the Minster Yard was then in an enfeebled state, having dwindled in numbers to about forty, under a headmaster more interested in theology than discipline. In January, 1843, the assistant masters, replying to a com-mittee of enquiry appointed by the Dean and Chapter, testified 'that the Grammar School of St. Peter has declined to such a state of inefficiency as no longer to possess a character of utility answerable to its endowment, or justifying the actual expenditure of its funds.' The upshot was an amalgamation with the recently founded Proprietary School at Clifton, where, on a healthy site, the new school prospered: after twenty years it had 150 pupils. Munby moved with the rest to Clifton at Midsummer, 1844, but he did not stay long at the school (nor apparently make any mark there), leaving at Easter, 1846, to join a private tutor in preparation for Cambridge.[2]

Munby's boyhood had been comfortable; there is no reason to doubt it

---

[1] The information in this and the preceding paragraphs is derived from the memorial booklets of Joseph Munby and F. J. Munby; from A. J. Munby's *A Few Records of the Name and Family of Munby* (1881); and from a letter from A. J. Munby to W. Robertson Nicoll in Dr. A. N. L. Munby's collection.

[2] *History of St. Peter's School: York*, by Angelo Raine (1926), Chapter XI; and information from the Librarian of St. Peter's School.

was happy. He grew up to become a patriotic Yorkshireman and an expert on the local dialect. Some Praed-like lines in his poem 'Auld Lang Syne' (included in *Verses New and Old*, 1865) suggest the grandeur, almost feudal, of the family's annual expedition to Scarborough:

> Do you remember, Rosa dear,
> The days when we came jaunting here—
> Long, long, before these rails were down,—
> In that old carriage of our own;
> That chariot, built with antique art
> In the great times of Buonaparte,
> And rocking on its lofty springs
> As lightly as the thrones of Kings?
>   O'er its gay panels, as we rode,
> Mamma's heraldic lozenge glow'd;
> The round imperial on the roof
> Kept her stiff dresses waterproof;
> And Jane so fair and Ben so kind,
> High perch'd above the wheels behind,
> Guarded the sword-case, amply stored
> With vast umbrella, and with cane
> The sordid offspring of the sword.
>
> . . . .
>
>   'Twas thus of old we used to roam,
> In annual splendour, from our home;
> Nor unannounced; for on before
> The chaise had whirl'd our little store
> Of country cream, and country maids
> Who gossipp'd with the rural blades,
> While Taffy,[3] trotting loose beside,
> With no one but himself to guide,
> Had room enough to prance and toss—
> A puny pert σειραφόρος.[4]

Munby was coached for Cambridge (as he noted many years later in his diary for 1883) by the Rev. A. W. Brown, Vicar of Pytchley. In marked contrast to his schooldays—on which he had nothing to say—he always spoke with the greatest enthusiasm of his time at Trinity College, Cambridge, where he matriculated at Michaelmas, 1847. As his name does not appear in the Tripos lists, the implication is that he was a 'poll man' and took an ordinary degree, requiring simple classics, mathematics and theology. Although there is no record of his performance, it is clear he was not academically gifted in the conventional sense, but was a slow starter,

---

[3] Taffy was Munby's pony, who lived to the age of 40.   [4] 'Trace-horse.'

showing the promise of an original mind. He occupied L5 New Court for three years from 1848.

At Trinity he was appreciated and formed a wide circle of friends, to whom he remained faithful for the rest of his life. Coming from a Christian home, and being himself a sincere though not unquestioning believer, Munby naturally found his companions among the religious and devout. Many of his Trinity contemporaries became Church of England clergymen, including R. S. Borland (his best friend), Cuyler Anderson, Alfred Kennion and F. J. Moore. His tutor Michael Angelo Atkinson, like most of the Fellows at that time, was a clergyman. Munby himself might possibly have taken holy orders, as an uncle and two of his younger brothers did, had it not been for his father's wish to make him a barrister, an ambition common to solicitor fathers, and often attended by unfortunate results—as it was in the case of Munby, who detested the law.

Among other Trinity friends, often to be mentioned in Munby's diary, were H. A. James, who became a lecturer and coach; William Ralston, the Russian scholar; Vernon Lushington, eventually a county court judge; and R. B. Litchfield, who was to work with Munby at the office of the Ecclesiastical Commissioners. Such names imply a firm moral nucleus, reinforcing his father's philanthropical ideals, which must have helped to direct Munby to a life of social purpose. Litchfield, in particular, became an important influence inspiring him to teach at the Working Men's College. Both Litchfield and Lushington had been drawn by the Cambridge booksellers, Daniel and Alexander Macmillan, into the movement of Christian Socialism, led by F. D. Maurice. Munby, too, was influenced by the movement, though not politically; individually, he had acquired, by the time he left Cambridge, a compassionate concern for working women which was to remain a lasting personal obsession.

How he acquired it is perhaps primarily a psychological problem. He was hardly the flirtatious Cambridge undergraduate of Calverley's poem:

> Poising evermore the eye-glass
> In the light sarcastic eye,
> Lest, by chance, some breezy nursemaid
> Pass, without a tribute, by.

Most of the poems in his first volume of verse, *Benoni*, published in 1852, were written while he was an undergraduate (the Prologue is dated 1850), and there is an earnest moralising strain about the whole book, including the romantic poems. 'Alma Mater' features Munby 'pillow'd in the mateless student's nest', while the poem that follows envisages 'The

Poet's Bride'; but 'Pachys: or, The Man of Substance' sings the praises of farm-girls and fisherwomen, hints that true chivalry must not be conventionally reserved for 'Beauty in distress', and urges a crusade against the exploiters of poor women. One can only speculate whether it was Munby's concern for a delicate mother, or some early experience involving a servant or nurse, that turned his sensitivity into this channel.

Cambridge established Munby's liking for long country walks and nocturnal masculine conversations. He was not a games-player, but read widely in English literature and devoted himself to the study of poetry. He was already becoming a bibliophile: the collection of some six or seven hundred books which he bequeathed to Trinity library contains rare seventeenth and eighteenth century works, and is especially strong in classics and poetry. It includes volumes by Clough, Beddoes, Browning, Tennyson and Wordsworth which were published in his undergraduate years. We know that at this period he was indebted, above all, to Tennyson, but also in a lesser degree to Clough.

The happiness of his undergraduate life is attested by the regular visits he paid to Trinity in later years, and by frequent nostalgic passages in the diary. A photograph of him (Plate 6) taken with his younger brother Joseph, probably at the latter's matriculation at Trinity in 1858, suggests how thoroughly and piously he identified himself with his old college. The Cambridge revelation had been intensified by the Great Exhibition of 1851, which acted as a strong stimulus to Munby's intellectual curiosity and love of the arts.

Meanwhile there had arisen at Clifton in 1850 a solid serviceable residence equally imbued with the early Victorian spirit, called Clifton Holme (Plate 4). It was a house proper to a successful citizen of York, with a fine view from the twenty-acre grounds across the river to York Minster. Joseph Munby laid the foundation stone in 1849, having approved an architect's plan showing three handsome reception rooms on the ground floor; a breakfast room and a waiting room, a servant's hall, a butler's room, and a coach house, stables and saddle room opening on to a large kitchen courtyard. This was to form a splendid and beloved home for the Munby family for the next thirty years.

It may have been as well that Munby's Trinity friends were mostly in the professional class; his contemporary Christopher Sykes was financially and morally ruined by his association with the Prince of Wales, who made a butt of him by his coarse practical jokes, which he bore with long-suffering dignity. Years later, Munby saw him in Hyde Park: 'I observed Christopher Sykes, seated aloft in gorgeous mailphaeton, overpoweringly aristocratic to behold. Him, now M.P. for some place, I remember as a reputed ass at Trinity. Yet he deserves great credit; for he has contrived to make himself look like a man of sense' (2 June, 1870).

Munby was impressed, as we shall see, by the Prince of Wales when he observed him at Trinity in 1861, and being something of a snob, as well as a loyalist, might have been in peril if he had come under his influence. Fortunately, his intelligence was not put to that test.

Information on Munby's years as a Bar student is no less meagre than for his Cambridge years. He graduated B.A. in 1851 (and M.A. in 1856), and was admitted to Lincoln's Inn, 11 June, 1851. More than four years elapsed before he was called to the Bar, 17 November, 1855. The long delay suggests he was not strongly attracted to the law—an understatement, as it proved.

From subsequent references in his diary, it appears that Munby's London lodgings were in University Street, and that for a period he was a pupil in the chambers of Hugh Cairns, the future Lord Chancellor. R. D. Blackmore was a fellow Bar student who became a life-long friend. One of the few reviews of Munby's *Benoni* was written by Blackmore for *Woolman's Exeter and Plymouth Gazette* (3 July, 1852). It was a friendly, quizzical piece, in which Blackmore made it clear that he lamented a tendency to obscurity in the verse—with some justice, for Munby's discovery of the language had rather gone to his head; perhaps he took Blackmore's admonition to heart, obscurity not being one of his later faults.

Although Munby was not one of the eight official founders of the Working Men's College in 1854, he subsequently wrote: 'My recollections . . . begin with the inaugural meeting in Red Lion Square, at which I was present, and with the letters and talk that preceded it. I remember a good many social evenings in one of the upper rooms of the old house.'[5] Having made friends at Cambridge with supporters of Christian Socialism, he naturally found himself involved in discussions concerning the embryo College, but probably did not put himself forward as a possible teacher while he was working for his law exams and trying to establish himself at the Bar.

On 10 November, 1857, he began his tenancy of the first floor of 6 Fig Tree Court, Inner Temple, the annual rent of fifty pounds being paid by his father; he remained the tenant for the rest of his life. (This beautiful little seventeenth-century building was destroyed by a land mine in 1941.)

[5] *Working Men's College Journal*: July, 1905. The public inaugural meeting was held in St. Martin's Hall, 30 October, 1854; but by then preliminary meetings had already been held at 31 Red Lion Square for some months. (Harrison: *History of the Working Men's College*.)

By 1857, however, it must have become clear to Munby that his success at the Bar was, at least, doubtful. His family connections put him in the way of a certain amount of conveyancing and other business, but he had time and energy to do more. We find his name figuring for the first time as a voluntary unpaid teacher at the Working Men's College (then at 45 Great Ormond Street) in the programme of studies for the term beginning 31 May, 1858. He was to be responsible for a two-hour class in Latin ('easy translation, &c.') on Thursdays. In the same list, Litchfield is down for Arithmetic and Vernon Lushington for English Composition. Rossetti and Ruskin were both members of the council.

Munby was now also beginning to send articles and poems to the magazines. His earliest anonymous article appeared in *Chambers's Journal* in 1857; he subsequently wrote another, in collaboration with his friend William Ralston, for the same magazine. But he was too fastidious and scholarly a writer to earn much as a freelance journalist.

There was a need to acquire an income, not only to appease his father, and to continue the foreign travel he had begun to enjoy, but because he was already in the throes of the extraordinary clandestine love affair which was to occupy him for the rest of his life. The love poems in *Benoni* suggest that Munby had undergone one or two romantic trials before 1852, probably of a most elementary kind, and it was predictable that the poet would fall seriously in love before long. His poem 'The Bride to Come' virtually announced his intention of doing so:

> I know thee not; yet ever in my soul
>   Some strange prophetic dearness eddies round
> A vacant centre, whirling to their goal
>   Whatever of love or hope in me is found:
>
> And some day, haply, in the march of life,
>   That dark, unquicken'd void instinct shall be
> With sudden Being, and the ideal wife
>   Warm into shape, and mould itself to thee.

It would have given Munby an easier, though perhaps less remarkable life, if 'the ideal wife' had 'warmed into shape' within his own social class. But as a young man in London he soon found himself looking with much more interest at the working girls than at the 'young ladies'. And thus preoccupied, he walked to his fate near Grosvenor Street, in May, 1854, at the age of 25.

The girl was Hannah Cullwick, a servant born at Shifnal, Shropshire,

13

on 26 May, 1833; in fact, by her own account, she met Munby on the day after her twenty-first birthday. According to her certificate of baptism, her father was a saddler. Her mother was a housemaid, and Hannah told Munby 'even when she rose to be a lady's maid, she only had 12 pounds a year wages' (recorded in his diary, 9 April, 1874). Another time she declared: 'Ah, I remember my mother saying how thankful she would be if she could be sure of eight shillings a week—and she never could be sure even of *three* shillings. And that with five children to keep!' (13 March, 1874). Later, Munby investigated some of Hannah's relatives in the hope of explaining how she came by the personal distinction which she undoubtedly had; but for the moment all that need be said is that Hannah at twenty-one was an unusually intelligent, affectionate, and highly strung working girl (Plate 7).

In one of her manuscript autobiographies headed 'Hannah's places', Hannah described her first twenty-one years. She was taught at the charity school at Shifnal until she was eight, then left to do occasional housework for Mrs. Phillips, a friend of her mother. Mrs. Phillips 'give me one of her old straw bonnets trim'd with a plaid ribbon—& a new print lilacfrock from Birmingham what i thought was the loveliest could be'. Her next job was at the Red Lion, where she 'clean'd the tables & floors & even waited on the Farmers dinner of a Market day, & they gave me always 2ᵈ or a penny each on the plate as i carried round o'purpose, after the cheese, making a curtsy to them as give the most. . . .' Soon both her parents died, within a month of each other; and after two or three intermediate jobs, Hannah at seventeen went as a housemaid to Lady Boughey of Aqualate Hall, Newport. She enjoyed 'running along the splendid halls & gallery & rooms at Aqualate' and 'Jim the postilion was such a good looking little fellow & used to take me for a walk in the park'. Unfortunately she and a friend were caught 'playing as we was cleaning our kettles', and were immediately dismissed. It was a come-down to have to take a post as scullion with Lady Louisa Cotes, daughter of the Earl of Liverpool, at her two country houses, Woodcote and Pitchford Hall, the latter a fine timber-framed manor-house. But it was some compensation for Hannah to be brought to London with the family for the season. On one of these visits, in 1854, she met Munby. Hannah endowed the encounter with some mystical significance, believing she had seen his face beforehand in the fire. This street meeting was a scene for one of the Pre-Raphaelites:

. . . At home the kitchenmaid & me had our meals alone in the kitchen & at tea one day i saw a man's face as clearly as could be in the fire, & i show'd it to

Emma—she said '*Ah* one of us will see somebody like that some day'—it was such a nice manly face with a moustache—i little thought *i* sh^d see such a face, much less to love such a face, but in 54 i *did* see it—it was the day after i'd turn'd 21 & i was took to London again. My brother had been to see me & i walk'd with him part of his way home—i'd my lilac frock—a blue spotted shawl & my black bonnet on, & an apron. When i had kiss'd Dick & turn'd again & was crossing for the back street on the way to Grosvenor St. a gentleman spoke to me, & i answer'd him—that was Massa's face that i'd seen in the fire but i didn't know it again till a good while after. . . .

When she wrote this account, many years later, Hannah was calling Munby 'Massa', the abbreviation of Master in negroes' English. That was to be her way of acknowledging she was his servant for life—and it seems it had always been her ambition to love someone above her own class.

Fifty years later, at 'the Jubilee of our love', Munby also described their first meeting. Not surprisingly, he then saw it as having happened on Hannah's 21st birthday, not the day after:

For, on *the 26th of May, 1854*, she was brought to me, a surprise of all surprises, by Him who brought Eve to Adam. A country girl, she was, a scullion at the Squire's: and to her and her mother, that was a great distinction; for she had worked in the fields, and had been pot girl at a village inn.

A tall erect creature, with light firm step and noble bearing: her face had the features and expression of a high born lady, though the complexion was rosy & rustic, & the blue eyes innocent and childlike: her bare arms and hands were large and strong, and ruddy from the shoulder to the finger tips; but they were beautifully formed . . .

A robust hardworking peasant lass, with the marks of labour and servitude upon her everywhere: yet endowed with a grace and beauty, an obvious intelligence, that would have become a lady of the highest.

Such a combination I had dreamt of and sought for; but I have never seen it, save in her. And from that day to this, my love for her, and hers for me, has been in each of us a passion and a power that has stimulated and ennobled Life, even through the very contrast of our lives. But I did not know till after long, that she had seen *Sardanapalus*[6] acted, and had been charmed by the character of Myrrha. 'If I ever have a sweetheart', she thought, 'he shall be some one much above me; and I will be his slave, like Myrrha.'. . .

Hannah soon took another job—at Lord Stradbroke's house, Henham Hall, Suffolk. His Lordship's mother, the Countess, was very kind to her, and gave her a new cotton frock, half a sovereign, and some good advice: 'And be sure Hannah' she said; 'be careful whom you choose for a

---

[6] By Byron.

15

husband.' But Henham was most inconvenient from Munby's point of view: 'Massa came to see me in Suffolk & lost his way on the road back to his hotel at Halesworth & he told me if i stopp'd there he wouldn't come again.'

By the end of 1858, Hannah was working in London; and Munby was educating her, and exhorting her—all too successfully—to bear her life of service with humility. He may well have quoted George Herbert's lines to her:

> A servant with this clause
> Makes drudgery divine;
> Who sweeps a room as for Thy laws
> Makes that and th'action fine.

Munby himself approached 1859 professionally unsuccessful but sporting some large whiskers as well as the moustache which, if Hannah is to be believed, he was wearing in 1854. The new year was to bring two important changes: he grew a beard, and he started the diary which was to become his main claim to fame.

2

THE DIARY OPENS

1859

Little is known about Hannah's life, or Munby's, between 1854 and 1858. Munby began his diary on 1 January, 1859, while staying at Clifton Holme after the Christmas holiday. Several members of his family were successively taken ill; and a public execution which he chanced to witness on 8 January while walking to York can hardly have cheered him, though 'there was little of horror in the sight'. On the 12th Munby himself succumbed to 'atmospheric fever'. 'In bed & upstairs for a week or more, tenderly nursed & kindly tended. One may be thankful for sickness, when it comes with an "entourage" of cosy warmth & comfort, and an atmosphere of dreamy thoughtful quiet. Selfish, perhaps, to feel so.'

In ten days he was again out and about. On the 22nd he learned of 'my poem on Burns being one of the first six, of the 621 competitors at the Crystal Palace, & recommended for publication along with the prize poem'. The fifty-guinea prize, offered by the Crystal Palace Company for a poem on the centenary of Burns's birth, was won by Isa Craig; Gerald Massey and F. W. H. Myers were others in the first six. The news helped to revive Munby's poetic hopes, temporarily at least; he 'went to York to telegraph about it'.

On Friday, 28 January, a long walk in the neighbourhood of Clifton afforded the sight of a local Amazon whom he described with typical admiring reflections:

Back through Upper Poppleton: and behind one of the farms in the village, pumping water in the yard, appeared a creature worth seeing. A farm servant girl really worthy of the name: tall & strong as a man—short thick neck and square massive shoulders—square broad back, straight from shoulder to hip with no waist to weaken it—stout, solid legs, & arms as thick as legs, bare and muscular throughout. . . .

Altogether, a noble creature, refreshing to behold: simple & unconscious—thinking only, if she thought at all, that she was very dirty & not fit to be seen: and yet possessing all the charms of contour and colours that ladies strive for, and a large sinewy grace besides, that were neither proper nor possible for them. A noble creature, bred in healthy useful toil, & growing in strength & endurance from rosy youth to stalwart womanhood: a helpmate fit to labour—a vigorous fruitful mother of English sons. Blessed is the land whose peasant women measure four feet round the waist, and have arms as thick as a bed post! Those who prate of woman's rights, if they knew their own meaning, would honour such mighty daughters of the plough as much at least or more than the 'strong-minded females' who have neither the shrinking graces of their own sex nor the bold beauty of ours. To be a *strongminded* woman indeed, and share the purely intellectual work of men, is a thing to be striven for, since it bringeth place and fame: but to be an *ablebodied* woman, using the strength of her honest arms un-seen and unapplauded—hath any man heard them say that *this* is an honourable thing? And yet, are not the fishwomen of Boulogne better than all the Minervas of Yankeedom?

On the following day, Saturday, 29 January, Munby returned to London to his chambers at Fig Tree Court:

... cab to Temple: found the rooms looking very warm & bright, with lamps & fire, and a warm welcome from Miss Mitchell the housekeeper: felt however for the first five minutes a new sensation—nympholepsy of the period—the longing for a wife. Probably the result of cheerful family life and endearments, and the tenderness which sickness brings about. Dined at the Cock, and (of course) got rid of it. . . .

The next two pages of the diary are excised, an indication that they referred to a meeting with Hannah. These are the first of many excisions in the early volumes. It is clear that Munby took fright at some point, possibly from fear that the diary might be discovered by members of his family. In a note dated 19 June, 1894, later inserted in the fourth volume, Munby declared that 'all the excised passages' referred, 'so far as I can remember, to my darling Hannah'; 'they described the hours we spent together; the training and teaching that I gave her; and the work, often of the lowest and most servile kind, which she—a maid-of-all-work—of her own accord did for me, to show her love in her own way.' Fortunately, after 1861 there are no more excisions; Munby seems to have accepted the risk.

The entry of Tuesday, 1 February, describes missionary visits to two other girls. Mary Anne Bell had lost her nose after an accident, a tragedy in which Munby took a sympathetic if insistent interest:

... she hopes to get a false nose at the hospital. Our conversation was amusingly peculiar: 'Well Mary, your face looks quite nice now'—'Yes Sir it's a deal better, if only I get a nose put on'—'And when you've got a nose, what will you do?'

'Well Sir, when I've got my nose, I think I shall go into service.' 'How? But wont they find out that you've got a false nose?' 'No Sir, I expect not—they wont see the joining. My nose will be fastened on with a hook, and I can take it off when I like!' 'And how long have you been without a nose?' 'Four years Sir: it'll seem quite strange to have one again.' 'Yes, & you dont feel the want of it after all?' 'Oh no Sir, it's only the look!' She is very sensitive about it however, & looks forward with pride and joy to the possession of a nose: I hope her project may succeed . . .

In the diary Munby discloses a somewhat morbid fascination with the female anatomy, especially the skin, the hands and their tactile sensations and any disfigurements or abnormalities; he lingers, for example, over 'two tanned human skins, male & female', which he discovers at an 'Institute of Anatomy' later in the year.

The second visit of 1 February was to a middle-class milliner-girl whom he had tried to help. Munby's comments on her social situation, though determined by the rigid framework of mid-Victorian class distinctions, are sufficiently shrewd to retain some relevance.

. . . I went up to Euston Road to see what had become of Louisa Baker. Found her still at her lodgings, & within: she came down, asked me up, and was honestly glad to see me. She is much improved in circumstances and appearance —has a good front room on the first floor, instead of the wretched back places she had before. She paid me what I lent her in the days of her poverty, and told me of her present state. She has £50 a year from one milliner, & a promise of £100 from another: but talks of going to her uncle in Australia. I had a quiet tea with her, and we sat a long time talking of her life and plans, and her chances of a husband in Australia. She does not like her fellow milliners: like all others, she says their talk is chiefly of their 'gentlemen friends', who give them presents & take them to Casinos. My impression is that the morality of the milliner class is lower than that of any other: they have all the temptations and none of the safe-guards of the classes above & below them. Louisa herself, though a virtuous respectable girl, has not—nor can any such a girl have—that *ignorance* of vice which one desires in a lady. Her life seems the ideal of grisette life: a comfortable room, a neat bed in one corner with washhandstand at the foot: a sofa on the other side of the room, a round table with work, in the middle, a neat dressing-table trimmed with gauze; a bright fire, pictures, and bonnets & dresses on the drawers. All the arrangements her own too: she makes her own fire and boils her kettle in a morning before going to work, & dusts the room into tidiness in the evening when she returns. Nevertheless, as she made the tea or floated about in her blue silk dress (they must all dress handsomely in the shop) one could not help feeling that young women were not, except for religious purposes, intended to be *bachelors*. Her landlady's son had made her an offer of marriage, which she

had declined on pecuniary grounds. She is just twentytwo. We sat long over tea
& talk, & it was eleven before I left. Such interviews are a curious proof of the
independence of female virtue upon mere conventions. Here was a young woman
sitting in her bedroom for a whole evening, alone with a man! Is her modesty
injured thereby? Not at all: for Conscience is no Casuist, until it be tutored by
prurient Propriety. She receives him innocently as a *friend*: for it is in such cases
only, that mere friendship is possible between man & woman. And it is curious
to see the result, when a middle class girl, modest by instinct but not by rule,
goes out to live alone and earn her living. She has no home sympathies, no
family life: she cannot confide in the girls her companions—most of them are
frivolous or worse, and all are mere acquaintances: ladies she only sees as
customers & superiors: with the men of her own class it would be indelicate to
associate as friends; for modesty is an affair of *class* as well as of sex, and with
them, such intercourse would certainly be misconstrued. There remains then,
only men of the class above her—gentlemen. Here lies her danger, and their
responsibility: all the better parts of her nature, as well as some of the worse,
are attracted towards their higher education and manners, and if they are unworthy of her confidence, the end is what we know. If however they be honourable, in such a case friendship & trust may grow up between him and her of a
kind she could not in her position get elsewhere: sisterlike, & yet with just enough
of sexual consciousness to make it romantic without being unsafe.[1]

Saturday, 5 February . . . After dark in Oxford St, met a child of 8 years old
seeking his way home to Brompton! Had no money—'no, but had a *top*.' Been
in an omnibus once, 'when he was a little boy.' Put him into one & sent him
home . . .

Tuesday, 8 February . . . Dined at the Pearsons[2] in Hyde Park Square. . . . My
beard much reviled.[3] Walked home, & tempted to go into the Cider cellars—a
ribald place, the vice of which cures itself by its want of refinement. One's
spirituality & love of what is Godlike and pure never rises so high as in presence
of these temptations: yet it is a dangerous method of reviving one's good things:
for only to have been there is a thing to repent of before God.

Wednesday, 9 February . . . In the evening at our musical meeting—the Howlers
—at Stewart's rooms in Stone Buildings. After the glees were over, gymnastics
& pantomimic evolutions by Danny Henfrey & other young barristers of the
period. Good fun: anything too, is pleasant, which shows that man cannot be
wholly professional.

[1] Re-reading the diary at a later date, Munby noted: 'She afterwards married a Greek
merchant in London, & became a "lady".'

[2] Cousins of Munby, whose grandfather married Jane Pearson.

[3] The first indication that Munby had grown a beard, perhaps during his illness at Clifton
Holme in January. 'The typical mid-Victorian of all classes was a man with a beard and a pipe'
(G. M. Trevelyan).

Thursday, 10 February . . . Walked round S. Jameses Park. Foreigner talking to respectable looking girl, trying to seduce her to some brothel—exit without success. She a servant, aged 18, just run away from her place by reason of ill-treatment: didn't know London—didn't know what to do. Knew her danger, but verging towards it from sheer idiotic insouciance. Typical example of the way such girls come to grief. Put her by help of peeler to respectable lodging: offered help, but probably useless.

In the evening at the Working Men's College: resumed my Latin class, which Godfrey Lushington[4] had taken for me. Warmly received—seventeen men.

Friday, 11 February . . . went to look for the girl above mentioned (Louisa Flatman by name, from Thetford) at the coffee house where we placed her. Sell, of course: she had never slept there after all: engaged a bed but never came: so much for her. Called at Harrison's the publisher, and received from him one pound two, for the unbound copies of Benoni[5] which were sold as waste paper, to line trunks or be reduced into pulp again. Amusing and instructive incident! It disposes satisfactorily of the amiable delusion that one has 'a work to do' in the world: God having put his veto on *that* kind of work, & I being fit for no other . . .

Munby adds here that 'humour indeed is the salvation of the cynic—the religion of the disappointed man.' He cultivated humour, certainly, as a means to overcome bouts of depression, often induced by the tedium of the law and his failure to make money at it; but his many friends, his Christian concern for others—especially for the working women of the lower classes—and his persistent artistic, musical and antiquarian enthusiasms kept him generally active and curious.

Monday, 14 February . . . In the evening went to a concert of Mendelssohn's chamber music at S. James's hall. Began with the posthumous quintet, which is exquisite, especially the andante. Still, one cannot quite away with the wiriness of even the best violin playing. Music, to be perfect, should have no artificial medium: or at least the medium should not obtrude itself upon one's notice. Yet in fact one cannot help thinking of *it* as well as of the music: and there is no more subtle problem in acoustics than to find what is the value of different media, & their influence upon pure sound. . . .

It is rather sad to see how mere physical comfort, or discomfort, is able to weaken & destroy the purest spiritual, & highest sensuous, delight. At first, the music was all in all to me: then I began to have a sense of being comfortable, &

---

[4] Godfrey Lushington (1832–1907), Fellow of All Souls, Oxford, became Permanent Under-Secretary in the Home Office and was knighted. He and his twin brother Vernon were both actively concerned in the Working Men's College. They were distantly related to Tennyson, whose sister married a Lushington.

[5] The original publisher of Munby's *Benoni*, in 1852, was John Ollivier of 59 Pall Mall.

the music ceased to be absorbing, & became the accompaniment and the ground-tone to a melody of reveries: then again, after long sitting, one began to have a sense of being *un*comfortable, and it seemed an insult to the music to stay longer . . .

Thursday, 17 February.   In all day. In the evening my class at the W.M. College. Afterwards went with Litchfield[6] to Macmillan's in Henrietta St. Had supper, pipes, & a long tête-à-tête with Macmillan,[7] on various subjects, e.g. 'Out of the Depths',[8] the autobiography of a prostitute, by a young parson—a plainspoken healthful book, it seems, which with judicious boldness he is bringing out: the Burns business: and old Maurice,[9] his greatness & his doctrines. However obscure these may be to such as only understand, & do not feel, it is quite pleasant to see what an influence they have on men who, with clear heads, have also sound loving hearts: how as in MacM. they build up in a man a living, loving, practical creed, all the better if perhaps it is wanting in logical symmetry.

Litchfield, fastidious & desponding, kicked & remonstrated in vain: for M., warm & genial, talked one into a glow irrepressible . . .

Friday, 18 February . . . Went with Moore[1] in the afternoon to see over the Bank of England. . . . The clerk, as usual, put into my hand a bundle of notes—a thousand, of £1000 each—remarking that I had now in hand a million of money: certainly an admirable way of reducing to its simplest expression, & bringing palpably home to one's senses, the worthlessness of gain as an object for any human soul to pursue. My first impulse was to put them all in the fire (had there been one) as *my* solution of the theorem. Yet by such worthless things all life, all death, is fashioned & determined. Had I a few of those bits of paper, I might do—so & so: not having them, my life—not merely my sensuous, but my moral, intellectual, spiritual life—is wholly altered: for the better, we'll hope . . .

Saturday, 19 February . . . went in for a short time to Caldwell's[2]: the only representative we have, that I know of, of the German middleclass dancing-rooms. Lots of young men, clerks & apprentices, dancing with young women of the same class—shopgirls & milliners—also respectable, but not very attractive.

[6] Richard Buckley Litchfield (1832–1903), friend of Munby since Trinity days, and a founder and mainstay of the Working Men's College. A barrister, he joined the Ecclesiastical Commissioners' office in 1859. Taught a singing class at the College from 1859.
[7] Alexander Macmillan (1818–96), the publisher, held weekly 'tobacco parliaments' for congenial literary men, in the firm's office.
[8] *Out of the Depths: The Story of a Woman's Life.* Anon., but by Henry Gladwyn Jebb.
[9] Rev. Frederick Denison Maurice (1805–72), the Christian Socialist who was a founder of the Working Men's College in 1854 and became its first principal.
[1] Rev. Francis Joseph Moore (1826–96), a Trinity friend of Munby, curate of St. John's, Fulham.
[2] Caldwell's, or? Caudwell's; a house partly in Dean Street and partly in Frith Street, Soho; well known as the Dean Street Music Room in the eighteenth century.

1. Arthur Joseph Munby, aged about 32

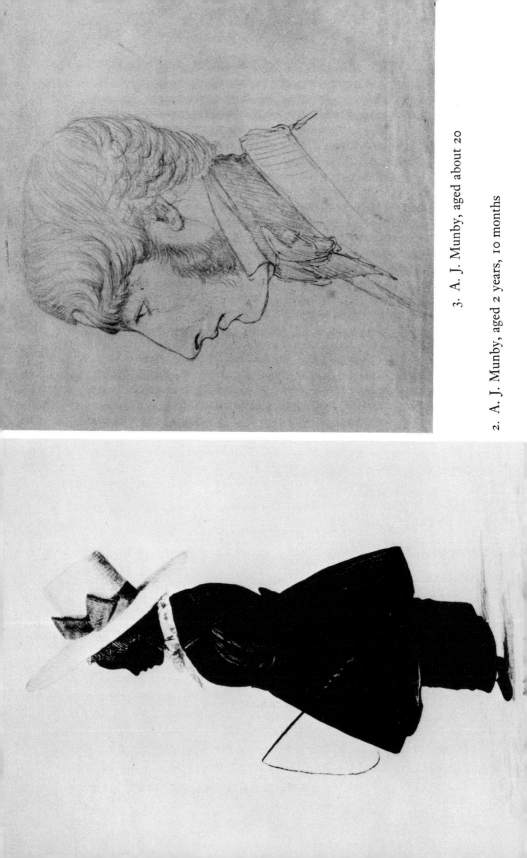

3. A. J. Munby, aged about 20

2. A. J. Munby, aged 2 years, 10 months

Things carried on in an easy & unconstrained but virtuous manner: for fast girls & prostitutes think the place 'slow'.

Monday, 21 February . . . to Dean's Yard to the Cayleys—Found George C.[3] at home, also Henry Coke (Lord Leicester's brother) and young Worsley of Hovingham—We sat long, having Spanish cigarrettes & café noir in cups of crackled china, and talked of many things, as the Burns poems, the merits of Browning & of Kingsley as song writers, the shallowness of Bulwer—by the way G.C. who knows Robert Bulwer (Owen Meredith)[4] says he is a fashionable vapidlooking fellow of 25, with a languid brokenbacked air & manner—affecting indolence & insouciance though really working hard for ambition—who in his place of attaché has had many liaisons with *married* women & come to grief thereby, physically & mentally: altogether a contemptible Byronic sort of account, shockingly at variance with the tenderness & half-devotional purity of his poems: which, let us hope, reflect his better self . . .

Sunday, 27 February.   Bright lovely day, warm as spring. Had Stokes,[5] Ormsby,[6] Litchfield, and Wadham to breakfast. Rossetti[7] could not come, being engaged. After breakfast we sat till near two, over pipes & talk. Talked of philology (of course, Stokes being present) books, and so on to creeds & Theology. This last however I speedily discouraged & put out, finding Litchfield assuming, in his usual offhand way, that Matthew or Luke never dreamt of the Divinity of Christ, and Stokes maintaining the contrary 'but without committing himself' to any belief.

It breeds in me ineffable sadness and despair, to see truths that are to me of solemn & impregnable beauty, the very centres of all spiritual life, thrown aside altogether out of the lives of men whom I love and admire. For, I think, the undergraduate days of doubt and argument are over for us; there is nothing left but to let the heart stand up & answer, 'I have felt'; to keep, as far as one may, the *instinctive* faith of childhood. . . .

Monday, 28 February . . . In the evening, with Litchfield and Furnivall[8] at the Haydn & Weber Concert at S. James's Hall. Most delightful: Haydn's

[3] George John Cayley (1826–78), a contemporary of Munby at Trinity, Cambridge, and winner of the Chancellor's English medal, 1848; barrister of the Inner Temple and author.

[4] Edward Robert Bulwer Lytton (1831–91) poet, and son of the novelist. Viceroy of India, 1876–80. First Earl of Lytton. Ambassador at Paris, 1887–91. As a young man served as private secretary to his uncle, Lord Dalling, at Washington and Florence, and as paid attaché at The Hague and Vienna.

[5] Whitley Stokes (1830–1909), B.A., Trinity College, Dublin. Celtic scholar and Inner Temple barrister.

[6] John Ormsby (1829–95), B.A., Trinity College, Dublin. Author and translator from the Spanish. Entered Middle Temple, 1848.

[7] Dante Gabriel Rossetti (1828–82), painter and poet. Taught art at the Working Men's College from 1855 until 1858, and then occasionally until 1861.

[8] Frederick James Furnivall (1825–1910), scholar, editor, oarsman, social reformer, and a founder of the Working Men's College. A man of violent temper, he became an agnostic, like Litchfield, and increasingly antagonistic to F. D. Maurice.

child-like simplicity and Weber's half feminine refinement showing off each other. Sat in the orchestra on chairs, close to the performers: & the physical conditions of one's position being equable & satisfactory, enjoyed it undisturbed by indolence or by discomfort. . . .

Wednesday, 2 March . . . Went to Ralston's[9] rooms, & walked out with him. At seven, dined with Edward[1] & George Cayley in Dean's Yard. After dinner coffee & pipes & some etymological talk—also E. brought out the pedigree & papers of the Wiltshire peerage case, which he is conducting for the Scroopes. Towards eleven G. took me to the Cosmopolite,[2] in Charles St. Berkeley Square: talking by the way of protestantism & prostitutes, and of the character of Evil . . . The Cosmopolite was formed out of the Sterling, White Cottage, & other clubs, and is now the arcanum & the Parnassus of literary swells. They meet in a large lofty room, or rather hall, formerly a studio & still hung with pictures & cartoons of great size and some of considerable value. Round the fire a large inner circle was formed of ottomans & sofas, bounded towards the door by a huge folding screen of Chinese pattern. Coffee & tea on a table in the outskirts: on another (much more frequented) soda water, spirits, & punch-ingredients: long clays also, & a tall jar . . . of real Turkish. So much for the entourage: the men were few when we arrived, but came in thickly about midnight, from parties or the House. Soon the room was half full of groups: on one sofa Jacob Omnium (Higgins)[3] was lounging, huge, fat & sixfeet four, with smooth grey hair & sleek dimpled face, selfsatisfied but pleasant; talking to Lord Wodehouse,[4] a rather plain man with scanty beard & weed in mouth: near them Robert Lowe[5] the great Albino, shading his pink eyes from the light, & warding in his Times secrets from that puppy Vernon Harcourt.[6] Reeve,[7] the editor of the Edinburgh, a big sandy man

[9] William Ralston Shedden-Ralston (1828–89). Another of Munby's Trinity friends. Assistant in the printed book department, British Museum, 1853–75. A distinguished translator from the Russian.

[1] Edward Stillingfleet Cayley (1824–84). Also of Trinity, and elder brother of George. Inner Temple barrister. Author of books on European history.

[2] The Cosmopolitan Club, founded in 1852, occupied a former studio of G. F. Watts. It had a distinguished life for about fifty years.

[3] Matthew James Higgins (1810–68), successful journalist, frequent contributor to *The Times* and other papers. Known as 'Jacob Omnium' from the title of his first published article.

[4] Lord Wodehouse (1826–1902) was then Under-Secretary of State for Foreign Affairs. Created Earl of Kimberley, 1866. Colonial Secretary, 1870–4. Kimberley was named after him.

[5] At this time Robert Lowe (1811–92), later Lord Sherbrooke, combined a political career with leader-writing on *The Times*. He was subsequently Chancellor of the Exchequer and Home Secretary.

[6] The 'puppy', a contemporary of Munby at Trinity, became Sir William Harcourt (1827–1904), an outstanding Chancellor of the Exchequer. He was to expound his knowledge of international law in a series of articles in *The Times* during the American Civil War.

[7] Henry Reeve (1813–95) had virtually controlled the foreign policy of *The Times* for fifteen years under Delane. He was the first editor of the Greville Memoirs. His *Times* colleagues called him 'Il Pomposo'.

of not unkindly look, stood talking to George Venables,[8] the supposed original of George Warrington but in manner at least more genial than that good old cynic. Layard[9] too was there—a short man (I was surprised, on Homeric principles, to find myself a head taller than the hero of Nineveh) of bulldog make, big head & grizzly beard, & of restless irritable look—apparently not much sought after: Sir Henry Rawlinson[1] too, a stern sourish looking man with scrubby black moustache: Monckton Milnes[2] & Tom Taylor[3] also, to whom I was introduced. Both were very civil: T.T. hoped to see me, that I may renew my acquaintance with his wife, as soon as they have moved to their new house at Clapham—an invitation which will probably however be forgotten; and M.M. (by way I believe of showing his approbation of my poem) asked me to dinner next Wednesday. He showed much more interest in the Burns poems than T.T. who is harder & more 'practical'. T.T. is a short man with crisp black beard and keen spectacled eyes, & with an air of selfpossession and compact strength—well knit in mind & body, & critical in look. M.M. on the other hand, is plain, loosely made, corpulent: a genial chatty man, unpoetic both in face & figure. The cleverest looking man in the room, to my mind, was Mr. Stirling[4] of Keir—'Velasquez' Stirling—a man with shapely bald head, penetrating eyes, & versatile but satirical mouth. Bright & humourous in talk, he told most graphically how the scoundrel Palmerston was mobbed by foreigners, coming down from the House on Monday night: also how Lord Cardigan,[5] being at Gibraltar in his yacht, was asked by the Governor to dine: how he replied that *Lady* C. also was on board: how the Governor said in answer that he invited Lord C. alone: how Lord C. in return sent a *challenge* to the Governor, who for reply straightway sent a steam tug, which towed Lord C. out into the middle of the straits and left him there!

There were present also several of those amiable young gentlemen with downy moustaches who condescend to represent mankind in Parliament. On the whole it was a pleasant & instructive evening: and of course I watched the

[8] George Stovin Venables (1810–88). *The Times* contributor, and Inner Temple barrister. George Warrington is a character in Thackeray's *Pendennis*.

[9] (Sir) Austen Henry Layard (1817–94) had excavated Nineveh in the forties, and had since gone into Liberal politics. According to T. H. S. Escott (*Club Makers and Club Members*), he is supposed to have suggested the establishment of the Cosmopolitan!

[1] Sir Henry Rawlinson (1810–95), the Assyriologist, had recently been knighted and was eventually raised to the baronetcy. He sat as M.P. for Reigate, 1858–9.

[2] Richard Monckton Milnes (1809–85), later Lord Houghton, the politician and poet who had written the biography of Keats. Esteemed for his encouragement of literature, and for his advocacy of mechanics' institutes.

[3] Tom Taylor (1817–80), civil servant; prolific author and dramatist; art critic of *The Times*. Subsequently edited *Punch*. Tended to heaviness, but was a friendly host at Lavender Sweep, Clapham. His wife had poetic ambitions, but Munby described her as a 'cold hard intellect' (see 19 June, 1862).

[4] He became Sir William Stirling-Maxwell on succeeding to the Maxwell baronetcy, 1865. In 1859 he was sitting as M.P. for Perthshire. A pioneer in the appreciation of Spanish art.

[5] James Thomas Brudenell, Earl of Cardigan (1797–1868), the eccentric soldier who led the Charge of the Light Brigade.

distinguished party with deep humility, reverently beholding their long clays, and taking a respectful interest in their brandy & water. It was near two when they broke up, & Cayley & I walked homewards together.

In that entry Munby provides a valuable cameo of the literary and political establishment that had its focus in *The Times* of Delane. Munby's success in the Burns competition had given him a right to consideration; his agreeable manners made him acceptable in society at all levels—though just how low those levels could be would have surprised the majority of his intellectual acquaintances. In whatever company he found himself, this watchful moralist observed shrewdly, sceptically, and sometimes despairingly. The Working Men's College served as a bridge between the two worlds in which Munby moved. With his tolerant Broad Church principles, he refereed continual wrangles between the believers and non-believers who administered the College:

Thursday, 3 March . . . My Latin class in the evening. Went to Macmillan's afterwards, & found him with Litchfield, Furnivall & Vernon Lushington,[6] discussing one of those College jars which *will* occur: how Furnivall wants to read Mill on Liberty with his class, & Maurice objects to it as a contemporary book on an unsettled question. F. will kick, but Maurice will conquer: for all submit to him, not because he is *Principal* but because he is *Maurice*. Inevitable, & quite right too. Then the talk grew towards Genesis & Geology: Macmillan holding that Maurice had fully explained Chap. I—Litchfield & Furnivall laughing to scorn (though with full recognition of Maurice's greatness) his, or any, reconcilement—Vernon mediating in his clear earnest way—I as usual, watching. As if all this, like astronomy, will not right itself in time: as if the necessary spiritual truths of God could be affected by Moses & his erroneous physics! And hearing such talk of Maurice, one feels most the brute folly of the Evangelicals, who persecute as infidel & traitor a man who is to many their only hope for loyalty and faith, & whose only crime, with others, is that he believes too much, & holds too strongly what he holds.

Wednesday, 9 March . . . In the evening called for George Cayley in Dean's Yard by appointment, & we went to dine with Monckton Milnes in Brook St. Pleasant intelligent party of ten. M. Louis Blanc[7] was the 'lion', a little man about four feet six or so with a round face & a merry humour: he talked a great

---

[6] Vernon Lushington (1832–1912), twin brother of Godfrey, and a close friend of Munby. A scholar of Trinity, Cambridge, who became Secretary to the Admiralty and later a County Court Judge.

[7] Louis Blanc (1811–82), French political leader and historian, had fled to England after the defeat of the workers in the revolt of June, 1848; he did not return to France until 1870. His ideas greatly influenced the development of socialism.

deal (in French) and told several good stories from his political experience, with much spirit & a little egotism: Rees[8] of Lucknow was there too—a German looking man with foreign accent, agreeable but scarcely a gentleman in manners: I had much talk about the siege with him, but learnt scarcely anything new. Tom Hughes[9] also, Walter Severn,[1] Borland's friend (son of Keats's friend), and Clough[2] (the Bothie of Toper-na-Fuosich) with his wife: a grave gentlemanly man, handsome, greyhaired, with air of fastidious languor about him. Mrs Milnes[3] a fine elegant woman, an accomplished artist. . . .

Date uncertain owing to excisions, probably Tuesday, 15 March: a gathering 'at "Little Parker" the publisher's'[4] . . . Blackstone—Clark of Trinity . . . Robert Bell, & others: Froude[5] too, whose look & manner pleased me much: a tall man in clerical dress, with a grave sweet face full of thought and tenderness, & a manner saddened by struggle & suffering . . .

Wednesday, 16 March . . . After dinner went to a private rehearsal of certain socalled Creole Serenaders: seven women in fantastic half Spanish dress, their faces coloured brown: the fair creatures having too much vanity to blacken themselves in the true Ethiopian manner. By this means they destroyed the character of their entertainment, besides disfiguring themselves more than need be; for brown, to a whitewoman's face, is much more destructive of beauty than black. The entrepreneurs were two elderly men of highly respectable grave appearance—looking like welltodo solicitors: to see the serious interest they took in the colouring of the women's faces and the trivialities of their comic songs, was ludicrous not to say humiliating. The songs were 'nigger' songs, and the performance very commonplace: but it was a good opportunity of seeing the inner life of such peoples & places. It was hardly a satisfactory experience, though everyone seemed very moral and respectable. After all however the business is not more absurd than others, to the judicious observer: it is well to see

[8] L. E. Ruutz Rees wrote *A Personal Narrative of the Siege of Lucknow* (1858), an invaluable first-hand account. He was a Calcutta merchant unexpectedly involved in the siege while on a business trip.

[9] Thomas Hughes (1822–96), staunch Christian and author of *Tom Brown's School Days*, was already known to Munby as a founder of the Working Men's College, where his hearty athletic approach had proved an important factor in its success. He later became its Principal, and a Liberal M.P. and County Court Judge.

[1] Walter Severn (1830–1904), the watercolourist, who worked in the Privy Council Office. Robert Spencer Borland (1826–1910) was the closest of Munby's Trinity friends; a barrister, but ordained Church of England clergyman, 1865.

[2] Arthur Hugh Clough (1819–61), the poet. His *Bothie of Toper-na-Fuosich* (1848) had influenced Munby. It was reprinted after Clough's death as *The Bothie of Tober-na-Vuolich*.

[3] She had been the Hon. Annabel Crewe, younger daughter of the second Baron Crewe.

[4] Presumably John William Parker (1792–1870), whose London business was sold to Longmans in 1863.

[5] James Anthony Froude (1818–94), historian; Carlyle's disciple, executor, and biographer. See 2 February, 1864.

how even the merest trifles of amusement can become real *work* to a human being—how too (to take the other side) they acquire—everything acquires—a factitious seriousness & importance when taken up as a profession, and lose too whatever airy grace & spontaneity they have: not that law or conveyancing ever had any.

Thursday, 17 March . . . My Latin class in the evening—first night in the new term. Vernon Lushington walked home with me from the college, & came in for half an hour: we talked of Burns, of poetry generally—he holding that nowadays it is time for a poet to leave introspection, & analysis of feelings & mere love of Nature, & to become Homeric and Shakespearean, & deal with & celebrate the facts & events of his time. A noble plan certainly: but I held & feel that the very tumult of events nowadays, & the splendid supremacy of physical science, is enough to drive the imaginative & contemplative soul into the society of himself and of nature: for here he finds the quiet & the permanence & the spiritual meanings which are the food of his poetic life. But when the first whirl & flash of engines and telegraphs & revolutions is over, & the poetic soul—which is slow to change & clings to familiar loves—has learnt to keep pace with them, and to see the poetic side of all such things, *then* we may have a Homer of the railway and a Shakespeare of the Ballot. Vernon is a dear old fellow—his devout & earnest talk always does one good.

Saturday, 19 March . . . Today an unusual bout of law work made me feel, as usual in such cases, wretchedly anxious & unsettled, as one who has grown hopeless of life and finds not any work to suit him or to do good to others. But I hate to write about such feelings, which must for the sake of present duty be overcome or borne in silence. Fiat voluntas Tua.

Sunday, 20 March. Breakfasted with Litchfield. Ormsby being there also. Talk chiefly of the comparative morality of this generation and the last, and of the advantage or otherwise of repressing street vice: as to which on the whole I side against the puritans, & am in favour of the unmolested street walker—provided she be sober, well dressed, & not too importunate. It is certain, as Ormsby said, that the clearance, socalled, of the Haymarket and Casinos produced a large & still flourishing crop of secret dens & night haunts all about . . .

Tuesday, 22 March . . . Today, after an auction yesterday, they began to pull down the old buildings on the south side of Figtree Court, opposite this house. After standing more than two hundred years, these old houses are coming down at last, to be replaced no doubt by some wretched modern improvement . . .

Friday, 25 March. Fine day. In till five. Went by boat to Chelsea, & thence walked to Moore's at Walham Green. The piles are now laid for the new railway

28

bridge, just below the other new Chelsea bridge. The whole right bank of the river from Vauxhall or rather Pimlico to Chelsea Hospital has been embanked, streets & terraces laid out & built, Battersea Park enclosed & the old Red House & Mill pulled down, the Crystal Palace railway & station completed, & Chelsea bridge begun & finished—since I first knew the place in /52. Well may I envy the navvies their retrospect of work! . . .

Saturday, 26 March . . . About 2 p.m. I went down to the Crystal Palace with Fred,[6] to hear Fidelio, the music of which was performed straight through, & that beautifully. The music soon overcame my illhumour & impatience at the crowd & want of room, & by shutting my eyes & representing to myself from memory each scene as the music rolled on, I was able to enjoy it intensely, & to feel how thoroughly the strains interpret themselves, without words or scenery. To me, the dramatic beauty of the story, & the wonderful tenderness & preternatural power and glory of the music, make up perhaps the highest emotional delight on earth: not to be enjoyed without something very like tears. And yet Fidelio is never performed!

After it was over I rushed away to calm down among the courts & orange trees & greenery: a most delightful resource, for the beds by the water tanks were full of brilliant flowers, & the creepers & shrubs were all in bloom. Crowds of people 'swelling' up & down the nave: but I liked it not: in such places the company of one's equals is hateful to me—it arouses vanity, selfconsciousness, ogling, small talk, & every creeping thing that creepeth upon the face of the earth. One sees many lovely & well-dressed girls: but, save for them, better is Monday the people's day, and the sandwiches & porter & the prentices & strapping servant maids . . .

Friday, 1 April . . . after dinner dressed & went to the Princess's to meet Miss Stott & Mrs Tarleton, to whom I was to be cavalier. The play was Henry V.— The chorus exceeding well spoken by Mrs Kean—the play a series of brilliant spectâcles, strung together by 'appropriate Shakespearian readings': scenes & speeches being left out by whole sale. The siege of Harfleur really wonderful— the rush and shouting of innumerable armed men, the flights of arrows, discharge of cannon, onslaught of catapults, blazing of fireballs—the volumes of smoke & dust, & especially the absence of anything to betray the limits or the 'properties' of a stage, made it by far the most real thing of the kind one ever saw. The Episode too of Henry's reception by the Londoners, was extremely beautiful. After all the result impressed me not so much with Kean's[7] merit as an actor, as with his surprising power of discipline: every man & woman of the crowds of supernumeraries . . . seemed thoroughly animated & full of individual interest in their work.

---

[6] Munby's brother, Frederick James Munby (1837–1914), who eventually succeeded his father as head of the firm of Munby and Scott, solicitors, York.

[7] Charles John Kean (1811?–68), son of Edmund Kean; married to Ellen Tree.

Coming out of the theatre & sending the ladies home, I met Henry James,[8] come up to pass an examination for a lectureship on Physical Science at Cheltenham Training College: an agreeable surprise—we walked together some distance, & I then went on to Belgrave Road to Alex. Munro's[9] the sculptor, whom I had not seen since his return from Rome. . . .

Monday, 4 April . . . Dundas Holroyd[1] came & sat some time, to take leave of me, going to Melbourne on the 10th of May, to practise at the bar there. Certain solicitors there have guaranteed him £2000 a year, to be shortly doubled. Visits and talk such as this make me horribly despondent: they bring me to a sense of my position. . . . I am sure it is something more than mere indolence that keeps me from working earnestly at indifferent matters—at anything that does not help forward my convictions, whether literary, artistic, or religious. With all other work, there comes over me a shuddering sadness that I can neither explain nor get rid of . . .

Tuesday, 5 April . . . Yesterday, as I forgot to mention, Litchfield and I went by invitation to see some pictures of Inchbold's,[2] an excellent young painter—one of those whom Ruskin[3] has created . . . all painted with most patient accuracy, most delicate finish, & most vivid truth: and this man Inchbold is only one of many whom we owe to Ruskin.

Sunday, 10 April . . . In the afternoon I walked up to Kilburn.[4] On my way home, being importuned by a girl in the Strand to come home with her, I replied by way of excuse 'but it's Sunday': on which she exclaimed 'What, are you so *froom* as all that?' *Froom*, she explained, meant *religious*: but query the word, which is new to me.[5]

Wednesday, 13 April . . . Before one, called at Whitehall for Litchfield, & we went in a Hansom to Ruskin's at Denmark Hill. Mrs Elwes's carriage, with Miss Kennion & Miss Spottiswoode, drove up to the gate as we did. We were shown

[8] Henry Alfred James (1827–98). Became lecturer in physics at the Normal College, Cheltenham. At Trinity with Munby. He, Borland, and Vernon Lushington were Munby's most intimate friends.

[9] Alexander Munro (1825–71).

[1] Edward Dundas Holroyd (1828–1916), contemporary of Munby at Trinity. Q.C., 1879. Justice of the Supreme Court of Victoria, 1881. Knighted, 1903.

[2] John William Inchbold (1830–88), landscape painter, who had been Ruskin's guest in Switzerland, where these pictures were painted.

[3] John Ruskin (1819–1900), author, artist, and social reformer. He had taught drawing at the Working Men's College from 1854 to 1858, and still did so intermittently. Munby had apparently already visited him at his family home at Denmark Hill. See 13 April, 1859.

[4] Where Hannah was then in service.

[5] '*froom* or *frume*. Religious in the orthodox sense: Jewish colloquialism: late C. 19–20. Ex. Ger. *fromm*.' (Partridge's *Dictionary of Slang*).

into the charming morning room, from which you look over the lawn & across a beautiful parklike country to Norwood: not a house to be seen, though it is only three miles from London Bridge. Ruskin came down, & being introduced to the ladies, proceeded to show us the Turners in the room: removing the green calico covers in which he hides them, & taking down each picture to be looked at. I had seen them all before, but can never see them too often—The Coblentz, and the Lake of Zug, a new one, bought at Windus's[6] sale—one the loveliest, perhaps, in the room. After seeing these & hearing his wise appreciative talk about them, we went into the dining room to luncheon. There, the talk, in which Ruskin of course took the lead, was chiefly of his political economy book—how he could not get people to listen to nor appreciate what he had said in it—especially of the folly of paying people to produce ugly or inferior things. I hinted that his wild advice about buying Italian palaces might have injured the influence of the book—he agreed with this, & regretted he had put it in.[7] I asked what he thought of the attempts one seems to see in every new building to carry out by colour & by carving, his advice: he scarcely thought them sincere, or adopted from any other motive than to please a growing taste. After luncheon he showed us the pictures round the room—two large Turners in oil, a Sir Joshua (Angelica Kauffman), several charming W. Hunts,[8] & others. Apropos of a capital head of a village girl by Hunt, which Ruskin took me aside to look at, I spoke to him of my favourite project—namely that some one ought to paint peasant girls & servant maids as they are—coarse & hearty & homely—and so shame the false whitehanded wenches of modern art. *These* have been painted as they are, but *women*, never: spurious refinement & false delicacy prevent it—as if a housemaid was not as well worth painting as a lady—& as if, being painted, she ought to be idealised & varnished with the halfgentility of a lady's maid! I reminded him of that picture of the garden scene in Faust, where Margaret says 'How can you kiss my hand—sie ist so *garstig*, ist so *rauch*'—and yet the hand is as white and soft as a lady's! I was much pleased to find that Ruskin cordially agreed with me—and after talking some minutes & saying that Hunt was the man to do it, he thanked me for mentioning the subject: so I hope it may bear fruit.

He then took us into the drawing room, and being obliged to go into town, left us to enjoy the remaining Turners, which include the Goldau, the Gates of the Hills, & others engraved in Modern Painters. We stayed in the room an hour or more, & lingered last & longest over three—the Lucerne, the Constance, and the

[6] B. Godfrey Windus, an 'enthusiastic retired coachmaker of Tottenham' (Finberg), had built up a large Turner collection.

[7] *The Political Economy of Art*, here referred to, consists of two lectures Ruskin gave to a fashionable audience in Manchester during the Art Treasures Exhibition held in that city in 1857. In the second lecture he urged his hearers to acquire and preserve buildings in Italy, a gesture he preferred to the transportation of art treasures to Manchester. The sole motive was to be that they should take pride in their Italian houses—'only a noble pride'.

[8] William Henry Hunt (1790-1864), the watercolourist who specialised in rustics, fisherfolk, and still-life subjects.

Brunnen (on Lucerne), which, and especially the last, are marvels of colouring . . .

On the following Saturday, 16 April, Munby left London with his knapsack, having decided 'to take advantage of the trains by which one can now go to the *Isle of Wight & back for three & sixpence*'. He spent the week-end walking through the island, and joined up with two friends on the way. Returning on the Monday evening, he noted that the whole trip had cost him one guinea. The following Friday, 22 April, was Good Friday; Munby went to services at St. Dunstan's in the morning, and at Lincoln's Inn Chapel in the afternoon. On the Saturday he attended 'the Easter Even service at All Saints, Margaret St.,' and bought some Easter Eggs in Soho on the way home. On Easter Sunday he went to early Communion at All Saints; to the 'morning service at S. Andrew's'; and to an evening service at Holy Trinity, Vauxhall. Munby was always extremely conscientious in his religious duties (his churchgoing has had to be neglected in the excerpts from his diary entries). All Saints, Margaret Street, originally Margaret Chapel, professed an Anglo-Catholic churchmanship; so that Munby's religious views, though strongly anti-Papist, were apparently High as well as Broad. On Easter Monday he felt able to relax:

Monday, 25 April . . . to the Crystal Palace. None but holiday people there: ten thousand of them. They showed more interest in the art Courts and other refinements than usual: but I doubt the advantage, the rightness, of offering them such exquisite food. . . . They are not refined, but blunted and vulgarized still more, by eating sandwiches (and they *will* eat sandwiches) on the tombs of Kings, and drinking pots of porter in the Courts of the Alhambra: these are mighty influences for good, wasted altogether by being exercised upon those who have never been taught to feel them. Today I heard a wench exclaim, standing by the avenue of Sphinxes, before the statues of Rameses the Great, 'Come on Bill, let's cut: I'm sick of this place—there's nought to do' . . .

Monday, 2 May . . . Went to the W.M. College to hear Ruskin's 'talk' about Switzerland. The room was full, many of the teachers there. Ruskin had brought one or two of his best Turners, and photographs & maps. He spoke well and in his usual free pleasant way: with as usual a little too much *infant school* humour—like the funny papa telling stories to the good boys. His lecture was historical & geographical chiefly—without book, he standing before the fire with hands under coat tails, or whisking about in his airy way. At the end he broke out into politics—saying, to the surprise of Lushington and me, that we ought to have trusted Louis Napoleon and joined the French at once! No:

Austria is infernal, but we don't care to turn out Beelzebub for the sake of Moloch.

By the way, last Wednesday night the Austrians crossed the Ticino, & the war began.[9] . . .

Monday, 16 May . . . Went to the British Museum—Found there some things of mine in 'Beautiful Poetry'—Met Borland at Club Chambers, & dined with him there. We then walked to Severn's in Eccleston Square—Mr Severn,[1] the friend of Keats, in whose arms Keats died, does not look more than fifty even now: a quiet man who scarcely spoke at all—but one could not look at him without deep interest. Miss Severn[2] a sweet unaffected girl, loving and impulsive— an exquisite artist. Her drawings, specially her portraits, in pencil & in water colour, are charming. She painted the Duchess of Kent & the younger Princesses: & the Queen would sit by her for hours looking on, or go & fetch clean water for her colours, in a most simple and kindly way. Walter Severn[3] showed us his sketches in Spain too, which were capital: he draws excellently well, and is besides a very genial good fellow, handsome and with an air of 'ton' which the others dont possess . . .

The fine Spring weather now induced Munby to spend long week-ends walking in the country with his friends. In London he went out nearly every night, and was obviously not overburdened with work. Charles Keene might appropriately have attended, and drawn, some of his parties:

Wednesday, 25 May . . . at 10.30 went by [Walter] Severn's invitation to one of the wellknown parties given by Vaux[4] of the British Museum in Gate St. Lincoln's Inn Fields. A very enjoyable bachelor's party: the rooms—uncarpeted and lined with books and pictures—were full of groups of men more or less known or distinguished: music in one room, food in another, and cigars and pipes in all. Some admirable partsinging by members of Leslie's choir: songs, serious & comic: piano-sonatas, and duets and trios with violin and violoncello, all splendidly played. Everything as pure and refined, too, as if there had been women there: whose absence was more than made up for by the freedom of dress and of smoking which it made possible. It was pleasant to see a man sit down to

[9] Napoleon III had declared war on Austria with the aim of liberating Italy. The war was short and inconclusive, but prepared the way for the success of Garibaldi. Napoleon's erratic foreign policy was making him increasingly distrusted by Britain, his former Crimean ally.

[1] Joseph Severn (1793–1879), the painter.

[2] Mary Severn (1832–66), portrait-painter, daughter of Joseph Severn. As will appear later, Munby was considerably attracted to Miss Severn, but his liaison with Hannah inhibited him here, as elsewhere; she married in 1861 (Sir) Charles Thomas Newton, the archaeologist, and died five years later. See Plate 10.

[3] Brother of Mary. See 9 March, 1859.

[4] W. S. W. Vaux (1818–85), antiquary; Keeper of Coins and Medals, British Museum, 1861–70.

the piano, and draw the loveliest music from it too, in morning dress & with a weed in his mouth, a crowd of bearded smokers standing round in listening attitudes: to see also many a short meerschaum & long clay meeting over portfolios of exquisite drawings. Jones of the 18th Hussars was there, who was so desperately wounded in India—looking as well as ever, but for the loss of one eye. Edward Palliser of the Staff College, too, a splendid Irishman, six feet four, with the longest moustache I ever saw—yet as pleasant and gentle as a child, and a singer of tender songs: and many other pleasant men. Severn came home with me about two, and we sat talking till three—I gave him my spare bed.

Monday, 30 May . . . Wretched & hopeless again of late, owing to the state of things at home,[5] and my inability to see any way of making money. Tried 'Once a Week' without success.

Wednesday, 1 June: The Derby at Epsom . . . the views from the course of heath and woodland and rich plain country were charming. 'Musjid' won the Derby: a very good race, which we saw from the hill among the carriages. . . . The crowds, and the joyous excitement, were as great on the course as ever: but I saw much less fun, and fewer amusements, than usual. No drunkenness either, no rows nor fighting, and not many prostitutes: everything quiet and orderly . . .

Thursday, 2 June . . . went, about 12, with Severn to a Bachelor's Ball at S. James's Hall: to which we were invited, at Vaux's party, by a pleasant gentlemanly man named Lewis,[6] the son and partner of the *mercer in Regent St.*— Lewis, being modest & accomplished and having the wisdom not to be ashamed of his position, is much liked in good male society. The ball was a most sumptuous affair: the great Hall thrown open for dancing, to Coote & Tinney's band —and the whole Suite of the S. James dining rooms being given up to supper and refreshments. But the guests looked unworthy of all this luxury: the women were to a striking extent wanting in beauty, in grace of motion and manners, & even in the fine symmetry of make that one sees in real ladies. They were all splendidly dressed: but the old ones had no dignity, and the young ones no ladylike ease or selfpossession. I never saw so clearly that there is a real difference in physical and mental breeding, between these rich tradesmen's families— for they were all of that class, nearly—and those above them. Their equality in wealth, dress, and circumstance only makes the true inferiority more evident. The men were better than the women: but this was only because a good many gentlemen, properly so called, were present. One noticeable thing was, that several actors and actresses were among the guests—and these not of the noblest

[5] Munby's father had financial worries, because of the expenses of Clifton Holme (and also perhaps of the upkeep of A.J.M.).

[6] Arthur Lewis, of Lewis and Allenby, who later married Kate Terry, and became the host of Moray Lodge, Campden Hill; he helped to found the Arts Club.

kind. Old Keeley[7] and Mrs K. for instance—it was great fun to see them todd-ling or romping about, in the wellknown Adelphi style. Mary Keeley was there too, with Albert Smith, who looked horribly coarse and vulgar. On the whole, comparing the people and the place, one could scarce help thinking of the Crystal Palace on Easter Monday: but commend me to the honest roughness of a stolid maid of all work, rather than to the hybrid fineladyism of Miss Swan & Edgar.

I walked home about 4 a.m.—broad daylight. The street scenes at that hour, especially at the top of the Haymarket, were quite Hogarthian. The last stragglers were just reeling out of the 'Pic',[8] & talking or squabbling outside: two gentlemen in evening dress, a few unwashed foreigners, several halfdrunken prostitutes, one of whom, reeling away, drops her splendid white bonnet in the gutter, & another dances across the street, showing her legs above the knee: languid waiters in shirt sleeves stand looking on from their doors: two or three cabmen doze on the box behind their dozing horses: and a ragged beggarwoman skulks along in the shadow of the houses. Beyond them all, looking out for a *dignus vindice nodus*,[9] stands with dead calm face the Rhadamanthine peeler.

When I got into the Strand the market waggons were beginning to come in, and a servant maid had already taken down the shutters of her master's eating-house, and was shaking the mats in the street. To bed at 5.

Friday, 10 June ... Went in to the Circus in Leicester Square for a while on my way home, to see 'Ella'; a splendid creature, tall and well made, with large bright eyes, fine features, and dark abundant hair. She is said to be a man in disguise: but there is nothing to favour such a suspicion except her height and the boldness of her riding: which, like herself, is the most admirable thing I ever saw in a circus. . . .

On Saturday, 11 June, Munby went up to York with his brother Fred: 'The mother and all looked well: and if they were but happy & secure, one would have been in perfect peace—All in good spirits today however. . . .' He returned to London on the following Wednesday, after recording: 'The father in better spirits than I had hoped, but still talks of leaving Clifton—If one could but help him to stay there!'

It was a warm summer; and for Munby trips into the country were interspersed with entertainments in town.

[7] Robert Keeley (1793-1869), the celebrated low comedian, admired by Dickens. His wife, Mary Ann Goward (1806-99), was outstanding in pathetic parts. Their daughter Mary married Albert Smith (1816-60), the popular one-man entertainer and humorist, but he died soon after-wards. Munby's attitude to the family is what we might call highbrow.

[8] The Piccadilly, a supper house.

[9] *Nec deus intersit, nisi dignus vindice nodus inciderit.* (Neither should a god intervene, unless a knot befalls worthy of his interference). Horace: *Ars Poetica.*

The Diary Opens

Monday, 20 June . . . This was the first day of the Handel Festival at the Crystal Palace: to which Fred, Joe[1] and I went together, having exchanged a guinea ticket for *four* five shilling tickets. Our place was just under the corner of the N.E. gallery, & from it we saw the whole of the transept—and nearly all the orchestra. The sight of an amphitheatre of 4000 singers & musicians, seen at due distance, with the great organ standing among them like a rock at high water, was very grand: the floor also of the building being crowded with people—all the ladies in white muslin, with adornments of violet and purple. But though unequalled as a spectacle, to the ear it was not so glorious, and to the spirit still less. The solos indeed were audible with a far off clearness; and the choruses were accurate and brilliant: but none of them—not even the Hallelujah—had a volume of sound equal to 4000 voices. And the devotional effect of the music was, to me at least, quite lost: especially, when the audience, after the Descent into Hell, dispersed in search of ices and bottled stout . . .

Thursday, 7 July. A brilliant hot day. My father's fiftyfifth birthday. How I wish I were supporting him instead of being even partially dependent on him! And just now I feel almost as far removed from youth as if I were a father myself. If to look backward and not forward be the characteristic of old age, I am already very aged. . . . Met Markham Spofforth[2] in Piccadilly, who offered me the chance of making £1500 without risk, if I would give my name as prosecutor in fifteen actions for bribery at the Beverley election: the penalties being £100 in each action. Felt somewhat excited at the prospect of so large & much needed a sum, but desired a night to consider, not being satisfied that it was quite right or prudent . . .

Friday, 8 July . . . Ralston came to breakfast, & declined to share the £1500 with me. I went out at ten and consulted Warner & George Cayley, and then to Markham Spofforth and declined his offer, as being likely to imperil one's good name, even if not slightly tinged with dishonour—So ends my only chance of making money. . . .

On Saturday, 16 July, Munby went off by himself to spend a long weekend in Boulogne, repeating an excursion he had made the previous year. With its Proustian undertones, this was one of his characteristic forays in search of the working woman, which he was later to extend to many areas of Britain and part of the continent. Settling into a room on the fourth floor of a hotel facing the harbour, he filled his diary with pages of

---

[1] Munby's brother Joseph Edwin Munby (1839–67), then at Trinity, Cambridge. Took holy orders and became curate of Leeds parish church before his early death. See Plate 6.
[2] Markham Spofforth (1825–1907). Principal Conservative agent for twenty years. Senior Taxing Master in Chancery from 1876.

description. 'If I had the means,' he wrote, 'I would investigate, being now old enough to do so without misconstruction, the moral & physical statistics of labouring women all over the world.' But, alas, the motives of the vigorous Munby—only thirty, after all, though he sheltered behind his bushy beard—could still be misconstrued, as he strode along the beaches interviewing any female who struck his fancy.

. . . The quay, open to the afternoon sun, was as usual full of life & picturesque costume. No where, I think, can so great a contrast to the deadness of English outward life be got so rapidly as at Boulogne. After washing & dressing, I walked down by the Baths, and then back along the quay. The strong brown bathing women—not wizened hags like ours—sat on their benches by the road-side knitting: for the bathing hours were almost over—their bare wet legs crossed idly, their big feet buried in the sand—their only garment a brown flannel blouse, & a brown kerchief wrapping the head . . . Also of course I met on the quay numbers of women & girls, in short striped or short red petticoats, in bare legs, or blue stockings & strong shoes, in white frilled caps or caps of the modest ancienne môde; each with her big basket slung behind her; each carrying, or having carried, or preparing to carry, a load. Women stooping under a weight of fishing nets: women—female porters of the Customhouse—bearing on their backs great English trunks, which John Thomas would not touch with one of his lumpish fingers: women with burdens of wood, of sand, of fish—with baskets only asking to be filled. How distressing to the humane & sensitive cockney! . . .

. . . After dinner, I walked down to the sea, & along the shore to Portel. . . . As I neared the ridge of rocks before you come to Portel, the white caps & red skirts of a number of picturesque Portelaises appeared amongst them, bobbing up & down as they washed & wrung their linen at the little cliffstream. Here they are always to be found at low tide, kneeling at work by the pools: peeping suddenly over the rocks, like antelopes over a hill top, or bounding away in glimpses of red & blue colour. . . . I went a little further, & by a rude path up the cliff: half-way up was a small quarry; where the men were hewing sandstone: & women, with frames fitted to their backs, carried the stone by a steep stair to the top. . . . The industry of these busy Portelaises is admirable: & yet they are not coarse or masculine or unusually strong. Feminine to look at, clean & neat and (by comparison) fairskinned, they stand aloof from the brown robust & ragged pêcheuses-de-crevettes of Boulogne. Whether from contempt or not I don't know, but they never associate: and it is odd that though the shrimp & mussel grounds lie close to Portel, the Portelaises never fish for them, while the women of Boulogne come all the way on purpose. 'It is not our métier—voilà tout'—said a Portel woman to me. With all the excellence of these peoples, however, I am bound to say I met one black sheep among them: a girl of ten or twelve, who followed me for 'un petit sou' near an old fort on the cliffs toward Boulogne. She was bolder & less clean than the other children—and after teasing me long for sous she at length, saying something in her patois which I could not understand, faced about & lifted her skirt to the waist, exposing her body. And at my reproof & signs of disgust the creature only laughed—so I had to drive her away. However as she herself said, she was an orphan & uncared for . . .

Sunday, 17 July . . . went to the large church at 9.30, the principal service. . . . After this I walked back again to the quay & the douane. The Folkestone boat had just come in: the female porters were all astir, some in the hold hoisting up luggage along with the sailors, others carrying the trunks to the cart and piling them there, others steadying the shafts (and sometimes carried off their legs) while it was filling. . . . When the hold is empty, the women go round and sit about in the yard behind, knitting—for they are never idle—till the luggage has passed. Each woman has a brass badge hung on her breast with the word 'bagages' thereon: and each has her number painted in large white letters on the big basket she carries behind her. As I came round, a douanier was calling them over by their numbers: 'Numero trente-six?' 'Ici!' says a stout fille, looking up from her knitting. And so each in her turn enters a door inscribed 'Femmes pour porter les bagages,' and reappears with a load on her back. . . .

. . . an Englishman assumes that because the women work, the men must be idle; which is false; the husbands of these porters are all working, either at sea, or in the army, or elsewhere . . . the wife is a licensed porter, and the husband may not interfere with her duties. And why shouldn't she be a licenced porter? She is helping to keep the family; and her calling is neither immoral nor unwomanly. For it is absurd to say the work is too severe. . . .

Monday, 18 July . . . I met the mussel gatherers . . . returning from the rocks . . . to stand in the midst of a knot of fine young women with brown bare limbs, coarse wet seafaring clothes, faces full of health and spirits, and nothing about them to remind you of the women you have met in London drawingrooms, is refreshing. . . . Last year walking on this beach, I found my path to the cliffs cut off by a large saltwater pond which was rapidly widening as the tide came in. An old fishwoman came up, & proposed that her daughter, a stout pêcheuse de crevettes who was wading with her nets close by, should carry me across. I declined, from delicacy or masculine pride, and went on: but being unable to get off my island without a wetting, I hailed the old woman & accepted her offer. The daughter was called, & came striding out of the waves to us. She took off her creel and laid down her nets, and replied with bland contempt to my fears that I should be too heavy for her to carry. Only she hoped I would sit firm on her hips, & clasp her shoulders with both hands. Whereon I sprang into my seat with much agility, and grasping her chest with each hand, settled into a graceful attitude on her back. Her strong legs stood the shock like pillars: and throwing herself forward and folding her arms under my knees, she plunged through the water, which was up to or above her knees, with the firm easy tread of a carriage horse. She was neither breathed nor sweated when I jumped off on the other side: with a smiling 'Non non' she assured me I was no weight (alas, I am ten stone) and taking her franc walked back again into the water. Among the groups today was one very fine handsome girl, tall & straight, largelimbed but shapely, the belle of all the matelottes I had seen: a most picturesque creature, with smooth dark hair, black piercing eyes, and a rosy bloom enriching her sunbrown cheek. Her name is Elise. . . . She had with her her elder sister. . . . As she stood there leaning on her shrimp net (for she had been fishing) wet through from the arm pits downwards, the water dripping from her red kilt and glazing the brown of her shapely legs, I regretted much that I had not brought my sketch book. The sister, who evidently liked to show her off, bade me observe that Elise was a fine girl: and when I replied that she was a regular beauty, Elise did not blush & simper—she smiled frankly, and looked full at me with her large eyes. Your rustic likes to be told pointblank that she is pretty. . . .

. . . dined at a restaurant, and along the quay at dusk. . . . I walked down the deserted pier, & saw the moon rise from dark clouds over the town. Coming back, a fishwoman walking alone in the shadow came up to me, & to my astonishment proposed a walk and 'pleasure' on the beach. Was she married? 'Oh yes: but he is away, & will never know—que voulez vous?' Whereupon I gave vent to certain appropriate remarks, and the fishwoman vanished quickly. This is the only case of the kind I met with: & I daresay it too is due to us English . . .

Tuesday, 19 July . . . walked along the beach towards Portel. . . . One tall woman, who was standing up to her waist in the water, transferring her last haul of shrimps from her nets to her creel, recognised me, and came splashing & striding to the rock where I stood, to offer me some shrimps. It was Elise's elder sister. . . . And now Sister to Elise was anxious for sous—I had promised them yesterday, she said. Presently, I replied—when you have done fishing. Ah, but you'll go away while we are in the water! Nothing of the kind. Well then, will you be *sure* to wait for us, & not give anything to the other women, but only to us? Pacified at length on these points, Marie (so I may call her) and her companion grasped their nets and took to the water. . . . When it was done, the two shouldered their nets, and without caring even to wring the water out of their clothes, moved off with me towards home. I had fulfilled my promise, and yet every few minutes Marie kept asking for more sous; till at last I sharply refused, & added 'Let us walk together to Boulogne as friends.' To this the fair fishers assented: sous were mentioned no more; and the talk at once became free & unconstrained. Soon two other shrimpgirls joined us with their nets, and we walked on abreast over the hot silent sands. It was a strange group, I suppose: in the midst, an Englishman of the period, smoking a cigar: his dress is 'civilized'— he wears gloves, he steps gingerly among the pools to save his boots, he carries an umbrella, for the glare is tremendous. On either side of him are two of the 'softer sex': yet these young ladies have no veils & parasols to keep the sun off, no gloves to nurse their hands, no dainty boots to protect their feet from the rocks. . . . And each of them wears a rough pea coat with big wooden buttons: and round her ample waist each has a coil of nets or lines, and bears a burden on her back & another on her shoulder: and below the waist, save a short kilt, she wears—nothing! . . .

. . . went on board the boat soon after one. . . . We reached Folkestone soon after three. . . . I walked up through Folkestone to the junction. What a contrast to the scene we had left! No life, no beauty, in place or people: a dull street of brown brick houses, and a few sleepy stragglers in black cloth coats or faded tawdry bonnets. So we got back to London by seven, and the stench of the Thames gave me a sick headache, & destroyed at once all the blessings of the pure sea air. I shut my windows to keep it out: had tea, and stayed in all the evening.

Monday, 25 July . . . to Vauxhall. It was the last night: dense crowds of people filled the gardens: the circus, the ballet, the dancing & concerts, the supper-rooms, the rifle shooting, the fortunetelling, the coloured lamps and the statues in the long walks—all were there as usual; there was no sign of dissolution: there was nothing in the noisy gaiety of the people (except perhaps that noisy gaiety itself) to show that they knew they were meeting there for the last time. But over all, in large letters formed of coloured lamps, hung the words 'Farewell for ever.' *These* were the moral of it all. . . . It is indeed much for a thoughtful man, to have seen the last of Vauxhall: to muse for the last time in those dim lighted alleys, and cry Vanitas vanitatum, and call up melancholy shadows of Kings & Court ladies to put to shame the living laughing crowd: but the real sting is, that *it is all over.*[3]

Saturday, 30 July . . . Going to the Opera, I met in the Strand one Sarah Tanner, who in 1854 or 5 was a maid of all work to a tradesman in Oxford Street: a lively honest rosyfaced girl, virtuous & self possessed. A year or so after, I met her in Regent St. arrayed in gorgeous apparel. How is this? said I. Why, she had got tired of service, wanted to see life and be independent; & so she had become a prostitute, of her own accord & without being seduced. She saw no harm in it: enjoyed it very much, thought it might raise her & perhaps be profitable. She had taken it up as a profession, & that with much energy: she had read books, and was taking lessons in writing and other accomplishments, in order to fit herself to be a companion of gentlemen. And her manners were improved—she was no longer vulgar: her dress was handsome & good, and she was, & is still, a fine looking girl, with good features & brunette complexion, &

[3] After two hundred years, Vauxhall Gardens was closing owing to the rioting and disorders provoked by its frequenters. The site was to be built on.

fine hazel eyes, remarkably large & bright. With these advantages and the education she was giving herself, she thought she might get on: for she was not extravagant—she cleaned up her own lodgings, she said, before taking her professional walk. And the girl was as quiet and honestlooking and selfpossessed as ever. So, after giving her a glass of ale—which she did not ask for—we parted. During the next two or three years I saw her twice or thrice at intervals *on duty*, and generally stopped to talk. She was always well but not gaudily dressed; always frank and rosy and pleasant, and never importunate: nor did I ever hear her say a vicious word. Yes, she continued to like it—she had some good friends, & was getting on nicely. After this I never saw her till tonight, when I met her in the Strand, walking with another young woman. She was stouter & healthier than ever, and was dressed, not professionally as a 'lady', but quietly & well, like a respectable upper servant. She stopped with a frank smile, & shook hands; and How is this? said I again. 'Well, I've left the streets & settled down,' she said quietly. 'Married?' I asked. 'Oh no! But I'd been on the streets three years, and saved up—I told you I should get on, you know—and so I thought I'd leave, and I've taken a coffeehouse with my earnings—the Hampshire Coffeehouse, over Waterloo Bridge.' I laughed, incredulous. 'Quite true,' said she simply. 'I manage it all myself, & I can give you chops & tea—& anything you like: you must come & see me.' 'That I will,' said I; for her manner was so open & businesslike that I saw it was true: and with a friendly goodbye we parted. Now here is a handsome young woman of twentysix, who, having begun life as a servant of all work, and then spent three years in *voluntary* prostitution amongst men of a class much above her own, retires with a little competence, and invests the earnings of her infamous trade in a respectable coffeehouse, where she settles down in homely usefulness and virtuous comfort! That the coffeehouse *is* respectable, is clear I think from her manner: that she *did* invest her earnings in it I believe, because she was not fashionable enough to be pensioned, & if she were, men do not pension off their whores in that way. Surely then this story is a singular contribution to the statistics of the 'Social Evil' and of female character and society in the lower classes.

Thursday, 4 August . . . My Latin class in the evening: Furnivall will take it for the rest of term. Came back round by Waterloo Bridge, to seek for the Hampshire Coffee House: A small decent house just over the Bridge. I asked a policeman about it: Yes, it was quite respectable: never heard anything against it: didn't think bad women went there at all. I went in, & found a little room with supper-boxes: neat & newly painted: through an open glass door appeared a little kitchen, where sat an elderly woman, & before the fire stood Sarah Tanner, with her sleeves turned up, cooking chops on a gridiron. She came forward, neatly dressed and ruddy: was glad to see me, but so busy just now, cooking supper for people upstairs: would I come again? So I said goodnight, satisfied with the truth of her story so far. . . .

For much of this hot August, Munby stayed at the parsonage, Rocester, Staffordshire, with his brother George,[4] a newly-ordained clergyman who was tutor in the Church Missionary Society's College, Islington. He saw the sights of the neighbourhood, among them Dovedale and Jacobean Wootton Lodge; he was greatly touched by the memorial to little Penelope Boothby in Ashbourne Church. But his ruling interest was always with him. In one day (Saturday, 13 August), as he reported magisterially, he had 'seen & spoken with eight examples of the female peasantry of the district . . . on the whole very satisfactory. . . . Unfortunately, I forgot to ask about their wages.' And there was an athletic cheese-maker (Thursday, 18 August) who won his heart by an energetic demonstration of her skill. 'She suddenly sprang on to the edge of the tub with her knees, and from thence nimbly flung herself upon the sieve, kneeling upon it with her whole weight. Arching her straight back & gathering her limbs together, her head bent down till one could see the dimpled neck behind, she kneaded the wet curd together with all the strength of her knees and her hands, till it was compressed below the rim of the sieve. . . .'

Munby's sentimental attitude to village maidens, about whom he gushed so fulsomely both in prose and verse, can be contrasted with the less reverent approach of his contemporary and fellow-Classic C. S. Calverley:

> The farmer's daughter hath soft brown hair
> (*Butter and eggs and a pound of cheese*)
> And I met with a ballad, I can't say where,
> Which wholly consisted of lines like these.

Whether owing to the continuous heat or for some other reason, Munby's diary for 1859 peters out at the end of August, in the midst of a visit to the colliery girls of the Wigan coal district—one of his favourite hunting grounds, to which he often returned. From then until the close of the year, his record consists only of the rough notes which he habitually enlarged into diary form. These reveal that most of the remainder of the summer was spent with his family at Clifton Holme, where on 1 September he was photographed with his favourite old pony Taffy. But in late October he paid a visit to a friend at Stonehouse, Gloucestershire, and there, as always, enjoyed country walks with an observant eye for the peasant women. Travelling on by himself, he came to Newport, Monmouthshire, where he discovered a woman who had roughed it all over the place wearing men's clothes: 'Didn't know why she took to men's c. but

---

[4] George Frederick Woodhouse Munby (1833–1911), Rugby and Trinity College, Cambridge. Ordained deacon, 1856. Later Rector of Turvey, Bedfordshire.

father behaved badly. Wore 'em more than 10 years, never had long hair in her life. . . . Was ostler at an inn . . . slept with her master's son 7 weeks & never found out . . . been at sea 18 months—can go aloft like any chap . . . twice wrecked, cast away on iceberg. . . . Will never wear woman's clothes again, not if I live 50 years. . . .' Such excited jottings are interspersed with descriptions of scenery and churches.

By November Munby was back in London and had resumed his teaching at the Working Men's College, where he was now a member of the Council of Teachers. On Wednesday, 23 November, he found drunken women in the streets at night and took one of them, 'Annie Hill, milliner', back to her home; however, the sequel is: 'A. Hill out again and follows me home.' Two brief entries suggest that he was searching desperately for a remunerative job. On Friday, 16 December, he went to the office of the Royal Agricultural Society to discuss 'the editorship' (presumably of the society's journal and publications). Nothing came of this approach, but on Monday, 19 December, he noted a visit to the Ecclesiastical Commissioners' office, adding the important comment 'accept appointment'.

These jottings do not reveal any enthusiasm on Munby's part for his future as a civil servant; nor, when he returns to York for Christmas, is 'the father's' reaction described, though it must presumably have been favourable. A 'sad want of devotion' is observed in York Minster on Christmas Eve—'dilemma, protestant bigotry, popish trickery'. The last entry of 1859 includes the words: 'Disturbance of mind, going away tomorrow. . . .'

3

AN OFFICE IN WHITEHALL
1860

He was a simple Barristere,
Unknown to wealth or fame;
In Figtree Court his chambers were,
And Munby was his name.

Munby prefaces his diary for 1860 with this sprightly quatrain, but his
entry for Sunday, 1 January, is disgruntled. He did not like travelling on a
Sunday, still less on New Year's Day. He always relished 'the quiet musing
and solemnity of feeling' which he thought appropriate to the turn of the
year, and felt aggrieved that he had to take the train from York to London
in order to start work at the Ecclesiastical Commissioners' office on the
Monday. However, 'it can't be helped. . . . I smoked in my corner, and
looked out on the long changing panorama of hill and dale & fields of
Sunday quiet. . . .'

In 1860 the Ecclesiastical Commissioners were still a controversial
body, as G. F. A. Best shows in his excellent history *Temporal Pillars*:
distrusted as bureaucrats, they were criticised as an anomalous semi-
independent power whose growing authority was widely resented. Within
the next twenty years, however, they were to win in large measure the
confidence of clergy and laity.

They had been established by Act of Parliament in 1836 with the duty
of supervising the redistribution and reduction of episcopal incomes, of
re-drawing the boundaries of dioceses and forming new dioceses, and of
remedying abuses in the organisation of the Church of England. In 1840
the separate estates of Deans, Canons and Prebendaries were vested in the
Commissioners, and they were given power to negotiate agreements with
the Deans and Chapters for the commutation of their corporate estates for
money payments. In 1860 the estates of the diocesan Bishops were similarly vested in them. The Commissioners had also received authority in
1843 to constitute and endow new parishes—a power which had only
recently become effective after the necessary funds had accumulated. Thus
Munby entered the office—where his friend R. B. Litchfield was already

employed—at a time when extra staff was needed to cope with its increasing activity.

Munby's was not a legal appointment, though his legal training provided a qualification. At first his views on the work varied from despair to resignation, with infrequent bursts of enthusiasm. In 1861, as we shall see, he actually made an attempt to escape. Nevertheless, beginning humbly—at the age of thirty-one—as a supernumerary clerk with £120 a year, Munby was to prove in the long run a successful civil servant, and when he retired nearly thirty years later had attained the rank of first-class clerk with a salary of £600, which gave him a pension of £340 a year. The job had its advantages; the office hours were short,[1] and having shown himself conscientious his time-keeping was not required to be exact. As a churchman and antiquarian, he came to find some of the work rewarding, despite its sad confirmation of the parochial distress already exposed by Trollope, while he had the consolation of knowing that his experience of the law and conveyancing—bitterly though he disliked his profession—would not be entirely wasted.

Munby still pursued his busy social life and philanthropic interests. His practical research into the lives of working women continued and was often, not surprisingly, misconstrued; he talked to them in the street or wherever he came across them; he questioned the women, encouraged them, advised them, often gave them small sums of money; he followed up interesting cases with pertinacity; and, as time went on, he made journeys throughout the country, especially to colliery districts, in search of new specimens to record in his diaries. He used some of the material thus acquired in his poems, notably those about working women in *Vulgar Verses*, by 'Jones Brown' (1891).

Monday, 2 January, 1860.   Got up at 8: a dull morning. Had breakfast, and walked down to 11 Whitehall Place, to begin my experimental career at the Ecclesiastical Commiss[rs] Office. Saw Pringle the Assistant Secretary, & was by him introduced into my sphere—the Estates Department. My companions three—Pigott the chief clerk, an Oxford man, scarce as old as I; Gregson, a ditto ditto: and an amiable pleasant youth named Ottaway. Was initiated very civilly by them into certain mild formal work: and employed myself thereat industriously enough till five p.m. when we leave. Walked away & dined, somewhat stupified by my new situation and employment; depressed too rather at the nature of the work and of my position there—among my juniors. For me, and at my age, to find a precarious clerkship of £120 a year the best work in life to do, may well be depressing: nevertheless, so little have I earned, that this

---

[1] At first they were nominally ten to five for Munby; subsequently, ten to four.

annual £120 looks like a fortune: the sacrifice of one's days too will make the rest of time more precious, and the compulsory work will create habits of regularity and early rising. To earn the money too, & that quietly and regularly, is a great thing: and on the whole it is clearly right to put oneself into this subjection and harness. After all, one's *life* does not lie *there*.

However, finding Ralston out, to get rid of my moody confusions of thought, I went, as the way is of weak minds, to the theatre—Covent Garden. . . . The opera, Mellon's[2] *Victorine*: thin and fâde. . . . The pantomime, *Puss in Boots*: remarkable only because the Cat was played by a woman—Miss Craven. She wore no garments, but was disguised from head to foot in catskins: her face painted or masked to look like a cat's, with feline whiskers and bristling ears and fur: a red collar and pad-lock round her neck. Her body and her legs and arms— or rather her fore & hindlegs—were those of a cat: her hands & feet were clawed, and she had a long pendent tail. She is first seen lying asleep on some sacks: she mewed, and purred, and ran at times on all fours, and climbed, and caught and devoured a mouse with accurate gusto. All this Miss Craven did: showing I conceive a commendable boldness in throwing off her womanhood and be-coming a thorough cat . . .

Tuesday, 3 January . . . Walked to the office at ten & worked fairly enough till five, initiating myself into the mechanism of official letters, minutes &c: for this, the youngest of the offices, is as much wedded to precedent as any. Felt less depressed than yesterday; but dull and headachy towards five. . . . Dined & walked homeward: on the way fell in with one Amy Dixon, a well dressed young milliner, one would say, tall & of good face and figure. No delicate selfstyled 'lady' she, however. I work at Lack's in the Strand, she says: make shirts, collars, gloves, anything. Sixteen shillings a week! Bless you Sir if I could earn that I should think myself a lady! I can earn nine or ten perhaps. 'But your smart clothes?' Clothes! why this bonnet I made myself & this frock was given me and this cloak I made out of a gentleman's old one that the lady his wife gave me when I went there to clean the paint. 'Clean the paint!' 'Yes, that I do: why I cant make my living by needlework, so I go out charing every Saturday—scrub floors & black grates and any dirty work. . . .' Good: good for the power of doing honest hard work, and for the absence of false shame in speaking of it . . .

Friday, 6 January . . . met Marion Gibbs the needlewoman, still in a state of great trouble about money. . . . Why didn't you tell your mother? 'Oh, what could she have done for me? Father couldn't afford to keep me at home; and I was ashamed for mother to know I was so bad off.' This utter want of mutual intercourse, & even interest, between the members of a family, & especially between mother & daughter, strikes an observer of another class as the strangest of phenomena. . . . I am persuaded that it goes far to explain the misdoings of

---

[2] Alfred Mellon (1820–67), violinist and musician of the theatre.

lower class girls. . . . Marion did not know what to do: couldn't pay her rent nor get work: wanted to keep from going on the streets: *must* do something to get out of this wretchedness. I gave her the addresses of some of the 'Homes', which she gratefully accepted.[3]. . .

Thursday, 12 January . . . Office 10 to 5. . . . Dined, & home till 8. Then to my Latin class—first day of new term: 12 or 15 men, not bad now that we have advanced into Caesar . . .

Saturday, 14 January . . . Came home till 7.30 and then went to the Gurgoyle supper at Coates's rooms, 6, Gray's Inn Square . . . we ranged ourselves round the comfortable room . . . and the stories began. . . . I produced some verses in the Locksley Hall metre on the Gurgs & the Gurgoyle glories, which were most favourably received; though it was a humiliating discovery, to be told that I had 'surpassed myself' in writing them. After this, supper appeared, at 9.30: which being despatched and cleared away, we settled down again in a ring round the fire, the bowls of punch & 'Cardinal' were placed steaming on the table, the glasses were filled & the pipes relighted, and each man as best he might took up his parable in song. . . . On the whole, a not unfavourable specimen of Templars' orgies in the Victorian age . . .

The next entry is the sort of passage—perhaps less suggestive than others—that Munby excised from his diary at a time when he was worried lest written evidence of his love for Hannah Cullwick should exist. We owe its survival to sentiment. It was an episode that had touched him particularly; 'I have not the heart to destroy these two leaves, even now,' Munby wrote in 1882; in fact, he inked in the name Hannah over one of the pseudonyms that he habitually used for her in these early diaries—in this case Juno, other aliases being Una and Reine.

Monday, 16 January.   Fine & cold. Office 10 to 5. Dined, and then my craving drove me up to Kilburn. I rang the bell; it was answered by my Hannah, radiant in clean cap & apron and dark frock; for she had been waiting at table. Then came a little flutter of surprise & joy: and as her master & mistress & fellow servant were, so it happened, all going out, she asked me in, and like Policeman X, I followed her into the kitchen: content to be a kitchen visitor at a house where I would not condescend to appear in the drawing room. So do we cheat ourselves into the appearance of humility! In the capacity too of a servant's 'follower', I begin to take a new view of the question of kitchen courtships—the hardship, both to the servant and her sweetheart, of compelling an honourable love into deceit and darkness. In my case of course, frankness is hopeless; her

---

[3] See 9 November, 1860.

credit and my own pride keep me away: but tonight, how could the poor girl see any harm in receiving me into her kitchen, if I would condescend to come there? She, poor darling, knew her place too well to sit down in my presence, save on a little stool at my feet: and as we sat there by the warm homely hearth, I on a kitchen chair & leaning on the deal table hacked with many choppers, she on that little stool beside me, with her cottage bonnet on, and her mistress's baby (for she had to turn nurse for once) lying in its nightgown across her lap, and she looking down on it or looking up at me, smiling, and blushing to be kissed—as we sat thus, what did I think & feel? N'importe! Perhaps of that picture of Lee of John's,[4] inventor of the stocking loom; perhaps (for the crickets & the kitchen clock were the only sounds) of John Peerybingle & Dot:[5] perhaps I wished that baby were mine, and she its married mother: perhaps I just enjoyed the homely loving picturesqueness of the scene, and thought it better not to think at all. And so we sat till nearly ten; and then I kissed her face once more, and she whispered 'Goodnight, dearest Master!' and I came away, and thoughtful home at 11.

Monday, 6 February ... I have hitherto been in the Estates Dept. of the E.C. Office: in which schemes for the rearrangement of Church property are prepared, and all manner of applications to the Commissioners as landlords & patrons are dealt with. The schemes appear to be fair enough, though the E.C. always bag a large share on all capitular sales: as to the rest, their contributions to parochial wants are, as far as I can judge, niggardly—seldom exceeding five pounds; and various rules apparently arbitrary exist, e.g. as to never subscribing to clothing clubs. . . . A most complex system of registration and management has grown up also in the Office, inversely proportioned to its age: 'forms' for everything, accurate queries and setting forth of facts: very judicious doubtless, but highly exasperating to the applicant, who cant get his chancel rebuilt for want of a straightforward answer.

Today however I have gone into the Augmentation Department, where there is a pressure of work. Here are received and answered all applications from clergymen for increase of poor livings and building of parsonages. The work apparently is less formal and systematic, being strained down (or up) to the level of the unpractical parsonic mind: sad enough in its revelations of clerical straits. . . .

Wednesday, 8 February. Fine and cold. Office 10.15 to 5.33. More disappointed parsons, writing humbly for help year after year, passing away unbeknown, and leaving the hopeless task of appeal to one successor after another: sending pathetic statements, with much quite unofficial talk about 'Divine

---

[4] William Lee graduated B.A. from St. John's College, Cambridge, in 1583 and invented the stocking-frame in 1589.
[5] The married couple in Dickens's *The Cricket on the Hearth* (1846).

blessing', 'neglected poor', and the like, to Commissioners who will never see them . . .

In the years 1859–60 the volunteer movement was established on a practical footing in many parts of the country. For twenty years there had been periodic scares over the possibility of a French invasion. Public distrust of Napoleon III's intentions reached a climax with the publication in 1859 of Tennyson's poem 'Riflemen Form!'—the agitation having been fed by innumerable jingoistic verses from Martin Tupper. As a result, official permission was given for the formation of groups of riflemen and artillerymen. The movement advanced rapidly during 1860; Munby, though not himself eager to get into uniform, approvingly recorded its progress; the corps of the Working Men's College, incorporated in the 19th Middlesex, flourished exceedingly, and Munby wrote a poem, 'Invicta: A Song of 1860', for the College magazine.

Friday, 10 February . . . went by [Walter] Severn's invitation to the Argyll Rooms, where was a meeting of the newly formed 'Artists' Rifle Corps. It was a picturesque scene: Phillips, manly with great black beard, in the chair, behind a long table of rough deal; near him several tall handsome fellows—Cockerell, Stirling, Leighton—broadshouldered, goldenbearded, in the newly chosen uniform of the corps; a frenchgrey loose tunic, foraging cap, & trousers, without facings; & belts & gaiters of unblacked leather. Behind sat Woolner with his shaggy brown beard & round bright eyes; Dickinson, Luard, Barwell, & Millais, leaning back in sublime repose, striving to appear unconscious of his own greatness. His features are well cut, symmetrical, and very handsome; but his face wants manliness—it seemed to me weak and selfconscious; a Narcissus face, with the bloom of youth already supplanted by the blueness of a shaven chin.[6]. . .

Monday, 13 February . . . at seven to Maurice's, 5 Russell Square, to the W.M. Council Meeting. Found Maurice, Ludlow, Hughes, Westlake, Furnivall and several others at tea. We discussed the Committee's Report on Examinations;

[6] Munby's unfavourable first impression of (Sir) John Everett Millais (1829–96) was to be modified but not entirely effaced. Perhaps his marriage in 1855 to Effie Ruskin, after Ruskin's divorce, still disturbed Munby. The other figures at the meeting may be identified as Henry Wyndham Phillips (1820–68), portrait-painter; Frederick Pepys Cockerell (1833–78), architect; William Stirling (later Stirling-Maxwell) (1818–78), art-historian, whom Munby had noted at the Cosmopolitan Club in 1859; Frederic (later Lord) Leighton (1830–96), painter and P.R.A.; Thomas Woolner (1825–92), sculptor, poet, and Pre-Raphaelite; Lowes Dickinson (1819–1908), portrait-painter and a founder of the Working Men's College; John Dalbiac Luard (1830–60), subject painter; and Frederick Bacon Barwell, genre and landscape painter, a close friend of Millais.

and Maurice read a letter from the Rev. H. Chester, urging our union with the Society of Arts—Discussion thereon postponed.[7] I walked home at nine, dressed, and to a musical party at Miss Warren's 14 Harley St.... Walked home about one: bitterly cold night. In the Haymarket was a youngish woman, quite drunk: it was pleasant to see the interest which the group of prostitutes around took in her—one offering to subscribe for a cab to send her home in, which the police wouldn't allow, another picking up her shawl & running after them with it; all pitying her, yet showing a feminine disgust at her drunkenness.

Tuesday, 14 February ... Office 10.20 to 5.24. Letter came in containing curious account of a marshy place called Canvey Island, on the Thames between Tilbury & Southend: originally a *Dutch Settlement*, but of late the inhabitants petitioned to have their Dutch chapel converted into a church. Query, what the history of this Dutch settlement? The last curate, with some £40 a year, died there from want of means to buy necessary food and stimulants! But so many sad cases of clerical hardship come before me, that I have begun a book to record the worst of them. And ever one 'has the honour to state' that nothing can be done! After hours I walked down the Mall and up Constitution Hill. Met the gangs of dust-women returning from Paddington, and had a specimen of their manners. Two respectable workmen were passing a group of these women along with me. Two or three of the group were fine big women, and one, a broadshouldered creature in a thick brown great coat, carrying a sack of perquisites—odds & ends from the dustheap—on her back. One of the workmen, pointing to her, said to his fellow 'What a strong woman that is!' And indeed she was taller than he, and broader in the back. The women however, taking this for 'chaff', felt aggrieved: and the whole gang set up a volley of hard names, hisses, and horse laughter against the two workmen. These did their best to reply, and shouted and hissed at the women in a strain of good-humoured contempt: but their feeble assaults were quite overpowered by the big voices and huge laughter of the gentler sex. The shouts of the women pursued them down the streets of Westminster, but at length merged in cries for beer—a tacit confession of their own inferiority. As they parted at the corner of two streets, 'I say', shouted a grimy girl of nineteen, standing in the middle of the street.... 'I say, stand us a pot now! We're precious dry after our day's work.' But the men refused with scornful laughter, & left their female antagonists hallowing after them in vain. Looking on at such scenes, one ought of course to feel properly shocked at the rudeness of the two workmen, and saddened at the coarseness & vulgarity of the dustwomen. ...

[7] Frederick Denison Maurice was the revered leader of the Working Men's College, and Tom Hughes and Dr. F. J. Furnivall were both active and forceful extroverts of marked individuality. J. M. F. Ludlow (1821–1911), modest but practical, was the real founder of the Christian Socialist movement and a figure of influence in the College next to Maurice himself. John Westlake (1828–1913), a Trinity contemporary of Munby, who thought him a considerable bore, was an eminent international lawyer. Harry Chester had pioneered the examinations of the Society of Arts, but his proposed amalgamation did not happen.

But what struck *me* most, was the piquancy of contrast between such manners and those of the civilized classes. . . .

Monday, 20 February . . . to the Council Meeting at Maurice's. A very full meeting: we discussed and settled the Examination rules for the College, and Hughes brought on for consideration the Rifle Corps, now some 230 strong—so large as almost to swamp the College. Martineau,[8] a very tall handsome fellow, moved a scheme for keeping it within bounds. Westlake, that oracular mummy of a man, Ludlow & Litchfield, chief speakers on the other matters . . .

Tuesday, 21 February . . . the other day at the Pearsons, Julius mentioned a Mr Lock, a tradesman (music seller) at Tooting, whose maidservant was actually the daughter of a clergyman! Being anxious to do something in such a scandalous case, I took the omnibus at 5.30 today for Tooting, to see if it were true. After a cold ride of an hour I found out the shop, saw Mrs Lock (herself considerably reduced in the world, being in fact a *lady* who married beneath her) and found to my relief that the 'clergyman' was only a dissenting preacher. Service however is rather a degradation even to the daughter of such a man; but the girl had married a workman, & was comfortably settled. Waiting for the return omnibus, I discovered some pretty Gothic schools, new, on the green . . .

Friday, 24 February . . . Office 10.7 to 5.37. Another very sad case: a clergyman in Wales, with eight children and a sick wife; obliged to mortgage his effects to pay his Christmas bills; his daughter apprenticed to a dressmaker! Afterwards, I walked up to the Female Employment Society in Langham Place about this, but without much present result . . .

Wednesday, 29 February . . . Came a note from Hannah, asking me to go and see her, her mistress being out and she all alone. I went up . . . and sat with her till after nine in her kitchen, she on her stool at my feet. I found her dirty and unkempt, as she had been all day, she said; and the poor child evidently thought I liked to see her so. I made her wash herself at the sink—her only toilette place!— and stood by, among an entourage of foul pots and pans, which it is her work to clean. Most sad, to see her wearing out her youth in such sordid drudgery, her only haunts the kitchen the scullery the coal-cellar! She unconsciously increased this sadness in me, by bringing out a portrait of herself, taken five years ago, and looking all tenderness & refinement. Then, if I had had the means, she might have passed into a drawingroom at once: now, it is too late. I looked at the portrait and then at her, and seemed for the first time to see the change that five years of exposure and menial work have made in her: five years of scrubbing & cleaning, of sun & wind out of doors and kitchen fires within. And she was pleased with the change—*pleased* that she is now 'so much rougher and coarser'

---

[8] John Martineau, pupil and friend of Charles Kingsley.

—because it pleases me, she thinks. Truly, every smear and stain of coarseness on her poor neglected face comes of love. And now, it is high time that all this discipline should cease: but I have no means of ending it! To be a smart parlour maid even, or a lady's maid, are distinctions far above her reach: she would smile incredulous, if I proposed them. Che sera, sera.

I got home about ten. Found one of Miss Severn's charming notes, so sincere and yet so flattering: about a lady who wishes to meet me and knows my unhappy book by heart, and about what she herself thinks of that book. Had any human being, much more any clever imaginative person like her, felt and said the half of this seven years ago, how different might my life have been!

This exposes Munby's chronic dilemma. Having gone out of his way to admire and encourage Hannah as a hard rough worker, he is beginning to realise that she had taken his exhortations only too literally. She was working like a slave to please him. Even on her visits to Munby in the Temple she came as a servant as much as a lover. Munby now reluctantly understood that his parallel aim of elevating and educating Hannah had somehow gone awry. His painful situation is underlined in the final paragraph; for he sees that Mary Severn, with her open appreciation of his talents and of his 'unhappy book', *Benoni*, is the sort of attractive, gifted girl whom he might have hoped to marry—could perhaps still marry, if he renounced Hannah's devotion. Indeed, by harking back seven years to 1853, Munby seems almost to be saying that he wished he had met Miss Severn before he had met Hannah.

But the diary, endlessly reflecting changing moods, makes more cheerful reading after Hannah's next visit to Munby's chambers, on the following Sunday, 4 March, when he 'read to her simple bits out of Kingsley and Allingham, which she seemed to enjoy'. Munby adds: 'One wishes, of course (if love & intellectual friendship *could* co-exist), for the electric sympathy of an equal mind: but it is much that a maidservant should care for such things at all. Moreover, her notion of love is *doing* things: a useful, practical notion! "You see" she triumphantly exclaimed, after some new service—"I can do *everything* for you!" Surely a most pure unselfish triumph!' Perhaps things were not so bad after all, Munby may have reflected, as he lay back in his arm-chair having his feet washed.

Thursday, 1 March . . . The father and mother's wedding day: thirty three years. Would that they, or rather he, were happier! Fortunatus nimium, sua si bona nôrit.[9]

9 'Only too happy, did he but know his happiness.' Virgil: *Georgics*.

Tuesday, 6 March . . . After posting a letter at Charing Cross, I bought a copy of the 'Standard' of a sharp dirtyfaced little girl who plies there among the boys, selling, as they do, the penny papers, running with her freight after the omnibuses, or calling 'Star!' 'Telegraph!' from the kerb stone. The creature is a perfect 'gamin', and carries off the trade from her male companions—rivals rather—by her superior quickness. With her bundle of papers under her arm, she rapidly counted out the halfpence into my hand, and then, saying 'Thankyer Sir', she did not curtsy, but 'touched her hat' smartly and made a leg, as the street boys do. What manner of woman will grow out of such a child? A coarse one, but not necessarily a vicious, I think. I walked down the Mall, and so to Eccleston Square, and dined tête à tête with the Severns: Mr and Miss & Arthur,[1] Walter dining out. . . . At and after dinner much bright animated talk about art and poetry, made pleasanter by Miss Severn's charming enthusiasm and her modest naive expression of it . . .

Friday, 9 March . . . Looking in at the window of a print shop in Bedford Street, over the heads of three dirty little street boys, who were gazing at the pictures, I heard them discourse thus concerning the 'object they had in view'. It was a print representing a Spanish peasant family at their cottage door—an old priest blessing the little children of the house. 'What is it?' asked one of the boys. 'Why, don't you know?' replied the biggest of the three, 'it's Jesus Christ to be sure, a blessing of the little children, which they brought 'em to Him, and "of such is the Kingdom of Heaven", that's what he said.' 'But what did He do to 'em?' persisted the first boy. '*I* don't know' said the other 'but I know *He burns 'em when they're wicked*!'

What an affecting commentary upon the Protestant teaching of the period! They did know something about the *facts* of the New Testament, however.

Saturday, 10 March . . . to the 'Ramblers', a small club of literary men who meet at the Mitre. . . . Scoble[2] told me many things about America. . . . Vulgarity and affectation are he says universal. . . . A race of mincing puling ill-favoured women, fed on pumpkin pies and reared in heated rooms: not a native woman in the land who can show the bright healthy complexion of an English lady, or the strong helpful roughness of an English peasant girl. What will the children of such mothers be? Scoble added that, the insecurity of life & property, and the amount of crime & bold immorality of speech & act, in their large towns, is incredible. . . .

So hopeless is nobleness of character and a lofty national life, among a people who have never learnt humility and obedience, nor to reverence some central

---

[1] Arthur Severn (1842–1931), Joseph's youngest son, another talented artist. Married Ruskin's cousin and tended Ruskin in his later illnesses, as his father tended Keats.

[2] Perhaps Andrew Richard Scoble (1831–1916), whose father came from Canada: a barrister of Lincolns Inn, later K.C., K.C.S.I., and Privy Counsellor.

majesty, whether it be Law or Law-giver—whether it spring from themselves or not. So possible it is, for a nation to go on increasing in wealth & numbers, while all virtues are oozing out of it, till nothing is left but greed & procreative power. Which of our English politicians perceives these truths? The debasement of the English Character in America, and the probable influence for evil of America upon England, will soon be among the most serious questions of the time.

Sunday, 11 March . . . This is not a Diary of moods and 'experiences': else I might say much of the wretchedness & selfdespair I have gone through this week—and all, or chiefly, because of some law business I have had in hand! The practice, though not the grand general principles, of Law is most hateful to me, from natural inaptness & from the miserable associations of home. Perplexed among its dry hideous subtleties, ever afraid to bring one's little knowledge to bear, for fear of some unsuspected trap which nothing can evade—one feels degraded by this, and by the hypocrisy one has to maintain: from which my only refuge lies in my poor £120 at the Office, and in the far-off possibilities of literature.

Monday, 12 March . . . met my Juno[3] at the Haymarket Theatre, to see Tom Taylor's ingenious & spirited piece, the 'Overland Route'. We went to the gallery, of course: Hannah has never been to any other part of a theatre, except once, when 'William the groom' took her with an order to the boxes—actually the *boxes*! at 'Astley's'. Poor child! she did not presume to recognize me in the street, but waited alone in the crowd. As for me, to stand in the mob at the gallery door in the Haymarket, to sit in the gallery among the 'roughs' by the side of a maid of all work, & drink with her out of the same bottle between the acts—is not this the very nadir of vulgarity & degradation?

Is *this* the companion and the sphere I have chosen for myself? Ah, if she were native to the sphere, I should not be near her or it. Self analysis helps one here also: looking over the rail, down upon my equals in the stalls and boxes, I am sensible of a feeling of placid halfcontemptuous indifference: but how if they were to look up and see me thus? Should I feel ashamed, worthy of *their* contempt? I think not: yet if not, would it not be only because I know that she is worthy to be one of them? And so we get back to class distinctions: I love her, then, because she is *not* like her own class after all, but like mine! But this is too large to dwell on here. I perceive that at these times my first temptation is, to think myself a hero. One thinks, 'what condescension this is of me, to come here with her!' One is buoyed up with a comfortable sense of superiority to those around: one says to oneself 'how noble, how romantic, for a man of your &c to stoop to such a creature & her ways!' Oh base and selfish thoughts! But below them, I am thankful to believe, lies much of love & of selfsacrifice; much of pure delight in her artless tender simplicity. Certainly, my chief pleasure all the while

[3] Hannah.

5. Joseph and Caroline Munby, parents of A. J. Munby, c. 1860–65

4. Clifton Holme, near York: the Munby family home

7. Hannah Cullwick, aged 20, in her Sunday dress, when a kitchen-maid at Pitchford near Shrewsbury

6. A. J. Munby with his younger brother, Joseph Edwin, probably at Cambridge in 1858

was to listen to her childlike questions, to watch her kindling face, to mark all her little sayings & exclamations of delight—so naive & unconsciously refined, so different both from the languid constrained whispers of the boxes and from the boisterous vulgar utterance of the women around us. She told me, in her simple way, of the 'odd things' an elderly gentleman had said to her in the omnibus as she came. He looked hard at her, asked her some indifferent questions, and then said bluntly 'I suppose you are very low?' (He could see her bare hands, poor thing, & her common clothes!) 'Yes Sir' she answered meekly, unwounded by the words, 'I am a maid of all work.' 'Ah, I thought so' said he 'but you have better blood in you than you know of.' She stared, scarce understanding, and he went on 'I can see by your profile that you have good blood in you. Has nobody belonging to you ever been better off than you are?' 'No Sir' she answered 'I never knew of anything but what I am.' 'H'm—perhaps', said the old gentleman; 'but that profile doesn't belong to your class in life—you have blood in you, I tell you!'. . . It was good to hear the wondering blushing way in which she told me of these 'strange sayings'—afraid that I should think them such nonsense!

Well, I don't care to find ancestors for *her*, nor to love a kitchenmaid because she is *not* a kitchenmaid: yet it makes one glad to think of this little story; glad and sorry—that being what she is, she should have a 'sweetheart' like me, who is yet so helpless to raise her above the kitchen . . .

Wednesday, 14 March . . . Office 10.12 to 5.55. Great excitement there, the Commissioners having at length discussed the Treasury scheme for the revision of places and raising of salaries: which they passed, but with such curtailments & alterations as to disgust everybody. Loud complaints of the 'impracticability' of the Bishops: the old feud of laymen & ecclesiastics. As for me, I abjure hope & stifle expectation, and thinking of a curate's salary, can scarcely grumble at mine. The Archbishop of Canterbury[4] came into my room—a mild patriarchal old man, whom one cannot look at without affection and respect. The Bishop of Oxford[5] was with him—but his appearance is not prepossessing. . . .

Saturday, 17 March . . . Went into Evans's[6] on my way home & supped there, in a hubbub of nigger howlings, such as are in vogue in these times. I went, not so much for the supper, however, as to try and dispose of a song of mine, 'My Mother-in-law'. In this I was of course unsuccessful; but it gave me an opportunity of observing a kind of man whom one chiefly knows through Thackeray. The comic singer, to whom I addressed myself, read through the song in a businesslike manner, praised it, but remarked that he was 'full of matter' for the next two months, and added, apologising for his professional language, that the

---

[4] John Bird Sumner (1780–1862) had been Archbishop of Canterbury since 1848.

[5] Samuel Wilberforce (1805–73), sometimes known as 'Soapy Sam'. See 23 July, 1873.

[6] 'Evans's Song and Supper Rooms' in King Street, Covent Garden, were then at the height of their fame. Thackeray had already immortalised this all-male preserve as 'The Cave of Harmony' in *The Newcomes*. They closed in 1880.

'tag' was not strong enough. 'You see Sir, said he, I look to have something at the end that I can rely on to raise a laugh: now there's that song of mine "The Temptations of S. Anthony" (I wrote it myself, I generally write my songs); the audience keep looking for a hit, and at the last it comes, & then they burst out, and I make my bow and go off with a round of applause. That's what we chiefly look to—a good tag. And then there's the mildly virtuous style, like that song about Opinions, you heard me sing just now: I take care to put 'em in a good humour at the end, by saying "I hope we shan't quarrel, though we differ in opinion"; and then they feel pleased and applaud, and away I go—don't you see Sir? Oh, we have to consider all these things, I assure you,' said the man, with a grave businesslike civility. So there is a philosophy of comic singing, also . . . so to the parson his sermon, to the painter his picture, to the musician his oratorio, is half 'tag' and business, and only those who know nothing of the machinery can purely enjoy the result. The poet, thank goodness, can scarcely as such be professional. This being so, it would seem better to choose some occupation, such as law for instance, which cannot possibly have any real value or interest. . . . Yet here again one thinks, why waste so much of life on that which is both distasteful in itself, and deadening to those very tastes which we seek to cherish by its aid? . . .

My 'comic' friend suggested that I should apply to certain 'niggers', who had just bowed themselves off the stage through that magnificent portal with the gilded cornices and the twelve-foot mirrors. Accordingly, stooping through a low door and half creeping under the stage, I found a wretched dingy stair, leading to the miserable den into which that gilded portal opened. In this den were two or three men with blackened faces, taking off their shabby nigger costume. The bare floor was littered with old 'properties', and scraps, and slops of beer; and the plaster walls were scrawled over with chalks and smeared with candle smoke. This was the apartment out of which those elegant persons in evening dress had emerged to sing and play. The niggers at once said that they sang only songs of their own making: but they said it most civilly and courteously, and I left them with a feeling of pathetic sympathy that was worth coming for . . .

Sunday, 18 March . . . I called on the Markham Spofforths. Sat and smoked in the little conservatory with Markham, and his wife joined us there. A successful man is he: shrewd & clever, versed in the bustling intrigues of politics and parliamentary committees: to him these things, and the sort of life they imply, are all in all; and they have made him prosperous, a member of an eminent firm, & the trusted agent of the Conservative party. If I had any of the necessary tastes or talents, I could probably obtain from him briefs, and grow to a thriving Parliamentary counsel. But alas! I feel no interest in bribery transactions or Reform and Carlton conflicts, and have no boldness or readiness, to hold my own in struggles for the issue of which I care not a straw . . .

. . . Mrs Markham . . . told an amusing story of Markham's gaucherie, at which he laughed too. She had asked Mrs Crowe[7] the authoress to a tête à tête dinner, & explained to M., who knew nothing of her, about her books &c. He, thinking of business, had heard but not listened: and so at dinner, when his wife reproached him for abusing literary people, since there was one at table, he exclaimed 'Why, Mrs Crowe, you dont mean to say *you* ever wrote anything?' The old lady's look of polite contempt was superb . . .

Sunday, 25 March . . . Walked to S. Paul's Churchyard, and took an omnibus to Brentford. No better place than the box seat of an omnibus for seeing English life on Sunday afternoons—In Fleet St. and the Strand, small tradesmen strolling with wives and children, servant maids with their sweethearts, clerks in gorgeous pairs: westward, 'genteel' people, gentry, 'swells' & ladies, till the tide of fashionable strollers breaks on Hyde Park Corner: then, beyond Knightsbridge and all the way to Brentford, middleclass men & women staring idly over the blinds of their suburban windows, and slinking back when you look that way: lower class ditto ditto standing & staring at their doors, equally idle, but much more frank and at their ease; staring openly & boldly, having purchased rest and tobacco by a good week's work. I walked on from Brentford past the grounds of Sion House. . . . I reached the Borlands' house before 7.30 . . . and to bed at two.

Saturday, 31 March . . . The Oxford and Cambridge boat race came off at 8.30 a.m. today, Putney to Mortlake. I put on the Cambridge colours, & felt a boyish delight in meeting so many light blue rosettes in the Strand, and in hearing that Cambridge had won by two boats' lengths. This is not merely fellow feeling & esprit de corps: it is the pathetic joy with which one clings to anything that recalls a younger and lovelier life, now gone for ever.

    I have now seen for three months the working of the Ecclesiastical Commission: and with respect to its relations with the general life of the age, three things have been very fully revealed to me by it. First, the vast and continual increase in the population of the country. Letters from parsons and laymen everywhere speak of it: their parishes have doubled in ten years—new villages or towns are rising, old ones rapidly outgrowing themselves. This occurs first of all in manufacturing & mining districts, next & consequently (for a great increase of wealth is also observable) in the fashionable watering places. But even in quiet rural places, almost every one speaks of an addition of hundreds to his people. Secondly, I see an enormous energy and devotion exhibited for religious purposes all over the country. The amount offered to the E.C. by private individuals during the last twelve months in the form of Benefactions to the Church, is £225,000! Every where churches, schools, parsonages, are building. . . . New districts too are assigned, new clergy set agoing; struggles made in all quarters to keep pace with the growth of the nation . . .

---

[7] Mrs Catherine Crowe (1800?–76), novelist and writer on the supernatural, who translated Justinus Kerner's *Seeress of Prevorst*.

Thirdly, I see more clearly than before the great amount of sorrow and distress among the clergy. *Their* incomes have not risen along with the others, but their obligations have. . . . Reading their pathetic letters, one fancies how the struggling father of a family sat in his bare room writing his painful appeal to the Commissioners—fancying, poor man, that they were men, and not, ipso facto, machines—how he talked it over with his weakly wife; how they waited weeks and months in hope and fear; and then when the answer goes, one fancies —nay sees—the weary disappointment of a whole family, if it be unfavourable; the joy the gratitude the mutual embraces, if it brings the news of £10 or £15 a year . . .

Wednesday, 4 April . . . Walked to the Bank of England soon after nine, and got my cheque cashed.[8] . . . It was too early for the City men, and too late for the work girls—who, elegant welldrest young persons, were kneeling within the plateglass windows arranging their wares. . . . I came home, paid my rent for the first time out of my own earnings, & went on again. Office 10.22 to 6.28—The last day before the Easter holidays. . . . Coming homewards, I observed my name in print at a shop door, and found they had inserted my 'Après' in 'Once a Week'. . . .

Munby spent the Easter week-end at Gillingham, where his delicate friend Cuyler Anderson was now a curate. He read the new novel *The Mill on the Floss* and made long solitary walks in the neighbourhood. He returned to London to find conversation divided between Tom Sayers's fight with the American John C. Heenan and the ever-increasing mania for the Volunteer movement. Ralston was looking 'very well and martial' in the scarlet uniform of the Volunteer Guards; another friend offered to propose Munby as a member of the Victoria Rifles; but Munby's 'patriotic, picturesque or vain fancies' were overwhelmed by the 'irritation, depression, and shrinking' that he felt 'on committing myself to act with other men'. He called this 'an unfortunate idiosyncracy—but I can't help it'. His father came up to town unexpectedly (23 April), and sent in a note to him at the office, saying 'Forty years today since I met your Mamma'. 'So deep & vivid are such sacred memories in the hearts of those who seem only cold grave men of business,' commented Munby.

Wednesday, 25 April . . . Walked up to Hyde Park. . . . The South Middlesex Volunteers were to be inspected by Lord de Grey—or rather by Col. Mac-Murdo—on the site of the old Crystal Palace, one of the dearest and most sacred spots in this neighbourhood to me. The ground was kept by the Civil Service Corps, and was surrounded by large crowds of welldressed people, including

[8] His first quarter's salary from the Ecclesiastical Commissioners (£30.)

many volunteers of other Middlesex regiments. At one time I stood in the throng near to Thackeray,[9] and spent some minutes in studying him. His face at first sight looks cold and bitter, as his works do: but in it, as in them, there comes out as you read such tenderness and grave sad pity! It is a noble face. The regiment went through its movements on the whole extremely well, and did not leave the ground till eight. As it marched off headed by its band, the Civil Service formed and marched off too, to the drums and fifes of the Fusiliers. I saw Tom Taylor energetic at the head of the corps . . .

Thursday, 26 April . . . with Litchfield and Vernon L. to Macmillan's. . . . Tennyson[1] was there last Thursday—if one had only known it. He had written his name in capitals on the rim of the big round table. I had much talk with a clever American named Stillman:[2] a tall lean man, with the lanthorn jaws, keen profile, and scanty peaked beard of his nation. Their physiognomy is almost as marked as the Jewish: a remarkable instance of a national character & characteristics formed in less than a century! It was satisfactory to hear the other side, from an opponent full of respect for institutions and manners which one loathes or despises. . . . But he talked politics, which I don't care about, and not social life, which I do. . . .

Tuesday, 1 May . . . One or two Jacks-in-the-Green appeared in Whitehall Place. One a very good one: two clowns, a man or two in laced velvet coats and cocked hats, and a tall stout girl dressed as a shepherdess, dancing to a drum & fifes round the Green . . .

Sunday, 6 May . . . Walked up to Bond Street to see Holman Hunt's 'Christ in the Temple',[3] he having reserved today for the Working Men's College, of whom there were many present. As for the picture, I cannot trust myself to speak of it, writing hurriedly; it is unique, and simply wonderful . . . one should sit before it in quiet, and for hours. . . .

Date uncertain owing to excisions, probably Friday, 11 May: a ball in Inverness Terrace . . . Walking up the noble street as I arrived, a kitchenwench was washing dishes in the scullery under the hall steps of a house, within a few doors of where the sumptuous young ladies, my future partners, were disembarking from

[9] William Makepeace Thackeray (1811–63), the novelist.
[1] Alfred, later Lord Tennyson (1809–92), appointed Poet Laureate in 1850, had been worshipped from a distance by Munby since the publication of *In Memoriam* in that year.
[2] William James Stillman (1828–1901), landscape painter, journalist, art critic, and diplomat; friend of Ruskin and Rossetti; settled in England *c.* 1870, and later became *The Times* correspondent in Rome; died in Surrey.
[3] 'The Finding of the Saviour in the Temple' had been bought by Gambart, the dealer, for 5500 guineas. It is now in the Birmingham Art Gallery. William Holman Hunt (1827–1910) had been one of the founders of the Pre-Raphaelite Brotherhood.

their carriages at the Prichards'. I stopped to look at her and them, and speculate on the probable results and values of the two methods of training. Again, as I left to walk home at 2.30, when it was still dark, I saw before me a woman dressed like a coster girl, with a large empty basket on her arm, striding heavily along. . . . I asked why she was out so late—she answered respectfully—To her it was not late, but early: she had had her night's rest already; had gone to bed at half past six, and got up at two; and was now walking in from Shepherd's Bush, a mile beyond, to Farringdon Market, to buy watercresses—She would then walk back, be at home between 6 & 7, have some breakfast (she had had no food as yet) and go out to sell her cresses from house to house. . . . She could not understand that a party—'parting' she called it—should be so late: could scarcely believe that my night's rest was yet to come, any more than I could that hers was already over. . . . And could any difference be greater, than between this girl & the girls I had just left in the ballroom? But her companionship in its way was as interesting as theirs. . . . It was broad daylight when I left her, nearly half past three; and the orange girls were all trudging to Covent Garden with their baskets, to buy their stock of fruit for the day. The baskets were thrown in a heap under the piazza; 'this is Kitty's basket, and that's Mary's, and that's mine'; and one girl sat on her haunches, watching them, while the others went off to bargain. To bed about 4.

Tuesday, 15 May . . . Went up to Mudie's, and coming back, turned into S. Martin's Hall to see and hear John Bright,[4] who was to speak at an 'Indignation Meeting' against the House of Lords, about the paper duty. . . . J. B. a stout burly man with massive English face: spoke very fluently, and with much heartiness & zeal, but rose scarce at all into eloquence. The enthusiasm of the audience for him was tremendous: I sat and read my book quietly, and enjoyed with much private laughter the vehement delight of my republican friends—respectable welldressed clerks and artizans—all round me, who sprang to their feet & hurrayed for J. B. whenever he said anything against anybody . . . there is a strong element of humour, and of brotherly fellowship too, in the thought that all these people are frantic with excitement about something for which you cannot persuade yourself to care twopence. . . .

Monday, 28 May . . . about eleven I went to see a masquerade of a very singular character at the Victoria Theatre. The ball took place on the stage, the house itself being densely crowded with spectators of the lowest class, many of them young women—orange girls, coster girls, servants, and the like. The masqueraders, whose costumes when they wore any were absurd enough; were of a somewhat better class. I was in a private stage box (price sixpence!) and to me entered two uninteresting young women, rather tawdrily dressed, one of whom,

[4] John Bright (1811–89), orator and statesman, subsequently a member of Gladstone's governments.

though not at all immodest, paid me the most unnecessary & undesired attentions. They were hat trimmers, working for Christy the hatter; earning some 15/ a week: all the linings and braid of hats are made up by women, it appears. They said that most of the young women masquerading were envelopefolders and bootbinders,[5] earning from 15/ to £1 a week: these have the reputation, said the hat trimmers, of being 'fast' and fond of dancing. . . .

Tuesday, 29 May . . . In till near four: then took an omnibus to Kew, and walked alone in the gardens, and especially the quiet wooded parts near the river. I heard the cuckoo and the song birds: the rhododendrons were coming into flower, the chestnuts were full of their saffron-white bloom: there were breadths of spring grass, with nests of hyacinths about the roots of the elms; and there were the large matronly curves of the beeches, smooth boles of lichenclouded grey. Alas, it is not good to be here: for, walking among them, the old transports of love & joy, the old imaginative triumphs, come feebly back again; and I think what might have been—what might be even now—had I been allowed to be, in my humble way, a poet, and live among such things. . . .

Thursday, 31 May . . . Passing through Kensington on Tuesday, I saw a man of all others worth seeing—Sir John Lawrence.[6] He was riding down the street alone—without even a groom: and no one knew or noticed him. A large loosely made man; sitting grave and quiet on his horse; with sallow wrinkled face and grizzly moustache: riding along, an unappreciated king of men, with such keen eyes and such a stern solemn face! All one's memories of 1857 were revived by the sight of him.

And he all unnoticed, and still a commoner, while Vernon Smith[7] is a peer! But idiots are proverbially the favourites of fortune.

In June, Munby suffered the 'humiliation', duly lamented in his diary, of having to take an examination to qualify for the Civil Service—this being in itself a concession, as he was over the prescribed age. ('In the afternoon, had "English Composition"!' he records with pathos on one of the examination days.) But he passed well, and was commended for 'marked proficiency in all the prescribed subjects'. His parents came up to town for a week, staying in rooms in Jermyn Street; they were, Munby thought, 'the most distinguished looking people' at 'the Ellises' ball at Clapham'; but his mother told him that his brother Fred had 'requested of the father permission to marry Miss Latimer the governess!'—a

[5] Thus in MS.

[6] John Laird Mair Lawrence (1811–79), the 'saviour of India' and hero of Delhi, 1857. He was to become Viceroy of India, 1863–9, and to be raised to the peerage in 1869.

[7] Robert Vernon Smith (1800–73), Sydney Smith's nephew, was President of the Board of Control, 1855–8, and had been created Baron Lyveden in 1859.

poignant proposal certainly, yet a far more acceptable alliance than his own secret romance with Hannah, which Munby had always realised would horrify 'the father'. (Fred married Elizabeth Jane Latimer two years later.)

Sunday, 10 June . . . I breakfasted with Litchfield, where were Stokes & Ormsby and Furnivall, and Brett[8] the painter of the charming Val d'Aosta and the still better 'Hedger' of this year—A bright-eyed modest fellow with a flaxen beard. . . .

Thursday, 14 June . . . I went in to the Haymarket theatre. Just opposite in the stage box were two quiet ladies in black, and a smoothfaced man of forty, looking somewhat like a thriving solicitor. Shades of the Crusaders! it was the Count of Flanders.[9] The Queen was with them, half-hid by a curtain, but laughing consumedly at the farce. The ballet was one of negro life, and the men were properly blackened; but the negresses were all white, & like Swiss peasants. Such is the contemptible vanity of women. . . .

Saturday, 23 June . . . A holiday, this being the Volunteer Review.

At 11.30 the band of the Rifle Brigade began to play in the Temple Gardens, and the Inns of Court Corps dropped in by groups, till the gardens were filled with men in uniform, ladies, and officers of the regulars, listening to the music and all a-stir with excitement of preparation. . . . At 1.15 the bugle sounded to fall in; and I walked on through the crowded Strand to Adelphi Terrace, when the London Scottish and the W.M. College corps were forming. Thence again through the crowd—flags waving, windows filled with people—& along the Mall to the Park: regiments marching into the main street from every quarter, with their bands playing: and so to the enclosure in Hyde Park. . . . I walked all round the vast area, densely crowded on every side, and took up a position at first on the west edge under the trees, on the right of the line; where the cavalry and corps d'élite were. Across the park from every point the regiments converged, marched into the ground, took their places, & piled arms. This, and the march through the streets, was perhaps the most spiritstirring part of the business. The 1st Surrey light cavalry, in scarlet blouses & rifles slung behind, the horse artillery with two field guns, and above all, the Huntingdonshire mounted rifles, in scarlet tunics, buckskins, hessians, black helmets with floating white horsetail plumes: large bearded men, on magnificent horses, riding in at a gallop amidst huge cheering, & looking, in their picturesque novel grandeur, like some relic of the cavalier days. Then came the Artillery Company, the

---

[8] John Brett (1830–1902), a painter attached to the Pre-Raphaelites, and particularly influenced by Ruskin—to the detriment, in the long run, of his artistic development.

[9] Philip, Count of Flanders (1837–1905), son of Queen Victoria's uncle, Leopold I of Belgium. Old for his age, if Munby's evidence is accepted.

Volunteer Guards, the Middlesex Engineers, the foot artillery, the Queen's, the Inns of Court, the Robin Hood Rifles—600 men in Lincoln green—and all the endless line of rifle regiments.

Having piled arms, they stood at ease, strolled in groups, smoked pipes, and snatched some luncheon: and the crowd watched them, quiet & goodhumoured; and all the park to Kensington gardens was black with people gazing. And then the Queen arrived, with cheering and salute, & brilliant surrounding of horsemen in uniform; and the review began, with thunder of captains, and shouting. The marching past took one hour & a half, & seemed endless. . . .

Wednesday, 27 June . . . Office 10.7 to 5.20. At 8, went up to our conversazione at the W.M. College, to which Mr & Miss Severn came as my guests. A large cheerful party. . . . We had a tent for tea in the garden, and sang on the terrace under Litchfield's baton, and afterwards in the large room. Some capital photographs of Maurice Ruskin Hughes & other teachers including my unworthy self, were exhibited. I read Miss Severn some of the best passages out of Ruskin's new volume, and had a good deal of walk & talk with her. . . .

Friday, 29 June . . . I met Stokes in the Strand & Fitzgibbon a friend of his, and walked up with them to Mudie's. S. says that Tennyson is becoming very shaky and feeble in body: can scarce walk. Like Kingsley, he smokes too much. . . .

The publication in 1859 of Darwin's *Origin of Species* had convulsed intellectual and theological England; neither Tennyson's *In Memoriam* nor Tupper's *Proverbial Philosophy* any longer provided, as they had done for many in the Fifties, acceptable reassurance. The British Association's meeting in Oxford this summer was held at the centre of a whirlpool of controversy. In the course of it, Munby paid a Sunday visit to Oxford with R. B. Litchfield that enabled him to write a first-hand report. Here are Temple, the great reforming churchman, who contributed in 1860 to the Broad Church *Essays and Reviews*; the Bishop of Oxford (Wilberforce) who attacked those essays—and challenged Huxley on evolution; Clerk-Maxwell, the outstanding Victorian physicist (a close friend of Litchfield); and Holman Hunt, painter of meticulous religious pictures. A disturbing yet rewarding day.

Sunday, 1 July. Brilliant morning—warm sunny day. Got up at six: Litchfield came to breakfast at half past, and we started soon after seven for the Paddington station. Left there at 7.45, and arrived at Oxford at 9.40. We walked down to All Souls, and found that Godfrey Lushington had gone to breakfast at Merton. . . . I went at eleven to the University sermon, preached by Temple[1] of

---

[1] Frederick Temple (1821-1902), then Headmaster of Rugby, and Archbishop of Canterbury, 1896.

Rugby. S. Mary's was full of dons and savans, for whom the sermon was intended: it being an essay on the old theme—science v. revelation. Eloquent, learned, forcible—yielding much, but not preserving the remainder: confessing the horrid hiatus, and yet flinging across it his airy bridge—which fell, alas how short!

We all walked home to Godfrey's rooms together: G. & Vernon, Maxwell[2] of Trinity (now Professor of Natural Philosophy at Aberdeen), Litchfield, and I. And straightway began a great talk about the sermon and the controversies which had led to such preaching: and Godfrey and L., especially, cried bitterly 'And this is all! We go to hear a great divine, proving before these savans that science and revelation are *not* at war; and we come away misdoubting worse than ever! "Identity of tone and sentiment"—"spiritual struggles"—"promptings of conscience"—will all this do away with the facts of astronomy, geology, and Darwin?' And so the blankness of unbelief grows more hopeless than ever.

Even the proprieties of the [British] Association have been outraged: the Bishop of Oxford coming forward, somewhat imprudently, as the champion of Christianity, and the savans making war on him. Yesterday in a speech before the meeting, the Bishop ended by appealing to Professor Huxley[3] whether he would not rather have for his father a man than an ape: Huxley replies fiercely, that, having to choose between a genuine ape, and a man of abilities who used his talents for purposes of evil, he would prefer the ape! To such straits have we come! It's no use, cry L. and Godfrey—defence is no longer possible—the controversy has been pushed to the last point; and that will soon be given up. Nous verrons: meanwhile, I ask, is it worse than in the days of the Encyclopaedists? Facts indeed look far more alarming now: but spiritual consciousness is more widely awake, the need of a Father much more keenly felt. For me, as I said, let any number of insensate laws and necessary God-excluding developments be proved for nature: the moral world, then, shall for me be cut loose from the physical: even if Love be not Power, I will yet believe in Love: I must & will have a Father in heaven, and a Christ too, if I have even to create them out of old memories and tottering beliefs. In religion, at least, let us be allowed to live through the Imagination, if we can find no stronger aliment.

How saddening this sermon was and all our talk about it, and its subjects, which recurred again & again all day! What grim laughter it provokes, to see, here and at Cambridge, one's friends, fellows of colleges and the like, living in the midst of a system which they fret at & despise and think rotten to the core! Dear, loveable men—wise and thoughtful, full of love and good works, and yet hopeless—in appearance, but not surely in reality, without God in the world.

What would Archbishop Chichely have said to see us, fellows and friends of his college, sitting, under the shadow of S. Mary's and looking on that grey

---

[2] James Clerk-Maxwell (1831–79), former Fellow of Trinity College, Cambridge; discoverer of electro-magnetic radiation.

[3] Thomas Henry Huxley (1825–95), the scientist.

solemn court, and talking not heresy merely but absolute unbelief? Unbelief, not loud and defiant, but reluctant and very sad—yet alas! no better for that. And so the young blood of the universities sets this way: and the old divines cling instinctively to their denunciations, and the younger ones try compromise, and make things worse. Here in Oxford, it is the reaction from 'Puseyism': but, what contempt and scorn it arouses, to see the puritans fighting their petty skirmishes with the high church, when struggles like these are going on! Doubtless, there shall be a dayspring someday: but not yet...

Maxwell showed us an ingenious instrument of his on which he had read a paper, for mixing at pleasure in any combination the colours of the spectrum.[4] About 3.30 we all turned out, and called on Dr. Acland, to get the key of the new Museum,[5] to which we then went. The details of the building are admirable, and especially the flower carvings of the capitals round the arcade, and the woodwork, of plain deal, but pierced with leaf shapes, and so at once made light and beautiful. Munro's statues were there, and Woolner's Bacon—a repulsive but clearly truthful rendering of him,—but only quà man of the world. We all agreed that the least successful thing is the ironwork, elegant as it is: the shafts and arches have nothing for roof but glass, which gives no background and seems to need no support.

From outside, the buildings look very rich and graceful; but they lose in light and shadow and in grandeur, for want of buttresses and projections—one flat wall surface everywhere. We walked on to the Clarendon Press, where lives Mr Combes[6] the manager, a self-raised man of energy, who buys good pictures and means to leave them to the University. With him are staying Holman Hunt and Woolner, who came out to greet us, and took us up into the pleasant drawing-room. Round the walls hang the Light of the World, the Return of the Dove to the Ark (Millais), the Persecution of Christians by the Druids (Hunt), Collins's Nun ... a subject of Rossetti's from the Vita Nuova, and several others. A snug paradise of art round one's own fireside. We talked over the pictures, and then went out into the green pretty courtyard; a large basin of water full of gold fish in the centre, and round it a lawn, & overhanging willows and acacias. Here, on the stone edge of the basin, we all sat down, and lighted pipes, and talked together for an hour in the sunny afternoon. I had a long talk with Holman Hunt, who is a most unaffected, goodnatured, and gentlemanly fellow, about his great

---

[4] Munby later noted: 'This was the beginning of Spectrum Analysis, which has since done such wonders.'

[5] The University Museum in Parks Road, designed by Benjamin Woodward in Ruskinian Gothic, was formally opened in 1860.

[6] Thomas Combe (1797-1872) was Superintendent of the University Press from 1838 until his death, and senior partner in the Oxford Bible Press, 1853-72. The 'Patriarch', as he was called, made so much money out of the Bible business that he could afford to give generously to the Church and to buy important works by the Pre-Raphaelites. According to his wish, his art collection was left to the Ashmolean Museum, Oxford, by his widow, with the exception of 'The Light of the World' which went to Keble College. For a good account of Combe, see *Wolvercote Mill* (1957) by Harry Carter.

picture.[7] The Jews, he told me, were all painted in Palestine, though he did not tell his sitters the subject of the picture: for which reason the figure of the Saviour was finished in London from a Christian boy—a son of Toby Prinsep's, I think—though studied in Judaea. The Virgin, he said, was painted from a Mrs Mocatta, a beautiful Jewess in London. . . .

Friday, 6 July . . . In the evening went to Prince George Galitzin's[8] Russian Concert at S. James's Hall. The Prince, a very tall large man, with black beard and massive face. His conducting is marvellous: *facing* his audience, wielding his stick with a supple quickness and a vigorous staccato movement quite new to us, & meanwhile using his left hand, conspicuous in white glove, as a kind of expression-stop; he ruled and modulated the band and chorus as if they were but one pulse of sound. All the music unknown to me . . . Glinka very fine, and his own things strikingly quaint and original . . .

Monday, 9 July . . . a young woman came behind me and begged for charity in a timid way. She was a beggar to look at, and her face was hidden by a dirty white cloth, tied tightly across it and fastened behind her head under her bonnet; covering all the features but the eyes, and showing by its flat surface that some of them were all but gone. It was Julia Slingsby—a poor girl who was in the hospital with scrofula, & left with all her face inflamed into sores, her lips dried & stiffened, & part of her nose destroyed: nothing could be done. . . . One would think such a life would be intolerable to the vanity and the sensitiveness of any the humblest woman: but in most disfigured girls that I have seen, there is a quiet sadness, & a resigning of themselves to the consciousness of being ugly and abhorred, which is very pathetic. Love of dress too and feminine vanities seem to die out, when the hope of pleasing is for ever gone. This poor Julia would like of all things to wear a mask, and would be so grateful if I could get her one, to hide her face![9] . . .

Sunday, 15 July . . . I went from Waterloo at 10.15 to Guildford, to visit Borland, who has gone there to sketch. . . . walked up the quaint quiet High Street to the White Hart . . . the congregation were leaving the parish church close by; and I watched from the inn steps the militia staff with their band marching down the street with the crowd . . . but amongst the people I saw no pretty faces, no rustic pleasant costumes; always excepting the old men, who came out of church in clean white smocks & gaiters. The same thing was to be noticed everywhere: it was sad to see standing at an old time-honoured cottage door, a grey old peasant in his Sunday smock, with his strong hearty wife beside

[7] 'The Finding of the Saviour in the Temple', which Munby had seen in Bond Street on 6 May.

[8] Prince George Galitzin (1823–72), son of Beethoven's patron, had founded a choir of seventy boys in Moscow, and maintained his own orchestra.

[9] This meeting took place while Munby was returning from Walham Green after calling on his friend F. J. Moore. Munby obtained a mask for the girl and later visited her more than once.

him, in her high cap and old-fashioned russet gown, whilst a couple of pert flimsy girls, in worthless garments of a pseudofashionable kind, stood talking to them, gaudy with ribbons and crinoline. Such a contrast is depressing not from an artistic point of view merely: for what social elevation, what habit of reading writing and gadding about, can make up for the change from those old people with their grave solid self respect and their picturesque and honourable class-costume, to these young ones, all sham from head to foot—ashamed of what they are, yet awkwardly conscious that they are not what they would be? Here as everywhere in such matters, the women are fifty times more evil than the men. It is the dark side, among many blessings, of our railway days; which will ultimately destroy all the refreshing ruggedness, all the valuable folk lore, of our rural dialects, and all the charming differentia—or what little is still left—of our rustic dress & manners. God forbid that one should live to such a time, when all England shall be one dead level of Americanised halfeducated vulgarity! . . .

Tuesday, 24 July . . . Office 10.23 to 5.21. . . . Went to the newsroom, and home 8.45. Found my housekeeper Miss Mitchell and a policeman in anxious talk: my rooms, at 4 p.m., had been broken open and robbed.

It is curious to observe one's own behaviour under such a new sensation. My first impulse was to laugh; and I accompanied the friendly peeler upstairs with a cheerful calmness which was perfectly heroic. The sight of the empty plate basket, cupboard standing open, housekeeper aghast, and real policeman, struck me as really 'good fun'—the realization of a drama which hitherto one had only read of. My loss was only seven spoons, four forks, sugar tongs, a coral pin, and a favourite coat: had it been greater, perhaps I should not have felt so jolly: as it was, I felt a sort of grotesque admiration for the ingenious protestant who wrought the deed of darkness.

I fancy him 'swelling' about in my coat, with my pin in his gorgeous scarf, and the product of my slender plate in his pocket: I feel a magnanimous pity for the wretched miscreant: I will enjoy my triumphs over him, if he is caught: and if not, I know—blessed thought! that he will suffer for his doings in a future world. On the whole therefore, my position is rather pleasant than otherwise, and I entertained a series of intelligent police inspectors during the evening, with a delightful sense of the novelty of the situation.

Presently, however, more serious feelings will come: a consciousness of home security disturbed, and a real anger against the thief . . .

Wednesday, 25 July . . . Came back in the afternoon, but no news (of course) of the thief.

Blackmore[1] met me by appointment at Prince's Gate at five, and drove me out

---

[1] Richard Doddridge Blackmore (1825–1900) had yet to write *Lorna Doone* (1869). He and Munby were old friends, having met when they were both studying for the bar. Owing to ill-health, Blackmore had abandoned his practice as a conveyancer by 1858, and was established as a market-gardener at Gomer House, Teddington.

to Hampton Wick in his dogcart. . . . Mrs B. had dinner ready at seven, and afterwards B. and I walked in the garden and talked of classics & literature, of which a good deal to be said, as I see him so seldom. After tea, prayers, and bedtime, B. and I lighted pipes by the kitchen fire, and he read me his poem on Franklin—much of it very good—and talked over some few translations of Horace and Virgil of mine. To bed after 1.

Saturday, 28 July . . . I went to the newsroom, and up to Porchester Terrace at 7.30 to dine with Markham Spofforth. . . .

The Spofforths' dinner was a snug sestett: Charles Landseer,[2] Edwin Ward R.A.,[3] Goodenough Hayter, a nephew of Sir W. H., and I. Ward is a big gross man, kindly and weakwilled, one would say, but a loud incessant talker: and his conversation not cultivated or brilliant. Landseer is quiet, smug, middle-aged: crossgrained probably, but in talk sensible and rather amusing. He had a good story of his brother Sir Edwin: how that lately, being at the South Kensington Museum, Sir E. stopped before one of his own pictures, and removed a speck from it with his finger. Straightway appeared a peeler. 'What are you a doin of, touching that picture?' says he. 'Why,' says Sir E. mildly, 'you see I've often touched it before.' 'Have you though? replies the peeler: more shame for you then—you come along with me!' and forthwith hands him before the Museum authorities . . .

Saturday, 4 August . . . to Hampstead, to see the local sham fight. Overtook the North Middlesex corps, and walked up with them—band playing, and Crimean sergeantmajor with Victoria Cross and splendid beard leading regimental goat at their head. . . . Lines of carriages, and thousands of people scattered over the wide ground. The combat came off in that large amphitheatre of broken hillocks that looks N.W.—most of the volley firing was very good; and the sight of that green hollow, its breadth of tall ferns interlaced everywhere with waving lines of human faces, and masses of bayonets among the gorse bushes, and wreaths of blue smoke floating above, was very interesting: but far more so, as I stood on the ridge that looks down into the vale of Hendon, was the look of its moist woods and fields, and their ever-varying innumerable green. . . . Surely this London is blessed in its neighbourhoods—Standing here, and, looking down, on one side upon the illimitable city, and on the other upon a land rich with all rural joys, one somehow feels that each explains & justifies the other . . .

The affair was over about 8.30: . . . All the way through London were volunteers—regiments & companies marching home. . . . So it is every day, and specially on Saturdays, in this town and all over the land: and boys do not jeer nor even smile at them now; for it is felt that they have won respect, and have a

---

[2] Charles Landseer, R.A. (1799–1879), historical painter, elder brother of Sir Edwin Landseer, the great animal painter. Keeper of the Royal Academy, 1851–73.
[3] Edward Matthew Ward, R.A. (1816–79), historical painter.

heart of reality in them. So much the cautious Briton, intolerant of humbugs, now confesses concerning this Rifle movement . . .

Munby did not enjoy spending August in London, 'not a single carriage or person of fashionable guise being visible about Pall Mall'. The news of Mary Severn's engagement to Charles Newton was also in a manner depressing. Munby and Miss Severn had got on well; they were both romantic, religious, poetic young people. Charles Newton, by contrast, was classical, exacting, and by no means religious; he was sixteen years older than Mary, but he was handsome, insistent, and made a devoted suitor and husband. Munby had realised that Mary was a rare being, one of the few girls of his own class whom he could have contemplated as a wife. However, his own peculiar temperament and predilections having kept him silent, he was left to make the best of it.

Saturday, 11 August . . . walked to Eccleston Square . . . Miss Severn away in the country. One feels a selfish pang, perhaps, hearing of her engagement to 'Halicarnassus' Newton;[4] though of course I should never have proposed to her: it is only the thought that someone very loveable has given herself wholly to another. However, her society will be still as charming, when she is married . . .

Friday, 17 August . . . In Oxford Street a fashionable prostitute accosted me who once before had begged me to go home with her; & she now explained her importunity by saying 'All my gentlemen have left town, and I really am so hard up—I shall have to give up my lodgings!' 'Then why not go out of town too?' 'I've nowhere to go to!' This, spoken by a girl who though not interesting was elegant & well-dressed, gives one a sad sense of the loneliness of such a life—and a glimpse also of the embarrassment which besets these London butterflies when the season is over. She was a farmer's daughter from near Chesterfield; & came to town, nominally to be a draper's assistant, but really to become of her own accord what she is. N.B. *After nine months*, her family still think she is at the shop.

Sunday, 19 August, was Munby's thirty-second birthday. Hannah came to bring him a birthday cake she had baked. They had recently had a row (unexplained in the diary); but Hannah, says Munby a trifle unctuously, had 'quite regained my confidence; for it was impossible to withhold it long, or to believe that that outbreak was anything else than the expression, in words learnt from a coarse mistress, of a passion which one may well bear with in a creature so loving and so untaught. And does she not pray

---

[4] Charles Newton had identified the site and recovered the chief remains of the mausoleum at Halicarnassus.

every night in her attic, that she may "be a good girl and obey her master?"'

It is not surprising that Hannah, childlike as she still was at twenty-seven, should occasionally have reacted violently against the frustrations of her relationship with Munby—Eliza reacted similarly against Higgins in *Pygmalion*; for Munby was both her 'master' (or 'Massa', as she called him) and her lover. As a master, he was kindly enough, yet insisted on the principle of salvation through hard manual work (i.e. for Hannah; he himself would not have considered cleaning his own boots). As a lover, Munby might have exasperated many women.

Probably Munby, living comfortably as a bachelor on his small income, was not yet sure that he wished to *marry* Hannah—the very idea had shattering implications for a mid-Victorian gentleman of his pretensions; however, he did not doubt that he loved her, as she loved him, nor that she personified the sense of admiring sympathy for working women that was becoming the main motive force of his life. He had given up trying to teach her *everything*; and when on this birthday she sat with him 'making and mending and prattling', and asked 'What was the *Conquest*, Massa?' he was content to draw on his pipe and say 'My dearest, I like you better because you do not know'. But the diary entry for the day is significant: 'let me at least work out some of my theories upon this tender servant: let me be refreshed and comforted by a mother's love, and by that of one so different: let me look on this hardworking simplicity, this humble un-selfish devotion, which finds its highest expression in the doings of a sweep or a lapdog, and feel, unreservedly, what I always meant to prove—that the veriest drudge, such as she is, becomes heroic when she truly loves. I told her she was my blessing—and she is.'

These lines show that Munby still viewed the association as a social experiment as much as a love affair; that attitude never altered; and in both aspects he was sincere. Munby was a romantic, and attractive to women, but the evidence of the diary suggests that his masculine urges were less powerful than the average. His reference to Hannah's as 'a mother's love' reflects his lasting devotion to his own delicate mother. In Jungian terms one might suppose that his 'Anima', or psychic image of the Female, was split. Partly, Munby viewed women as weak creatures requiring chivalrous help (which he tried his utmost to provide); and in this aspect there was apparently little erotic drive. But partly, also, he was drawn to those features in working women that were more male than female—the hard hands and reddened muscular arms obsessed him to the extent, perhaps, of becoming, in analytic terms, a 'fetish'. Munby himself called this his 'hobby'. His interest in trousered, grimy, even disfigured women, suggests the same tendency to 'defeminise' the opposite sex. If there was a latent homosexual trend, it is unlikely that this will have been openly expressed with any of Munby's numerous men friends; more probable that it was diverted towards the tough working women, whom he generally preferred to society beauties.

For Munby, of course, the implications were unconscious; psychological hindsight in no way detracts from his altruism and concern for the unfortunate, based as they were on strict moral and religious principles. One cannot but admire Munby, who despite an acute social consciousness, was ahead of his time in crossing the barriers of sex discrimination and class distinction. But it is not surprising that some of Munby's female acquaintances should have found him a puzzle, while his complex orientation left poor Hannah with a difficult rôle to play. Read in this light, the diary excerpts that follow deepen our understanding.

Tuesday, 21 August . . . by train to the Crystal Palace, to see something of 'the Foresters' Day'. . . . Last year at this time there were 63,000 present, and now it was thought there were still more. This Foresters' anniversary, to which thousands come up from the country, is of all others the scene and the time to see the English working classes. . . . Here I would bring a foreigner, to show him whatever of picturesque or of mirthful is left among us.

. . . I passed a tallish young woman, evidently a servant, who was noticeable for the size of her gloveless hands. She seemed to be alone in the crowd, and (with a view to her hands) I asked her if she meant to dance? No, she couldn't dance at all—only liked to look on: for which I was not sorry. So after a little chat we walked away, and I (still with a view to my hobby) proposed to rest on the bank near, under the trees. She gave me her hand to help her up—and, oh ye ballroom partners, what a breadth of massive flesh it was to grasp! She sat down by me, ready to talk, after the blunt fashion of such maidens, but not forward. . . . She was a maid of all work at Chelsea, it seemed. . . . I looked at her hands, and spoke my opinion of them. 'How can you like them?' she says, like Margaret in the garden; 'they are so large and red, I'm ashamed of them.' 'They are just the hands for a servant,' say I: 'they show you are hardworking, and you ought to be proud of them. You wouldn't wish them to be like a lady's?' 'Yes I should!' said she, bitterly: 'and I should like to be a lady, and I wish my hands were like yours!' And she looked enviously at my hand, which was quite white and small by the side of hers. I could not then understand her vehemence: but remembering the difference between my fist and those small taper ladyhands one sees in drawing rooms, it did seem pathetic that this poor wench should envy my hands, and fancy that if her own were like them, she would have reached a ladylike pitch of refinement. Her right hand lay, a large red lump,

71

upon her light-coloured frock: it was very broad and square & thick—as large and strong & coarse as the hand of a sixfoot bricklayer . . . the skin was rough to the touch, and hard & leathery in the palm: there was nothing feminine about it in form or texture . . . and yet she was only nineteen. . . . I lifted it too—it was quite a weight, heavy and inert. . . . My companion's name, it appeared, was Sarah Goodacre, & she was born at Grantham: father and mother died before she was a year old. Did she know what her father was? 'Yes,' she only said, looking down, and seemingly strangely confused . . . hesitating long, at last she said, looking another way—'He was *Curate to the Vicar of Grantham.*'

I turned to her in amazement: there was nothing suspicious in her stolid face —'Impossible!' I said: 'your father a *clergyman*! You do not know what you are saying.' 'Yes I do', she answered quietly . . .

Sarah Goodacre bounds off to a game of 'Kiss in the Ring'. But Hannah is never long absent from the diary, which now approaches a moment of truth.

Saturday, 1 September . . . Met Hannah in Oxford Street and had several photographs taken of her in working dress and attitudes. With what meakness she submitted to be posed, and handled, and discussed to her face; the coarseness of her hands examined and the best mode of showing them displayed! She came home with me, for the first time to *stay*: a dangerous experiment, which I had much considered, & almost feared. For on Tuesday, in her innocence, she begged me to stay with *her*; 'for then she could get my breakfast and clean my boots in the morning!' and it took some self-control to refuse. And now, when after a quiet evening together, she melted into the full tenderness of artless endearment, I learnt somewhat of physical temptation and of resistance. But *she* never knew what I was learning—I had not miscalculated myself. And when she had gone to rest, under my roof, in a bed that was not mine, I went in & kissed her rosy face as it lay on the white pillow and smiled; and thought, as well one might, that 'God do so to me and more also, if I harm her anywise.' And so, I left her to her virgin sleep.

Sunday, 2 September. At six I was awoke by a kiss: and looking up, a cold thrill of excitement ran through me, to see Una[5] standing over me, unconscious of all harm. But the worst was over; I got up, she lighted the fire and made breakfast, and we walked down to London Bridge. At 8 we started by train to Eastbourne, and arrived there at 10.40. . . . We climbed the cliff, for three miles to the right of the town, and so, after a length of breezy down, found ourselves on the summit of Beachy Head . . . we strolled, & gazed, and sat, and fed, & dozed, and—thought? till evening: would that we could have *talked* too! But there is no other alternative—meditative loneliness, or *intelligent* companionship.

[5] Hannah.

To be alone yet not alone, in the worst sense of the words—who shall say how depressing it is! And yet, how hatefully unjust, how unkind, to the simple creature with you! She is full of mute untaught admiration: she opens her store of sandwiches on the cliff, and thinks she has made you happy. And you *ought* to be happy. Alas, the result is other than happy, is very disheartening, as you walk down to the town with her in the ruddy evening, watching how meek and gentle she is, and yet how hopelessly cut off, in all but heart, from you. Heart: is that all, is it enough? It seemed so, as we came home in the train. . . . We got to London Bridge about 10.30; and as it was so late, she came here for the night again: but 'obsta principiis'[6] had done its work.

Saturday, 8 September . . . Every morning of late, as I pass the end of Cecil Street, I see a group of young well-dressed men, waiting to be enrolled as volunteers to serve under Garibaldi. How one would like to go, to serve under *him*! So, one yearned for India in /57: & meanwhile one's life smoulders & one's youth decays, for want of that money which is freedom of action. In Gordon Square yesterday, I saw an apple woman seated at her stall, reading the Life of Garibaldi . . .

Monday, 10 September . . . About 8 I walked down to Eccleston Square. Found Mr and Miss Severn, Walter, and two Oxford men. . . . Miss S. looked more brighteyed and rosily regally beautiful than ever: was as frank and as earnest too as ever. She actually told me that in writing to her betrothed, she gets from my book expression for her feelings! From another, one would not believe it: being absolutely true from her, it is the more humbling.

It is the first time I have seen her since the engagement: I felt a half selfish pang—not that she was not mine, but rather that Hannah had never been made such as she is. I showed her Hannah's picture, as that of some stranger; 'What a fine face! & how ladylike!' she and her father cried. Yes, poor child: she *is* a maid of all work and a chimney sweep; and she *might have been* like you! . . .

Beginning his month's holiday on 12 September, Munby set out for Cromer to spend a week with his Pearson cousins. Being an agreeable intelligent bachelor, he had no lack of such invitations, and constituted a continuing challenge and source of speculation for the marriageable girls.

At Sheringham on 15 September he arranged a distribution of sweets to the village children, who soon blocked the street. A woman ran out of a cottage to ask Munby to look at her son's bad finger: 'I looked and sympathised, and the mother was quite satisfied. It seems they have a belief, the reverse of the mal' occhio, that the gaze of a stranger, & especially of a gentleman, is a cure for disease.' It was for Munby the perfect assignment.

---

[6] *Principiis obsta* (Resist beginnings), Ovid.

73

At Sheringham Hall Lord Suffield was to be seen watching a cricket match 'in a suit of black velvet, with buff leggings: Velasquez-like'. On 18 September Munby moved on to Thursford Hall, East Dereham, to stay with a Trinity friend, Scott-Chad.[7] He then travelled across England to his friend James at Cheltenham, where he met Sydney Dobell (1824–1874), the poet of the 'Spasmodic School'. Delicate, nervous, hyper-sensitive, idealistic, intensely and singularly religious, Dobell had something in common with Munby but had already made a reputation as a poet, which Munby despaired of doing. Like Munby, Dobell thought deeply about women—especially on the contrast between womanly simplicity and the emancipated 'strong-minded' woman. In financial and domestic circumstances, Dobell was better placed than Munby; he was a competent manager of his father's wine business, and had been happily married to Emily Fordham since he was twenty.

In 1860 Dobell was living at Cleeve Tower, a bracing but bleak little house on the hillside of Cleeve Cloud, near Cheltenham, rich in ancient remains, some of which he had attempted to excavate.

Monday, 24 September . . . walked up the Winchcombe Road, and up the wooded lane . . . among the trees is a modern Gothic tower, and a high embattled wall lining the lane, and an arched gateway in the wall, giving entrance apparently to a quasi-baronial mansion: but within is simply a kitchen, two miniature sitting rooms, a spiral staircase in the tower, and a kennel and garden-house on the second side of a half square. The house being only one room deep, all these open like cages upon a little square lawn, a terrace of the hill, from which is a fine view of the valley. In this house lives Sydney Dobell—about to leave it however—and James took me in to call on him. His wife, whom we saw first, is a handsome delicate girlish creature, and very agreeable—She reminded me strongly of Hannah, in spite of the contrast between her delicate features and rosepink complexion, and Hannah's poor coarsened face and red sunburnt skin. Dobell soon came in, and talked with me: of Scandinavian mythology—apropos of some Danish or Roman fibulae he had found in a barrow on the hill—of Matthew Arnold's poetry, and similar subjects. His talk showed much intelligence and research. He is a tall man of 35, with thick long hair, slight beard & moustache, and refined features—thin nose, broad forehead and keen deep-set eyes. A thoughtful, grave, but not unkindly face. Here, one thought, is a man not much older than oneself, who is recognised as a poet, has done a definite work as such, has leisure and means to do it, and such a wife to boot. And wounded vanity and envy made themselves felt; but were repressed out of hand. . . .

[7] Joseph Stonehewer Scott (1829–1907), who had assumed the additional name of Chad on succeeding to his great-uncle's estate, 1855.

On 27 September Munby went to stay at Knutsford, Cheshire, with his brother Fred, who was clerk to a firm of solicitors there. The next morning he got up early to visit an 'ancient protégée, Mary', a housemaid at Bowdon now showing some grey hairs. 'I talked to her at the gate: neighbouring housemaids look on and giggle—cook comes up, is told I am a "friend". Position trying, but maintained with serene firmness.' Munby did not linger; he took the train to St. Helens, to tour its collieries, which he already knew.

Since Lord Shaftesbury's Act of 1842 women and girls had been excluded from the mines, but Lancashire 'pit-brow lassies' ('broo-wenches', they called themselves) still worked on the surface. As an admirer of the rough muscular female, who deplored the pale shop and factory girls in their would-be ladylike finery, Munby held the reactionary view that women should be allowed to work below ground, if they wanted to. An 'overlooker' supported him strongly, telling Munby that the reform had been 'the worst thing that could be for both masters & workers. Can't get the work done, hardly, now, even with profuse wages: has thrown many a poor family out of work—parents don't know what to do with their girls, now. Work was not too hard for the women—*they* never disliked it.'

This was a male managerial view; but much of what he said was true; the Act had brought great financial distress, which had not been fully alleviated. Munby found his informant supported by older women who had formerly worked below and now worked on the brows. One told him she 'liked it reet well—would like well to work below again—used to draw with belt and chain—liked it better than working up here.' Another agreed she had been 'like a horse or a dog', but said the surface work was harder 'and we was warm in't pit'. 'I only wish I was at it again,' she added: 'No, the chain never galled me between my legs, nor when I was in't family way, for I used to leave off at five months.' Even Munby thought this remarkable from a married woman; and indeed the Mining Commissioner's Report of 1844 had contained evidence to the contrary. However, summing up his day's work (28 September), Munby noted that the four women interviewed who had worked below 'were unanimous (as well as their superiors) in favour of underground work'. All told, he had seen sixty 'broo-wenches' and found them 'nearly all, much above the average of women for strength, health and robustness, & quite equal to it for sense & character. . . .' He had not been asked for money, and 'though a few giggled at first—which considering my beard leggings and knapsack was not wonderful—every one of the sixty was civil, modest, and womanly, in speech and gesture. I pronounce, therefore, decidedly, for pitwork at S. Helen's.'

Munby stayed the night at the Victoria Hotel, Wigan, to resume his one-man commission the next morning.

Saturday, 29 September . . . I went out at 9.30: and first to Mr Craig the photographer, a very civil man, about obtaining a photograph of a pitwoman in costume. There was one he said, who came, as a messenger from Ince Hall pits, every morning to a shop in the marketplace for letters & parcels. I went up with him to the shop, and waited outside the door: presently one of those wellknown figures came up the street—a woman in flannel trousers, waistcoat (with livery buttons, in this case) and pink shirt; and lilac cotton bonnet. A very comely woman she was; about thirty, & married: hair yellow, complexion golden brown, with brilliantly rosy cheeks; arms plump and strong, & rich in colour. She was quite clean, for besides working at the pit brow she is employed to run errands about the town from the coal office; and her dirty work had not begun yet. Mr Craig had photographed her before; and she readily came with us to the house, and he took a full length of her. She was very anxious not to be exhibited in the window: 'If mah feller should see it, he'd about kill ma,' said she. A quite respectable woman: Elizabeth Fairhurst by name. Her dress was not noticed in the streets: in Wigan, a woman in trousers is not half so odd as a woman in crinoline. Barbarous locality! . . .

At the various Wigan pits, Munby found ample confirmation of his observation that the women who had worked underground had liked their work. But even the surface 'broo-wenches' were now being increasingly replaced by 'strange skinny Irishmen'; and it irked Munby to see young potential Amazons being seduced from healthy outdoor work by the higher wages paid in decadent factories. At Lancaster's pits, Munby 'scrambled with difficulty' up plank ladders to a wooden gallery where the women worked, and shook several hands that were 'black and hard'; he missed a former friend Jane Mercer who used to chaff him about 'getting a Missus'. Women's wages there were 1s 6d a day, the hours 6 to 5.30.

The Haigh Moor Brewery provided a change from coal, and was a place dear to Munby's heart, being entirely run by young women, apart from three senior men. Girls were taken on for training there at eleven or twelve by the manager, Mr. Sumner:

. . . I saw several little girls in tiny trousers, in the cleaning house: and . . . he has a constant supply of female prentices. They all dress alike, and their dress is the same as the collier-girls'; a loose cotton shirt, a waistcoat, and flannel or

76

fustian trousers (petticoats would be in the way, as Mr S. says), with skirt pinned up round the waist. Cotton bonnets are worn for the outdoor work. Such a dress is very picturesque and serviceable; and being perfectly clean—not blackened as at the pits—is extremely becoming. . . . When the women were turned out of the pits in 1843, Mr S., seeing the injustice of that measure and the distress caused by it, took some of the excluded pitwomen to work in his brewery. These of course brought their costume with them: and the dress and its wearers answered so well, that ever since, Mr S. has continued to employ female labour, and has ended by putting his whole business in the hands of women. 'They are quite capable of doing all the work,' he says, 'and they do not, like men, drink more beer than their labour is worth' . . .

Munby's collection of photographs of working women was a principal concern on these expeditions; throughout his life he entered innumerable cottages to buy photographs or persuade women to come to the local photographer's. In Wigan, he triumphantly escorted another pitwoman, a 'quiet respectable hardworking person', Margaret Hunter, to Mr. Craig's studio. As a model she received his usual fee of one shilling. 'When it was all over, I found her still sitting there, patient, unquestioning. I said, it was time to go; and she rose to depart without a word, never knowing or asking what it had all been about.'

What *was* it all about? One can only say that Munby's vision of the labouring woman remained so strong that he followed it as one entranced. Was his benign perversity influenced, one wonders, by the androgynous women of the Pre-Raphaelite painters and poets he knew? Yet Munby's convictions were founded on an elementary if distorted truth; and they led this ardent feminist to reject much that the woman's movement accomplished. In the twentieth century he would have found himself most at home in Soviet Russia. Nevertheless, Munby was to become a founder of the Working Women's College, and had his hopes of reconciling brawn and brain.

What is rather surprising is that he made no use of the mass of information about women in his notebooks, except as material for some poems and articles. Life was too full of women to be watched, admired, encouraged.

Munby returned to Knutsford from Wigan on Sunday, 30 September, with all his 'old good impressions of it confirmed; regretting only the apparent diminution in the number of female labourers at the pits: which diminution however is I fancy confined to the district lying just round the town, within the range of factory temptations and maudlin philanthropy.' He carried with him an apron and petticoat bought for Hannah in the market. He spent the next two days exploring fourteenth-century Tabley Old Hall, on its island in a lake; on his first visit (Monday, 1 October) he was alone, and wandered unperceived through the deserted house in a state of enchantment, being mistaken for a ghost by the housekeeper.

The Munby Syndrome. A 'young lady' contrasted with a collierywoman greasing truck wheels. Undated drawing in Munby's sketch book of 1853–70

Munby's second visit to Tabley was made more prosaically next day in the company of W. A. Walker, the local clergyman, with whom Munby and his brother Fred dined and spent the evening; 'Mrs W., formerly I believe a flirt at the York balls, resuming her occupation with singular zest.'

Wednesday, 3 October ... At breakfast, Fred having just gone out, Mrs W. called, to my surprise. It soon became obvious that I had the honour of being her motive. She talked with much empressement—paid me the strangest compliments—asked earnest questions about my 'influence over women', and such things; and finding me unimpressible and not to be pumped, sat looking at me with great eyes, declaring that I was a 'puzzle'—'unfathomable'—and so on.

I began to feel extremely uncomfortable, especially as her husband is a quiet kindly man—but she insisted on accompanying me in my walk towards Tabley. On the road she talked as before, admiring also my costume, & stopping to handle my watch trinkets; keeping me in fear for her reputation—for we met parties of the Cheshire Yeomanry, trotting down to their review, and among them Lord de Tabley and his son, with whom she must stop to chat. At length she left me and I went on into the Park . . .

Knutsford did not appeal to Munby—'a dull shabby 18th century place of three or four streets, noticeable only for Knut, who is said to have forded the stream there, and for being the original of Cranford'—and on 4 September he made a somewhat desperate expedition to Northwich. At Marshall's salt works there he found '8 women & girls employed'; Higgins's Works did better with 'perhaps a dozen'.

Leaving brother Fred, he travelled on to York, to end his holiday with a week at Clifton Holme. He returned to London on 15 October.

Wednesday, 17 October: Mary Wright, a bookbinder . . . A quiet girl, virtuous in manner, and apparently in habit. Elegant, pretty, and well but simply dressed. . . . She excited my interest by her love of reading and desire for education: specially by her love for music and poetry. . . . By way of seeing what was in her, I asked her, after considering the rights of the thing, and she agreed, to come with me for an hour to my rooms; whither no strange woman—save once in a similar case long ago—has ever penetrated. She behaved very modestly and simply—though she *did* smoke a bird's eye cigarrette straight through, it did not seem in her unfeminine—and talked intelligently and read with enjoyment the Tennyson which I showed her. So she spent the hour: and at 8 o'clock I gave her a glass of sherry, went out and saw her into an omnibus, and came in again. After all, however, though the case is interesting, I am not disposed for a repetition of this incident, even if it were desirable. Her tastes and her character may be above her class; but the companionship of a *half* educated girl, who has the form of ladyhood without the substance, is of all things irritating & unsatisfactory. . . . And she is certain to be vulgar. . . . A true peasant girl, servant girl, is too low and too genuine to be vulgar. . . . Had I brought in 'Miss' Wright for the very purpose of realising the truth that lowest is higher than low—that an inferior kind may be chosen, but inferiority in the *same* kind, never—I could not have felt this more. . . . For me, I have chosen long since. But why should you choose either? That were long to tell: but at least, you see, I can look in Hannah's simple trusting face and think that here at least is a woman who knows nothing of the doubts and problems, of the pursuits, deep or trivial, that agitate *our* classes—who never heard of High Church & Low Church, of Maurice or Buckle, of Ruskin or of Thackeray; who never wore a white kid glove, and never saw a visiting card, save haply on the table she was dusting; whose deepest study is a child's history book, and that all new to her; who calls the Italian Masters 'pretty pictures', and Mendelssohn's music 'a pretty tune'! And if, for all this, or rather *with* all this, she be neither gross and vulgar nor stupidly simple, but quite the contrary of each, then I say that the sight of such a maiden (and the hearing too) in her peasant's garb, is like a cold plunge in summer.

Wednesday, 24 October . . . About seven most of the remaining members of my Latin class at the W.M. College—now the senior class—came to tea: viz. Tansley (draper's assistant), Maher, Brock (shoemaker), Coldric (telegraph clerk), & Rapkin (engraver): all very good & pleasant fellows, and, especially the three first, intelligent and apt. After tea, I showed them photographs & pictures and books, and we talked—of the Mort d'Arthur and the Idylls of the King, of Norse mythology, whereof I told them something, and of general social subjects: I reading out stories and poems now and then to illustrate the talk. After ten Litchfield came in, and we discussed the future of the class: all were anxious to go on with Latin, and kindly desirous that I should still be their teacher: which cannot be unfortunately, as it seems best that I should begin another elementary class. So at 11.30 they departed, shaking hands with me all round in friendly regretful manner.

The evening was a very pleasant one. . . . My two years with them, and my year with a former class, have given me quite as much as I have given[8] . . .

I saw a very pleasant incident in the Strand as I came home this evening. A crowd stood round a doorstep on which lay a woman at full length, motionless & senseless: and the women were all anxiety, for in her unconscious arms was a little baby. The peeler, a fine manly fellow, came up, and calmly adjusted himself for action, with halfcontemptuous look—as who would say 'It's the usual thing—drunk!' He shook & called her in vain: with help he lifted her up, loosed the baby, and gave it to a workgirl standing by, one of many women who claimed the charge of it: and seeing her dead face and the foam on her lips, his manner changed all at once. 'She's as sober as I am,' he said: 'it's a fit; get some burnt brown paper & some water.' A shopman from next door brought out water: rough dirty men, cabmen and costermongers, laid her down tenderly and held her softly, and gave her drink, while the peeler waved the burning paper in

---

[8] Munby's pupils having left, Litchfield told him how 'a week ago' he had rescued two young girls from a brothel in Exeter Street, Strand; taken them to his rooms for the night; and paid their fares back to Manchester, where they were barmaids, the next morning. After Litchfield's death, Munby contributed an account of this or a similar incident to the *Working Men's College Journal*, March, 1903, and it is reproduced in *Richard Buckley Litchfield: A Memoir* (1910). The details differ; Manchester becomes Liverpool; and the date is given as 'about 1857'. (Of Munby's pupils here mentioned, one, George Tansley, was later to play an important part in the administration of the College.)

her face till she revived: the crowd stood back that she might have air: the plain shabby workgirl nursed and kissed the baby, and she and all the women were full of anxiety for it and its mother. The mother was raised & brought round at last—a nice respectable young married woman: she moaned for her baby, and the workgirl laid it kindly in her arms. She dropped a quite rustic curtsy when I suggested a cab: no, she could walk quite well home to Drury Lane, though she could only just stand. I sent the peeler for one of course, and he went off with her in it: and I went home, thanking God for a sight of so much tenderness & helpfulness among a crowd of London poor and strangers. Truly, when one is sick at heart for selfishness and isolation and scornful thoughts and utter lack of brotherhood among men, a sight like that is worth a thousand sermons.

Thursday, 1 November . . . To the W.M. College at eight, and began my new Latin class (elementary). There were twenty-two men—a room full. Finished soon after ten . . .

Thursday, 8 November . . . Office 10.25 to 5.21—Home after dinner, and to my class at 8. Met Godfrey and Vernon Lushington in coming out. V. and I went upstairs to the drawing classes, and found Ruskin talking with Litchfield—telling him of a letter of sympathy which he has had from Carlyle,[9] in reference to his articles on political oeconomy in the Cornhill.[1] No wonder the grand old prophet approves of any protest against that which appears to regard human souls simply as 'hands', and to rest on the sovereignty of dead laws rather than of living wills. But Ruskin continued preaching away at us, & especially at the incredulous L., reviling the science of Adam Smith and his successors as 'the damnedest devil's lie, my dear Litchfield' with huge emphasis and pointing of finger 'that ever was'! And so he went on, loud and selfsatisfied, assuming that the object of the science was to make men rich and that by setting them against each other; speaking approvingly of 'Plato, Aristotle and *Solomon* (!)', saying many harsh things, which he declared he would have said in the Cornhill, 'only Thackeray wouldn't let him': so he means to put them into his forthcoming book on the subject. He described J. S. Mill[2] as 'a fine fellow, but whose brain was full of confused fancies (!): which I will show!' cried he conclusively, rising up & down on his toes, after his manner, with his hands in his tailpockets, and finally jaunting downstairs in the same springy fashion, with the prim smile of

---

[9] Thomas Carlyle (1795–1881), the historian.

[1] Ruskin's essays appeared in the *Cornhill* for August, September, October and November, 1860, the series being then concluded by Thackeray, as editor, under pressure from his publisher George Smith. They were collected into the volume *Unto this Last* (1862). Ruskin's 'heresies', widely condemned as 'socialistic' in 1860, read as familiar doctrine a century later. Munby was out of his depth in political economy, but not unsympathetic to many of Ruskin's views on social reform. Like others, however, he could be profoundly irritated by his manner of speaking and writing.

[2] John Stuart Mill (1806–73), the philosopher, had published *On Liberty* in 1859.

Sir Oracle upon his dry lips. Whether one agrees with him or not, nothing can be more offensive than his scornful selfsufficient manner—filliping away with his flippant abuse the careful work of three generations! As usual, he did all the talking himself: Litchfield listened and chafed, covertly defiant; Vernon was gentle & reverent as always; I looked on, observant and indignant. Here is a man vastly one's superior in intellect: and yet where is the grave dignity and modesty & manly reserve, without which a man can neither be truly great nor be revered? This Ruskin, courteous and kindly as he really is, makes you feel, not only in his oracular vein but even more by the demure & pharisaic condescension with which he listens to you, that he looks upon your view as wholly contemptible, and his own as simply impregnable because it is his own. Every honourable and intelligent man must resent such conduct; and the more deeply, because he would fain admire and respect. Those who only know Ruskin in the beauty & worth of his books, had better look no further: the doubts of his virility, and his appearance which confirms them, are alone sufficient to make one feel strangely in his presence[3]. . .

Friday, 9 November . . . In the Strand, some one laid a hand on my arm, and looking round, I saw Marian Gibbs, a nice looking quiet girl of 23, whom a few months ago I persuaded to enter—or promise to enter—a 'Home'.[4] She was a workgirl, but had been living with a medical student, who died; and she had lost work & character. She went, it seems, being downhearted one evening, to one of the 'Midnight Meetings' at S. James's Hall: was much affected there, and entered a Home—9 Portland Road. There were about 20 girls there, she said. How did they behave? Well, two or three were discharged every week, for bad language and so on. She did not think the girls were sorry generally, or wanted to change: they come chiefly for shelter. For herself, she stayed there three months, and then they gave security and got work for her at her old master's shop: so now she works as a tailor, making waistcoats, at home. Lives by herself in a little room near Gray's Inn Road; earns 12/6 a week, & pays 4/ for lodging, so keeps herself, living frugally. Finds it very dull . . .

Sunday, 11 November . . . In till 3. Litchfield came in. He has had a letter from Ruskin about his explosion the other night; wherein he distinctly claims for himself superiority over J. S. Mill. He encloses a copy of Carlyle's note, who says in it that R's arguments 'go down into the system of the political oeconomists like a dose of Epsom salts'![5]. . .

---

[3] Could there be an unconsciously projected self-criticism in Munby's stern attitude to Ruskin's sexual inadequacy?

[4] See 6 January, 1860.

[5] Carlyle actually offered a different choice of aperients. 'You go down through those unfortunate dismal-science people like a treble-X of Senna, Glauber, and Aloes. . . .' (Letter to Ruskin of 29 October, 1860: *Works of John Ruskin*, ed. Cook and Wedderburn, Vol. XVII, p. xxxii).

Monday, 12 November . . . Ralston came in to tea, and we talked of the case[6] and of his sister's remarkable forensic efforts. She has made a great sensation, as any young lady might well do, after speaking in full court for three days, four or five hours each day, and examining witnesses! And all the while she is so ill that Ralston fears she may at any moment be prostrated in Court, & even die there.

Tuesday, 13 November . . . Went down to the Probate Court at Westminster Hall during the day, to hear something of the Shedden case. Miss S. was speaking: simply dressed in mourning, she stood within the bar, holding in hand now her brief, and now some book or document of reference; and consulting at times with her father who sat near. Her voice was clear & calm, her utterance distinct, her manner as easy and selfpossessed as that of a leading counsel; speaking in language correct and elegant, she stated her facts and arranged her arguments with admirable skill and force; and withal she never for an instant forgot the quiet dignity and gentleness of a woman and a lady. It was a noble display of female power: one could scarcely regret that she had been driven to make it. The court of course was crowded; various ladies being there, simpering hugely, as not knowing what to make of such a sister . . .

Friday, 23 November . . . Dressed in Litchfield's room,[7] and went to Clapham to dine with the Ellises. Georgie as usual intelligent and charming, and Alice piquante & laughingly sarcastic. I look on Georgie with interest and affection, because *they say* she would marry me if I asked her. And truly she would make a wife to be proud of. Two pleasant Miss Johnstones were staying there: and all these young ladies, white bosomed, fairylike with muslin and flowers, found a foil for their elegance in a pretty but coarsemade rustic & redhanded waiting maid. Gentle, and beautiful in face as they—and her name *Laura* too—why should she have a life so different? Why should she wear a cotton frock and a cap and hand me dishes—why should those imperious misses order her about so? . . . This girl's large eyes have glanced at me furtively before: and tonight, as the young ladies crowd to the hall door and I am helping grandmamma to her carriage, Laura, waiting in the background, says low 'Let me carry your bag, Sir'—and I give it her; and in the dusk outside she holds the carriage door open for me—and as she closes it and gives me the bag, somehow her thick broad hand comes more than once in contact with mine, and does not retreat. Oh ho! Here we have a scene for a novel: the hero from his chariot bows farewell to the elegant imperial creature who thinks she has him captive, but meanwhile his real

---

[6] Ralston's whole life had been affected because his obstinate father had dissipated a large fortune in seeking, unsuccessfully, to prove that he was heir to certain property in Ayrshire. Ralston's real name was William Ralston Shedden; he called himself Shedden-Ralston to free himself from the associations of the surname. As a last attempt, his sister Miss Shedden was now presenting their case before a House of Lords committee; a gallant but unavailing effort.

[7] At the Ecclesiastical Commission.

83

adieus are given, in secret pressure of her working hand, to the humble serving maid who hands him to the door! . . .

Saturday, 24 November . . . Dined, and walked down to Eccleston Square to the Severns. Found Mr and Mrs at home, Miss S., Eleanor, and Arthur. . . . We were soon in full talk—about Ruskin,—whom Miss S. had of late been discoursing with, and he has been copying a picture too by her side at the National Gallery. It was a head, and he couldn't do it at all, and gave it up—and about art and poetry and novels; Miss S. with her gentle earnestness, taking the lead as usual . . .

Saturday, 1 December . . . I heard today of the death of my old pony Taffy—aged 40 or more—whom I rode when I was five years old. Out of the house at Clifton, no death of human being in *that* neighbourhood could affect me so much, or make the gap in my life so wide. He was the last of the vestigia juventutis.

Friday, 7 December . . . Going into a shop to buy some photographs the shopman, who was also photographer, brought out by way of temptation various portraits of nude & semi-nude women, which he himself had taken. I enquired what manner of women they were, who were willing to have pictures of their naked bodies taken, and sold to strangers at 2/- each: of course they are virtually prostitutes? 'Not at all, Sir!' cries the worthy photographer, indignant: 'this one' (holding up a stark naked figure) 'is herself an artist, and was a *governess*. No, No—they wouldn't do anything of that: a girl has no need to go on the streets when she can earn *five or six pounds* a week, by this sort of thing & sitting to the Academy!' Nearly £300 a year to be earned by simply sitting in a chair without any clothes on: no wonder such a trade is preferred to the hard and selfaccusing life of a prostitute! Nevertheless, one would say on the whole that these delicate gradations of female modesty are somewhat inexplicable to the coarser masculine mind . . .

Two episodes of the next few days well illustrate the complications in which Munby was continually involved by his quixotic gallantry and curiosity regarding the opposite sex. On Saturday, 8 December, he escorted Mary Ann Ireland, aged nineteen, from the Strand all the way to Mile End. She was a sewing machine hand, who earned 16/- a week by 'working from 8 to 8 with an hour for dinner' ('she keeps the machine going with her feet'). Munby left her at her door and walked away; he had 'scarce lighted my pipe' when the girl came running after him: 'Oh, mother says I ought to have asked you to come in!'

'Ours is not a grand house,' she remarked; 'it's homely, you know!' So she led me down a dark low passage, opened a door, and ushered me, with a sort of pride as who should say 'Look what *I've* brought!', into a small neat kitchen-parlour. By the fire sat her mother, a respectable but querulous looking woman, and on the other side her sister, a neat slight girl in a brown frock, resting from work. On the hearth crouched an idiotic old aunt, with cropped hair and an old man's face, who played with a bag of nails. . . . The woman got up, came forward, held out her hand, which of course I took: 'How d'ye do?' said she: 'Mary Ann, get him the armchair—sit down Sir, sit down!'. . .

The conversation 'became general' and touched on local murderers, especially one Mullins—'they had been privileged to know Mullins in the flesh, but only distantly', noted Munby in his Dickensian vein. After half an hour he rose to shake hands all round, the mother saying 'Well, I hope you'll pay us another visit', and Mary Ann conducting him to the door and inviting him to 'come and see them again'. 'Curious!' commented Munby. 'I suppose my next visit would be that of an accepted suitor!'

Annie Stuart was a gamble from the start. Having heard of an intriguing 'female sailor' of that name, Munby inserted a guarded advertisement in the personal column of *The Times*, 12 December, mentioning the 'news-room'[8] he habitually frequented: 'ANNIE STUART late from Liverpool—If you want help, SEND your ADDRESS to F. P, West-end News Room, 76 Strand, London W.C.'

Thursday, 13 December . . . Went to the newsroom, to give directions about any letters for me relating to Annie Stuart, the female sailor of whom I received an excellent account from the Master of the Liverpool Workhouse, & for whom I advertised yesterday in the Times. To my surprise, I found that a young woman had already been enquiring for the advertiser, had seemed anxious to see him, had left a note—'Dear Frend, ask for Annie Stuart who will be glad to see you at Holman's Coffee house 143 Fleet Street', and had said she would call again. Singular—and too good to be true, apparently! However, though according to my rule I assumed the worst, I felt extremely excited and desperately anxious to get off going to my duties at the W.M. College. Mastering all this at length, I went home after dinner to prepare—having first called at the coffeehouse, a clean respectable place, and learnt that Annie Stuart *was* there & would be in by ten—and went to my class at eight. After this, which of course was all the pleasanter for my stupendous moral victory, I went to the coffeehouse again, found that Annie Stuart had come in, was shown into a clean homely parlour up stairs, and waited, prudently repressing expectation. Presently entered a strong

---

[8] These 'newsrooms', originally called 'Cigar Divans', offered the facilities of a modest club for a small fee. They were mostly to be found in the area of the Strand.

bony hardfeatured young woman, dressed like a milliner or tradesman's daughter: a sort of person who would be commendable as a maid of all work, but who was wholly uninteresting in the class to which this 'female' evidently belonged. I looked instinctively at her hands: they were square & masculine, and yet in spite of this and her figure, she clearly had not been a sailor—was not *my* Annie Stuart. That was her name, though; and like her namesake, she came from Liverpool and was born in Glasgow. Very odd! as she truly observed . . .

After condoling with each other on our mutual disappointment, we parted. . . . The fiasco was rather amusing. . . .

Tuesday, 18 December . . . Dined, and going up to Mudie's afterwards, I was shown his new hall, or library and offices combined, which he inaugurated last night with a grand literary fête. A big ambitious hall, skylighted, corinthian-columned, with gallery all round: lined with new books up to the roof, and at present adorned with busts statues and pictures—among the rest a cast of Woolner's noble Tennyson, and a fine statuette of Cromwell by Leifchild.[9]

Such is the latest developement of this Mudie,[1] whom I have seen year by year enlarging his phylacteries and adding house to house, from the time when he kept a small shop in Southampton Row. That is but seven or eight years ago: but such rewards are vouchsafed to any man who can promote and satisfy a salient want of his time . . .

Thursday, 20 December . . . Carry[2] arrived by the Brighton train, which was full of schoolgirls and schoolboys, with a dozen other girls under charge of a governess. We drove off in a cab, and on the way I had, almost for the first time, some talk with her, from which one could guess how good it would have been for me to have had a sister in my youth. She is improved and developed, and really thoughtful and tender.

We stopped at Brandon's the great shop in Oxford St. to choose a new bonnet for her. A resplendent turkey carpeted drawingroom, or suite of such, was the place, full of showy or tasteful female handiwork: many Mammas and daughters making purchases, and elegant young women in silks flitting about. Under guidance of one of these, I chose a structure of the period; ugly in all but colour and material (which are left free to the worshipper's choice, who is thereby the more enslaved as to the *form*) and destined to look ridiculous ten years hence. Colour, 'Magenta': price, 25/; cheap, I am told! The place was quite a Hogarthian study . . .

. . . went and bought a trifle for my Hannah. 'A nice present for a servant, Sir,' said the man: so *he* knew too! . . .

[9] Henry Stormonth Leifchild (1823–84), sculptor.

[1] Charles Edward Mudie (1818–90), founder of Mudie's Lending Library, had moved in 1852 to 510 New Oxford Street, where his new hall and library had just been opened. His financial resources now began to be overstrained; Mudie's became a limited company in 1864.

[2] Caroline, Munby's only sister; sixth of the seven children, of whom he was the eldest. She was at a Brighton boarding-school.

9. The hand-coloured photograph of Hannah admired by Rossetti (Diary, 22 June, 1862)

8. Hannah in men's clothes, 1861

10. Self portrait in oil by Mary Newton, née Severn

11. Helen Faucit, a detail from the portrait by

Snow covered the country as Munby returned to Clifton Holme on 22 December. Train journeys were too rapid for his taste. 'To emerge from the train at the end of such a journey, with no greater newness of sensations than you would feel in leaving an omnibus at Brompton—this is a sad result of railway travelling. Travelling, to be really worth much, should be a gradual process. . . .'

It was very cold but fine, that Christmas. 'Household unity' had been preserved, reflected Munby before leaving on 30 December, 'by a careful avoidance of religious topics'; and they had all, 'parents, brothers, sister, wife and child, realised for once the sacred family life which only Christmas, with snow without and warmth and love within, can give.' He was alone in his Temple chambers when 'the calm deep bell of Paul's . . . finally buried the dead year'.

4

WORKING WOMEN OF LONDON
1861–2

By the beginning of 1861 Munby had completed seven red diary note-books. He now began an additional record of his correspondence, shopping, calls, and parties. He obviously intended to keep his more important material and best literary style for the main diary; but sometimes, not surprisingly, he failed to 'write it up'; so that henceforth, for a few years, the two diaries must be read concurrently. In 1861 Munby filled no less than 780 pages of the red notebooks, as well as 100 pages of his concise version. In fact, he had become an addict; he could not stop writing his diary.

Preceding chapters have sought to establish Munby's bachelor routine by fairly extensive excerpts. In future, quotation must be more sparing. To follow him regularly in his continual encounters with working women would take too much space and involve too many repetitive themes; some of the interviews will be quoted, but much of this material must await the possible future attention of a social historian. Similar considerations apply to the diarist's busy life in society; for despite the discipline of office hours, Munby found the lure of theatres, concerts and evening parties irresistible. He was not only punctilious and polite but highly energetic, arriving at his office about 10.20 each morning, however late he had got to bed the night before.

As a poet he was now feeling more cheerful; his poems were obtaining a modest success with magazines such as *Fraser's*, *Macmillan's*, *Temple Bar* and *Once a Week*. He did make one desperate attempt this year to get away from the Ecclesiastical Commission, but his application for the Middle Temple librarianship failed. He still taught Latin each week at the Working Men's College and played his part in its management. The usual sequence of country expeditions and periodical visits to his parents continued.

With Hannah, the situation remained static. Munby visited her often at her place of work at Kilburn and took her out walking and canoodled with her in green meadows long since built over, during the brief intervals she could snatch from her chores. Whenever they met out of doors, rigid class

88

distinction demanded that Hannah should walk apart from him until they could safely recognise each other. By special arrangement, Munby would sometimes watch her approvingly from a discreet distance as she furiously cleaned the front steps or scrubbed the flag-stones. Nearly every week-end, Hannah, in her turn, arrived at Fig Tree Court, when she would put Munby's chambers to rights, cook his supper, and sit with him while they read to each other—for he had taught her to read very well. Munby took care of her small savings and invested the money. He reproached himself that he could not afford to do more for Hannah, but he did not intend to sacrifice his comfort on her account, nor to curtail his considerable expenditure on photographs, or on sixpences and shillings for the other working women he met.

A female mudlark drawn by Munby from life. Undated, but similar drawings are dated 1855

Wednesday, 9 January . . . Went across Hungerford Bridge and round by Blackfriars bridge at 3. . . . It was bitter cold. Yet some divers—noble looking fellows—were working at the piles of the new bridge, & down by Blackfriars several female mud-larks were wading, barefoot and thigh deep, under the barges through the frozen ice covered mud. One, a young woman, with simious face and creel on back, stood by me as I looked over the rails down the Whitefriars dock, considering her chances of stray coal; then . . . she waded through mire and water, among dead cats and broken crockery, towards the river, until, stooping almost double, she disappeared in the mud and darkness under the side of a coal barge. . . .

Friday, 25 January . . . W.M. College: Council meeting on the dance question, Westlake in the chair. Furnivall defended himself: Hughes and Ludlow were severe and indignant, the Lushingtons Litchfield and I were for compromise and peace. The resolutions being confirmed, we went upstairs to conference with the assembled students, one of whom was put in the chair. Speeches were made, chiefly by students, pro and con: the general feeling being good and orderly.[1]. . .

Monday, 4 February . . . Mr. Severn appointed Consul at Rome! Lord Lansdowne supposed to have done it, out of regard for Miss S. A Whig job anyhow, and likely to bring a row in the House, coming so soon too after Newton's appointment at the Museum.[2] For the Severns's sake of course one is glad.

Tuesday, 5 February . . . Went out about two for an hour, & saw the Queen pass & repass to and from Parliament: in ermine robe & diamond coronal, looking well and young. Great crowd, & more cheering than I have heard before—one workman near me very enthusiastic, shouting 'England's crown for ever!' as he held his cap up . . .

Wednesday 13 February . . . Walked up to Fink's in Oxford St. & met Hannah there by appointment, and had three photographs taken of her—Bust only, in bonnet & shawl, full length with me, and do. in men's clothes[3]. . .

Thursday, 14 February . . . Dined, and home till 8: my Latin class till 10. One of the men came up to me afterwards, to say how much clearer he found my teaching to be than that at King's College. Shook hands with Ruskin. . . . I went

---

[1] Dr. Furnivall had promoted a successful series of dances at the College, which had been strongly criticised by members of the Council as opposed to its objects and likely to disrupt the work of the students. The dances were condemned by the Council with one dissentient (Furnivall).

[2] Mary Severn's *fiancé*, Charles Newton, having given up the Rome consulship, had been appointed Keeper of Greek and Roman Antiquities at the British Museum.

[3] See Plate 8. No photograph of Munby and Hannah together seems to have survived.

to Macmillan's: found Masson[4], Dallas of the Times.[5] ... Furnivall, & several others. Dante Rossetti came in, hot from the capture of Farrell Hogg,[6] whom he had lodged in the station house: he & F. went off thither ...

Sunday, 24 February ... In till 3. Stokes came, & chatted philology awhile—then we both to Dante Rossetti's by Blackfriars bridge. ... R's book, early Italian poems—his wife's drawings—R., S., & I dined together at the Cheshire Cheese, then back to tea at R.'s—who read us his sister Christina's charming poems, some of his own, a sonnet of Stokes's, R's memoir of Guido Cavalcanti, W.M.R's Ugolino from the Inferno, &c. So talk and look at sketches till 10.30—then S. & I home.[7]

Monday, 11 March ... Dined at Rouget's,[8] where were Sala,[9] Blanchard,[10] and a party of such as they, laughing, & talking loudly all at once, to the astonishment of waiters and guests, till the place rang like a pothouse on Saturday night. Sala, inter alia, told how, when some one wrote from America to ask for his autograph, he wrote back 'Sir, I don't see why I should be troubled by people asking for autographs. Yours truly, Nothing.' 'So the fellow'll have *nothing* to show for his pains, ha ha! Damn his impudence!' He is a coarse beery redfaced man, with a circlet of short black hair round his mouth. ...

Thursday, 21 March ... to Macmillan's ... very pleasant evening. Had some talk with Hughes on Essays & Reviews,[1] which he discussed with his usual cheerfulness of sentiment and his usual sturdy dogmatism, and with Rossetti and Dobell on the methods and reasons of loving, in man and in woman; apropos of Patmore's 'Faithful for Ever'.[2] ... Holman Hunt was at M.'s too. His great

[4] David Masson (1822–1907) was editor of *Macmillan's Magazine*, 1859–67.

[5] Eneas Sweetland Dallas (1828–79), celebrated for his literary criticism and as the author of *Poetics* and *The Gay Science*.

[6] Farrell Hogg, cashiered from the army, was an incorrigible young swindler and thief who had once been given 'some small literary employment' by *Once a Week*. I cannot find Rossetti's name in *The Times* reports of the proceedings against him, but nearly a hundred letters of complaint were produced at Middlesex Sessions, 17 September, 1861, when he was sentenced to six years imprisonment (see *The Times*, 18 September, 1861, and preceding weeks).

[7] This entry is in note form in Munby's secondary diary; one regrets that he did not enlarge on it. Rossetti was then living at 14 Chatham Place with his ailing wife. His book of 'early Italian poems' was a collection of translations, *The Early Italian Poets*; its publication in 1861 was made possible by Ruskin's generosity. Rossetti included an essay on Dante and Guido Cavalcanti in this volume, which was republished under another title in 1874. His brother William Michael Rossetti was engaged on a blank-verse translation of Dante's *Inferno* (Macmillan, 1865).

[8] In Castle Street, Leicester Square: 'provide French dinners at moderate rates' (Murray's *Handbook*).

[9] George Augustus Sala (1828–96), prolific journalist and author; then editor of *Temple Bar*.

[10] Edward Litt Laman Blanchard (1820–89), journalist; writer of Drury Lane pantomimes.

[1] The collection of Broad Church religious essays published in 1860.

[2] Coventry Patmore (1823–96), poet and associate of the Pre-Raphaelites, had published 'Faithful for Ever' in 1860.

picture[3] has had a narrow escape. The hangings over it caught fire: the attendant sprang up to smother the flames, and begged some one to throw him a rug for that purpose: none was at hand, & the fire had gained the canvas, when a lady— Lady Seaton—threw him her Indian shawl.

At Easter, Munby went over to Paris for a week. He was initiated into the 'notorious cancan' at the Salle Valentino (28 March), but did not find what he saw as bad as he expected—'In the midst of the quadrille she suddenly gathered up her dress to the knee, and springing forward, flung her right leg into the air & with the point of her toe knocked her partner's hat off. This occurred several times, and each time the leg was covered again in a moment, so that the action though startling could hardly be called indecent.' In general, he found Parisian immorality 'concentrated in a few foul spots, and those for the most part kept out of sight'. His deepest indignation was therefore reserved for the despotic Napoleon III and his son:

Friday, 29 March, Good Friday . . . into the Bois de Boulogne, chiefly to see the promenade of Longchamps.

On the broad road near the gate a close carriage with escort of dragoons met and passed us. Standing up against the window was that wretched little being known as the Prince Imperial: a healthy chubby child, with commonplace features & intelligent but illtempered look. He is driven about every day and kept constantly in view; in the futile hope that he may someday inherit.[4]. . . After a while, in a miniature Rotten Row by the side of the drive, we saw the Tyrant himself among the horsemen. He rode between two of his minions, two grooms behind. We on the path were close to him as he passed: and it was tantalising to reflect, as I looked him in the face, that he was within reach of the butt end of my trusty umbrella. Nevertheless, this villanous atheist goes his way unharmed and works out his doom: and it is right. Great is the sacredness of life, and the supremacy of law . . .

Thursday, 16 May: London . . . called by request on the Editor of the Morning Chronicle, who proposed to me to write articles for the paper . . .

Friday, 17 May . . . Dined at Rouget's, and met Dante Rossetti there, & his young disciple Algernon Swinburne.[5]. . .

[3] Presumably 'The Finding of the Saviour in the Temple', already praised by Munby.

[4] In 1861 the Prince Imperial, usually described as delicate rather than healthy, was five years old. Munby could not foresee that he would die fighting for England in the Zulu campaign in 1879.

[5] Algernon Charles Swinburne (1837–1909), the poet, was an Oxford undergraduate when he was first introduced to Rossetti in 1857.

Saturday, 18 May ... I went at 12.30 by train from Shoreditch—3rd class excursion: whereby more than any way I know, one learns the ways of the working classes ... in the next seat opposite me, sat a rosy country wench with a child brother on her knee, travelling alone. ... Her neighbours were three young men, who smoked their pipes and paid her little half facetious attentions. These soon broke what little ice there is on such natures as hers; and for the rest of the journey it was pleasant to see the frank simple way she talked to them ... telling them about herself, and laughing at their mild jokes with fresh open-mouthed unrestrained laughter. What an artificial product the modern lady is! Is not *this* type of woman, also, valuable & interesting? And *is* there any advantage in seeing beyond the end of your bezom?

We reached Cambridge about three. ... I sent my luggage on to Trinity, and got down & went on to Parker's Piece, where the review was going on—the Inns of Court Corps having come from town to be reviewed with the University corps. ... The Prince of Wales[6] was on the field, in plain clothes ... & was much cheered by the crowd as he rode away. The University corps marched first off the ground ... the difference of individual age between them and the D.O.[7] was not nearly so great as I had expected. The latter corps followed, headed like the other by its band, and more than twice as numerous. All my legal friends were there, and I fell into the rear, just behind Private Fitzjames Stephen,[8] and marched with the corps between the crowds of people ... to the Senate House, where the D.O. dispersed to the different colleges to dine. I went on to Trinity, and to Joe's[9] rooms in the great Court ... Hall was to be at five, and all the Trinity men of the D.O., to the number of 210, were to be feasted by the college. ...

Sunday, 19 May ... I went to Hall, having put my name down yesterday, as this is a scarlet day, and the grand feast day of the year. A group of dons—of doctors in scarlet & pink, and undergraduate noblemen in full dress gowns of purple & gold, and Masters—of whom I was one—stood together at the edge of the dais, waiting for grace: and I was admiring the manly sunburnt face of the youth in purple & gold who stood next me, when a sudden likeness to his mother struck me: it was the Prince of Wales.

I had been admiring him for some minutes, as he stood at my elbow: and the discovery was most agreeable, that I had been admiring *him*. He stands apparently about 5 feet 7; is manly and well made; and his frank intelligent face (with a good deal of fun and animal vigour in it too) has a pure rich sunbrown tint, which his soft gold hair and large blue eyes make all the more artistic. The full underlip, receding chin, and prominent eyes, are Brunswick all over. His

---

[6] Later King Edward VII (1841–1910); then an undergraduate at Trinity College, Cambridge.

[7] 'Devil's Own', i.e. the Inns of Court Corps (Munby's note).

[8] Later Sir James FitzJames Stephen, Bt. (1829–94), the famous judge.

[9] Munby's brother Joseph.

hands, I observed, are square & strong, & neither white nor delicate; but suggestive of healthy outdoor use. A brave manly boy, & worthy of his mother— worthy to be a King. He spoke to the dons he knew & shook hands; and was treated with respect, but no ceremonial whatever. I could not but admire the way in which we of Cambridge have combined authority and selfrespect with due regard to his future claims. Presently the Master[1] came up, his bearish old face warped into a courtly grin; and shook hands with the Prince, and led him to his own right hand, after himself taking part in the Grace. Two boys of the Prince's age—the Duke of S. Alban's (who is strangely like Charles II)[2] and Lord Pollington, were present: both far inferior in vigour & good looks to the Prince. . . .

Tuesday, 21 May . . . Commencement Day. After breakfast I walked down to the Senate House . . . got a very good place near the rostrum. The house was densely crowded, & the undergraduates in the galleries kept up incessant thunders of cheering & groaning, on every possible subject. Much enthusiasm was shown for Lord Derby, a good deal for Garibaldi & Italy; a divided applause to Gladstone, & unanimous dislike for John Bright . . . at twelve the Vice Chancellor appeared, with the Prince, who was placed at his side, and the young Duke of S. Albans. Clark,[3] as Public Orator, then introduced, one by one, in very apt little Latin speeches, the recipients of the honorary Doctor's degree, who appeared in scarlet. First, Lord Elgin,[4] who, with his white hair and large eyes and earnest loveable face, only wants height of figure, to be very noble; then Sir R. Murchison,[5] stiff and portly, wearing orders (the others wore none); then Lord Stratford de Redcliffe,[6] thin, silverhaired, refined & selfpossessed in face & manner; then Sir W. Hamilton,[7] a short stout loosely made old gentleman, smiling, amiable, and simplicity itself. He it was who accosted me in chapel on Sunday, and talked with a childlike frankness about his coming degree, and the copy in gold of Newton's statue which the Royal Society sent him. Then came Gen[l] Sabine,[8] in uniform, short and spare & benign looking; Dr. Robinson[9] of

[1] William Whewell (1794–1866), mathematician and philosopher, had been Master of Trinity since 1841.

[2] The first Duke of St. Albans was the son of Charles II by Nell Gwyn.

[3] William George Clark (1821–78), the Shakespearean scholar; endowed the Clark lectures at Trinity.

[4] James Bruce, eighth Earl of Elgin (1811–63), son of the seventh Earl who secured the Elgin marbles; diplomatist, Governor-General of Canada, envoy to China, and finally, in 1862, Viceroy of India.

[5] Roderick Impey Murchison (1792–1871), the geologist; knighted, 1846, and created baronet, 1866.

[6] Stratford Canning, first Viscount Stratford de Redcliffe (1786–1880), the eminent diplomatist.

[7] William Rowan Hamilton (1805–65), the Irish mathematician and astronomer; knighted in 1835.

[8] General Sir Edward Sabine (1788–1883), more distinguished as scientist and explorer than as soldier; President of the Royal Society, 1861–71.

[9] Thomas Romney Robinson, D.D. (1792–1882), astronomer, and Rector of Carrickmacross.

Dublin, a strange ghastly old man; Motley[1] the American, who to my surprise is a handsome 'swell' of forty, Englishlike & aristocratic—indeed, with his trim beard and moustache & curled hair parted in the middle, I had taken him for an equerry of the Prince; and finally, George Grote.[2] The tall grave largefeatured historian of sixty ought not to have been postponed to Motley—ought to have had his honour long ago. And so thought the undergraduates, who cheered him to the echo. Lord Elgin too was much cheered; the others had a succés d'estime. . . .

Then came the Greek & Latin poems, read by their authors from the rostrum; & finally, the English poem, by Myers[3]; the subject being 'The Prince of Wales at the Tomb of Washington'. This was much better than the average, and in some parts extremely good. The metre, that of 'The dream of fair women'. Every allusion in it to the prospects of the Prince (who was cheered immensely as he came in, and as he retired at the end) and to the virtues of his mother, was received with thunders of applause: and, allowing every thing for youthful enthusiasm & for social influences, the great and unanimous love which not here only but everywhere is shown for the Queen & her children, is most delightful. Never, so far as her dynasty can effect it, was the political happiness of England so great as now. . . .

Wednesday, 22 May . . . Dined in Hall; walked up the lime avenue and along the backs, where crowds of gay people filled the grounds of King's; then up the parallelogram a little way, for auld lang syne; then back through the avenue, lingering a little on the bridge, while the boats shot under and the mellow afternoon light was on the river and the trees; and so to Joe's rooms at 5.30. The Ellises were there, invited to coffee, which had been set out in Henniker's[4] rooms overhead: but the Prince of Wales, coming in from the flower show, had just gone upstairs, and finding the board spread, had expressed to Mary Ann his intention of staying to share what he supposed to be his friend's provisions. The faithful bedmaker, however, preferring her master to her prince, secretly removed the coffee pots & muffins, and sent for Henniker, who when he came was more distracted than even the Ellises, who were waiting for their meal in Joe's rooms below; for he could neither ask the Prince to stay & partake of what was not his, nor explain to him that he ought to go away. So the Prince stayed and Joe and his party waited and the bedmakers fretted outside: & thus I was obliged to leave them, after snatching a cup of coffee, and take the omnibus for

---

[1] John Lothrop Motley (1814–77), the historian, author of *The Rise of the Dutch Republic*. Became American Minister to Great Britain, 1869–70, and henceforth lived in England.

[2] George Grote (1794–1871), historian and reformer, whose masterpiece was *The History of Greece* (1846–56) in eight volumes.

[3] Frederic William Henry Myers (1843–1901), poet and essayist; then still an undergraduate scholar of Trinity.

[4] The Hon. John Major Henniker-Major, later 5th Baron Henniker (1842–1902); Lord-in-Waiting for several periods, 1877–95. His rooms were M3, Great Court, in the range on the south side along Trinity Lane.

the station. . . . So ends another visit to Cambridge: and the charm of it and the good of it who can tell? Who, indeed, can appreciate, even for himself, the results upon him of a pilgrimage—each time longer than the last—to the spot where his youth lies buried, and with it, all that was or is most loveable and memorable for him?

This Cambridge visit is significant for an understanding of Munby. His account combines two favourite themes—an immense nostalgia for Trinity and for his lost youth (usually accompanied by regret for wasted opportunities); an equally strong loyalty to the Crown and to patriotic causes. In worldly terms, Munby might be termed a snob, of a naïve kind; yet the man who travelled up from Shoreditch by third-class excursion could appreciate a country wench in the railway carriage almost as much as he admired the Prince of Wales in hall at Trinity. Respect for tradition and social standing went with a corresponding reverence for innocent simplicity.

The Prince of Wales appeared a knightly paragon in Munby's eyes. He would have been horrified if he had known that, before the end of this same year, the Prince's exacting father would travel to Cambridge to discuss with 'Bertie' an unfortunate affair he had been having with an actress; that the Prince Consort would return depressed and exhausted, to die three weeks later; and that Queen Victoria would then write of her son: 'I never can or shall look at him without a shudder.'

Monday, 27 May . . . Went with Litchfield to Covent Garden, to hear Patti,[5] the new soprano, in Lucia. She is not a Jenny Lind, but she is certainly a great triumph, her voice being more powerful & of wider range than poor Bosio's.[6] It is however a little thin & metallic, & wants mellowing and rounding into fuller tone. But it is a brilliant voice; and her vocalization is wonderful—yet she is only eighteen! . . .

Friday, 31 May . . . Dined with Cuy[7] . . . and went with him to the Princess's to see Fechter[8] in Hamlet. Never having seen Hamlet on the stage before, I could not compare this with other renderings of the character: but Fechter completely satisfied, and indeed ennobled, my own conception of Hamlet; nor can I

[5] Adelina Patti (1843–1919) had made her English debut as Amina on 14 May.

[6] Angiolina Bosio (1830–59), a great favourite in London, had died suddenly at St. Petersburg; the Russian climate was too much for her.

[7] Cuyler Anderson.

[8] Charles Albert Fechter (1824–79) was a French actor who made a success in Paris before coming to London, where his highly original interpretation of Hamlet in 1861 created a sensation. He went to America in 1869 and opened the old Globe Theatre, New York, as Fechter's. He died on a farm near Philadelphia. See 2 February, 1864.

imagine a more truthful and noble view of that subtle imaginative questioner—that sensitive soul, warped by constant yearning towards the awful riddles of life, which he states so eloquently, which he is too irresolute ever to solve by action.

Fechter has a fine presence, a beautiful hand, a grand strong-featured face full of expression; and with his flowing golden hair and slight beard (a novelty in stage-traditions) he looked like the portraits of the face of Christ. His masterly delivery of English, with almost no accent, was wonderful ...

Saturday, 1 June ... At five, I went to the Horse Guards to see the distribution of Colours to the Queen's, who are now 2000 strong. The gates were guarded; but I met Walter Severn, who took me up to the top of the building. Here was a group of ladies and officials, and amongst them Millais, with whom, being introduced, I had some talk. He was very civil and agreeable, & is certainly singularly handsome in feature, and noble looking. ... He and his wife[9] did a thing the other day, which ought to exclude *her* at least, from all society. Ruskin was in the middle of his lecture 'on a Twig' at the Royal Institution, when these two actually came in, and sat down in a front seat before him. Poor Ruskin (and it is the first trait of human feeling I have known in him) at once turned pale and ill, and had to 'hop the twig' of his discourse and retire. Now, such an act on Millais's part is atrociously mauvais gout—though he is very absent and careless; but on *her* part, it is about the most shameless, barbarous, and unwomanly thing that she could have done. A divorced adulteress & her paramour would not do it ...

... at 8.45 met Walter again by appointment, and went with him to 37 Gower Street. Here live Newton and his bride Mary Severn, settled in a fine substantial old house, with a garden and *rookery* behind. She looked well and happy; and he too, as he well might ...

We left about ten, and walked down to the Junior United Service, to call for Capt. Green, a friend of Walter's. ... I was persuaded to go with Severn and his friend to the 'Alhambra', where some thousands of people had gathered to see a man fling himself, in a highly dangerous & thrilling manner, from one swing to another across the building. The man himself, Léotard,[1] was beautiful to look upon; being admirably made & proportioned; muscular arms shoulders & thighs; and calf ankle and foot as elegantly turned as a lady's. His feat also was wonderful and done with ease & grace ...

The summer months in London were propitious for Munby's encounters with the working woman. This year he gives accounts of a

[9] Millais had married Effie (Euphemia) Ruskin in 1855, after her marriage with Ruskin had been annulled. The lecture 'On Tree Twigs' was not one of Ruskin's best.

[1] Jules Léotard (1830–70), the Frenchman who gave his name to his acrobatic costume, now regularly used by dancers at schools or rehearsals.

brickmaker, a telegraph clerk, a shirtcollar-maker, a porter in Hungerford Market, a consumptive embroiderer, and a mid-Victorian draper's shop:

Sunday, 2 June: evening, Hyde Park . . . Many, and I among the rest, took refuge under the trees from a long shower . . . and I fell in talk with a neat pleasant looking young woman who stood next me . . .

. . . Her father, it gradually appeared, is a farmer near Lutterworth; & she, his only daughter, is a draper's shopwoman. . . . I offered her my arm & umbrella . . . and I found she was ready to tell me all I wanted to know about the life of the shop. . . . Her employer, whom she called 'the Master' and 'our old gentleman', is a bachelor, and keeps eight attendants for his shop, four male, four female. These all, except one man, live in the house, but not with the master. They have a common sittingroom for meals, down stairs in the cellar next the kitchen; and a common drawingroom parlour, at the top of the house. In these they all, young men and young women, sit together, the men however breakfasting & dining at a different time. There is no elder person present, but the cook downstairs has a certain authority. 'We have to get our meals as we can', she said: 'sometimes when you've gone down to get dinner, the shopbell rings, and up you've to come without tasting a thing. . . . The "young ladies" begin work at eight, and go on till nine at night—you don't go out of the shop all day except downstairs for meals; . . . I stand behind the counter—we have one counter & the men the other. Our customers is chiefly ladies; and *ladies* are so tiresome . . .'

'We've not many gentlemen customers', she went on, 'ours is mostly a ladies' shop: but sometimes a gentleman might come in for gloves or that. Yes, if he asked me to put the gloves on for him, I should, of course; but not without. And if he wanted to joke me, I should say "one of the young men'll attend to you, Sir". Our old gentleman is very particular about us joking with the young men, or the travellers . . . he's very particular who you go with: if I was to stop out meals of a Sunday without asking, he'd have ever so many questions about where I'd been when I got home. "Eliza",[2] he says sometimes, "what 'ud your father an' mother say to me if I didn't keep an eye to you?". . .'

. . . 'We go out for a walk sometimes after shop hours, from halfpast nine; the men don't often go with us; they try to, but we don't want 'em. I think we like 'em very well, but there's no sweethearting between us. We sit with them of an evening upstairs after supper, and work and talk; yes, we talk about the customers a good deal, what's happened in the day; that's the chief of what we talk about, I think. I never go out to any amusements hardly; not dancing rooms, no! our old gentleman *would* be in a way if I was to go to them. On Sundays we all dine with the master; we go to church, and have to be in at meals, unless we ask leave; but we have the evenings to ourselves, from half past six till eleven; and then I go and see some friends in Pimlico sometimes, or else for a walk, like tonight. . . .'

'Yes, we're prenticed first; it's according the premium you pay; I was prentice

2 The girl's name was Eliza Close. She was 23.

two years, but some's three. I don't get so much as £20 this year, but I shall get more, next. They rise you every year, according; if they didn't rise 'em, they'd go. And of course there's board & lodging besides. Yes, it's much better than service; but the men get a deal more than us. We have to dress nicely for the shop, of course; but he dont like us to be too smart.'

. . . It seemed strange enough that Eliza should prefer such a life as she described, to the freshness and freedom of a farm: that however is the foolishness of half educated girls: and I was much pleased, not only with her story but with herself.

We shook hands and parted excellent friends, in Southampton Row; and she ran home up the street, for the rain was coming on. I walked homewards, and got in soon after nine.

Wednesday, 5 June . . . London Bridge, more than any place I know here, seems to be the great thoroughfare for young working women and girls. One meets them at every step: young women carrying large bundles of umbrella-frames home to be covered; young women carrying wooden cages full of hats, which yet want the silk and the binding; costergirls, often dirty and sordid, going to fill their empty baskets; and above all, female sackmakers. These last are peculiar to London Bridge, for they all live in Bermondsey and fetch their work from the warehouses some where near Billingsgate. These girls have a yellow oily look, and are many of them slight & delicate; but they carry immense loads of sacking on their heads. I saw an unusually fine one today, on the Middlesex side . . .

There is here the feeling, so familiar with Munby, of acquiring a new specimen; but he was a compassionate collector who loved his discoveries. Of all the working women of London, the milkwomen were his favourites.

Tuesday, 11 June . . . in Trafalgar Square, I noticed a young milkwoman who was just commencing her career under the auspices of an old one, probably her mother. The débutante was standing by the railings of the Union Club. She was a ruddy blooming wench of eighteen or so, scarcely formed yet, but clean-limbed and muscular. Her large hands were in colour a glowing red; the skin coarse and rugged without, showing no vein or dimple, and tough & leathery in the palms, hardening into yellow callosities—*corns*, she would call them—at the roots of the fingers. Can a girl of eighteen possess such hands and have a lover? I should think so! She wore the usual plain straw bonnet, woollen shawl, and clean cotton frock: but her bonnet wanted the thick white cap, her boots were effeminately thin—hardly so strong as a shooting boot—and her frock came down to her ankles! Can it be that fashion is infecting the London milkwomen, noblest of conservative caryatides? So she stood, awkward and happy, a picture of ungainly strength. A lady came mincing past at the moment, with tiny hands cased in lavender kid: the contrast was delicious. Then her mother returned, and the daughter, with her help, adjusted the yoke upon her own square shoulders. It was a brand-new yoke, with her master's name in large letters upon it; whereby as she walks all the world may know that she belongs to 'Sims, 122 Jermyn St.' She walked thus away between her heavy cans, the old mentor keeping at her side and guiding her to the next customer's on the milk walk. Doubtless, she felt happy, when after being hired she was sent to the cooper's to fit herself with a yoke. Doubtless, when she first walked along the streets this afternoon, she felt proud of wearing a new yoke with big letters on it, and clean brown straps and bright hooks and buckles; as proud as a cart horse in his Mayday harness. Long may she feel such pride! She will work in that year out of doors six hours a day, in all weathers, with never a holiday from year's end to year's end: she will nevertheless be as merry as a lark, yet stronger and healthier every year, and marry and breed us sons strong and fullblooded like herself.[3]

On 16 May, Munby had been encouraged to contribute to the *Morning Chronicle*. It appears that he did write an article; but nothing more is heard of the experiment. Munby lacked the adaptability and political expertise which made a barrister-poet like W. M. Praed so useful to the *Post* and the *Chronicle* thirty years earlier. If he was being tried as a leader-writer (perhaps the only department he would have felt appropriate to a gentleman) then it is not surprising that Munby failed; yet he might have made an excellent descriptive reporter. Like all good diarists, he had the knack of being in the right place at the right time; he was returning, for instance, by the last train, from one of his loyal excursions to a volunteer-review—this time at Leatherhead—when he got his first sight of the Tooley Street fire, the worst in London since 1666. Such scenes were not to be witnessed again in the capital until the burning of Munby's beloved Crystal Palace in 1936 or the air raids of 1940-1.

Saturday, 22 June . . . Between Epsom & Cheam, we saw from the train a great fire in the direction of London. A pyramid of red flame on the horizon, sending up a column of smoke that rose high in air & then spread, like that over Vesuvius. At Carshalton, where the villagers were gazing in crowds, as at all the stations,

---

[3] Munby, as we have seen (11 March, 1861) rather disliked George Augustus Sala at first sight; but Sala was a capital observer of London life. Like many Victorian men, Sala also admired the milkwomen, though he seems to have been more sceptical of their marital prospects than Munby—'. . . I have a great affection (platonic) for milkwomen. . . . What clean white stockings they wear, on—no, not their legs—on the posts which support their robust torsos! How strong they are! There are many I should be happy to back, and for no inconsiderable trifle either, to thrash Ben Caunt. Did you ever know any one who courted a milkwoman? Was there ever a milkwoman married, besides Madame Vestris, in the "Wonderful Woman"? Yes:—I love them—their burly forms, their mahogany faces, handsomely veneered by wind and weather; their coarse straw bonnets flattened at the top; their manly lace up boots, and those wonderful mantles on their shoulders . . .' (*Twice Round the Clock* (1878), p. 72).

we heard that it was by London Bridge, at Cotton's wharf. At New Cross the reflection of the firelight on houses & walls began to be visible; & as we drove along the arched way into town, the whole of Bermondsey was in a blaze of light. Every head was thrust out of window, and the long black shadows of train and telegraph posts made the bright road look brighter.

The fire was close to the station: dull brickred fumes & showers of sparks rose high between it and the river. The station yard, which was as light as day, was crammed with people: railings, lamp posts, every high spot, was alive with climbers. Against the dark sky southwards, the façade of S. Thomas's Hospital and the tower of S. Saviour's stood out white and brilliant; and both were fringed atop with lookers on.

A few of the regular omnibuses had got, but hardly, into the station: men were struggling for places on them, offering three & four times the fare for standing room on the roofs, to cross London Bridge.

I achieved a box seat on one, and we moved off towards the Bridge, but with the greatest difficulty. The roadway was blocked up with omnibuses, whose passengers stood on the roofs in crowds; with cabs and hansoms, also loaded *outside*; with waggons pleasure vans & carts, brought out for the occasion and full of people; and amongst all these, struggling screaming & fighting for a view, was a dense illimitable crowd, which even surged in heaps, as it were, over the parapet of the bridge. From my perch I overlooked the whole scene: and what a scene! For near a quarter of a mile, the south bank of the Thames was on fire: a long line of what had been warehouses, their roofs and fronts all gone; and the tall ghastly sidewalls, white with heat, standing, or rather tottering, side by side in the midst of a mountainous desert of red & black ruin, which smouldered & steamed here, & there, sent up sheets of savage intolerable flame a hundred feet high. At intervals a dull thunder was heard through the roar of fire—an explosion of saltpetre in the vaults, which sent up a pulse of flame higher than before. Burning barges lined the shore; burning oil & tallow poured in cascades from the wharfs, and flowed out blazing on the river. A schooner was being cut from her moorings, just in time, as we came up. And all this glowing hell of destruction was backed by enormous volumes of lurid smoke, that rolled sullenly across the river and shut out all beyond. Just above the highest flames stood the full moon in a clear blue sky: but except a pale tint in far off windows, not a gleam nor a shadow of hers could be seen. But the north bank, where she should have shone, was one fairylike panorama of agitating beauty. Every building from the Bridge to the Customhouse was in a glow of ruddiest light: every church tower and high roof shone against the dark, clear in outline, golden in colour: the monument was like a pillar of fire: and every window and roof and tower top and standing space on ground or above, every vessel that hugged the Middlesex shore for fear of being burnt, & every inch of room on London Bridge, was crowded with thousands upon thousands of excited faces, lit up by the heat. The river too, which shone like molten gold except where the deep black shadows were, was covered with little boats full of spectators, rowing up & down in the overwhelming light.

So, through the trampling multitude, shouts and cries & roaring flame and ominous thunder, the air full of sparks and the night in a blaze of light, our omnibus moved slowly on, and in *half an hour* we gained the other end of the Bridge. All along King William St. and Cheapside the people were pouring in to see the fire, and eagerly questioning those who had seen it. And even far away in the dim streets where the houses were all in shade, every church tower that we passed reflected back the light of the conflagration. Bow Church was ruddy bright: the dome of St. Paul's was a pale rose colour on its eastern side . . .

No such fire has been known in London since *the* Fire of 1666: which, by the way, began at a spot exactly opposite this. Two millions, at least, of property destroyed: near eleven acres of ruin: many lives lost, among them the chief of the Fire Brigade.[4] The fire was at his height two or three hours after I saw it: but it is still (Wednesday afternoon) burning furiously . . .

On Sunday, 30 June, Munby recorded that even then 'people were looking at the black smoke that rose thick from the ruins of the fire'.

Friday, 5 July . . . went to a ball at the Prichards' in Inverness Terrace. . . . My interest in balls as such is fast dying out: they enable one to draw out & study the characters of women, and to blow off one's superfluous bitterness under the guise of polished deference: that is all.

But always, to be thus among the sparkling froth atop of Society has one sad delight, in that it keeps vividly before me that gentle misplaced creature who lies grovelling among the dregs; that toiling maid of all work who might have been a drawingroom belle, and is a kitchen drudge. Her love, her humble devotedness, are more than ever valued in the presence of their opposites . . .

Tuesday, 9 July . . . Went over in the afternoon to the Geographical Society's rooms, to see the great gorilla which has been prepared & stuffed—and most admirably—by Wilson of Sydenham. It did not appear more than five feet six or eight in height; but the body is of immense size, three times the bulk of an average man's. The legs very short and weak; the arms of great length and power. The hands, which must be four to five inches across, reminded me of the huge coarse hands of Amelia Banfield[5] and other labouring wenches whom I have observed in farmyard or in colliery.

---

[4] James Braidwood. He was succeeded by Captain (later Sir) Eyre Massey Shaw in command of the London Fire-engines Establishment maintained by the insurance companies. In 1865, as a consequence of the Tooley Street fire, the force was reorganised as the Metropolitan Fire Brigade, and in 1904 became the London Fire Brigade. Munby's estimate of the damage at two million pounds was not exaggerated.

[5] 'A workhouse girl & farm servant near Yeovil' (Munby's note).

Many fashionable women were there, and talking to Du Chaillu[6]; though he has just disgraced himself by grossly insulting a hostile critic, and in the presence of ladies . . .

Wednesday, 10 July . . . I went down to the Crystal Palace at five . . . then up to the slopes under the little wood, where a large circle had been formed for Kiss in the Ring.

The women were chiefly shop girls and servants . . . a nicelooking girl came up, & saying 'Are you in the ring Sir?' offered me her favour—a leaf. I acquiesced; I caught and led and kissed her: and stimulated by the feat, we joined the game; a young woman next me linking her hand in mine with much simplicity, whereby I became a part of the circle.

I remained passive at first: but soon, one pretty girl after another, and several who were passées and plain (cooks, probably), came up, threw me the leaf in passing with an arch look and a smile, and dashed out of the ring and down the slope. These I had to pursue and reclaim; and good fleet runners many of them were, though others yielded at once to my wish for a speedy settlement: but some again had to run after me, till I chose to be caught: and often, one would see a girl pursuing her flying swain up and down, in and out, with the perseverance of a young lady pursuing, not half so innocently, an eldest son. For the rule is, that when a girl has chosen you and you have pursued and caught her, you acquire the right to choose another and be pursued and caught. The original right of choice is thus secured to the fair sex. It is interesting to see how far things that would in a higher class be counted 'liberties' are tolerated here, and even expected, without suspicion of evil. When, after a chase, you bear down full sail upon your partner, you may seize her any how so as to detain her—for she is apt to break away—; and the collision very often brings you both to the ground together. Again, when this romping has ended in her submission, you place your arm round her waist, & lead her tenderly back to the ring: and when you get there, your kisses may be numerous, your embrace somewhat fervent; and if she is pretty, interlopers very likely rush in and snatch a kiss from her— male pertinacem—in passing, as she rests on your arm.

The behaviour of the girls too at the supreme moment, varies with their character. Some—the plain ones chiefly—walk demurely to the place of execution, cast down their eyes, and quietly offer you one cheek: but the greater number approach with simple frankness, look full in your face, and expect to be kissed upon the mouth.

And if they are veiled, you must lift the veil from the shrine for yourself, before you kiss the relics. You are expected however to take your hat off and to

[6] Paul Belloni Du Chaillu (1835–1903), African explorer and author, was exhibiting the collection he had formed in the Ogowé basin, 1855–9. Munby had already seen the exhibition on 11 June, when he described Du Chaillu as 'a slight wiry little man . . . tanned and sinewy, plain of feature but candid and unassuming. His specimens . . . look truthful like himself.' Du Chaillu's veracity had been questioned, but was eventually confirmed.

adopt a certain respectfulness of attitude during the operation: after it, you shake hands warmly, and retire each to the ranks.

There was one tall buxom wench, a servant maid from Islington, who played with great vigour and abandon, and was immensely in demand. For greater freedom she had taken off her shawl. . . . She evidently enjoyed the game intensely: it was the satisfaction, in a rude & sensuous kind, of a long repressed and half unconscious desire: to be let loose, from the solitude of her kitchen where no followers are allowed, into a circle of young men prepared for unlimited kissing—quel bonheur!

I took her large hand and led her up to the centre for 'only one more': her hot but comely face was radiant with joy and soap, as she looked at me with innocent eyes and put up her large lips to receive the reward of beauty. As I handed her back to her place, I said 'and how many kisses have you had?' 'Oh, *thousands*!' she replied with triumph. She had been playing two hours and more, and was not tired: none of them were. To some girls the kisses seem more serious. One simple young creature was heard . . . to say to her friend very solemnly, 'Do you know, *I've been kissed*!' 'And what of that?' laughed the habituée; 'Surely, it didn't hurt you, did it?'

After this contribution to Victorian social history, Munby felt it appropriate to strike a more serious note. He strode, metaphorically, to the rostrum in his M.A. gown:

To me, apart from its own pleasurable but somewhat too youthful excitement, the game of Kiss in the Ring is the most cheering of all lower class amusements. I am convinced from much observation that it both proves and maintains the purity of English working women: it promotes a rustic politeness on the one hand, and on the other a healthy familiarity, between the sexes: it is almost the only relic of the uncouth & hearty outdoor merriment of old England: and last and chiefly, it is a standing protest against the conventions of a false civilization. Let any man in Society consider, whether such behaviour as I have sketched is not more blameless than the flirtations of his own youth. Young men and women can do all this & be pure—can do it (the women at least) because they are pure. And so, the servant girl who rather enjoys being kissed in the hayfield or claspt round the waist behind the pantry door, is not therefore indelicate: the want of that 'personal dignity' which makes young ladies revolt at such horseplay, is no shame to her; for, even with them, it is a feeling induced by training (as in some countries by character) in order to bring about the reserve and isolation which belong to cultivated life. Even my Hannah was not ashamed to tell me—though she hid her face in telling it—that the cook whom she served (the same who used to bring his friends down to see his pretty scullion in her den, and who regretted that he could not think of her, because she was so low) would sometimes unbend from his dignity, and snatch a kiss as she waited on him . . .

104

One cannot help wondering what Munby's father would have made of all this. The authorities agree that 'Kiss in the Ring' is basically a 'marriage game'—the 'marriage' moreover being one of free selection. When children play it, no such significance arises; but as played by strapping Victorian shop girls and servants, it must have been charged with emotional overtones—was indeed a rough and ready matrimonial agency. The scholarly Munby should have known this; yet his eulogy of 'hearty outdoor merriment' and 'rustic politeness' omits the essential point. Munby could be free with his kisses, because for him they were mostly devoid of sexual content; moreover, he had a servant girl-friend of his very own; he was not, then, a sound guide to the theory and practice of adult 'Kiss in the Ring', and one fears he was playing under piratical colours and arousing, not for the first time, some false hopes. Munby's excuse must be that, as usual, wherever the lives of working women were concerned, he was entirely devoted to research.

Monday, 15 July . . . Went, by request of the benchers, to the Middle Temple Hall at 4.30. Out of nineteen candidates for the Librarianship, the six best had been selected for choice.

The other five were assembled in the subtreasurer's room where I joined them. All were apparently gentlemen, but the difference of character among them was amusing under the circumstances. No. 1., older than the rest, was a serious melancholy looking man, in black of antiquated cut, and specially characterised by a large gingham umbrella. He said little, but spoke well and with information when addressed. No. 2 was a gentlemanly well dressed but hard looking barrister of thirty. No. 3 was a parson, of accurate costume and sensible looks. No. 4 was a quiet gentle but somewhat weak looking young Oxford man. No. 5 was an Inner Temple student, drest fashionably, a lively intelligent forward youth, who did most of the talking, and made jokes appropriate to the situation. After a time, I went out in my turn, and was introduced into the fine old parliament or combination room, where some fourteen benchers sat in really venerable conclave round a long oak table. Seated by the president, I was addressed by that functionary, all eyes being upon me. 'Pupil of Sir Hugh Cairns, I think, Mr. Munby?' he said. Yes. 'Yes', added an assessor; 'Cairns says so in this letter.'[7] The magic words 'pupil of Sir Hugh Cairns' were passed down the table, and the reverend Masters put on their glasses and looked at me with a respect bordering on devotion.

[7] Hugh McCalmont Cairns (1819–85) became Lord Chancellor in 1868 and was created Earl Cairns in 1878. Munby had earlier recorded in his diary (8 July) that he was indebted to him for 'a very kind note' in support of his application. Munby had been pleased to find him 'better than he seemed', and concluded that his previous judgement of him had been tinged by envy. This great lawyer was, however, generally thought a chilly character.

After a few formal questions—the real object being to look at one—I rose and retired, the ancient whiteheaded worthies turning round each on his timeworn posterior, to scrutinise me and to return my parting bow . . .

Wednesday, 17 July . . . I went to the subtreasurer of the Middle Temple, and found that the librarianship had been given not to me but to an Oxford man, Smith of Exeter, No. 4 in my list.

I took up my wasted testimonials; walked away with a careless and smiling air, and tried to think first of the pleasure success would bring to that amiable looking fellow. Moreover, had I not determined that I should fail, now as always, and refused to think of success?

But even thus, it will not do: imagination has dwelt unconsciously upon the forbidden prospect; and I felt and feel it a great disappointment.

. . . For the thought of being freed so opportunely from the miserable illpaid & hopeless subordination of Whitehall Place, where the Ecclesiastical Commissioners have behaved to me with the folly & falsehood of their profession[8]; the thought of attaining, at length and for good, to independence, and of saying so to those at home; the thought of entering at last upon congenial work, and in a place so quiet convenient and picturesque; all this has to be given up wholly. And I am tempted to reflect, that this was not a brilliant or wealthy post that I sought, not one that offered hopes of marriage and a settlement, even; but only an obscure and modest income, which might barely enable me to see at last the foreign lands I long to see, might bring to an humble end the dependence & disappointments of ten years, and might help me after all to do some little thing for *her*.[9] . . .

To those who do not know, I shall say nothing; to those who do, I shall lightly speak of this matter as a trivial one . . . but for myself, in parting with this glimpse of hope and competence I shall sink back to my normal state; from which it will be hard, if I ever have the chance, to rise again to the loathsome task of begging for certificates of merit from men who have long ceased to need such things themselves . . .

Friday, 19 July . . . I walked up to the New Road, and had a long talk with the old ballad seller opposite S. Pancras church. A very respectable intelligent man, of some education: said he had been there twenty years and brought up a family of nine children on the proceeds of his stall. The trade, he said, was never so good as now: the public concert rooms have created a large demand for popular songs of the day, and the old fashioned ballads sell well too. Has customers of all classes, but mostly young men, shopmen and artisans, who buy comic songs, tradesmen's daughters, who buy sentimental parlour ditties, and servantmaids.

[8] This is not fully explained in the diary, but Munby, having passed his examination with credit, had hoped for more consideration.
[9] Hannah.

These when they first come to London buy the old ballads they've heard at home in the country; but afterwards they choose rather the songs—from English operas and so on—which they hear young missis a playing upstairs . . .

Saturday, 20 July: Grosvenor Square . . . I saw a tall graceful woman cross the road in front of me, walking between two milk cans. . . . It was Kate O'Cagnay, the queen of the London milkwomen. And she is so still; though the soft complexion of her handsome face is changed, as I saw today, into a weatherbeaten brown, & though the full curves of her sumptuous form are sharpening into lines of strength. It would not be so if she had been a lady—a well-preserved beauty of that Mayfair through which she passes daily, a rustic contrast; but we must work, nous autres—and Kitty is seven and twenty now, and for nine long years she has walked her rounds *every* day, carrying through London streets her yoke and pails, and her 48 quarts of milk, in all weathers, rain or fair. Long before the Crimean war she did so; and she does so still . . . she never had an umbrella or an illness in her life . . .

Looking down at her large hands, redder now than ever, I saw with surprise no wedding ring there. 'Well, Kate!' I said in passing; & the stately wench turned half round but did not stop or start. 'Oh, Sir!' she exclaimed, opening wide her mouth and her large grey eyes. 'So you are not married, after all?' 'No Sir' she answered, with a sly shamefaced smile and a downcast look. To stop and talk to a milkwoman in Grosvenor Square, is a test of moral courage which I was prepared to undergo; but it might have compromised poor Kitty's unsullied reputation: so after one and two enquiries about her, made by me without looking at her (vile subterfuge!) and answered by her from behind, I walked away, and Kitty descended into the area of Lord Tom Noddy's house[1]. . .

Monday, 29 July . . . I went up at five o'clock to the Paddington Station. Hannah came there by 6.30: and after a word in private, we separated. She waited, walked about the platform, leaned on a rail, stood close by me: but always we were strangers: no look betrayed her; she neither expected nor wished me to notice her. Base necessity—which she does not feel the weight of, but I do. Other women would think it an insult to be thus ignored: she accepts it, takes it for granted, absolutely prefers it. She is content to pay for an actual nearness with an apparent contrast, which after all is natural on her side. And yet, in her straw bonnet and brown shawl and pink cotton frock (given her ten years ago by her mistress) she looked, not indeed a conventional lady, but something quite as refined. Her bare hands were absurdly white and small: the lithe grace of her tall figure—the free unconscious simplicity of her manner—and the frank maidenly look of her noble face—for it is noble still: all these things I watched intently and long. Strange perennial grace of true womanhood! . . . Sometimes her face and

---

[1] In 1881 Munby added a footnote: Kitty was then married with six children; but she was still a milkwoman.

hands look coarse, and they and all her ways show signs of work and age; but again, the hands grow white, the step elastic and young, the face as soft and bright as in her teens. One moment, she is the very pattern of a kitchen drudge, awkward and strong, hard at work in sweat and dirt: the next, she is the perfect image of a still and stately queen. . . . At last the train came, and in it her sister, whom she had not seen for four years. Ten years and more between them, & yet she hardly looked the older. I watched the sisters' greeting, and saw them walk away together; not without many meditations & thoughts of heart. Then I walked homewards . . .

Thursday, 1 August . . . to Eccleston Square to dine with the Severns. Mrs. Severn was unwell & invisible, so Eleanor and Walter and I dined together. Eleanor is greatly improved, and is a graceful gentle creature, intelligent and kind, not unworthy to take her sister's place. It was probably my last visit; for next week they are going to the south of France, and so on to Rome to reside with Mr. S. And thus this charming household is broken up, to my great regret.[2] . . .

When Munby passed his Civil Service examination in June, 1860, he noticed on the list of successful candidates the name of Eliza Harris, who carried the letter-bags between Cobham and Stoke d'Abernon. Subsequently he discovered that she was the only female postman in England appointed under the Civil Service rules.

On Saturday, 10 August, 1861—over a year later—Munby went to Leatherhead, on one of his country excursions, and thence walked through Stoke d'Abernon to Street Cobham. He does not admit in his diary that he was seeking anything more substantial than fresh air, but it comes as no surprise that, on the way to Church Cobham, he 'met a tall young woman, who did not seem to belong to any of the ordinary classes of village girls':

. . . She had on a battered green velveteen bonnet, a shabby black cloak, and a brown stuff gown of milliner's design. . . . I asked her 'Are you the postman?' 'Yes, Sir', she replied readily; 'I'm going to Stoke now for the letters'. Whereon I turned back and walked with her. 'Your name' I said 'is Eliza Harris, and you are the rural messenger from Cobham to Stoke?' 'Yes Sir,' she said with a smile of surprise: and taking me perhaps for an emissary of Sir Rowland Hill, she answered my questions with most cheerful eagerness. . . . 'I walk eighteen miles everyday Sir,' says she, 'except Sundays, and then I only walk four or five miles. . . . I like the work, and can do it very well. . . . It's rather lonesome,

---

[2] Eleanor Severn (1842–1912), Joseph Severn's youngest daughter, married Henry Furneaux. Her daughter Margaret married F. E. Smith, first Earl of Birkenhead. Munby bought Joseph Severn's piano: 'Paid in £25 at Herries & Farquhar's to Mrs. Severn's account, for piano' (Concise diary, 17 August 1861).

that's all . . .' . . . I shook her hand—which was large and thick, though soft—& complimented her upon her vocation, & exhorted her to persevere in it; which indeed she will certainly do . . .

After spending the night at Cobham, Munby walked on to Teddington, Sunday, 11 August, to visit Robert Borland and his family. Approaching Molesey, he met 'a respectable brewer's clerk from London' who accompanied him for a while. 'We spoke, among other subjects, of the Queen, and how she is beloved, and of the exceeding happiness and peacefulness at present of this nation; which indeed may well strike a man with gladness who looks on history, made or making.' Re-reading this passage of the diary in 1894, Munby added: 'Yes. The decade which began with 1860 was the happiest portion of the 19th century.'

On 17 August, Munby set off for a holiday in Devon, where he made the acquaintance of two female ploughmen and harrowers who may have helped to inspire his poem *Dorothy* of twenty years later. He went on into Wales and contrived a flying visit to Wigan before going home to York early in September. He returned to London on 5 October; and after only a fortnight (long holidays obviously being one of the advantages of the Ecclesiastical Commission) he left again on 19 October to spend a few days in Boulogne, where he repeated many of the experiences of his visit in 1859.

Thursday, 7 November . . . Went to Bow Street Police Station to enquire about the two young ladies who were tried yesterday at Clerkenwell Sessions (under the names of Long & Murray) for stealing books, and who I find are sentenced to nine months' imprisonment with hard labour[3]. . .

Thursday, 14 November . . . Dined in Hall, where I saw one of the two Hindoo (or at least Indian) gentlemen who have become members. This one is an envoy for some Nawab: an intelligent man he is, of pleasant looks: dined in a red turban: ordered a cab in excellent English.

The two bring each his own cook, but sit at the same mess with the other students. They must have joined only for the honour of the thing; for the Bench have decided not to call them to the Bar.

To the newsroom, & home till 8. My Latin class, and then to Macmillan's, where were Masson, the Rev. F. Garden,[4] H. Kingsley, D. G. Rossetti, Hughes,

---

[3] On 30 November Munby visited Tothill Fields Prison and saw 'Murray' in her cell. Munby found her 'commonplace'; he would not have taken her for 'a lady born and bred'. He admired the 'Matron' of this large prison—which held 800 women convicts, and was entirely run by women (except for two gate-porters and 'the oakum master'); but he felt that, compared with male convicts, the women were treated too lightly.

[4] Francis Garden (1810–84), theologian and sub-dean of the Chapel Royal.

Litchfield, and others. A very pleasant evening. Mr. Garden, who is a genial man of his discourse (a college friend of Tennyson's, by the way), held forth a good deal about miracles &c . . . not perceiving (as parsons never can) how several of the laymen were only restrained by his cloth from speaking their minds . . .

Tuesday, 19 November . . . Went out to the Westminster Police Court, to the examination of Mary Newell, the maid of all work who robbed her master last week, went off in man's clothes, travelled down to Yarmouth, took lodgings there, smoked cigars, & made love to her landlady. Assuming that she had as I was told done it only for a lark, I admired her pluck skill and humour, and wished to observe her person & character. But the inspector who helped to catch her showed me that she was probably a practised thief and a dissolute girl. . . .

At noon the court opened, with a great rush of people to see the prisoner. As a barrister, I had a reserved seat in front of her. She was led in and placed on high in the dock: a sullen but fairly good looking girl, of moderate height, and not unfeminine. Drest in shabby finery: her hair, which she had cut short, hanging over her forehead. Her hat, coat, trousers, and the rest of her male clothing were exhibited on a table. . . . After she had been committed for trial at the Sessions, I walked away with her master—a surveyor—and his pupil, the young man whose name & garments she assumed. She was a dirty and untidy servant, they said; was in the habit (they now found) of stealing out to low theatres alone, hiring cabs to go in and smoking cigars with the cabmen . . .

Tuesday, 26 November . . . rode to Kilburn to see my Hannah, according to promise. I rang the servants' bell, and she came running out, her face full of smiles, & tolerably clean, and bonny withal as it ever is. She couldn't stir, being full of work; but begged me to come in and round to the back of the house, that I might through a window see the kitchen and scullery where she spends her life, and the pots and pans which for my sake she loves to clean. All which I did; going carefully along with her, that none might hear: and brought her out again into the street, where when I had kissed her she had to run & leave me—all along of them partridges. Ha ha! and Alas! . . .

The talk at Macmillan's on 28 November was 'chiefly about the atrocious Yankee outrage on the *Trent*, of which news came yesterday'. At the outset of the American Civil War, the U.S.S. *San Jacinto* had stopped the English steamer *Trent* and seized the Confederate envoys Mason and Slidell, who were on their way to England. It was now that Prince Albert, already seriously ill, averted possible war with the North; as his last political act, he re-drafted a government dispatch in more conciliatory terms, his revision being accepted by Lord John Russell. For the remainder of 1861, the *Trent* incident and the tragic death of the Prince Consort dominated the thought of the nation.

Sunday, 15 December . . . This morning came the astounding news of Prince Albert's death: so unexpected and sad and ominous, that people are struck dumb with amaze and sorrow. The news-offices in the Strand were open and besieged by anxious folk; a strange gloom was upon the town; in church, the preacher spoke of it, and an aweful silence there was, with something too very like sobbing, when his name was left out from the prayers . . .

Saturday, 21 December . . . Went up Regent Street in the afternoon, shopping. Every one in mourning; all shops boarded across with black; even brass door plates covered with crape. Crowds round the photograph shops, looking at the few portraits of the Prince which are still unsold. I went into Meclin's to buy one: every one in the shop was doing the same. They had none left: would put my name down, but could not promise even then. Afterwards I succeeded in getting one—the last the seller had—of the Queen and Prince: giving four shillings for what would have cost but eighteen pence a week ago. Such facts are symbols of the great conviction of his worth & value which the loss of him has suddenly brought to us all . . .

Monday, 23 December: York . . . a dull grey funereal day: the burial of the Prince Consort. . . . The day was to be celebrated by a funeral procession through the town and a service in the Cathedral. . . . The pageant was strangely solemn & impressive, and seemed from the behaviour of actors and spectators to express a grief not formal merely. So also in the Minster. . . . When all was over, the troops marched away and the crowd retired in silence . . .

The whole of the proceedings were projected and arranged by my father; and were most creditable to the town . . .

Friday, 27 December . . . I started by the 9.45 train for London . . . the pleasures of one's home grow more sadly precious as age and the widening asunder of our mature lives suggest that they cannot last for ever. And to me there is besides, the thought that *she*[5] can never share them . . .

Tuesday, 31 December . . . Looked out over the Thames while the clocks struck midnight, and sat musing over the fire far into the new year.

The close of this year is notable for two events: the *Trent* outrage, and the death of Prince Albert: and is still more notable for the result of these events upon public feeling. For the end of the former is not yet known: and meanwhile, the whole nation seems to be sublimed by a noble sorrow and a noble anxiety, into a purity and oneness that I never remember to have seen before. Party

[5] Hannah.

III

strife is for the moment dead: even the private life of ordinary men is subdued and toned down from its frivolity by the awe of apprehension and of regret. And England, knit together as one man by grief and indignation, has poured out its heart, as the heart of one man, in a passion of sympathy and love and veneration for the Queen, for which mere loyalty is a cold name indeed. It is much to have seen such a time, and felt, as only such a crisis could make one feel, that after all, we of this land are one family and brotherhood. But it is still more, to have lived and been young through these last twenty years of calm good government and social peace: years of ever increasing affection and respect for her and him, to whose wise ways and pure life and serene domestic happiness we have owed so much of that government and peace. . . .

*   *   *

The daily life of Munby in 1862 was extremely full but far from methodical. Apart from office hours, on which he has less and less to say, his actions were governed largely by chance meetings with women. He could not walk a mile, the diary suggests, without talking to one or more women—and these encounters might lead to conversations of several hours, during which Munby could tramp half across London escorting his 'fair friend' to her destination. Often all went well; the girl, usually in such cases described as frank, homely or honest, had no expectations, chatted away about her occupation to their mutual satisfaction, and was finally well pleased to be rewarded by a cup of tea or a sixpenny tip.

Other acquaintances could be dangerously embarrassing; among them a young woman encountered near the British Museum (Tuesday, 7 January, 1862), 'tall welldrest and handsome', whom Munby took for 'a shop-woman or milliner of the best class' and who looked at him 'in a grave and diffident way'. No sooner had they set off together than 'her whole behaviour changed. She put her arm through mine, unasked, & throwing off her reserved & ladylike demeanour, she grew all at once lively and amorous: a turn for which I was scarcely prepared.' This lady proved to be an artist's model. She scandalised Munby by describing a party at which the guests, male and female, including herself, had all disported themselves entirely naked—this in the hearing of passers-by, to Munby's 'frequent discomfiture'; so that it was a relief to bid her goodbye. One must conclude that in these matters Munby was a determined innocent, perhaps unwilling to learn.

It is, on the whole, a happy idealistic life the diary reveals. There were always trusted friends to be turned to: men such as Borland, Ralston (now a busy book-reviewer for several journals), Litchfield or Stokes. Munby also had the gift of enjoying simple pleasures—the purchase of a new meerschaum pipe, for instance (6 January), which he 'noticed the other day, but refrained from buying till I had considered the matter, and justified to myself the indulgence'.

The very persistence of the diary evinces an inner strength in Munby that sustained him in his constantly fluctuating moods. On 8 January the threat of an American war receded; 'the news, that the Americans have yielded & given up Mason and Slidell, was published in third editions of the evening papers. Newsboys crying it in the street; people gathered round the news offices, where "The Answer" was posted up in large letters, the ink still wet.' On 10 January, though, he was left with 'a certain horror, new & unexpected' after his brother George had told him a family secret, that their grandfather, 'driven wild by calumnies about some business of accounts which was afterwards honourably explained', had committed suicide. But three weeks later (3 February) a visit to the Law Courts enabled him to give thanks that he had *not* succeeded as a pleader in wig and gown; 'the dulness & dreariness of the matters in hand, the hustling and bustling of attornies and other heated persons, and the need there of a briskness & countenance which I have not, turn my brain and sicken my heart; and I rejoice that, being as I am a dreamer and observer merely, I seem to have escaped from court-work.'

And always the diary brings evidence of the eagerness with which Munby sought fresh experience in art or entertainment, and nourished his contacts with writers and artists:

Wednesday, 15 January, 1862 . . . went into the London Pavilion in the top of the Haymarket. . . . A nicelooking young woman, one Miss Catherine Parkes, dressed herself in pantomimic characters, appearing finally as a clown, with face bedaubed and broad grin, & thus dancing a clumsy dance. She apologised to the audience for not standing on her head or doing the other clown's tricks; saying 'I, being a lady, turn my toes in instead.' This at least shows a certain propriety of taste, in her and them: and indeed she seemed respectable as well as pretty. From my seat I caught glimpses of her mother, behind the scenes, arranging the cockscomb and chalking the cheeks of her clown-daughter . . .

Thursday, 16 January . . . To my Latin class. Ruskin was there, having returned to his class. I did not stay to speak to him, but went down to Macmillan's; where were Masson ∴ . . Rossetti, Ralston, Leslie Stephen.[6] . . . and others. Stayed

[6] Leslie Stephen (1832–1904), the writer, mountaineer, and first editor of the *Dictionary of National Biography*, knighted 1902; younger brother of Sir J. F. Stephen, the judge; father of Virginia Woolf.

talking till late; and found to my surprise and delight that M. has discovered & bought up the copies of Clough's charming 'Bothie'. I instantly bought one. Few books are more precious to me than this. My theories of women, my love of college reminiscences, of scenic description, of hexameters, are all satisfied by it to the utmost.

A female clown at the London Pavilion, January, 1862

I could not help telling poor Clough this, the only time I ever had the good fortune to meet him—which was at Parker's, some years ago.[7] It is a selfish satisfaction to think that such a book as this, too, never reached a second edition —'fell dead on the market'. Rossetti Ralston and I walked home together, talking of the former's new book on the Early Italian Poets. . . .

Saturday, 18 January . . . I walked past the South Kensington Museum and along the Cromwell Road to see the Exhibition building. When I was here last, some three or four years ago, all this country was a tract of market gardens, with bridleroads between & footpaths, where sweethearts walked for privacy, be-

[7] According to the diary, Munby met Clough at Monckton Milnes's house, 9 March, 1859. Clough had died in 1861.

tween Brompton & Kensington. Now, broad streets of lofty houses; and further on, roadways terraced on arches in all directions; the wretched grass of the old fields still visible below, with here & there a doomed tree, where the houses have not yet been begun. Crowds of welldrest people hanging about, looking at the Exhibition: a vast building—hideous enough, of course, but having a certain massiveness, as of good masonry . . .

Sunday, 16 February: Munby returns from spending a night at Gillingham with Cuyler Anderson . . . I changed at the Crystal Palace, and reached London Bridge at 5.30.

I found Hannah waiting for me at the station, by appointment. I had meant to take her to church, but it was too early, so I told her we would go home. She would not take my arm—for it was still daylight & many people were about—but walked apart, till we got down into the empty streets about the Borough Market—for I led her that way to avoid observation; and even then she hung back, and whispered, 'You know I have no gloves on'! Gloves, indeed! I took the poor child's bare hand and laid it on my sleeve; and so we walked arm in arm in the dusk along Bankside and over Blackfriars Bridge. 'And how would you like, dear, to be servant at one of these old houses by the waterside, where the coal agents and foremen of timberyards live?' Oh, she would like it very well: and it 'ud be near me, too!

I left her for a few moments to call in Chatham Place and enquire after Rossetti, whose invalid wife, I was shocked to hear, died on Monday, through an overdose of Laudanum. He is in a sad state of grief; Ruskin says so, who has seen him.

I rejoined Hannah and we went on to the Temple together. She unpinned her coarse shawl and took off her simple bonnet, and rolled up the sleeves of her Sunday frock—a black stuff one, old, and rent in places—as usual: but her manner was sad & spiritless, and she looked weary & workworn. It was bitter too to see her bonny tender face all roughened and red, and her hair, that was once so soft and beautiful, all foul with dust & overheat, that she cannot get it clean. 'Oh, it's dreadful!' she said: 'they can see it for all my cap, and every one stares at me so! And Sarah says she shouldn't wonder if my face was to break out all in blotches, in the Spring, with overheat!' Presently she broke away from me, and hid her face, and began a long low cry that ended in sobs and tears.

I drew her down toward me, wondering and anxious; and she lay and cried softly against my knee, while I tried to soothe her and learn what was the matter. At last it all came out. 'Everybody hates me!' she sobbed; 'I'm so dirty and shabby! The missis did look so upon me this morning when I waited at breakfast —and I know it was because I was dirty. And Neal[8]. . . sent me a nasty Valentine, of a cookmaid scrubbing . . . and Mary says I'm ragged, and talks so of my

---

[8] The gardener at the house where Hannah worked.

dirt . . . and Ellen[9] . . . wouldn't hardly walk down the road with me the other night, she said she was so ashamed of me, in my bonnet and shawl—and she *knew* I hadn't a better one to put on!' This was the very bonnet and shawl in which she had just walked home with me. Yet who could blame her, poor innocent, if even the knowledge that I loved her in spite—nay because—of all this, was not enough to counteract the taunts of the foolish women her equals? . . . 'tis hard in practice, even for a maid-of-all-work . . .

I set myself to still her half-hysterical weeping & to comfort her; and after awhile she made her cup of cocoa, and sat on her hassock on the hearth, & listened with childlike interest—though her eyes were still red—to a story of Miss Mulock's,[1] which I read to her out of 'Good Words'. 'Mistress and Maid', it was called: but though it professed to be a servants' story, I had to translate it, as I went on, out of a most involved and magniloquent style into homely English. . . .

So she grew cheerful; and got up when I had done and fetched the ewer and towel, & knelt down and washed my feet in her own handy helpful way. . . . I have left out one thing that was characteristic. After sobbing out all the griefs she endured from taunting fellow servants, 'And yet,' she added 'I don't think I *could* be less dirty if I was to try, with all my dirty work'.[2] . . .

Sunday, 23 February . . . near S. Martin's Lane, I met W. M. Thackeray; 'tooling' along quietly, alone, with hands in pockets and absent air; evidently on his way to the Garrick. . . .

Thursday, 27 February . . . To my Latin class; Taylor, the young baker, came to say farewell. . . . He is setting up a wife . . . as well as a shop: . . . He thanked me in a frank manly way for my teaching. 'Though I've been away,' he said, 'my mind's been here—thinking of the Thursday evenings; and I do feel to love the College—every one is so social and pleasant.' I shook hands with him as he left with regret, and hopes of meeting again. . . .

Friday, 7 March . . . to Upper Belgrave Place, to a gathering at Munro's: the first he has had since his marriage. It was all the pleasanter for this new element. . . .

After music and pictures upstairs (there was some good photographs of the Brownings, given to Munro in Florence lately by Robert B.) I went down to the men. Sala came in late, with whom I had some talk for the first time. He looks horribly bloated and rednosed; but his manner is frank & pleasant, and his

---

[9] Hannah's younger sister.

[1] Dinah Maria Mulock (1826–87), author of *John Halifax, Gentleman*. In 1864 she married G. L. Craik, a partner in Macmillan's.

[2] Munby had reckoned for Hannah's benefit that she had cleaned 1023 boots in the course of 1861 (entry of 19 January).

conversation spirited and full of amusing anecdotes. He told me of Mudie the Autocrat, who actually wrote to him this morning suggesting that he should write a 'country novel', & adding that *Mrs.* Mudie was sure it would be delightful! . . .

Friday, 21 March . . . After dinner I went up to Mudie's; and at a bookstall on the way, fell in with that strange incarnation of PreRaphaelitism, young Algernon Swinburne. He told me that Rossetti is calmer & better; and that he has given up the lodgings he has had for so many years in Chatham Place, and taken a house at Chelsea with some of his own family.[3] . . .

Saturday, 22 March . . . I crossed Westminster Bridge by the temporary wooden footway; at the Surrey end of which I found a group of dustwomen, resting on their way home. . . . It occurred to me that this was a good chance of obtaining a photograph of a woman of this class in working dress. Knowing however that the creatures would be simply astonied if I made such a request in person, I asked a photographer's doorsman close by,[4] if he could persuade one of the women, whom I pointed out, to come and be taken. He went off to do so, and returned to the door with her: but seeing me, she quickly ran away again. 'She's a stoopid!' cried the doorsman; and rushing off once more, he brought her back; and grinning and wondering, she tramped up stairs like a ploughman. I followed; and in a little room that served as showroom & parlour, I found the photographers, two respectable young men, and two girls, their sisters apparently, who were seated at needlework. The dustwench, all in dirt as she was, had plumped herself down in a chair by the door, and sat silently staring: and the disgust and astonishment with which the two milliners looked at their coarse masculine sister, was very amusing. Rapidly noting the contrast, but speaking as if the whole affair was a matter of course, I said to the young men. . . . 'Can you take me a portrait of this woman?' They agreed; and 'this woman' was marched on up to the glass house.

. . . She put on her jacket at my desire, and sat down, holding her tin dinnercan in one hand, and thrusting out her strong feet before her: and when I had posed her thus—which I did with my gloves on, seeing how dirty she was—the lens was uncovered.

They kept her several minutes, for the light was very bad; and wonderfully still she sat, not moving even her eyelids. But when it was over, she drew a long breath and said 'Eh! Well, that *is* a punishment! that's wuss than a day's work, that is.'. . .

A second picture was taken of her by the photographer for his own satis-

---

[3] Rossetti left Chatham Place after his wife's death, but did not move into Tudor House, 16 Cheyne Walk, with his brother William, until October, 1862.

[4] This was the hey-day of popular photography. On 29 March Munby counted seventeen photographers' shops on the New Road between Judd Street and Albany Street in north London.

faction; and then 'Now I think we may dismiss her' I said. She understood me, and quickly exclaimed 'Ain't you a goin to give me nothin Sir?' and then, having received a shilling, she huddled up her things, tramped downstairs in her rude manlike way, & exit. . . .

I came away when the picture was ready; leaving behind me, as I thought, no other impression than that of wonder at my bad taste, in desiring to possess the portrait of a clumsy dustwoman rather than of (say) an elegant young milliner in costume of the period. But, as I gave the doorsman a fee for his trouble, he remarked that he had 'another young woman' close at hand—'a beautiful specimen.' I asked what he meant; and by way of reply, he plunged into a publichouse next door, and produced in a twinkling the damsel in question, who had evidently been in waiting: a tall palefaced girl in mourning of fashionable make though somewhat shabby. He set her before me in the passage, adding by way of introduction 'She's an envelope maker Sir—there's lots of 'em hereabouts'. The girl looked quiet and modest; & what I was expected to do with her I could not conceive. I passed on therefore, simply telling her that she was not the sort of hardworking person whose portrait I wanted. The doorsman however came forward & whispered that he had brought her 'to have a picture of her taken *with her clothes up*'. Here was a revelation, indeed! The fellow, finding quickly enough that he had made a mistake, took to vehement apologies—'he was an old soldier' (he wore a medal) 'and no doubt I was an officer—and he thought &c— and he meant no harm.' I walked off in disgust; but the scene was not yet over. A shabby-genteel young man who had been lingering about now came up to me bowing. 'Beg pardon Sir—but was you in want of any ballet girls or poses plastiques?' I stared and answered No: but . . . added 'What have you to do with such matters?' 'Sir,' replied the seedy one 'I am a theatrical agent: I can supply you Sir with girls, for ballet or poses or artists' models, at an hour's notice, if you honour me with an order.' And he offered me a dirty envelope containing his address.

I thanked him coldly, and so got away at last; wondering why on earth a dustwoman's portrait should have produced these offensive results. There had been no appearance of evil in the matter; the photographer had seemed respectable; and I can only conjecture that Astley's theatre, and the crowds of mean workgirls who live thereabouts, may have been local causes for the annoyance . . .

. . . Went to Dickinson's—his last gathering this season. . . . Among the men there whom I knew more or less, were H. W. Phillips . . . Millais . . . Holman Hunt. As usual, the difference of character between Hunt & Millais was well seen: Hunt talking genially with all his acquaintance; Millais holding himself sublimely aloof, except for a few juvenile worshippers. Me, who am by no means juvenile or adulatory, he affected to ignore: while Hunt cordially shook hands, though I know him but slightly. If a man would escape envy and heartburnings with himself in such encounters, he must learn to be silent & selfcontained . . .

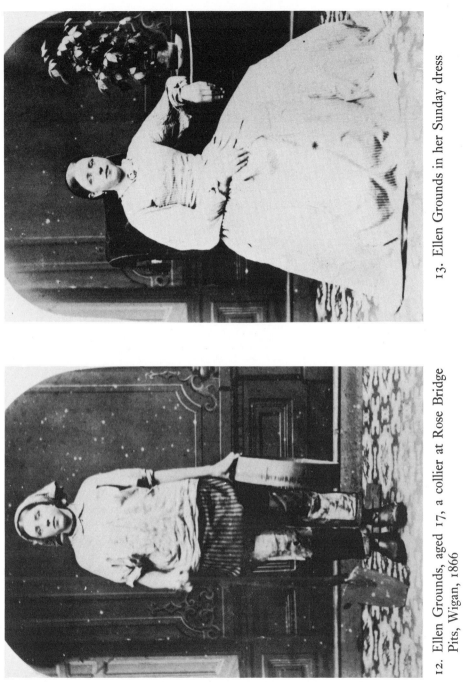

13. Ellen Grounds in her Sunday dress

12. Ellen Grounds, aged 17, a collier at Rose Bridge Pits, Wigan, 1866

14. A. J. Munby with Ellen Grounds at a Wigan photographer's, 1873

Sunday, 23 March . . . Ralston came in, & also Bailey: whose visit disturbed me somewhat, for I was expecting every moment my Hannah's single knock at the door. It *is* hateful to be reminded thus, that one cannot show one's chiefest treasure to any living soul, because of that very homeliness and lowliness which is one of its best charms to me. . . . She stayed with me till nine o'clock, very happily . . .

Thursday, 27 March . . . to my Latin class till 10: then to Macmillan's. . . . Macmillan gave me a copy (for Ralston to review) of Christina Rossetti's Poems,[5] which are not yet out. Home by 12, and read them with strong admiration & pleasure. They include those charming ones—e.g. My Secret—which Dante read in MS. to Stokes and me a year ago. They are vigorous, sensuous, keenly observant.

The craze for photography coincided with the rise of the London music-halls, of which more than twenty were established by the eighteen-sixties. Munby ministered to the former enthusiasm, but he was sceptical about the latter, so far as the large West End halls were concerned. On Saturday, 29 March, he visited 'The Oxford' in Oxford Street:

. . . The great gay glaring hall & balconies were crammed in every part; there was barely standing room in the crowd, which was chiefly made up of men; business men, clerks, & others, of no very refined aspect. . . .

Socially speaking, the audience were a good deal higher than those I have seen in similar Halls at Islington & elsewhere. One result of this was, that the women present were whores, instead of respectable wives & sweethearts. Therefore, another result was, that there was nothing wholesome or genial in the folks' enjoyment: they drank their grog staring gloomily or lewdly grimacing; and the worthless dread of your neighbour which halfeducated respectability creates kept them silent & selfish. At Islington, for instance, the whole audience, men and women, joined heartily in the chorus of wellknown songs, to the amusement of the singer: here, on the other hand, the popular favourite 'Sam Collins'[6] did all he could to persuade the people to sing the chorus of his ditty, and yet scarcely a voice responded. As for the musical entertainment, it was exactly the same as at similar places of a much lower grade. Comparing these Halls with other and far nobler places of recreation, I am inclined to think that their sudden rise & immense popularity is simply due to their being free and easy, and yet having a certain pretence of refinement and splendour. The amusements are agreably varied: your real taste is gratified by nigger songs & acrobats; & betweenwhiles, 'operatic selections' put you for the time on a level with your

---

[5] Christina Rossetti (1830–94), D. G. Rossetti's sister; this book, *Goblin Market and other Poems* (1862), was her first.
[6] Sam Collins was, in fact, the founder of Collins's Music Hall, Islington Green.

betters, and please your vanity. Besides, you are not compelled to sit silent &
cramped as at a theatre or a concert: you drink & smoke pipes alongside your
woman or wife, and chat & 'chaff' to your heart's content. . . . It is a great thing
to know that, for sixpence, you may command admission to all this display of
gilding and statuary and Trovatore-singing, and not be called upon to stint your
own vulgar desires in the least . . .

Sunday, 13 April . . . Brett the painter & Litchfield breakfasted with me. . . .

Brett has been spending a year at Florence; and his account of Italian affairs
is, that the old nobility and even the professional classes are awed or crushed by
mob rule; that the lawlessness is as great as ever, and the unity no nearer. But
then he praises the Pope's government, and holds Louis Napoleon to be an unselfish hero. Able and intelligent as Brett is, his love of paradox and his chivalrous proud devotion—self-opiniated too—to unpopular causes is very pleasantly
provoking. Litchfield asked what he thought of Raffaelle after a year's study: he
replied calmly 'I think he is the worst painter I have known;' and proceeded to
show à la Ruskin, that Raffaelle was all wrong in colour, and could not draw . . .

Hannah's present master owned a house at Brighton; she was now sent
down there to put it in order for the summer. Munby followed her on
Easter Sunday, 20 April, and on Easter Monday she accompanied him (in
the usual surreptitious fashion which Munby deplored) to a volunteer
review on the Downs. 'Tom Hughes passed me at a trot,' wrote Munby,
'—the most genuine & business-like of volunteer officers, to my mind.
During the march past, as he rode by at the head of the 19th, he caught
sight of me in the crowd, and shouted to me a cheery welcome. Hannah
was sitting at my feet.'

The incident emphasises the emotional isolation into which Munby was
forced by his love for Hannah. They had already known each other for
eight years, and their association was to survive its ups and downs for
another half-century. What it cost them both to preserve their innocent
secret from the world at large—as they did to the end of their lives—
cannot be contemplated without respect and amazement.

Munby's mother never knew about Hannah; he did tell his father about
her, six months before his marriage (see 26 August, 1872), but his father
was so horrified that Munby pretended to abandon the idea of marriage,
and it seems safe to assume he never knew his son had a wife. The
full extent of Munby's interest in working women of all kinds would have
astonished his parents. Did they suspect that there were mysterious areas
in their eldest son's life to which they were not admitted? It is possible
that his mother, in her simplicity, did not look beyond his obvious

affection and habitual kindheartedness; 'the father', however, may have been disturbed. He was pleased that Arthur had inherited some musical talent; he appreciated his poems, and had probably reluctantly accepted his lack of enthusiasm for the law; but he would, beyond doubt, have liked to see him happily married to a woman of his own class.

Returning from his Latin pupils on the night of 24 April, Munby 'was surprised to hear my piano at work, and on entering I found my father, who had unexpectedly come up today'. On 25 April they dined at Clapham with the Ellises, where Munby's sister was staying. 'Walking homewards, my father in his cautious kindly way—as if one could not see it all, good man!—hinted that he would not object to my marrying Georgie Ellis, if I wished to ask her.' Munby then closed the entry abruptly with 'Home 12.30'.

Wednesday, 7 May . . . at 10.30 . . . walked down to the Cosmopolitan,[7] to meet Walter Severn, by appointment. I found him chatting & smoking with a quiet unaffected man of about thirty, wearing a little moustache and of slightly foreign aspect, though he spoke English with scarce any accent. He turned out to be Prince Frederick of Schleswig-Holstein, a nephew of Christian VIII. of Denmark. Severn however introduced me to him—or rather indeed *him* to *me*—without any ceremony; and we then talked awhile freely & pleasantly; the Prince describing to me his enjoyment of the Thames from the deck of a penny steamer. It was obvious that he was on terms of easy equality with all the club. He is a quasi exile, being mixed up in the interminable Schleswig-Holstein business: is living here by literature, and has become quite an Englishman.

There were not many of the Club present when I got there; but they kept dropping in till nearly one, from the House and from parties. There was . . . Jacob Omnium (Higgins) lounging, huge & venerably handsome, on a sofa, talking to Layard, who looked waspish as ever, and greyer. Monckton Milnes strolled in late; more gross in figure and strange in manner than when I saw him last; looking in fact rather drunk than otherwise. He is given to telling lewd stories; and at a breakfast party of his the other day, Severn told me, the drawing-room table (his wife was away) was found covered with photographs & engravings of naked men and women in foul postures: the pictures being bound up in rich morocco covers, stamped with his arms. . . .

Saturday, 10 May . . . at nine, to the Alhambra . . . to see my female gymnast what she was like—the 'elegant daring and beautiful' Nathalie Foucart . . . the applause . . . was immense . . . the people were simply astounded . . .

I learnt from the proprietor of the Alhambra that this girl Nathalie is but ten years old; that she took to gymnastics of her own accord, from four years old

---

[7] Compare Munby's first visit to the Cosmopolitan Club, 2 March, 1859.

and upwards; that she has a passion for such feats of strength and suppleness as I saw her do, and means to devote herself to them as a profession. . . . And, said he, she proposes to fly from one trapeze to another, like Leotard, and to turn two somersaults in the air between, and not one only, like him. As he spoke 'Here she is!' he said; I looked, and saw in the crowd a quiet little schoolgirl in a brown frock and straw hat, walking between her father, and her mother who was a quiet respectable youngish woman of about thirty. I complimented the father on his daughter's exploits: he was radiant, and insisted on shaking me by the hand and 'remerce'-ing me mille fois; being evidently charmed with her success.

I shook hands with the child herself too, and her hand did not feel unusually large or hard at all; but her arms are full of muscle as a big boy's, I was told. A simple modest child she seemed . . . she saluted me gravely as she left, kissing her fingertips & bowing.

. . . Modesty being secured, let us watch and welcome all new capacities of her sex . . . it would be curious to see whether puberty will affect the taste or powers of this strange fearless child . . .

Thursday, 15 May . . . To my Latin class, and on the way, met Wickcliffe Goodwin,[8] who offered me work on the Parthenon, the new successor to the Literary Gazette, of which he is editor. But I know not: I write so slowly, have so little confidence in myself. . . . It was my examination, the last night of the term: and while the men did their papers, I lost myself in the new edition of de Quincey, which one of the class, an engraver, is taking in. That story of his London life and his fruitless search for Ann[9] is so profoundly pathetic and tragical, and so closely fits in with some of my own experiences, that I never tire of it . . .

Saturday, 17 May . . . The streets of London . . . are now on Saturdays and Sundays almost . . . as lively and picturesque as those of a continental town. Beards, knickerbockers, volunteer uniforms, and a greater laxity and individuality of costume, have done it. . . . I went down to Tothill Street, to examine a place there which advertises itself as 'The Albert Saloon.'

I expected a large music hall, but found myself instead in a small room, like the parlour of a village cabaret. 30 or 40 people—as many as the place would hold—sat on benches, drinking porter & smoking . . .

At the end of the room was a cracked square piano. . . . A young woman sat on a broken chair, with her back to the audience, strumming on the piano with an unmeaning monotony. Three other young women, without bonnets and wearing cheap muslin gowns & jackets, sat among the people. . . . There was no curriculum of entertainment: every now & then one of the young women would

---

[8] Charles Wycliffe Goodwin (1817–78), Fellow of St. Catharine Hall, Cambridge, and barrister. Became acting judge in the supreme court of China and Japan. Died at Shanghai. Contributed to *Essays and Reviews*, 1860.

[9] In *Confessions of an English Opium Eater*.

say, 'I think I'll sing a song,' and would mount . . . to the stage, and warble some 'Aunt Sally' or other harmless popular thing; the pianist strumming ever as usual. Sometimes the daubed canvas dropscene was raised, and a stage of about 6 feet by 10 was displayed, where one of the ladies performed a few conjuring tricks, or—on one occasion—a statuesque group of very mild & unexceptionable kind was represented by a woman and a child . . .

I came away . . . much gratified with the rude picturesqueness and propriety of the place . . .

The warm-hearted, hot-tempered Dr. F. J. Furnivall was a memorable character at the Working Men's College; his robust vitality and enthusiasm stood out even in a company that held Maurice, Ruskin, Rossetti and Tom Hughes, although increasing agnosticism separated him from Maurice, and he was often the dissentient at College meetings. An ardent feminist, he was in advance of his colleagues in advocating the introduction of women on all College occasions; and he set what seemed to them a dubious example by falling in love with, and marrying, the sister of one of his students. A splendid oarsman himself, he organised a succession of rowing clubs for the College and outside it devised a women's sculling eight. He founded societies in honour of Shakespeare, Browning, Shelley, Chaucer and Wyclif; he founded the Early English Text Society and the Ballad Society. Yet he is best remembered for his work as secretary of the Philological Society; in which capacity he initiated the collection of the material that eventually provided the foundation of the *Oxford English Dictionary*. Munby's description of Furnivall at work with his helpers in 1862 offers an intimate glimpse of the prime mover in the great Dictionary, which was not to be completed until 1928:

Monday, 19 May . . . After dinner, I went to Ely Place by appointment, to see Furnivall. Found him in a strange dingy room upstairs; the walls & floor and chairs strewn with books, papers, proofs, clothes, everything—in wondrous confusion; the table spread with a meal of chaotic and incongruous dishes, of which he was partaking, along with 'Lizzy' Dalzell,[1] the pretty lady's maid whom he has educated into such strange relations with himself, and for whose sake he has behaved so madly to Litchfield & others of his best friends; & her brother,[2] a student of our College. F., who was pleasant & kindly to me as ever, was enjoying a vegetarian banquet of roast potatoes, asparagus, & coffee! Presently came Hantler, the jovial goodhumoured builder, in his uniform as a Captain of the 19th Middlesex . . . and William Sutton, also of the College. After the meal, which lasted from 7 to 9, all four of them set to work, arranging

---

[1] Furnivall and Eleanor Nickel Dalziel were married later in the year.
[2] W. A. Dalziel, afterwards secretary of the Early English Text Society.

and writing out words for the Philological Dictionary, of which Furnivall is now Editor in place of poor Herbert Coleridge.[3] 'Missy', as F. calls the girl, is his amanuensis and transcribes: takes long walks too with him and others, of ten and twenty miles a day; which is creditable to her: and indeed she seems a quiet unassuming creature. . . .

Tuesday, 27 May . . . Dined, came home, dressed, and to Ralston's by appointment. . . . With him to a ball at the Wornums' at the National Gallery. Danced once with Miss Wornum, a pretty plump rosy girl: but her special fascinations I failed to discover.[4] . . .

. . . Severn told me many things of his sister[5]; and said that, as I expected, a selfish tufthunting husband is fast spoiling her clear and artless nature . . .

Wednesday, 28 May . . . Breakfasted with Litchfield. I hear from several quarters that Ruskin's Calvinistic faith is fast going, and leaving him in a state of great spiritual desolation. No wonder that a creed so anomalous in his case, and so out of keeping with his aesthetics, should fail him at last . . .

Tuesday, 17 June . . . I went down at 5.30 to the Victoria Station, and saw Hannah arrive from Brighton with her master and his family: stood apart and saw her, as one of the servants, attending to the ladies and helping to carry the luggage: & felt accordingly.

Plainly drest as she was, she looked more like a lady's maid or a governess than a mere kitchen drudge; and her bare hands were miserably white.

I was annoyed at this change; annoyed at seeing her thus without being able to notice her, and after so long; annoyed at the revelations which such scenes bring of our difficult position. I walked away homewards, and trained myself to a calmer mood, lest I should do the poor child injustice. Dined, and home by seven, unwell.

Stokes came in to tea, and brought me an invitation from Helen Faucit to meet Browning and Thackeray, on Thursday: which I could not resist, so when Ralston appeared afterwards, I got him to undertake my Latin class.

Munby's friend Whitley Stokes knew Helen Faucit well; she had been a devoted friend of his father Dr. William Stokes, F.R.S., since her acting days in Dublin. It seems that Munby himself already had some slight acquaintance with the leading 'straight' actress of her time. Helen Faucit (1817–98) was now 45; she had been married for ten years to Theodore Martin (1816–1909), part-author of the *Bon Gaultier* parodies, who was

[3] Herbert Coleridge (1830–61), philologist and grandson of the poet.
[4] Ralph Nicholson Wornum (1812–77) was Keeper of the National Gallery. Ralston had fallen madly in love with Miss Wornum.
[5] Mary Newton, *née* Severn. Munby's informant was Walter Severn.

destined to be remembered for his Life of the Prince Consort, for which he was knighted in 1880. In the course of her career she had come to know the outstanding authors, artists, politicians, and actors of the period. During the many years in which her husband was engaged on his biography, the couple were often at Court. An invitation to their house at 31 Onslow Square was a passport to distinguished society; its hostess was more than famous; she exerted an unusual attraction based on refinement and sympathy. To George Eliot she was 'the most poetic woman I have seen for a long time' with 'the ineffable charm of a fine character'. Thackeray, for years a neighbour in Onslow Square, called her 'one of the sweetest women in Christendom'. Robert Browning had long been grateful for what she had done for his ill-fated plays.

Henceforth Helen Faucit (Plate 11) filled for Munby the rôle of the superior woman of talent who could be romantically admired without risk of serious involvement. She took the place Mary Severn had held before her marriage; and this time there was no hint of a personal challenge in the situation. One notes again that Munby's taste in women was for the highest or the lowest. At the upper end of the scale, they preferably had to be strikingly gifted, charming, acceptable at Windsor; but, finding such geniuses rare, and anyway beyond his reach, Munby had settled for the long courtship at the area railings. What simply would never do was the conventionally eligible young lady of the middle class, whom Munby thought affected and ineffective; uninteresting, unpoetic.

Thursday, 19 June ... At ten I ... went down to Onslow Square to Mrs. Martin's party. A very pleasant party it was. Imprimis, the house, as I knew of old, is one of the most charming in London. It has a lofty spacious hall, made more beautiful by pictures & statues; and a noble staircase, sloping up round three sides of it, leads to a suite of drawing rooms furnished with costly and most fastidious elegance. The whole interior of the house, I believe, is due to the taste and the professional gains of Mrs. Martin herself. She too, secondly, was extremely cordial, and as charming & spirituelle as ever. The grace of all her movements has once, perhaps, been studied, but is now habitual and instinctive; and the expression of her mouth and eyes in conversation is, from long tragic habit, so intense, that it requires some selfpossession to speak to such a listener. I never saw a face that seemed, as it were, to come so close in upon one's own soul. By way of contrast, I had a little struggling talk with that cold hard intellect, Mrs. Tom Taylor. Thackeray's daughters were there also, and Miss Anna Blackwell (sister I think of Dr. Elizabeth B.), a literary spinster with grey hair and a fine intelligent face; ... After a while, the older men came up from dinner. They were, Martin himself, and Thackeray, Robert Browning, Tom Taylor,

W. G. Clark of Trinity, and 'Dante' Pollock,[6] son of the Chief Baron. I had never met Thackeray in society before; and I was greatly charmed with him. None of the photographs do him justice: his face, which in repose is melancholy, lights up, when talking as tonight, into a sort of glow of gentle humour and venerable pathos, that would make him a most winning talker, even without the charm of his words and of his piquant manner. Conspicuous for his white hair and tall portly figure, he lounged about the rooms in an easy smiling way, chatting or murmuring to himself, and every now and then stopping before some friend, such as Ormsby, and with raised forefinger and head on one side gravely giving out one of his irresistible little jokes.

At another time he sat and did a little quiet badinage with Miss Blackwell and her friends: starting strange paradoxes and maintaining them with apparent earnestness: as, that avarice is the purest source of pleasure, and that the happiest character would be his who should be able to weep for sorrow at every tale of distress, but should not care twopence for anybody. I saw him at his best: all said he was in full health and spirits. He has lately built himself a large house in Kensington Park Gardens.[7] He told us tonight that he was going to take his daughters to *Russia* this summer.[8] Browning has just returned from Florence, to settle near London. He is a short man, with a crisp grizzled beard, and a keen restless peering face, not specially attractive. I had no opportunity of talking with him, and but little of hearing him talk.[9]....

The days that followed the Martins' party were fraught with emotion for Munby. His mother, staying in lodgings in Craven Street on a parental visit to the International Exhibition, became 'exceedingly ill with weakness and hysteria'. She lay on Munby's shoulder, moaning for 'her dear dear home' and saying she had only come to see his brother George and him, 'whom she never sees'. Munby was overcome; but fortunately, after a rest, Mrs. Munby began to recover.

Almost equally distressing was the long-drawn leave-taking of Whitley Stokes on his departure for India, where he was to pursue a successful legal career, Sir Henry Maine's influence being exerted on his behalf. Stokes had been a close friend of Munby since they were fellow pupils of Hugh Cairns; he was highly popular with many other members of their literary and artistic set.

[6] William Frederick Pollock (1815–88), eldest son of Chief-Baron Sir Jonathan Frederick Pollock, Bt., became Queen's Remembrancer in 1874. He published one of the many Victorian translations of Dante (1854).

[7] A mistake for Kensington Palace Gardens; the house was actually called 2, Palace Green.

[8] Unexplained, but they did not go.

[9] Robert Browning (1812–89), the poet, had returned to England this year after the death of his wife. By praising Munby's *Dorothy* in 1881, he was to become his chief literary benefactor.

Sunday, 22 June . . . Stokes, Dante Rossetti, Ormsby, and Ralston, came to breakfast with me by invitation: Litchfield could not come. It was my farewell gathering for Stokes: but Rossetti asked us all to his rooms tomorrow. He seems to have recovered, outwardly at least, the loss of his wife. We sat at the open window looking on the gardens, and smoked and told stories and discussed various books and men, till after two. Then I walked down to Craven Street, and found my mother better and on the sofa . . .

. . . Rossetti this morning, to my delight, dwelt with warm admiration upon the portrait[1] of my darling—little suspecting who or what she was. 'It is a beautiful face' he said 'a remarkable face indeed'; & he was anxious to get a copy. 'I should like to know that lady' he added. Yes: *that lady*, who is wasting her beauty in drudgery, and who looks no higher than to clean one's boots!

Monday, 23 June . . . at ten, to Rossetti's new rooms 59 Lincoln's Inn Fields. House of the old Earl of Chatham: lofty immense rooms, which R. has adorned with antique furniture and with his own masterly drawing. His brother was there, & Stokes, & C. B. Cayley,[2] Madox Brown,[3] Ralston . . . and others, including the intolerable little prig Swinburne. I stayed till after supper, and came home by 1- . . .

Tuesday, 24 June . . . At five I went down to Manchester Buildings, and found Walter Severn in, with Joyce of the Privy Council Office. Severn was making a large drawing of the view from his window, which looks out upon the river. It is a noble view, and in the fitful sunset light was full of picturesque effect. The river and its banks from Westminster almost to Blackfriars; and the dome of S. Paul's for a central mass, bosomed in purple mist. He told me by the way, as a thing told to him by Millais, how the fine picture of 'Trust me' in this year's Academy was done. Millais, staying in the country, saw an elegant girl in a brown silk dress: got her to sit to him, and painted her figure in, without background or companion, and without any purpose. Coming to town afterwards & wanting a subject for a picture, some one suggested that he should add a man's figure to this canvas. He did so accordingly; but still without any definite aim; in so much that he knew not what to call the picture, till a lady said 'Call it Trust me'. The execution is wonderful: but this is not the way in which great pictures are conceived!

. . . at ten I went to Lower Belgrave Place to a gathering at Munro's.

. . . Ralston Rossetti Sotheby Stokes and I walked home together: but Stokes and I tête à tête—for it was our last talk. We discoursed—or rather he did—of Celtic mythology and the old Irish legends; some of which he related to me, in his passionate poetic way—and beautiful they were. He lamented his departure

---

[1] This is Hannah's photograph, hand-coloured by Munby, reproduced in Plate 9.

[2] Charles Bagot Cayley (1823–83), the translator.

[3] Ford Madox Brown (1821–93), the painter, of whom Rossetti had once been a pupil.

from the study of his 'beloved philology'; & many here and in Germany—Max Müller among them—lament it too; for Stokes has few equals in the knowledge of Celtic speech & history. And we talked, arm in arm, of all he will do in Madras: just like a couple of boys building castles in the air . . .

Wednesday, 25 June . . . about ten, went to Dick's,[4] where some of Stokes's more intimate friends entertained him at a quiet supper. . . . After the supper, which was simple and unpretending, we had punch brought on; and sat smoking and discoursing in groups—earnestly enough, but with little jollity; for everyone felt that a friend was going away.

Stokes Rossetti Swinburne & I had a good deal of talk about old French literature, with which, in spite of his priggishness, Swinburne seems to have a considerable acquaintance, though not always of a reputable kind. Rossetti brought as a parting gift to Stokes (I gave him the Opium Eater) a copy of the poems of François Villon, a contemporary of Louis XI, who besides being a famous poet, was also a thief and a pimp, and would have been hanged as such but for his genius.

Rossetti read out some of the poems, which are full of vigour and pathos & descriptive power.

So passed the night till 2.30: and then our party broke up, and it was pleasant and affecting to see the warmth and tenderness with which one after another wrung Stokes's hand and bade God bless him and Goodbye. He and I and Rossetti Ralston & Swinburne walked down to the Middle Temple Gate; & there I parted from my friend of ten years, with that heartiness and lingering but not unmanly sorrow which one feels at such a time, when recollections of one's intercourse rush in, as it were, into the gap that opens between your life and his; and he is going into a far country, from whence when he returns, years and years hence, who knows what will have become of all of us? . . .

Munby later added two footnotes to this passage. In one he recalled a characteristic gesture of Swinburne's at the parting by the Middle Temple entrance: 'And Swinburne ran off to get "Sordello" for Stokes; exclaiming "What—go to India without Sordello!"'[5] In the other, he recorded that Stokes returned to England in 1882 as a member of the governor-general's council.

Saturday, 28 June . . . Rode down to Brompton . . . and called in Onslow Square on Mrs. Theodore Martin. Found her just going out—in a very elegant toilette, by the way, for her taste in dress is admirable—to the Exhibition, with some Miss Dalrymples, bright fresh girls, to whom she introduced me. I walked with them to the building, & then bowed myself away, thinking I might be de trop.

[4] A Fleet Street eating-house.   [5] 'Sordello': Browning's poem of medieval Italy.

This was my first visit to the 'International Exhibition of 1862'. The first Exhibition coincided with the end of my college career, with my entrance into London, with the change from youth to manhood in me. The crude imaginative years that went before led up to it—to the rapturous surprise of its unique and exquisite beauty: and through such a portal I entered upon the dull & pathless commonplace of life. Therefore I look back to it as to the daylight at a cavern's mouth; and it is to me an almost sacred memory. The very presence of such feelings, and the impossibility of gaining others like them, has made me utterly indifferent to the second show. The contrast between the blank ugliness of this building and the vivid grace of the other is for me painfully symbolic. I go to this as it were, because others do: to examine a museum, not to revel in a fairy-land . . .

I . . . went off to the machinery 'annexe', where amongst other things cotton spinning and muslin weaving were going on. I went carefully through the whole annexe, and counted the number of women at work: they were twentyfive; about half employed at the cotton machines, and half at the muslin. . . . All were quiet decent and modest; but the muslin weavers showed no sign of a country origin, and were drest like ordinary London work girls.

The factory girls, on the other hand, were unmistakeably Lancashire; and I took to them accordingly. They mostly wore short cotton frocks without sleeves: but a few were in their proper bedgown and striped kirtle. It was not bad, to see these homely strenuous lasses, with bare rough arms and soiled hands, oiling the machinery or minding the bobbins as they would at home, quite regardless of the elegant ladies and gentlemen who stared with vapid curiosity at their work. . . . I had a talk with two of the several girls whom I found buried here among the looms. The first . . . said she earned 24/ a week here, and worked from 8 a.m. till 7 p.m.—Her master at Manchester paid her expenses and those of her fellows to London and back, and she was glad of the work of course, for at home mills was stopped and a wench couldn't make more than 10/ a week at most. But she didn't care for London or for the Exhibition: 'Oi'd reyther be i'Lankishire' . . .

. . . It was after 7.30 when I left: the carriages were all gone from the Cromwell Road, but a few male & female servants of the exhibition and other folks were strolling about. The look of the roads round about is curious. Highways built on arches cross the country in various directions: between them and ten feet below, is the natural level of the soil—the poor remains of grass fields and orchards gone for ever. Lines of big houses already fill up these here and there; but near the Exhibition the roads are fronted by temporary buildings. . . .

This year Munby intended to take a holiday in Switzerland in September; and while he remained in town throughout July and August, the claims of society on him were minimal. He paid several more visits to the

International Exhibition; took part in entertaining some workmen from Leeds at the Working Men's College ('they are all staying in one big house, rented by Cook the excursion monger'); and busied himself in helping two women with grave facial disfigurements. One of these, Harriet Langdon, he had encouraged throughout a long period in hospital; he now tried to find employment for her—no easy task. Despite an element of morbid obsession, Munby's interest in such outcasts was unselfish and charitable; to the sufferers themselves it brought fresh hope— rarely fulfilled, unfortunately, in those days before plastic surgery.

Sunday, 13 July . . . I went in the afternoon to Shadwell, thinking it would be a good opportunity of seeing the people of that district turn out in force. For I had seen in the papers that a young Irish prostitute, one Nora Scannell, who was murdered there lately by a Spanish sailor,[6] was to be buried today with professional honours: fourteen of her fellow harlots walking behind the coffin, seven in white and seven in black.

I walked along Ratcliff Highway and the neighbouring streets as far as Rosemary Lane, where the body lay. The streets were all sunny and quiet, and in any other country would have been picturesque: for the roadways and doorsteps and windows were full of loungers—sailors of all countries, and crowds of women, young but hard featured, strolling about in light cotton jackets and gowns, without bonnet or shawl. Near the house where the corpse was, the crowds became more dense and more wide: the report I had heard about the fourteen mourners was true, I was told, and the people were waiting to see them come out. No one seemed to see anything odd or unusual in such a procession. However, a rumour began to spread, and it was confirmed to me privately by the policeman on guard at the house, that the funeral would not be till Tuesday at noon: 'the girls had been disappointed—the dressmakers had not yet sent their mourning things home.' This being so, I came away. I was nearly an hour among these crowds, in and about the notorious Ratcliff Highway; and I did not meet a single policeman, except the one I have mentioned, nor see a drunken person, nor hear an evil word . . .

Saturday, 19 July . . . I went down, by a train crowded with gaily drest people, to the Crystal Palace by 3.30, to see the Dramatic Fête which is now annually held there. The building was crowded; and it being a half crown day, 'elegant toilettes' prevailed everywhere. . . .

After dinner—a very bad one—in the Palace, I walked down the crowded nave and went up to the gallery of the central transept. . . . Flags and streamers of all colours—remains of the Rifle festival of Monday—were hung aloft; the lines of airy creeper-plants and pendent baskets of flowers were lit up by slanting

---

[6] A Spanish bricklayer, according to *The Times*, 7 July; he committed suicide.

sunlight from the west; and below, troops of brightly clad people were walking to and fro, whilst the great Handel organ opposite filled the air with a sort of reverie of soft fugitive music.

This was sensuous enjoyment of the highest; it did not enervate, but soothed one—stroked down as it were the bristles of one's discontent: so that when I went into the upper balcony overlooking the grounds, I was able to receive the full blessing of that sunset view. The golden light moved & moved upwards among the clumps of elm and cedar, and over the valley and the slopes beyond Beckenham. . . . I sat thus, non sine fumo, till the twilight came on and the sky grew bare and blue; and soon afterwards left the now quiet Palace, and walked down to Anerley, among the ruins of Penge Wood, which is now half-felled, and ready for the neat modern publichouses and flimsy whimsy 'villas' which are rising all round . . .

Wednesday, 23 July . . . Home to the Temple at 6, and to Mudie's. Coming thence along Oxford Street, I saw before me, striding along in company with an Italian organgrinder, a tall young man in full Highland costume; wearing a Glengarry bonnet, a scarlet jacket, a sporan and a tartan kilt & stockings, his legs bare from the knee to the calf. It was not a man—it was Madeleine Sinclair the street dancer, whom I used to see in a similar dress a year ago. She and her companion turned into a quiet street, and she danced a Highland fling to his music, in the midst of a curious crowd.

For no one could make out whether she was man or woman. Her hair and the set of her hips indeed were feminine; but her hard weatherstained face, her large bony hands, and her tall strong figure, became her male dress so well that opinions were about equally divided as to her sex. 'It's a man!' said one, confidently: 'I believe it's a woman', another doubtfully replied. One man boldly exclaimed 'Of course it's a man; anybody can see that!' I gave her a sixpence when she came round with her tambourine; and she told me she had been in Paris five months for pleasure, and was now living on Saffron Hill, and dancing in the streets every day, always wearing her male clothes . . .

Friday, 25 July . . . About ten I went to a ball in Great Cumberland Street, at Mrs. Bonner's, wife of a retired Major General of the Madras Artillery. A very handsome suite of rooms—two houses, in fact, thrown into one; and a really agreeable company, including several very elegant & brilliantly drest girls, some decorés Frenchmen, and a Bey in half-oriental costume. I stayed somewhat late, and danced, finding a good many people I knew there (the two charming & frank Miss Grants, for instance) and partners of more than average intelligence. The best of these was a Lady Rollo—I think—a young married woman of thirty or so, loftily handsome and thoroughly sensible and unaffected. After dancing with her, we talked sometime on general subjects, she conversing with that refined yet strenuous simplicity of manner and language, which marks, I think, the very perfection of female training. I had some talk also with Tom Brassey,[7] who was here, & his piquante and sumptuous wife. He is, thanks to his sturdy character and his university education, by far the best specimen of a *nouveau riche* that I have known . . .

I walked home by 3.30. By way of special contrast, I had a letter tonight from my Hannah, who says that 'Ann and me went to the Princesses last night by ourselves, to the gallery, & enjoyed ourselves capittaly, and a young man & his sweetheart got friends with us, and he gave us ale and gingerbeer & oranges.' And this from a girl who for beauty and grace, and intelligence too, might—but now never *may*—vie with any of those I met at the ball tonight! . . .

The diary at this period affords fresh evidence of the unusual relationship that had grown up between Hannah and Munby. On 29 July, a day of 'special drudgery' for Hannah, Munby made a trip to Kilburn to 'see her in her dirt' (Hannah's 'homely phrase'). Where another girl would have beautified herself for her lover, Hannah's great joy was to show herself to Munby as dirty as possible. In so doing, she hoped to fulfil his prescription of salvation through toil and degradation. 'If there were, as I would there were, any more excellent way in sight,' writes Munby, 'how loftily she would walk in it, who has thus overcome the vanities and weakness of woman's nature. . . .' Munby reveals (3 August) that long ago he had ordered Hannah to climb and sweep chimneys not merely to prove her love, but also to demonstrate his theory of redemption. He explains this in an entry later in the year (16 November): 'It is the old Socratic theory inverted . . . it is not desirable to be a chimneysweep, for instance: but she who becomes one in the course of her work, as Hannah did, and from such a motive, is potentially a heroine, and is capable of all noble doings.' And when she whispers into his ear (3 August), not for the first time: 'I love you, Master—and I will be your faithful drudge and slave!' Munby adds: 'Will be, my child? Have been—and alas still are: Will be, I trust, something more than that, if devotion may have its due.' It appears from this that Munby now envisaged marriage with Hannah as a probable, if distant, prospect.

While he looked forward to his Swiss holiday, Hannah had been planning something more modest:

Sunday, 20 July . . . 'The family' go away soon: and then, 'May I ask Missis for a week's holiday?' she says. 'And what shall I do with it? must I go somewhere

[7] Thomas Brassey (1836–1918), son of the railway contractor of the same name; Liberal M.P. for Hastings, 1868–86; civil lord of Admiralty, 1880–4; K.C.B., 1881; first produced *Brassey's Naval Annual*, 1886; Governor of Victoria, 1895–1900; created baron, 1886, and first Earl Brassey, 1911. His wife Anna, *née* Allnutt (1839–87), published *Voyage of the Sunbeam* (her husband's yacht) and other accounts of long sea voyages.

with you, Massa?' This is put rather timidly: her next enquiry, more timidly, for it is a strange one. 'I couldn't go with you drest in my own servant's things— we couldn't be together: and of course I couldn't go like a lady—' 'No dear: you've no lady's clothes, and if you had, they'd see you was only a servant, of course.' '*Of course*,' she answers gravely, with full acceptance of the awful truth: 'And so' she went on 'I thought—if I could go with you *in men's clothes!*' There! it was out now—and she had been thinking of this, she confessed, for some weeks.

Well: the same dilemma and the same mode of escape had occurred to me too, though I had not mentioned it. Her nature is so genuine, and in spite of her rough life so womanly, that I doubt if she could play such a part: and I would not have her learn to act & to conceal. Besides, is it safe? possible? *right?* . . .

Munby decided against Hannah's scheme, though as an opera-goer he might have enjoyed it. In fact, all that happened was that Hannah spent two innocent nights at Fig Tree Court and went with him on a day trip to Southend.

Saturday, 2 August . . . One seizes, with a sort of melancholy pleasure, upon the many little proofs she gives of what she might have been. One night lately, for instance, as I held her ready to depart at the door, she suddenly exclaimed with a fair accent 'Dépêchez vous! ouvrez la porte, s'il vous plait!' Seeing my surprise, she added with a blush and a smile that when she was a nursegirl, fifteen years ago, she once heard the governess say that to her pupils, and guessed or discovered its meaning . . .

On the next Saturday (9 August) Munby met Hannah at the studio of the Oxford Street photographer 'who has so often taken her before'. He found it difficult to write about what followed or to do justice to Hannah's 'selfsacrifice' in going through with it, or to his own motives 'for allowing and desiring, it'. For this was to be a record of Hannah 'in her noblest guise—that of a chimneysweep', and it involved her blackening herself 'from head to foot' and standing 'almost nude' before 'that phlegmatic little German'. 'Do I respect her less,' asked Munby, 'because I allowed such degradation?' His own answer would, of course, have been No; psychologically, these photographic charades may have stemmed from his persistent subconscious urge to 'de-feminise' the opposite sex: even on occasions to un-sex Hannah.

Photography provided some outlet for the inhibitions of another Victorian idealist, Lewis Carroll, who specialised in portraits of little girls, some of them nude or nearly so. But Carroll was his own brilliant photographer; Munby was a good amateur draughtsman but his photographs were taken for him by others. Munby insisted that the photographs he commissioned should be entirely respectable (they did, however, include a number of gruesome records—which have not survived—of the features of disfigured women).

Other poses were assumed by Hannah that Saturday afternoon:

... she was taken in the same black and forlorn condition, crouching on the ground at my feet—I doing my best to look down upon her like a tyrant! That was for 'the contrast': contrast indeed—but which the nobler?

She wished to be photographed also in an attitude of her own: and this being granted, she sat down on the floor, with only her shift and serge petticoat on, & thrust out a bare foot, leaning on one knee and clasping her chain[8] with the other hand. She was so anxious about this pose, which was very happy, that I enquired its meaning when we were alone. It was 'the way I sit on the floor when I'm going to bed, and—think of you!' We came home together, or rather she followed me home, by halfpast seven. She had leave to stay out a few nights during her mistress's absence: and she wished to spend them with me. In her innocence and confiding love she wished it: ought I to refuse? Her coming would compromise neither herself nor me, because it would not be known to any one: she who washes dishes and makes beds can remove all traces of her own presence. I remembered the temptation of last time: but I had overcome it: and now also, when the hour came and she had said her prayers between my knees, I was able to kiss her with due selfcontrol, as she lay alone in my spare bed, and smiled 'Good night Massa!' She had trusted her honour to me: voilà tout.

During the excursion to Southend on 10 August, Munby was determined to

have no more of that vile underhand affectation of walking apart, I proud & unregarding, she meek and furtively attendant. So I took her arm, and we began by having beer together like the rest; and then walked down through the town, and out along the beach & little cliffs towards the Nore.

... our walk to Shoebury Ness was pleasant & refreshing. We went through the lines and the artillery barracks ... to the little hamlet of Shoebury.... We went down to the beach, and sat among the long sandy grass (a lizard ran out between my feet).... An hour or more of this, and then we walked back by the fields ... to Southend at about six. Here we went into a publichouse (how could I take her to my hotel?)[9] and in the sodden parlour *she* had porter & *I* had tea.

At this place and every where, people stared at our being together, and

---

[8] Hannah wore a chain which was somehow intended as a symbol of her loving servitude to 'Massa'. She had also worn a strap on her wrist ever since she had sprained it 'a-liftin the pigtub' while a young girl; the strap had acquired the same significance as the chain.

[9] Where Munby had previously stayed in Southend.

addressed me with respect, while they spoke bluntly to her as an equal. Walk with a lady or even a quasi-lady, and you find her feminine delicacy recognised by all in little acts of courtesy and deference: but here, such acts are reserved for me, while my companion, who deserves them as much as any lady, if she only knew how to claim them, is known for a mere servant, and treated as such. She however sees no irritating anomaly in this: 'They may well stare, with such a difference between us,' is her only comment.

We left Southend about 6.30 . . . and home together by 9. Hannah slept here again as before: and it was easier to me than last night. . . .

Monday, 11 August . . . Awoke by Hannah again: who left me early, after her rough & ready breakfast, to spend this her last holiday at the Exhibition, all by herself; and then—'there's the boots and knives waiting for me to clean!' Pure she came and pure she went: and for her, the strange visit was one of simple affection merely and unmixed enjoyment.

But for me it was very different: and I scarcely know how far it is right thus to strain one's own endurance, and allow her to cheapen, though from very love, her maidenly reserve of charms, and permit oneself to discount the quiet freedom of domestic life, because her humble and obscure position makes it possible to do so. However, the affair is one of difficult conduct; and I see no way of honest intercourse, except this of taking advantage of that difference which keeps one apart in public, but makes more possible a private nearness . . .

Munby appreciated the homespun morality of the Lancashire factory women at the 1862 Exhibition. These women were the chief attraction of the exhibition for him; he did, of course, study the works of art conscientiously, and heard a mechanical bullfinch and nightingale in the Swiss Court, but he tended to sneak off to 'the machinery annexe' (though his interest in machinery was minimal) for conversations with the millworkers, who were shrewd and independent:

Saturday, 16 August . . . Many, she said, of those about her held that conduct, bad or good, didn't matter, inasmuch as, for all they could see, there might well be no God at all, and no futurity; and at any rate, we know of nothing after death. 'But Ah tells em, supposing all that—suppose there is naw God and nowt for us when wa' dee; wah then, Ah says, we mun gaw by this life only; and it's cheaper, for wer awn saak, te do right nor wrang. Cheaper? Why, it's pleasanter: it dont pay, to be wicked.'

From lips like hers, the Paleian philosophy sounds creditable: and it is truly something, that our *women* of the labouring class can think and speak on such questions at all . . .

Sunday, 17 August . . . My Hannah came about four, and stayed till nine. She had scarcely gone when she returned, to say that it was pouring with rain, and

—could she stop here all night? Of course she could, and she must not be sent away in the wet: so she has stayed, and is at this moment calmly sleeping in my back room. The most unpleasant part of such a proceeding is the necessity for its concealment—for hiding her, for the sake of her own reputation & mine, while the housekeeper is upstairs. She submits without a thought of degradation: but it makes one burn, to see her go away instinctively, when I ring, and crawl under the bed—where she lies, still as a mouse, till the room is clear. And yet this wretched but inevitable expedient does not seem to lessen her self-respect, or sully her nature in the least.

By the end of August, Munby had had his 'walking coat' lined with flannel; his knapsack had been altered; he had gone to Bradshaw's about his passport and 'to the Circus in Piccadilly for information about the tidal trains'; Hannah had paid him a farewell visit to sew on his buttons, blacken his boots and polish his flask. On Saturday, 30 August, he wrote 'She did not ask me a single question about the journey; how should she? It seems natural to her, poor child, that I should go anywhere and she nowhere: she does not know what I do or where I am, but she knows that I am hers and she is mine; and so she scours her floors and blacks her grates from day to day, in patient waiting and in peace.' He took the 8 p.m. train that night for the continent.

It was, like most of Munby's excursions, a 'busman's holiday', so far as female employment was concerned. From Calais he went, by way of Lille and Brussels, to Charleroi, where he explored the coal-mining district of Mambourg. He then travelled through Germany into Switzerland. During a strenuous tour he filled his diary with appreciative descriptions of scenery, but kept an observant eye on the working women. His most interesting piece of research was accomplished in the diligence on the road between Chamonix and Geneva:

Friday, 19 September . . . I took the trouble of counting and arranging by sex the labourers in the fields, during the whole way from Chamonix to Geneva.
Their numbers, & the proportion of male to female labourers, were as follows:

	Women	Men
Vale of Chamonix to Ouches—	40	10
Ouches to Servoy (rocky)	22	11
Servoy to Sallenche	49	27
Sallenche to Cluses	79	53
Cluses to Bonneville	43	50
Bonneville to Geneva	73	84
Totals	306	235

These figures speak for themselves: as far as Cluses, the valleys being narrow, they include *all* the field labourers in sight: afterwards, those only whose sex was distinguishable from the road. According to English views, the people & country ought to have improved in appearance at every step of the above scale: but in fact, they both degenerated in an inverse ratio: and as female labour decreased, the women grew less robust & comely, less picturesque, till near Geneva they became utterly uninteresting: whilst at Chamonix they were strongest and best looking . . .

Munby returned to England by train through Paris and Boulogne, where he paid his usual visit to the fisherwomen, and reached London on Wednesday, 24 September. Arriving at Fig Tree Court, he was startled to find that

. . . my father, not knowing of my return, was coming to occupy my chambers. And I had appointed my Hannah to come at 5.30 and welcome me home. Inconsistent and mutually unintelligible visitants: rencontre impossible, not to be thought of. And at 5.30 accordingly came the lowly single knock, and she was again with me . . .

Hannah sat at his feet in her blue cotton frock, checked apron, and scullery bonnet. She read to him 'bits of her simple diary' (kept at his request). Munby had written to her twice on his journey 'in the strain of affected simplicity one uses towards a little child. For she did not know where I was: could not attach any meaning to names of which she had never heard.' He now told her something of his adventures; but in the circumstances the affectionate reunion was anxious and curtailed.

. . . She stayed with me thus till half past seven; and then my father came; and she, poor child, had to be hidden away as usual, willingly enough! and then to be dismissed with secret kiss, to find her way back alone: comforted & happy, but with bitterness of heart to me.

Munby's holiday was not yet over. He soon left for a fortnight at York: where he played croquet on the lawn; where his mother played her harp in the drawing-room; and where Munby encountered on the Skelton road a lusty young woman who had long been accustomed to drive the plough, which she did in men's clothes (a rare and heartening find). A visit to Cuyler Anderson at Gillingham followed; so that it was not until the end of October that he resumed his London life.

Thursday, 23 October . . . to my Latin class, the first night of the new term: eleven men—a very good muster after two years' wear.

Thence to Macmillan's, whose 'evenings' have begun again. There were Masson, Henry Fawcett,[1] Edward Dicey[2] who has returned from his mission of whitewashing the Yankees; and various others.

The two last named absorbed all the talking. Fawcett is a man of very pleasant manner; his blindness was caused by a shot from his own father's gun, as they were shooting together . . .

Friday, 24 October . . . After dinner I walked up to the Edgware Road, where I had written to Hannah to meet me. It is hard to say which is the worse; to speak to her openly in the street, and be stared at for it by strangers and misunderstood and slandered by any passing acquaintance, or to pass her by (the safer plan) as if I were too grand to speak to a servant . . .

She however, poor child, showed no sign of recognition, but meekly followed till I should choose to stop and speak to her; thinking it the most natural thing in the world that I should be ashamed to do so before others. . . . I made her take my arm at length, and we walked up and down a back street, where I heard one boy say of her to another, as they stared, 'She's a milkwoman, she is!' and then we went to Paddington Green, where much against her will I made her go into a little shop with me to buy a bonnet. The shopwomen knew not what to make of our conjuncture; and indeed it was an experiment on my part; and, as such, a failure. Hannah is too downright and sincere to act as if she were *merely* my servant; and to pretend that we are socially equals, is useless and impossible . . .

So the shop girls stared & tittered; saying 'Sir' to me, but affecting a chill superiority—superiority, indeed!—to her; and wondering when she tried on the bonnet I chose, a black straw of plain oldfashioned shape, and they saw her short cropped hair.

We came away, she carrying the bonnet: she went back to her master's, & I home by 9.

Sunday, 1 November . . . I went down . . . to the Exhibition. It was its last day. . . . I went, although it was dusk, through the Colonial and Scandinavian courts, and then returned to the nave and the western dome. This last was densely thronged, and two of the great organs were pealing out God Save the Queen, which was sung by the Sacred Harmonic Choir, with a multitudinous chorus from the thousands below. I made my way to the gallery around the dome; and in the dim evening light (it was 4.30 p.m.) the sight of that great crowd under the dome, and the works of art among which they stood, and the dusk nave beyond, and the music and the shouts and cheers rolling over all,—these things

---

[1] Henry Fawcett (1833–84), political economist; Liberal M.P. from 1865; Postmaster-General, 1880; F.R.S. 1882. He had been blinded in 1858. Married in 1867 to (Dame) Millicent Fawcett, *née* Garrett (1847–1929), the suffragist leader.

[2] Edward James Stephen Dicey (1832–1911), author and journalist; worked for *Daily Telegraph*, and edited the *Observer*, 1870–89.

went to make a remembrance not wanting in solemnity and grandeur. 'Partant pour la Syrie' followed, and then, after a clamorous demand, Rule Britannia: and then the crowd, I among them, walked slowly through the nave, lingering and unwilling to go. Long time the police, who were very civil, exhorted folks in vain: and even when the nave was cleared and it was dark, but for a few stray jets of gas, the reluctant people stood round Minton's fountain in the Eastern dome, & cheered wildly and incessantly; every one glowing with intense good humour. Hundreds were still there, when I took my last look backward down the nave, and left the building at 5.30. So ends the Exhibition of 1862: which I part from not without regret . . .

Sunday, 2 November . . . Going out in the afternoon, I met Vernon Lushington, and had some talk with him of Maurice's[3] resignation, now happily revoked, and of Bishop Colenso's[4] new book. I wrote to Maurice the other day about it, begging him, as all other friends have done, not to resign. It was a noble error, but a great one. From Blackfriars Bridge I observed that they are digging the foundations of the new railway bridge just below it, and are also driving the piles, above it, for the Thames embankment. . . .

Friday, 14 November . . . I came home to the Temple at 5.30, and found Hannah loitering about waiting for me, but careful, poor child, not to be seen by any of my people. Hateful care! That tall figure, awkward and bent with work but meant to be far otherwise, shambling under the dark wall, with its mean clothing and gloveless roughened hands, what is it to me? I pass it without notice: it turns, and silently, humbly glides in at the doors behind me. Alas, it is everything to me— . . .

Saturday, 15 November . . . I walked down to Brompton, and went to see Harriet Langdon; only to give her my usual halfcrown, for work I had none to tell her of. And she also could hear of none. She was sitting moodily alone in her sister's room; her face looking horribly hideous in the red firelight. Names survive things for long: and she poor creature continues at times to speak of her nose, though she has not had a nose for near twenty years. But she is fully and cruelly sensible of her own ugliness and her outcast condition; which last seems more hopeless than ever: my schemes for getting her employment having all failed, because as one lady said 'the disfigurement is too great.' . . .

Wednesday, 19 November . . . Litchfield came to breakfast. We had some talk of Kingsley,[5] who is suspected of playing the wordling, and of withdrawing in

[3] F. D. Maurice's deep sense of humility was a weakness in his leadership of the Working Men's College. He tended to offer to resign, to avoid faction and disagreement.

[4] John William Colenso (1814–83), Bishop of Natal, a radical and controversial theologian.

[5] Charles Kingsley (1819–75), the author, had been one of the first Christian Socialists and an early promoter of the Working Men's College, though not strictly a founder.

some measure from fellowship with Maurice—who it appears seldom sees him now—in order to get a reputation for orthodoxy and a chance of more loaves & fishes! I hope not: yet fear he is not to be depended upon ...

Wednesday, 26 November ... I dined with Ralston at Rouget's, where was William Morris, the poet and painter. He and I went home with Ralston, and sat some time, looking over R.'s books for review, & talking chiefly on light literary matters. Morris is simple & unpretending in appearance & conversation, and does not express by either the power which his book[6] shows him to have. We walked homeward together; Morris to the 'Co.' in Red Lion Square; and I home by 10.15.

Friday, 28 November ... During the day I went by water to S. Paul's on business. I found the choir of the cathedral crowded; many parsons in their gowns, and a lay multitude, curious and quiet, but certainly not devout: morning service going on. It was the Bishop of London's[7] Visitation. A verger placed me in a quiet aisle opposite the pulpit, where I heard the whole of a sermon, preached by Mr. Kempe[8] the Rector of S. James's Piccadilly: a concio ad clerum: vapid and wordy, it seemed to me; vaguely hinting, but with affectation of candid superiority, at Colenso and the essayists, and the 'frightful infidelities' of Strauss and Hegel. Coming down the aisle into the dome afterwards, I met the Bishop, in his robes, straggling along pellmell with the crowd, a few other dignitaries following in similar fashion, all scurrying off to the vestry. Neither reason nor taste consulted here! Paul's itself, though it is cold and cheerless and worldly, has yet the stern & masculine beauty which is not wanting to a businesslike and selfenwrapt but honest and downright character. A temple vacant of deity, but full of Wren and British gold ...

The next entry, about Ruskin, is of particular interest because no adequate record of the occasion exists. Ruskin had not taken regular art classes at the Working Men's College for some time—but he had retained the habit of paying occasional visits to the place which had largely inspired his interest in social and economic questions. He was now in a disturbed state; he had not only reached a religious crisis, but had conceived a sentimental obsession for the child Rose La Touche which was to have far more dangerous implications than Lewis Carroll's friendship for Alice Liddell; moreover Ruskin's devoted father had been in critical disagreement with his son on these and other matters. To escape from all this,

[6] William Morris (1834–96) had published *The Defence of Guenevere and other Poems* in 1858.
[7] Archibald Campbell Tait (1811–82), subsequently Archbishop of Canterbury.
[8] John Edward Kempe (1810–1907), Chaplain in Ordinary to Queen Victoria from 1864.

Ruskin decided to live in Switzerland. Before he made the final move, he consented to speak to the College for the last time.[9]

Saturday, 29 November . . . After dinner went to our College, where Ruskin had promised to give a farewell talk. I had a few minutes' tête à tête with him, and he described to me the house he has taken, on the further slope of the Grand Salève near Geneva, looking towards the Alps. Here, he says, he means to live, quite alone among the peasantry—except for his intelligent English man, and think, and take his two hours' climb to the mountain summit. As we were talking, Litchfield came and said the men were ready; so Ruskin went to the dais—the rooms being crowded with teachers and students—and began a friendly & familiar discourse. He suggested that any one who chose should ask him questions; and accordingly Furnivall and several others did so: on art, on political economy, & several other subjects. To all these enquiries he replied with wonderful readiness; with great power and aptness of language, and with thoughts always deep and clear; and, as usual, with an intense dogmatic assurance, as one who sincerely believes himself an oracle. On political economy he spoke thus for half an hour or more; giving the same ingenious and amiable but as I think fallacious views of it, that he has put forth in 'Fraser'.[1] As to art, he admitted—without cause, I thought,—an imperfection in his teaching. He had taught the men to *see* rightly, but not to reproduce what they saw, direct from Nature: and he was going to consider in his seclusion how to do this latter. After more than an hour's talk from him, Furnivall (not knowing, I think, what he did but merely anxious that nothing should be unsaid) asked Ruskin if there were any other subject he wished to speak on. I and a few others knew what was coming, when Ruskin gravely and with hesitation said there *was* one thing he had hoped to be asked about; but as no one had mentioned it (as if they *could!*) he would speak unasked.

And then it all came out. He did not indeed say aught of a change of opinion in himself: but those who believed him still an artistic Calvinist (!) must have been astonished when he began. He spoke of the grave religious doubts and searchings of nowadays; and said that he for his part had been greatly enlightened therein by a recent suggestion from a friend (Helps, Vernon thought it was[2]); which was, that the *attempt to combine religion & ethics* was foolish and fatal. On this text he preached for half an hour with intense earnestness; a

[9] Ruskin referred to his address at some length in his book *Time and Tide* (1867); it was briefly reported in the *Daily Telegraph*, 1 December, and was mentioned in the *Morning Star*, 4 December, 1862. See *Works*, ed. Cook and Wedderburn (1905, Vol. XVII, p. lx and pp. 324–5, and footnotes).

[1] Ruskin was then contributing a further series of 'Essays on Political Economy' to *Fraser's Magazine*, a sequel to his *Cornhill* essays. Essays appeared in June, September and December, 1862. With subsequent essays, they were published as *Munera Pulveris* (1872).

[2] Arthur Helps (1813–75), Clerk to the Privy Council, knighted 1872, was an earnest but not particularly original author, whom Ruskin admired. The suggestion was Vernon Lushington's.

mixture, as it were, of unitarianism and positivism: speaking, as he himself said, in an 'audacious and impudent' way of God: not that he was the least irreverent —far from it—but apostlewise, as if he were telling out a new revelation. God, says he, hates you to be unhappy: hates selfdenial therefore: will have men *not* pry into another world and sacrifice everything to that; but will have them look at this world, enjoy and fulfil their being here, be manly and brotherly, and take delight in, when once they have comprehended it, the unique nobleness and splendour of Humanity. All this and much more that he said is full of profound truth; but it is not *all* the truth; it leaves out of count, makes no provision for meeting, the sadness and the struggles of our double nature. It is with Ruskin somewhat as with Colenso (only Ruskin is infinitely abler): having escaped from the pit of Calvinism, he has swung himself up into the free air, and thinks it is always sunshine there: and it was just like his strong selfconfidence and fearless candour, to speak out what he felt and thought just because he could not bear to hold it in. A solemn thing and significant, truly, to see a man like him stand up in such a place, and give out a creed absolutely opposed to so much of what we call Christianity. Neither Maurice nor Hughes was there, happily: and the tremendous *implications* in what was said would not be thought of, at least at first, by his audience; who would simply be rejoiced to see and hear (as Litchfield afterwards expressed it) a great soul who, after all doubt or even disbelief, had attained to so much clearness and freedom and tranquillity. And though I know that his present posture of mind is not permanent, and though I differed much from some of his sayings, yet what he did say was so manly and sincere, and showed him to be so much better off for convictions than I had thought, that in saying farewell when it was over I could not but grasp his hand and thank him heartily for saying it.

Vernon Lushington and I walked down to the Temple together, talking of what we had heard, and specially of that backhanded blow to Christianity conveyed in the maxim about religion and ethics. Vernon thought, with his usual kindliness, that Ruskin should not have spoken so freely before the students, lest haply the faith of some should be disturbed or wounded: and if they *did* see all the purport of his speech, I should say so too. But quaere, are they not also in like case?

Sunday, 30 November . . . A thick yellow fog all day. . . . My Hannah came at five & stayed till nine. Her presence is like a cooling sedative, after such distractions of thought as those of last night. She comes to me like a creature of some other world: she never heard of, could not comprehend, even the *words* enquiry and doubt: to her ignorance is bliss, because it is not of stupidity but of labour. How all intellectual conflicts fade out of hearing, when I take her face between my palms, and see its loving intelligent simplicity!

A refuge, this; homely, but as far as it goes, certain, divine.

Wednesday, 3 December . . . Litchfield came to breakfast. We talked of Saturday, of course.

It seems that Ruskin and Carlyle have, apropos of the Church of England, come to the conclusion that 'the poor old thing' cannot exist much longer. May be: but a rash conclusion, I think, when one remembers how long, in such matters, the machinery can go on after the engine has stopped. And indeed the engine has *not* stopped: a greater motive power, moral and social, does not exist . . .

Munby travelled home to York for the family Christmas celebrations on 23 December. Over the holiday, he walked through the neighbouring villages and as far as the battlefield of Marston Moor. In York he bought 'a new striped scouring apron and three red and blue cotton pocket handkerchiefs for Hannah'. Back in London on 28 December, he heard from Hannah herself of her Christmas enjoyments, which 'seem to have consisted of work harder than usual, and one stealthy peep "through the crack of the door" at the dancing party "upstairs" (i.e. on the ground floor) in the drawingroom'. But Hannah had found an admirer in the nephew of Sarah the nurse; he had kissed her, she confessed, under the mistletoe, and she was going to a pantomime with him. 'Here is a case for the greeneyed Monster!' commented Munby; but he accepted it philosophically as 'a salient instance of the freedom of manners which her class enjoys'; after all, he had himself played 'Kiss in the Ring'. His own rejoinder was to take Hannah to a 'Music Hall'.

There is no set piece in the diary to wind up this year; but from the heart of London comes a sketch of a young girl, clear as a Baxter print, to mark the passing of 1862:

Tuesday, 30 December . . . A girl named Margaret Cochrane is a crossingsweeper at Charing Cross, and has been so, to my knowledge for several years. She says she is but fourteen, but she looks much older—quite a young woman, indeed. She sweeps a path from King Charles's statue to Spring Gardens; the densest part of the wide throng of hurrying carriages. She plies her daring broom under the wheels, which bespatter her with mire as they fly; she dodges under the horses' heads, and is ever ready to conduct the timid lady or nervous old gentleman through the perils of the crossing; she is wet through her thin clothing when it rains; she is in the street all day, the lowest and least protected of that roaring buffeting crowd. And she is a wellgrown and really pretty girl; with a delicate complexion and refined features and bright eyes: her mudstained frock and bonnet are neat, though shabby; and even in her dirt she is attractive, as she drops you a quiet curtsy and says 'Please Sir', holding out her hand and leaning on her wellworn broom. Yet I never—and I have often watched her among her companions—saw any rudeness, levity, nor immodesty in her behaviour: nor did I ever see her insulted by any passerby. Tonight in giving her a penny I asked her if she meant to remain a crossing sweeper; and she said 'No Sir—I think I shall take to selling oranges when I grow up.'

Whether it be modesty or love of change, it is the fact that crossingsweeper girls seldom stay at their calling after they pass the age of puberty. . . .

5

PUBLIC AND PRIVATE OCCASIONS
1863–4

The diary excerpts for 1863 are taken from Munby's full diary; but his concise diary, in note form, requires some attention. Munby prefaced this shorter diary for 1863 with a careful summary of 'Journeys and Excursions' in the year; he did not go abroad, but visited many places on his bachelor rambles near London, went to Cambridge in April, and in August made a tour of the Midlands, the Lake District and Northumberland. Another feature now appearing in the concise diary is a daily record of letters sent and received; this makes one regret that Munby's correspondence, with few exceptions, has not survived.

The new year brought a welcome amenity for Londoners. On Saturday, 10 January, Munby returned from a visit to Hannah at Kilburn 'by the Underground Railway, which is opened for the first time today. I travelled the whole way; from Paddington to Farringdon Street. Except that the carriages are lighted with gas, and that the stations as well [as] the line are obviously underground, there is nothing outwardly remarkable in the journey.'

Love affairs, even marriages, between Victorian gentlemen and maid-servants or other 'inferior' women, were by no means unknown. Munby gossips with feeling about such *mésalliances* from time to time in the diary; and in July, 1863, we find him gravely discussing them with a society lady during the Eton *v.* Harrow match at Lords. They were often sudden, passionate affairs, the reverse of his own long-drawn liaison with Hannah. The case of Lord Robert Montagu (1825–1902), the second son of the sixth Duke of Manchester, was more singular. He had been five years a widower, with four young children to bring up, when on 18 October, 1862, he married, according to the reference books, 'Catherine, daughter of William Wade', who was to add five more children to his family.

Sunday, 11 January . . . Hannah came to me at five, and stayed till nine. From her I learn the other side of the Great Montagu Case. Robert Montagu—Lord Robert—whom I remember at Trinity, has positively gone & married a house-maid! Of which event one Davis, a nurse who knows the cook as lived with her

—which her name was Betsy Wade, was the housemaid's—has preserved the details for kitchen ears.

Cook & Betsy was a walking in Kensington Gardens; a gentleman unknown picks up Betsy's parasol (parasol indeed!) and follows the two home, unbeknown, to their master's house in Westbourne Grove. Not long after, when Betsy was on her knees in the street, cleaning the steps, one morning, the same gentleman goes by; speaks to her—but then it was early & no one was about; says, Would you like a better place? I think I could get you one in (sic) Lord Montagu's nursery. She, taking him for a butler or other man of eminence, says Yes Sir, I should; he then calls in person on her mistress for Betsy's character: and Betsy becomes a nurse in that noble household.

There, her master's favour grows daily towards the humble maiden; and in few weeks, the astonished servants, all but her, are discharged en masse, and Lord Robert proclaims his terrible resolve. But Betsy Wade, though her hands are still rough with blacking grates when my lord claims her for his bride, comports herself with grave propriety: being indeed far less sensible of her new honour than a girl of the middling ranks would be. She goes to see her old friend & fellow servant. 'Hollo Betsy,' says the Cook, 'what, have ye left already? Ye must be a going to be married, or somethink!' 'Why yes', says the fair Griselda, 'I *am* a going to be married'; and she says no more. Would Miss Sugarplum, or even Miss Bolus, have kept such a secret so? The judicious Betsy then retires for a few days to her mother's cottage in some Suffolk village; receives the blessing of her astonished unpresentable parent; and on her return, is made Lady Robert Montagu at once, without any educating or refining preliminaries whatever. 'Which there was five & twenty baskets of flowers went from Jobstick's to the wedding', says the excellent person from whom we in our kitchen derive all this news.

Now I happen to have heard lately the views taken by Society of this fatal deed: I have heard from ladies of the shocking degradation of poor Lord Robert, and of his hopeless exclusion from family and friends by reason of this inexplicable depravity; and have of course expressed my deepest sympathy & horror.

It is therefore amusing to hear what Betsy's friends & equals say. There is envy among housemaids; there is increased yearning for the fortuneteller's promise to us, of being 'a lady'; there is the conviction that we are as good as she is. And among the elders, like Mrs. Davis (née Gamp) there is the proud patronising thought that she did well, as a champion of her class. It is scarcely necessary to remark, that Betsy had a sweetheart of her own rank, whom she discarded for her noble lover: and upon this theme, Mrs. D. is eloquent & full of praise. 'Sweethearts be blowed!' says that matron: 'why' she adds with scorn, apostrophizing our Hannah, 'if *you* had a chance to marry a gentleman, would you be such a fool as to let a sweetheart stop you?'

Her kitchen auditors laugh, and applaud the good woman's saying: but she to whom it was addressed does not laugh: she answers with an indignant affirmative; and is emboldened by her kindling heart to such a degree, that for a moment she forgets her own inferiority to the speaker, who never condescends to notice her when other than servants are by. 'Look here, Ma'am', she exclaims over the deal table; and enters upon a simple defence of love and honour, which draws down upon her the contempt of all these her fellow women. N.B.

Monday, 12 January . . . I went to Stoke Newington in the afternoon on business. . . . I went and came in a hansom. If a man want to meditate in and on London streets, let him take a hansom. Like a hero of old with his cloud and his guiding deity, he is in the midst of the roar and the conflict, but he is safe and quiet: it is an excitement that does but breed & colour reflections. Reflections on the crowd of hard isolated men, intent on gain or on duty, each one, in spite of himself, the centre of some little circle of loves and interests; and on the crowd of women, frivolous and flaunting, or honest and singly self reliant, & womanly—

Tuesday, 13 January . . . to Covent Garden, and heard Wallace's 'Love's Triumph'[1] one of the best English Operas I have heard: graceful though slight; the melodies not very salient, but the orchestration often bold and massive: the whole, for an English Opera, fairly original. The audience was a crowded pantomime audience: and I stayed with the rest, till the harlequinade began.

The transformation scene was really beautiful; a maze of moonlit tropical woods & streams, with the usual nymphs concealed among the flowers. On the right, there shone a stream of intense golden light, supposed to represent the dawn; and in the midst of this blaze, high up at the back of the stage, on a level with the topmost galleries, hung the form of a young woman. It soon appeared that she was attached by her waist & legs to the nearer end of a framework of iron, shaped like the handles of a plough and apparently twenty feet long, which projected at first almost vertically upwards, but soon, moving slowly into its arc, brought her down into full view, and into a light so strong that every detail of her face and limb was visible to the whole house. She wore only fleshings, and was therefore apparently nude, except for a short skirt round the loins, which, as she was hung so high, did by no means fulfil its decent office. There and thus she remained suspended for a quarter of an hour, waving her one free arm, but otherwise rigid and helpless as the knob on the end of a barber's pole; and all eyes and glasses converged upon her in her flood of glory.

The situation, if you consider it, seems both degrading and immodest: yet certainly neither the young woman nor the audience thought it so . . .

Thursday, 22 January . . . Home till 8; then to my Latin class till ten: then to Macmillan's, where were Masson, Tom Hughes, Lowes Dickinson, Fitzjames Stephen, Ralston, Deutsch,[2] and others.

[1] By William Vincent Wallace (1813–65).
[2] Emanuel Oscar Menahem Deutsch (1829–73), the Semitic scholar.

I had some conversation with Macmillan—on the word *gentleman*—wherein he told me that his father was a small farmer near Glasgow, and his mother a typical Scotch peasant woman; and that he himself began life as a shopman at thirty pounds a year, & was afterwards usher in a little school . . .

Sunday, 25 January . . . I was asked to join a new literary and artistic club which Severn and others are about founding,[3] to be called the Greco—after the Caffé: but some object to the name, and I was requested to think of a better. I however approved of Greco . . .

Sunday, 1 February . . . I went . . . by the Horse Guards down to Westminster Bridge, & crossed it: the first time I have done so since it was completely open. Its great width and its low quatrefoil parapets give it an air of extreme lightness and elegance; and, with its brightcoloured Sunday crowd of people on foot, it reminds one of the Seine bridges—on a large scale. I came back by the south bank & Waterloo Bridge, and home by five.

Hannah came soon after, and stayed with me till nine. I cut her hair, which has now for nearly a year been as short as a man's. Under her servant's cap the loss is hidden, and the few who see her never know it: and though I should never have proposed the sacrifice—which she made of her own accord—it adds one more to the outward contrasts between her and fine-ladyhood, & so I like it. My skill in haircutting is about as great as that of the prentice hand that crops the workhouse boys: but this does not matter, to one who never went to a 'barbers', as she simply calls it, except once, in her life . . .

Hannah is omnipresent in the diary throughout these months. She is chidden for not writing her own diary, as Munby had insisted (18 January), and she admits: 'I like cleaning boots, but I *hate* to sit down and write.' Nevertheless, she did write enough to leave a thorough and intelligent record of the life of a Victorian maidservant (it can be sampled only briefly in this volume). She is described (2 February) trying on her mistress's evening dress of black tulle, and blushing at the sight of her uncovered shoulders. And always Munby insists on his enjoyment of the hours of domesticity—all too rare—that her fleeting visits afforded. 'Tea alone, with a book, is delightful: breakfast in like case is not bad: but to me, at least in my present mood of disappointment & restlessness, dinner alone is the very type and realization of loneliness, of estrangement from family life, of the yearning, in short, for husbandhood' (3 February). Munby lingers affectionately over Hannah's 'kitchen errors of speech'—though he

---

[3] The club Walter Severn was founding was 'the present Arts Club in Hanover Square; of which I was a member' (Munby's later note). It is now in Dover Street (1971). Munby joined it in 1866. The Café Greco was an artistic centre in Rome.

did not regard them as errors: '. . . when she says "It *lugs* so" or "I'd as *lief* do it" or "never did *nothing*" or the familiar "she says, says she", the phrase sounds precious as an epigram. . . . "Them taters", also: she sat on the hearth in the fireglow, and peeled them deftly into her blue checked apron' (8 February). There can be little doubt on whose account he went to buy a Valentine, though he doesn't admit it.

Friday, 13 February . . . To shops, and among others to Rimmel's to buy a Valentine. The perfumed shop was full of staid ladies and middleaged gentlemen, busy with the same apparently absurd errand. And nothing *can* well seem more absurd, than to describe to the comely young woman behind the counter the particular variety of sentimental fondness which you wish to have. Most of the purchasers however were evidently intent, like myself, upon some pleasant surprise for young folks or practical joke upon elder ones. As for the young shopwomen, of whom there were several, all drest in a uniform or livery of black; they plied their amorous trade with the most businesslike coolness: which would have been amusing, only it was so sadly inappropriate to their sex and age. But it is to be feared that the yearning of the female heart for Valentines is checked in them by overmuch fruition. 'You must be quite tired of valentines?' said I: 'I am that, Sir', replied the civil kindly girl who served me. . . .

Romantic sentiment was strongly fashionable. For more than a year, since the death of the Prince Consort, England had been starved of royal ceremony and the emotional release that it brings. The whole country, London in particular, looked forward eagerly to the arrival on 7 March of Princess Alexandra for her wedding with the Prince of Wales. Much has been written of this famous welcome, but Munby is an eloquent eyewitness in the crowd.

Sunday, 1 March . . . The streets were unusually crowded, with people who had evidently come out to see the preparations for next Saturday. I hear of shopwindows let for that day at 22 guineas each: and of men at Windsor, who have let their houses—opposite the Castle—for the four days, for £150. . . .

Tuesday, 3 March . . . The preparations for celebrating the Princess's arrival go on at a wondrous rate. All the way from London Bridge, and probably from the Bricklayer's Arms, to Paddington, every house has its balcony of red baize seats; wedding favours fill the shops, and flags of all sizes; often the banners are already waving, & the devices for illumination fixed. In Pall Mall this evening, rows of workmen were supping on the pavement, ready to begin again by gaslight, with their work. The town seems as full as in the height of the season: one may say that the carpenters and gasfitters are all working day and night, while the rest of the population spend their time in watching them. . . .

Thursday, 5 March . . . I went down the river by boat at 4.30, to see the doings in the City. The steamer and the piers were crowded with provincial folks of the highly respectable kind: mostly women.

As we approached London Bridge, the parapets were seen covered with work-men and a confused array of statues scarlet cloth and scaffolding; and when I got on to the bridge itself, the scene was very striking. A great triumphal arch, as big as Temple Bar, was being rapidly adorned with pillars and drapery: through it, an huge mass of people of all kinds was struggling to and fro: seats and scaffolds were being hammered together on all sides: in every recess of the bridge stood massive draped pedestals, surmounted by mediaeval Knightly figures: rows of tall Venetian standards with gilt Danish elephants atop were being fixed along the parapets: and between the standards, great tripods of seeming bronze, from which incense is to rise. . . .

Friday, 6 March . . . The Strand was scarce passable this morning, what with crowds and workmen: and was all en grande tenue, like the rest of the town, with waving flags. But clouds came on at noon, and a storm of wind and rain followed, bitter to the hearts of thousands who are expecting tomorrow. . . . I came home, not without difficulty of passage, by five; and found Hannah waiting.

Her mistress had offered her leave to go and see the sights: and she came to me instead, as I wished her to do. *She* has no holiday tomorrow, poor child; but is left alone to guard the house; and means to have a 'good day'—a day of hard scrubbing and dirty work—while all London is out to see the Princess. She tells me that her master has given near £100 for a single room for that purpose.

At nine, I walked down with her to Farringdon Street, avoiding the crowd by byways; and sent her home by the underground railway. From thence I went on by Newgate and Cheapside to London Bridge. Crowds all the way, and banners pendant, and illuminations: the crush increasing, till at the Monument I found I could get no further; being indeed borne backward helplessly by the mass of people coming the other way. The roadway was jammed with vehicles, brought to a standstill in the midst of a sea of human heads, and themselves, whatever they were—coalwaggons carts or omnibuses—filled and covered with sightseers. Beyond all this rose the great unfinished triumphal arch; and flaring gas jets showed its columns and its white seahorses and its throng of workmen busy all day & night upon the scaffolding. The house fronts on either side the street were busy and lighted also; and standards waved dimly above in the darkness; & a confused noise of shouts went up continually from the swaying multitude, in the midst of which I was pinned fast. A good place to study the philosophy of panics: which perhaps may be summed up in the old words Corruptio optimi pessima: worse than that of bisons or elephants is the rush of the human herd in an irrational unanimity. . . .

Saturday, 7 March.   Fair day, with occasional showers: rain at night. An universal holiday. . . .

About one o'clock I went out of the Temple—which was blockaded except by the side gates, and those were closely guarded—into Fleet Street & to Blackfriars Bridge. The street was given up to Pedestrians, who filled the whole of it as far as one could see; a dense goodhumoured crowd of men and lowerclass women, in which one could just move along and no more. They were quietly waiting; looking at the flags and garlands which embowered the roadway overhead, at the welldrest folks who had long since taken their places in the red cloth seats & balconies at every house window, and at the artillery troopers who were to keep the line.

I took the steamer at Blackfriars for London Bridge. When we got there, it was impossible to land on the Surrey side, by reason of the crowds; and we tacked across to Middlesex, looking up at the crimson battlements and waving pennants and roaring throng on the Bridge. All the steamboats of course were crowded; and when I landed every side street was sending in a stream of people towards the main thoroughfares. The steps at London Bridge were blocked up: every avenue to it was barricaded with vehicles full of sightseers. At last by happy chance I got into King William Street, which like all the line of the Progress was full of human beings only.

The mass of these however was far denser than it had been in Fleet Street an hour before: and it was with much difficulty that I gained a place of vantage on the slope facing King William's statue. Around the statue were ranged the mounted battery of the Artillery Company: every visible window and housetop on every side was filled with gay people, wearing (as did many of the crowd) wedding favours or Danish colours: a vast and compact multitude filled the streets: banners and illumination devices appeared everywhere: the triumphal arch on the Bridge, now finished, was glorious with white & gold and bright colours. I waited with the rest about an hour; during which time the civic procession passed, with many struggles, down to the bridge to meet the Princess . . . .

At last, about 2.45 pm, bands were heard approaching; handkerchiefs innumerable waved from all windows; the sound of deep hurrahs came nearer & nearer; the great crowd surged to and fro with intense expectation. The glowing banners of the City procession reappeared and passed; and the countless carriages full of blue robes and scarlet robes and Lord Lieutenants' uniforms; and the Volunteer bands and the escort of the Blues; and the first three Royal carriages, whose occupants—at least the Danish Princesses Thyra and Dagmar,[4] for the rest were only officials—were heartily cheered. But when the last open carriage came in sight, the populace, who had been rapidly warming to tinder point, caught fire all at once. 'Hats off!' shouted the men: 'Here she is!' cried the women: and all those thousands of souls rose at her, as it were, in one blaze of triumphant irrepressible enthusiasm; surging round the carriage, waving hats

---

[4] Princess Alexandra's younger sisters; Thyra married Ernest Augustus Duke of Cumberland, and Dagmar married Emperor Alexander III of Russia.

and kerchiefs, leaping up here and there and again to catch a sight of her, and crying Hurrah with such oneness of heart & universality of utterance as I had not known before. There was no moving on for her: her carriage was imbedded in eager human faces, & not the scarlet outriders with all their appeals nor the mounted Equerries with their good-natured authority, could make way one inch.

She meanwhile, a fair haired graceful girl, in a white bonnet & blush roses, sat by her mother, with 'Bertie' and her father opposite, smiling sweetly & bowing on all sides; astounded—as she well might be—but selfpossessed; until the crowd parted at length. . .

Tuesday, 10 March: Gillingham, the wedding day of the Prince of Wales . . . In the lane I met one girl returning from fieldwork to dinner . . . she was the only person I saw out at labour today; and it soon appeared both to eye and ear that this was a great Festival. . . . The bells of Hoo church, miles away across the river, could be heard ringing a peal: the bells of Gillingham answered them before long: there was a distant roar of cannon, at intervals from the Forts at Chatham: and as I came into the road, farmer folks were going by in taxcarts, village children with medals and favours on their breasts were toddling along to Gillingham, and the wayside houses, especially the Publics in the Hamlet of Grange, had flags hung out over the path. All last evening, schoolgirls had kept coming to Cuy's,[5] with 'Please Sir may I go to the Feast?'

. . . I went . . . to the Green to see the festivities. Long deal tables were ranged all round the open; & at these 500 schoolchildren were already waiting for their meal, while banners were hung from the houses, and the villagers crowded to look on. In the centre, within the lines of tables, the Glenies and Troughtons, Cuyler and I, and several others, busied ourselves in distributing wedges of plumcake out of huge baskets, and in ladling cups of tea from pails and cans, in which the mixture had been brought from the vicarage. It was a pleasant & rather gay affair, with the green churchyard and tower—on the top of which floated a white ensign—for a background.

At church there had been before tea a special service, which was crowded: all the dissenters of the parish had been there with the orthodox: the Shining Light of the Methodists, and the preaching spinster of the Baptists, had for once become liturgical: & the tea fight afterwards was the saecular expression of the same unique harmony.

I said goodbye to Cuyler & the rest; went back for my knapsack, and walked to the New Brompton Station by 6. When the train came up, the engine was decked with flowers and evergreens, and nearly all the passengers wore wedding favours . . . every station on the line was dressed with flags and flowers, and at every place we passed there were sounds of guns and blazing of fireworks. We got to town about nine, & saw the brown sky over London lit up with reflected light. I buttoned up my coat and plunged into the crowd at London Bridge. The

[5] Cuyler Anderson.

bridge itself, with its parapets topped with tripods of burning incense and statues with rings of light round the pedestals and tall pennons that waved dimly above, was very beautiful: a lane of brilliant fantastic colour, and full of eager struggling human beings; and on either side, far down, the dark water of the Thames, its ripples faintly gleaming here & there, but still and solemn every where. Life, bustling and blazing for awhile; and the great mute eternity lying unheeded below it.

The dome of Paul's too was visible in the night, with a lurid zone of red lights across it; and from the top of the Monument a stream of electric flame shot across the sky before us. The whole effect was not unlike one of Martin's wildest pictures. I went on with the stream, under the illuminated triumphal arch at the north end of the bridge; up to the Mansion House, which with the Bank & Exchange made a splendid group, the façade of each being traced in light: along the midst of Cheapside, S. Paul's Churchyard, and Ludgate Hill. Almost every house was lighted up: the streets were as bright as day: pavement & roadway were packed with a dense mass of people, slowly but freely moving on foot between two rows of helpless and motionless vehicles. Men of all classes, and women of the lower and lower middle, made up the crowd; and more women than men: but the ladies—luckless beings—were rooted in omnibus & carriage.

On Ludgate Hill, a young woman, bonnetless & dishevelled, was carried past me on a stretcher upon men's shoulders. Drunk, I thought: *dead*, it afterwards proved; for she was one of the six poor creatures who were crushed to death near that very spot and time. A minute or two after, I was in the middle of the press that killed them. A tremendous throng, at the four cross streets; two broad *torrents* of people, meeting and striving among a confused mass of carriages.

I saw no one hurt; but the crush was severe and increasing, and I had only one free arm, having my knapsack with me; so with much difficulty I retreated, and went round by the passages into the quieter stream that filled Fleet Street; and so to Temple Bar, which stood up against the dark, one sheet of dazzling gold tissue and of crimson.

It had taken me about an hour and a half to reach it: writhing and squeezing, one of many atoms, through a crowd that was at every point dense enough to hide every stone of the street from one who had seen it above. And such a crowd extended also to Paddington, to Brompton, to Camberwell: two millions and a half of souls, they say. . . .

On 14 March, Munby completed his loyal homage by visiting Windsor, with a trainload of excursionists, to see 'the temporary wedding rooms, all of wood, built on to the west end of S. George's Chapel. There was a central Hall, not ignobly proportioned, & gay with coats of arms; and on either side, rooms with doors wide open—"The Bride's Chamber", all rosepink & gold and lace, and opposite it, "The Bridegroom's", of a sterner splendour. . . .'

Sunday, 15 March . . . Hannah came to me at five . . . she begged to lie down; it was all she could do, she was so tired. She did lie down, and was asleep in a moment.

I stood over her & watched her—good heaven, with what feelings! There was her hair—once massy and flowing, now cut short like a man's for mere cleanliness' sake: there was her fine face—once girlish and blooming, now reddened and soiled with work and weather: there were her hands—delicate & shapely by nature, but grown broad and coarse & unseemly, in so many years of scrubbing: there were her clumsy boots & her homely frock, all splashed with mud—for she had come through the rain, as usual, without any shelter. And yet, she 'cannot bear the thought' of leaving her hardworking place: and yet, if she could, I have nothing better to give her. . . .

Thursday, 17 March . . . to Harrison's in Pall Mall, to make at last a settlement about my unfortunate book,[6] of which the eleven remaining copies were sent to me the other day. 'There is no greater hell' says some one, 'than the failure in a great object': or in an object that *seemed* great. But perforce one gets accustomed to the brimstone in ten years; and forgets oneself if possible in the light studies of the flâneur—if a flâneur can be supposed to care about milkwomen, or about the comparative coarseness of servant maids' hands. So I took a grim sardonic pleasure in noting the contrast between my own bitter inward regret, and the businesslike calmness of manner with which I saw the proofs of failure put before me by the shopman. He was the representative of the bankrupt scoundrel Ollivier: & therefore I exacted from him without scruple the *nine shillings* which formed the final balance in my favour. . . .

Thursday, 26 March . . . to Macmillan's, where a very good meeting. . . . Garnett[7] and I had a long talk with Woolner (who is a great friend of Tennyson's) on English style in poetry & in prose. Woolner is certainly one of the ablest talkers I ever met. His opinions & judgements are always given with bold calm decision; he sets them forth in words which one feels to be, what so few are, the adequate and accurate expression of a clear thought; and he gives marvellous point to all he says, by a delicate sculptorlike use of his hands and by the power of his face. For his face, with lionlike hair and crisp chestnut beard and deepset keen eyes & cleancut features, has a manliness & intellectual might in its look, such as one seldom sees. . . .

Thursday, 2 April . . . I reached Cambridge before seven, and Trinity by 7.30. . . . I wrote to my old bedmaker, who is still alive and well, and so I have got,

---

[6] *Benoni.*

[7] Probably Richard Garnett (1835–1906), man of letters; eventually Keeper of Printed Books in the British Museum.

not my own rooms, but the set next to them, at letter L, New Court. Four generations of men have inhabited those rooms since I left them. . . .

Saturday, 4 April . . . to our Chapel at 6.30. It was, of course, a surplice night: and for the first time I wore my grandfather's M.A. hood, now mine, over my surplice.

It is a trivial matter, going to chapel thus clad, or walking through the streets and college grounds in one's Master's gown; but there is a powerful charm in the symbolism of the thing: it is a visible sign of membership, of being at home. . .

Friday, 10 April . . . About noon I went to call by appointment on Miss Stanley, at her 'Repository for Work' in York Street Westminster. It is a mean house like the others near it. The door opened straight into a small narrow shop, in which there was barely room to stand: for the floor was piled high with heaps of cotton shirts. Behind a counter, also full of shirts in progress, sat Miss Stanley, stitching away at a wristband, and two women who were doing the like.

She is that Honble Miss Stanley,[8] who was with Miss Nightingale in the Crimea: and here she now sits, day by day, looking after the making, by poor needlewomen at their own homes, of some thirty thousand soldiers' shirts per annum. A quiet selfdevoted woman of forty or so: slight and worn, with traces of past beauty in her calm & ladylike and unpretending face. A woman worthy of deep respect; and of a certain desiderium too, when one looked at her busy hands—thin, uncaredfor, dignified by no wedding ring.

She very kindly promised to give immediate work to Harriet Langdon, upon my undertaking to be responsible for the safety of the materials: and added that as Langdon was so much disfigured, she might come for the work privately, & not with the crowd.

To the newsroom at four: and at 5.30 dined by invitation with Walter Severn. I found him and Arthur both etching.

After coffee Walter said he would like to go and explore Caldwell's[9]: and it was agreed that we should do so at once. Now Caldwell's is one of the few public dancing rooms in London, which is frequented by respectable women and *not* by prostitutes. These think it 'slow': for the 'swells' who pay for their embraces are not to be found there. When we arrived, the relâche was begun. We took off our hats and coats, as the women do their bonnets and shawls: & it is worth notice that the doing of this forms the differentia between vice and virtue.

As we went upstairs I asked one of the girls who were standing about the door of the ballroom, When dancing would begin again? She did not know. 'I've only just come in', she said (it was 10.15 p.m.): 'I came straight from business'. Struck by such a phrase in a woman's mouth, I insinuated the enquiry, What

---

[8] Mary Stanley, a convert to Roman Catholicism; her friendship with Florence Nightingale did not last.
[9] In Dean Street, Soho. See 19 February, 1859.

business? And in reply, was informed that she 'had been *writing* all day'. This answer was so singular, that I at once proposed to dance the next polka with her: a penalty which it seemed necessary to pay, in order to gain her confidence and so obtain the information I wanted.

The dance—which was a perfect bore to me, especially as I really could not spin round with the rapidity which she required—gave me the right to a subsequent tête-a-tête: so taking her downstairs to the rude & simple refreshment room, I gave her what she asked for (sherry & sodawater) and got in return, by dint of judicious management, an account of her business and her habits. It was well worth the effort: for she was *a merchant's clerk*!

A bonâ fide female 'city clerk': a copying clerk, in fact, at a mercantile house in Old Broad Street. It was interesting to know the details & results of such a phenomenon. One of these results was, that she had none of the frippery and giggling frivolity of other girls of her class. She had spoken to me frankly at first, and now she talked soberly and gravely, just as a young man might have done, about her affairs. She was twentytwo, and had been three years a clerk under her present employers. It was the only business she had ever been engaged in: and it took a good deal of interest to get her her place.

There were only three or four other firms that she knew of, who have any female clerks. In the office where she is, there are several other girls; & their work is the same as the men's. 'We are instead of gentlemen', she said.

The girls however are all mere copying clerks, and have nothing to do with the accounts. She knew nothing of accounts: but 'it requires you to have had a good plain education', she said, 'to do our work'. There is one German girl in the office, who copies the German letters: and she herself is able to copy French ones tolerably. There is no matron, but 'a head gentleman-clerk who is over us'; and the male & female clerks all sit together in a large room. For herself, she sits on a high stool, at a desk, with the others, copying invoices letters or whatnot, all day: 'our sleeves get worn with leaning on the desk, & our white cuffs get dreadfully inked', says she. The male clerks are pleasant companions enough; but there is no flirting: 'when you're all in business together, it's different; and besides, we've no time.' As to the relative commercial value of the two sexes, her view was that the firm liked the 'ladyclerks' best: for they do the work as well as the 'gentlemen', *and are paid less*. As a woman of business, in fact, she looked upon some of her male companions as poor creatures at their work: and her opinion of the 'headgentleman' was not high. Our employers, however, she said, are very kind, and do all they can to make us comfortable. As to the salaries: the head female clerk, who is young like the rest, gets thirty shillings a week; and none of us get less than a pound a week. Our office hours are, eight hours a day: from 9 to 5, or from 10 to 6, or from 12 to 8, according to circumstances. 'I've been on late duty this week', said the fair copyist. . . .

The two Severns had by this time come to us: and I introduced Walter, in the fashion which seemed most appropriate, saying to my clerkly friend 'Here is a man who will dance with you to your heart's content': and straightway he did so, when we had all gone upstairs together.

The dancers were all shop-girls, milliners, & the like, & men of the same class: and though several of the women were pretty, the Broad Street clerk was decidedly the finest girl in the room ... bright-eyed, whitetoothed, ruddy lipped; a complexion glowing with rosy health (strange to say), and a countenance expressing strong sense and lively resolution. . . . Her hands, too, would have delighted Rossetti; they were large, and brown with exposure, and somewhat thick and heavy; but they were well shaped, longfingered, and by no means coarse. Her easy way of showing them, and her superb indifference to coquetry, in general, was itself a charm ... she looked a most queenly self-reliant young woman, able to make her way in the world, & neither diffident nor over-bold. . . . It was now 11.30 pm, and her fellow clerk was anxious to go. . . .

I offered to accompany them; to the disgust of Walter, who was struck with the tall beauty, especially when I told him her occupation; and tried in vain to persuade himself that Oxford Street was on the way to Westminster.

So he and Arthur shook hands all round; and the two clerks, who had frankly accepted my guidance, each of them as frankly took my arm. . . . Presently her companion retired to an omnibus, and she and I walked on together towards the Tottenham Court Road, where she said she lived, at home with her parents. She began to express a fear lest she should 'catch it'. . . . 'I have to tell so many fibs!' said she 'when I'm out late. I tell my father I've been kept at work at the office: and then he says what a shame it is to keep girls working till such hours, & why don't they put the men clerks to it? So they do, I tell him. But my mother suspects I cant be at business till eleven o'clock at night, & she dont like it at all. . . .' We had now got to University Street; & here she stopped, saying she was close at home. Like a prudent girl as she was, she abstained from telling me either her name or her address; and shaking hands with me as if she had been a male acquaintance, she departed, again exclaiming that she would be sure to 'catch it'. I returned home, by 12.30. . . .

Saturday, 11 April . . . I . . . walked down to Brompton, to see Harriet Langdon and tell her of the work I had got for her. . . . I told her of Miss Stanley's kindness, and how she was to go and fetch the work on Monday: she listened eagerly, and I knew that the ghastly death's head grin upon her raw and noseless visage was meant to be a smile of gratitude.

And so, after a year's effort, I am able to gladden this poor creature with the hope of earning—five shillings a week! . . .

Wednesday, 15 April . . . Passing through Scotland Yard about noon, I saw a large crowd, in the street, & heard the banjos of some Ethiopian Serenaders. But there were surely female voices as well as male: and going up, I was astonished to see that two of the five 'niggers' were young women. Yes: there were two young women, drest in fantastic ballet costume, and with shining black faces & necks & hands. Their heads were bare: their hair decked with network and rolls of scarlet cloth: they wore pink calico jackets, petticoats of spangled blue, ending a little below the knee: and red stockings and red boots. One of them came up to me, when the singing was over, with her tambourine; and earned a sixpence for her courage in blackening her face.

Street singer, 15 April, 1863

For she and her comrade were both very decent and modest in behaviour; and were protected by their male companions, if they needed protection. They were the wives, she said, of two of the men; they go about with them through the west end, performing always out of doors, & both in the daytime and at night. They dance as well as sing—and they sang very well. They wash the black off every night.

I remarked to her that this was the first time that I had ever seen female niggers (except one, & that long ago) singing in the open street. 'Yes Sir' she said 'it's a new thing; but we mean to stick to it.' I watched these two selfmade

negresses going through the crowd by turns, collecting money after the performance. They did it very quietly and simply; appealing in silence—with not
even a smile, for the lampblack varnish disguised whatever good looks they had,
so smiles would have been useless—now to some contemptuous swell, who
looked another way; now to some honest workman, who made a wry face as he
stared at the black girl's face before him and the black hand that took his penny;
and now again to the female spectators, who evidently could not understand
how any woman could make herself such a fright. . . .

Thursday, 23 April . . . Home till eight: then to my Latin class till ten: then to
Macmillan's.
　　A small party; but Dr. Kingsley and his brother Henry was there, & Ralston,
and Allingham the poet[1] also, whom I was glad to meet again after so long.
　　He has settled in London, and is in the *Custom House*. No wonder he hates
it . . .

Early in May, 1863, Munby stayed with an artist friend at Ripley, and
was immediately attracted to this part of Surrey. He discovered the neighbouring village of Pyrford for the first time; its ancient Norman church
and the wide view from the churchyard over the Wey valley, with the
ruins of Newark Abbey in the centre of the landscape. He wandered
through the meadows and came to the lock at the junction of the Wey
canal and the main river. Munby did not then realise that this was the
beginning of a long association, and that he would eventually make his
home at Pyrford; but, as he noted, he 'spent such a pleasant time, it almost
seemed as if in some such nook one might work out the long sad problem,
How to live with Hannah & do justice to her love and my own'. In fact,
Hannah was never to live with Munby at Pyrford, but he was to undergo
a distressing emotional experience there four years later with another
sweetheart.

Tuesday, 5 May . . . Met Ralston . . . who told me that Brett's pictures have
been rejected at the Academy!
　　R. and Coventry Patmore and others are getting up a separate exhibition of
them. I promised to help and to be one of the guarantors of two guineas each for
expenses.

Wednesday, 6 May . . . At 4 p.m. I went to Walter Severn's rooms, to tell him
of the Brett project. He and Arthur were there, and Richmond the painter's two
sons; both gentlemanly fellows, one of them a parson. . . .

---

[1] William Allingham (1824–89).

Tuesday, 12 May . . . At 4 p.m. I met Cuyler by appointment at the Academy.

So far as the R.A.'s are concerned, the exhibition of this year is contemptible: Pickersgill, Hart, Cope, Charles Landseer, A. Cooper, Witherington—all of them simply humiliating and distressing to look at, if you are to think of them as painters honoured and successful.

Millais's three pictures—the First Sermon, the Wolf's Den, and the Eve of S. Agnes—are the most admirable in point of expressiveness and colour that I saw: except indeed Holman Hunt's Dr. Lushington, and Mrs. Newton's charming portrait of herself[2]—but it does not do her justice. . . .

We left at seven, and dined at Rouget's; Ralston meeting us there as arranged. Afterwards Cuyler went to the Olympic, and R. and I together to Chelsea, to see Rossetti, by invitation, at his new abode, 16 Cheyne Walk.

The house, which even on the outside is noble, having a fine Queen Anne front and elaborate scrollwork gates, perfectly astonished me by its historical interest and by the sumptuous way in which Rossetti has filled it with antique furniture. It is, he says, the remaining wing of a palace built by Henry VIII as a nursery for his children; and it remained in royal hands till at least the time of George I, whose monogram is carved throughout the interior.[3] There is a fine pillared diningroom, now a studio, which looks upon the spacious gardens behind: but the great charm is the drawingroom; a splendid apartment, forty feet long, having seven windows, the centre one a bay, all of which look out through the ancient elms upon the river. This room, hung with curtains of old Indian chintz from end to end, and quaintly furnished with Japanese cabinets and Italian & Dutch pictures, was so utterly unlike the commonplace comfort or splendour of London houses, that I was never wearied of walking up and down it, absorbing as it were the aroma of its manifold romance. Tea, too, was served there (absolutely with thick cream!) in antique china cups, upon a carven table, and by the light of massive Elizabethan candlesticks.

But all this, and the still greater pleasure, as it ought to have been, of a fireside talk with Rossetti, was marred by Rossetti's own intolerance. For when we came to talk of Brett, about whom he knew Ralston and myself to be interested, he spoke with so much unfairness & malignity of Brett as a man and as a painter, that Ralston's warm hearted sensitive nature closed up at once into silence, and I was as indignant as he.

Brett is opiniative and entêté; true: therefore Rossetti called him insufferable, ignorant, and (with unconscious irony) the very opposite of himself (!): Brett paints landscape & Rossetti ideal portraiture; therefore Rossetti called

---

[2] See Plate 10.

[3] This ambitious history of the house was wishful thinking on Rossetti's part. Even the site of Henry VIII's manor is uncertain, and no significant traces of it remain. In fact, Rossetti's house was built in 1717 for Richard Chapman, an apothecary of St. Clement Danes. His initials R.C. on the wrought-iron gates were once mistakenly interpreted as C.R., *Catherine Regina*, standing for Queen Catherine of Braganza, Charles II's Queen. They may also account for the alleged G.R. monogram 'carved throughout the interior'.

him a stupid literalist, and said that he had 'no more eye for colour than a pig'.

Truly, a melancholy example not only of the jealousy and bitterness of artists, but—for Rossetti is much more than artist only—of the inability of even the ablest men to understand or care for any excellence outside of their own range of sympathies. But Rossetti has been much injured by the constant toadying of that clever little prig Algernon Swinburne, who was present, echoing all his master said. He, and George Meredith[4] who was out, live in the house also.

The conversation was happily turned by the appearance of Street[5] the architect, whom I had not met before. An agreeable modest man, but in appearance somewhat vulgar.

We were shown round the house; the old and rare beds and cabinets & tables with which it is stocked; and declining supper, R. and I came away. Rossetti wanted me to dine there on Saturday; but I declined.

We walked back to town, lamenting together over this seeming impossibility of finding a society which satisfies both heart & intellect.

The genial & goodnatured, whether men or women, are foolish or superficial: the able and imaginative are hemmed in by prejudice, and make as if their very largeness excluded, instead of *in*cluding more intensely, the homelier interests of life.

But so it is, for men like Ralston and myself: to hang like Mahomet's coffin between heaven and earth, and draw full sustenance from neither; that is our portion.

It is interesting to observe Munby's changing reactions in the diary to the varying moods and manifestations of those men of genius, such as Ruskin, Rossetti and Swinburne, with whom he was closely acquainted. In course of time he managed to reconcile himself to Ruskin's more irritating characteristics, and latterly he wrote of him with devotion. He eventually contrived to view even the 'little prig' Swinburne with compassion.

But Rossetti's love of poetry, of the mediaeval, of London life, and especially of the working-class, set him apart in Munby's affections—as one whose enthusiasms he endorsed, and whose failings he condoned and preferred not to mention. There has been no hint of criticism of Rossetti in more than four years of the diary; but some such clash of temperament as is recorded in the last entry was probably inevitable over a period of time. That Munby was such a warm supporter of John Brett is a tribute to his heart rather than his head. Munby could not have chosen a more dangerous subject for conversation with Rossetti; not only were Rossetti

---

[4] George Meredith (1828–1909), the novelist and poet.
[5] George Edmund Street (1824–81), the architect of the Law Courts.

and Brett poles apart as artists, but the very mention of Brett must have served to remind Rossetti of Ruskin's didactic patronage, which he himself had enjoyed and come to distrust. But Munby's disagreement with Rossetti was temporary; we are to see them again as friendly as ever.

Saturday, 16 May . . . In the afternoon I went to Farringdon Street, to make enquiries at the Victoria Press. It is much enlarged in influence since Miss Faithfull showed me over the Coram Street house some years ago: but it is no more a *female* press than it was then. Fifteen or sixteen female compositors are all the women they have on the old premises: and the actual printing, which is done here, is all done by men. The clerk in charge, whom I saw, was a man: the office boys *were* boys. This, I apprehend, is little better than trifling with the female labour question. We dont want—at least *I* dont—to disturb the 'wages fund' by making women printers or clerks or what not: that which I want is, liberty for any woman who has the strength and the mind for it, to turn her hand to any manual employment whatever. . . .

Wednesday, 20 May . . . A damp grey morning: but soon after ten a hope (delusive like other hopes) of fine weather appeared, and I determined to go to the *Derby*: not to see the race, but to see those who go to see it, and to observe the humours of the course, which I had not visited since West Australian's year, whenever that was.[6] Moreover I was in a moody and despondent condition: and a race course or other suchlike place is to me the best resort at such times. Not that I am pleased at all by its pleasures, but that the study of them and of those who are pleased by them calls out one's power of observation and one's love of reverie into a set of subjects other & better than one's self. I went down by a crowded train from Waterloo Station, and got to Epsom at 12.30. The rain had fairly set in by this time, and Epsom town was deep in yellow mud. However I walked up to the course: the roads being at times almost ankle deep in mire: but like most other men—and there were few women to be seen—I was clad accordingly in great coat and leggings. . . .

I saw . . . three lusty bold girls alone, playing and singing together, with organ tambourine and so on: two female ballad singers, young, each accompanied by a man with an instrument: two female trumpeters, girls, who belonged to a German band: and two young female acrobats or stiltwalkers—also with a man—who looked forlorn and pitiable in their satin shoes & spangles, struggling through the dirt.

. . . So the time passed till after three; and then the multitudes gathered up for the Derby. I saw both the start and the goal, from the shoulder of the hill. After *thirty one* false starts, the horses went off with a bound and a roar of hoofs at five minutes to four: and Macaroni came in first, beating Lord Clifden by a hair's breadth. Whether the awe be divine or devilish, the unanimous enthusiasm of

[6] It was 1853. But Munby forgot that he had been to the Derby in 1859. See 1 June, 1859.

fifty thousand human beings, the thunder of their voices and the swaying to and fro, *is* in a high sense awful: is perhaps the most tremendous expression of an unseen force that one can conceive of, except a storm at sea. . . .

Thursday, 28 May . . . to the Working Men's College by seven p.m., to the Council meeting, where the new student members, elected under our recent resolutions, were present for the first time. They are three in number: and to the great surprise of every one, they signalized their entrance into membership by violently repudiating the terms of their own election, and making use of that very election to propose certain other rules, which would swamp the old council with innumerable students, who were all to be permanent members like the teachers. It was curious to see the lasting antagonism between the gentleman and the snob, the educated and the half-educated, breaking out among us, of all bodies; & all our liberal 'radical' members suddenly changed to conservatives & aristocrats in spite of themselves. Probably the Girondins felt just as oddly, when the Jacobins took the helm out of their hands.

But, worst of all, these men had been caballing; trying to create parties, and set student against teacher, 'university-men' against their own class: or tending to do this, if they did not try.

Maurice at the head of the table had been chafing for long under his sense of this: and at length he rose, as chairman, and losing not indeed his temper but his judgement, broke into one of his most fitful, earnest, pathetic harangues. He was no longer Principal, he said; the College was at an end; class had been set against class, the very principle of cooperation and brotherhood on which we—all men —stood, had been violated; let us confess to the world that we were a failure, a sham—that there was no divine centre of unity among us! He sat down, his frame quivering (I was next to him) and his face electrical with noble but un-reasonable emotion.

With him, the fellowship of men with each other in Christ is not merely a creed; it is a passion. Then Hughes spoke, manly and blunt, but too much surprised, like the rest of us, to be very clear: and Ludlow, vehement & illogical, took the part, impromptu, of the malcontents, Furnivall of course assisting; & Vernon tried to bring things round, and Westlake was cold and selfpossest as usual. The only man who had got hold of the right, and who put it clearly, with perfect temper and justice, was Litchfield: whose comprehensiveness and ease of expression I always admire. By his aid, things were somewhat calmed and cleared, and the Council being adjourned, we all went upstairs to the large rooms, where the students & some strangers were assembled for the general meeting.

Ralston came to it, and brought three young Russian noblemen, who are studying in England such phenomena as this of ours. They were all promoters of the Sunday schools which were put down by the Petersburg government a year or two ago, after being attended by hundreds of the people. One of the three had fought against us at Sebastopol as an artillery officer: another was a very fine young man, and he when called upon made a pleasant little speech, in English. They were all cordially received, and seemed to enjoy and appreciate what was going on. Ralston and I left at ten, and walked down to Macmillan's: where we found Dr. Kingsley, Lowes Dickinson, Edward Dicey, and others. Amongst the strangers were two Yankees, with one of them I had much talk of his country and ours. A man not only intelligent, but, strange to say, wellbred and even modest. This was the last night of these weekly gatherings: the thriving Scotchman, having now founded a London 'house' and become publisher to the University of Oxford, finds it necessary to come to town and take a villa at Streatham, where he hopes still to see you.

I shook hands with him at the door, regretting the loss of these pleasant and unceremonious meetings, where friends personal & literary and old college acquaintance have used to come together for so long. . . .

This crisis in the government of the Working Men's College is bound to recall the student unrest in London a century later. It was due to F. D. Maurice's insistence on the authority of the teachers and of his own casting vote as Principal. Having no sympathy for democracy, Maurice inevitably clashed with men like Furnivall and Ludlow. The outcome of the discussion on 28 May, 1863, was a decision 'that at no time should more than one-third of the Council be members who had entered the College as students. This was little different from the previous arrangement, and it neither improved the efficiency of the Council as an instrument of government, nor satisfied the desire for a real measure of student representation. The only benefit which came out of these 1863 meetings was the formation of a small Executive Committee, designed to handle the current business of the College more efficiently'.[7] In fact, little could be done to reorganise the College until the death of F. D. Maurice in 1872.

Tuesday, 2 June . . . Passing Savile House in the afternoon, I went in to see a Polish giantess who is being exhibited there. She proved to be a young woman— aged 20, she said—standing just seven feet high, but her figure so well proportioned that at a distance she scarcely looked remarkable. Coming near, however, I found that the crown of my head was on a level with her shoulder. I talked to her, in French and scraps of German; craning back my head to do so. She asserted that she was, as the bills said she was, a 'Countess'—a Grafinn and a *Von* Lodoiska; if those two words can go together.

She was a fine girl, not ill looking . . . & seemed wholly indifferent to her position as a 'curiosity'. . . .

[7] J. F. C. Harrison: *A History of the Working Men's College*, p. 94.

Wednesday, 3 June . . . dined in Hall, at six: it being Great Grand Day. . . . The Chancellor, the Archbishop of York, Lord Brougham, and the Bishop of Lichfield, were the lions of the Benchers' table. Lord Brougham, who looked grim and grey and vigorous, was loyally cheered on retiring after dinner: and the Chancellor (Bethell[8]), after his manner, made as though he thought the cheers were meant for himself; until the delusion became impossible, and then he slunk away. As for Lord Brougham, he went out backwards, curtsying rather than bowing his acknowledgements, with quaint gravity.

Dinner was not over till nine; and then I went home to dress, and went with Litchfield to Campden Hill, to a party at Mrs. McCallum's.[9]

A pretty house, and a good many people I knew there: amongst the rest Miss Wornum & her father. She looked very bright and charming; and I carried her off into a quiet spot, and delicately 'trotted her out', so to speak, for half an hour or more seeking to know what it is that has wrought infatuation for her in such a man as Ralston.

A lively goodnatured very pretty girl of nineteen: voilà tout! Yet there is something noble in that worship of beauty and girlish weakness, which makes a brave highminded man fall down before such an object in despite of his own judgement. Alex. Munro was there, and his wife; & J. C. Jeaffreson[1] & his wife; and James Stansfeld[2] also, the new Lord of the Admiralty (a keen Yankee-faced man with a sweet but selfconscious smile) and his wife: whom I took in to supper; and a fussy young woman she was. . . .

Saturday, 6 June . . . I took boat to London Bridge, and so by train to the Crystal Palace by three p.m.: there being a concert there of unusual brilliancy, to celebrate the Queen's birthday. The Thomlinsons had asked me to drive down with them; & being unable to do so I appointed to join them in the transept: but the crowd of gaily drest folks filled the whole transept and overflowed down the nave on either hand; so that my search for them was vain. During the concert, as I stood on the skirts of the crowd listening to Adelina Patti, whose rich ringing soprano was audible beyond all other voices, the man whom of all others I should have wished for came up: Ruskin. He had just come back from Switzerland, where he is building himself a house on the further side of Mont Salève looking toward Mont Blanc. I walked up and down with him for near an hour among the courts and in the nave, talking on many subjects, or rather suggesting them for him to talk on. For whatever we spoke of, he was always overvehement, onesided, paradoxical; gliding over objections in his bland and persistent way, .stating strange opinions with an air of quiet naïveté as if they were the most natural things in the world; and yet pouring out his thoughts with all that pure

---

[8] Richard Bethell, first Baron Westbury (1800–73).
[9] Wife of Andrew MacCallum (1821–1902), the landscape painter.
[1] John Cordy Jeaffreson (1831–1901), novelist and anecdotal anthologist.
[2] James Stansfeld (1820–98); Liberal M.P. for Halifax; became President of Local Government Board; G.C.B., 1895.

unworldly eloquence which charms one quite away from the influence of commonplace or merely clever companionship.

We talked of the Crystal Palace itself: it was a base and formless shed; compare yon 13th century tomb with these ugly & monotonous girders! Of portraits, apropos of the fine copies of Venetian pictures in the courts: there were no good portraits now a days, because there were no faces worth painting. Of vanity: which with much ingenuity he maintained to be a charm in women and a necessary part of every noble character; and thereafter of humility and self-abnegation, which were utterly bad, and of the innocent unconsciousness of girlhood, which, he affected to hold, was a sign of immaturity merely, if not a thing contemptible. And so on! At last we were joined by old Mr. Ruskin, a dry antique little man in a lean frockcoat of old-world shape; and by Litchfield and Pearse. Ruskin and his father departed; & having lost L. and P. again in the crowd, I strolled for awhile in the nave, where two streams of gauzy gorgeous women, and their cavaliers, were moving up and down listening to the Guards' band and depreciating one another's dresses. I dined in the building, and came home by 8. . . .

Sunday, 28 June . . . Hannah begged me last night to come this morning: she would be alone in the house, and it would be 'such a chance' to show me 'the places what I clean'!

I went therefore about noon: most unwillingly; and yet with much desire to see her for once in her kitchen. I found her in a clean Sunday lilac cotton frock and white apron and cap, standing with a tub before her on the deal table, shelling peas. Her arms, of course, were bare; and the work was wholesome and homely. Nevertheless I did not care for it, thus. But she, pleased & smiling, led me to see the scenes of her daily scouring. . . . And then insisted on my going upstairs, to see the dining room that she had dusted, and the pretty things in the drawing room. But to see her stand in a drawing room in her servant's dress, and know that she *is* a servant, and that the piano the books the pictures belonged to her *mistress*, and were all utterly beyond her comprehension and outside and above her life, though so near to her; that she was not even brought among these things and their people by errands of service, but remained below in the kitchen out of sight evermore: this I could not endure; and I left the house not unkindly indeed but hurriedly and sadly, much to her surprise and disappointment. If only she could have understood: but how *could* she understand? . . .

Wednesday, 1 July . . . Walked in the Green Park and Hyde Park from five to six p.m.; and eastward through May Fair. Near Grosvenor Gate, where carriages full of languid perfumed ladies were as usual flashing by, and other misses, less languid but not less sumptuous, sat or strolled elegantly in the quasi-private garden, I passed a milkwench, going home with her yoke and her emptied pails to the Grosvenor Dairy in Mount Street. A tall clumsy creature, with feet of inexpressible bigness. Looked at from behind as she moved heavily along, she seemed a brawny woman of middle age; so large and burly she seemed, so dull and listless as to all the gay life around her.

But I passed, and saw her honest ruddy face; and she was a girl of twenty. The same age as those novelreading charmers & those reposing beauties in the barouches and on the garden chairs, between whom and herself so great a gulf is fixed. In South Audley Street, another milk woman (there were dozens in sight) was collecting all her small supplementary cans and placing them in and around the empty big ones, before she yoked herself to these for the last journey homewards. The small cans are of all capacities, from quartsize downwards. I counted them as she moved off: they were *twenty three* in number, besides others in the depths of her pails, which I could not see. And yet she was not proud, either of her power of carrying such a weight of metal, or of the grand inscription which was painted across her shoulders upon the yoke; 'Stevens, By appointment to the Queen'! . . .

Friday, 10 July . . . Brilliant hot day. Went up to Oxford Terrace by 3.30: for Miss Williams had asked me to go with her party to the Eton and Harrow cricket match at Lord's. . . .

The Miss Williams's carriage was at the door; and with us went Mrs. Foulger, a lady whom I used to see at the Prichards' at Harrow. The ground at Lord's was said to be more crowded than had ever been known. Not less than 10,000 people, I was told, were there; all well drest folk and more or less fashionable. We drove all round the ground without being able to find a place in the solid ring of carriages, three deep at least: so taking campstools we all got out, and settled down within the barrier among an equally dense circle of ladies and their squires. Mrs. Foulger has a son at Harrow; and our party like everyone else wore the colours of the players, in knots of ribbon atop of their parasols. By some chance, the conversation turned on Lord Robert Montagu's recent marriage with a housemaid. Other cases of the kind were mentioned, and that with due contempt and abhorrence, by the ladies: and at length Miss Williams drew me into a keen tête à tête discussion on the subject of such mésalliances, which lasted nearly all the time we were there. If she had known how nearly the question touched me, and how all I said had a secret reference to a certain maid of all work, I fear that the respect and preference with which she has lately honoured me would quickly disappear.

For she spoke with such bitterness and scorn of all servant maids and suchlike, that I half fancied she had some private reason for doing so. She refused to believe that any such woman could by possibility be refined in nature, or be companionable for a man of education. She knew them by experience: their faces might be pretty and their manner modest, but within, they were full of baseness & vulgarity. And no man of refinement & gentlemanly feeling could *ever* degrade himself by such an union. *That* was absolute: there was *none* exception!

To try her, I mentioned that Lord Robert first saw his housemaid as she was on her knees in the street cleaning steps; and that he stopped to look at her. No words could express Miss Williams's disgust at that proceeding. 'You, for instance' said she 'I am sure *you* never would stoop to look twice at such a being!' Ah me! But my rôle throughout was that of an impartial critic: explaining Montagu's conduct, but lamenting it. . . . I left my fair friends' carriage at Hyde Park corner: dined at 8.30: and at ten, home. There I found, by way of commentary on our talk, a letter from that menial drudge, that vulgar female servant.

Saturday, 11 July . . . I walked up to Kilburn by six, to see Hannah: but though she was out, in her old bonnet & working dress, expecting me, it was impossible even to exchange a quiet word with her. All down the side roads, & among the unfinished houses, I sought in vain for some place for talk: she following, and I half beside myself with the thought that she could only follow. Everywhere there were prying eyes, and folks who might know her as Mr. So & So's servant, and who at any rate would stare if they saw us together. And in the end we had to return; she walking off the path and somewhat behind, that she might not seem to be with me, and I talking to her hurriedly over my shoulder! The increase of pity and tenderness that all this begat in me, is certainly bought dear with such a bitter experience. Without one kiss or one touch of the hand, the servant goes back to her kitchen, and I to whence I came. . . .

Sunday, 12 July: Working Men's College excursion to Burnham Beeches . . . each of us had brought his or her dinner from home: so, after tea had been ordered for five o'clock, we went down into the glades, and settled on a space of sweet sward under a ring of the beeches. . . . We all went back to the cottage at five, and found snowy tables spread on its little lawn under the apple trees: tea, and fresh eggs, and jam of this year's preserving, & butter and bread without stint: all which was fully and quietly enjoyed, in all heartiness and kindly goodhumour. And before seven, a great farm waggon which our host had purveyed for the women's sake, came up to the gate: and as many as might—of whom I was one— got in, and the rest went laughingly after. We and our waggon went thus at a foot's pace back to Farnham Royal; . . . From Farnham we walked to Slough as before: but in one bright green meadow we stopped and had a final concert. We sat and lay in a circle close to the path: the parents with the children, the sweethearts and friends close together, the men who were no singers, smoking; and Litchfield kneeling in the centre, with his baton and his music books. And some of the youths played ball in the further parts of the meadow. It was a lovely summer evening; the music, which was chiefly Mendelssohn's Elijah and old English madrigals, was charmingly sung, and was heard to perfection in that still pure air. . . . A haha belonging to somebody's grounds overlooked the path. At the first notes of our voices, children and maidservants appeared on the top of it

& stared with all their eyes. Soon an elderly squire with his boys came by; and two young 'swells' of the neighbourhood; and some farmers & their wives, and cottagers & their wives, and boys and girls to match. All these, in various attitudes of well-bred or rustic wonder, stood listening and looking; & stood the whole half hour that we sang. They might well wonder: a strangely clad hetero-geneous company of young men and young women and children, evidently be-longing for the most part, but not altogether, to the working classes, sitting and lying at ease upon the grass on a Sunday evening, singing such music, and sing-ing it so well! Whatever they may have thought, I never saw the blankness of utter astonishment more plainly than in the faces of our motley audience.

. . . The train left Slough at 8.30, and all the way to London our compart-ments rang with glees and chorales. . . .

Saturday, 8 August . . . I walked and rode down to Putney, & thence by rail to Teddington. The new line is now open all the way, and so my riverside walks are ended. . . .

. . . I went to call on Blackmore—scholar of Exeter, barrister, novelist, poet, and marketgardener. Found him in his gardens, among (for instance) five acres of strawberry beds: & he took me through his vineries, and fed me on luscious grapes; among others the more aromatic Muscat. We adjourned to the house close by, & in the drawingroom, besides his odd goodhumoured insipid little wife, was his aunt Miss Knight, a lady of perhaps fifty; so handsome and refined and courtly, and withal so grey and delicately worn, that one fancies so sweet a spinster must have a tender history. I sat awhile with them, and back by train to London by 8.45. . . .

Wednesday, 12 August . . . Went to shops and the newsroom, and home by 5.30, when Hannah came, to spend this last evening before I go. She helped my pack-ing, and did a thousand useful things; and moreover looked bonny and kindly all the time. She had been peering into shopwindows as she came, and had seen a picture of Our Saviour and some sheep. Was that 'Etchy Homo', she wanted to know? And what did them two words mean?

She guessed Homo must mean *man*: because she knew that I.H.S. meant 'Jesus *Hom*inum Salvator', 'Jesus, saviour of *men*'. No bad induction that, for a maid of all work! How came she to know all that? said her master, who showed neither his pleasure nor his regret. 'Dont know! But I can always pick up bits of things, if I chance to see a book!' . . .

Munby was out of London for the next five weeks on his summer holi-day. He went straight to Dudley in the Black Country, and soon heard the 'well loved sound of clog shoon' going past his hotel window. Here and in Wolverhampton he interviewed many colliery women. At Wednesfield Heath (14 August) he first learned 'of a late Act of Parliament' forbidding 'females' to come within seven yards of the shaft. 'I must enquire about this notable enactment,' he commented indignantly; but he soon discovered more about it when he got to Oakengates and observed that some of the women 'were not so civil and communicative as all others had been'. It appears that two overseers had been watching him, and had taken him 'for an *informer*, under that same detestable statute . . . the Lilleshall Company, whose pits these are, were grown cautious. . . . It was cruel; an enthusiast for female labour to be suspected of informing against it!'

At Shifnal, Shropshire, the scene of Hannah's childhood, Munby, *incognito*, visited the homes of her relatives. The dwelling of her father was 'a poor house with a mean little shop in front of the 18th century type'. He found Hannah's uncle and aunt at the Crown beershop in Madeley. 'Good, humble, struggling people: they little thought how much I knew about them, how strangely near they were to me.'

Munby went on to Manchester, and paid a visit to his brother Fred at Pendleton. Wigan was his next objective, where the ground was already familiar from previous years. At Lancaster's No. 1 pit (20 August), he expected to find the 'lusty laborious lasses' he had known of old, but their platform and little hut were empty; he was told the pit was 'getting worked aht'. At one of the neighbouring Ince Hall pits, he asked: '"Dus Jaan Brahn work here?" "Yah!" said some of the maidens: "Aye!" said others. . . . "Tell her Ah axed after her, will ye?" I shout to them; and they shout back a volley of "Yahs".'

A week of tramping in the Lake District followed. Its highlight was a climb of Skiddaw. At Grasmere churchyard on 24 August Munby 'found the wellworn graves of Wordsworth and his kin, and Hartley Coleridge; and sat down on the low wall by them. . . . It is good to be here: but also, it is not possible to stay long, for stress of feeling'. On 28 August he reached Hexham by train from Carlisle. He then explored the Tyne valley and the Roman Wall. The Bay Horse at Stamfordham was, he noted, 'one of the best inns I ever entered'.

At the end of the month, on his way home to York, Munby added some remarks on the main object of his Northumbrian tour, those legendary figures—the Bondagers. Munby's research was confirmed by the report of the Commission of 1867: 'Generally speaking, the old organization of labour still stood, hardly shaken by the agitation of ignorant demagogues against this "system of villeinage".[3] . . .' But during the past century the number of women working on the land has decreased steadily, even in Northumberland.

[3] W. Hasbach: *A History of the English Agricultural Labourer* (1920), Appendix VI.

Monday, 31 August . . . I came into Northumberland mainly to observe these so called female serfs: and herein my brief visit has certainly been a failure. For owing to the uncertain weather, I have seen but some twenty of them in all; and most of these were too far off to speak to or examine. Those whom I did see moreover were not to be distinguished from other women-labourers, either in dress or mode of work. They were just reaping binding or weeding, in groups, or singly among men, like any other country lasses.

However, I have had talks with a good many farmers, labouring men, and so on, about them: and this is the long and short of such talks and of my own observation.

Area of employment. Bondagers are in general use all over Northumberland, and in parts of Cumberland also. They are fewest about Newcastle: they increase and become universal as you go north and west from thence: they are most numerous in the country about *Wooler*. They are to be seen all down the vale of the Tweed, on the Scotch side as well as the English; and that is their northern limit. . . .

Sex and Age. Bondagers are always *women*: there seems to be no such thing as a male bondager. And they are all young, & unwed: a girl may be bondaged at ten years old, and there are stout strapping bondagers of thirty: but a married woman, apparently, is hardly ever a bondager. . . .

Hiring and Wages. The hind is the farmer's servant, and the bondager is the servant of the hind, which he is bound to keep for his master's use. She is hired by him at the statute fairs, yearly or halfyearly: is fed and housed by him, and paid wages at the rate of eightpence a day or £12 a year; though she has more in harvest time. But often she is his own daughter; and then he saves her wages. . . .

Kinds of Work. The bondager is strictly a servant in husbandry: she is hired to do outdoor work, and that only. If there is nothing to do in the fields, she often helps to do the dirty work of her master's house or her master's master's; just as at Halton I saw the bondager busy at the washtub: but she is not bound to such trivial tasks: she may lounge about like a lad & whistle or snooze, until she be ordered afield. Once afield, she is put to any thing, except ploughing and ditching . . .

Times of appearing. The best times of year for seeing bondagers are, the statute fairs at *Whitsuntide* and *Martinmas* in the market towns; and, to see them at work, *June* and *July*, when they are all out hoeing turnips, especially in the district about Wooler; and late *August* or early *September*, when harvest is going on.

I indeed saw very few: but that was owing to the weather. . . .

Numbers. On the small farms, about the Wall, there is often but a single hind, who has one or two bondagers. The large farms of the Wooler country employ, I am told, six or eight hinds apiece, so that one farm may have sixteen or twenty bondagers. In any case the bondagers work in gangs, either by themselves or under a male overseer. . . .

Generally. Every one has told me, that although on the large farms it is often hard to find as many girls for bondagers as you want, the system is in full vigour, & is approved. 'And the wenches like it, bless you Sir: they know they're a deal better off than in a town-place. It's healthier for 'em, & freer, and they earn more money, too'. Me judice, it has at least these advantages:— it leaves the married women to their home duties: it trains up the wenches to be hardy and lusty and familiar with outdoor ways: and it keeps up a wholesome protest against the Mollycoddlers, to see a whole countyful of stout lasses devoted to field-labour only. . . .

Munby reached York by way of Durham, where at the Cathedral, he had a glimpse of Henry Phillpotts, Bishop of Exeter,[4] the notorious High Churchman and reactionary of the Reform Bill period. Considering that Phillpotts had inspired Praed's satire *The Red Fisherman* as long ago as 1828, his survival comes as a surprise.

Tuesday, 1 September . . . Morning service was just over and the procession of choristers was leaving the choir, headed by the Bishop of Exeter and another Canon, who turned round both of them and bowed to the altar as they left. There are some, I believe, who look on this act as a sure mark of Antichrist: there are others, who regard it as a blessed indication of orthodoxy: others, again, who find it a picturesque and reverent old custom: others, who Dont care twopence about it: others again, who think it Damned Humbug, or (to vary the expression) Beastly Rot: others finally, who know so little—like your Jew Turk or Infidel—of the matter, that they would not even notice it. Such is the value, or no-value, of symbolicks. I had never seen this staunch and fiery old Bishop before. A tremulous grandsire of eightyfour, moving feebly along leaning on a crookt stick; and looking, in his lawn sleeves and black skull cap, exactly (barring the moustache) like a prelate of James I's time. His thin wide lips and wrinkled face kept working continually, as he looked straight before him. Upon the whole, an aged volcano, by no means extinct; and worthy of admiration, veneration, for his volcanic feats. . . .

Munby spent a few weeks at Clifton Holme with his family, reviving old acquaintances, and returned to London on 21 September. He did not enlarge on the notes in his concise diary for the rest of the year, which was not particularly eventful. He contributed some verse to periodicals, and on 10 December visited Bell and Daldy's in Fleet Street, probably to discuss a new collection of his poems. He paid his usual Christmas visit to his parents, and was still at home on 31 December, when he heard the 'Minster bells ringing out old year. Amen'.

[4] Henry Phillpotts (1778–1869); Bishop of Durham, 1806, and of Exeter, 1830.

The new year sees the full diary again in spate. The concise diary contains an analysis of Munby's correspondence in 1864, when he received 547 letters and sent 505. May was his busiest month for letter-writing, with 76 received and 70 sent.

In London on 4 January he bought 'the original edition of the Newcomes'. He 'grudged the cost; but it is one of my pet books'. The incident reminded him of Thackeray's recent death, at Christmas, 1863, and he felt grateful that he had 'met him once or twice in society: seen his tall figure and venerable grey head: stood close by and heard his kindly voice, his childlike humour'. He returned to the theme more than once in the ensuing weeks, noting (23 January) that F. W. Burton[5] had told him that 'most of Thackeray's intimates think that he has died at the right moment for his fame; that himself even confessed to such, of late, that he had "said all he had to say" to the world'. Thackeray's friend John Ormsby also mentioned to him (24 January) that Thackeray 'had a presentiment of his end . . . and told Martin that one day "it would be just one spasm too much"—and so it was. His face and his clenched hands, when the corpse was found, showed that his kind soul had gone out in pain. And whither?'

Thursday, 7 January, 1864.   A dense fog all the forenoon: cold and hard frost continually. To shops, and dined at the Mitre at 5: then home 6.40 to 8. Then to my Latin class, at the College: the first night of the new term. Walked home thence by 10.40.

Just as I was turning in to Mitre Court this evening, I noticed two young women, struggling across Fleet Street through the crowd of vehicles, and carrying between them a large box & several smaller ones. They passed down the Court before me, straining at their load, which they set down near the Mitre, in order to 'change hands'. Each of them stood up with a grunt of relief, and wrung her fingers, which must have been almost glued by frost to the iron handles of the big box; and they sat down upon the burden, to rest. They were both homely respectable looking wenches, drest like servants. As for the box, it was a large heavy ironbound clothes-trunk; the rest were band-boxes and the like.

I stopped: 'You have a great load there!' 'Yes Sir,' says one, simply. 'And how far are you going to carry it?' 'To Lower Marsh, Lambeth, Sir.' 'Why, that's beyond the Surrey Theatre—a mile and more over Blackfriars Bridge!' 'Yes Sir.' 'And where have you carried it from?' 'From Holborn Sir; near Weston's.'

And then it appeared that they were sisters; and the younger, a fancyboxmaker living at home, had come to help the elder, who was a maid of all work in Holborn and is leaving her place, to bear her luggage to 'mother's'. And why

[5] (Sir) Frederic William Burton (1816–1900), painter, and Director of the National Gallery.

not take an omnibus? 'The conductor couldn't lift my box to the roof, Sir': no more he could, indeed, for I tried the weight of one end myself. A cab, then? Ah, a servant out of place and a boxmaker out of work can't afford cabs. I produced the money to pay for one; and the fair coolies, with infinite expressions of gratitude, took up their load again & followed me back into the street. A passing cab was hailed, & a bargain struck; but when the cabman gallantly tried to carry up the box alone, he could not raise its weight. The stout servantgirl had to help him and do half the task; and between them they hoisted it to its place, and half filled the seats inside with the smaller things.

Then the two lasses came back to thank me again, and each frankly held out her hand as she said 'Good night Sir'. I took off my glove (*they* had no gloves!) to grasp the broad palm. Both, and especially the maid of all work, had large thick hands, infinitely suggestive to the touch and sight. And so they got in; and the cab drove off with them, smiling and bowing at the window. It is something to find a case where one may do a stroke of good in the street without fear of imposture. . . .

Saturday, 9 January . . . Last night a first child, a son, was born to the Prince of Wales. At noon the Princess was with him on the ice at Virginia Water: at 9 p.m. she freely produced her baby. This is something like a young woman!

About seven tonight I heard a most charming ring of bells across the Thames; churchbells on the Surrey side, ringing a peal in honour of the child-prince. They rang for near an hour; the sound rising and falling in faint sweet modulations over the water. Soon I shall neither hear nor see the things beyond the river. A month ago they began to dig, and are still digging, foundations for a building opposite my windows.

Now that the times of /48 seem returning in Hungary and Italy, and the Germans and Danes on the Eider bring back thoughts of the perriwig-wars of old, one thinks somewhat of the destiny of that baby-Guelph at Frogmore. About the year 1900 or so, when my skeleton is fast decomposing and the butterman who bought up my verses is himself a corpse, that same Prince will (let us say) be ruling, or at least presiding at levées.

The memory of his grandmother will still be green and fair: but he too will see squabbling Germans, agonised French, oppressed Poles and Venetians, plotting Hungarians; and will witness the swellings of a yet more bloated Yankee; and will see his land corrupted, from the reaction of that Yankee's ways and from every other influence that is growing now, by that curse that looks like blessing: an everdecaying individuality.[6]. . .

Monday, 11 January . . . The new Railway from Charing Cross to London Bridge was opened today. Beginning of a new chapter in London history. So I

[6] In fact, in 1900 Munby was still alive, and so was Queen Victoria (who died in January, 1901); but the 'baby-Guelph' (the Duke of Clarence) died in 1892.

went by it, at 4.40. Temporary stairs, a temporary platform: the great building in the Strand being yet unroofed, yet unmasked by stucco.

Our train went out of what lately was Hungerford market, over what was Hungerford Bridge: instead of the graceful curves of that, we have now a horizontal line of huge gratings, between the bars of which the folks on the footway stood to gaze at us. All the rest of the way, our Asmodeus-machine looks over the roofs of poor men's houses which it has made horrible to live in, and passes across the sites of infinite dwellings destroyed: two other unfinished destroyers are seen on the way: then we stare impudently *down* upon the glorious old church of S. Saviour, lying in the pit which we have made for it: and finally crawl into the miserable makeshift station at London Bridge. No words are strong enough to condemn the scandalous & irretrievable ugliness which has spoilt the old Station & the entrance to the Borough. Leasehold houses are ugly, but they are built to fall down at the end of the lease, so their baseness will at least have a speedy end: but these railways are meant to last; and who are we, that we should decimate the population and defile our children's minds with the sight of these monstrous and horrible forms, for the sake of gaining half an hour on the way to our work or our dinner? Few things of the kind are more distressing than the absolute divorce of strength and skill from beauty, which such buildings speak of. I walked back through the crowds, passing on my way another tremendous excavation on each side of Ludgate Hill. . . .

Friday, 22 January . . . Last night and tonight I have observed for the first time the noise of the new Charing Cross Railway. Even as I write the dull wearing hum of trains upon the Surrey side is going on: it goes on far into the night, with every now & then the bitter shriek of some accursed engine.

I almost welcome the loss, which I had been groaning over, of my view of the Thames; hoping that the new building when it rises may keep out these sounds. No one who has not tasted the pure & exquisite silence of the Temple at night can conceive the horror of the thought that it is gone for ever. Here at least was a respite from the roar of the streets by day: but now, silence and peace are fast going out of the world. It is not merely the torture of this new noise in a quiet place: but one knows that these are only the beginnings of such sorrows.

Our children will not know what it is to be free from sound of railways.

Saturday, 23 January . . . Went to shops and the newsroom, and home before six; where, as arranged, I found Spencer-Perceval and Williams just finishing their first aromatic brew of 'Bishop'[7] for this evening. We went up to Dick's together at six, and there the annual Gurgoyle dinner came off pleasantly; after which all adjourned to my rooms, to sit round in an easy circle, and consume the hot purple Bishop and the Bird's Eye, and read successive plays and stories

---

[7] 'A warm drink of wine, with sugar and either oranges or lemons.' Obsolete by 1890. Partridge's *Dictionary of Slang*.

prepared for the occasion. Married men with three children—fellows and bursars & L.L.D.s—rising barristers, professors, editors of papers—how old and grave one used to think such folks must be! Yet here we all are, as apt for mirth and nonsense as if we were undergraduates still. Yes: *once a year*. . . .

Sunday, 31 January . . . I walked back to Lincoln's Inn through the Russell Square country; and in the still, twilight streets a row of lighted windows in the basement story of each house attracts one's attention.

The maids had not yet drawn down their blinds; and in house after house and street after street the scene, as I looked down in passing, was just the same. A warm cosy kitchen, with stone floor partly carpeted, and clean deal table & dresser and tins and china gleaming on the wall, and often a joint roasting at the fire; and for human, a female servant or two, in white cap and apron and cotton frock, moving about at some task of cooking, or lazily seated basking on a wooden chair at the hearth.

That was the picture, hundreds of times repeated; so many young women, living thus in homely comfort, homely work, and *alone*. . . .

Tuesday, 2 February . . . home from 7.30 to 9. Then to Onslow Square, to a large mixed party of young & grown up folks at the Theodore Martins'. As I entered the tea room, there were Millais's three eldest children, just going away. I had never seen them before, but, as I said to Martin, there was no mistaking their likeness to the pictures of last year, the 'Wolf's Den' and the 'First Sermon'. Effie, indeed, had on the very hat and red cloak that she wore on that occasion. She is a pretty child, with retroussés features, & bright and selfpossessed, and she frankly accepted my kiss. 'And did you sit for that picture of Papa's?' 'Yes, and I sat very still, too!' 'Not so still as I did, Effie, when I was the wolf', cried one of her brothers. Millais himself was upstairs, lounging en grand Seigneur about the rooms as usual, and talking occasionally with his lady-admirers. . . .

Froude was there also; whom I have known by letter for sometime but never met before.[8] John Ormsby introduced me to him, and I had a pleasant bit of talk, for his manner I believe is always kindly. He is a tall loosely made man, with dark hair and darkshaven chin; his features large & roughly shaped: altogether, a plain man in the sight of John Thomas. But there is that in the brightness of his large eyes and the subtle movement of his wide and by no means firm-set mouth, which shows that he is a man of mark.

Talking to you, he leans his head forward & sideways, and looks softly through you, and smiles with a wavering sardonic smile, and speaks with a gentle languour that yet does not want animation. His whole manner gives one the idea of sadness & quiet self-repression.

He asked me among other things what I thought of 'My Beautiful Lady'.[9] I answered that knowing Woolner somewhat, I had thought the measure of his

---

[8] But see 15 March, 1859.   [9] The poem by Thomas Woolner published in 1863.

power would have been greater than that book implies: to which Froude said truly, that his highest power only comes out in marble. I asked if the story were imaginary, & he replied Yes, wholly: & then he spoke of a sketch of David by Woolner, which was purposely made *mean*, to express Woolner's view of the Psalmist's character: '"sinning on like that, and yet writing his puling psalms", he says', added Froude, his lips writhing with that strange smile. *I* knew what the smile meant, and I just mentioned the closing act of David's life: but it was a dangerous subject, and a Cinque Cento salver on the sideboard produced a happy diversion.

Later in the evening, Fechter the actor came in, fresh from his performance of Bel Demonio. A gentlemanly goodlooking man he is in plain clothes, apparently about 35, but, Mrs. Martin says, 40 at least. His three children were already there, and his wife, a dark handsomely drest Frenchwoman of mature age.

Taking Mrs. Martin down to supper, I had speech with her about the Shakespeare celebration. 'The Mayor of Stratford has been with me today about it,' said she, 'and I have promised to act—in Cymbeline—upon condition that I approve the rest of the cast'. She looked well, and as young and graceful as ever: and when the party closed with Sir Roger de Coverley, I had for the first time the pleasure of dancing with her—with Helen Faucit.

I walked thence with Ormsby and Edmund Smith, talking of Thackeray and much else: and so home by two o'clock a.m.

The next entry records the inauguration of the Working Women's College, an institution in which it is no surprise to find Munby involved. It was established in Queen Square, Bloomsbury, as a counterpart of the Working Men's College; but in the long run did not prove equally successful and, having changed its name to the College for Men and Women, was wound up in 1901.

Friday, 5 February . . . After dinner I rode up to Marlborough Hill S. John's Wood, to the friendly meeting which Mrs. Frank Malleson had convened at her house, to talk over her project of a Working Women's College, on the plan of our Working Men's.

Teachers, shopgirls, and even servant maids they (I can hardly say *we*) hope to collect as members & pupils. . . . The party consisted of Messrs. F. and W. Malleson, Professor Seeley,[1] Litchfield, Tansley, and myself; of Mrs. F. and the two Miss Mallesons, Mrs. Tansley, and six young ladies who had offered to teach. Mrs. Frank, who is gentle & womanly as well as energetic and earnest, was much distressed by a letter from Ruskin, who in his wild way vetoes the whole thing.

---

[1] (Sir) John Robert Seeley (1834–95), Professor of Modern History at Cambridge from 1869; author of the controversial *Ecce Homo* (1865).

After tea we formed a half circle in the drawing room and the talk began. Imprimis, as usual, comes the religious difficulty. Shall we have any parsons or any ministers, any religious teaching? Wide and wholly irrational suspicion if we dont: infinite confusion if we do. Then, shall we have a Principal, and who shall he—or she—be? John Stuart Mill is too extreme, Mrs. Somerville is old and absent: Harriet Martineau (who wrote approvingly) would never do! Stanley too, in his degree, is a bugbear; Maurice is preoccupied. All which and much more had to be discussed. It reminded me somewhat of the meeting in Red Lion Square ten years ago when our College began. At last they simply settled provisionally a council of teachers, of whom I am to be one.[2] ...

Munby had been persuaded by his friend G. J. Cayley to contribute to a new periodical, the *Realm*, and during the past fortnight had worried himself into a state of nerves over this commitment; (Litchfield, incidentally, had become music critic of the shortlived *Reader*, a job which was equally too much for him, on top of his work at the office and the Working Men's College).

Tuesday, 9 February ... First thing this morning, comes another proof, to be corrected & sent on at once.

Here have I, malgré moi, written two leading articles, a piece of theatrical criticism, and a book review, all in one week! This state of things is inexplicable, & cannot last. I do not seek the work; it is offered me, and I take & do it, for money's sake: but the interest of this work is small; is as nothing, compared with that of writing one poor verse, or one bit of narrative, about female labour, for instance.

Apropos; I have just got a ton of Kirkless Hall coals, for the sake of my Wigan friends. Every skuttleful I now use, was brought from the pit's mouth, and placed in the railway trucks, by women; & women, too, whom I have seen & known, heartily working away in their suitable jackets and trousers. Mysterious bond of sympathy! This big lump of coal, which I daintily put on with the tongs, has lain, perhaps, in the broad black hand of Jane Brown or of Bumping Nelly! Every lump has thus its individuality, its history; and I cannot mend the fire without being reminded of days spent with those brave rough lasses of the north, on their pit broos and by their rude cabin fires. ...

Wednesday, 17 February ... In King William Street about 5 o'clock, I met Queen Kitty with her pails. ...

... after dinner on my way home I went round towards Buckingham Street ... for Kitty is my sole interpreter of milkwomen, and I have yet much to learn of her, if haply it may be honestly learned.

[2] The others included Octavia Hill, George Tansley, R. B. Litchfield, and Alfred Grugeon, who taught botany.

At the corner of the Strand close by, by happy chance I found her; standing alone at the turning, waiting, as she said, for her fellow servant, whom she had just left at the dairy. So they employ *two* milkcarriers there.

Meanwhile she talked with me, simply and quietly, and told me a few things about herself. She liked her new place, where she has been about two months, very well; but not so well as the West End work.

"Yes, sir, I are very black; it's a Saturday, sir, you see. . . ."
From Munby's poem about this Wigan friend, 'Boompin'
Nelly' of John Lancaster's pits, in his *Vulgar Verses*, 1891

Was she living near here? 'No Sir—I'm still living where I always was; in Duke Street Manchester Square': that is, in some court out of Duke Street, in lodgings—half of one room. And she walks from Manchester Square to Charing Cross every day and back, besides her rounds with the milk.

And what time have you to be down here at the dairy of a morning? 'At half-past five, Sir,' said my maiden, simply. Halfpast five! impossible! 'No Sir'—she answered 'its true, upon me wud'; with the same grave open-eyed look that she always had. And you work till now—after seven o'clock? Yes. Nearly fourteen hours a day; and another hour at least spent in merely trudging to the scene of labour and from it.

Well then, surely they give you your meals, besides your nine shillings a week wages, Kitty? 'Oh yes Sir, they do *that*'. And holidays: I have it down that from [18]52, when she came to London, till [18]58 inclusive, she never had a single holiday, Sunday or workaday. Had she had one since then? Yes, and it was two months' long: but how spent, I had not time to ask. At any rate in all the ten, nay, *twelve* years she had never been home once. . . .

Speaking from memory, I had said ungallantly enough that she 'must be thirty now'; and she had protested that she was only twentyeight. But either way, her face, as I saw it thus closely, is sadly significant. Her delicacy of feature and complexion is gone; utterly marred by twelve years of rough work & weather. Weather! Why, *now*, she had on the same wet shawl and bonnet that I had seen her in two hours before. And yet she is still queenly. If Kitty had been a lady, she would now be a stately young matron, with beauty scarcely yet mature, and whole drawing-rooms at her feet. . . .

In the next entry Munby revives the memory of Jean Ingelow (1820–97), a Victorian poetess now almost forgotten except in Kensington, but in her hey-day thought worthy of Calverley's parody:

> O if billows and pillows and hours and flowers,
> And all the brave rhymes of an elder day,
> Could be furled together, this genial weather,
> And carted, or carried on 'wafts' away,
> Nor ever again trotted out—ah me!
> How much fewer volumes of verse there'd be!

Tennyson and Rossetti (and Munby) were, however, more appreciative. In 1864 Miss Ingelow's fame was recent. It dated from the appearance of her *Poems* in two volumes in June, 1863 (an earlier anonymous collection, *A Rhyming Chronicle*, having fallen flat). The new *Poems* sold so well, both in England and America, that they went through 26 editions in a few years. When Munby met her, Miss Ingelow's reputation was at the crest of its wave.

Thursday, 18 February . . . to my Latin class, which I dismissed at 9.30, in order to go to a party at the Pattisons' in Guildford Street, where I was to meet, among others, Miss Jean Ingelow the poetess. Her poems, many of them, seem to me second to no woman's poetry except Mrs. Browning's, and sometimes scarce second to hers: and besides curiosity & admiration, I had certain reasonings with myself before I went. Here was one, a woman, who has gained at once the recognition as a mover of the hearts of others which I, a man, hoped for ten or twelve years ago and have never got at all. But then, she deserved it far better; and she *is* a woman; and we unsuccessful ones are broken in by long endurance. Therefore, said I, let there be no envy nor bitterness: let us gulp down the *amari aliquid* in silence, as usual.

But when I was introduced to her, I found that I had done her injustice in thinking one could need such brave resolutions. She sat in a low chair near the fire: a woman of six & thirty[3] (so Pattison told me), who looked her age, and yet looked as if she were passing out of youth without losing any of the noblest parts of its beauty. Of middle height & ordinary figure; of face somewhat full and rounded, somewhat florid in complexion; with features not coarse, nor yet regular or refined; with quiet soft brown hair. . . .

I sat down by her, charmed at once with her unostentatious simplicity of looks and manner; and then it was that her soft low voice and sensitive mouth and large expressive eyes revealed to me things in her which her features would not have gained credit for. I spoke—delicately, of course—of her book and its success: 'It was all a very great surprise to *me*', she said; and I felt that she spoke truly. And then we talked of art-criticism, and Woolner and Palgrave; and of Patmore and Allingham; and of Longfellow, whom she thinks, as I do, under-rated by clever folks; and thereafter of the Americans, and their anomalies in taste & character. . . .

Throughout, she talked in the same simple unaffected and yet clear & intelligent fashion. 'I am no critic', she kept saying: 'I cannot give reasons for liking what I like': and she even spoke at times with a diffidence and, almost, nervousness, that was quite touching because it was so wholly undeserved by *me*. There was no doubting that she is a pure and tender woman, disciplined and strengthened by household sorrows; abiding quietly among her own thoughts, and as yet half timid at being drawn out thence by prosperity. . . .

F. W. Farrar of Harrow[4] was there too; and his wife, to whom I was presented: graceful & ladylike & rather pretty. Farrar came across the room very frankly and pleasantly to talk with me. I had not seen him for some seven years: then, he was the brilliant young parson, great with youthful looks & intellect, and interesting by reason of his unhappy passion & his lover's complainings. Now, he is growing stout & has lost his beauty; and he has married *another*.

Oh my Thackeray, how such things remind one of you! Have I not read the ardent & despairing poems which this my friend wrote concerning Miss A.? And here he is with Miss B. for his wife, and looking as if he had gained pounds of solid substance to his slight limbs by the change! . . .

The following passage is one of the most revealing in Munby's diary. Outwardly Munby's health was good, with neuralgia and toothache his

[3] She was actually 44.

[4] Frederic William Farrar (1831–1903), scholar and fellow of Trinity College, Cambridge, was then a master at Harrow, and had published *Eric, or Little by Little* in 1858. He was a successful preacher, and latterly Dean of Canterbury.

worst troubles; but this entry suggests something of the subconscious
strain he suffered from his double life:

Sunday, 21 February: misdated 22 February in MS . . . Last night I had a
dream; and it was this. I was at the foot of a great mountain-slope: great sheets
of steep smooth snow went up as high as one could see, and towards the foot of
them were vast moraines, not of stones but of black half-frozen mud. I and my
guide sought in vain among these for some place to ascend: the mud gave way
under us, and there were deep yawning pits in it. I turned away at last, and—
went straight to a grand dinner party in the neighbourhood. After this I found
myself, in full evening dress, at another house near: seated in the drawing room,
alone with a hardworking rustic maiden, who nestled on a low stool by me. She
was a servant there, and I was her sweetheart: and seeing we were so different in
station, she had received me in the parlour and not in her kitchen.

She wore, I remember, a large white cap, a lilac cotton frock, a bluecheck
apron: her arms were bare & brown, her gentle face was roughened by toil and
weather. As we talked thus (for the family were out) a noise was heard. 'It is the
Master!' she cried, and would have hidden me and crept, herself, under the
table. But I prevented her; and at that moment the door opened, and in walked
a man of tradesmanlike aspect, in Quaker dress; her master.

He stared. '*You* here, Hannah!' he cried 'in the parlour! and with a gentleman
—a stranger!' She trembled and was silent: I stood up, & felt ashamed at first,
but not for long. 'Do not blame her' I said 'nor me: I must apologize for being
in your house; but I mean no harm; *I am honestly your servant's sweetheart*'. 'It
is impossible!' he answered: 'come with me and explain; and Hannah, you go to
your kitchen'. 'No' I interposed: 'where I go, she goes; but I will go with you &
tell you all'.

So we went into the dining-room: he sat down on a sofa, I on a chair opposite;
and the servant on the floor beside me, leaning her cheek on my knee. Then I
told him of my long love for her, & hers for me; of the cruel discipline by which
I had educated her, of the degradation which had purified her spirit; & how all
that she had done & suffered for me had (as I knew it would) increased my love
tenfold.

And as I was speaking she had softly withdrawn from my side, and crossed
the room and gone behind her master's seat: and suddenly I saw her reappear
from *under* the sofa, crouched upon her hands and knees. Her face was pressed
against the floor, between her outstretched arms; she moved forwards towards
me, crawling on allfours, prone along the ground, as if she would abase herself
to the utmost. I knew what was in her heart: I trembled with indignation at
myself for letting her lie so low, with love and intense delight at the loveliness of
her humility. So she crept up to my feet, and flung her lips upon them, and
would have *licked my boot*.

Oh divine condescension to me unworthy! Her humiliation is glorious—my lordliness is tyrannical and base. I know it, and rejoice in her triumph over me. So I lift her up and embraced her; and said to him—who had sat amazed the while—'*Now*, do you think she loves me? do you think I owe her any love?'

Her master stood up: 'Take her' he said 'I understand it all now'. And just then a bell rang. 'It is the bell for prayers', said he: and he went out into the hall, and I with him. But she went too: my arm was round her, and her face was hid against my shoulder; for the hall was full of people, ladies and servants, who stared and gibed & tittered to see us so: was not I a gentleman resplendent in evening dress, & was not she a kitchenmaid in homely working clothes? Yet I remember how proud I felt in confessing her thus before them all; in humbling myself a little, in return for her unselfish love.

We reached the parlour, and all that company were ranged for prayers. The ladies sate loftily aloof;—and her fellow servants scowled upon her, as she sat lowly by me and clasped very close; and one of them said aloud 'Sir, you cannot love her—you never mean to *marry* her!' 'I do!' I cried defiantly, & sealed it with a kiss upon her forehead. But at that very moment she fell back on my arm: something unseen had smitten her head behind: her brown hair was dark & wet with blood: she had fainted.

All was confusion; I bore her up, and implored help; and her master ran for a surgeon. Meanwhile I lifted her in my arms, to carry her to her bed. What a journey it was, what suspense and horror, bearing her thus alone up flight on flight of dark & winding stairs, kissing her cold cheek, waiting and praying that the help might come.

At last it seemed that she had been taken from me unawares, and laid in the garret where she slept: and I was called in to see her. She was stretched on a chair, hidden by some coarse servant's bedding: her master and the doctor sat by. I rushed in—'Tell me—' I began: but they looked up and said quietly 'Dont you know? *She is dead*'. I tore off the bedding and looked at her, lying stark and still: I sat down and flung my head between my knees, & wept with the passion of one whose life and all has passed away for ever. Then at last I woke: woke and found that I was crying like a child, and all my pillow wet with tears. It was still dusk—I shuddered to think, in the dim twilight of my confused consciousness, that it might still be true: I went on weeping hysterically, uncontrollably, till I had sobbed myself to sleep again.

That is my dream; thing for thing, as I have set it down: and if it *had* been true, I might indeed have wept & sobbed.

'Life, what is it but a dream?' In Munby's nightmare, dream and reality were closely blended. On the preceding 28 June, Hannah had 'insisted on my going upstairs, to see the dining room that she had dusted, and the pretty things in the drawing room'. Observing her in those surroundings had distressed Munby; but the awkward dénouement occurred only in his dream; '*You* here, Hannah! . . . in the parlour! and with a gentleman—a stranger!' Behind the dream's agony lay the ever-present risk of exposure and embarrassment in daily life. In this respect Munby was lucky; yet the dream anticipates later occasions on which Hannah was sacked: one such crisis, involving Munby, did not arise for several years; but another, which did not involve him, occurred only a few days after the dream. The story of the latter can be told in Hannah's own words from one of her diaries, headed 'Hannah's Account of 1864'.

When this year began i was general servant to Mr. Foster the beer merchant, at 22 Carlton Villas. i was kitchen-servant like, & did all the dirty work down stairs, besides the dining room & hall & steps & back stairs. There was 12 steps to the front door, & it took me ½ an hour to clean 'em crawling backwards, & often ladies & that come in while i was a doing 'em & their feet close to where my hands was on the steps. i liked that, & made foot-marks wi my wet hands on the steps like they did wi their wet feet. it made me think o the contrast. i clean'd all the boots & knives & some o the windows & the grates belonging to the dining room, kitchen & the room down stairs what the children play'd in & the nurse sat in to work & that—i had 3 or 4 pair o boots of a day & about 2 dozen knives & six forks—& i clean'd the watercloset & privy & the passage & all the rough places down stairs & my wages was 15 lbs a year. All that is my sort o work what i *love*, but i had to wait at breakfast, what i couldn't do well, cause there was no set time & i couldn't keep myself clean enough to go up any-time i the morning —to go before my betters & be star'd at, & the Missis told me once or twice of it. But i *couldnt* be clean, & besides i'd liefer be dirty, & no grand folks to stare at me. at last i got warning. the Missis said to me when i was clearing away the things 'Hannah, your Master & me think you'd better leave & get a place where you've no waiting to do'—i look'd surprised, & she says 'you're a good hard-working servant she says, & we like you, but that strap on your wrist your Master cant bear to see it nor yet your arms all naked & black'd some-times & you so dirty'. i felt a bit hurt to be told i was too dirty, when my dirt was all got wi making things clean for *them*, & as for the leather strap i couldn't leave *that* off, when it's the sign that i'm a drudge & belong to Massa. But after all, i was glad i was to be sent away for been dirty, for then Massa may know i *am* dirty. and i thought of what May the housemaid said to me, as i wasn't fit to be a gentleman's servant. Still, i *am* a gentleman's servant, & one that wont turn me away, however low i may be. i left in February & Misser's Foster give me a very good character—i was there 3 years come March—& i went to Massa, but i was very down about it all, so sudden, & got to go & earn my living again among strangers as a servant. And I lay on the hearth rug & cried a bit—but Master sat down by me & kissed & comforted me, & said how gladly he would keep me there always if he could, & told me how my home is with him wherever i go—& so i got better. . . .

It was on Sunday, 6 March, that Munby listened to this story and heard Hannah say 'It's impossible to please everybody!' He lamented that he could not afford to seize the opportunity 'of taking her away from her slaving'; but the day before he had used his Saturday afternoon to inspect the Female Servants' Home in Clement's Lane which offered a refuge for 'ten servants-out-of-place'; 'she listened and thought it "beautiful" to go there' he recorded, but her own diary says 'i stopp'd at Mrs. Smith's' (in Clerkenwell).

Saturday, 26 March . . . went by Regent's Park to Ormonde Terrace and called on the Golds. Drove back to Mme. Tussaud's, to show them the waxwork.

I had not seen this for many years; and what struck me chiefly now was, the absolute worthlessness of these figures for any high purpose of imaginative realization. Your waxwork dummy of Edward the First or Oliver Cromwell, to wit; excellent as waxwork—with fleshlike cheeks & glass eyes, with real hair, real coat & breeches: what notion does reality of this Teufelsdröckh sort give you of the *life* of such a man?

You stand before him unawed; you would not mind pulling his garment or twitching his beard, though he stands there rotund and vraisemblant: but the eyeless marble and the flat canvas express the power of the man's face and form —and they *do* awe you and help you to understand him. . . .

. . . at 9.30 I . . . went to Langham Chambers—the last of Lowes Dickinson's evenings. . . . John Cordy Jeaffreson, who was there, introduced me to Mr. Winwood Reade[5] the African traveller, whose clever book I have just read. A slight young man of five or six & twenty. I had a long talk with him about Africa, apropos of his statements in print. He told me that among the warlike tribes— not in Dahomey *only*—the women are warriors; among the trading tribes, the women are commercial travellers; among those that are given to politics and negotiation, they are envoys & diplomatists. And among all, they are also labourers & burden bearers. . . .

Saturday, 9 April . . . I walked across S. John's Wood and through Regent's Park, and went into that land of children's joy and grown men's wonder—the Zoological Gardens. Very few people were there, & the animals were mostly resting after food or sleeping: which was all the pleasanter for me. Elephants & camels, giraffes & hippopotami—such as these simply bring back the awe of one's childhood, one's boyish love of the marvellous East: but why are the Carnivori so horribly human—why does the lioness lie on her back & stretch her great arms & yawn; why does the lion clap his broad hand to the side of his mouth & tear down his horse-bone, just as Hodge does that of his mutton chop? And that infinite variety of smaller animals & birds—what is the meaning and

[5] William Winwood Reade (1838–75), a nephew of Charles Reade, the novelist.

use of their ten thousand little differences of structure and habit? Are they only toys, upon the making of which a divine intellect has spent its prolific fancy? . . .

This was the year in which London welcomed the Italian patriot, liberator, and guerilla leader, Giuseppe Garibaldi (1807–82), at the height of his fame after his triumphs in Sicily and Naples. Predictably, Munby left the office early and stood for hours to greet him. The crowd's enthusiasm expressed a fervent radical sincerity which made it most memorable.

Monday, 11 April.   Bright warm spring day. All the afternoon, the neighbourhood of Whitehall was in a bustle; bells ringing, music playing, every one getting ready to witness the entry of Garibaldi into London.

I went out about 3.40. Scotland Yard was full of loungers, & mounted police from the country, in felt helmets, riding in to reinforce the native peelers. . . .

By four o'clock the crowd was impassably dense as far as one could see, from Trafalgar Square to Parliament Street. It was a crowd composed mainly of the lowest classes; a very shabby and foul smelling crowd; and the women of it, young and old, were painfully ugly and dirty & tawdry: indeed in all the evening I only saw two who could be looked at without pity or disgust; and they were stout yellow haired lasses, costergirls, with bare heads and broad shoulders; in short cotton frocks, and picturesque red & yellow kerchiefs across the bosom.

Yet for three hours, from four till seven—for I stood on the steps of a tobacconist's shop all that time—this coarse mob behaved with the utmost good humour and peacefulness, though their patience must have been taxed to the utmost. They had come to see what was worth seeing; drawn, however unconsciously, by something of noble within them, & not merely as sightseers. The procession, such as it was, came in sight at 5, and went on continuously till 5.50. Then it suddenly ended, re infectâ. No one could tell—not even the very few police who were present—what was become of Garibaldi himself or why he did not appear. Still there were no cries of disappointment or impatience: the mob waited calmly, as before, for another hour. Then at last the rest of the procession struggled up: more banners of Odd Fellows and the like, more carriages and cabs, filled with working men and foreigners, who looked all unused to the luxury of riding; more trades unions on foot, from all parts of London; a young lady on horseback (who was she?) riding calmly alone; a small bodyguard of Garibaldians; and the General himself, seated on the box of a barouche, in brown wideawake and what looked like a blue blouse. The excitement had been rapidly rising, and now, when this supreme moment came, it resulted in such a scene as can hardly be witnessed twice in a lifetime. That vast multitude rose as one man from their level attitude of expectation: they leapt into the air, they waved their arms and hats aloft, they surged & struggled round the carriage, they shouted with a mighty shout of enthusiasm that took one's breath away to hear it: and above them on both sides thousands of white kerchiefs were waving from every window and housetop.

There was an ardour and a sort of deep pathetic force about this sound that distinguished it plainly from the shouts of simple welcome which I heard given last year to the Princess Alexandra.

And He, mean while, sat aloft, sometimes taking off his widewake or gently waving his hand, sometimes sitting quiet and gazing around and upwards as if he could scarcely believe that this great greeting was meant only for him. I was not near enough to see his features closely. But one would have known that heroic face among a thousand: and in his bearing and looks there was a combination utterly new and most impressive, of dignity and homeliness, of grace and tenderness with the severest majesty.

Others who saw him nearer have since told me this most emphatically: Ralston for instance, who was converted on the spot by that grand countenance, and who says it was 'by many degrees more beautiful than any face he ever saw'.

This of today has been the greatest demonstration by far that I have beheld or, probably, shall behold. No soldier was there, no official person: no King nor government nor public body got it up or managed it: it was devised & carried out spontaneously by men and women simply as such; and they often of the lowest grade. It was the work of the rough but lawabiding English people, penetrated with admiration for something divine, and expressing themselves as usual in a clumsy earnest orderly way. Contemptible as a pageant, it is invaluable for its political and moral significance, and for the good that it reveals in the makers of it, and for the good they themselves receive by reverencing a guileless person. How rare, and how beautiful, to see hundreds of thousands of common folks brought together by motives absolutely pure, to do homage to one who is transcendently worthy! . . .

Wednesday, 13 April . . . I had chanced to see an advertisement of a masked ball tonight at some pleasure gardens in Camberwell: admission *one shilling*. Who would be attracted by such a ball? It was a fine starlight night, and I resolved to make it the excuse for a walk, and go and see.

I set off at midnight: the low moon, still gleaming on the river, was setting over Somerset House as I crossed Blackfriars Bridge, and the night air was fresh and almost pure. I walked on about three miles through the quiet dull suburban streets and through Camberwell Gate. In the broad lonely road beyond the Gate I found with some surprise a respectably drest young woman vainly trying to relight her cigar, which she had already smoked halfthrough. I offered my aid, and she in return told me, as I intended her to do, somewhat of herself: to wit, that she was an ironer by trade. She lived 'down 'Erne 'ill way'; but must now get a bed somewheres about, for it was too late to go to her lodgings. She had been to the ball, alone; in costume, as a 'debadoor'; she had hired the dress on the spot (for 'three 'alf crowns') and left it there. 'It aint often as I can afford to come out on the spree, Sir', says she 'it comes so expensive; and I've got myself to keep and all, you know'.

Well, but ironing pays better than sewing? 'Why yes—I earn 14/ a week; but then it's harder work'. A few more such words, and she said 'Goodnight Sir', and quietly went her way, with the cigar well alight between her lips. She was perfectly sober, and wellbehaved towards me: a decent and commonplace girl, taking her little recreation after her kind. I went on; found the gardens, & went in; to a large wooden shed, not unlike the Barrier ballrooms of Paris, but bigger. Only about fifty or sixty people were present; most of them in fancy dresses of a tawdry kind. They seemed to be people of the class I expected to see: young artizans, and workgirls.

Several of the girls were drest in men's clothing, as sailors and so on: one, as a volunteer in uniform, I took for a man until somebody called her Jenny. Moreover, not a few of the youths were elaborately disguised *as women* of various kinds; and some so well, that only their voices showed they were not girls—and pretty girls. This is a new thing to me, and is simply disgusting. Nevertheless it was clearly 'only a lark'; and the youths affected a quiet & feminine behaviour. Of the women, I should conjecture that very few were professional harlots, but that many were more or less immoral, though like the ironer they all had a trade to live by.

I looked on for about half an hour; during which time I saw no indecency whatever: and the childish eagerness with which every one played Kiss in the Ring between the dances, is a point in their favour. . . .

Friday, 15 April . . . On my way home, went to look at the great mound of earth, now an acre in extent, which carts are outpouring on Thames shore at the foot of Norfolk Street, for the Embankment. . . .

Then walked awhile in the Inner Temple Gardens. A wall of scaffolding in midwater already impedes our view across the river. Never more after this year will any one look down from our walks straight into the tide. Oh Public Good, what private wrongs are committed in thy name! . . .

Monday, 18 April . . . Today Garibaldi was to receive addresses at the Crystal Palace . . . The grounds, just bursting into leaf & flower, were strewn with groups of people, thickening into a great crowd by the time I got upon the lower terrace. Almost every one had a ribbon of the Italian tricolour, or a Garibaldian medal, on his or her breast: for the women were decorated as well as the men. Bands were playing, Italian flags were flying, and the crowd moved up and down quietly, in vague expectation of the hero. The great steps on both sides were full of such seated expectants; and the topmost terrace before the main entrance to the building was densely thronged. Just as I got into the midst of this throng, Garibaldi appeared in the balcony immediately above, along with the Dowager Duchess of Sutherland and others. He wore his grey and scarlet cloak and his wideawake. The moment he was seen, all hats were waved aloft & all voices cheered wildly; he doffing his hat & bowing and gently waving his brown sinewy right hand.

The great Fountains—chief 'attraction' of the place—began to play behind us in the grounds; but not one person took his eyes off Garibaldi to look at them. *He* looked at them and at the multitude below him, and chatted with those roundabout: standing thus for ten minutes, with his long hair blowing in the wind; so that I could look well upon his grave and kindly face. All that he did was watched by the spectators with an almost ludicrous eagerness. He bent forward a little, and 'Hush!' they cried, 'He's going to speak': he smoothed the wrinkles of his wideawake with his sleeve, and even that trivial action called forth a fresh cheer, because it showed that he was simple and could fend for himself.

At length, with a parting shout and a final crash of music from the bands, he bowed and retired: and then I and the rest were borne madly up the stairs to catch a glimpse of him inside the building. All that I saw however was a band of police, vainly struggling against the press of those who hustled and hurrahed across the centre transept and up to the doors on the other side where the carriage was waiting for him. He departed, and the people dispersed themselves to saunter or to feed. But from the balcony where he had stood I saw one or two incidents pleasant to look at. The Swiss who had come to greet him formed four abreast with the white cross banner at their head, and marched along the terrace singing the Ranz des Vaches: and the British Garibaldians, in loose scarlet blouses, with tricolour and band of music, swept up the steps and away through the palace; and the Italians followed in like manner. These Britons of the Garibaldian legion were mostly slight young men, the best of whom looked like undergraduates, & the worst like medical students. They were some thirty or forty strong. As for the crowd generally, it was of a somewhat higher class than that of an Easter Monday or a Foresters' day. There were very few people of fashionable aspect, & no rustics nor noisy jokers: the folk seemed to be chiefly tradesmen and artizans, with their women: but the women were much fewer than the men. . . .

Even the very scullion wenches of the palace kitchens ran out 'in their dirt' from their dens under the great orchestra to see Garibaldi go by. . . . It was to be noted, also, that the people did not when all was over go off to squat round pots of beer on the slopes, nor to play kiss in the ring. There was nothing of this kind today. They had come to see one man and welcome him; and having done so, they quietly went away. . . .

At the next weekend Munby went to Southend and tramped round the neighbouring creeks and islands, returning to London by the 8.20 train, on Monday 25 April, 'in a luxurious moveable drawingroom, where well-drest men lounged round the table and smoked, and thus sitting, found themselves (as it were casually) in Fenchurch Street before ten'. He then obtained leave from the Ecclesiastical Commission—tolerant employers, at least in this respect—to go to Alton the following day to act as best man for his old friend Alfred Kennion at his wedding. 'A staid and simple choice,' he found the bride; he would have wished 'something a little more stately & swanlike' for 'Alfred, once the handsomest man of his year'. The bell-ringers faced the best man with his most serious decision, by asking two sovereigns for their services, instead of the one sovereign for which he had budgeted. 'It depended upon my giving or withholding that single coin, whether the eight bells of Alton church should ring out the glad tidings to the country round—or shouldn't.' Munby paid; but the incident inspired the following lines:

> When I come thus to pay my heart's full fee
> To that true maid who lives and works for me,
> No gauzy dames I'll have, no gorgeous Swells,
> No loud acclaim of mercenary bells.

It was as well that he felt that way; for his was going to be a quiet wedding in any case.

Wednesday, 27 April . . . At the breakfast was an ancient Vicar, who was interesting as a specimen of the fastfailing school of 'Evangelical' clergymen, the immediate disciples of Wesley or Scott; men who clung to and preached a few strong and effective tenets, and under the honest pretext of 'knowing Christ alone' remained ignorant of most other things. This old gentleman, who looked like a dissenting tradesman of other times, made a speech about the persecutions he had gone through for his doctrines, and told meagre anecdotes about the regard shown by his Quaker 'brother' Jonathan to him, Samuel the persecuted.

It was curious to observe the emotion which his speech, rambling and pointless, even vulgar and ungrammatical, aroused even amongst those of his audience whom I knew to be most refined and most sensitive to the ludicrous.

But it was sincere, his speech was; and at such a time, tears easily gather to the eyes. The odd thing was to see Gunter's men (for the universal Gunter pervaded all) standing mute & impassive, while this very undignified and inelegant old preacher expressed his hope of speedily wearing a white robe & singing with a palm in his hand. . . .

On 1 May, Munby came back to Pyrford, Surrey, a year after his first visit; and now he saw for the first time the 'grey old gabled farm, with quaint little garden in front', which eventually was to become his home for thirty years (Plate 25). He talked to widowed Mrs. Carter, who lived in the house, Wheeler's Farm—'a gentle and almost ladylike woman'—and she showed him 'a pleasant old parlour, with a view of the Abbey and the meadows'. He made tentative inquiries about lodging there on some future occasion. ('But if one came to such a place,' he ruminated in his diary, 'how could one ever get away?') He was more than ever attracted to the old church with its wide view from the churchyard. Even a visit to Shere and the Tillingbourne Valley, which he paid on the same day, failed to shake his preference for Pyrford; Shere 'has not the freshness and quiet, & the sense of infinitude . . . that the remote heaths and meadows of the Wey can give'.

There were several famous contemporaries whom Munby would have liked to know but never met, notably Tennyson, Gladstone and Dickens; but of these he made the best from chance observation. Charles Dickens (1812–70) was 52 in this year. Munby greatly admired his work, although Thackeray was more congenial to his taste:

Tuesday, 10 May . . . Near Covent Garden this afternoon I met Charles Dickens, walking along alone and unnoticed. A man of middle height, of somewhat slight frame, of light step and jaunty air; clad in spruce frockcoat, buttoned to show his good and still youthful figure; and with brand new hat airily cocked on one side, and stick poised in his hand. A man of sanguine complexion, deeply lined & scantly bearded face, and countenance alert and observant, scornful somewhat and sour; with a look of fretfulness, vanity; which might however be due to the gait and the costume.

Thus he passed before me, and thus, in superficial casual view, I judged of him. Anyhow, how unlike the tall massive frame, the slow gentle ways, the grave sad selfabsorbed look, of Thackeray!

The building of the Thames embankment made these months of 1864 depressing for a Temple dweller. From the Middle Temple garden the embankment was 'outlined by the scaffold beams and dredging engines ranged far out in the river opposite; whilst above the steamboat pier, acres of made land already appear above high water, shapeless and slovenly. . . . And the old steps of the Temple stairs have been carried off to make way for the monster' (12 May). At the same time Munby was now seriously contemplating a new collection of his poems: 'Heavens—to think of publishing again and being mentally handled by that miscellaneous mob of strangers—the erudite men, the novelhunting women!' (13 May). Another regrettable sign of change in the Temple was the departure of the watchmen; he had thought them 'the last of the race', but walking down Bond Street late one night, he 'espied a figure before us, in a slouched hat and long drab coat with cape—the very dress of the old watchmen. Just as I was about to say so, he opened his mouth and cried "Past twelve o'clock!" ...' (17 May).

On 21 May Munby spent his first weekend with Mrs. Carter and her friendly family in Pyrford. It was a great success; and though in the ensuing weeks he explored the country between Edgware and St. Albans, and the Thames valley at Cookham, he found nothing to challenge Pyrford as his favourite spot for a country refuge.

His sustained and highly creditable efforts on behalf of the tragically disfigured girl Harriet Langdon reached their climax when she was accepted by the Royal Hospital for Incurables.

Friday, 27 May ... Went to the London Tavern by 12.30, to the election of candidates to the Royal Hospital for Incurables.

... A couple of large rooms, handsomely built and decorated in the rich eighteenth century style, and hung with full length portraits of that time: and these rooms, and the staircase that leads to them, hung with election-placards— such as mine, 'Vote for Harriet Langdon; a case of great disfigurement'—and crowded, with a few men and a great number of quietly drest ladies and other women, intent each on the case of her choice. An admirable safety valve for feminine excitement. The patients however are elected not upon their merits, but according to the amount of money & votes that A or B can beg or buy for them: the Hospital folks pocketing all receipts with admirable impartiality.

The poll closed at two, & the elderly gentlemen who sat at the receipt of custom retired to get at the result.

I went out to a newsroom, and dined in Cornhill: & came back to the room at 3.30. But it was near 5 before the scrutiny was over: and meanwhile those women, with their plain but kindly faces, sat in groups about the table, quietly sewing as their manner is. At last the awful procession appeared: every one stood up, produced a pencil to note down the successful numbers, and listened breathless while the Chairman read them out. Harriet Langdon was among them ... she got in as a pensioner, by 575 votes, the smallest number of any that succeeded. And so my two years' effort on her behalf ... is ended: and this poor penniless object, this hideous unpresentable young woman, is made for the rest of her life happy. Happy? Yes, for she is to have twenty pounds a year. ...

I dismissed Langdon's sister, and wrote on the spot to announce her success[6]: and then—it was a lovely evening, and I wanted a walk. Therefore I went to the London Bridge station, and by train at six to Spa Road, among the market gardens. ... I went down the Deptford Road ... and along Blue Anchor Lane, and across the alluvial flats beyond the Brighton railway. ... I discovered a new

[6] Munby added as a subsequent footnote that Harriet Langdon enjoyed her pension for eighteen years and died at Swansea, aged 50, in May, 1882.

form of female labour. In the fork of the two railways, in a road just beyond the buildings & near Blue Anchor lane, a dreary lonely way, I met a very strange looking girl, without a bonnet or a shawl, wearing a soiled ragged gown, and boots to match; having her arms bare, & her throat wrapped up in flannel; for she was very hoarse. A tall hulking wench of eighteen, rolling along like a sailor. . . .

Considering her in vain, I asked her if she worked in the market gardens. No, she did not, she answered civilly. Then, said I, what is your trade? 'Sir', she meekly replied, looking me straight in the face, 'I *scrapes trotters*'. The answer was so comic and the speaker so serious, that I hardly forbore to laugh: but perceiving that this was a 'find', I went on to ask particulars. The trotter-scraping institution was close by, and full in sight: a group of low wooden buildings, standing suspiciously alone in the field. And straightway a second girl, of the same age, came out of it and joined us . . . she was a stout buxom lass, rosy and healthy; with wavy black hair, & bright eyes, and pleasant sprightly face. . . . I learnt from her (and afterwards from the tollkeeper near) that these Works are Glue, Offal, Bone, works, & belong to a Mr. Brier or Bryant: and that forty or fifty girls and women are employed there. 'We scrapes' said this belle of the Boneworks, not only trotters, but also 'bullocks' feet, Sir, and horses' feet. We scrapes the hair off 'em, and steeps 'em in lime, & prepares the hoofs. We makes a place in the lime for ourselves to sit down in: it do burn one's clothes so (this is lime on my frock),—and we has to wear these old boots': and she held up her prodigious chaussure. And is it nice work? 'Well Sir, it's nice for them as likes it': & she, for all her comeliness, seemed to be one of them.

We earn *two shillings* a week, but you *can* earn as much as three: it's piece-work, and we begin about 8 or 9 of a morning, & leave off when the foreman lets us.

The smallness of the wage seemed almost incredible: but each girl stated it thus, out of hearing of the other. . . .

Tuesday, 31 May . . . Today I finally lost my view of the Temple Gardens and the Thames. Week by week and day by day the hideous new building has been slowly rising, shutting one in, like the man in the Venetian prison, from all that I have looked on so long. For nearly five years, if I remember right, I have had from these windows an open view of the green gardens and trees, & of the Surrey shore and the hills of Penge in the distance, & of the broad river. The little steamers have darted to and fro, brisk & noiseless; the stately hay-barges have swept upwards with the tide, and the sun on their brown sails and grey-gold freight and green hulls: & at night the line of wharfs and warehouses on the further bank have seemed like a long façade of Italian palaces, lit up by many points of red and saffron tint, with vertical beams shooting down into the dark water, & traversing the moonlight with deeper & more brilliant colours.

All this I have seen and dwelt on for so long: and now it is gone for ever, not from me only but from all the Temple. For the Embankment is coming.

Public and Private Occasions

Wednesday, 1 June . . . Walked across the Park and in Kensington Gardens, and back by Rotten Row, which of course was crowded with fashion and milliner-constructed beauty. By way of absolute complete contrast to this (and it *is* the most striking contrast I know) the gangs of Paddington dustwomen were struggling through the equipages in the open near Apsley House. I stood by the rail awhile & watched this phenomenon. Close by, at Fools' Corner, a troop of exquisites sat motionless on their welltrained steeds: very elegant persons, in faultless gloves and sumptuous attire and aristocratic moustaches. Who shall describe their haughty idlesse, their refined & lofty ease, as they spoke & simpered languidly with the yet more languid belles who lay supine under a cloud of pink and white fluff in the barouches that waited near? And meanwhile among the wheels of those barouches & under the feet of those steeds the mob of coarse and ragged and ablebodied wenches were creeping and darting, anxious only to save their limbs and their loads of cinders. No one took heed of them. Just beside me, one strong black-faced lass . . . popped up from below the railing, and disappeared. Her stout grimy arms were bare; her fustian jacket was slung over her shoulder; her creel was on her head: the sleek and gentlemanly horses disdained to notice her. . . .

Friday, 3 June . . . to a somewhat large party at Dr. Roget's in Upper Bedford Place. C. W. Goodwin was there; and being early, I fell in talk with him about the Colenso business, & ultimately into a long tête a tête on religious matters at large. He goes, I find, a good deal further than anything he has said in print: and he thinks that Colenso will at last do the like.[7]

The company crowded in, and broke off our talk . . . Miss Roget, still young, piquante, and of charming courtesy: and the old Doctor,[8] whiteheaded, wiry, wizened, learnedly affable, held in evident respect by the F.F.R.S. and other savants present. . . .

Saturday, 4 June . . . In the afternoon I went to shops, and to enquire about trains at the new Blackfriars station on the Surrey side, which is opened (I think) today. I crossed in going the new temporary wooden bridge, whose footways are some fifteen feet above the level of the carriage road. This difference of height gives one a wide & a far-extended view up and down the river.

Returning, I came over old Blackfriars Bridge, for the last time: on Monday or Tuesday it is to be closed and pulled down. Many a noble sunset have I seen from thence: and other very different sights too: for ten years ago the miry shore was crowded at low tide (it is not now) with female mudlarks; and many a time I have seen them, young women and matrons too, crawling out of the darkness

---

[7] Bishop Colenso of Natal published a book on *The Pentateuch and Book of Joshua* which was condemned as heretical by both Houses of Convocation in 1864.

[8] Dr. Peter Mark Roget, F.R.S. (1779–1869), of 'Thesaurus' fame, had served as secretary of the Royal Society, 1827–49.

between the barges, and wading, up to the knee & far deeper, in the black mud, even when it was thickly filmed over with ice. . . .

Meanwhile Hannah had gone to work in a Margate boarding-house, at Munby's suggestion, to get some sea air; and there Munby visited her, meeting her by the 'great iron pump, with massive handle', at the end of Union Crescent:

Sunday, 5 June . . . Standing by it, I presently see a figure approaching from a hundred yards off, up the middle of the street: a tall young woman, in a close white cap, and short frock of lilac cotton, and coarse sackcloth apron, and strong boots. Her hair is blown about by the wind, for it is cropped like a charity girl's: her arms are bare servile arms, touched with redness and roughness: she carries a pail in either hand. She is but a servant maid, and one of the lowest kind: yet look at her face, as the light of a recognizing love spreads over it—*it* is not peasantlike, in feature or expression. She comes to the foot of that lofty pump, and easily with her strong arms works the ponderous handle; unaided; for Sam Weller could help his Mary to shake carpets, but we must not help her.

This is she whom we have come to see: this is the noblest and sweetest-natured woman we have found in the world. . . .

Some lines from Hannah's own diary, written while she was working at Miss Knight's in Margate at this time, may be interpolated to support Munby's view that this was an exceptional servant:

. . . i often thought of Myself & them, all they ladies sitting up stairs & talking & sewing & playing games & pleasing themselves, all so smart & delicate to what i am, though they was not real ladies the missis told me—& then *me* by myself in that kitchen, drudging all day in my dirt, & ready to do any thing for 'em whenever they rung for me—it seems like been a different kind o creature to them, but it's always so with ladies & servants & of course there *is* a difference cause their bringing up is so different—servants may feel it sharply & do some-times i believe, but it's best not to be delicate, nor mind what work we do so as it's honest. i mean it's best to be really strong in body & ready for any sort o rough work that's useful; but keeping a soft & tender heart all while & capable o *feeling*. How shamed ladies'd be to have hands & arms like mine, & how weak they'd be to do my work, & how shock'd to touch the dirty things even, what i black my whole hands with every day—yet such things must be done, & the lady's'd be the first to cry out if they was to find nobody to do for 'em—so the lowest work i think is honourable in itself & the poor drudge is honourable too providing her mind isn't as coarse & low as her work is, & yet loving her dirty work too—both cause it's useful & for been content wi the station she is placed in. But how often poor servants have to bear the scorn & harsh words & proud looks from them above her which to my mind is very wicked & unkind & certainly most disheartening to a young wench. A good hard day's work of cleaning with a pleasant word & look from the Missis is to my mind the greatest pleasure of a servants life. There was two Miss Knights, & one was always in bed, & couldn't bear a bit o noise, so it was tiresome often to be stopp'd doing a job when i was doing it as quiet as ever i could, but i bore it patient knowing she was ill & that it vex'd the Missis so to have her disturb'd, & Miss Julia (the Missis) was the first real lady that ever talk'd to me, & she doing all the light part o cooking was a good deal wi me in the kitchen—she lent me a very nice book (The Footsteps o St. Paul), & said she was sure i sh^d not dirty it & I read it through wi a bit of paper under my thumb & give it her back as clean as when she give it me. She used to tell me things too about the moon & stars & fire & earth & about history that I knew not of & it surprised me, & she advised me to read the Bible now i was got older for that i may understand better than when i was younger—But she said it was difficult in some parts even to her & she'd study'd a great deal having bin a governess—And so I enjoy'd Miss Knight's company in the Kitchen & she sat one day ever so long seen me clean the paint, & she said she could watch me all day, there was something so very interesting in cleaning & that i seem'd to do it so hearty & i said i was really fond of it. But the poor thing couldn't wash a plate or a saucepan or peal a tato, nor even draw a cork of a bottle, which was unlucky for her, been so poor in pocket—& she *did* wish she could afford to give me more wages. . . .

Saturday, 11 June . . . A day or two ago, M'Lean sent me two photographs of Sim's milkwoman: so excellent and so typical, that I insert one of them here,[9] to illustrate and justify very much speaking about milkwomen. Look at this one: she is an English girl, about twentyseven years old, unmarried: look at her strong figure (though she is *not* one of the strongest), her homely easy attitude, her large solid feet, her large brown shapely hands; observe how the thick harness and heavy yoke sit home upon her shoulders; note the comfortable grace, the picturesque neatness, the utter freedom from fashion, of her rustic dress: she is one who lives in the heart of London, and yet can be like this! She is one who knows how to carry milk and scour pails, and probably knows little else: and yet, with all this, look at her face, how full of beauty it is—of sweet expression, of noble sincerity, of calm strength and modest selfreliance. . . .

Sunday, 26 June . . . At 6 p.m. I walked up . . . to Munster Square, and went to S. Mary Magdalene's church, to hear a sermon from Brother Ignatius,[1] the young Oxford deacon who has started, mero motu & without ecclesiastical sanction, what he calls The English Order of St. Benedict. His monastery is at

[9] See Plate 23.

[1] Joseph Leycester Lyne (1837–1908), otherwise Father Ignatius, after being ordained in 1860, had studied at Bruges, assumed the Benedictine habit, and formed a monastic community at Claydon, near Ipswich, which removed to Elm Hill, near Norwich, in 1863. He moved to Llanthony in 1869, but his community eventually dwindled.

Norwich; and he goes about preaching (having a gift that way) on its behalf, whenever he can get a pulpit; which is not often, even in high church places. The large church was densely crowded tonight; every alley & standing place being full, as well as the seats. I, knowing Vaux, got by his favour a place to stand in, near the vestry door; & the Monk Ignatius passed close by me: a small spare youth with attentuated earnest face of no very lofty type, wearing black cowl and robe and cord, and tonsured almost from forehead to nape of neck. Another Brother in similar guise was among the congregation; a bearded gentlemanly quiet-looking man.

To see a tonsured monk preaching in a protestant or Anglican pulpit was of course odd, and slightly amusing: but the main thing was to notice what he said, and how the people received him. His sermon was about the love of Christ, & the abjuring of pleasures here in order to escape hellfire. And I observed in it, more than ever before, the close rapprochement of the extremes of Calvinism & Catholicity. The same coarse & vigorous threats of torment; the same denunciations of trivial fooleries—balls, new bonnets, and the like—the same austere creed: but with the usual Roman differentia—symbolism and symbolic associations, love of ceremonial and therefore (in a sense) of beauty, admiration for conscious physical purity.

This man was rudely humorous like Latimer: vehement like Knox; plain-spoken & forcible like the preaching friars: he asked his elegant fashionable hearers if they had not committed fornication last week; asked the ladies why they had not been helping prostitutes out of sin, instead of decking out their own contemptible bodies, as if they were not worse, instead of better, than the prostitutes.

The onesidedness, roughness, exaggeration, of such language is obvious: still, it may be a wholesome reaction from the mincing ways of the world.

The fashionable hearers, however, were too wellbred to show any signs of emotion, whether of repentance or disgust: and the whole scene almost realized one's notion of what would happen, if some old Apostle were to set to work upon the supercilious Athenians of this period. In coming out, a sweetvoiced lady behind me remarked that 'he seemed to think the bad people were best off, after all'; and her husband replied that Ignatius's doctrine was 'only an idea'. A truly British sentiment.

Ignatius has been proscribed by Bishops and parsons; & he will probably add one more to the causes of the disintegration of the Anglican Church. He is also a fresh proof of the utter inability of this church to assimilate and use any new forms of devout energy that may offer themselves to her. This monk, judged by his sermon & his doings, has not eloquence or great ability: but he has fervour and sincere enthusiasm, which deserve respect and sympathy all the more, because they are certain to be thrown away. The sermon lasted an hour, but did not seem long to any one, that I could see. It was after 9 o'clock when I got out of church. . . .

Wednesday, 6 July . . . by underground railway to Westbournia, to a party at Mrs. Cunliffe's in Saint Stephen's Square. Here I had again, involuntarily, the opportunity of seeing that strange and on the whole sad phenomenon, a woman making love to a man.[2] Not a budding miss, with mere openeyed admiration; but a fullgrown, accomplished, elegant person, knowing the world and living sumptuously in it, with carriages and so on of her own. With what a marked preference she discards others' talk for his, and reminds him of former conversations, and takes pains to show that she has remembered and dwelt on his casual words, and asks about his writings (*his*, indeed!) and begs his opinion on this and that: and by her ardour and earnestness shows too well that she feels. He thinks the Rhine will be safe this year, after all? Then she will certainly go, & not mind those dreadful reports. She offers him a seat in her carriage to the Cricket Match tomorrow: there is excuse for declining that, & he declines: but presto! She has arranged that—if he would not mind—he should escort her and her friend Lady So and So to those garrison theatricals; because she remembered he was so fond of theatricals, you know. A lady's demonstrations of attachment must be delicate & subtle, & come by glimpses only; else what would Society say? But if in her case they mean as much as a man's more open ways would mean, it is alarming & saddening to cause such lost labour & inspire such pain. Yet on the other hand it is hard for a man to believe that he does create so much longing in a woman. Avoid her he cannot without rudeness; and who can help talking, with an intelligent listener hanging on his words? But as he stands by her, perhaps he thinks something like this: You, with your ladylike presence, your handsome dresses, your carriage and horses, & what not, might be mine for the asking: and instead of you, I choose one who has nothing in the world to give but herself, & who has given *that* with an absolute unsurpassed devotion. It costs me no effort to make the choice, & to give up *you* for an illiterate maid of all work, who is now blacking grates in a Margate lodginghouse. . . . The choice (says he) was made long since, and shall not now be revoked: but still, twenty years hence it may be well to recollect that I had this chance—and more than this—of revoking it.[3] . . .

Friday, 15 July . . . Walking through S. James's Park about 4 p.m., I found the open spaces of sward on either side the path thickly dotted over with strange dark objects. They were human beings; ragged men & ragged women; lying prone & motionless, not as those who lie down for rest & enjoyment, but as creatures worn out and listless. A park keeper came up: who are these? I asked. 'They are men out of work, said he, and unfortunate girls; servant girls, many of them, what has been out of place and took to the streets, till they've sunk so low that they cant get a living even by prostitution. It's like this every day, till

---

[2] The woman may perhaps be identified with Miss Williams (10 July, 1863).

[3] Re-reading this passage in 1886, and again in 1894, Munby re-affirmed his belief in the choice he had made.

winter comes; and then what they do *I* dont know. They come as soon as the gates opens; always the same faces: they bring broken victuals with 'em, or else goes to the soup kitchen in Vinegar (?) Yard; and except for that, they lie about here all day. The girls herd with the men, whether they know 'em or not: and at night they leave, and sleep on steps or anywhere, and comes back next morning. It's a disgrace Sir (said he), to go on in a City like this; and foreigners to see it, too! Why Sir, these unfortunates are all over the place: the ground (he added with a gesture of disgust) is *lousy* with them'. I looked and looked; it was Dante and Virgil gazing on the damned; and still they did not move. The men were more or less tattered, but their dress was working dress, & so did not seem out of place. But the girls were clothed in what had once been finery: filthy draggled muslins; thin remnants of gay shawls, all rent and gaping; crushed and greasy bonnets of fashionable shape, with sprigs of torn flowers, bits of faded velvet, hanging from them. Their hands and faces were dirty & weatherstained; and they lay, *not* (as far I saw) herding with the men, but singly or in little groups; sprawling about the grass in attitudes ungainly, and unfeminine, and bestial: one flat on her face, another curled up like a dog with her head between her knees; another with her knees bent under her, and her cheek on the ground, and her arms spread out stiff and awkward, on either side of her. Every pose expressed an absolute degradation and despair: and the silence & deadness of the prostrate crowd was appalling. I counted these miserable lazzaroni, as I went along; and on one side only of one path (leading from the lake to the Mall), there were *one hundred and five* of them. 105 forlorn and foetid outcasts—women, many of them—grovelling on the sward, in the bright sunshine of a July afternoon, with Carlton House Terrace and Westminster Abbey looking down at them, and infinite welldrest citizens passing by on the other side. The Keeper said he had no doubt there were more than 200 of these folk in the Park at that moment. . . .

Wednesday, 20 July . . . back across S. James's Park; and I counted 79 of those forlorn prostrate outcasts, in half the space I observed last week. I went up to one group, all girls, and some of them healthy and ablebodied. Two or three raised their heads from the ground as I stood over them; stared blankly, not boldly, & said nothing, asked for nothing. One girl lay in her rags at my feet, her face hidden between her outstretched arms. I spoke to her: but it was at least a minute before she heeded. When she did lift her dirty sodden face, she seemed halfmazed: answered, that she was about twenty; a shawlfringemaker; out of work; no father nor mother; no home; comes here to lie down, every day; wouldn't come if she had anywhere else to go to, of course not. She answered wearily, grudgingly, observe: and as soon as I stopped asking, she covered her face again and curled herself up as before, without a word.

Park Keeper meets me: says (ut supra) these are degraded prostitutes, and so on: adds, We have orders now to keep the women awake—prod them a bit with sticks, & that—that they may go away: have orders too to keep men & women apart—but we can't. It's not the men, so much; it's the women; they *will* run to the men. . . .

Friday, 22 July . . . Passed through S. James's Park at 4.30, & there were the outcasts again, though not quite so many of them, the day being damp & cool.

A mass of broken hoops and frowsy crape and napless velvet lay huddled on the grass where I passed. I spoke to it: no answer. Spoke again: a movement ran through the heap, as of one tormented before the time, and anxious to be let alone. Said once more 'Is anything the matter with you?' Then she lifted her face a little: for it was a young woman. A soiled, gloomy-eyed young woman: a kind of female Jack Sheppard to look at: for under her tawdry bonnet you saw that *her head was shaven.* And yet, for all her rags and desolation, she had tried to conceal in part the loss of her hair, by wearing the usual netbag behind her neck, and stuffing it with horsehair.

What is your trade? I asked. 'Have no trade Sir—only *cleaning*: am a charwoman out of work, in fact. Am going to see my sister, if she've got anythink to eat. Have had a fever: not been in prison—oh no, never was'.

She, too, asked for nothing, relapsed into deadness at the first pause. And why not die? . . .

. . . In Pall Mall I happened to meet Mr. Gladstone,[4] walking along unnoticed and alone. He looked at me in passing, and so enabled me the better to notice his brilliant flashing eyes and the stern and somewhat cynical melancholy of his mouth. At once, one said to oneself That is by far the most powerful face I have seen today.

Tuesday, 9 August . . . Dined after a warm bath; and went for ten minutes, about 7 p.m., into the 'Alhambra', to see one Margaret Douglas, an Australian, who is there walking 1000 miles in 1000 hours. A boarded stage, $\frac{1}{19}$ of a mile in circuit, has been built round the centre of the hall, high enough aloft to exhibit the performer: and upon it the woman was pacing as I entered. A stout sturdy little woman of 43; drest in a wideawake, a loose white shirt, a red kilt with a pair of knickerbocker breeches underneath, and red stockings: no petticoats. Round and round she went, like a wild animal in a vast cage; walking about four miles an hour; taking no notice of any one. A dozen visitors or so were looking on: at every round the umpire called its number: at the 19th he called 'Up!' and Margaret Douglas marched straight off the stage & disappeared—for an hour. She has been walking for a week: a monotonous, almost ludicrous performance: shows power & last, however, & that is why I went to see it . . .

The next day Munby set off by himself for a holiday in Brittany. His concise diary contains a list of things he took with him, viz: 2 pairs of

---

[4] William Ewart Gladstone (1809–98) was then Chancellor of the Exchequer.

trousers, 1 pair of leggings, 2 flannel shirts, 1 night shirt, 3 pairs of socks, 1 pair of boots, 1 pair of slippers, 16 paper collars, 2 linen collars, 2 silk and 3 linen pocket handkerchiefs, 1 lb tobacco, ¾ lb tea, 1 teamaker, quinine, Gregory powder, Court plaister, soap, sponge, tooth and nail brushes, hairbrush, leather drinking cup, hand looking-glass, and luggage labels. He stayed in Jersey, and at Avranches was in his element consoling the fille de chambre—the inevitable comparison with Sterne being resolved rather in his favour.

Saturday, 13 August . . . I went to my room at ten to pack; and straightway Marie came up to fetch my luggage. She looked worn and I had noticed how constantly she was afoot and on service. But now, she no sooner entered the room than she flung herself head foremost upon the drawers, and buried her bonny face in her large coarse hands, and sighed as if her heart would break. What is the matter, ma fille? said I, looking round in surprise: vous avez beaucoup de travail, n'est ce pas? 'Oui, oui!' she cried, without looking up; 'le travail est trop fort! moi seule, je fais toutes les chambres, Monsieur!' And this room was No. 23: and the hotel is three houses thrown into one. She went on, sobbing, 'Oh, j'suis malade; j'ai mal à la tête; j'n'puis pas faire des travaux pour tout le monde!'

I looked at her; at her strong young figure; built for toil, and suffering toil to the utmost; at her neat frock and snowy frilled servant's cap; at her smooth hair and brow, and the pathos of those two rough hardworking hands. And without more ado, I went up to her, and stooped and kissed her forehead.

She raised her eyes then; with a little surprise and a pensive weary look; and straightway without speaking she stood up, and gently laid her head on my shoulder.

Somebody had pitied her; and she shut her eyes satisfied, & rested on him quietly, though he was a stranger. And he, having her rounded girlish face, her brown & coarsened face, so close to him & so trustful, he kissed her cheek also, & pressed her once; and says so to this pure page without shame. Nothing more passed, except that I placed a franc in the broad palm of this overworked maiden, and she thanked me for it eagerly. But after this scene, there was a certain respectful tenderness in Marie's manner to me; and she grew bright and alert again, and hastened of her own accord to gather up my luggage She laded herself as before with the knapsack and the portmanteau and the rest; & marched off with them lighthearted, and carried them out into the street, and placed them in the voiture.

And I shook hands with her warmly, and parted from her in the presence of her mistress; she with her face glowing and smiling—frank honest smiles, mind you, and such as dwell pleasantly with me. There are women and women, Mrs. Grundy. . . .

After this emotional beginning, it was not a sentimental journey that followed, but a Baedeker tour that took in St. Malo and Dinan, Rennes and Carnac; and which Munby greatly enjoyed. He returned to England on 3 September, making straight for his home at York. Almost immediately, while out riding the mare, he was unlucky enough to have a serious accident, from the effects of which he was to suffer for many months.

Wednesday, 7 September ... There is a certain little hill, in view of Castle Howard woods, where the shady road leads down to the lowest point between Terrington & Ganthorpe, & meets another road going to Malton.

The mare was timid in descending; but I had her well in hand, as I thought; and I had just reached the bottom at a walking pace, when without any warning, she dropt forward like a stone, and sent me over her head. Starting up again, I found two streams of blood of very respectable force and volume gushing from my face, which was clearly swollen up like a pugilist's. My hat was off, my clothes stained with dirt: & the mare stood by uninjured, looking on in mild surprise. All which led me first of all to give way to a fit of laughter.

The suddenness & strangeness of the incident; the complete overthrow of all my plans which it had effected in a moment: and finally the ludicrous ignominy of continuing my journey in this plight; all this made up such a grimly farcical illustration of l'homme propose et Dieu dispose, that I regained my self-possession & even my spirits, at once. With the aid of a friendly labourer, I washed my face at a stream; mounted again, and with the blood still flowing rode at a gallop the remaining four miles over the hill to Hovingham. Reached the parsonage at seven, in a sanguinary & dilapidated condition. Presently comes the doctor, and sews up my gashed lip & monstrous nose; and I am put to bed, thankful that things are no worse, but also secretly enquiring why on earth such a trivial far-reaching bouleversement should have happened at all.

It was fortunate for Munby that an uncle and aunt lived near. After a few days' rest, he returned home. On 19 September, 'about noon, under remonstrance of doctor, I with patched nose and shaky brain, take leave of home, drive to York, start by Great Northern for London'. Soon it appeared that the doctor's remonstrance had been justified; 'what with headache & general lack of power & life, I half regret that I came back to town so soon' (20 September). On the following day he went 'to the Gray's Inn Road Hospital, & saw Mr. Hill, who "dressed" my face and prescribed extreme quiet' (21 September).

But 'extreme quiet' was not easily found in London, especially if you opened *Once a Week* and read 'a paper of John Plummer's ... abusing the Wigan colliergirls':

Thursday, 22 September . . . I knew the abuse must come some day; but now it has come, it annoys me beyond expression. Am I to brave public opinion in this matter and try to show the fools that a woman may wear trousers and have coarse hands if she likes? or must we let this healthy simple labour be ended also, as other good things are daily ended? It is monstrous, the fond philosophy of these shallow philogynists.

Came from Hungerford to the Temple by steamer. The embankment grown a more horrible chaos than ever.

Dined early at the Cheese, & home from 5.30 till 8. Then to my Latin class: & reading over old Cato's speech to them at the close, I felt the 'trouble of the brain' that my accident has caused, so much that I could hardly get on. . . .

Friday, 23 September . . . to the Hospital to see Mr. Hill.

It seems I have got, in slight degree, concussion of the brain: and as these London noises worry me, I am to return tomorrow to the blessed quiet of home, which I left too soon. . . .

Munby's accident had proved, in fact, more serious than he had thought —if perhaps less dangerous than Hannah stated in one of her auto-biographical papers: '. . . poor M. was riding at home & the horse slipp'd & threw him off & cut his face so badly that he was afraid it'd kill him—i didn't know the worst till after. . . .' Anyway, he had to start again at the beginning and 'mooned about the terrace or sunned himself by the lawn' (25 September). He took short walks, moving with unaccustomed slowness; but his nervous temperament and restless mind made him an awkward convalescent, especially as he still insisted on writing poetry, and on 27 September, while out walking, he 'finished my first Seatonian[5]; hurriedly, and with brain throbbing'; after which, 'it was so hot that I was obliged to put up my umbrella'. Later he 'read at intervals my friend Blackmore's clever novel, Clara Vaughan' (30 September). When he tried a longer walk, 'throbbings came on again afterwards' (5 October). The diary is for some time a record of pure domesticity.

Sunday, 9 October . . . This evening at nine we had prayers in the library as usual: my father sitting at the centre table & reading for the twentieth time one of those good sincere old sermons, full of the simple Calvinistic Protestantism of thirty years ago. I am on the sofa by my mother: at the far end of the room the servants sit in a row against the wall: last and lowest in rank, and next the door, sits Maggie the kitchenmaid. She is directly opposite me: let us observe what effect the good old sermon has on her. At first she sits bolt upright: her white

---

[5] The Seatonian Prize at Cambridge for religious poetry.

cap is relieved against the paper on the wall; her smooth black hair is neatly combed behind her large red ears; her rosy wholesome face is bright & clean; she wears a brown plain 'frock' and black apron; her ruddy hands lie folded in her lap. Her big round eyes are wide open, staring at nothing, or glancing sometimes with vague interest up at the busts on the top of the bookcases.

But it is seldom she sits on a soft chair like this: & it is so strange to be sitting down at all, & having nothing to do: and then the room is so warm and pleasant: and thus before long her eyelids begin to droop, her full under lip loosens & drops; she is just asleep, when her own heavy nodding awakes her. She starts a little, & looks stealthily round, to see if any one had noticed that crime: she puts up her hand & rubs her eyes & twitches her collar; she shakes herself up with a good jerk against the back of the chair: and so manages to keep awake—for five minutes.

Oh kitchen-Maggie! The long grave periods, the Calvinistic protestantism, of that excellent sermon, how little they are valued by your rustic mind! And so, perhaps, it is more or less with all of us. Yet do we think the reading of these sermons useless? Certainly not. The formal good they do may be small. Their value comes from the scenes they create and the associations they leave behind.

The master of the house, every year more reverend & more worthy, sitting in the same room amidst his family and servants, reading thus gravely and with un-doubting faith: such a scene so long repeated gains from habit and affection a sacredness and sublimity which has little to do with the merit of the things read, though it reflects a certain beauty upon them also.

By deepening our understanding of his Early Victorian background, such an entry reinforces the likelihood that youthful observation of the family servants had originally inspired Munby's obsession with working women. This thorough scrutiny of young Maggie argues not only keen perception and sympathy, but also much practice; perhaps we owe Munby's lifelong preoccupation to his father's habit of family prayers?

Monday, 24 October . . . For exactly a month now I have led a sort of interlunar life in this quiet green home of ours: never moving further than a mile or two on foot from the house, and cut off even from my favourite riverside walks. Sudden unexpected unwished-for retreat: plans disturbed, occupations circumscribed or cut off, by partial illness. Yet, when once put aside with a strong hand, desires, earnest or feverish, succumb, and plans that will not keep are quietly allowed to die: so that the influence of place & season is soon felt, and one enjoys to the full and profits by the little incidents of home, & the novelty of this dreamy lotos-eating time. Moreover, not to speak of original thought, the recollections of travel are a source of infinite pleasure in such donothing days. My remembrance of Brittany is, of all things, invaluable.

His parents took him to Scarborough on 25 October for four weeks, and there, at the end of October, his main diary petered out. On 28 November he again left Clifton Holme, to make a further attempt to renew his London life. He returned to work at the Ecclesiastical Commission, and attended council meetings at the Working Women's College, as well as the Working Men's. He went twice to music halls and looked up Walter Severn, Ralston and other friends. The strain still proved too much. An entry in the concise diary for 12 December tells the tale: 'To Dr. Budd, Dover Street, 12–1.30, "not to work in an evening, & to go away till Easter".' Hannah meanwhile had left Margate, and tried the Servants' Home in Clement's Lane for a time, 'but the beds was so hard'. She was offered work as a general servant at St. Leonards, '& as Massa was going away for some months he said i'd better take the place. . . .' She earned there, 'more nor i've had afore—18 lbs'.

And so 1864 ends on an uncertain note. At York the Munbys assembled as usual for Christmas, and on a cold, frosty, foggy Christmas Day Munby received a letter from Hannah and wrote to her in return. On New Year's Eve he heard a distant peal of cathedral bells ringing out a year of mixed recollections.

6

ROMANTIC COMPLICATIONS
1865–7

At the close of 1864, the long series of Munby's twenty-eight red leather-bound diary volumes came to an end. For five years he had filled five or six of these plain note-books annually with his copious careful prose. Henceforth, he confined himself to the yearly octavo book he had recently been using as a concise diary and record of correspondence. He now proposed to cover his activities as thoroughly as possible in the single volume.

Although the new system was presumably easier for Munby, it has drawbacks for an editor. The printed Letts's diary allotted space for three days on each page, with a tiny allowance for Sundays at the foot of every second page. The constriction compelled Munby to write very small on occasion, and obliged him to continue particularly long entries in any odd corners or spare pages of the book that happened to be free. Thus, reading him can at times resemble a game of snakes-and-ladders. Fortunately, Munby's handwriting was fundamentally so clear that the text, however microscopic, is rarely in doubt.

Looking back over the year 1865, Munby wrote: 'Thanks to my illness, this year has been one of unusual enjoyment, and varied with a rare succession and interchange of rural delights.' For Munby the diarist (who was at his best in London) this meant a quiet year. Clifton Holme in January produced only a set of ploughboys dancing the sword dance in the fore-court and stable-yard; and Scarborough, to which he soon removed 'by doctor's advice', meant drinking spa water, walking to Cornelian Bay, and making train journeys to reach Filey, Flamborough Head or Robin Hood's Bay. There was a continual interest for Munby in the activities of the girls who gathered winkles and mussels, or who were let down over the cliffs of this coast to collect sea-birds' eggs, and get bait for the fishermen. Interviews with 'flither-lasses' filled pages of the diary; girls of 'noble rugged nature, scorned of men, but loved by me as passionately as I love the grand country where they dwell'.

During March he spent a week among the Lancashire colliery-women, and another week at Trinity College, Cambridge, where he noted

Woolner's bust of Tennyson installed in the library. He was back in London to resume work with the patient Ecclesiastical Commission on 1 April, his office hours henceforth ending soon after 4.0 p.m. At the Temple he found that 'the embankment is now above the level of the

Munby's drawing of himself on the high road above Haydock Gate, near Wigan, 5.30 pm, 17 March, 1865, 'walking home with Mary Harrison, aged 20, a waggon filler at Pewfall pits, and a very good and gentle girl.'

gardens: a wild mass of earth & rubbish, with scaffolding & cranes beyond: our broad pleasant river terrace turned into an inland walk, with flower-beds on the *outer* side, and rude palings shutting all in' (3 April). He now concentrated on finding a publisher for his new book of poems.

Monday, 17 April, 1865 . . . At 4.30 p.m. I went by appointment to call on Macmillan in Bedford St. And whereas in 1851 I used to find him serving customers in his retail shop at Cambridge, now I found him seated upstairs as

Eminent Publisher, in first floor drawingroom office, with obsequious gentle-manly clerks who call him 'Sir'. He was very friendly & agreeable, & chatted away for 3 quarters of an hour, although busy. Talked about C. Rossetti's book & Allingham's & so on—Could not share risks, you know, but would publish for me on commission, which he wouldn't do for everyone, observe: but thought that Bell & Daldy, who of course know your name, would take the risk. Nous verrons. Parted from him with much cordiality, & not without a sense on my part of the humour of the scene. . . .

After calling on Bell and Daldy on 29 April 'about my M.S.S.', Munby had another relapse, and spent the next fortnight in bed. By 13 May he was a little better, and went out to explain his difficulties to the Ecclesias-tical Commission, 'but brain still weak & blurred by noise. Oh the horror of London street-faces, when one is sick & longing for pure rusticity, and for fellowship!' All this time he had not seen Hannah, though they had written to each other; but on Sunday, 14 May, she paid him a visit from St. Leonards and to his delight 'repeated the Greek alphabet quite right, picked up from hearsay 17 years ago!' After this, he improved.

More convalescence followed, at Hastings and in the Isle of Wight. On 23 May he walked reverently past Tennyson's house at Farringford and talked with a countryman about him on the road: '"We never see him," said he; "he does his poetry work at night on the downs".' But Munby, after he had walked on to Yarmouth, proved luckier.

Tuesday, 23 May . . . At 4.30 by steamer (3 or 4 times a day) across Solent to Lymington, Hants. Dirty weather, sea & downs hung with mist. On board with us went Tennyson & (I suppose) his wife. T. about 5 feet 8, largely made, hands big & muscular: wore odd careless dress, tall wideawake, camlet cloak, loose blue trousers, frock coat & open shirtfront—no gloves. Long wild curling hair: beard thin on cheeks, full & wild round lips & chin. Complexion sallow, finely cut acquiline nose, veined: mouth grave & subtle in expression, face deeply lined: eyes hidden by blue spectacles. Voice deep & slow: gait stooping & heavy, almost aged.[1] I watched him talking with a fat parson: round him other parsons, tourists, sailors; and his face supreme in manliness & mental power. . . .

In June Munby was able to resume his usual daily work, and on 15 June he had a 'long talk' at Bell and Daldy's 'about my book and the manner of arranging for it'. He now had the task of preparing the MS. of his poems for the printer, and engaged a copying clerk, the equivalent of the latter-day typist, whom he studied as an interesting object in her own right:

---

[1] Tennyson was 56. He was taller than Munby estimated, being over six feet.

Saturday, 15 July . . . She was a young woman of 23 or so, respectable and decently drest; a Cockney girl however, with something of the pertness and sham-gentility of the species: she took off her bonnet & cloak (or overcoat rather), flung them on a chair, pulled out a pen, stuck it behind her ear, through the braids of her hair, and sat down at once to write. Having started her, I went to another table & wrote, smoking also, which she rather liked. She kept on writing, in a hand like an office-boy's, quietly & steadily, coming to me now and then for explanation, till 6; then declared she was not at all tired, thought the time had passed very quick; & so wrote away till 8—four hours in all, and after her day's work. Said she liked copying very much; had worked for Kerr the law stationer, who keeps 29 female hands, & earned 20/ a week; more than she gets now, but Kerr's girls were low and 'larky', she did not like them. Her name is Morley, & she lives with married sister in Pentonville. After 8, she put on her things & went; but will finish her work on Monday. I gave her a ticket for the Working Women's College meeting next Thursday: would like to go: means to learn *mapping*. Her quiet unconcern at being in my chambers was amusing.

Monday, 17 July . . . Back to Temple 4.30, and at 5 the law stationer's clerk came again to finish her copying. She took off her bonnet &c as before, set to work, wrote steadily till 8, when it was done: then she cast up the 'folios', drew out the bill, 5/9, and signed it: I paid her, and she put on her things *before the glass*, said goodnight, and went away. . . .

Munby delivered his MS. to the publisher, and a few weeks later received his proofs. He does not mention seeing his copyist at the *soirée* of the Working Women's College, where there were 'about 100 young women, of the milliner & shopgirl kind: all good & respectable, but fatally uninteresting' (20 July). He now gave up teaching at the Working Men's College, though he continued to attend meetings there; and in the autumn began to teach Latin to the working women—a transition which causes no surprise.

Munby had been successful as a teacher. J. Rigby Smith, subsequently secretary of the Working Men's College, testified: 'My pleasantest recollections of the College are connected with Mr. Munby's Latin class. . . . The class was small, but it was a very happy weekly gathering. We read the "De Amicitia" of Cicero, Virgil, etc. Mr. Munby was an excellent and most patient teacher. . . .'[2]

Wednesday, 2 August . . . to the W.M. College, where a meeting was held to congratulate T. Hughes on his election for Lambeth. Maurice, Layard, Louis Blanc, & the college men: a good modest speech from Hughes, full of manliness

[2] *Working Men's College Journal*: July, 1905.

and feeling. Home 10.30: Walter Severn came & sat till near 1, talking. Said the Prince of Wales has joined the Cosmo,[3] and does his pipe & chat affably and friendly, like a man.

Munby spent each weekend during August at Pyrford with Mrs. Carter and her family, who had proved to be Canadian in origin. He 'came to love that charming valley and the simple kindly Canadians', he wrote in his retrospect of the year, 'with a strength of affection which I never felt

'A quiet moment' at the Dowlais Works, Merthyr Tydfil: Jane Matthews, aged 20, 'mending her stocking, seated on a heap of ironstone. Pencilled on spot, 26 September, 1865.'

before for anything near London'. On his last visit of 1865 he described them as 'a simple, graceful, Godfearing family of women: not ashamed to cook & clean & wait on me, yet cultivated, artlessly refined, in taste, in dress: knowing nothing of the world and its ways, yet loving its best things —music & books & flowers' (11 September). He noted especially a girl in her early twenties, 'fair Sarah, who sat in the broad old window seat, with the morning light playing on her curly clustered amber hair & on her sober pearlgrey gown'—a picture as idealised as an illustration by Marcus Stone; Munby could not have foreseen that this gentle creature would soon give him one of the biggest emotional jolts of his life.

[3] i.e. The Cosmopolitan Club.

In September and October he travelled again, making a tour with his sketch-book in South Wales, 'introducing me to the grand hills & vallies of the mineral country, and the splendid chaos of the iron works, and above all, the picturesque ways and frank modest charms of the robust and fearless girls who work at those mountain-mines'. He also spent a few more days in Scarborough before he returned to work in London on 23 October. The same day he called at Bell and Daldy's, his publishers, '& got an early copy of my book, which is to appear on the 28th'. He added gloomily: 'It will fail, of course.'

Wednesday, 25 October ... by 8, to the Working Women's College, Queen Square, to begin (with trepidation) my Latin Class of young women. Found Miss Harrison, the pretty superintendent, at her desk, with rosecoloured ribbon in her hair; and student girls lounging in the saloon-like coffee room; and Mrs. Tansley, duenna to my class. Neat & comfortable was my classroom; neat tables & papers; neat little table for me, well-arranged with neat penwipers, inkstand, name books & so on. Woman's careful eye & facile hand everywhere; whilst we of the men's college, after ten years experience, are rough & careless and untidy as schoolboys. There were seven pupils, all girls of 20 or so; respectably & plainly drest; probably shopgirls & the like. Most had left their bonnets & shawls downstairs. They sat facing me, & answered questions & took notes; behaving with quiet frankness; not giggling, nor yet too grave. Not one (they said) knew anything of Latin: so I discoursed of the why & wherefore, & they seemed interested & fairly intelligent ...

Thursday, 26 October.   Funeral of Lord Palmerston (who died Wed. 18th).[4] Saw cortège in Pall Mall & at Abbey West door. A most *poor* & mean business: nothing noble or solemn or religious in the aspect of it or of those who thronged to see it. Only a dull & brutal curiosity among the spectators: few even raised their hats when the ugly hearse, daubed with blazon, went by. I saw no one of either sex who was at all noteworthy, except one, & that was a servant maid belonging to the Guards' club. A kitchen wench, she was; the word 'Kitchen' or 'Kitchenmaid' was stamped on a corner of her coarse apron. With two commonplace fellow servants, she had come up from the cellars, & stood within the railings, holding on thereby, in her humble dress of lilac cotton frock and coarse clean apron, while some of her moustachio'd masters lounged on the steps above. A robust countrylooking lass of good height, pleasant to behold in such a spot ... thus she stood, gravely gazing, while sumptuous ladies, silked & furred, looked down from balconies all around. Note, that no clergy met the coffin at the Abbey gate: men took it on their shoulders; a tawdry pall was thrown over; they disappeared, without a prayer or a note of music, into the

[4] Henry John Temple, third Viscount Palmerston (1784–1865), had died in office as Prime Minister.

cold crowded nave. A child's funeral in a village churchyard is pathetic, impressive: this was pitiful, even as a show. . . .

Saturday, 4 November . . . Dined in Hall, & then to Her Majesty's by 8, to hear Der Freyschutz: but no sooner seated there than, opening note which to my astonishment from H[annah], just come, I up again and hurried back, to find her waiting. Her, so large and lusty, so healthful & ruddy & strong: alas, no ladyhood, save that of a gentle loving nature, now possible for her. With her right arm, all but 14 inches round the raised muscle, and thicker than her neck, she lightly lifts the big wash-hand basin full of water, and holds it out horizontal at arm's length, with ease, and smiles. Such youth and vigour is yet in this true woman. I walked part of way home with her . . .

Thursday, 9 November . . . At 4.50 p.m. today I went by train to Teddington—a place miserably changed and all melancholy now to me: a village awkwardly sprouting into a town . . . & to Blackmore's; who with his wife bade me stay all night, which I pleasantly did, & smoked & talked with B. till 1 a.m. on books & his novel 'Cradock Nowell'. . . .

Saturday, 11 November . . . To Daldy's & saw him. To Ludlow's[5] chambers in Lincoln's Inn & saw him, & home, & walked westward, sadly enough, for Daldy was not satisfied with the London Review article on me, and urges me to speak of the book among my friends: & Ludlow, though I merely went to ask him who 'does' the poetry for the Spectator, received me with chilling roughness & bearish discourtesy. No popularity could make up to me for the humiliation & loss of modesty which would result from such a course of adverting oneself as publishers prescribe. My book, whatever it be worth, represents the best part of me, the happiest & holiest hours of my life: and the coldness or apathy of socalled friends, and the business-necessities of the bookseller, would turn me into a puffing-agent—an auctioneer of my own quiet thoughts. . . .

Munby's embarrassment at being asked to solicit publicity for his book will be recognised by authors. *Verses New and Old* was unlikely to make money—and did not[6]—but was an improvement on his *Benoni*. It is a good example of mid-Victorian minor verse and shows off Munby's variety and craftsmanship. His nature poetry, when it transcended conventional imagery and sentiment, could attain an effective simplicity; his poem 'T'Moosel Getherers' was a *tour-de-force* in Yorkshire dialect; and 'Woman's Rights' championed the rough worker in vigorous polemical

---

[5] J. M. F. Ludlow, Munby's colleague at the Working Men's College, was not only a barrister and social reformer but also an author and journalist who founded and edited the *Christian Socialist*.

[6] After two months about 100 copies had been sold, and the book was eventually remaindered.

stanzas—Munby writing here freshly on a theme which he later over-worked, and briskly satirising the usual feminist argument:

> 'Hard hands! and oh, a dirty face!
> What sad indelible disgrace
>   For this soft sex of ours!
> *We* want them to be nice and clean;
> With tasteful dress and gentle mien,
>   Like nymphs among the flowers!
>
> 'If those poor souls are so degraded
> They fancy they can work, unaided
>   By our wise counsellings,
> We must, we really must, present
> And pass a Bill through Parliament
>   To stop such dreadful things!
>
> 'Why were they never, never taught
> To scorn their labour as they ought,
>   And feel that it is wrong
> Thus to use strength and gain by it?
> It doesn't signify one bit
>   That they *are* well and strong:
>
> 'We're bound to *show* them what they want;
> To say they mustn't and they shan't
>   Destroy their fair complexions
> By doing work that *men* should do:
> Great, big, ungrateful men like you,
>   Who raise these weak objections!'

The book slowly collected a fair number of reviews. A favourable notice in the *Athenaeum* persuaded the great Mudie to order copies for his library, and he told Munby he was 'always so pleased to get a volume of good poetry' (8 January, 1866). Two of the poems are given in the Appendix. Particularly gratifying was it for Munby to learn, a few months later, from his mother, that 'the fisherfolk of Filey have had my "Moosel Getherers" read to them at a Penny Reading, & were "so delighted that they begged to have it again next time"' (20 June, 1866).

Tuesday, 14 November ... to 5 Blandford Square, by invitation to Mme Bodichon's.[7] ... As I went up Regent Street about 8 p.m., two fashionably drest

---

[7] Barbara Leigh Smith Bodichon, *née* Smith (1827–91), the wife of Dr. Eugène Bodichon, was an important figure in the women's movement and the virtual founder of Girton College, Cambridge.

young women, crossing the Circus, passed me close, & one looked hard, & leaving her fellow, came up to me & said in a very sweet voice 'Dont you know me?' Pretty & brighteyed she was, with nez retroussé and roselipped mouth; in velvet cloak, in veil and handsome bonnet; tall, roundly formed, graceful. The light was dim; I could only bow & say I knew her not. But she tried all ways to recal herself to my recollection; 'Oh I'm *sure* it's you!' she said with innocent earnestness: 'Dont you remember me in Liverpool Street, near King's Cross, ever so many years ago? Oh yes, and I saw you on Waterloo Bridge—and you would not take me to your chambers—dont you remember Nelly?' Nelly? She looked up at me with all the eagerness of one who strives to bring back into her own face the old familiar expression—'I remember the name well' said I 'but surely—' 'Yes Yes!' cried this richly drest ladylike beauty 'it's me—*I was a servant, you know*!' 'What? and you were cleaning the steps one morning as I passed—?' 'Oh yes! *now* you know!' she cried, almost dancing in her pretty delight; 'but I've *grown* so!' I seized both her hands: 'Nelly, is it *you* then? Oh how often I've thought of you, & how you've weighed on my con-science, you poor child, since you told me you'd go to the bad if I wouldn't take you home that night!' For it was Nelly Turner, gamekeeper's daughter from near Blandford in Dorset, & maid of all work in London at sixteen; sweetest brightest little rosy delicate maiden that ever scrubbed a floor. And now? 'Let me walk with you up the street', said Nelly; and she did; and she had lost a glove, so I took her to a shop & bought her a pair; and her hands were so soft & white; but I said 'Nelly, they were better when I saw them first, red with dipping in your pail!' And then she told me, how she went to be servant at a lodging house, and some one there seduced her; how her brother came to town & sought her, & she went home for 2½ years & was good; how she came back, became a nursemaid, got 'gay' again, went awhile on the streets, nearly fell into the hands of the harpies of Wych Street, when she saw me once (and I her) and ran away for shame: how a gentleman, a Major in the 3rd Buffs, took her and is a 'friend' to her still; how her sister, a ladysmaid, married her master's son, 'a real gentleman, a Captain in the army', and they live at Yarmouth, & she has been with them, but the Major has sent for her to see him en passant: 'but I'm going to be married, I think', said she; 'it's a very respectable man, a collar & harness maker near London, & he knows all, but he'll marry me if I like. I wouldn't marry a gentleman I think, cause I'm not used to it. Oh, I was awfully fond of *you*', she went on: 'stupid little thing that I was—and of course you couldn't have married me, you know! And have you that diamond ring you used to wear—little diamonds all round your finger?' I pulled off my glove and showed it. What a lesson! All this minute remembrance, passionate girlish shadowlike fondness, welling up in a woman after years of mercenary folly, and springing, too, from so slight a source—from those few talks and walks that seemed so harmless & that led to nothing! She gave me her address, & begged me to go & see her: 'Ah, Nelly' said I 'could I do that *now* to you, when I would not do it *then*? But you will give me one kiss, for peace?' And she did; and she ran back, when I had said Goodbye, still smiling, & saying 'You will come?'

'What a lesson!' he writes; but he had been slow to learn that a well-meaning naïve approach to working women could carry dangers different in degree but no less real than those threatened by society ladies. Teaching them Latin in a class-room was safer than questioning them in the street.

Wednesday, 22 November . . . by 8, to the Woman's College. After the class, I went through the book in which the women enter their names, occupations &c, in Miss Harrison's office downstairs. There one reads of 'Kate Appleton, *Telegraph Clerk*': 'Emily Holdsworth, *Corrector of the Press*': 'Charlotte Frank, *Medical Student*': 'Jane Orris, *tobacconist*': 'Louisa Cooke, *bootmaker*': 'Emma Wilson, *barmaid*': 'Lucy Gearing, *waitress*': 'Ann Smith, *domestic servant*'. But most are milliners, shopgirls, or 'at home'. There are 2 medical students, 2 barmaids, 1 waitress; and 4 servantmaids, all of whom however are sent by mistresses interested in the college. Not a few married women too. 310 names entered since the College opened: 170 now at work there. Home by 10. Many of the girls come from far—as from Pimlico, Islington, &c; and many walk home alone after class.

Wednesday, 6 December . . . By 8, to my women's class. Bright and pleasant all these girls are; anxious to learn; and, as learners, very like the men of the other college. One has to remind oneself that these are girls, sitting a row in front of one, writing or repeating their latin; that this is for oneself a new relation of the sexes: and after all tis hard to realize that it *is* new; it seems so natural, so independent of sex. Yet I could not but smile inwardly tonight, seeing how pretty tremulous Laura Favenc, the belle of my class, sat with her large eyes fixed on me or on the fire, biting the plume of her pen, trying to recollect what was the dative plural of *puer*! . . .

After the traditional Christmas holiday, the express from York brought Munby back to London on 2 January, 1866, through a strong gale that reduced its speed to 15 miles an hour. Early in the new year, he was elected to the Arts Club, and also to the Pen and Pencil Club which met at Aubrey House; both were to provide material for his diary. But the year opened sadly with the news of the sudden death after measles of his old, admired friend Mary Newton.

215

Wednesday, 3 January . . . to the Conversazione of the Working Women's College. Miss Garrett[8] the female doctor was there: I was introduced to her whilst she was busy tying up the toes of a live frog, whose foot was to be inspected under the microscope. It was amusing to see how the women around watched the process; partly horror stricken at her cruelty to the poor beast, partly admiring her surgicall skill. She is a young woman of 25 or so, well drest in black silk, with soft full chestnut hair & an open pleasant face, with, one fancies, something of a professional look about it already.

Maurice was present too: I had some talk with him, of Ruskin and his present strange transitional state . . .

Thursday, 11 January . . . Snow: the first of the year & of the winter. . . . The main streets all day, and at night too, ankledeep in snow and watery mire: no attempt made to cleanse them, in this metropolis and centre of self-government. Walter Severn called on me in the afternoon, and we walked up together to Gower Street about 5 . . . Newton was away; only Arthur Severn at home: we went into the melancholy house, into the drawingroom—her studio. Mary Newton, Mary Severn, is dead! With face most sweet and bright, with violet eyes and soft brown hair; with a naiveté and winning grace of manner that one never saw the like of; with such an eager beautiful soul, such supreme skill & delicacy of hand and propriety of taste in drawing and in colour; a woman-artist the best and the most womanly that I have known: with all this, she is gone to the grave at thirty three; & Lady Jones and Mrs. Brown live long, to cackle small-talk and torment a foolish husband. How well I remember her, in the old days in Eccleston Square; talking with modest yet rapturous ardour on questions of art, on the relations of Beauty and Truth, making masterly sketches before us all, in her open artless way, of him who wooed & won her! She died lamented by all, from the Queen—who has written through Lady Augusta—to the brave Yorkshire nurse who nursed her in her brief delirious illness. We looked at her last drawings; sketches taken in the East—of Syrian women, of Scutari burial-grounds—lovely all of them, and they are going soon to the Dudley Gallery. And on the walls hung her great picture of Elaine, by far the best rendering of that subject, and her exquisite Sebaste . . .

Saturday, 20 January . . . Severn mentioned today that Ruskin has written a letter to Newton, bitterly & savagely lamenting the death of Mrs. Newton, whom he knew well: saying that 'the gods' have made him angry with them by doing this, which he for his part cannot make out nor submit to. So this is what 'evangelical' teaching has led John Ruskin to.

[8] Mrs. Elizabeth Garrett Anderson (1836–1917), as she was known after her marriage to J. G. S. Anderson in 1871. Her Marylebone dispensary for women and children was opened in 1866. She supported her sister Mrs. Millicent Garrett Fawcett in her campaign for women's suffrage.

Wednesday, 24 January ... at 8, to my Latin class, and afterwards to Aubrey House Notting Hill, to one of a series of undress evening parties given by Mrs. P. A. Taylor, wife of the member for Leicester. The house stands on the hill top near the water tower, & with drive and gardens in front and parklike grounds behind, is thoroughly rural. But then, once outside the gates, you are in a town. It was amusing to see how rooms and hall were made to express the owner's politics. Busts of Cromwell, portraits of Mazzini, memoirs of Abraham Lincoln, instead of Landseers & so on; which, after all, have no particular meaning in most houses. M. D. Conway[9] was there ... & J. R. Seeley—with whom I had a talk about dreams—and Henry Fawcett, who stood and talked politics in his fullvoiced statuesque expansive way, making you forget his blindness in the expressive compensation of his smile, and the *look*, so to speak, of his whole face. He maintained, & so did others, that J. S. Mill has a wider influence on the working classes than Bright, who is 'suspect' because he takes an employer's view of things ...

Tuesday, 30 January ... to Northumberland Terrace beyond Primrose Hill, to an evening party at Westland Marston's.[1] Chiefly a literary party ... and to my great amusement, Buckstone[2] (with his young wife) and Sothern,[3] the actors. A clever charade, written by one of the company, was acted, & well acted; and Buckstone *before* the curtain, as auditor, in high collars & decorous elderly white choker, was as comic to look at as if he were on the stage. At supper he enjoyed savoury pie and champagne in a snug corner, avec empressement. The party was a good illustration of the advantages of intelligence, even in small social matters, over mere wealth: the house is small, and at first the women, many of them, looked dull and commonplace: but the clever charade, and a free sparkling flow of talk, soon showed that the people were capable of giving and receiving higher enjoyment than those who frequent an ordinary soirée. Sothern, who is a gentlemanly man, apparently about forty, left when I did, & kindly offered me a seat in his dashing brougham & pair—result, one may suppose, of Lord Dundreary: but he was going to Kensington, so I walked home, by 1.30.

Saturday, 3 February ... to Aubrey House Notting Hill by 8.30, to a meeting of the Pen and Pencil Society,[4] which Mrs. P. A. Taylor, who founded it, has

---

[9] Moncure Daniel Conway (1832–1907), the American author and preacher; then pastor of South Place Chapel, Finsbury.

[1] John Westland Marston (1819–90), dramatic poet, and critic of the *Athenaeum*.

[2] John Baldwin Buckstone (1802–79), comedian and manager of the Haymarket Theatre, 1853–76.

[3] Edward Askew Sothern (1828–81), the actor, who played Lord Dundreary in *Our American Cousin* for nearly 500 nights.

[4] The Pen and Pencil Society (or sometimes, Club) included among its members William Allingham, Edmund Gosse, and Austin Dobson. Two poems by Munby are published in *Auld Lang Syne: Selections from the Papers of the 'Pen and Pencil Club'* (privately printed, 1877). They are 'Autumn Leaves' (May, 1866) and 'Things Gone By' (May 1869).

asked me to join. Everyone has to contribute something in prose or verse or in painting or sculpture. People sat round the drawingroom & listened to the stories, and then looked at the drawings &c afterwards. The subjects of the night were 'Suspense' and 'Witchcraft': there were two good eldritch stories, one by Miss Adelaide Manning[5] . . . & the other by a Miss Keary,[6] also a novelist. . . .

Tuesday, 6 February . . . Today the Queen opened Parliament; the seventh Parliament of her reign. Very stout, very red in the face, she looked, bowing at the carriage window—not the old state carriage—within a sort of bridal veil of white, that flowed round her head; and her younger daughters sat opposite, with ruffs on à la Marie Stuart. She was well received; but not so warmly as the Princess of Wales, who followed . . . it was a goodhumoured crowd. . . .

Sunday, 11 February . . . to Onslow Square by 6.30, to dine with the Theodore Martins. When I arrived, Mr. Arthur Helps was there, but he had to go away, to dine with the Prince of Wales. I was introduced to him: a fine face he has, grave, calm, well cut; with short smooth beard and hair, both grey. A face not unlike the portraits of Mazzini. The party consisted of Mr. & Mrs. Martin, the two Miss Thackerays,[7] Miss Susan Durant[8] the sculptor, and myself. . . . Miss Durant is a very striking person: she was alone; she sailed in upon us—Mrs. Martin & me—a tall & very comely young woman, apparently under 30, well-made, with rounded limbs, full bust, flashing face, and massive rippling chesnut hair; erect, high-couraged, and superbly drest. And her talk was worthy of all this: she dwelt with airy ease, but without parade of learning, upon art works, art subjects, upon Italy and Dresden & the like; upon Michael Angelo, and Gian Bellini, & whether Benvenuto Cellini ever worked in marble; upon Roman & Pompeian art, and the 'points' of that new and noble Sileno, a copy of which in bronze stood in the centre of the dinner table; and on that exquisite missal, you know, of the Brentano family at Frankfort; and so on. And whithal she was full of graceful fun, and told happy stories of the Queen & Princesses, with whom it seems she is a favourite. The Queen, she says (& so did Helps) is so exceeding nervous, that even when her husband was living she could scarcely brace herself to speak her speeches and for days beforehand could not eat, for apprehension: & now, when she opened Parliament the other day, she had arranged to say 'My Lords, be seated', but fearing her own nervousness, she told the Chancellor she would make him a sign at the moment, if she could *not* say it; and she did make the sign, so he said it. Miss Durant was interesting to me, because she is a refined type of that character which is so noble in low life: a strong & handsome

[5] Anne Manning (1807–79) was the author of *The Maiden and Married Life of Mary Powell.*
[6] Annie Keary (1825–79), author of *Castle Daly* and other novels.
[7] Anne Isabella Thackeray, later Lady Ritchie (1837–1919), the novelist and essayist; and Harriet Marian ('Minnie') who married Leslie Stephen in 1867 and died in 1875.
[8] Susan Durant, a talented sculptor who exhibited at the Royal Academy from 1847 until her death in 1873. She specialised in portrait busts.

woman, dignified and self-reliant; and moreover, ladylike, highbred, blazing, as it were, with talent, and sleek with cultivation; just the person to impress some men with awe & admiration. Yet, in a drawingroom creature, such selfasserting strength looks somewhat masculine and out of place: whereas the form it takes in working women is simply heroic. I hold, for instance, that Kitty, queen of milkmaids, with her calm lofty endurance and her grand silent ways, is a nobler being than Miss Durant, though the one is a sculptor, with queens to sit to her; and the other only carries milkcans through the rain. As for Thackeray's daughters, 'Annie and Minnie', they are charming girls; plain—for their faces pleasantly recal their father's—but so bright, so naive & eager, so kindly and affectionate: no wonder Mrs. Martin kissed them warmly.

We looked over the original MS., beautifully written & sketched, of 'The Rose and the Ring', which Mr. M. has had bound for them. 'Oh Mr. Munby' said 'Annie' 'we have a little MS. of yours that Papa used to like so much!' Was it 'Five & Thirty'? 'No, I remember 'Five and Thirty' well; Papa liked it too very much, & so did we: but Mr. Smith used to be so afraid, & wouldn't let Papa put things in, you know'.[9] Habet solatia tempus: it may be vanity to put this down, but I will. Miss Thackeray asked me to call at their house; & yet the two girls live alone, and 'What do you think, dear Mrs. Martin, we offered Mr. Tennyson a spare room & said to him Do come!, but he shook his head and said "My dears, what would the world say?"' I walked home by 12.

Friday, 9 March . . . by 7 to Queen Square, to a Tea at the Working Women's College. The Mallesons, Mrs. P. A. Taylor, others of the teachers, & about 30 of the girls. A pleasant hour or two of talk, music, & pictures, in the antique Queen Anne's Parlour: for one thing, Miss Lucy Harrison, buxom & βαθυκολπος,[1] who looks like a more intelligent dairymaid & is goodlooking withal, *whistled* an elaborate accompaniment of a song which her sister sang and played. Her whistling was sweet & clear & did not writhe her pretty lips in the doing. I have heard colliergirls whistle at their work on Wigan pitbrows; & heard Sally Mainprize whistling to the sea, as she sat swinging her legs on a bit of rock halfway up the cliff face at Brail Head: but I never heard a lady whistle before. . . .

Saturday, 17 March. At 1 I went to Dean's Yard by appointment to George Cayley's, & with him to call on Lord Houghton,[2] at 16 Upper Brook St. Lord H., it seems, has been 'exclaiming' (kind man) that I never go to see him. We found him in the small drawing room which is also his study. 'Glad to see you!' says he, shaking hands: 'take a chair' and seating himself next me, & looking full at me with his odd wrinkled eyes & compressed mouth 'I am delighted' says he

[9] George Smith (1824–1901), of Smith and Elder, was the publisher for whom Thackeray edited the *Cornhill*, to which Munby had apparently submitted 'Five-and-Thirty'. The poem appears in Munby's *Verses New and Old* and seems unobjectionable, though rather long.

[1] 'Deep-bosomed.'

[2] Richard Monckton Milnes had been created Baron Houghton in 1863.

'with your poems': and asked questions which showed that he had been reading them. Apropos, he showed me Prince Lucien Buonaparte's Song of Solomon in the several Yorkshire dialects, & suggested that I should ask the prince for some, using his name. Prince L., it seems, is living quietly at Paddington, doing the Bible into Basque.[3] He spoke of Swinburne: said he has been S.'s only friend (true enough, but what has he done to check S.'s drink & bawdry?): that 'the evangelical old Admiral', S.'s father, is at last getting proud of him: that he, Lord H., thinks S. 'will beat Alfred' i.e. Tennyson. Then the accomplished old Silenus turned the conversation to his favourite subject—venery: he produced out of a secret drawer R. Payne Knight's 'Worship of Priapus', a book full of antique obscenities. . . . Then he discoursed (arranging letters & newspaper cuttings all the time) of παιδεραστια; how the ancient world was based upon it, saw nothing unnatural in it—which, however, is not true as to the Romans at their best, nor (as I said to him) as to the Teutonic nations; how Grote had said to him that on this account it is *impossible* to draw a true picture of Greek life: . . . And then he went on to speak of other subjects more loathsome still.

This is not the first time, by many, that I have observed the peculiar attitude taken by men of high genius—poets, politicians, painters—towards the things of the spiritual life. To such men nowadays, purity, love, passion that is noble, are terms of art merely: they see truly & admire keenly that which is beautiful; but it is only in an intellectual sense; & thus they admire and enjoy, just as much, fastidious villanies & exquisite subtleties of lust. Of course, as I know well, these capacities are complementary of the other; & they are a protest against respectable dulness. But, instead of striving to keep them down (and a poet should feel towards purity as a woman or a truly devout man does) these men give way to them: & respectable pure readers delight in their books, knowing little of what is behind.

There is nothing noble in Lord Houghton's face: it is sly, sensuous, and potentially wicked. After sitting two hours with him, & drinking brandy & seltzer (which he insisted on our doing) we left, about 3.45. . . .

Thursday, 22 March . . . At 3 p.m. I went down to the House of Commons, to enquire about the Committee on Mines; & found to my surprise that it was sitting, & taking evidence. I went to the room: there were no spectators, except about 6 or 8 men, all of whom looked liked miners or miners' delegates. One delegate from Lancashire . . . was just finishing his testimony, & declaiming against the employment of women. Another followed, on a different matter.

I waited, in a state of feverish mental vertigo, till they rose at 4, & then spoke to Fawcett, who is on the Committee. He seemed to think that no evidence but that of local people would be taken; and he was by no means cordial about it.

---

[3] Louis Lucien Bonaparte (1813–91) spent much of his life in England, studying English dialects. He also published some notable works on the Basque language. He was the fourth son of Napoleon's younger brother Lucien.

The prospect of another false & foolish measure against women is simply distracting to me.

Henry Fawcett, the Liberal—shortly to marry Millicent Garrett the suffragist leader—may well have been embarrassed by Munby's determination to defend a woman's right to do heavy work if she wanted to. It was a point of view then unfamiliar in left-wing circles, and was opposed by the men's trades unions for a number of reasons. Fawcett probably did not realise that Munby knew much more about working women than he did; he may have thought him a pure reactionary.

Munby's life in the spring of 1866, complicated as it was by the sittings of the Mines Committee, was even busier than before his riding accident. He still wrote frequent notes in his diary about milkwomen; he still called on the deformed girl Harriet Langdon, recording the problems of her masks and false noses at length; and he joined the committee of a newly formed 'Housework Society', 'for training and employing destitute girls as charwomen' (28 March). Hannah remained in St. Leonards throughout 1866, and was at Margate for much of 1867, a fact which may have had some bearing on Munby's distressing emotional involvements during this period. Although they corresponded regularly, Hannah's letters hardly compensated for the loss of her week-end visits.

On 9 April he received a letter from D. G. Rossetti, and on 10 April he replied to it; the sequel was a trip up-river:

Friday, 13 April . . . by steamer to Chelsea—40 minutes from the Temple. The walls of the Embankment begin to appear: piles for new bridges block up the Thames everywhere. As we steamed into Chelsea the clear sun sank over Cremorne in an open fair sky; a glaze of white light was on the river. The old Don Saltero Tavern in Cheyne Walk is being turned into a private house. So by 6.30 to Tudor House (No. 16) and found the Rossettis, Gabriel & William, in the studio, with Ralston, Scott[4] of Newcastle, & a young half-Portuguese named Howell.[5] We dined upstairs in the long state-room: the table, almost covered by a great silver plateau, with tall red waxlights above, standing in the middle of the dim lofty ancient chamber, hung with Indian chintz on one side, and a blazing fire opposite on the antique hearth, and pictures & ebony cabinets and large silvergilt dishes and flagons gleaming strangely all around against the dark wainscot. A weird impressive scene, worthy of our friend's genius. After dinner

[4] William Bell Scott (1811–90), poet and painter, an early friend of Rossetti, who had recently returned to London from a teaching post at Newcastle and had resumed their friendship. Munby was to become friendly with him.

[5] Charles Augustus Howell, the witty rascal who served Rossetti as secretary and art-dealer; and who was to recover Rossetti's poems from his wife's grave.

we went down again & smoked & had coffee in the studio, which is lumbered with all strange rare things, and with large easels whereon stood some of Gabriel's unfinished pictures; heads of splendid melancholy women, with long hands clasped and aureoles of thick hair. He showed us too a lovely picture, painted when he was 20, of the Virgin's youth[6]: he wrote for it that sonnet which I have. S. Anne & the Virgin—noble faces both, and painted from his mother & Christina—sit together; and Mary is broidering a lily on a frame, & a little angel holds the live lily she is copying, and among trellised grapes behind sits a white dove on a nimbus of opaque gold. 'That' said I 'is the *Paraclete*, I suppose?' 'No my dear fellow' answered Gabriel quite seriously 'It's not a *parakeet*'. For somebody had thought it a parrot. Huge laughter followed this odd mistake. After much talk, Ralston and I left together, and walked home in a starry night by about 12.

Saturday, 14 April . . . I met Walter Severn, & went with him to the private view of the new National Portrait Exhibition, in the remnant of the 1862 Building, overlooking the Horticultural Gardens. The collection is one of supreme and exquisite interest. . . . Today, the privileged crowd of spectators was almost as interesting as the portraits. There was Lord Grosvenor[7] with his handsome wife, superb in glowing Indian shawl; & many were shaking hands with him, & congratulating him on having 'saved the country' by his amendment on the Reform Bill. There were the two Archbishops; Canterbury with his daughter, & York with his fair wife; there was bluff & handsome Sir F. Grant,[8] the new P.R.A., talking to the yellowfaced Bp. of Lincoln; & Thompson our new Master of Trinity; and lofty Jacob Omnium, & hundreds of the like. We spoke with Lord Houghton, who asked us both to breakfast tomorrow. . . .

Sunday, 15 April . . . To Pall Mall Place at 10, & thence with W. Severn to Upper Brook Street, to breakfast with Lord Houghton. 3 other men. . . . Talk at breakfast chiefly about art: Lord H. and the rest agreeing that Rossetti is the greatest painter of the day for poetic genius. His unfinished Venus Verticordia, which he showed me on Friday, was much spoken of: a wondrous woman's face, looking out through a mass of roses & honeysuckles. In the drawing-room afterwards, Lord H. showed me the privately printed Letters & Remains of A. H. Clough, and pointed out in it a poem of his on Easter Day, full of solemn irony & nobly-pathetic despondency. The party broke up about 1. . . .

Tuesday, 17 April . . . Went from 3 to 4 to the House, to the Mining Committee, & saw & spoke with a Mr. Day of Barnsley & a Mr. Peace of Wigan (agents for

---

[6] 'The Girlhood of Mary Virgin,' Rossetti's first picture, painted in 1849: now in the National Gallery.

[7] Later first Duke of Westminster (1825–99). Then Liberal M.P. for Chester, he had opposed the government on the franchise question.

[8] Sir Francis Grant (1803–78), the portrait-painter.

the coalowners in this business) about the women's labour. They of course wish it to be retained; & the men have been telling lies against it: but I see no one who will deal with the thing *on principle*, and in that great bustling strife of business men I grow saddened & maddened to think that the strength & purity of womanhood which I have seen at the pitmouth in Lancashire & Wales, may be about to vanish for ever. . . .

Saturday, 21 April . . . to her Majesty's 8.30, to refresh my soul with the divine beauty of Fidelio. . . . Boyse[9] the painter sat next me; we walked home together, and he came in with me & we talked art & so on till 2 a.m. I showed him some photographs, & when we came to the portrait of my Hannah, 'What a fine expressive face!' he exclaimed. 'Yes,' said I tentatively, '& one wonders what class in life its owner belongs to'. 'Oh, she is a lady, undoubtedly,' said Boyse. . . .

Wednesday, 25 April . . . Tonight I went to the Cosmopolitan (Charles St, Berkeley Square) as Cayley's guest. Got there about 12, and found the large room . . . full of men, smoking, & chatting in groups within the great Indian screen. . . . Mr. Stirling of Keir, who has lately assumed the baronetcy of Maxwell of Pollok, joined our group in humorous talk; a subtle mouth he has & a keen eye, and an odd sharp laugh like the crowing of a cock. Lord Stanley[1] was there, sedate & selfpossest; & Jacob Omnium, who brought his long legs & handsome face into our corner awhile; and Anthony Trollope,[2] cracking jokes before the fire. . . . Towards one o'clock Mr. Davenport Bromley came in, a grizzled eager man with a temper: with him I had some talk about the pitwomen, for he is on the Committee; and Lord Houghton arrived too, & began to loll about & talk in spasms, after his manner. I wanted to speak to him too about the women; but the worthy peer was maudlin with drink, & spake not the words of wisdom. Seizing my arm, & twisting his strange face in a ludicrous manner, he remarked that membership of the Athenaeum (where he is not popular) was 'unm'stak'l sign'idiocy'. We assisted him downstairs. . . .

Saturday, 5 May . . . Today, in a book of etchings called 'By the Loch & riverside', I saw a picture entitled 'Fair fishing; what is sometimes seen in the North'. A young lady, in a wideawake, jacket, & (apparently) knickerbockers, is salmon fishing; standing up to her hips in the stream, in the act of throwing. Another young lady, in a sailor's hat, a jacket, and knickerbockers—in men's clothes, in fact, like the first—is smoking a cigar at the water's edge, leaning on a rock; and a gentleman, brother to both, stands ready to land the fish. There is no caricature, & no disapproval exprest in the drawing: the thing is perfectly simple,

---

[9] Perhaps George Price Boyce, the watercolourist, who was an old friend of Rossetti.
[1] Lord Stanley succeeded in 1869 as fifteenth Earl of Derby (1826–93); and was foreign secretary under Disraeli.
[2] Anthony Trollope (1815–82), the novelist.

natural, modest. But lor bless you, if a colliergirl wear flannel trousers to do her work in, how dreadful *that* is! . . .

Sunday, 6 May . . . Out about 4 p.m. and walked to Onslow Square Brompton & called on Mrs. Theodore Martin, who was out; then down the old Brompton road, whose windings & trees & modest old red brick rural dwellings are over-looked & hemmed in by armies of streets & squares that are building on the market gardens; & so round to Onslow Gardens, & called on Thackeray's daughters. Both the naive charming girls were in. . . . We talked of Froude, of Fitzjames Stephen, of the Malvern ways, of characters & conversation in society, & many other things; Miss Thackeray especially being as ever delight-fully genuine, fresh, and buoyant in manner & thought. She was deeply in-terested about the drowned villages of the Holderness coast, which I told her of, & exclaimed 'Oh, that is a story—that is a poem!' and began to sketch the plot. Thus it came to pass that I sat a whole hour enrapt there. . . .

Tuesday, 8 May . . . to the club,[3] where a table d'hôte party had been made up to dine at seven, consisting of Lord Houghton, Cayley, Severn, Mr. Hamilton a new member, myself, & one or two others. Lord H. took the chair, and talked sensibly & agreeably—Conversation on Capri, Venice, & art subjects; and after dinner more general talk over coffee upstairs, when Swinburne joined us—I had a good deal of talk with him, & liked him much better than of old—We spoke of Rossetti's pictures, of the Travailleurs de la Mer, & so on; & with all his flighty restless manner, he talked without his old pretentiousness & paradox, & showed simply such pure enthusiasm as a poet ought to have: which pleased me, after all one has heard of his 'bumptiousness' of late. He told me that Rossetti, when his wife died, actually, in a fit of lamentable madness, threw the M.S.S. of all his own poems into her grave! Our party broke up about 11. . . .

The next day, 9 May, Munby met a cultivated young Swiss lady who was to complicate his existence during the next few years. She was a friend of Cuyler Anderson named Julie Bovet, and he was introduced to her at one of the gatherings at Aubrey House. 'Mdlle Bovet,' he wrote, 'is very bright and pleasant'; she was also a friend of Mazzini, whom Munby wished to meet.

Munby was now thirty-eight, and his long-drawn affair with Hannah still drifted indecisively. Although he had pledged himself, he was unable to put a term to the contract; and meanwhile he felt increasingly his failure to achieve a settled domesticity—a failure underlined for him in 1866 by his bachelor friend Walter Severn's engagement to a sister of Sir James Fergusson, Bt., M.P., the Under-Secretary for India.

[3] Arts Club.

In these circumstances Munby allowed himself to be drawn into romantic situations both with sophisticated Julie Bovet and with innocent little Sarah Carter of Wheeler's Farm, Pyrford. They represented distant extremes of his extensive female acquaintance; neither affair brought him happiness. If only subconsciously, these contrasting relationships were probably tokens of a last attempt to achieve the normal sex life which had evaded him.

Fastidious, scholarly, chivalrous, sentimental as he was, we have seen Munby in perpetual contact with an interminable succession of women— society ladies, intellectuals, servants, milkwomen, down-and-outs. But his innate and complex inhibitions, no less than his individual sense of the poetic in life, drew him always to the labouring woman, and so back to his idealised vision of drudgery: Hannah. The ensuing years were to show finally that his dilemma had only one solution.

Tuesday, 15 May . . . Went about 1 p.m. to the Oxford & Cambridge Club & called on Mr. Neate,[4] & talked with him for half an hour about the pitwomen, & he expressed a wish that I should give evidence. He said some large coal manager who was strongly in favour of female labour told him the pitgirls were 'mules, not women': & I protested against this. Mr. N. said, for himself, he thought the work undesirable, but not bad enough to legislate about: & when I spoke of principles, he actually said in so many words that he was in favour of 'mere despotism' over women; we were the stronger sex & they were to do what we let them do; would not hear of rights of labour for them. And this from a Professor of Political Economy, a man of mature age who sits in Parliament as an 'advanced Liberal'! 'What do they want to learn Latin for?' said he of my class at the W.W.C. . . .

Wednesday, 23 May . . . by ten to Notting Hill, the P. A. Taylor's. . . . I had a talk with . . . Mlle Bovet & her brother: with buxom Mme Bodichon, fresh from Algiers, who was in great request & earnest about a petition to Parliament to grant votes to women; & let them vote by all means, if they will also *work.* . . . Frederic Harrison[5] was there, whose petit-maître face, now growing red & coarse, belies his intellect. . . .

Saturday, 2 June . . . by 8, to Notting Hill, to the Pen & Pencil Meeting at Aubrey House; the last of the season. A small meeting, but pleasant. After the readings, I had some talk with an American lady from Boston, a Miss Allcot[6]; a

---

[4] Charles Neate (1806–79); Drummond Professor of Political Economy at Oxford, and M.P. for Oxford City, 1863–8.
[5] Frederic Harrison (1831–1923), the author and positivist.
[6] Louisa May Alcott (1832–88), author of *Little Women* (1868).

woman of about 30, simply & elegantly drest, agreeable, quiet, intelligent. Still, she had a je ne sais quoi that was unEnglish about her, & even something of the Yankee drawl. She knew my acquaintance Mr. Edward Hale of Boston. We talked of Theodore Parker,[7] for she is a 'Parkerite' in a quiet way; & of women's labour. She said that on the farms of Kentucky & elsewhere away from cities, the farmer's daughters & servantmaids milk & tend the cows, make hay, even hoe turnips. She knows of a good & modest girl, a farmer's daughter in New England, who is a horsebreaker by trade.

Thursday, 7 June . . . To the Privy Council Office, & thence to Bond St. On the way met W. G. Clark of Trinity, & walked with him down Pall Mall talking of Whewell.[8] Met also Gladstone, in the Mall, walking down to the House, alone; going to propose a dowry for the Princess Mary. A slight man of moderate height, with sprightly tremulous gait; a face of great power; hard, yet pathetic, worn with struggles & thoughts: the cheeks deeply lined, the mouth set & compressed, the eyes halfclosed, looking inwards. Severn met me at the German Gallery, for Mme Bodichon had sent me an order to see her skilful Algerian sketches. . . . S. and I dined together at Rouget's, & then home, he with me, & I dressed, & with him to the Club, & then I on to Notting Hill about 9, to a small party of women (Mr. Shaen & I the only men, for Mr. Taylor was at the House) at Aubrey House. There was . . . Miss F. R. Cobbe,[9] round and fat as a Turkish sultana, with yellow hair, and face mature & pulpy, but keen & shrewd & pleasantly humorous, who sat talking lively unpretending talk to a circle of admirers. The women's petition for the franchise, which she & Mme Bodichon & Mrs. Taylor have got up, was presented tonight by J. S. Mill. They say it has 1500 signatures. . . .

On 14 June Munby was privately assured by Charles Neate, M.P., that the parliamentary Mining Committee 'do not intend to interfere with female labour'. He rejoiced, though he remarked that 'the end is not yet'.

Through his friendship with Mrs. Taylor, Munby was now closely involved in feminist circles. The suffragists may have thought that, because he taught Latin to working women, they had his unequivocal support; this was not exactly true. From the level of the milkwomen and colliery-women, on which Munby placed himself, he looked critically at some of these strong-minded women's leaders. Bessie Parkes,[1] for instance, whom he met at one of Mme. Bodichon's 'evenings', received the comment

---

[7] Theodore Parker (1810–60), the American theologian and Unitarian clergyman; a reformer who influenced Lincoln.

[8] William Whewell, Master of Trinity, had just died.

[9] Frances Power Cobbe (1822–1904), the philanthropist and religious writer, prominent in many women's causes.

[1] She married Louis Swanton Belloc and became the mother of Hilaire Belloc.

'clever hard American hatchetface, she has'. The working girls themselves remained his real interest, the unfailing object of sympathetic study:

Wednesday, 27 June . . . by 8 to my Latin class. As my girls were dispersing, the next class, a dozen of neat fair maidens, came into the room; a pretty sight. Home 9.45, & on the way I saw a costergirl whom I always find at the same spot in Lambs Conduit St. She was standing as usual in the gutter, opposite a certain publichouse, where she could be well seen under the gas lights, & where customers might stop as they went out or in. She wore an old strawbonnet & light cotton frock, & a shawl tied round her waist, so as to leave her shoulders cool; & a soiled coarse apron. A well-grown comely girl of 20 or so, with feminine face & small hands. Her large basket stood on the flags before her, full of lettuces & onions: & with a strip of bass in her mouth she was tying up the onions in bunches & wiping them clean with her apron; every now & then looking up to cry 'Nice lettuce a penny Ma'am!' or 'Penny a bunch onions Sir!' . . .

Leaving nothing to chance with the Mining Committee, Munby wrote them a formal letter which he handed to Neate, the chairman; and when Neate repeated 'We have quite made up our minds not to interfere with the women's labour', he felt he had discharged his conscience.

These summer months brought a continual round of evening parties. Munby attended them assiduously, and derived some unexpected lessons; as at the Theodore Martins', on 6 July:

. . . There were two very fine girls there whom at first I did not know; both tall, ladylike, & quietly beautiful; one with a rose in her bosom, a nimbus of white gauze floating round her shoulders, a classic face & delicate complexion, & massy pale gold hair loftily tired & tressed, with a single lily upon it, looked like a masterpiece of Sir Joshua. I got to know her afterwards & talked with her & found her worthy of her face; & also I took down to supper her mother, a pleasant elderly lady, of quiet gentle manners, ladylike, selfpossest: might have been a Bishop's wife. And who was this nice old lady? Why, she was Mrs German Reed —Miss P. Horton[2]; whose legs, as Ormsby said afterwards, used to be familiar objects, when she danced & sung at the Haymarket, years ago! Nay, she is 'entertaining' still. Does this prove the versatility of women? or not rather their wellkept purity in many cases where fools allow it not? And her daughters, so dignified & free from what is theatrical & meretricious—*they* prove something too, I should think! . . .

And after the social round, Munby regularly refreshed himself, this summer, in his Surrey refuge. On Saturday, 7 July, he looked in at a

---

[2] Priscilla Horton (1818–95), talented actress, mimic and comédienne, wife of Thomas German Reed (1817–88), with whom she appeared very successfully in their popular musical 'entertainments' at St. Martin's Hall.

garden party of the Mallesons at Wimbledon, meeting 'Arthur Hughes[3] the painter, with his gentle subtle face, which it is a pleasure to watch as you talk to him', before taking the train on to Woking and Pyrford. On 25 July, when his Latin class 'broke up' until October, he 'shook hands with the girls all round'. His own holidays did not begin until September, but he now had all the more time to record rural adventures in his microscopic handwriting; and on 2 August he made a special expedition to Rushey Green, near Lewisham, to congratulate Ann Parker, a farm worker, whose exploit in rescuing a child from molestation had been reported in the newspapers. She had knocked down the offender, 'a tall, powerfully-built fellow', three times 'with her fists'. After a long interview, Munby gave her half-a-crown.

Munby's triple romance matured slowly. At the farm-house in Pyrford, he looked down on 'sweet Sarah's' fair head and turned the pages of her music as she played the piano. But Julie Bovet was also in the picture: 'called on the Bovets in Victoria Street; found Mdlle Julie at home, & sat an hour with her tête-à-tête' (14 August). On 25 August Munby sang 'The Brook' to Sarah; and she sang to him 'I know that my Redeemer liveth'. Sarah Carter was 'ladyborn', having only become a farmer's daughter owing to economic circumstances; she had 'long shapely hands, but thicker & larger than a lady's; with a russet-apple texture and a warm apricot hue which were well seen as they moved on the white piano keys': a serious combination, for anyone of Munby's susceptibilities.

On 1 September he travelled to Harrogate, where his mother was staying for her health. 'My dear mother was so weak & so overborne by excitement', wrote Munby, 'that she had to be carried upstairs by my father: rather a distressing commencement of holiday time!' After a week of Harrogate, he went to Wigan, spending several days talking to women at the various pits and breweries in the neighbourhood. On 10 September he found a foreman who declared that pitgirls were 'more moral & healthier than millgirls'. He filled a special sketchbook with a long account of this visit and several excellent drawings. His skill as an artist now becomes increasingly evident; one of his drawings, made on 11 September, shows a girl from the Haigh brewery receiving orders from her top-hatted master.

Next, Munby crossed from Liverpool to the Isle of Man to spend a fortnight with a family friend, and was sea-sick on the six-hours' passage. He enjoyed 'the pleasant days of peace & stillness & kindly comfort at Rhenass Lodge', but it was another 'wild stormy day' for the return crossing on 25 September. Arriving at Whitehaven, he visited a friend in

[3] Arthur Hughes (1832–1915), one of the most distinguished of the Pre-Raphaelite painters.

Wastdale before making his way home to York. He was back at work at his office in London on 15 October, bringing with him some old clothes of his mother's for his unfortunate protégée Harriet Langdon.

Ann Smith of the Haigh Brewery and her master, in the Balcarres Arms, Wigan, 4 pm, 11 September, 1866

He pronounced his Latin class promising with '3 new girls', one of whom, 'a tall goodlooking young married woman brought me an exercise with only 3 mistakes' on 31 October, 'though she declared she had never known anything of Latin until a week ago. No one had helped her to do it, she said'.

Friday, 2 November . . . dined in Hall, with Everett, Piffard, & Horton Smith, all of whom are doing well at the bar; and so the talk was of who is to have silk presently and make way for us rising juniors. Everett talked of getting up at 5 to work; of having his briefs read to him in bed; of making his notes in pencil there, as he lay; he would not go to India for £8000 a year—for, says he, running his fingers through his hair in his bland quick way, 'we look for better things'. And Piffard again is great as a Privy Council man, as a Director of Companies, & so on: everything implies a busy prosperous battling life, with judgeships & social success as its crown and goal. Meanwhile I acquiesce, affect an interest, in all this; yet wonder also whether it be wrong, that the dusk of a ferny copse, the curl of a wave at height, the words of an old poem, the talk & life of fishergirls and colliergirls and Shropshire serving maids, are more to me than all such lofty things. After dinner, to a Council meeting at the Working Men's College; Maurice, just made, to our joy, Professor of Moral Philosophy at Cambridge, in the chair. . . .

Sunday, 4 November . . . to Onslow Square & called on the Martins, who were at home, just come from Manchester. Theodore Martin was in his library, & I sat with him there sometime, talking de omnibus & especially of the appalling future which Trades Unions are preparing, of the foul tyranny which they exercise, & of the false position of those liberals who defend them & those philosophers who palliate their injustice. T.M. was very strong hereon: as for me, nothing but co-operation, I thought, could work a cure. Presently Mrs. Martin came in, drest to go out, & looking young, & in the highest sense charming, to an unusual degree. She was in great force, and most friendly and agreeable: sat down and talked with me about her acting at Manchester last week; how good & hearty the folks there are, & yet how unable to seize the finer humour of Shakespeare, in As You Like It, for instance. She said the Germans of Manchester were her most appreciative audience. She had been doing Iolanthe, in King René's daughter,[4] which 'draws' greatly there; and I begged her to play it here next month, for no one living could so vivify that exquisite creation. With a touch or two, indeed, she made me see it; throwing into her large grey eyes the strange purposeless look of the blind girl, and with light waving of her slender subtle hands making the whole thing clear to me.

But managers here say the play is too short, she says. We talked too of Miss Thackeray's 'Village on the Cliff' in the Cornhill: Is it not a charming story? said she & her husband too; as who would not? Reine, she told me, is sketched from a Norman servant maid the T.s had there last year; a remarkable creature—a lady among gentlefolk, though among her fellows, she slapped the men on the shoulder & bustled about like any other peasant girl. I went on about 4, after a very pleasant hour, to Onslow Gardens, & called on that same fair Thackeray & her sister. They were at home, 'Annie & Minnie', in their elegant little drawing room; en séance, at afternoon tea, with callers—a daughter of Mrs. Gaskell's, and her husband, Mr. Holland. 'Annie & Minnie' too were most frank & cordial, as ever: playfully reproached me for not having called on them in their Surrey

---

[4] Her husband had adapted *King René's Daughter* from the Danish for her, in 1849, before their marriage.

farmhouse this summer. 'Why did you never come & see us?' said the charming creator of Reine, giving me her hand, and looking infinitely bright & spirituelle, in her pearlgrey dress with necklace of massive amber. Soon, the Martins came in; and while Mr. Martin talked with Minnie, we three others got into an animated conversation, about men & women and the ways of married folks, their pettiness & little mutual cruelties of word & look, & the wrong & sadness of all this. 'Oh, dearest Mrs. Martin!' cried Miss Thackeray with all her ardour 'I often think if it were not for you & Mr. Martin I could not bear it—it makes me so unhappy, seeing all this among so *many* people one knows!' and then at her questioning Mrs. M. told of her own ways with her husband, sitting together in loving silence, or reading aloud one to another such passages as seem worthiest in some book. For they are indeed loftily & purely happy together, this couple. There was to me a delightful contrast in the different modes of beauty & interest belonging to these two fair women. Helen Faucit lay back in her chair in graceful repose, tall, like a slighter & milder Juno, looking on with calm delight at her young friend's sallies; while Annie, all lithe and tremulous, leaned forward or moved rapidly to and fro, her face & limbs as it were gleaming and flashing perpetually with the impulse of thought and strong feeling. Once, when I said that the woman can *sting* more cruelly than the man can sting *her*, she turned sharp round at me, held up both her hands toward me, & with her great eyes & her white teeth shining with enthusiasm, said '*Oh!*' with such longdrawn intense emotion that she suddenly broke off, & laughed & made us laugh at her own impetuosity. Surely there is not another girl in England, so artless & intense, with such a charm of love & of power!

Anyhow, this afternoon was the most delightful for interchange of thought, that I have had for a long time, and wrought me up to such a level that for once the calm of Pyrford, which I had regretted, was well missed. . . .

Tuesday, 13 November . . . I went up to the club till 6.30; then walked down to Victoria Street Westminster, to dine with the Bovets, meeting Cuyler there by appointment. A partie carrée; Mdlle Julie, her brother Charles, & we two. The Bovets had a box for Der Freyschutz at Her Majesty's, and we all went after dinner. . . . Box on the grand tier, near the stage; but it is one thing to sit thus, lounging with opera glass, counting acquaintances in the stalls, & having the poor illusion on the stage continually destroyed by the nearness of paint & powder, & the sight of workmen behind the scenes; it is one thing to enjoy this languid afterdinner amusement, & quite another thing to sit alone in the amphitheatre stalls, & study and worship from afar, as I do at Fidelio. Tonight however there was something better than fashion: Mdlle Julie, scanning the boxes near us, exclaimed 'Oh, there is *Mazzini!*'[5] He was with the Ashursts & Mrs. Stansfeld; and presently Mr. A. came to our box, and took la Bovet & me back to theirs; and la Bovet introduced me to Mazzini. I had often wished for this:

---

[5] Giuseppe Mazzini (1805–72), the Italian patriot and republican.

whatever may be his extravagance of opinion, the patriotism of this man, his lofty unswerving purpose, his noble selfsacrificing poverty, the romantic & historical interest of his character, made me feel it to be an honour indeed when the Dictator, bowing with dignity, came forward and gave me his hand. A poor man, look you, to the outward eye: slight and meagre, clothed up to the throat in mere undistinguished black: but with life & genius in all his face; in the high forehead and keen deep eyes, & clear-cut slightly curved nose, and thin lips and sharp-edged jaw: and his grey thin hair, and grey smooth beard, suited well the melancholy composure of his looks. But he talked with her and with me in gentle subdued voice, with calm smile & graceful simple manner: speaking English well, talking simply on ordinary general subjects. He shook hands with me again at parting, and I escorted la Bovet back again. She was once nearly arrested at Berne, on suspicion of being a spy of his. . . .

It might have been thought that Julie Bovet had advanced her cause that evening; but at Pyrford on the following Sunday Munby noted ominously: 'as for Sarah, standing there bareheaded, with a shawl round her, & the moonlight full on her bright upturned face & amber hair, a man young and heart free might well have fallen in love with her' (18 November). And the next week-end: 'I sing with her Juanita, which I have just bought for her' (24 November). Helen Faucit was a safer object of his admiration:

Monday, 19 November . . . I dined in Hall, and then met Cuyler at Drury Lane Theatre, to see As You Like It. Though I have known Mrs Martin for ten years, it was the first time I ever saw her on the stage, as Helen Faucit: and I expected that it would be a shock, and a strange thing, to see one whom you know as a highbred accomplished lady, moving in good society & mistress of a fine house, to see her appear in public as an actress, and in men's clothing. But her Rosalind is so graceful and natural, so pure and transporting, and withal so like her own self off the stage, that one forgets the publicity and indeed everything but the part. And Helen Faucit plus Rosalind makes a delightful compound result, for those who know both Shakespeare and Mrs Martin. She looked so young too, so arch and lively: with her beautiful tall figure, her lithe limbs, her expressive face, it was hard to believe oneself in presence of a woman of fifty. . . .

Friday, 23 November . . . To Onslow Gardens 7.30, to dine with the Miss Thackerays. A partie intime: 'Annie & Minnie' . . . and Mr. Charles Collins & his wife[6] (née Kate Dickens, daughter of Charles), and a young Etonian, Walter

[6] Charles Collins, artist brother of Wilkie Collins, designed the mysterious cover of *Edwin Drood*. He died young, and his widow re-married; as Mrs. Perugini, she had some critical things to say of her father in conversations with Gladys Storey, published in *Dickens and Daughter* (1939).

Pollock, a grandson of the Chief Baron, and I. K.D. is a lively pretty little creature, piquante & clever; I took her in to dinner; a very nice little dinner, where Miss T. presided with all her arch simplicity of manner & her naive humour—She dared not carve the grayling (which Millais had sent) for fear it should *bark* or something. . . .

On 27 November, Munby read the following advertisement in *The Times*: 'A Lady, through the death of her husband and failure of business, is anxious to Place her Daughter, age 16, in service as Under Housemaid or Under Nurse'. Excited at the possibility of 'a young lady about to become a housemaid, phenomenon unprecedented', Munby called on 29 November on A.B., the advertiser, at 48 George-street, Blackfriars-road. She and her children proved not to be 'gentlefolks', however, and 'she said frankly that she feared I had "expected more than there was". . . .'

. . . she had thought it best to word her advertisement so, having to get her girl out with only a character from herself. Her husband, she said, was a *surgeon-dentist* at Chelsea; who died some years ago, & then she kept a confectioner's shop which failed—voila tout! Here the daughter of 16, *Lydia Martin* her name, came in: a nice honestlooking girl, poorly drest, with cold red hands, poor thing, and not at all superior to many maidservants, apparently. She did not mind being a servant, she said; she knew she must earn her own living; she can do housework—yes, she can clean grates, & has done. And her education was 'very limited', owing to her father's early death; in fact she can 'only just' read & write, & knows not summing. Under which circumstances, it is after all the wisest thing to become a servant; & there is no disgrace in it. These truths being enforced by me & heartily accepted by Mrs Martin & Lydia, I shook hands with mother and daughter and departed, amid amiable adieux. . . .

Sunday, 2 December . . . Walked up to the Club, & dined there. . . . Going up-stairs afterwards I found Swinburne, & had some talk with him about Poe's Raven, Walt Whitman (whom of course he frantically praised) and Bourdelaire,[7] a certain ribald French poet, whom he declared to be '15 million times' better than Tennyson. He spoke of 'my unfortunate book'[8] and its resemblance to Walt Whitman. He was obviously drunk: he sat waving his arms & writhing his little legs after his manner, & talking loud and wild. He ordered a cab; counter-manded it; jumped up & down, shook hands with me, with glazed eyes, & tottered out of the room, saying he 'must make a call'. Presently, when Bailey, F. W. Burton, I, & one or two others, sat quietly reading & talking, Walter Severn came in, crying 'What a sad business! Here is Swinburne come into the club again, dead drunk!' and he described the scene downstairs; and every one

---

[7] Charles Baudelaire (1821–67). *Les Fleurs du Mal* had appeared in 1857.
[8] Presumably the first series of his *Poems and Ballads*.

looked grave and sorrowful, but hardly a word was said. Truly it is sad enough to me; to see this young poet, with so much rare knowledge, & so much more of the θειαμοιρά[9] than ever I could claim, belching out blasphemy and bawdry & prostrated by drink. . . . About 10. p.m. I left the club with J. C. Jeaffreson, & we took a hansom & went up to Westland Marston's. Found there . . . the great Hepworth Dixon.[1] That Eminent Person, unbending from his lofty height, talked much & pleasantly about America, from which he has just returned. Longfellow, he said, told him that one of the great social dangers ahead is that the women of the wealthy classes *refuse to bear children* to their husbands, & defend the refusal. Of the Mormons he seemed quite enamoured: an earnest laborious race, he says, under a kind of Mahomet; all Christian and believing; earnest to replenish the earth & subdue it. He advised Brigham Young to migrate en masse to the Holy Land, if they be again disturbed . . .

Wednesday, 5 December . . . This morning in the Strand I saw a servantgirl—a maid of all work—cleaning a shop entrance on her knees. . . . Again, tonight down in a cellar kitchen near Holborn I saw another servant; a roughlooking girl with rough hair, alone in a dim poor kitchen, kneading dirty clothes with her bare arms in a washtub.

Mean creatures these, mean things: why should we give them a thought?

The year drew to its end with renewed signs of emotional danger for Munby. As late as 8 December, he made his way to Pyrford to give French lessons to Sarah Carter, who thought of becoming a nursery governess or lady's companion. Meanwhile, he was writing letters to Julie Bovet, and on 15 December 'sat *two hours* tête à tête with her' (Munby's italics) at her home in Victoria Street. The voice of honour and duty was, it is true, represented by a visit from Hannah on 7 December, who came up from St. Leonards after many months, looking like a milkmaid 'rosy and blooming and bright, and with a lady's eye and smile'.

Christmas was celebrated at Clifton Holme as usual. On the morning of Christmas Eve, Munby 'walked round the garden & grounds, & to see the horses & cows, the new ducks, the calf, the pigs, & so on'. Christmas Eve supper was at nine, with a Yule log and 'frumenty'.[2] 'The servants also had theirs—but my mother complains that servants now do not so much care for Christmas matters: the mistletoe in the servants' hall, which we used to have yearly, with its paper of verses written by the footman & addressed to the Master & Mistress, is now a poor & unregarded affair.'

[9] 'Divine providence'.
[1] William Hepworth Dixon (1821–79), editor of the *Athenaeum*, 1853–69.
[2] 'Hulled wheat boiled in milk & seasoned with cinnamon, sugar, etc.' (*Concise Oxford Dictionary*).

Munby corrected this somewhat after the servants had had another party on Christmas Day, 'and one could hear female voices amongst them singing hymns. There is a new housemaid, who sings at her work in a pleasant way'.

Back at Fig Tree Court by 31 December, Munby heard 'the midnight clocks sound, and the New Year's peals begin':

But within the room, there is warmth & light, & signs of comfort & culture; selfish comfort which may vanish, profitless culture which leads to nothing. So on the whole we begin the new year with prayer, I and love; for love is artless & innocent, and in giving up itself, gives a blessing that can lighten much darkness.

'I and love . . . artless & innocent.' Munby's phrases this New Year strike a hazardous, prophetic note. And he concludes: 'Prayer or no prayer, however, the new year will move upon and over us; relentless & biting and swift, like the old.'

Tuesday, 1 January, 1867 . . . at 8 to a children's ball, given by Mrs Senior & Miss Thackeray, & held in the Vestry Hall at Chelsea; a large convenient room. Some 200 people, including many grownup folks. An agreeable party, but the fair Annie was unwell & could not be there, so her sister Minnie, who is engaged to Leslie Stephen, did the honours with fairhaired Mrs Senior. Anthony Trollope was there with his wife. . . . George Macdonald,[3] with hair diffuse and tender imaginative face; Mrs Millais, in sky blue, elegant of figure but worn, & *not* tender; her children, & many other children too of her husband's painting, in the costumes they were painted in . . .

Wednesday, 2 January. Since midnight, snow had silently fallen, to the depth of 6 to 8 inches; by breakfast time it was all over except a slight flaky dropping, & the day was calm & very cold. Nothing could be more beautiful; no change more complete & charming. The trees around the fountain near Garden Court were loaded with snow: an exquisite tracery of white branches, relieved against the dark red housefronts. But in the streets the transformation was greatest. All traffic, except afoot, was stopped; no cabs, no omnibuses, no waggons. The snow lay in heaps in the road; men were scraping & shovelling the footways; & people in thick coats & wrappers stepped noiselessly along. The Strand was as quiet and empty as a village street at nightfall; even the footpassengers were far fewer than usual. Here in the heart of London, & at midday, there was absolute cleanliness & brightness, absolute silence: instead of the roar & rush of wheels, the selfish hurry, the dirt & the cloudy fog, we had the loveliness & utter purity of newfallen snow. It fell without force or sound; & all things huge & hasty & noisy

---

[3] George Macdonald (1824–1905), the poet and novelist.

were paralyzed in a moment. I walked along enjoying the wondrous lovely scene, the long perspective of houses, all grown picturesque & antique; their gable roofs white against a clear sky, & every salient cornice & lintel in their outline picked out in brilliant white; and beneath them, the tumbled & tenantless pavement of snow. It was like the quaint still London of old; one might have been arm in arm with Mr. Pepys, or even Mr. W. Shakespeare. And this state of things lasted all day. There were many crossing sweepers about: I noticed one near S. Clement Danes, a girl of 17 or so, in ragged but warm shawl, & a bit of an old bonnet, whose dark rough hair was covered with snow, & hung in a tangled *white* mass, like the foam of a waterfall, over her brown bonny face, as she stood with her broom under her arm, stamping & blowing her fingers.

. . . at 8.30 to the Working Women's College, where there was a Christmas Party. . . . I had to read 'Five & Thirty'. . . .

Friday, 4 January. The cold out of doors at ten this forenoon was more intense, to my apprehension, than I ever remember. My beard froze, the nape of the neck, & the heart, seemed paralyzed, headache came on, & at the end of the short walk from here to Whitehall I was almost helpless. At 4, I walked westward, thinking to call on the Thackerays. The Horseguards Parade & the Mall were one sheet of snow, with paths trodden but not swept: a thick brown fog brooded over it, deepening the twilight; muffled spectral figures hurried to & fro across the slippery ground. . . . In Victoria Street a girl begged of me: a ragged tall lusty girl of 19, by name Caroline Randall, by trade an ironer; who has no home; who slept last night on a step in a sheltered corner, & felt 'as cold as a frog', she said.

Wednesday, 9 January . . . At 8 to my Latin class at the Working Women's College: first evening of new term. Two new girls, one of whom knew nothing of Latin, but *begged* to join because she is employed at Powell's glassworks in painting inscriptions on churchwindow glass, & she wants to know what they mean: the inscriptions being mostly in Latin. . . .

Saturday, 12 January . . . near Ormonde Terrace, there was a cornerhouse with tall flight of steps & showy portico; and in the side wall of the steps, a little window, opaque & iron-barred. As I passed it, I heard within the scraping of a knifeboard, & the sound of a girl's voice. An unseen scullerymaid was cleaning knives; and as she cleaned, she sang: 'I love Robin' she sang, 'and Robin he loves me!' Down in her dark hole beneath the doorsteps, the scullion scrapes and sings: and over her head, young ladies trip & tattle at their ease.

Saturday, 26 January . . . Going out at noon today, I saw the first pair of Landseer's lions, supporters of the Nelson column. One of them had arrived yesterday, & was already in its place: the other had but just come, & was about to be heaved into position. Both were cased all over in white Calico, tightly wrapt; through which their proportions showed visibly grand and massive. . . .

Tuesday, 5 February . . . Dined at Rouget's, and walked thence down to Brompton about 7.30, to give Harriet Langdon her month's money. Attracted by pity and repelled by horror, one looks with strange emotion on this poor girl, without a nose and with only one lip, who comes forward with a grin of welcome to the door. A rude, narrow, irrational nature, too, makes it hard to deal with her. She 'thinks she shall go mad'; which a lonely outcast, without work, without features, might well do! 'I am the only friend she has near': she would so gladly hear from or see me oftener: she disdains pity, yet says 'You neglect me— you dont feel for my wretched lonely condition!' and the tears run down.[4] . . . She even complains of the false nose I got her from Paris, & she would not wear it. . . . Still, she threatens to reward my help by becoming a kind of Frankenstein monster, exacting sympathy from me in proportion as she feels herself cut off from it elsewhere. This scene took so long that I did not get home till about ten.

Saturday, 9 February . . . at 8 drove to the Working Women's College, to preside at a Conversational Meeting: the subject was, 'The beauty of manual labour, and the weakness of being ashamed of it'. We met in the coffeeroom (Queen Anne's Parlour) and sat about in groups: three or four ladies, 20 or 30 of the girls, and myself, the only man present. I opened the talk with a short speech about the nobleness & noble effects of robust and hardhanded labour, for women as well as for men; and read an apropos passage from the Bothie: and then they, or rather the ladies & one or two only of the students, commented & questioned: the net result being, of course, that these lower middle class London girls showed themselves quite unable to realize the charm of rustic women & rustic work, or even to see that of service and its work & dress, though they professed not to be above working. But I put it very feebly and ill; partly because they are not the right sort of girls, being but weakly stitchers and strummers; & partly for that I could not say out frankly all I knew. . . .

Wednesday, 20 February . . . About noon today I went to the Southwark Police Court, to hear the case of one Thomas Walker, barman at a publichouse in the London Road, who the other day turned out unexpectedly to be a young *woman*. The Court was densely crowded outside & in, with roughs, male & female: but I had a place near the magistrate & not far from the prisoner, & saw & heard with ease.

It did not appear who or what Thomas Walker really is; but there she stood, alone in the dock, conspicuous and central: and to the outward eye she looked a bluff and brawny young man, of four or five & twenty. A broad bronzed face, fullcheeked & highboned; well cut straight nose, sharp eyes, determined mouth:

[4] Munby's conduct towards Harriet Langdon deserves nothing but praise. He saw her regularly, wrote to her, and sometimes took her out for excursions.

rough dark hair, short as a man's, and evidently worn in man's fashion for a long time past. Her head was bare, and so was her strong bull neck: about the waist, she wore nothing but a blue sailor's shirt, with the sleeves partly rolled up. Standing there, with broad shoulders squared and stout arms folded on the dock rail, she seemed just such a fellow as one may see drawing beer at an alehouse, or lounging about a seaport town; and it was almost impossible to believe that she was not a man. No one suspected her, indeed; she confessed her sex to avoid the prison bath. . . .

She was a ship's steward two years, before she was a barman: and before that again, she was errand boy, & afterwards light porter, at a cheesemonger's in the New Road. When I arrived, the cheesemonger was charging her with not repaying him some of her receipts as his porter: . . . And thus poor Thomas, who only said 'Nothing Sir' in a low tone when asked if she had ought to say, was committed for trial; and the ruthless Peeler hauled her down through the crowd; whereby one saw that she was of average woman's height & no more. The magistrate was pompous and petulant and grandiose, as one might expect. . . .

Thursday, 21 March . . . in a Brompton omnibus . . . opposite to me sat a big robust damsel, smartly drest in round hat and odd outré ornaments. Not 'improper', and not absolutely vulgar; but remarkably cool and selfpossessed; evidently one who was wont to fend for herself and move about alone. She talked loudly, but with perfect staidness, to a gentlemanly man next her, who after a while shook hands with her and got out. 'Jolly supper we had last Saturday week,' said she: 'wish you'd been there. By the way, I went to a concert the other night in Park Lane; Wandering Minstrels, you know; guinea tickets & all that; but I didn't enjoy it a bit, among all those swells. Clever fellow though, that Seymour Egerton; conducts uncommonly well. There's a man Hughes too, plays violin capitally. Know any of 'em, eh? I was introduced to one of 'em— heard him asking "Who's that jolly girl?" but it was only his chaff, you know!' So she rattled on, with the air of one young man talking to another: and after he had gone, 'Robert!' said she to the conductor, 'I say, if any of you fellows want an order, I can always get you passes, you know'. When we got near the Haymarket Theatre, 'I'll jump out now', she called to Robert; 'you'll take so long, getting round; so I'll just run across, the near way'. And she did jump out, and ran down street at full speed to the stagedoor.

'One of the actresses at the theatre,' Robert explained: 'name of Thornton; Miss Thornton; lives at Brompton; a many of 'em do'. . . .

Saturday, 23 March . . . called on Mrs Theodore Martin. . . . We talked of acting; & I was a little amused to see however Helen Faucit is not above the usual jealousies of the profession: she spoke with an airy laughing scorn of Phelps's[5] acting, & could not remember the name of the girl who played Celia

---

[5] Samuel Phelps (1804–78), for many years at Sadler's Wells.

to her Rosalind. . . . I walked up to Knightsbridge and into the Park; and found a long line of carriages near the Achilles statue, waiting to see the Queen go by to Windsor. . . .

And then the Queen drove past us, with outriders & hussars; in open carriages, her younger children with her; looking plump & matronly and pale, in widow's weeds; and that John Brown, of whom there is so much foolish talk, sat behind, a big man in livery. . . .

As the weather improved, Munby filled pages of the diary in minute writing about his weekend excursions to Pyrford, where the piano recitals and French lessons he was giving to Sarah Carter and the duets they sang together, were proving increasingly distracting. On 6 June, he took Sarah and her younger brother, Eddy, to see the Royal Academy exhibition, where he contrived to introduce her to his other friend Julie Bovet: 'they were such a contrast too: Miss Bovet, a cultivated lady, drest elegantly & in perfect taste, in costly silks of fashionable cut; and Sarah, a lady too, yet only a poor & rustic maiden in attire'. Miss Bovet's 'admiration' of her innocent rival 'was evident' (according to Munby), and she took charge of 'little Eddy', while 'I gave Sarah my arm, for the rooms were crowded'. The expedition included a visit to Munby's chambers in the Temple, and was all too successful. When Sarah told Munby, on their way home to Pyrford, that his rooms were 'just like what I fancied them', he began to be alarmed. 'Then, she has been "fancying" them,' he wrote; 'she has been dreaming about me. A new thought and a new dread came to me when I heard that, & has never left me since.' The next morning Sarah cleaned his boots, a gesture of gratitude which transported Munby 'to the very limit of selfcontrol'.

Friday, 7 June . . . I left at 8; all things were cool and charming, and opal-grey, in the cool sweet morning; the church green, & the lane & copse, and the elm-walk, & the heath; but a horror of great darkness was upon me. What if between this dear innocent soul and mine, there is a danger of too close attraction? Music and French lessons, must they be repressed? Pyrford itself—but that will not bear thinking of. This is a great evil that I have seen under the sun; when the enthusiasm of admiration for a worthy object begins to be actually injurious to that object; and virtue itself, and all pure high charms, become temptations and instruments for ill. As I passed the cottage on the heath, there was pretty Sally Collings out as usual, with her pail, feeding her eighteen pigs. . . . She, pretty Sally, in her tattered peasant's dress, can talk to you of pigs & poultry as often as you like, and never be in danger of an affaire du coeur. . . .

Hannah meanwhile, after returning to London to an unsatisfactory job in Craven Street, had been 'out of place'; and Munby had decided that 'she shall go with me openly . . . & in all purity and candour, for one day's joy together, as if she were what someday . . . she shall be'. They went to Southend on 27 April, where the 'waitress-chambermaid' at the hotel gave them two single bedrooms, and said 'Ma-am' to Hannah, 'who followed her upstairs blushing, for no one ever called her Ma'am before, poor child'. It was feared that the waitress caught a glimpse of her working hands, which she tried to keep covered; but when she sat beside Munby that evening in an 'elegant silk gown', with a silver cross on her bosom, 'her smooth hair braided', reading 'intently the Life of John Clare',[6] she appeared 'calm and graceful & statuesque & charming'. Munby overcame temptation with the help of a misquotation: 'I should not love thee, dear, so much, Loved I not Honour more.'

In the middle of May, Hannah returned to Margate to work for her former employer Miss Knight, who liked and appreciated her—'& where the Missis *is* a lady it's like a *security*', wrote Hannah. Miss Knight had, however, moved to a new house, 17 Athelstan Road, where there was a dearth of lodgers. Hannah and her fellow-servant Mary, who slept together in the kitchen on a straw bed 'shut up in the daytime', were left with very little to do. The story of the comedy that followed is taken from an autobiographical MS of Hannah's, entitled by Munby 'A Servant's Life: 1866 to 1872':

3 Weeks went on or more—the Weather was fine but cold, & *no* lodgers came—i had clean'd all the house down on my hands & knees—laid the stair carpets & polish'd the furniture, & got the curtains up, & work'd out in the back garden when it was fine enough—setting potatos & things as well as some flowers, for it was a new place & had never bin laid out, so i dug it all up first. And i begun to feel very anxious for lodgers to come that we may have work, & to bring money in—my wages was to be 5 shillings a week, & the Missis couldn't well afford to keep me i knew, & her paying 50 lbs a year for rent & all, it made her low-spirited & me too, & i begun to feel like *idle* & not worth my keep, what i hate, & i never felt that afore in any place, being always full o' work. Then a way came into my head to get lodgers for i thought the house perhaps was too much out o' the way, but i didn't tell Missis, cause she wouldn't like it, being a *lady* tho' poor, but when i got out for my walk, & Miss K. let me go as before when i liked—i clean'd me & went out in my apron & plaid shawl, & walk'd about, & when i saw people i thought looking for lodgings, i spoke to them & said there was good apartments at 17 Athelstan Road if they wanted any, & i was servant there if they'd please let me show them to the house. I hardly liked doing so, but it was entirely from feeling for the Missis. Some spoke shortly to me & others not at

<hr />

[6] This must have been the biography by Frederick Martin (1865); and Munby was thus thoughtfully introducing the 'uneducated poet' to Hannah.

all, so i thought perhaps after all it wasn't prudent, & that lodgers would come in time, no doubt. . . .

. . . the first one as come was a Mr. Lineke, a Missionary from India, & he was ill with the yellow jaundice or fever—he took the room next the kitchen so it fell to me to wait on him & do the room entirely. Mr. L. was a german & a bit fussy, & he treated me as if i was a regular lodginghouse servant, & in an off hand way, telling me to do anything & never saying 'please' & hardly ever 'thankyou'—so i canna say i liked him, neither was it pleasant to wait on him, but he was a lodger, & better nor havin no one, beside, he was an *old* gentleman, & i've heard that being in India makes you illtemper'd & irritable, so i made allowances for him. . . .

. . . At Whitsuntide we had no lodgers in the house, & i had thought how much i s^hd like Massa to come & stay in the room next the kitchen—that i may wait on him, & also for him to see me as a lodging-house servant, & to see my Missis, & the house i lived in—if only it could be managed not to cause suspicion—And so M. agree'd to come on the Saturday[7] & to stay till Whit Monday evening. I took care to air the bed, but of course it was to come all unawares & i was all anxiety to hear the front door bell ring about six in the evening of Saturday—i was at work in the garden, & Mary had leave to go out, but i succeeded so far as to keep her with me till the bell rung—& she says 'Can't you answer that Hannah as i've got my bonnet on?' i said 'i'm not fit wi' these black hands, besides it might be people for lodgings & then you *must* take your things off'. And Mary went up & let the gentleman in to the dining room, & then went up for Misis to come & speak to him, & i still kept at work till she come running to me & says 'You was right Hannah, but it's only one, & thats a gentleman, & *such* a swell with a beard & Mustachios, & Missis has took him up to see the rooms'. i said, 'Oh, let's go in then, & stir the kitchen fire up—i hope he'll want some dinner or tea or something'. And by the time we got in the kitchen i could hear Massa's voice, & that Missis was with him in the next room, & i felt so overjoy'd you canna tell, but i was forced to pretend anything else but the right cause. In a Minute or so Missis came in & said 'Hannah, a gentleman has come to stay in the next room for a night or two, & he wants some dinner, so *you* go in, & tell him what you can get, & i'll put the sheets out for airing', & really Miss K. seem'd as confused as could be. i laugh'd to myself when i said 'Very well mam' & i went & knock'd once at the door & walk'd in, & there was Massa! i made him a curtsy & said 'Yes sir' pretty loud, & then put the door *too* but of course didn't shut it, & then i *think* i went up & he kiss'd me quietly, & then spoke louder about his dinner, giving me $\frac{1}{2}$ a sovereign to get what i thought best, & i came out again & told Miss K. & Mary what i was going out *for*—And Missis seem'd pleas'd at me managing it all myself & so went up stairs, & i put on my bonnet & shawl & took a basket to fetch the things, & i ask'd Mary to lay the cloth in the next room for me the while i was away. You may be sure i

---

[7] 8 June, 1867.

wasn't long a going to the butchers & fishmongers, but i was soon back again & got a nice little dinner for M. fish, cutlets, & an omelette. i thought it was best to let Mary wait on him the first night, anyhow at dinner, to save anything been thought—only as that was my room to wait on i didn't give it up, & so i lighted the fire & took coals in, & Mary *did* go out as she'd got leave for it—after the dinner was over, & Missis was safe up stairs at reading as she always did with her sister of an evening, & so *then* i went in & had a petting with Massa & talk'd about things. It was delightfully amusing altogether, for our having such a grand lodger at Margate was quite a new thing, that even the Missis seem'd pleas'd for she said 'He's *quite* a gentleman' & i thought 'Yes mam, *i* could tell you that'— And Mary was pleas'd too, & every time she come out o' the room at dinner time she had something fresh to tell me, & *i* listen'd eagerly & talk'd again & i wonder'd how ever he come to pick *one* house out from the rest. And so it was quite a bit o' new life for us, & there was no other lodgers in the house either. When Mary came in M. was out for a walk, which was good, & so i went in & got the tea ready, & put the bed ready & the candles & everything, so that i could easily go again last thing for *orders*, & just for the good night *kiss*. And Mary & me slept together on our bed in the kitchen & M. told me after he could hear us talking & laughing together being happy like. i ask'd Mary to call him next Morning, but i got the breakfast ready, & first thing i went in my dirt to do the grate up, & light the fire. i had a dirty face, & my arms was black too, on purpose for M. to see me as he had wish'd to, a lighting a fire of a morning, & i wore my striped apron, & Massa sat up in bed to look at me do my work, & when i'd done he call'd me to him for a kiss. . . .

There is something here of the charm of Daisy Ashford's *The Young Visiters*, with Munby as Mr. Salteena. Hannah's diaries help to explain her attraction for Munby, by suggesting how her robust humour cheered him in moods of depression. In fact, Munby was not at his best on this Margate visit; he was worried about 'sweet Sarah' at Pyrford; he even described Margate in his diary as 'the loathly town'. Nevertheless, he played his part loyally; the couple, meeting at a discreet distance from Athelstan Road, went for long walks, which Hannah at least enjoyed; and Munby spoke to Miss Knight: '"You are fortunate" I say to her mistress "in having such a respectable young woman. She seems quite a superior gentleman's servant." "Yes," replies the gratified spinster; "she came to me before, for the season, a few years ago; & I thought very highly of her." Just so, Madam' (10 June).

It was perhaps a situation that Hannah could appreciate more easily than Munby. Mary had told Hannah about her sweetheart, and Hannah thought 'what a surprise to her if I could tell her who was mine'. Hannah described the conclusion of the Margate week-end:

. . . i took lunch out & met M. as i did yesterday & we had a good long walk again in the fields & back along the cliff—We parting a distance off & saying the good bye there & then, & i got in by 5 o'clock & Mary went out directly after tea, & she had asked Missis for the gentleman's bill—Missis brought it to him herself & they were talking in the room a few minutes & then i heard 'em coming out to go up towards the hall & i look'd out at the kitchen door to carry the bag up & also to recieve whatever the gentleman might *give* me. i saw M. very politely lift his hat to Miss K. for her to go first, & then i follow'd with the bag & i open'd the front door & stood holding the bag—he wish'd Miss K. good bye, & then pass'd me giving me a shilling & said 'good bye' to me—i made a curtsy & said 'good bye sir' all the time wishing he had call'd me 'Hannah' as well, & not said good bye in such a proud way either—but i knew how lovingly we had parted a few minutes before, & i could forgive the other, & if Missis hadn't follow'd me down i s^hd have sat down & had a little melancholy as well as happy thought to myself about him—enjoying it too—still i was pleas'd & amused too, for Missis come into the kitchen & seem'd quite pleas'd with the gentleman & said 'Dont you think him very good looking Hannah' i said very *demurely* 'Yes mam, what little i've seen of him'—and so i'm certain she never imagined the truth for a moment. . . .

This charade was only a small-scale anticipation of what was to be required in later years. But Sarah at Wheeler's Farm, Pyrford, could not be appeased by play-acting; nor, one surmises, could Julie Bovet, who seems to have criticised Munby's sentimental entanglements freely. 'Sweet Sarah' asked for Munby's photograph for her album; and Munby played and sang for her; and gave her her French lesson tête-à-tête, 'to my dread, rather' (29 June); and they went together to Ripley Fair and watched a cricket match, Ripley v. Dorking. There had to be a reckoning before the summer was out.

Saturday, 3 August, provided the moment of truth with Sarah Carter. In the afternoon, Munby walked to the Pyrford churchyard, 'meaning to read there':

but as I came towards the edge of the cliff to look on the view, I saw there a ladylike maiden sitting, with long pale brown hair flowing loose down her back beneath her plain straw hat. She had her back towards me; & her face seemed to be buried in her hands. . . . I watched her some moments, but she did not stir. At last my step was heard, & she turned round. It *was* sweet Sarah. She rose, blushing celestial rosy red, & with an absent dreamy look in her eyes; & smiled, & gave me her hand. She had a book in her other hand, her music lying on the grave beside her. Her finger kept a place in the volume; and I saw at once that it was *my* book. This discovery, and her lonely sitting & sad attitude, gave me a shock not to be described. There is the fear of being vain, & attributing too much to slight matters: but there is the greater fear of doing irreparable harm; & there is the selfish & half passionate dread of losing sight of a creature so good & dear. Always, it seems, we must injure some one that we love: always we suffer most in Paradise. I apologised. . . . I reminded her that it was teatime, & she went homewards, & would not let me go with her. . . .

Sunday, 4 August. Beautiful day. . . . There was a melting mellow sunshine over all the valley; casting pale shadows only; diffused through a warm and fragrant haze. And the abbey, grey beyond a yellow belt of corn, and the elms and firs of Warren Wood, and the long waving lines of willows by the water, and under their green & their silver grey stood groups of red and white cattle, resting and switching their flanks with the slow sweep of a lazy tail. And snowy clouds in a blue sky above. All this was around me: ineffable delight, ineffable misery. Such calm and purity without: such a storm of griefs and longings within. For I knew what it must have meant, her sitting like that all alone by her father's grave: and this is the day when I had resolved to speak . . . we sat under the verandah for long, Sarah & Alice[8] & I: and at Sarah's request I read aloud things from the Christian Year,[9] her favourites, & one thing of my own. And after my dinner & their tea, I had a talk alone with the mother, in the garden. She, placid simple soul, had noticed nothing in Sarah; hardly knew what I meant. But she told me things that made me surer still: and as I had always told her everything, so now I told her what I would do. And soon after 6 Sarah and Alice and I set off for Woking, to the service at 7. We walked by the fields, and talked of many things, and sat together in a pew overlooking the wide expanse of ancient black oak seats in the body of the church. As the evening drew on, the great roof above grew dim, and the east window shone pallid & grey: and thinking of what was to come, regrets and longings uncontrollable came over me & shook my selfcontrol, that sweet yearning face sitting by me fearful and sad, & I took her hand in mine—for once. Nothing was said, as we walked homeward after, by the fields. . . . At the foot of the church cliff, when we got to Pyrford, I sent little Alice home at 9.15; and went with Sarah up the cliff and through the churchyard, and sat down with her inside the ancient porch. And there, in that beloved place, now tenfold sad & dear, I spent with that darling two hours as bitter, and as sacred, as ever I shall have or have had in this world.

The next morning, Munby sadly returned to town before Sarah got up: 'I walked away out of dreamland, out of an Eden which I may see again, but never as I saw it until now' (5 August). He did go back in November, when he was thankful to find Sarah 'gentle, and placid too, thank goodness' (11 November); but he then virtually exiled himself from Pyrford. It

---

[8] Sarah's younger sister.　　[9] By John Keble.

was only by a strange coincidence that he was able to return to Wheeler's Farm, after a long interval, and to live and die in that house of memories.

It is clear that Sarah had hoped she might marry Munby; she noted in her journal that 'she thought he cared for her', but 'that someone else had a prior claim & a promise had been given'. Apparently she never married.[1]

For Munby this disturbing year 1867 offered another romantic obstacle to be overcome. On 15 August he arrived at the Swiss watchmaking village of Fleurier, near Travers, to stay with Julie Bovet in 'the large & handsome house' of her family. His friendship with Julie was more sophisticated, and is less fully described in the diary, than that with Sarah Carter; but essentially it will have involved him in going over the same ground as he had done with her. After an excursion with Julie on 18 August, they 'had a lovely moonlight drive down the long valley . . . a drive never to be forgotten by me'. On 21 August he left the 'sad but charming house'; Julie went with him to the station; and on 22 August Munby reflected: 'What to do next I know not: after the things & thoughts at Fleurier & elsewhere, it matters little.'

Having revisited Grindelwald, Geneva, and other places, Munby returned to London on 1 September. He must have known then that he would never marry anyone but Hannah; and on 14 September he went down to Margate to see her, '& talked over the sad story of Pyrford & of Fleurier'. He also discussed the events of the summer with Mrs. Carter, Sarah's mother, in Kensington Gardens on 25 September: a reassuring conversation that did him 'a world of good'.

At the end of September, came news of a family tragedy: the sudden death from typhoid of his young brother, Joe, the curate at Leeds, aged twenty-eight. Munby attempted to console his mother, and after the funeral they all stayed at Scarborough, where he observed the opening of the 'flithering' season. By 21 October he was able to go over to Wigan: 'a moist drizzling day', good weather for seeing coal pits because the coaldust did not blow about. His entry of that date contains a catalogue of changes and movements among the women workers, with typical encounters: 'Oi know'd ye as soon as Oi seed ye; Oi was theer when yo was talkin' wi' Sarah Fairhurst, last year.'

The diarist was subdued for the remainder of 1867. He barely showed enough spirit to record the usual Latin classes and meetings of the Pen and Pencil Club. Julie Bovet was still on his calling list: 'We sat an hour in the

[1] This paragraph is based on two letters written to Dr. A. N. L. Munby by Sarah's niece, Mrs. S. Alice Millman, in February, 1950, after press reports of the opening of Munby's deed boxes.

twilight: a strange tête à tête, considering all that has passed; & requiring much selfcontrol on both sides' (31 October).

Monday, 2 December . . . Dined at the Club, in company with Deutsch and Swinburne—Deutsch is commissioned by government to go with the expedition to Abyssinia, as archaeologist: a wild & hazardous thing, and we dissuaded him from it, now too that he has just achieved a triumph here by his Talmud article.[2] He went upstairs, & then Swinburne and I had a talk about Shakespeare's sonnets: he upholding that hateful theory of their meaning, and talking of them with an air of high moral indignation which, in him, was amusing. 'If I, or Tennyson, or any man who has been successful in poetry' said this cool young person 'had dared to hint such things, we should have been scouted as utterly indecent.' After dinner, when I was alone in the back drawing room, he came to me, & kept up a long and earnest talk, or rather declamation, about the merits of Walt Whitman & W. B. Scott. Having taken a little wine—not much more than a pint—at dinner, he was off his balance at once, & absolutely raved with excitement; leaping about the room, flinging up his arms, blowing kisses to me, & swearing great oaths between whiles. He would hardly let me go . . .

Friday, 6 December . . . at seven, I dined with Col. Pearson at the Junior U.S.; . . . At 11, after a talk in the smoking room, we parted at the club door, and I walked homeward down the Haymarket, which was quiet & dark. But in Trafalgar Square, a strong red light was on all the eastern walls; & turning round, I saw volumes of bright smoke rising above Her Majesty's Theatre, which I had passed only two minutes before. I turned back; the street was still clear, though cabs & policemen were hurrying towards it; and from under the portico of the Haymarket Theatre I saw the whole of the fire, and the gathering of shouting crowds, & the galloping of steam-fireengines, & hurrying up of fire escapes, & gleaming of firemen's helmets and marching of police and of Coldstream Guards, who came to keep order. In about ten minutes, one vast body of flame rose out of the roof of the opera house, & swayed southward, with sparks innumerable, under a north wind, while the halfmoon, in a clear sky, shone pale *blue* by contrast. By 11.30, the flames had melted all the windows & burnt through the doors, & they rolled, or rather shot tonguelike, into the street, both above and under the colonnade. Before midnight, when I fought my way out through a howling mob, the fire was already sinking; for the theatre & all its contents were consumed.[3] Home 12.30.

.Meeting Swinburne at the Arts Club on 14 December, Munby remarked that 'being perfectly sober, he was as agreeable and kindly & rational as

---

[2] In the *Quarterly Review*.

[3] There is said to have been delay in getting the alarm call to the fire brigade. The theatre was rebuilt in 1869 but demolished in 1892. The present theatre, which cost £55,000, was opened in 1897.

Talk with Eliza Hayes, aged 25,
on Rose Bridge.

"A've niver done nowt else but this wark, all t' daas
o' mah laife."

15. Watercolour sketch by A. J. Munby of himself and a colliery girl at
Rose Bridge, Wigan

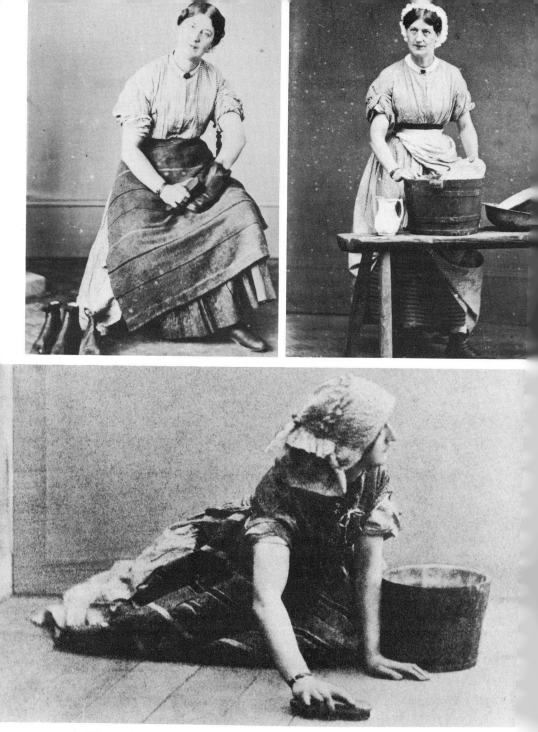

16. Three photographic studies of Hannah taken between 1857 and 1872

could be'. At York it was 'a sombre & melancholy Christmas visit; chiefly because of our dear mother, whose health of body and mind is altogether broken by poor Joe's death: so that instead of looking ever young and bright, she is become all at once elderly and tremulous in manner & looks' (28 December). The year ends with the entry:

Tuesday, 31 December . . . at eleven p.m. I went to S. Mary's Crown Street, to the midnight New Year service: a large congregation, all poor, and all quiet & apparently devout.

The last fifteen minutes before midnight was spent by all in silent meditation or prayer. Then sermon, & hymns in procession: and about 12.45 I came out with the rest, and home.

So ends this unhappy year: ending, for me, in inextricable mental misery, which is certain to grow worse and not better.

7

HIGH AND LOW SOCIETY
1868–71

During 1868 Munby's unpromising romance with Julie Bovet was slowly transformed into a rewarding friendship. She deplored Munby's association with Hannah, but was sufficiently fond of Munby to be able to give him some sound objective advice; we find him increasingly turning to her for a woman's opinion. She also kept in touch with Sarah Carter after Munby had parted from her, and passed on to him any news she acquired.

The diary yields little throughout January, and barely records the usual round of engagements; but Munby is always capable of surprises, and before the end of the month had set down a harrowing account of a mid-Victorian thieves' kitchen in the period between Oliver Twist and Sherlock Holmes.

Wednesday, 29 January, 1868 . . . Dined in Hall: home, & to my Latin class, 8 to 9. Afterwards, I met Police Sergeant 14E, by appointment, at the door of the Holborn Theatre: and we went to see the Thieves' Kitchen, in Fulwood's Rents. Up an alley, where the people stared at us: through an iron gate, down a narrow passage, down a rude old stair, across a rude lobby; and opening a door, we entered at the dark end of a large long antique cellar, low & uneven in the roof, walls irregular, and blackened with dirt and age. A large coke fire under a wide chimney, at the other end: long tables of rough soiled deal on each side the room, bare, except for a few pipes, and one bowl of savoury Irish stew: men and lads, perhaps 15 in all, lounging on benches. All thieves, man and boy; dirty & greasy & mean of face, but not otherwise repulsive. We passed through them (they were moody & silent) and went up another rotten stair, leading to the bedrooms: 180 beds here, at threepence a night. I entered one bedroom only; it was full of low truckle beds, side by side, eleven of them: nothing else whatever in it. One bed was vacant; a man having just drunk himself to death there. The landlord sat in a smaller cellar, huddled before a low fire, among lumber and dirt: a grey old man: very rich: owns land & houses: is worth, said the sergeant, not less than £200,000; all honestly made out of thieves. Home by ten.

Thursday, 30 January . . . Dined in Hall: home to dress, and then to Chalk Farm, to Westland Marston's birthday party. Hepworth Dixon was there; Sothern the actor; Swinburne; Sutherland Edwards[1]; Jeaffreson; the Duffus Hardys[2]; Maddox Brown; Robertson[3] the dramatist; and many other literary & artistic folk: notably, George Cruikshank,[4] wonderful old man, looking scarce more than 50; with grey restless eyes & shrewd face; dancing quadrilles vigorously, oddly drest in a queer *frock* coat. Swinburne, in his character of poéte réussi, received considerable homage; consequently the vain & self sufficient Dixon never noticed him. At the supper, Dixon made a pleasant speech, & Marston, as usual, a graceful epigrammatic reply: & then, after charades, the dancing began again. On the whole, & in spite of the women, who were mostly below par, it was a hearty & pleasant gathering, & such as Marston's popularity deserves. I walked home by 2.15 a.m.

Sunday, 9 February . . . to Onslow Square, & called on Mr. & Mrs. Theodore Martin. Found them both at home, & both spoke warmly of the kindness they met with at Osborne, after Mr. M's late accident, when he sprained his leg while on the ice there with Prince Leopold. The Queen came and sat by him & read to him every day, 'as if she had been his mother', he said: she sent for Mrs. M. after the accident, and welcomed her on her arrival and treated her as a friend: she sent a servant from Osborne to London with Mr. Martin, to see him safe home, and made him send her a telegram as soon as he got there. They were daily in close intercourse with her; seeing her in her room surrounded by the despatch boxes which come to her twice a day from London: for, it seems, she adheres to her husband's rule, & reads & understands a matter before she passes it: so that (said Mr. Martin) from 7.30 a.m., when she gets up, to 12 at night or 12.30, when she goes to bed, she is continually at work, except the hours of meals & exercise, and half an hour after dinner, when some one reads to her. We talked of her newly published Diary. They discussed it with her at Osborne: Helps, it appears, sends her all the critiques upon it, and the kindly and tender way in which it has on the whole been received (and even those who objected in private[5] are beginning to see that the 'abandon' of the confidence was judicious) has made her happier. 'My poor little book,' as the good Queen calls it, may turn out to have been, by its very artlessness, a masterstroke of art. Among other things, Mr. Martin said that the Royal household was the best ordered household he ever met with: every one was attentive and agreeable; every one knew what to do, and did it. . . .

[1] Henry Sutherland Edwards (1828–1906), author and journalist; first editor of the *Graphic* (1869).

[2] Thomas Duffus Hardy (1804–78), archivist and deputy Keeper of the Record Office; knighted, 1873.

[3] Thomas William Robertson (1829–71), famous for his latest play, *Caste* (1867).

[4] George Cruikshank (1792–1878), the caricaturist and Dickens illustrator.

[5] On 11 January, J. C. Jeaffreson had complained to Munby at the Arts Club of the 'injury' which *Leaves from a Journal of our Life in the Highlands* 'will do to private authors'.

Munby's pleasure in a little royal gossip (which could also be justified as research into the methods of a working woman) cannot conceal that he was restless and out of spirits during these months. He even inquired at the Colonial Office about a vacant appointment, 'the Rectorship of the Royal College in the Mauritius'—a way of escape, certainly, but, being 'a purely scholastic place', hardly a suitable solution, he decided, for his peculiar problems (10 March). Another day, he was glad to be able to go 'to the Club, to try and forget things awhile' (20 March). Perhaps his cousins the Pearsons sensed his depression, for they invited him to stay at Hyde Park Square for a few days. The change of neighbourhood gave him a chance of fresh observation in the life of London:

Saturday, 7 March . . . I was awoke before 6 a.m., by the clank of heavy pails in the street. The dawn was just breaking. . . . Down on the flags by the opposite houses, were the heavy pails I had heard, and their bearer was stooping over them—a strong stout milkwench, in warm shawl, and warm kerchief over her bonnet. She was alone in the cold dim street: she left her pails by the lamp post, took with her one of the smaller cans, and with her yoke still on her shoulders and the harness hooked together across her breast, she tramped down the street, her iron-shod boots ringing loud on the lonely pavement. And then I saw something new to me. This brave lass had been up and out of doors long before daylight, as she always is: but no maidservant was up yet, and the area gates of the master's customers were locked. Therefore she carries with her a coil of stout string, with a hook at the end. Taking this out of her pocket, she hooked it on to one of the little cans, and then rapidly unwound it through the railings, let down the can into the area, jerked the hook off, & drew up the string, leaving the can behind. This she would do at every house; so one may guess what a number of these small cans she must carry, besides her larger ones and her pails. . . .

Munby was soon up himself, and out for a walk; and in Gloucester Gardens he found a maidservant cleaning the steps and pavement in front of her master's house. It was Hannah, who had returned to London in October, when, as she wrote, Margate began 'to look dreary' and 'the niggers was gone'. As Munby approached, she seemed, in his words, 'to scrub and swill and crawl with double energy', and 'looked as if she would smile, but dared not'. Munby walked by, unable to speak to her, but reflecting: 'Yet this is she, this sinewy rustic lass, this laborious drudge, who has made the hearts of graceful and cultured ones unhappy, and has wrought such lasting influence on me.'

The servants of Bayswater came under Munby's eyes while he was dressing in the early morning:

Wednesday, 11 March . . . Six houses are visible at once from my window here: and when I looked out, 14 maidservants were visibly at work, at one or other of the 6: some dusting & sweeping parlours, in a perfunctory manner; some, hardier & more earnest, scrubbing steps & flags outside. Fourteen young women; all drest alike, in pale lilac frock, white cap, white apron, bare arms: all commonplace and indistinguishable, yet somewhat interesting, for their work's sake. Only one however worked really well: she was a lass with rosy arms, who after scrubbing her flags, brought out mats & carpets & shook them boldly in the mid-street. . . .

Thursday, 12 March . . . walked across the Park, in a fair still evening, to dine with Walter Severn in Warwick Street at 7.30. There I was introduced to his wife, née Mary Ferguson, a sister of Sir James; and to her sister Miss Ferguson. The new Mary Severn has not the unique and charming brilliancy & naïveté of her who is gone: but she is a gentle and most graceful creature, with clear intelligent face, its lines rather sharp & hard but its expression soft & genial, and a very slight elegant figure, which in a pretty antique demi-toilette made her look like a young greatgrandmother. Her baby is very bright too. Then there was Arthur Severn, and Eleanor, whom I last saw as a handsome schoolgirl before they went to Rome. She has lost her young contour, but is very pleasant & piquante, & reminds one rather of Mary. Walter has himself tastefully decorated his little house in colour. . . .

As Munby could not go to Pyrford, he found a new refuge this Spring at Edgware; henceforth places like Mill Hill and Stanmore appear often in his records of week-end excursions; and sometimes he would even go down there in mid-week. He was very conscious that all this countryside was about to be lost to 'London villas'.

The affair of Julie Bovet took time to resolve itself:

Wednesday, 22 April . . . by ten p.m., to Notting Hill, to the Wednesday evening at Aubrey House. She, whom for her own sake I so dreaded meeting, would be absent—I had ascertained this, as it seemed, conclusively. Yet she was there: suddenly we met face to face, in the intellectual crowd. So there was an end to such mental quiet as I had painfully attained. . . .

Sunday, 26 April . . . Yesterday, we had news that Prince Alfred,[6] in Australia, has been wounded severely by a Fenian: today, per contra, I found placards posted on the closed shutters of the newspaper offices, running thus: 'Great Victory—end of the Abyssinian war—Release of the captives—Magdala taken

---

[6] Prince Alfred, Duke of Edinburgh (1844–90), was Queen Victoria's second son. He was not severely wounded in Sydney, but his Irish assailant was executed nevertheless.

by storm, with 14,000 prisoners—Theodore killed!'[7] Which placards were being eagerly read by groups of people, who cried 'By Gad, what news!' And well they might: such a vindication of British prestige is refreshing, for a moment, in the midst of that decay of the English character, that dissolution of belief and of honour, which is rapidly going on around us.

Last night at the Opera God Save the Queen was played, in token of joy at Prince Alfred's escape: and so too at the Crystal Palace concert, where the telegram was read aloud, and the people stood up and gave three cheers for the Queen. . . .

Friday, 29 May . . . Went into Gatti's, idly enough, but with my own permission, for coffee; and so also into the Holborn Amphitheatre, where the pretty and girlish Pereira did the most unfeminine feats in a simple maidenly fashion: hanging head downwards, and by one leg, from the trapeze, for instance; drest, or rather without dress, like an acrobat; yet wearing her hair en chignon. After her, came a German girl, who rode a barebacked horse, leaping off and leaping on again at full speed. But she wore petticoats, though indeed very short ones: so that was proper, and the other not. . . .

During 1868 Munby acquired an interest in female acrobats that even threatened to rival his enthusiasm for milkwomen. The photographs of acrobats he now collected (see Plate 20) were, indeed, more in the nature of what were later termed 'pin-ups' than the rugged likenesses of colliery-women grasping shovels which he had tended to favour. He also made attractive sketches of 'La Pereira' and 'Mme Sinyah', and a good many other acrobats, in his diary. The Holborn Amphitheatre seems to have been the best place for such feats; and there Munby saw '"the wondrous Azella", in pink tights, leaping from bar to bar like a man' (Plate 22); while Pereira, hitherto known to him as a trapeze artist, showed herself to be an equally daring equestrienne (10 June). At the Alhambra, he watched Nathalie Foucart, whom he had congratulated for her precocious skill six years earlier,[8] appearing in an act with two younger sisters; all three performed feats on a rope which was at least ninety feet long, and Munby sketched the finale when they climbed the rope together, 'Papa, meanwhile, standing below in evening dress, looking up at his accomplished daughters with parental fondness, while the British Public cheered' (18 June). He thought of writing an article about female acrobats,

---

[7] A British force under Sir Robert Napier had been sent to effect the release of British officials imprisoned at Magdala by the Emperor Theodore, who committed suicide after the fall of Magdala, 13 April, 1868.

[8] See 10 May, 1862, when Munby described her as ten years old.

of whom he reckoned sixteen were appearing on English stages by the autumn (9 November), but apparently he never wrote it.

Saturday, 4 July . . . In the afternoon I went by train to Richmond, and walked by 4 o'clock to the Pagoda in Kew Gardens: the place where, in her sudden and startling mandate the other day, Julie Bovet had directed me to meet her. It was a lovely afternoon: warm & bright; grey clouds and fitful vaporous sunshine making a soft dreamy world of vague light and shadow in those lovely lawny groves and gardens. We met; and during a tête à tête of three hours under the trees, she told me of Pyrford and sweet Sarah, and of a strange romantic talk she has had with that dear soul, in the primrose copse that I used to love: and she consulted me too about her own plans for the future; plans which make one think more highly still of her strong earnest character and her wish for work and for affection. We went, incog., to a quiet tea garden on Kew Green; and then back to town by rail, continuing our talk in French. . . .

The holiday season opened with a week-end in the Isle of Wight.

Sunday, 19 July: Shanklin . . . Before going to bed I had a talk in the hall with Mrs. Hollier the landlady, on the evil effects of the new railway. I was about to light my candle, saying Good night: but 'Ellen!' cried Mrs. Hollier 'Light the gentleman's candle, Ellen!' And Ellen the chambermaid, who had been standing in the background, obediently came forward, took the candle, lighted it, and brought it to me again, with a slight reverence. A wellgrown and fairly robust girl of 23 or so is Ellen chambermaid: with an honest comely country face, and a rich sunbrown complexion, and light hair: and a blue ribbon in her neat white cap. She called me this morning: a knock at the door, and a soft voice said 'It's half past seven, Sir'—and Ellen came into the room, bearing a bath, and a can of water, and my boots. 'Would you like your bath the other side of the room, Sir?' she asked. If you please, I answered from my pillow; and she carried it round the foot of the bed and placed it by the open window. Dont pour the water out, please—said I. 'I must, if you please Sir; I've only one can, and there's such a many baths this morning.' So she emptied the can, and retired. All this time I was in bed: and though she talked frankly and moved about freely, as a servant, she refrained, with native modesty, from looking even once at me or at the bed. . . .

On Saturday, 8 August, Munby set off for the continent; the next morning a chambermaid at Calais brought in two cans of water, and 'talked with me as I lay in bed, and—being older than the maid at Shanklin— looked at me sans façon as she talked'. But this too seemed to Munby to suggest 'a frank and honest purity'; so honours were even. The object was the Belgian coalfield, and from S. Ghislain, Munby went on to Jémappes-Produits, his diary being illustrated by a drawing of a clean girl walking to the pit and a dirty one coming away from it. On 11 August he descended the S. Louis mine and 'saw at each getting place 2 girls, the bouteur, who flings up coal as got, into heap, with spade, & the chargeur, who loads corves from heap with spade'. Charleroy did not detain him, and he soon returned to England from Boulogne. The usual stay at York followed; and then came a visit to the Rector of Leconfield and his wife Sophy Whitaker, old family friends. Unfortunately, Robert Whitaker had a series of fits after the Harvest Festival, and Munby had to hold him down in bed, and 'was struck by the strange weird look of his face as he glared upon me: the eyes round and staring, the cheeks drawn in, the mouth rounded and protruding and emitting strange gulps of sound; the whole countenance full of insensate horror, & like a madman's.' Sophy wept, but kept 'his head cool with ice', while they waited for the doctor; and at midnight she came to Munby 'in her pretty white bedgown, to say good night', before returning to her husband's bedside (31 August). The next day, the Rector was better; and Munby set off to Scarborough, and then to Redcar, Salt-burn and Whitby, and so home again. A week later he was back in London; and, after noting that he had been elected a member of the Junior Athenaeum Club, embarked once more on the hunt for female acrobats.

Monday, 7 September . . . Went to Bishopsgate Street, with a view to a paper on Female gymnasts; for at the Cambridge Music Hall near Shoreditch Station, one such is performing, soidisant Zuleilah. The boxkeeper, a civil and very decent man, informed me that 'Zuleilah' is a Miss Foster, a publican's daughter of the neighbourhood; that she only became an acrobat 2 or 3 months ago, stimulated, like the rest of them, by the success of La Pereira; and that she is 'a very respectable girl'. I went in, and she appeared on the stage with her tutor 'Leopold', a fine muscular young fellow. Lizzie Foster herself was drest like a male acrobat, in tights, with spangled trunk hose and a sleeveless vest; her dark hair drest like a woman's, & with a rose coquettishly placed over one ear. A respectable looking lass of 18 or 20, not tall, but robust and well made; with a comely rustic face like a milkmaid's. Two 'trapézes' were hung high in air, and a third below them: she climbed up by a rope to one, and he to the other; and then she sprang or climbed, monkeyfashion, from each to each, and hung and turned and twisted to and fro and up and down, sometimes alone, sometimes along with him; for he would seize her now and then by the wrist or the ankle, and toss her about, head downwards very often, as if she were a puppet . . . a year ago, it would have seemed incredible that my sketch above is a faithful picture of an English girl, as she appears nightly, before an applauding London audience. . . .

Coming out of this place, about ten o'clock, I observed just opposite the Shoreditch Station a brilliantly lighted entrance to a 'Temperance Music Hall'. The admission was only *one penny*; and I went in, and found myself in the pit of a small and very dingy theatre, with a narrow stage. The pit was crowded with people of the lowest class; chiefly costergirls and lads, in their working clothes. There was no drinking nor smoking, as in the grander Music Halls; both, indeed, were forbidden. Rough as they looked, the audience were quiet and well-behaved; and two policemen kept strict order. When I entered, a man and a lad were on the stage, drest in tights as acrobats, and performing in a humbler fashion and on one trapéze hung low, feats such as I had just seen. The lad seemed to be about ten years old; a sturdy well knit little fellow, with broad shoulders, and a round plump smiling face, and curly hair parted on one side. He showed both pluck and skill; he climbed the rope, and hung from the trapéze by one hand or one foot, and sat astride his master's shoulder, and let himself be tossed and tumbled about, as the manner of street acrobats is with their young ones. There was nothing weak or feminine about the boy; but remembering how many female acrobats there are just now, I asked a girl who stood next me in the crowd—a shabbily drest but decent workgirl—whether the young performer were a boy or a girl. 'It's a *girl*, Sir!' she answered, briskly; and added 'She's only been at it three weeks, besides 8 days, that she practised at home. Who is she? Well, they call her The little Azella; but her name's Betsy Asher, and she's a Jewess, & only nine years old.' You know her, then? 'She's my little sister, Sir', said the girl, proudly . . .

In October, Munby contrived his annual brief visit to the Wigan pits, then spent a fortnight with his parents at Scarborough. The acrobatic theme continued: he went to Filey for a few days to meet an old friend and 'flither-lass' Molly Nettleton, to whom he had given a new rope of 24 fathoms, the year before, for the use of the girls on their climbs over the cliffs.

Thursday, 15 October: Filey . . . I went out at 9.30, and through the village and across the fields to Brail Head. Following the path at the edge of the great chalk cliff, I came to the point from which in autumn & winter weather I have so often seen the Flambro' lasses climb the rope. And then, looking down, I saw the new rope, my gift and Molly's treasure, hanging from the stake, & going down the whole height of the cliff, to the broad platform of table rock at the bottom. It was clear that Molly & her friends were below; . . . but as I looked down from the top (which here is about 250 feet up, I think) upon the black weedy scars and pools, I saw no one. . . .

Towards eleven o'clock, however, two bait girls appeared near the foot of the cliff, striding and stooping among the wet seaweed. Both were breeched up to the knee: and she, the tall one with the long legs, was evidently Molly. At that height, one could not hear their voices; but I saw them clamber up to the base of the rock, and there, Molly seized the rope, tried it with her own weight, and began to mount. Hand over hand, sticking her toes into the crevices of the chalk wall, she went up, as easily as one might walk upstairs; and having thus climbed some 50 feet, she turned round, and with her back to the cliff, worked her way along a level ledge that just supported her heels, to an overhanging point. There, stooping forward as coolly as possible, she hauled up her own full basket and her fellow's, which the girl below first tied to the rope-end. When the baskets came up, she just loosened them, and hoisted them up, with one hand, upon a broader ledge above her head: then, grasping the rope again, she climbed up to it, and sat down. It was the same windy corner-ledge on which Sally Mainprize used to sit and shout and whistle to the ships at sea: about halfway up the lower part of the cliff. For the whole ascent is like a house-gable; first the wall, and then the steep sloping roof above it. Meanwhile the other girl began to climb in like manner; and I went round and descended the rough 'trod' that leads from the cliff-top to the small flat summit of that lower spur of rock, from which the rope hangs down. From hence you see down the whole of the slope, but no further. The rope, knotted to the fixed stake at my feet, was trembling with some unseen weight; and very soon the crown of Molly's lilac hood-bonnet appeared above the lower edge of the slope. Thence, holding her basket in one hand and tugging at the rope with the other, she soon climbed up to the stake; grasped it, and then grasped my offered hand, and flung herself down beside me on the little platform of rock, panting for breath, but smiling. Her comrade followed a moment afterwards, & did the same . . . when the two had recovered breath, they began a talk, waiting for the others who were still below. . . . Dense mist clouds, borne by the strong southwest wind, had been sweeping over us, and beating on us with small searching rain, for some time: and the lasses, though they went down the Head at daybreak, had not brought their pilot jackets, and were getting wet through above as well as below. So Molly stood up for a moment and showing her tall figure at the cliff edge, shouted to the far off folk, 'Noo then, coom on, we're gahin'!' And at last the rope at our feet began to tremble again. Instantly Molly and Nan started up, and saying 'Wa min gan an' help 'em', these fearless lasses seized the rope, and before I could speak a word, began to run, Molly first, head-foremost down the dizzy slope of rock, until they both disappeared over the edge of the cliff wall below. I, the man of the party, was left in a ridiculous position; a useless spectator of these vigorous athletics. But before long, the climbers re-appeared, Molly as usual first, and carrying somebody's basket on one arm while she held on to the rope with the other. The other women followed, in single file. . . . After them came 3 fisher 'lads'. . . .

The little platform of rock was not big enough to hold us all, so the men wen on up the 'trod', and the women followed, after letting down their skirts &

Brail Head, Filey. Girl climbers on the lower part of the cliff

shouldering their baskets, each of which has its load of flithers[9] neatly covered with seaweed. Last of all, Molly, strongest and most agile climber of the group, stood by the stake, and hauled in the rope of which she was the owner. I offered to carry the coil, and did so, finding it heavy enough, until Molly insisted that Jan Beilby should relieve me. . . . When we reached the village, our party began to separate, going to their homes. Jan Beilby, when he dropt off, seemed inclined to take the coil with him; for 'them lads' are always after our precious rope. But Molly, brave and prompt, called to him to give it up; and placed it on her own shoulder, saying gaily 'It belongs to *me*'. . . .

This account of the Yorkshire cliff-climbers is one of many in Munby's diary. Their exploits, and those of the women colliery-workers and acrobats, have gone largely unrecorded in Victorian annals; so that Munby's descriptions help to fill a gap in social history.

At the end of October, Munby was drawn back to Pyrford, almost despite himself. Leaving the office early one Friday, he caught the 3.50 from Waterloo to Woking. He stood alone outside Wheeler's Farm in the twilight, wondering how everything could suddenly have gone so tragically wrong.

Friday, 30 October . . . The sun was just set as I crossed the border of Woking Common. . . . I went by the barn at Oldlands Farm; along the sheltered windings of White Rose Lane, and under the sandstone cliff where the martins build: the cattle were going home at White Rose Farm. I went by the road under the hill where the old tower stood; and met the papermill girls coming from work, as I turned up the avenue at Hoebridge Farm. Thus far, it was but a series of old associations, passages of tender pleasant regret: but once out of the avenue upon the hill, looking over the valley from the crest of Break Heart Field—*that* was the beginning of sorrows. It was dark; half past five; one could not see even the gables of Roundbridge Farm, though I knew where they were, below. . . . I stood for more than an hour on that high ridge, the night wind sweeping by, and the moon vaguely struggling to appear and shine. Should I go on, or turn across the field, by the wellknown path, by the common and the firwoods, and so back on foot to London? But I had got thus far, & who knew when I should do so again? Therefore at last I went on: down by the long line of elms, through the wild lonely copse, up the path of the cornfields into the road, and down the dark shadowy lane—after more than a year—into Pyrford. The Green was quiet and silent. . . . I partly knew what to expect at the church; for it is being 'restored', as the phrase is; and not unwisely, perhaps. It was lighted up, for carpenters were at work within. The interior was a heap of rubbish: all the old pews and seats gone, or waiting re-arrangement. A few scraps of rude old fresco, scraped

[9] Winkles and mussels.

bare, showed on the walls. Outside, the ivy is all gone from tower and gable and wall; and within the ancient porch, on the very seat where we sat during that terrible two hours, barrels of mortar were standing a-row. In the churchyard, my old tree, my darling haunt, was untouched; but the torn ivy from the church lay about in heaps, and lumber & workmen's gear were heaped upon the tomb of the old Vicar, whom I knew so well. And, as I stood near the edge of the cliff, I could see nothing of the abbey; nothing of the vale, except a waste of sombre grey, indistinguishable.

Yet after the first shock of all this, it seemed best to see things thus, so changed and spoilt; and not in that beauty which will again be theirs, but will never be ours any more. Standing in that churchyard tonight, I declare I did not know, nor much care, what to do next, or where to go: one felt inclined to lie down, and stay there. But at length I went back into the lane, and past the watermeadows (but still I could not see the Abbey) and past Master Collier's quaint old cottage; and so approached our house. The lane was very still and lonesome, as it always is; there were no shadows, for the moonlight was veiled and deadened by a watery haze of cloud; but it was fair and light. I passed the corner of the barn, and came in front of the house; I went near, & leaned upon the garden railing. There were the little grass-plots; Sarah's rosetree on one, the other flanked by her bower: my window, above, was open, & dark. Still, and cold, the long white gabled cottage stood in the cold grey ghostlike twilight of the unseen moon: I listened for voices from the parlour, for notes of Sarah's piano; but there was no sound at all, no light; and yet I knew they must be all within. Out of doors, too, there was no sound: the silence of the lonely lane was itself oppressive and painful. I stood there for a long time, as it were fixed and staring: then, seeming to hear footsteps far off, I woke and hurried away. What a mockery of all delights is this! Here in this house certain souls, I for one, have spent the very purest & happiest hours of their lives: here lives a family of almost ideal purity, piety, refinement; simple & loving and unworldly; dwelling too in this sweet secluded place. I come to them; I learn to cling to them and their home with a passionate, almost boundless, fondness; I love them and teach them, and they love me, and give me the higher teaching of their lives. No one of us has a thought of evil: and yet, suddenly all our fabric collapses with a shock that none of us can forget: one life of theirs is darkened for years; and I am selfexiled from the place and people to which I owe so much, and can never come again without sorrow and selfreproach.

It seemed to me, as I went away up under the trees of Warren Lane, that I had seldom had more to bear than this: why had I come back again to the place where this misery began? When I got to Walsham Lock, it was less acute; for the moon had come out almost clear, and above the long footbridge lay that still, broad, peaceful reach of the river, and the water falling over the lock made a soft lulling sound, as I crossed the meads into Love Lane, and so over Ripley Green to Ripley. It was 9 o'clock; too late to go back; so I went to the Talbot, where I write this. The fat landlady came forward smiling, and observed that she was 'jest enjoying a Onion, Sir'. Blessed are they who can enjoy their Onion, and ask for nothing more!

On the same day that Munby lingered disconsolately by her garden railings, 'sweet Sarah' wrote a letter to Julie Bovet describing her domestic life: a letter that Mlle. Bovet passed on to Munby. Sarah mentioned that she got up at six each morning, and continued: 'you would laugh to see my

Sarah Carter in her early-morning costume. (Diary, 2 November, 1868)

costume, while I do my morning work—making the fire, dusting, and getting the breakfast ready. It consists of a large pair of flannel drawers, into which I tuck my nightgown, a black jacket, an apron, a hoodbonnet (that Mr. Munby gave me) and a pair of gloves. Then when everything is done, I go and dress myself properly.' Munby made a drawing in his diary of Sarah in her early-morning costume. This sketch from memory is reproduced as it is the only available likeness of Sarah Carter; for the photograph that she gave Munby has not survived. The impression Sarah made on him was deep and lasting; meeting her unexpectedly at Victoria

Station, two months later, he recorded a 'sudden & fearful shock of duty and feeling' (19 December).

The faithful Hannah had meanwhile been trying to improve her status, and in May had taken a job as cook at a house in Norfolk Square, Bayswater, where she had a kitchenmaid under her. This was done with the belated encouragement of Munby, who at last decided that Hannah had had enough drudgery for her salvation. Hannah had been so thoroughly indoctrinated with his theory of humility, however, that she did not welcome the idea of promotion. 'Mr. Sanders's in Norfolk Square' was, she wrote in her autobiographical account, 'a large house where a big man was kept as footman, & several women servants—and the morning i went after the place i walk'd up & down in front o' the house feeling half afraid to venture, for altogether i felt unequal to being anything like "*upper*" not as i was afraid o' the cooking but from me always being under & never hoping nor wishing to think myself as higher nor the lowest servant in a house it was awkward & contrary . . .'

However, all went well for a time—despite the stupidity of Ann, the kitchenmaid, who once poured away the 'soup of the evening':

. . . It was ten minutes afore dinner time & then company coming—i had put the vegetables into the soup call'd 'Julienne soup' & set it for ready on the stove— she thinking to help me pour'd the vegetables in the cullender & the soup or gravy into the *sink*—without saying a word to me, & when she brought me the strips of carrot &c. i saw what was done & said, '*Oh Ann* you've thrown the *soup* away—get me the stock & more whites of egg to clear with as quick as possible'; the visitors bell was already ringing with the first comers, & i felt nearly mad, because i hated to keep the dinner back. Ann begun to cry, but i told her there was no time for that, & i clear'd more stock & sent it up very shortly. . . .

Hannah was liked by Mr. and Mrs. Sanders, and agreed to go with them to the Isle of Wight in the summer; but she made an enemy of the footman, Gower, by lifting him up and carrying him, in front of the kitchen servants.

. . . i was friendly with all the other servants—a trifle too free tho', as it turn'd out—i would have them all call me Hannah for i couldn't bear to be call'd Missis, & i joked & that along wi' the footman & all in the kitchen, & to show i was stronger nor any o' the maidservants i told Gower (the man) i was sure i could carry him easy, & before the housemaid & Ann i lifted him & carried him round the kitchen table, & i often wash'd the dishes up in the scullery to let Ann go out—but she was ungrateful, & talk'd in the pantry about my writing so much, & as i couldn't satisfy them who i wrote to, nor say i was writing diary, of course the worst was made of it & one Sunday Massa came & walk'd to & fro past the house waiting for me to come out, & this man had once lived at M's relations in Hyde Park Square & so knew him well, & again i gave my letters to the butcher boy to post when i couldn't get out, & it seems this Gower ask'd him to let him look, & *that* settled his suspicions at once, & he & the housemaid both told Mr. Sanders of it—what they said i don't know exactly but making out i was living dishonestly and so i was surpris'd & grievously hurt when i was rung for to see the Master, & he at once gave me notice to leave. I ask'd him *why*—he said, 'It's a painful thing to talk about, & I am very sorry, for Mrs. S. likes you so much in the kitchen', & he didn't seem to like telling me, but i guessed what it was about & wish'd to right myself if i could, so i ask'd him to tell me what was the reason for my having to leave—So he said—'You are keeping company with a gentleman—Gower has told me as *truth*'. I said 'Yes Sir, it *is* true—I have for a great many years, & he's a gentleman in every sense of the word, even as you are, & if you think a bit, & know how i've worked for my living as a servant, & had settled to go to the Isle O'Wight with you—right away from him, you'll know there is nor ever was anything wicked or wrong in him'. He said, I believe you, & think you perfectly honest, still if you went on & lived with us i sh^d feel you were in a false position. I said 'After this Sir, I would not go with you, & perhaps it has happen'd for my good, but I couldn't bear that you or Mrs. Sanders sh^d think me wicked or foolish'. He said 'No we shall not, I believe you are honest'. The Master had told me to sit down & there i was sitting ill at ease like a culprit almost & yet not feeling guilty . . . i made a curtsy to the Master when i went in, & when i was coming out i made another & said It's evident that Gower & Harriet have done what they could to injure me, but i will leave it alone, & i come away. . . .

This incident might have turned out worse for Munby, but it had an unfortunate effect on his attempts to persuade Hannah to 'better herself'. The following passage makes it plain that it had now become her dearest wish to remain a 'maid of all work', a theme that was to recur poignantly in later years:

. . . Massa seem'd sorry i was not going to the Island to live saying it was no further than St. Leonard's where I lived, but i think it was a blessing i didn't, for i couldn't have gone on again away from him & especially as a upper servant, for that is so opposite to anything he ever loved me for. I was got so tired of changing places, & also of that continual worry of writing to M. & in fear lest anybody sh^d know who i wrote to, & yet finding it so hard to keep the secret, that i really begun to feel so long loving was irksome & tiresome especially us not being equals. The morning after I had seen the Master Mrs. S. came down as usual, but she begun to cry & said how sorry she was for me to go away—i said 'i am sorry too Mam in one way but i think it's *best*'. she told me Harriet was not going with them, nor Ann either, but she said 'I shall always respect *you* & i wish you well'.

And so time went on and i had to think about getting another place. This was the first time i'd tried a bettermost sort, & the first time i got such high wages— 22 lbs with all found—still i saw it was no use me trying for another—indeed it was only nonsense for me. After being used to the lowest only, & M. teaching me to love rough dirty work, & this one place was quite enough, & so i resolved to go where only one was kept in the kitchen. And so this was the beginning & the end of me trying to be an upper servant . . . there's nothing like being a maid of all work—no one can think you set up or proud in that, & i'd liefer be despised than cause spite or envy from my fellow servants . . . i hope i shall always keep the same humble spirit—that of *liking* to serve others, & obeying instead of commanding. . . .

July, 1868, therefore saw Hannah installed in a small house, Mrs. Henderson's in Sunderland Terrace, Bayswater, with only a housemaid and a boy for company. As soon as she went into the dining-room there, 'i looked round & saw so many family pictures in oil that i concluded it was a *good* family tho' none of the ladies look'd pretty. . . .' In September she had moved with them to Gloucester Crescent.

During the last weeks of the year Munby found some comfort in walks in London, especially on the new Thames Embankment, now open for pedestrians, which had horrified him so much when it was building.

Tuesday, 10 November . . . To Westminster along the Thames Embankment, as usual. Here, for a time, there is a sort of quiet; there is the pale sunshine of a wintry morning; there is a great cope of southern sky in view, forms of large moving clouds, a visible sun; there is the river below the granite wall, swirling and tossing, streaked with white lights and deep shadows; and on it the brown sails of stately sliding barges, as well as the vulgar hurry of the steamers. It is better than nothing; a faint and languid reflex of the pure pleasures of a country walk.

Tuesday, 17 November . . . General Election today: polling; universal counting of heads all over England; with noise, fever of excitement, hurly burly of news-paper eloquence on one side and another; envy malice hatred and all un-charitableness (not to mention riots here and there) during the day; and at the end of the day, triumph or despair, ludicrous both, underneath the cool grey placid sky. Having carefully abstained from voting at all, I found a quiet refuge on the Thames Embankment; and dined in Hall, with Mark Hunter, and so home at 7.15: knowing this, for one thing, that J. S. Mill, thinker and logician, has been unseated for Westminster by Mr. W. H. Smith, universal newspaper-vendor, with money at command.[1]

Tuesday, 24 November.   Dined with Col. Pearson at the Junior U.S. Club at 7. Arthur Severn, and Walter Arnold, youngest son of Dr. Arnold; a manly frank intelligent man with a plain but candid and impressive face, not unlike his father's. Talk in the smoking room, after dinner, chiefly on Art, and on Gladstone's defeat today in South Lancashire.[2] We dispersed before eleven . . . and then to King's Bench Walk, to one of Sheldon Amos's[3] conversation parties. Several able talkers—among them F. D. Maurice's son—and the talk mainly on religion; disestablishment, Comtism, and coming bouleversement generally. . . .

Saturday, 12 December.   In the afternoon, went from Charing Cross to Cannon Street by rail, and thence walked up to certain old bookshops, beyond Finsbury Square. On my way back I rambled through the oldfashioned streets about Cripplegate; attracted first by the fine massive antique tower of Cripplegate church, which is a-repairing. In the quiet of a Saturday afternoon, when offices are closed and busy men departed, the world of modern life disappears for a moment, and these old 17th & 18th century streets and alleys, these deserted old churches, bring back something of the interest and delight with which one wanders through a mediaeval town abroad. Far better it is to ramble here, at such a time, than in some bustling suburb, mean, newfangled, fashionable or vulgar. I went, probably for the last time, through the mazes of old Newgate market: long low alleys, glazed in of late years, but walled on both sides with butchers' shops nearly as old as the Fire: open sheds, with massy beams and rafters and blocks, browned and polished by age and friction. Many of the alleys were closed and dark, for the butchers had removed to the new Market in Smithfield: but two or three were lighted up & busy with buyers and sellers—long rude vistas of meat and men . . .

On Christmas Day at Clifton Holme, Munby watched 'the red firelight making the old family pictures glow on the walls of the long dining room'; pictures that would have been proof positive to Hannah, who never saw them, that the Munbys were a '*good* family' (not that she doubted it).

For once Munby made no comment on the passing of the old year; he was soon back in London, walking through Blackfriars, and at a time of change in its history.

Sunday, 10 January, 1869 . . . In the afternoon, I rambled through some of the old backstreets of the City: the best possible substitute, on Sundays, for a quiet

---

[1] The election was a Liberal victory by 112 seats, and Gladstone became Prime Minister for the first time; but 'Pinafore' Smith won Westminster for the Conservatives.

[2] Though rejected by South-West Lancashire, Gladstone was soon returned for Greenwich.

[3] Sheldon Amos (1835–86), jurist and advocate of women's emancipation.

country walk. The course of the broad new street which is to run from Black-friars northeastward, is marked by heaps of ruin; but these were quiet and lovely, and full of meaning and pathos. The old houses that encircled S. Ann's Black-friars are gone, and the church stands high and bare above the open clearing. Just beyond it, are lines of tall costly buildings, facing at present nothing but ruined cellars and the débris of streets destroyed. Then came a mountainous hill, on the top of which a dozen withered trees, planted foursquare, stood out against the grey cold sky. They were almost all that remains of Doctors' Commons,[4] except a few broken archways, & the foundations of what was the Probate Court. These, and the trees, and the hill itself, will all be carted away: the Heralds' College is shorn of one side; the old churchyards near, and their corpses, have gone; the grim towers of City churches that have been spared for a time stand gloomily around: on doorplates in the dim old streets at hand, one still reads 'Faculty Office of the Bishop of London'—'Registry of the Arch-bishop of Canterbury'—and the like. Triumphant new things, and decaying old, are here brought into the sharpest saddest contrast. But, a little further on, in Great Trinity Lane, I found many quiet unmolested old houses, many silent unfrequented passages and little yards, with an old water tub at the far end, an old hooded doorway and mullioned kitchen window, an old whitecapped woman sitting peacefully before the fire within: places that are like rural England, that are hundreds of miles away from common London life. And so I came round over sombre Southwark Bridge, and back by the homely waterside streets to Blackfriars, where the river swirls through the half finished arches of the new bridge.

The Embankment had now firmly established itself in Munby's mind as one of the amenities of London:

Monday, 25 January.   The bright morning sun shone on the broad bright river, and on the white walls of the Embankment, which stretch away in a noble curve to Westminster, under the dark contrasting masses of the bridges. There is silence, except for the tread of passersby; there is life and movement, almost noiseless, on the water; there is infinite sky above. What a change from the vulgar riot of the Strand! Here is stateliness and quiet, and beauty of form and colour: one begins to feel that London is a City, like the cities of old, when men knew how to build. . . .

Thursday, 11 February . . . to a conversation-party in Blandford Square at Mme Bodichon's. A small & agreeable gathering of cultivated and accomplished women, such as Miss F. P. Cobbe, Mrs Lee-Bridell, Mrs Malleson, Miss Emily

---

[4] The former centre of ecclesiastical law, with its advocates, proctors and courts, had been dissolved on the establishment of the Divorce Court and Probate Court.

Davies,[5] & others. Had pleasant talks with several, as with Mrs P. A. Taylor on Women's suffrage, with M^rs. Malleson on hardworking hands, with Mrs Davies on the new College for Women, of which she is one of the founders. It is to open next October, at Baldock in Hertfordshire. . . .

Friday, 12 February . . . went to see the Siamese Twins, who are exhibiting at the Egyptian Hall, where they were forty years ago. It is strange to see a human being who is not completely rounded off from every other: but the apparent duality here is much less than I expected. You simply see two small elderly Mongolian men, grizzled & wizened, closely alike in feature & make & height, but each evidently in act and volition an individual. They lean on each other as they stand or walk, & the flesh bond that connects them (5 inches long and as thick as a strong man's wrist) is just seen through their open shirtfronts. With them was the daughter of one; a tall wellmade young woman, good looking, and like an English farmer's daughter, though her father is an abnormal Siamese. But her mother is an American of English descent.

Tuesday, 23 February Went to Hansard's in Abingdon Street about 5 p.m., and spent an hour there, studying the evidence in the First Report of the 1867 Commission on Employment of '*Children and Women*' (save the mark!) in Agriculture. Would that I had been one of these Commissioners! But the Northumberland Com^r, Mr. Henley, does full justice to those splendid lasses, the Bondagers. It is a comfort to me also, sitting here fastbound, to know that women so vigorous & so picturesque exist, and are at work, though far away. Home by the Embankment, where the grey mist gave one grand & sombre effects. . . .

Monday, 1 March . . . Tonight, Prime Minister Gladstone brought in his Bill for the Disestablishment of the Irish Church. This will be the prelude to the fall —in a similar sense—of the Church of England.[6] It is difficult to co-ordinate one's opinions and one's sentiments herein; when all one's interests, all one's earliest associations and tenderest feelings, are with the old régime. In this thing, too, one has to suffer & be silent; being allowed neither to share in any great work of these full times, nor yet to enjoy the peace that retirement among books and green fields can give.

Thursday, 4 March. After 5 p.m., went over Westminster Bridge—and really, what with the new Bridge, new Embankment and steamboat pier, new railway station, new Palace Yard railings, & Houses of Parliament over all, this bit of London now looks, as far as buildings go, almost like the Rue de Rivoli by the Tour S. Jacques—and walked round by the great open streets into the Borough

[5] Emily Davies (1830–1921), the unmarried sister of John Llewellyn Davies, helped to organise the College opened at Hitchin in 1869 and transferred to Cambridge as Girton College in 1873. She was its first Mistress, 1873–5.

[6] An example of unwarranted pessimism on Munby's part.

and High Street Southwark. One met numbers of working men and women, weary or sad or hard or gross, and shabby too—depressing to see: one picturesque dustgirl also, in dark boddice and lilac sleeves, and red-brown skirt, and scarlet kerchief over her shoulders; a creature unusually picturesque, who carried a great basket of broken wood on her head, and another upon her hip: and one pleasant group of dirty but merry children, dancing round an organ grinder in the street. My object was to look at the old Southwark Inns, and specially the Tabard.[7] All along the east side of the old High Street they stand, each down a covered entry; and several are now used as railway goods-offices.

I went into the yards of some, the Half Moon, the King's Head, and others. What is left of their buildings suggests the days of Hogarth, and sometimes those of Pepys; but outwardly, a few gables and overhanging upper stories are all. Lastly, by the aid of a policeman, I found the Tabard; just opposite the place of the old Town Hall, now gone and replaced by big warehouses. The narrow covered entry soon broadens into a wide roughly paved yard: on the S. side of this is a great old stable with mighty hanging roof of red tiles: eastward, a narrower yard leads away to other stables; and the N. and E. sides of the main yard are faced by all that is left of the historic Inn. Along these two sides runs the old open gallery, with wooden balustrades, projecting over the low ground floor story, and sheltered by the broad eaves of a lofty sloping tiled roof. Waggons stood below, and men were loading them; for the Midland Railway has a warehouse here; but in the galleries, linen was hung out to dry, in antique fashion; and on the east gallery was fixed a great old signboard, bearing the words 'The Old Tabard', and over them a faded picture of the garment. I stood long in the yard, recalling that old time: the Pilgrims defiling up the entry; Harry Bailey[8] shouting from that balustrade to his Knaves, Chaucer on his white steed below, the Knight helping my Lady Prioress upon her palfrey. The galleries indeed are not older than Elizabeth . . . and the railway men were bawling below: yet, how it all came back! And then I went into the bar, which is in the entry, a 17th century part of the house, and had a draught of old ale there, as a memento. The landlord said that there are 15 ancient bedrooms in the galleries, which he lets to folk by the night; and offered to show me them any day! . . .

Wednesday, 10 March.   To Salviati's, to buy some Venetian glass as a wedding present for John Liddon[9]; and to my tailor, apropos of the same wedding. What a bitter contrast to my own position in such matters! But he would be a shrewd carle who should find out that I feel it. Dined at the Arts Club, and had some talk there with little Solomon[1] the painter, an able and very pleasant fellow, quiet and unaffected. To my Latin class, and home thence by 9.45.

[7] Where the pilgrims assembled in Chaucer's *The Canterbury Tales*. It was destroyed in 1875.
[8] Henry Bailly is the host of the Tabard in *The Canterbury Tales*.
[9] See 8 April, 1869.
[1] Simeon Solomon (1840-1905) was a gifted artist whose career was to be ruined by dissipation.

Monday, 15 March.   To Negretti and Zambra's, and bought a double eyeglass: the first time I have ever needed an eyeglass at all. But my sight is growing near and dim; the first sign of advancing age—and one is not yet settled in the grooves of middle life.[2] Arthur Hedley dined with me at the Arts Club; and afterwards I went with him to the Egyptian Hall, to see the Giantess; Miss Anna Swan, of Nova Scotia, aged nineteen; a maiden eight feet high, and of vast but well-proportioned bulk; with a comely pleasant face (only it was twice as big as one's own), and a soft voice, and shapely hands—nine and a half, her gloves are—and gentle manners. She sat like a Colossus among the crowd, taller by a head than the men who stood around her; and when she rose, there seemed no end of the rising. 'I have not done growing yet, Sir,' said the stupendous maiden, looking *down* at me as she sat, and smiling. The exhibition was vulgar enough; for she stood on a platform, at intervals, while a showman described her to the people: yet she went through it all with a natural sweetness, an air of unconscious grace and dignity, as if she were Charles Lamb's Gentle Giantess, or rather some amiable Glumdalclitch,[3] unbending toward the Lilliputians. I looked up at her and spoke to her with great interest: even thus, it seemed, one might hereafter speak with some creature, like this, of a larger species, from another world; not human, yet belonging to a like grade of being. . . .

Tuesday, 23 March . . . In Scotland Yard about 5.30 today I met T. Hughes, smoking a cigar: He stopped and shook hands: 'Ah, you are going down to the House?' I asked. 'Yes, said he, this is *the* night, you know: about two in the morning, we shall have it all over.' Just so: about 2 a.m., the Irish Church Bill will have virtually passed; and Hughes, quietly smoking his cigar, goes down to vote for—well, let us say justice, in the abstract: but in the concrete, death to much that one holds dear, and possible poverty for me.

Apart from short-sightedness and frequent visits to the dentist, Munby's general health was still good. The word 'unwell' does appear occasionally in his diary, without explanation, but his energy is evidenced by his long walks in town and country. He was happy in his chambers at Fig Tree Court; 'there is an ineffable charm in this quiet ancient room: my favourite old books, my pictures on the dove-grey walls, the sunlight shining through the old panes or the green blinds, the stillness of the court without, the sound of church bells ringing: but I enjoy it all with trembling; in such a time as this, it seems—like Pyrford—too charming to last' (18 April). He contemplated a country retreat, but 'a pretty country cottage' advertised for sale at Ashford, near Staines, 'proved to be simply one of a row of new and petty "villas", without character or interest' (12 May). His

---

[2] The earliest indication of the serious trouble Munby would have with his eyes in later years.
[3] The farmer's daughter who attended on Gulliver in Brobdingnag.

social stamina remained exceptional: it was continually tested by the Theodore Martins, the Aubrey House côterie, the Working Men's College, and many more; and it equipped him not only for literary parties but also for the weddings of his bachelor friends, which now occurred with depressing frequency.

One of these was John Liddon, a colleague at the Ecclesiastical Commission, who was engaged to Annie Pennethorne, youngest daughter of James Pennethorne (1801–71), the 'government architect' responsible for New Oxford Street and many official buildings. Pennethorne was knighted in 1870; he lived in style at Worcester Park House, near Malden. Thither Munby travelled by train with H. P. Liddon, the bridegroom's brother, and other members of the wedding party.

Munby was to be 'grooms man', and Liddon was to marry the couple. Henry Parry Liddon (1829–90), a follower of Pusey and Keble, had already been mentioned in the diary as a cleric to be respected, and this wedding was to provide an occasion for Munby to study him more closely. For the next twenty years he was to become increasingly famous for his sermons as a Canon of St. Paul's.

Thursday, 8 April . . . drove from Worcester Park station to the house. In due course a large party of Liddons, Kings, Kinglakes, and Pennethornes, were assembled in the handsome hall, and we drove in procession to Malden church; a picturesque and pretty old village church, well restored. The floral crosses and monograms of Easter glowed above the rich altar; and the sun shone through painted windows upon these and upon the gay colours of the bridal party that filled the chancel and the nave. Henry Liddon, looking like a mediaeval monk of saintly character, stood at the altar and married them, the village choir singing the hymns and psalms: he went through the quaint plainspoken service with great simplicity and calmness, and also with a reverent earnestness that was very touching and effective. And then we took our bridesmaids, and marched out after the bride and groom, under arches of evergreen, and over flowers scattered by village children. And so back to the house: and then the breakfast, and the leavetaking and kissing in the hall, and the shower of old white satin shoes over the departing carriage. All was admirably managed; and there was, especially among the Liddons, a frankness and cordiality of family affection that was very pleasant to see. In the afternoon we broke up into groups, and went a walking in the grounds and the country near: I with my bridesmaid, a pretty Canadian girl, daughter of a Colonel Wainwright. Then came 5 o'clock tea, and needful repose for the girls, and a pleasant dinner at seven, and a carpet dance in the great drawingroom. I increased my acquaintance with H. P. Liddon and with Mrs King his sister, a handsome and kindly little woman, full of character and feminine ability. Henry Liddon is a remarkable man: a thorough priest in look

& manner, with an almost feminine suavity and tenderness, which captivates women and youths—and rightly, for it is both modest & sincere. The manners of a wily and unctuous confessor; but you see that the heart is that of a gentle and highsouled man. He is one of the very few men of first rate ability who continue to believe and preach as men did when Christianity was young.

We all went to bed early; and I slept in the room, full of pretty texts and pictures and books, where the bride had spent her last maiden hours.

Monday, 24 May . . . To the Arts Club . . . and dined. Had a pleasant talk with Boyse[4] about his pictures. After dinner, Swinburne tottered into the drawing-room, drunk and childish, yet capable of brilliant incoherence. . . .

Wednesday, 2 June . . . To the Arts Club, and dined there, with Alfred Bailey; and heard about Swinburne, who it seems the other day invited ex-Consul Cameron, the original author of the Abyssinian troubles, to dine at the club. Cameron, it appears is a disreputable fellow; and he and Swinburne both got drunk, made a scandalous noise in the diningroom and hall, and actually— incredibile dictu—embraced one another in some indecent fashion. The Committee have called on Swinburne to resign.[5]

Saturday, 5 June. Borland and I went down to Cambridge, to revisit the haunts of our youth: W. G. Clark having very kindly promised me rooms. . . . We reached Cambridge by 5. Drove down through the town to Trinity, and held converse with the porters in the lodge. It was 5.30, and the undergraduates in surplices were trooping to Chapel, just as we did twenty years ago! . . . After arraying ourselves in M.A. gowns, we went to dine in Hall, for dinner now is at 6.15. Munro presided at the high table; . . . Burn[6], who is growing grey already (as for W. G. Clark, he is almost whitehaired) spoke of the immense recent changes in the character and standards of university teaching, and said that college teaching too is on the eve of great change. He mentioned that there is talk of abolishing Fellow Commoners, and their quaint blue and silver gowns; and he pointed out several noblemen's sons sitting at the undergraduates' table with the rest, as pensioners. . . .

Sunday, 6 June. Brilliant summer day; cloudless sky. After leaving Borland last night, and walking awhile in the Cloisters, I went to New Court to sleep; and heard the 'boys who crash'd the glass and beat the floor' at supper parties in the rooms around; and saw a light in my old window—the room where I read,

---

[4] ?Boyce.

[5] Charles Duncan Cameron, consul at Massowah (1862), was imprisoned by King Theodore of Ethiopia at Gondar in 1864, an act which led to the Abyssinian War. He was released in 1868 and died in 1870. Swinburne remained a member of the Arts Club a little longer.

[6] Hugh Andrew Johnstone Munro (1819–85) and Robert Burn (1829–1904) were both classical scholars from Shrewsbury.

and wrote verse, and went through this and that spiritual or intellectual experience, so many years ago. But that time is not past, but is an immortal present. . . .

Monday, 7 June.   Up at 6 a.m., and crossed New Court in a brilliant morning, to breakfast in Neville's Court at seven. All the grand old college—our own college, mother of our souls—was sunny and calm, as we crossed the Great Court for the last time, and silently drove away. . . .

Monday, 21 June.   To Fenchurch Street, and went down by rail to North Woolwich, a place new to me. . . . I went into the 'Royal Gardens'; a dreary place of the Cremorne kind; with pleasant trees, however, and a terrace looking on the river. In a large hall or ballroom in the grounds, a farce, a concert, a ballet, went on successively, in broad daylight; the audience, some 200 respectable looking artisan folk, men wives and damsels. Then the hall was cleared, everyone standing around it; a couple of the new two wheeled velocipedes were brought in; and the 'French Female Velocipedists' appeared: two girls of 18 or 20, one of them very pretty, and both wellmade & graceful. They were drest as men; in jockey caps, and satin jackets and short breeches ending above the knee, and long stockings, and mid-leg boots. Thus clad, they stepped forth unabashed into the midst, and mounted their 'bicycles'; each girl throwing her leg over and sitting astride on the saddle. And then they started, amidst cheers; pursuing one another round and round the hall, curving in and out, sometimes rising in their stirrups (so to speak) as if trotting, sometimes throwing one leg or both legs up whilst at full speed: and after riding so, with the skill and vigour of young men, for a quarter of an hour, these girls halted and dismounted, and made their bow amidst thunders of applause. 'They're fine made girls,' said a respectable matron near me: and the man who had charge of their steeds observed 'They've got some English velocipede-girls at Cremorne, as rides astride like these here; but lor, they cant hold a candle to these two!' It seems that the fair cavaliers are circus-riders from the Paris Hippodrome, not unused, therefore, to bestriding a horse; and that they belong to a party of six female velocipedists who have been performing there. Before they rode, today, I had seen them in the garden, quietly drest in women's garb, walking to and fro: and in fine weather, they exhibit in the open air as well as in the hall. There was nothing indecent in the performance, or in the girls' behaviour; if once you grant that a woman may, like a man, wear breeches and sit astride in public. . . .

Saturday, 26 June.   Today the Queen was to hold a 'Grand Review' of troops in Windsor Park, in honour of her guest the Viceroy (as they call him) of Egypt. I went down; not so much to see the soldiering, as to see the spectators, and to enjoy the Park. . . . The review ground was that vast space of undulating lawn, between the Long Walk and Queen Anne's ride. On the side next Windsor, and on that next the Ride, the people stood in ranks, under the trees, to see; and carriages ranged behind them, and camp followers, 'niggers'—but no female niggers—and gipsy women brown and picturesque, and refreshment folk, behind that. Walking through the interminable crowd (for the line was so long that there was room for every one) I found little character, not much beauty of women, and no costume. Nearly all the folk looked like Londoners; few of the Berkshire peasantry were there; no smockfrocks, and no bright rustic lasses. There were numbers of maidservants from Windsor; going in twos or threes, without men, and quiet and stolid in behaviour. How do you know a maidservant, seeing her thus: Unless she be a lady's maid, you do know her at once, however smart she be. Her hands show work; and if gloved, you still see they are larger than a lady's: she has not the selfconscious selfrestraining dignity of a lady, nor the sprightly vanity of a milliner, nor the rude simplicity of a country girl living at home: her dress is less costly than a lady's, less tasteful than a milliner's; yet is an imitation of fashionable attire, which a country girl's is not, or hardly is. Her face shows comfort and animal prosperity, and does not show any culture or high intelligence; and her walk and ways have no method, no reserve; and yet, being artless, they are pleasant to behold. . . . But how incongruous to see such a girl, wearing a quasiladylike dress that well became her had she known how to wear it, to see her all gauche and careless, lolling about awkwardly, rubbing her nose with her red and bony fingers! More culture, such a girl wants, or more rusticity.

The Review, in the sunny afternoon, with a lovely background of rich foliage, and flashing helmets and gallopping horses and long walls of scarlet men, swiftly moving to and fro about that vast green lawny upland, was a pretty spectacle: 5000 or 6000 men looked few, absurdly few, to represent the British empire. Well, the empire is declining, as the race that made it disintegrates. I found myself at last near the Royal Standard and the Queen's carriage: saw the quiet little woman in her widow's cap, sitting there, with the Turk for a vis-à-vis . . .

Thursday, 1 July . . . Passing through Euston Square, about 5.30, I saw a yoke with its harness, and a pair of large cans, resting by the railings of S. Pancras church. The cans were inscribed 'J. Andrews, 16 Leigh Street': could these be Nora's cans, and J. Andrews her master? Yes! for looking round, I saw Rosyface Nora[7] herself, striding towards them across the road, her hands full of smaller cans. Seeing me, she nodded & smiled, in her blunt straightforward way; and I nodded and smiled at her: for, as for bowing gracefully, and taking off of hats, we know not of it. Both the great cans were emptied of milk; and one was nearly filled with heaps of smaller cans of different sizes. Nora put her handfuls of tins into the other, and placed her yoke on her shoulders, and harnessed herself, and lifted her load; and I walked with her homeward, in spite of grinning nursemaids and wondering ladies, and she told me of herself. 'It's three years since I've seen you, Sir,' said Rosyface; 'and I've been married two years.' And is your

[7] 'Rosyface' was one of Munby's favourite milkwomen, often mentioned in the diary.

husband sober? 'Well Sir, he does like the drink, a little. When we was keeping company, he didn't; but now, he's not exactly what I like.' And where have you been working? 'After I left Wreathall's, Sir, I was at a dairy in Marylebone 15 months; and then I was laid by, 5 months, afore I come to this place.' Why? 'Well Sir,' said she, looking down, 'I had a little baby.' And it came at the right time, I hope? 'Oh yes,' says Nora, with the pride of an honest wife, '*I* took care of *that*!' A milkwench can take care of herself in that way, mind you, as in most others. She is living with her husband in a court, Southampton Court, off the Tottenham Court Road: and her daily rounds of milkcarrying extend from Leigh Street up to the New Road and Somers Town: so she has not the honour of serving any aristocratic kitchens, poor thing! yet once, she was servant to the milkman of a Duke: that was Nora's highest promotion; but she was not proud, even then, though her master's title, 'Wreathall, milkman to His Grace the Duke of Northumberland', was blazoned on her shoulders, upon her yoke. 'It's nothing to me, all that, Sir!' she used to say. . . .

Tuesday, 6 July . . . In the afternoon I called at the Athenaeum, and then across the Green Park to the Junior Athenaeum in Piccadilly, and wrote letters and dined there: for the last time probably; for I withdraw from the club, having the U.U.C.[8] in prospect. Home to dress, by nine; and went for awhile to Sheldon Amos's chambers in King's Bench Walk; one of his 'advanced parties'; with ladies, as the Mannings, the Mallesons, &c. Talk about Mill and the 'subjection of Women'.[9] Thence by eleven I went to Onslow Gardens, to a party at the Theodore Martins'; pleasant and conversational, as usual, and some good singing, with Benedict[1] at the piano. Martin himself sang, with great feeling. Stanley[2] was there, in full costume as Dean of Westminster; clever looking little grey man, with cold cynical face but suave and catlike manner: Lady Augusta with him, and T. C. Bruce her brother: Sir John Simeon, the Thackeray girls too—Miss T. as gushing towards me and others as usual: with charming empressement, utilized me—to get her a cab! . . .

Friday, 30 July.   A soft still rain was falling when I got up; but the sky looked clearer, so I waited for the Stanmore omnibus, which passes through Edgware about 9.10: and on its box-seat I had a delightful ride to London.[3] Southward, the great grey rainclouds were lifting and soaring away, leaving a bright white horizon to the fair green landscape: the road was clear and quiet, and at roadside inns the village gossips sat on benches enjoying the cool fresh air, and the tankard. Ours is no vulgar London omnibus: we take up Farmer This and

[8] United University Club.
[9] *The Subjection of Women* by J. S. Mill had just been published.
[1] Julius Benedict (1804–85), the conductor; knighted, 1871.
[2] Arthur Penrhyn Stanley (1815–81), Dean of Westminster from 1864.
[3] Munby had been 'commuting' from lodgings at Edgware, several days a week, during this month.

Landlord That, and talk cheerily of rural matters: Saunders the driver is addressed by every one as Mr. Saunders, and the women at the inn doors enquire after his health when we stop to bait. At one pleasant house, which looks like some French house of mercy, we take up a lady in French straw hat and a cross on her breast: and the drive, one thing with another, reminds one of pleasant diligence rides of yore in France and Brittany. In London, we meet the milkwomen, going home after their morning rounds; and so descend at the Oxford Circus. . . .

Munby spent his summer holiday according to a familiar pattern—a few days talking to colliery women in and around Wigan (of which he committed a full account to a supplementary notebook); a week or so in the Lake District; a few days at York; and about ten days at Scarborough, where his mother went for her health. At Wordsworth's grave, he found

Lizzie Hodgkinson, collier at Bryn Moss pits, in Wigan High Street with the letter bag. August, 1869

an American lady 'reverently copying the inscriptions, and a fat Briton, with his wife, sat on the low wall and—whistled'. This afforded Munby a fresh insight into the American problem, and he commented: 'It will be the last humiliation for an Englishman, if hereafter reverence for English shrines is only to be found among Americans' (16 August). He drove the family carriage from York to Scarborough, with the groom sitting beside him, and stayed a night at the Talbot inn, Malton, breakfasting the following morning on potted salmon and pigeon pie: 'Apparently they had found out since yesterday who I was, and so gave me more honourable treatment' (25 August). The proprietor had probably discovered overnight that Munby's mother was a Forth of nearby Ganthorpe; his breakfast was therefore upgraded to the scale befitting a relative of a local minor squire.

The house they had taken at Scarborough, in Prince of Wales's Terrace, on the South Cliff, had a bay window from which they could see young people playing croquet in the terrace gardens; with the sea beyond, and the line of coast as far as Filey Brig. But anxiety about his parents' health, and how long they could afford to live at Clifton Holme, overshadowed his thoughts. Back in London, it persisted. The following entry emphasises Munby's lasting affection for his father; he never lost, perhaps, a feeling of guilt that he had substituted romantic ideals of his own for his father's more conventional ambitions for him. Although father and son were separated by an unbridgeable gap of confidence, Munby always loved and revered 'the father' for the good man he was.

Friday, 10 September.   Breakfasted at the Tavistock with my father; and afterwards walked with him down Southampton Street, where he stopped to look, as I have seen him do before, at the house, then Eastley's Hotel, where he spent the first days of his honeymoon with my mother.

In the Strand, I kissed his dear face and parted from him, and watched his receding figure: at such moments, it is hard to repress 'that child's heart within the man's' which cries, Come back! . . .

Munby had a rainy week-end at Gillingham and returned to London with a linnet, for which he bought a cage from a 'canine dealer'. 'Linnet, and rustic cage, and flowers in the window—how they brighten the still life of a room!' (13 September). 'Home early in the afternoon, & stayed there, with my linnet, my plants, and—a severe feverish cold' (14 September). It was a classically bad cold; Munby left the office early for the next ten days.

Saturday, 25 September.   Had a hot bath, and home unwell. In Craven Street I met Macmillan the publisher, rosy and plump, making thousands, son at Eton, & all that. He came up smiling and cordial, offered me card, so glad to see me at his country house at Streatham, would I come tomorrow? Talking of his original business at Cambridge, 'Do you know' says he 'I regret all that: I am not at all ambitious!' 'Just so' I replied: 'but some men have greatness thrust upon them.' Par exemple!

Wednesday, 29 September . . . returning from Dean's Yard, I saw at the busy end of King Street a crowd collected, listening to some musician who was play-ing a vigorous solo on the cornet. The player proved to be a young woman; and she was quite alone. A not uncomely English girl of twenty or so, respectably drest in hat & jacket like a milliner's girl; thus she stood in the street among the crowd, vigorously trumpeting. 'How odd!' said Walter Severn, who came up at the moment; 'what audacity!' Just then she left off playing, and went round among the people, soliciting money rather by her mere presence than by words or looks. She came and stood before us, the mark of the cornet still on her girlish lips; and we asked her a question or two. Three years, she has been playing thus: 'No, it does not hurt me, not the playing; but the standing and trudging about does.' At which word, Walter, fearful of the listening folk, hurried me away; and the trumpeted girl remains a mystery.[4]

Monday, 1 November . . . Every day now, and for weeks past, the river along by the embankment-wall is crowded at several points with strange craft, bringing sand or bricks for the underground railway they are making: barges and long canalboats from faraway midland waters; with rich brown sails and gaily painted sterns, and sailorlike men with picturesque wives on board: a scene of daily interest, helping one to forget the town. This morning as I passed, one of these country women, in lilac hoodbonnet & with brown bare arms, was standing in her empty barge, hauling it inshore by a rope, while the Londoners looked on from the wall above.

Saturday, 6 November . . . at 8 to Notting Hill, to the first meeting for the season of the Pen and Pencil Society at Aubrey House. 20 or 30 present: the subjects, 'Lighthouse', 'Vocation', and 'Shallows'. Amos read a good essay on Vocation: Mr. Dobson,[5] a clever young poet of vers de société, read a very bright & lively Theocritean Idyll of the Thames. Seeley, who did not contribute, thanked me warmly for my poem ('There was a man in days gone by') on

---

[4] A rare and revealing glimpse of a friend's reaction, born of long experience, to Munby's street conversations.

[5] The first mention in the diary of Austin Dobson (1840–1921), who, like Munby, was both poet and civil servant. He became a close friend and wrote Munby's obituaries in *The Times* and the D.N.B.

'Shallows' of school and creed, and hoped to see it again.[6] This from the author of 'Ecce Homo' was not unpleasant; for Seeley is a sincere man. . . .

Saturday, 27 November.   In the afternoon, I went to the 'Saturday Popular' Concert at S. James's Hall; chiefly to hear the new female violinist, Madame Norman-Neruda. The day being wet, I was able to walk quietly to a good seat in the orchestra, and so for once to enjoy the gracious blissful music fully: hearing, for instance, a Frenchman, a Hungarian, an Italian, all of them together playing out the thoughts of a German, to an English audience, who understood it all. An admirable audience, this: cultivated folk, studying the music from score, and earnestly sympathetic; yet quite simple in dress and unpretending in manner. Charles Hallé[7] played a sonata of Mendelssohn's in his exquisitely appreciative way. As for Mme N.,[8] she is a great artist, and she played without selfconsciousness. An elegant comely woman of 30 or so, drest in black velvet, she sat there, leading the Beethoven quartet as first violin, as calmly and naturally as a man would. That is the best of it; that she did not play as a female phenomenon, but was accepted simply on her merits. . . .

Wednesday, 1 December . . . Dined at the Arts Club, and by 8 p.m. to my Latin class; where a new student appeared; not a staid commonplace girl like the rest, but an elegant fashionable young person, of pretty face and serenely selfpossest manners; who exclaimed 'Oh how nice!' when any new fact was let in upon her maiden mind. . . .

Sunday, 5 December . . . to Chalk Farm, to the Westland Marstons' . . . the usual Sunday evening gathering of people literary & dramatic; the gentlemen smoking cigars, the ladies not minding that in the least. Dr. Marston and good Mrs Marston received me with all their old warmth of hospitality. I had talk with him, on novels; with young De Morgan[9]; with Mrs Lynn-Linton,[1] novelist and author of the wellknown 'Girl of the Period' articles in the Saturday Review; a quiet, keenlooking but gentle woman, with a soft voice, whom I have seen before, at Aubrey House. She was alone, and so she accepted my escort to her house in Gower Street. I gave her my arm & we walked all the way; having much pleasant talk en route, about the occupations of women, and about the

---

[6] It appears under the title 'Fallentis Semita Vitae' in Munby's *Vestigia Retrorsum* (1891).

[7] Charles Hallé (1819-95), German-born pianist and conductor, founder of the Hallé Orchestra; knighted, 1888.

[8] Wilma Maria Francisca Neruda (1839-1911), born in Moravia, was then married to Ludwig Norman. She married, secondly, in 1888, Charles Hallé, the pianist in this concert of 1869.

[9] Presumably William Frend De Morgan (1839-1917), the artist and novelist.

[1] Eliza Lynn Linton (1822-98), novelist and pioneer woman journalist, had married but was already separated from W. J. Linton (1812-98), engraver, poet, and political reformer (who became friendly with Munby at a later date). It was a long walk, at midnight, that Mrs. Lynn Linton was prepared to take with Munby, but each held highly independent views on 'the woman question'—which made them a curiously complementary couple.

theological tumults of the time. Huxley, she said, is the 'god of her idolatry': yet all her conversation showed a gentle, womanly, devout spirit. Home by 1 a.m.

Friday, 24 December . . . dined, and to King's Cross, and thence by the 5.25 pm. train for home. The streets and the stations were crowded with Christmas folk. In the carriage (2nd class) with me, were two youngish men, apparently clerks or shopmen employed in London, going to their homes near Knottingley. They talked together nearly all the way; talked of their shop doings, of their friends at home, how this one & that was getting on; of the girls & their sweethearts, of a thousand common things; and though their speech bewrayed them in trivial matters of style, there was not a trace of affectation or of real vulgarity in it; and all they said was honest and kindly and pure. There were two soldiers also in the carriage, representatives of the British Empire; one just home from Canada, a dragoon, the other an artilleryman, from Bombay. Each, with a travelled air, was glad to talk of what he had seen, and to exhibit the skins of beasts that he had shot; and the artilleryman was learned upon Telugu.[2] How did you get on with the natives? I asked—with a purpose. 'Oh very well,' said he; 'but of course I thought nothing of knocking 'em over. If a nigger didn't give me the wall, I'd knock him down as soon as look at him!' Here we have the British Philistine, & in Cambyses' vein. . . .

It was 'a perfect Christmas Day', but by New Year's Eve Munby's seasonal despondency had once more set in; 'at midnight the Cathedral bells rang out from far, in a dark & misty night, a night that well accords with the mental gloom and turmoil in which I close the year.' The habit of annual stocktaking always depressed him.

New Year's Day fell on a Saturday, which enabled him to remain at home over the week-end. Though his mother was far from well, she was not without 'help in the house'; not only did her daughter live with her, but she had a staff consisting of a personal maid (Munby's old nurse, Carter), cook, housemaid, kitchenmaid, groom, gardener, and needlewoman. 'Thus we live, for awhile,' wrote Munby, 'in this roomy house and fair garden so dear to me, on our own little estate of twenty acres: doing our best not to think of that Inevitable, which my mother's ill-health suggests with horrible agonising precision' (1 January, 1870).

Munby travelled back to London by the night train on the Sunday, and resumed work at his office on 3 January.

Thursday, 20 January, 1870 . . . at 5 p.m. went to audit the accounts of the Working Women's College, at the Mallesons' new warehouse (Fearon & Co.) on the Holborn Viaduct. This took me two hours and more; sitting with Mr. Frank

[2] The Dravidian language of the central and eastern portions of South India.

18. Hannah at Dorking, 1874, after her marriage

17. Hannah, 1872

19. Collier girls at Wigan between 1867 and 1878

Malleson up in the private parlour of the firm. The new warehouse is a great place, handsome with oak and polished brass and plateglass and marble; substantial, vast, with ranges of full cellars running under the viaduct; with clerks and mahogany desks below, and great vats aloft, visible through the walls of the parlour, which are glazed so as to place things well under the masters' eyes. And all this, for what? Why, for selling spirits. Last Christmas Eve, said Mr. Malleson, *fourteen-hundred pounds'* worth of spirits were sold by them on the premises, wholesale and retail. A hideous trade, a hideous life, it seems, to me: and yet these two brothers are both excellent and earnest men; and one of them at least is a man of culture & strong understanding, taking a lively interest in liberal politics. Both, too, give largely to such works as the Women's College. One of the parlourwindows looks down on the retail bar, where people come and carry away spirituous drink in bottles, though they do not drink it on the spot. Through this window I saw men and women coming & going in the bar, getting their bottles filled; and behind the counter stood two barmaids, of superior aspect; quiet young women, drest in ladylike fashion, who were pouring out whisky and gin as fast as they could. On Christmas Eve, said Mr. Malleson, they stood there, serving out spirituous drinks, from seven o'clock in the morning till eleven at night. That was *their* Christmas Eve; and both these barmaids are students at the W.W. College. . . .

This afternoon . . . in Waterloo Place I met a milklass of Sims's Dairy, who was not wearing a yoke and pails like the rest, but was—gracious heavens! taking round milk *on wheels*. She was pushing along a threewheeled cart, in the midst of which stood a gigantic milkcan, some four feet high, and around it a number of smaller cans such as a milkmaid carries hung to her big ones, and a basket for eggs. . . . How do you like wheeling *this* thing about? said I. 'Not at all, Sir!' she promptly answered. What, you like wearing a yoke and pails better? 'Yes, Sir, a deal! The yoke keeps you warm in cold weather'. . . .

Friday, 21 January . . . At ten, I went down to King's Bench Walk, to a conversation party at the chambers of Sheldon Amos. . . . I had some conversation there with Moncure D. Conway, the able American who preaches a transcendental Theism at the quondam Unitarian Chapel in Finsbury, where Huxley and other savants also hold forth on Sunday evenings about Science. He explained that 'having got rid of all superstitious notions about Christ, we are able to study him as the central religious genius of the race': and added his belief that in a century hence, Christians will be glad enough to retain *that* much of their Xtianity against the materialists. *We* shall know more, by then.

Munby had learned by bitter experience to avoid romantic involvements; and this aspect of his relationship with Mlle Bovet had now been transcended. She remained demanding, however, and Munby meeting her at Euston Square railway station, 'at her request I jumped in, and went as far as Willesden, discoursing of her affairs. I got out there, and returned by the next train. . . .' (22 January.)

Friday, 28 January . . . in Hanover Street I came up with Ann Bradley, warmly clad in her coarse clothing, a brown woollen kerchief over her bonnet: she was stooping over her great cans, and settling the yoke on her shoulders. Well, Ann, I've got your coalticket! 'Indeed and I thank you, Sir,' said she, standing up, ready harnessed; yet seemed hardly to realize the great fact. But you must give me your address; and I'll go into that house there, & write it, and you wait outside for me. 'Thank you kindly, Sir; but the master—' said Ann, looking scared—'it's my time to be in! If I could take my pails in, and come back—I've got to come out again wi' the cream, Sir?' And so she started for the Alderney Dairy, trotting roundly between her cans; & I went into the club, and wrote down her address, 7 Barrett's Court Oxford Street; the milkwomen's quarter. Coming out again, I descried our hardy Ann, running towards me up the street, and without her yoke and pails. I gave her the tickets; for a ½ cwt. of coals, and (what she did not expect) for 2 lbs. of bread: and when she saw, for she can read, that the thing was true and certain, she broke forth into thanks. 'The Lord spare you, Sir!' she cried 'the Lord spare you long! Nobody ever thought to do the like for me!' 'We've no coals,' she added, half to herself, 'I'll go and get 'em tonight!' So I shook hands with her, and she went away happy: girl of two and twenty, earning a living, out of doors, not only for herself, but for a consumptive husband and two children. . . .

Tuesday, 15 February . . . Today I dined, for the first time as a member, at the University Club; and afterward read—that charming new Life of Jane Austen[3] —in the smoking room and the library. The inner library of the Club is to me a delightful room: so quiet, so redolent of old memories, so fit for learned leisure; and reminding me of similar rooms in private houses and at the University. Somehow, one feels hardly worthy of all this: feels, also, that it might lead to selfish indulgence, to morose old bachelor habits. To me hitherto, the refinements of art and literature and society alternate, in piquant contrast, with the simplicity of country life, the robust and homely joys of intercourse with working folk; of which last, no one that I ever meet seems to have the faintest knowledge. . . .

Wednesday, 23 February.   To the Arts Club, and dined there, with Emmanuel Deutsch: thence to my Latin class at 8, and home from that by ten.

I had a long and interesting—painfully interesting—conversation with Deutsch at the Club. Beginning with the Moabitish Stone of King Meshech, the discovery of which he has just announced in the Times, we went on to the Jews, Deutsch affirming that in no other country has he found them so degraded as in

---

[3] The *Memoir* by J. E. Austen-Leigh.

England, and that this is the fault of the English, whose vices, and notably that of moneymaking, they exaggerate: and then came our chief talk, about Judaism and Christianity. Deutsch, himself a Jew by descent, said to me with almost passionate earnestness that the Jews, in the time of Christ, had so purified their religion by allegorizing it, had spread such pure and noble culture over all their own land *except Galilee*, that they might and would have done infinite service to the Roman and the modern world, *but for the triumph of Christianity*. And when I pressed him with the lofty teaching and high character of S. Paul and S. John, he said that their words were as far below the level of the Jewish thinkers 'as the Family Herald is below the Quarterly Review'. He, a learned theologian and Talmudist, reports *this* as the result of the studies which (as he assured me) he began with the desire of becoming a Christian. I was greatly moved by his discourse; and could not help laying my hand on his shoulder, almost affectionately, as we parted.

By the end of February, Munby had been worn down by a cold winter. He longed 'for health's sake' to go to Italy (24 February); and a week later was 'low in "tone", listless, oppressed with headaches' (2 March). He must have complained to Hannah, and perhaps blamed his liver; at all events, what he said was enough to bring Hannah to the Temple at full speed. She arrived about nine o'clock on a Saturday evening, 'so out of breath with running, and so flushed and overjoyed with the excitement of her escapade. . . . "I was sent out for the supper-beer, and I was so sorry to hear you wasn't well, so I thought, I'll just run down and see, and maybe they'll never miss me. And *that's* what I come for—to give you them two pills. Them pills" she went on "has took away my belly-ache, and I'm as strong as ever again; and they'll take away yourn! You take 'em tonight—they won't gripe you much, and they're *good*; better nor them as I give a penny a-piece for." I promised. . . .' Hannah was off again immediately. '"Goodnight, Master!" she said; "I'm so glad I come. . . ."' And I heard her thick boots ring along the silent courts, as she fled away to catch the train. . . .' (5 March).

Munby does not describe the effect of the pills, but they did not cure him, for he 'went to Cavendish Square, to consult Mr. Ashton the eminent surgeon about myself' (23 March).

Saturday, 26 March . . . I went, at 5, to the meeting of the Women's Suffrage Society at the Hanover Square Rooms. The large room was full: the audience chiefly welldrest women, old & young, whose carriages filled the square outside; but on the platform were many men. Numbers of my acquaintance of the Aubrey House set were present; and in the chair was my friend Mrs Taylor herself. I had thought it would seem strange, but it seemed quite natural, to see that gentle earnest ladylike woman acting as chairman of a public meeting, and to see other ladies standing up on the platform and making speeches. There was nothing 'bold' or unfeminine in their words or manner: and the two best speeches I heard (I heard four altogether, but not J. S. Mill's, who was sitting by Mrs Taylor) were made by women: Miss Helen Taylor, who did the rhetoric ably, and M^rs. Fawcett,[4] who was logical and calm. Many aspects of the question, however, were not touched at all. I left at 6. . . .

At Easter, Munby was able to get away to the New Forest:

Thursday, 14 April . . . Waterloo Station was thronged; the train crowded with welldrest folk, hurrying south; and on the platform at Basingstoke I found myself standing next to the Prince of Wales, whose three fair children were laying their faces to the carriage window close by, while the Princess sat within: all going by our train to Osborne. Prince, in billycock hat, smoking cigarrette, loudly laughs, jauntily walks up & down in the crowd, talking to this man and that. Thus does this Prince represent to us the long result of his race, the outcome of 800 years of English history. . . .

Munby stayed at the Crown in Lyndhurst, admired Leighton's fresco in the church opposite, and visited the Rufus Stone. 'The stone records the name of *Purkis*, the carter who carried off Rufus's body in 1100; and on the ground, leaning against the stone, I found one of the carter's descendants, sitting to be photographed. Mary Purkis, was her name; a servant (so they told me) in a family near here' (15 April). He explored the Forest as far as Lymington, and crossed to the Isle of Wight on a day excursion. Going on to Bournemouth, he met two Pearson cousins, and walked over 'bold and broken sandcliffs, with the wild moors atop, studded with new houses yet still wild' (18 April).

Monday, 2 May.　To the Arts Club, & dined there: and after dinner had a long tête à tête with A. C. Swinburne. He was reading his own article in the new Fortnightly on Rossetti's poems; of which poems, though they have only been out four days, he says that nearly a thousand copies are sold. Several of these poems were known to me long ago in MS.: and after discussing their beauties, we came naturally to Victor Hugo; 'my dear master Victor Hugo', as Swinburne calls him. Then came Newman's Grammar of Assent; and so, malgré moi, the wild poet got upon Christianity, and foamed and danced as his manner is; though certainly with less of irrational fury than of old. With him, as with all

---

[4] Mrs. Henry Fawcett (1847–1929), or Dame Millicent as she became, had made her first public speech on women's suffrage in 1868, and was soon the acknowledged leader of the movement.

freethinkers nowadays, the Church of Rome *is* Christianity: of direct communion between God and the soul, of the sense or the fact of *sin*, they seem to have no idea. The superstitions, wars, persecutions, caused by Xtianity, are all they think of: and Swinburne raved about these, and refused to hear of the other. 'Montalembert!'[5] he cried, and literally leaped into the air, clutching his hair with both hands as he did so. 'Ohoo! its glorious—he died *damned* by his own cursed set!' And yet he said, and truly, speaking of the character of Our Lord 'I always find myself an atheist among Christians and a Christian—I mean a philo-Christian—among atheists'. By 'atheists', he in his loose way meant freethinkers. 'When I was sixteen,' he added, 'I was a devout Christian; and I remember the intense emotion with which I received my first sacrament. But then, I believed it all, as my ancestors did!' And he blew kisses with his fingers; as he always does, ridiculously enough, to illustrate strong and keen delight. In the midst of his tirade, a clerical member of the Club came in; but Swinburne went on unheeding, till I turned him (variable and inconsecutive as his flow of talk is, it was easily done) into Shakespeare's sonnets. This however led to worse talk; he expressed a horror of sodomy, yet *would* go on talking about it; and an actual admiration of Lesbianism, being unable, as he confessed, to see that that is equally loathsome. When I expressed disgust pretty strongly, however, & regret at what he has written thereon, he took it very gently and quietly, instead of blustering, as he used to do. And at last, when he went down to dine, he wanted me to come too: 'Won't you come and finish our talk?' he said. But I declined: it had rambled on quite far enough. Without affecting to go beyond my tether, this man is to me an object of grave and pathetic study: a creature he is so reckless and childish & ungovernable, so far from all sobriety and restraint, from all ordinary moral sanctions and beliefs: and yet so full of genius, of noble enthusiasm for freedom and beauty; and so genuine, and kindly in his way, and unpretending.

Him also God has made and gifted; and though it is useless to guide or check him, one feels that God may do so.

I walked home by 9.30.

Wednesday, 4 May . . . At 4.30, I went to S. George's Hall, Langham Place, to my friend Ralston's (gratuitous) lecture on Russian Folklore. The Hall was crowded, and with people eminent in various ways. Near me sat *my* 'dear master', Thomas Carlyle, rarely seen abroad; his earnest reverend face looking worn & sad, as befits this troubled time,[6] and his figure bowed with age: around him were Sir Roderick Murchison, Owen, Huxley, Sir W. Stirling-Maxwell, A. H. Layard, George Macdonald, Sala, Hepworth Dixon, many more. All these came to hear my old friend, whose success was brilliant . . .

[5] Charles de Montalambert (1810–70), French Catholic historian of liberal views who offended the Ultramontanes.

[6] The worsening relations between France and Germany, in which Carlyle took the German side, may be what Munby had in mind. The Franco-Prussian War began on 15 July.

Thursday, 5 May . . . to Ralston's rooms: he is off soon to Baden, to meet Tourguenef[7] the Russian novelist and go with him to Moscow. Thence to the Arts Club, & dined there. . . . I read through, with judicious skipping, the first volume of Disraeli's Lothair, which is now the rage: & would not for worlds read the other two. One sees in it the craft of a practised writer, glib and epigrammatic and well varnished: but the so called 'great world' described in it, the arrogant Sybarites and sparkling politicians & voluptuous women, these I have seen and detested for myself: *they*, indeed, to make light of the grave and tender simplicity of Nature and her homely ones!

Coming home, a French harlot followed me, saying often 'Je ferai tout ce que vous voudrez, Monsieur—je suis aimable et polissante!' Sad pathetic words: for she looked womanly withal: and I saw her stoop down, in her fashionable finery, to pick up for a stranger his stick, which he had dropped in passing her. . . .

Today, in Whitehall, I saw a May Day band of chimney sweepers: Jack in the Green amidst, and a King in gilt cocked hat & gilt coat, and a Queen in a black velvet jacket with spangles and a round hat and short gauze skirt, gay with ribbons, & pink stockings; and a clown, & two or three others. All danced around the 'Green', & the Queen brandished the long-handled gilt spoon in which she gathers offerings. She was a goodlooking lass of 18 or so; and she danced vigorously down the street by my side, till I gave her something, not unwilling.

Saturday, 14 May . . . The gates of the Temple had been shut all the forenoon: and about 3.30, when I returned, the ceremony of opening the new Hall[8] was over, and the folk in their shining garments were driving away. Scarlet cloth to walk on and a pink striped canopy; flowers and shrubs lining the southern stairs; the band of the D.O.[9] playing in the Gardens close by; and a few laundresses and other familiars (for the public were shut out) looking on while the carriages drove up, and fat bedizened wives, and smiling daughters in false hair and flummery, drove off with Papa. Judges and Q.C.s and those barristers who had been present, wore wigs and gowns: but Lord, to see how gladly the judges did cast off their fullbottomed wigs, being entered into their coaches! Came Vernon Lushington Q.C., and I did greet him friendly, albeit he was clad in the gorgeous costume of a kind of British Admiral, with gold epaulettes, & cocked hat & sword, and shining white breeches of sattin, fair to look upon. . . .

Monday, 30 May . . . At ten I walked to the Blackfriars Station: for the railway beneath the Thames Embankment is opened today, from Westminster to Blackfriars. So by rail to Onslow Square, to a large musical party at the Theodore Martins'. While I was in the tearoom before going upstairs, J. E. Millais and his

---

[7] Ivan Turgenev (1818–83).
[8] Of the Inner Temple, by the Prince of Wales and Princess Louise.
[9] 'Devil's Own' (the Inns of Court Corps).

wife came in. She, the wife of two men, has lost the beauty that got her a second husband in the friend of her first; but looked well enough & was sumptuously drest. He is still a fine man; but red and gross in the face, and with his old vain and sneering expression changed for one of a coarser hardness. He spoke gruffly to his wife, who answered not: and so they went upstairs to smile. In the handsome drawingrooms I found as usual store of folk with handles to their names and folk with distinctions of their own, made as once I thought to make for myself: and gorgeous women old and young, in fluff and feathers and brilliant silk or gauze. There was a girl with a sweet unspoilt face, the daughter of some Irish Bishop, who sang with charming grace of voice and countenance: and a foreign tenor with an exquisite 'timbre'; and so on. One of the finest women present was M^rs. Brookfield, wife of the parson,[1] whose clever striking face was with her. She was Thackeray's great admiration; and tonight, D. G. Rossetti and I agreed in praising her; a lovely matron, ample and sweet and strong, in handsome but simple dress of black & blue, and hair all her own, simply worn, and still a shining brown. I had a good deal of pleasant chat with Rossetti; he is too great and too mature to be spoilt or elated by the success of his Poems: on the contrary, his nature seems to me gentler and more expansive than when I first knew him, some 15 years ago; and even then, he was famous. . . .

Tuesday, 31 May . . . went to a ball at Mr. Wornum's, the keeper of the National Gallery. There I had a long talk with Woolner the sculptor, about pictures and society. He asked me to see his Turner collection—for he is now rich and can indulge costly tastes—and had many stories of heaps of Turner drawings, heaps of Linnells & Mulreadys & Morlands, sold in little shops 30 years ago for a few shillings the bundle. His cinnamon beard is growing grey; but he gazes on you with the old fire, and talks with the old brusque rough force. Speaking of Rossetti, he would have it that R.'s is 'an Italian nature'; all for effect and dramatic point—not consciously insincere, yet highly artificial. Sélon moi, it is not so.

Munby spent the Whitsun holiday at Clifton Holme with his parents, returning on 10 June, to dine at the Arts Club and discuss with Edmund Yates and others 'the death of Charles Dickens, who died yesterday at Gad's Hill, of paralysis, aged 58'.

Saturday, 11 June . . . to the University Club and read there till 9.30; and coming home, went round by the Oxford Music Hall, to see another female acrobat, soi-disant Md^lle de Glorion. She came forward to the footlights hand in hand with two male acrobats; she was drest much like them; and she made a bow, and not a curtsy, to the spectators, as they did.

---

[1] William Henry Brookfield (1809–74). The Brookfields' married life had not been entirely happy, and Thackeray, who loved Mrs. Brookfield, had had to withdraw from their friendship.

A very pretty English girl, she seemed to be, of 18 or 20 years; trim and slight and shapely, standing about 5 feet 4. The only clothing she had on was a blue satin doublet fitting close to her body and having very scanty trunk hose below it. Her arms were all bare; her legs, cased in fleshings, were as good as bare, up to the hip: the only sign of woman about her was that she had a rose in her bosom, and another in her short curly hair. She began the performance by placing the nape of her neck in a noose at the end of a rope that hung over a pulley aloft; then, hanging so with her head thrown back, she cleverly hoisted herself up, by hauling at the other half of the same rope, to the triple swing or trapéze, some twenty feet above the stage. There she sat, side by side with her two male companions; and went through the usual gymnastics; hanging head downwards, hanging by one leg or one knee; sliding down headforemost over the body of one of the men, and then catching her feet under his armpits, and coming up again by grasping his body between her knees and his leg with her hands, whilst she brought her head & shoulders up by a strong muscular effort; and lastly, balancing herself on the small of her back upon the trapéze, till at a given signal the two men, who were hanging head downward on either side of her, each seized one of her ankles, and pulling her so by main force from her perch, flung her bodily forward and downward, and so held her upside down in the air, her limbs all sprawling apart. The shock to her brain and to all the joints and sinews of her body must have been tremendous: yet this is what she, and many other young women, do daily for a living; and she was rewarded with great applause by the crowded hall, as the men dropped their hold and left her to grasp and slide down a loose rope alone. But this was not all: for the 'chairman' got up & said 'Ladies & Gentlemen, Md^lle de Glorion will now take her daring leap for life, along the whole length of the hall'. And the fair acrobat went down from the stage among the audience, alone, and walked, half nude as she was, through the crowd, to the other end of the long hall, and there went up a staircase into the gallery. She passed close to me; taking no heed of any one; her fair young face all crimson with heat and wet with perspiration; and climbed the rope ladder that led up from the gallery to a small platform, just big enough to stand on, which was suspended high up under the ceiling. There she stood, in sight of all the people; intent on preparing for her nightly peril, and taking no thought (nor did they, I think, just then) of the fact that she was almost utterly unclothed. Two strong parallel ropes were stretched from hooks in the roof, fifty feet off, to the platform where she was: on the stage, far beyond that, one of her mates was hanging inverted from the trapéze, awaiting her; but he was wholly hidden from her by two great discs of paper stretched on hoops, which were hung near him, one behind the other, above the footlights. And she had to swing herself, high over the heads of the crowd, across that great space of eighty feet or so, and leap through the two discs and alight in his inverted arms, which she could not even see. A fair girl of eighteen, preparing in sight of all men for such a feat as that; perched up there, naked and unprotected, with no one to help her; anxiously testing the ropes, chalking the soles of her feet, wiping the sweat off her hands and her bonny face, and trying to smile withal. One must suppose that if she had not been an acrobat, every man present would have rushed to rescue or assist her: as it was, she had hired herself to do the thing, and they sat still to see her do it. She did it, of course; she leaped into the air, and in leaping, left the ropes that swung her, and dashed through the two hoops, and was seen hanging in the arms of her mate, grasping his body, her face against his breast. A moment more, and she had lowered herself by the loose rope to the stage, and was bowing and smiling amidst thunders of applause. And so I came away.

Ought we to forbid her to do these things? Certainly not, if she wishes to do them and if *men* may do them unforbidden: the woe is with those by whom such offences come. And, though it is not well to see a nude man fling a nude girl about as she is flung, or to see her grip his body in mid air between her seemingly bare thighs, I think that an unreflecting audience takes no note of these things and looks on him & her only as two performers. Still, the familiar interlacing of male and female bodies in sight of the public is gross and corrupting, though its purpose be mere athletics. Tonight, when the girl was sitting on the trapéze with her comrades, resting a moment after having climbed up there again from the grip of their hands or feet, she observed that one of their shoes had left a stain of dust on her pink thigh. And she called his attention to it, and wetted her handkerchief and wiped the place; just as nonchalante as if she had been in her own dressing room, and not there, aloft and under the gaze of several hundred people.

Wednesday, 15 June . . . In the afternoon I went to Westminster Abbey, and saw the place where Charles Dickens was buried yesterday morning so quietly, in Poets' Corner. The grave was filled in and flagged; but the floor was strewn with flowers, laid there for him by those who came to see. I walked up to the Arts Club, & dined & sat there. . . . Swinburne sat apart with a book; wildly kicking out, after his manner, at any passage that roused him. Thence at 8 to my Latin class. . . .

Saturday, 25 June . . . I went down by 3 p.m. to Twickenham by rail, and walked thence towards Isleworth (2 miles) to see the market gardens and the Shropshire girls, and find out if their ways are as of old. A short mile from Twickenham, a footpath leaves the road, and runs between hedges of market gardens, right into Isleworth. Following this, I soon was aware of many female voices talking together in a field on the left; and coming to the gate, I saw that the field was full of orchard trees, and gooseberry bushes beneath them; and a wide border of rough ploughed land around the orchard. And among the trees, one heard the sound of hoes smiting the ground, and saw figures of women and girls, rough-clad and picturesque, moving to and fro, half-hidden, and talking quietly together. These Dryads soon began to peep and peer at me; and one girl from her tree called out 'What's the time, Master?' So I opened the gate and went in, and talked with the nearest group; who were moving among the bushes, hoeing with long hoes the weeds there, and clearing the soil. They received me without any roughness or immodesty; with a little giggling at first, which soon toned down, being not encouraged; and each girl leaned on her hoe and looked at me and answered, and then went on with her work and her talk together. Half a dozen strong and hardy young women; all in rough decent clothing; and some, by speech and dress, distinctly Staffordshire or Shropshire. Which of you is Shropshire lasses? I began. 'I am!' cried one, and 'I am!' another, all round; and 'I'm a Cockney', said a girl who wore a slouchy gown instead of the Shropshire smock. One came from Wellington, one from Oakengates, and so on. And is there any pit-wenches among ye? Again came a shout of 'Yes!' and 'Aye, a many!' 'I've worked on pit bonk most o' my days', said an Oakengates lassie near me, Annie by name; a stout fair girl with sunny face and hands, who looked well in her cotton hoodbonnet and red neckerchief, and smocksleeves, and a short skirt made out of an old sack, on which the maker's name, & the word Flour, was conspicuous in large black letters. . . .

They come from the Black Country, these women, about the beginning of June, when pit work is slack; and work here in these market gardens for nine weeks or so, and then go back when the fruit is over, in August. Our Master has 48 women, and about 30 of us is Staffordshire and Shropshire, and t'others is Cockneys and Irish. . . .

Monday, 4 July . . . my brother Fred arrived from Manchester. He dined with me at Rouget's, & then we went to Westminster, and, as he wished it, we went into the Speaker's Gallery of the House of Commons. Education Bill going on, in Committee: W. E. Forster,[2] redbearded, affable, explaining to Hon. Members why we feel sure that Religion must be tabooed; redfaced Lowe, hat brim shading his albino eyes, sat silent; Gladstone, thin haired, with gaunt penetrating face, is restless; talks to this one & that; wipes his spectacles; unfolds clean pocket handkerchief suggestive of Womankind. Lowe, a parson's son: Gladstone, a trader's; Forster, a manufacturer; Stansfeld, a brewer. Mais il faut descendre encore, un peu! Meanwhile, here are 290 sleek prosperous men, kindly moulding the Future for us; sweetly persuading themselves that Revolution has *not* set in. . . .

Wednesday, 13 July . . . Today the Thames Embankment was opened, *not* by the Queen, but by the P. of W. and his sister Louise. Col. Pearson and I went and saw the procession, a miserable mean affair; but the noble outlines of the roadway were marked by brilliant pennons on high and banks of shrubs and tree ferns below. And all the afternoon, folk on foot and in carriages were enjoying the new wonder. . . .

---

[2] William Edward Forster (1818–86), Liberal M.P. for Bradford; successful sponsor of the Endowed Schools Bill and the Elementary Education Bill.

(25 Saturday, continued)
and one girl from her tree called
out "What's the time, Master?" So
I opened the gate and went in, and
talked with the nearest group; who
were moving among the bushes,
hoeing with long hoes the weeds
there, and clearing the soil. They
received me without any roughness
or immodesty; with a little giggling
at first, which soon toned down,
being not encouraged; and each
girl leaned on her hoe and looked
at me and answered, and then
went on with her work and her
talk together. Half a dozen strong
and hardy young women; all in rough
decent clothing; and some of speech
and deep, distinctly Staffordshire
or Shropshire. Which of you is Shropshire
lasses? I began. "I am!" cried one, and "I am!" another, all
round; and "I'm a Cockney," said a girl who wore a slouch
gown instead of the Shropshire smock. One came from Wellington,
one from Oakengates, and so on. And is there any pit
wenches among ye? Again came a shout of "Yes!" and
"Aye, a many!" "I've worked on pit bank most o' my

Part of Munby's diary, 25 June, 1870

The joys of the Embankment did not satisfy Munby as the summer heat
grew stronger; he longed for the continent but was prevented by 'the madness of the war surrounding us' (2 August) and by his mother's fears for
his safety; he thought of Norway, but was deterred by the sea voyage and
the expense; and so at every opportunity he made for Chatham, for Box
Hill, for Godalming, Haslemere and Hindhead. 'What news?' he asked at
Ludgate Hill, returning from Chatham on 7 August. '"Lots, Sir!" cried
the Guard: "great battle at Worth; 4000 prisoners; two Eagles!" he
exclaimed; taking it for granted, as I have done, that the Prussians were
victorious. So they are: which means, one may hope, the fall of the
Impostor.'[3]

Monday, 8 August . . . dined . . . at the Arts Club. There I learnt that Swinburne
is no longer a member of the Club: he has resigned, to save himself from expul-
sion, on account of his gross drunkenness. A sad case; far worse than that of

[3] Napoleon III.

Coleridge or Hartley Coleridge: for Swinburne seems to have no conscience, no sense of shame, at all. . . .

On Saturday, 20 August, Munby travelled up to York, noting the increase of girls selling newspapers in London streets, 'partly due to the war' which had led to a demand for the dailies as well as the evenings. He spent the greater part of the next day in the garden: 'that delightful garden which I enjoy always with a kind of tremulous awful enjoyment, as knowing not how long the joy may last. The lawn, with its borders of shrubbery and of bright geranium beds, and its bower of weeping willow in the midst; the long straight terrace, and its long laurel hedge; the low ground below, where our cows are feeding, and the lofty chestnuts beyond; the river meadows fair and dotted with trees; the red town-roofs far off and grey cathedral towers; the great ashtree by the house, above my seat; the face of my dear mother, looking out with a smile from her open window: ah, someday, how one will think of these things!' (21 August).

He soon set out again on the customary Wigan expedition, staying at the Victoria Hotel; the factory hands going to work woke him like the tramp of cavalry at 5.30 a.m. He now learned that some of the pitwomen had a nickname for him—'the Inspector'. One woman 'looked hard at me, and said "Why, it'll be th'inspector! We ca'u yo th'inspector, yo known—Ah was speerin' o'ye this last week, Ah was!"' (25 August). An account of this visit appears in a separate sketch-book, which contains some excellent pen drawings. Then Munby went north to stay a few days at Cartmell, where he had difficulty in getting a bath and was told 'ye're the awnly gentleman '*at iver spoonged*!' (31 August); he walked on through the lake district, again making his pilgrimage to the grave of Wordsworth, 'to whose soul I owe so much' (2 September). After a few days at York he returned to London on 18 September; and 'here in the crowded London streets, one lives for awhile, mind and body, on the memory of the country—on the scenes of Yorkshire and the Lakes: but even that will soon be lost, swallowed up in worser things' (20 September).

Friday, 23 September . . . to the National Society for Aid to the Sick & Wounded, in S. Martin's Place. The churchyard of S. Martin's was strewn with bales and boxes of lint, linen, &c, each marked with the red cross; and folk peered at them through the railing. An orderly bustle, too, at the office doors; ladies in carriages, ladies on foot going in and out, commissionnaires with the red cross on their arms, a clergyman and a gentlemanly official helping off a young officer, who was that moment starting for Sédan.[4] I went in, to ask if one could do anything: feeling sad & humbled enough. . . .

In October, Munby departed for another of his sporadic research expeditions—this time by train to Newport, Monmouthshire, and thence to the ironworks around Brynmawr, walking the last mile, 'right through the midst of those great furnaces, which were roaring and flaming around, while the moon shone clear overhead in a cloudless sky'. He soon found two girl ironworkers who complained that they were no longer allowed to work at night: 'It's a great loss to us girls, Sir, yes indeed! . . . we used to earn 8 to 11 shillings a week, and now we do earn only six'; and they added that the men had to be paid 'twice as much to do *our* work!' (4 October). Thus once again, as so often in his diary, Munby, writing on the spot, refuted the indignant Liberal view of women workers in industry. At the Griffin inn, Brynmawr, the house was full, but a bed was made up for Munby in one of the parlours, and the Welsh chambermaid asked 'Shall I pull your boots off, Sir?'

A fisherwoman at Llangwm carrying her
dredging spade

He went on to Haverfordwest, and is seen in an unusual rôle, for him, rowing down the Milford Haven estuary to the little oyster-fishing village of Langwm, a place he already knew and loved. Munby stayed in one of the village cottages, and was able to enjoy the sight of the fisherwomen at

[4] Where the French had been defeated and Napoleon III surrendered, 2 September, 1870. See 22 September, 1872.

work in their traditional costume—'the black wideawake, the white kerchief beneath it covering the hair and neck and bosom; the brown or darkblue sleeveless boddice, laced in front; the blue or white jersey sleeves; the short scarlet skirt'. And in the early morning, a day or two later:

Monday, 10 October . . . at the water's edge I found a strange and picturesque scene; a long line of fishermen and fisherwomen, standing in groups on the narrow beach, beside their mighty oars, which stood upright against the young oak trees overhead. Their boats lay out in midchannel. . . . 30 or 40 bright rustic faces, mostly fair and young, stood there in this oldworld fishing dress; strong girls, with folded arms, with workworn yet feminine hands. . . .

The boats were loosed at last, and brought to shore; there was a general orderly bustle; men and women took down the long oars, put their paniers and mussel-jars aboard, and settled to their seats, and pulled off; and so we started, soon after 8. What a sight it was, when our division of the fleet, some 30 boats strong, pulled out of the wide harbour in long procession upon the glittering waters of the haven! . . . and no one was there to enjoy it all, except us, the fisherfolk, with our black ships dotting the silver stream . . . till the Trinity wharf, and Neyland, came in sight, all too soon, and we drew near to Pembroke Ferry. . . . I stept out of the boat . . . and from the shore I watched them all dropping down below New Milford, to the oyster grounds, and saw the women heave the dredgenets over-board. . . .

Friday, 21 October . . . In the afternoon, went by rail to Kensington Gardens, and sat and read there in the shrubbery walk till near 5; the day being very mild and calm. Flowers still bloomed in the wayside beds; there was still a long vista of foliage overhead; and the sun was going down brightly, though in dim grey clouds. Close by was the gilded pinnacle of the Prince Consort's Monument, now all but finished[5]: tawdry yet interesting memento of an extinct monarchy, some one will say sitting here a hundred years hence. Walking back by the Round Pond and through the plantations, we have late Autumn at last on every side; bare branches overhead, feet rustling in dry or sodden leaves, cold dim mists hiding the fallen sun. And the roar of distant traffic prevents us from thinking ourselves really in the country. . . .

Saturday, 5 November. Tonight was the first meeting of the Pen and Pencil Society at Aubrey House. I sent a contribution, but could not go: mentally, physically, unable just now to face bright talk and happy faces in a sumptuous house.

So I went down to Gillingham, for fresh air and rustic quiet . . .

[5] The memorial was opened in July, 1872, but the statue of the Prince was not unveiled until March, 1876.

The death of an elderly Pearson cousin; the depressing effect of the siege of Paris; a sharp attack of influenza; the dirt of London—all combined to accentuate the November gloom:

Saturday, 19 November.   Still the influenza, the cough & dull headache & so on. Went out however by doctor's advice in afternoon: up and down the new unfinished terrace of the Temple Gardens; whence now we see and hear cabs and waggons, instead of the river craft and the lapping of the tide. A fine evening effect over Waterloo Bridge; misty amber light, showing the sun's place in the western vapour; and bold in front of it, one great lead-blue cloud.

In both the gardens, folk were looking at the show-chrysanthemums: handsome globes of dainty tints; but look close, and each petal is filmed with soot— even when under cover. So, I remember, did Ruskin once eloquently bemoan to us the griminess of his gardens at Denmark Hill. 'Today' says the P.M. Gazette, 'England is passing through her darkest hour since the time of the first Napoleon.' True: and don't we all feel that, in our murky recesses, and all our private griefs to boot? . . .

Sunday, 4 December . . . I went by rail to the Swiss Cottage, and thence walked across the fields (which begin close by) to Hampstead church and back. Open rural fields, with light snow lying in the furrows, and beyond them, the tower of the old church standing dark against bright palegreen sky, which changed to rosy red in the West. But all these fields are doomed: roads, houses, are closing in around.[6] . . .

Wednesday, 7 December . . . to my Latin class, and at ten, thence to Oxford Square, to a party at John Westlake's. A large gathering, of the advanced intellectual kind: Huxley, for instance, was there, stout genial looking man, with face shrewd and keen and ready: a brisk and bustling savant . . . among the rest, Miss Garrett, triumphant member of the London School Board. She looked quite youthful and charming—one of the belles of the room: 'tis amusing, to see this learned and distinguished M.D. moving about in rosecoloured silk and pointlace, with flowers in her hair, and receiving due homage, in both capacities, from the men. . . .

Writing on 31 December, after the usual family Christmas, Munby had nothing favourable to say of the old year:

So ends 1870: hateful and villanous year, bloody with wars still raging, treacherous with newly broken treaties; in which the hopes of human progress, cherished twenty years ago at college, have at length finally died out. Progress there may be, but not now in our time; hope there may be, but no longer for

[6] True; but Hampstead Heath was preserved by Act of Parliament in 1871.

us. And we even see our England drifting away from her colonies as well as decayed in Europe; hated by the Americans, who should have been our filial friends; barren of hope and large wisdom at home, where patriotism is dying or dead. And the Church to which we clung in youth, which to us represents every old association and family interest and distinction, is going; and I am gaining an income by administering obsolete laws, and a system which has in reality passed away.

Some may say, what matters it that the Church is going, when Christianity itself seems doomed; when Christ disappears in the tumult to which His name has given rise; when we who yearn for Him or His Father, 'we are most hopeless, who had once most hope, And most beliefless, who had most believed.'[7]

New Year's Day found him still in his leader-writing vein: 'German armies in sight of the Louvre: all France suffering and struggling, all England full of horror and pity, and full of alarm: England, which fifty years ago was the arbiter of Europe, and now counts for less than nothing.'

Monday, 30 January, 1871 . . . Yesterday, the news arrived that Paris surrendered to the German armies on Saturday, after a siege of four months. Today, close to Burlington House, I saw a French maidservant, in her pretty white cap, her homely frock and apron and cloak, standing in the bleak miry street, and in her arms her master's child, wearing a little red hood closedrawn. Many such redhooded babies one sees, carried by whitecapped bonnes, and following quiet French ladies along the miserable London streets: many French men, also, of all grades: yet not so many as I should have expected, considering the vast numbers who have fled hither from the war.

Wednesday, 1 February . . . Today I had before me,[8] for report, a characteristic letter from the Premier: a long autograph letter, in which the Right Hon[ble] W. E. Gladstone M.P., Prime Minister of England, writing in concert with a private clergyman, whose name he places before his own, sets forth an elaborate arrangement, and 'respectfully prays' that it may be sanctioned. And what is it all about? why, *pew rents!* the pew rents of the clergyman's church. Truly, this is the very man who was obsequious to the half barbarous priests of Corfu. And yet, if it be not the pride which apes humility, there is something noble and touching, in this profound selfabnegation.

On 9 February, Munby learned that Mrs. Carter and her family had left Wheeler's Farm, Pyrford, for Surbiton; and, moreover, that he could rent their house for £17 a year. 'Seventeen thousand would not replace the delights, nor cancel the sorrows, of that fair spot,' he commented in the

---

[7] Clough: slightly misquoted.   [8] At the Ecclesiastical Commission.

diary. He was tempted to accept the offer, but refrained; cheap as it was, seventeen pounds was more than he could yet afford.

Sunday, 26 February ... Today the so called Peace was signed, between Germany and France, at Versailles: a peace carefully arranged by the Germans for the purpose of making fresh wars inevitable, and inflicting a permanent injury on the Commonwealth of Europe. No more tranquillity, no more freedom, in my lifetime. And this is the end of our aspirations in 1848!

Late in February, Munby's mother suffered a slight stroke; he returned to Yorkshire in haste, to spend an anxious week at Clifton Holme; fortunately she made a good recovery.

Wednesday, 5 April.   In the afternoon I went by omnibus to Hammersmith, passing the newly opened Albert Hall, a noble but purposeless building. Opposite, men were railing off a piece of Hyde Park into Kensington Gardens, and making a wide approach to the Prince Consort's monument, now nearly ready. . . .

I had been 'summoned', for tomorrow, to the Hammersmith Police Court, for smoking at the station on Wednesday night the 22nd. To smoke in a quiet spot with no one near may be no great crime: but this was my first 'summons'; and it was with a keen sense of personal degradation, that I went and hired a lawyer to appear on my behalf. The court proved to be a villanous place. . . .

Saturday, 15 April.   Going to Hachette's this afternoon, to ask for Mme Roland's Memoirs, the French manager told me they are out of print and will not be reprinted as yet: 'I do not think' said he sadly 'that there is a reading public *anywhere* in France just now.' I went down to Hampton Court. . . . I walked on through Bushey Park to Teddington, and spent the evening pleasantly in the rural house and wide gardens of my friend R. D. Blackmore, classic and poet and novelist and market gardener. His 'Lorna Doone' has been a great success; and has had (what is the best success) the effect of arousing among the people on the spot a keen interest in their own legends. He employs, besides the men, half a dozen women young and old, as labourers in his gardens; some English some Irish; and he says that every season the two sets of women have a pitched battle on the ground. After much talk on books and on gardening, he came with me to the station. . . .

Friday, 28 April.   To the Arts Club, and dined there. Ralston was there, and spoke . . . of having spent last Sunday tête à tête with Thomas Carlyle in Cheyne Row. The old philosopher, returning about ten p.m. from his nightly ramble, seated himself *on the floor*, and poured forth his sayings; laughing too at Ralston's Russian folklore stories. . . .

The death of a second Pearson cousin—this time Julius Pearson, who was only thirty-two—meant another funeral service at the Paddington church, another interment at Kensal Green. Hannah came to show her sympathy.

Thursday, 4 May . . . Amongst the crowd of poor folks at the church door, there stood a tall young woman, humbly clad, with a gentle earnest face. She wore an oldfashioned black strawbonnet, with a milkwoman's frilled cap inside; an old grey cloak, a lilac cotton frock, a white apron. Evidently, she was a servant: her hands looked rough with work, and round her wrist she wore a common leather strap. As we drove solemnly away, she, meekly hiding, gazed at me with tender wistful eyes; and I at her, with eyes not less sad. Oh humble wistful face, how long shall it be thus with you and me? Here is another death, and our mutual life is not yet begun!

Friday, 5 May . . . walked to Albemarle Street by about 9, and heard Ralston lecture on Russian folklore, at the Royal Institution. An excellent lecture, and a crowded and brilliant audience. Tourguenef was there, a tall large man with white hair & heavy features, pleasant of countenance: Lord Houghton, ill-favoured & obese . . . George Macdonald, with shaggy locks and plaid . . . & many more. After some talk, I walked home by 11; glad to see my old friend winning the fame which he thinks it worth while to seek.

Friday, 26 May . . . went to Hampstead, to an evening party at Upper Terrace Lodge: the hostesses, Mrs James, Miss Coates, & Miss Marion James, authoress of 'Janet's Home' & one or two other novels. One of the pleasant old redbrick Hampstead houses; courtyard and row of tall limes on one side, and on the other, a garden looking over the Heath towards Hertfordshire. The party chiefly literary and artistic: among others, George Du Maurier,[9] and his rather elegant wife, whose figure one sees so often in Punch. Du M. himself seems a clever fellow; he sang several French songs extremely well, accompanying himself. I stayed till after twelve, and walked all the way home with Stone of the Chancery bar, son of Frank Stone and brother of Marcus. The freshness & fragrance of Hampstead was delightful.

Monday, 3 July. To the Arts Club, and dined there, and had a long talk with Ralston, who has just been paying another visit to Tennyson, at T's new house near Haslemere. Tourguenef has asked R. to stay with him at Baden; but R. declares he could not resist the gaming tables. He will have it, too, that the new book he is writing is simply the product of ennui; and that if I had not such a 'wholesome enjoyment' of life, I should bring out *my* book at once. . . .

[9] George Du Maurier (1834–96) had contributed drawings to *Punch* since 1860. He wrote his three novels, including *Trilby*, in the last years of his life.

This suggests something of the impression Munby made on an intimate friend. Ralston saw a man of wide interests, an extrovert who was always in society and enjoyed life, a writer who was apparently too busy to write. It is unlikely that even Ralston appreciated the extent of Munby's diary, still less the evidence of recurring depression that it contains; and he knew nothing of the problem of Hannah.

Another old friend, Whitley Stokes, whose departure for India was recorded at length in the diary in June, 1862, now returned on leave—to receive a warm welcome from the Rossetti circle.

Wednesday, 5 July.   To the University Club, and went to Chelsea by 7 p.m. to dine at 16 Cheyne Walk with Dante Rossetti, and meet my old acquaintance Whitley Stokes, now Legislative Secretary to the Government of India, who has come home on leave. I was the first to arrive, and found Dante and his brother William in the large quaint studio, full of great easels and hung with D.G.R's sketches—portraits of Browning & Swinburne among them. I was shown several pictures in progress; large idealized portraits of Mrs Morris, wife of William Morris the poet; a glorious heroic face, certainly, & Rossetti told me—what indeed is obvious—that most of his recent female faces are studied from her. While we talked, and Rossetti, looking like a younger Faust, in that weird chamber, was nursing his Canadian marmot in his arms, the others came in; C. B. Cayley the translator of Dante, and F. W. Burton the painter, and John Ormsby the critic, and Whitley Stokes, whose tall slight figure is now topped with a robust complexion and a flowing beard. After a hearty greeting all round, we went upstairs to dine in that large and lordly upper chamber with the deep half cylinder alcove, looking out on the river. But the wonderful figured Japanese curtains that line that side of the room were drawn; pictures and ancient china and grotesque bronzes and black carven furniture relieve the blue wainscot, and break up the vast apartment into spaces well arranged and harmonious; and in the midst is the white table, lit by red waxlights in silver candelabra, standing on a great antique silver plateau. The glass, the china, are all antique: the dinner, elaborate and refined, is handed round by a single female servant; a robust and comely young matron, whose large strong hands, used to serving, contrast with the small hands of her master, used to pictures and to poems. She offers the dishes with a quaint simplicity, pointing out to you the best part of each. And we, we talked as of old, ten years ago, about literature, poetry, art: and Stokes, with his old exuberance of spirits preserved by success and honour, told us his adventures—how, for instance, he was entertained by the Rajah of Kuppartoola, whose ladies adorned him with cashmere shawls and jewelled bracelets, and how he rode away on a white horse with jewelled saddle, the Rajah's gift.

Stokes and Ormsby left about eleven, after coffee, & Cayley too: but we with our cigarrettes went down to the studio again; and Rossetti read aloud some new poems of young Philip Marston's,[1] which all admired, and the more, because poor Philip is blind, and yet sees nature with marvellous fidelity. Then the talk turned on early memories; and the two Rossettis reminded each other of childish things; how Dante made drawings of his rocking horse, at the age of 4; how Christina, in those days, had such a dreadful temper; how they all talked Italian and English both. Dante mentioned that he was born in 1828.[2] At last, about 1 a.m., they opened the hall door and showed the moonlight shining on the river, through the lofty iron gates, between the ancient elms: and Ralston and I said Goodnight (he had come in late) and walked home together.

Wednesday, 12 July.   Breakfasted with Litchfield in Hare Court; and he gave me the first news of his engagement—only yesterday—to Miss Henrietta Darwin, aged 28, daughter of Charles Darwin the philosopher. Rejoiced to hear of my old and beloved friend's happiness, I yet have dwelt all day on his words, after speaking of her intellect and power—'She does not believe in a personal God'. How wide we have to stretch our sympathies, now a days! . . .

Friday, 21 July . . . to Spring Gardens, to an afternoon party at Vernon Lushington's. There I was introduced by Litchfield to Miss Henrietta Darwin his fiancée: a petite young woman of 27, with a face not unlike the photographs of her father, but very feminine and tender; with bright hazel eyes, and every feature full of life and expression, but subdued and selfpossest withal. . . .

Munby spent a week in France and Belgium at the end of August. He returned in time to attend Litchfield's wedding, but did not do so, noting in the diary: 'This is Litchfield's wedding day: a wedding which saddens and depresses me, for it takes away the last but one of my unmarried friends' (31 August). The last bachelor friend was probably Borland, but might have been Ralston; neither married.

On 9 September he paid his first visit to the Surrey village of Ockley, south of Leith Hill. On 23 September, he travelled back to his home at York. Most of the next three weeks was spent either in the Lake District, or with his family at Scarborough.

Friday, 29 September: Ambleside . . . The Salutation bears the date 1656; and though it is now modern looking and full priced, and rife with the things that 'civilized' tourists like, I was glad to find that Mrs Townson the landlady was homely & oldfashioned and spoke Cumbrian. She and her stout blooming daughter and her maids, all talking in the bar, next the smoking room, gave out

---

[1] Philip Bourke Marston (1850–87), son of John Westland Marston.
[2] i.e. the same year as Munby.

a rich music of broad a's and o's, and antique words, that was pleasant to hear. Mrs T. came in to welcome me, with a simple and matronly curtsey, and then sat down and talked. Born, and bred near here, she had known the famous residents of old. She was loud in praise of Dr. Arnold, that 'good man', who used to come and read to her when she was ill; and of Hartley Coleridge: eh, he *was* a dear kind man! and as for children, he was so fond of em he would catch em up and clasp em—like this—and feel in his pockets and say 'No, not a penny to give away!' 'for, poor fellow, they never allowed him money, you know Sir.' And reason good, alas! Of Miss Martineau[3] (who still lives, almost bedridden now 14 years) she spoke with respectful awe, as of something wonderful but uncanny. 'They do say, Sir, she believes in no God nor devil!' she said with a grim smile— 'Eh, I remember when she used to lecture here aboot her travels, and a waistcoat on and her hair parted a one side, looking like a wonderful *man* amost; but there —she's a deal wiser than me, I knaw—and the clergy was again her, and stopped it.' She was strangely severe on Wordsworth. You've often seen him? 'Aye, Sir, *too* often! A hard man he was—never gaave a sixpence to bury his old gardener 'at had lived with him 30 year, nor went [to] funeral neither—and was all for bringing down poor folks' waages. He got my husband turned oot on his plaace, (hinc illae lacrymae, perhaps) aye, he did Sir—but the Lord was with us' which means, that we took the Salutation, and made money. It is strange and annoying to hear such tales of him to whom one owes so much: but certainly, his exquisite soul lacked, not only humour, but the will or power of being en rapport with small folks in common things. Yet his epitaph in Grasmere church says that he 'never tired of maintaining the cause of the poor and simple'.[4] . . .

At Flamborough there was news of another wedding which had almost as depressing an effect on Munby as that of Litchfield and Miss Darwin. Molly Nettleton, the cliff-climber to whom he had given the rope, had married her sweetheart George White, and gone to live at Bempton. It was, commented Munby, 'another rustic idyll ended, another chapter of old associations finished & laid by' (13 October).

Saturday, 4 November . . . at 8, to the Working Men's College in Great Ormond Street. We, Council and Students, but specially the students, offered this evening a wedding reception to Litchfield and his bride.

The whole thing was managed by Tansley and the other students, with admirable vigour and enthusiasm: a great tent, with boarded floor, covered the garden, between the old house and the new lecture rooms; and after several choruses of wedding music, from the Huguenots and elsewhere, had been sung by the choir of students, men and women, in the circular hall, we went into the

[3] Harriet Martineau (1802–76).

[4] It is probable that the landlady of the Salutation had a particular grudge against Wordsworth, who is known to have shown consideration to several of his servants.

tent to supper, 200 and more in number. The Women's College were there as well as the men's; many of my old pupils at both, and many other friends and acquaintance; specially Professor Maurice, whose cordial and fatherly greeting is always charming. . . .

Munby's attitude towards the Prince of Wales had changed from early enthusiasm to caution and doubt. At a 'Special Promenade' at the Botanical Gardens in June, he had commented: 'Prince of Wales, sleek and thoughtless: Princess, in quiet ladylike dress, elegant & simple' (17 June). More recently, his Norfolk friend Scott-Chad, who had been to a ball at Sandringham, had 'said that the Prince & Princess of Wales are judiciously hospitable and kind to every one, down there: but spoke also of the Prince's ill-habits & gross practical jokes' (17 November). All these misgivings were, however, swept away, for Munby as for others, by the news of the Prince's dangerous illness.

Saturday, 9 December.   Every one last night was eager and alarmed about the Prince of Wales, lying ill of typhoid fever at Sandringham: for days past, telegrams of his state have been posted by the Home Office at Charing Cross and sorrowfully read by passers by: but last night and this morning there seemed to be no hope left. . . .

Tuesday, 12 December . . . Another day of public anxiety—shown more strongly in London than I ever remember. People asking for telegrams, listening for the passing bell; chance words heard in the street or elsewhere, showing that most men were thinking of the Prince. Home Office telegrams posted in our hall, as usual; at the Cheshire Cheese, the latest news written up in the dining parlour; in the Strand and Fleet Street, little details from the sickroom hastily brushed in with ink on large flysheets, which were stuck on shutters of newspaper offices; and crowds pressing to read them. As I returned from S. Paul's, at 9.30, crowds still reading; and the latest news somewhat better. . . .

Wednesday, 13 December . . . to my Latin class at 8, and home thence 10.15. Another anxious day: telegrams about the Prince posted up and read as yesterday, just with a glimmer of hope and no more. I said a few words about the matter to the women of my class, and they met them with an eager and spontaneous assertion of the interest which every one they knew of feels in it. 'It makes us feel like one family,' said one of the girls—Elizabeth Miller, metal-polisher and student.

Sunday, 17 December . . . In the afternoon I went by rail to South Kensington, and called in Onslow Square on the Theodore Martins. Mrs Martin was at home; and I had a long and interesting tête à tête with her, in the twilight, in the tasteful and luxurious drawingroom: she, drest in black but with some kind of white drapery about her head and shoulders—for she was not very well—sat graceful & statuesque, yet animated and earnest, by the fire, shading the light from her expressive face with a thin slight hand. She has just been with Mr. Martin at Manchester, giving her farewell there as Helen Faucit . . . she told me of the enthusiasm of the Manchester folk; how the house each night was crowded, and hundreds unable to get in; how, on the last night especially, crowds filled the street and cheered her as she left. . . . Then we talked of the degraded condition of the stage in London now: and she told me that it was in London she first appeared on the stage, and that in London she hopes to give her last farewell—'but it would be *impossible*, till things improve'. And then she spoke of her art—'my art', as she proudly called it. I had said something of the advantage that a poet or painter or musician has in being able to produce an effect without aid from other persons of the same calling: 'Yes' she said 'and that is so trying, so disheartening, in my art; I cannot command my instruments, nor make those who work with me intelligent or sympathetic, or even control such matters as scenery and so on. Even a musician can leave his music behind him and know that others will interpret it; but I must produce my result at once, if at all.' . . .

Seated thus alone with such a woman, conversing with her in the mellow fire-light on subjects that roused her to the full stature of her soul, one could not but feel penetrated with that sense of homage and divine respect which men owe to the great ones of the other sex. And I felt too, not for the first time, how ineffably superior this type of female greatness is to that which is current now a days; the hard political or social type, of which I meet so many examples.

In the midst of our talk, who should come in but Froude the historian, and the Rev. Charles Kingsley. I rose to go, but Helen Faucit, in her kindly way, bade me stay, & introduced me—to Kingsley at least, for Froude I knew slightly before, through Fraser's magazine. I was struck by the grave and tender respect which both of them, Kingsley in especial, showed to her. They began to talk about the Prince of Wales, who is recovering, and the wide and profound interest which his illness has caused. The silent multitudes, said Froude, have had a chance of showing what the real feeling of the country is; and the few mal-contents have been cowed. The working classes, too, have shown this enthusiasm at the very time when they were also showing their organization and power by winning the nine hours' movement[5]. Kingsley expressed great hope and con-fidence in the Prince of Wales's character; and Mrs Martin exclaimed 'After such a burst of enthusiasm, and from such a nation, what a King he ought to be!' 'I have heard it said' answered Froude in his halfcynical yet gentle way 'that no one ever got good from an illness.' Kingsley looked grave and said 'If the

---

[5] There had been a successful five-months' strike of Tyneside engineers in 1871 for a nine hours' day.

man who said that had been a parson for thirty years, as I have, he would never have said it!' . . .

A fortnight later, after a happy Christmas with his family, Munby took as much care to describe the hiring of a farm girl in York market as he had done to record the conversation between Helen Faucit, Froude and Kingsley. It is difficult to say which he found the more interesting.

If the diary in recent months had contained less than usual about Hannah, this did not mean that Munby was not thinking about her: rather the reverse.

8

MARRIAGE

1872–3

Pure Water, the emblem of Life,
  Has been chosen and blest from above:
Pure Woman, the maid and the wife,
  Is the source and the fountain of Love:
Pure thought, in the depths of the mind,
  Rises cool and refreshing and clear.
May you have all these blessings combined!
  One, at least, is awaiting you here.

A. J. Munby, *Poems* 1901:
'Fons Bandusiae: Inscription for a Spring.'

Throughout 1872 Munby grew increasingly preoccupied with the problem of Hannah. His failure to decide their future had already worried him deeply; now at last, and not before time, he began to show a refreshing determination to come to a decision. He spoke about Hannah to a few intimate friends; he introduced himself to her family in the character of a suitor; he seized a lucky opportunity to establish her as his housekeeper at Fig Tree Court. Before the end of the year, it becomes clear that a long-delayed marriage is imminent.

The established round continued: office work; Bayswater and Kensington society; the weekly Latin class for working women. As usual, Munby's London life was ventilated by week-end excursions into the countryside. But all these things no longer had quite the same significance for him; the diary is filled with meaningful references to Hannah.

His Cheltenham friend Henry James was one of the first to be given an inkling of the situation. Munby showed him his favourite photograph of Hannah, and when James responded with 'It is indeed a fine face—a remarkable face', Munby was encouraged to speak (24 January). A few days later, 'after much hesitation, I told my old friend all the story—at least all we had time for—of her whose picture he saw the other day: and he gave me hearing and sympathetic counsel, though he could not fully understand the position' (28 January). In 1872, it was difficult for a college friend to know what to say about such a disastrous misalliance as Munby proposed.

The diary entry of 15 February marks another important stage in Munby's journey towards matrimony; he annotated it, 'C'etait le commencement de la fin'. In that month, Hannah had to leave her congenial employment in Gloucester Crescent, for the familiar reason that the 'Missis' was dissatisfied about her mysterious relationship with Munby, which Hannah refused to discuss. Hannah applied for work as a charwoman at 25 Westbourne Park. Munby, meeting her outside the house, said: 'My dear, you shall not go—this sort of thing cannot go on for ever.' She took another job, all the same, at a different house.

In the meantime, public thanksgiving for the Prince of Wales's recovery occupied London's attention.

Saturday, 24 February.   Out and home by the Embankment, escaping thus the crowds in the streets: and stayed indoors from 3 p.m. all the afternoon and evening till near twelve, when I went out a while into Fleet Street, and found many people still abroad gazing: barriers erected to defend the footways . . . scarlet cloth fixed in a broad strip along the fronts of the houses at the first floor level, and workmen by gaslight decorating a triumphal arch at foot of Ludgate Hill, and many tiers of seats around.

Sunday, 25 February . . . In the afternoon . . . I went out for a stroll, with John Ormsby, whom I met coming out of his chambers. It was impossible to get out by the Inner Temple Gate: the gate-porters, aided by a policeman, were keeping it against a vast crowd of people on foot, who filled the whole of Fleet Street; come to see the scarlet tiers of seats and the great banners which already hung from the houses. We went out by Essex Street, & found the Strand equally crowded. Many of the people were evidently country folk. Workmen were still busy at one or two housefronts. The omnibuses, the company of Foot Guards marching to the Bank, were all driven on to the Embankment . . .

Tuesday, 27 February.   By 8 a.m. today I was at the West Door of St Paul's Cathedral; having made my way on foot thither, through back streets, among groups of well-drest people, going to their several points of view. My seat in St Paul's was close by the southwest pillar of the Dome, and just above the ground floor level. Immediately below me were the officers of the army, in full uniform: opposite to them, on the other side of the nave, were the navy and marines: and between the two services was the raised scarlet gangway, lined with beefeaters at intervals, up which the Queen and Prince, and all their array, passed to their pew on my right. Under the dome, below the royal pew, were the Peers and Commons, the Ministers & Judges. The Kings at Arms and Heralds, in their tabards, stood near the pew; and strange Orientals in turbans and jewelled robes passed up the gangway to their seats. One of these was a woman—the wife of Dhuleep Singh. She wore a hood and long cloak of stiff gold brocade. The service was scarce worthy of such an august assemblage: yet when the Queen & Prince & Court went by, and we all stood to our feet as one man, and the choir and the great organ burst into music, it was a thrilling moment: and the sun, too, broke out just then, and sent beams of slanting light down through the misty vault of the dome, upon the gold and scarlet and purple crowds below. . . .

In the afternoon I went through the Parks to Hyde Park Square, and dined at the Pearsons'; and home thence at night through the crowded and illuminated streets. Everywhere except in Oxford Street, vehicles were almost or altogether excluded: every street from wall to wall was filled with people on foot, quietly walking this way or that under the brilliant light of the illuminations on the house fronts. Nothing could be more admirable than the good humour and good behaviour of the crowds. Fleet Street, for instance, looked quite mediaeval again, its gabled houses bright as day with lights and colour—flags on the houses, flags festooned across the street, and legends, such as the Te Deum, stretching all down the way on either side, white letters on a scarlet ground nailed to the windows: and amidst all this, the working folk, men and women, boys and girls, merrily moving along; sometimes half-a-dozen decent lasses, arm in arm, dancing a row, and singing, while their prentice swains danced by them, playing the flute or the accordion. I never saw such a crowd, nor a sight so striking in England: it was like a scene out of one of Sir Walter's novels of ancient English life. So home about twelve.

On 9 March, a Saturday, Munby spent some hours looking at houses to let in Richmond and Twickenham. Nothing came of the search, which was perhaps connected with intimations of matrimony.

Tuesday, 12 March.   To the Club: home to dress, and to Hans Place by seven, to dine with Miss Marston & Miss Haworth. A party of ten; maiden ladies, dignified clergymen, and so on; all refined, fairly intelligent, and politely Conservative. One old gentleman expressed his pious gratitude for our deliverance from Mazzini, who died abroad yesterday.[1]

Thence at 10.30 I drove all the way to Chalk Farm, to a party at 9 Northumberland Terrace, at Dr. Westland Marston's, dramatist and critic. Marry, here was a contrast! The rooms full of professional littérateurs and their wives; nearly every man a poet or novelist or journalist; half the women novelists or actresses. I had some talk there with Dante Rossetti, Ralston, J. C. Jeaffreson, Garnett, and others: the immortal George Cruikshank was there, vigorous and sprightly as ever; the great 'epworth Dixon aired his own merits, with smug selfdeprecia-tion: Swinburne was there, too; but Swinburne, overcome by Mazzini's death,

---

[1] At Pisa.

arrived inebriated, and had to be concealed down stairs. One person new to me and interesting, was R. H. Horne,[2] the author of Orion: I was surprised to find him a small and feeblelooking *old* man, with thin white hair. People here, of course, were lamenting Mazzini. After a good deal of pleasant talk, I left about 12.30 (quite early) and walked home.[3] At dinner today I took down that charming Mme Jeannin, who with the best intentions gave me many a cruel stab in her discourse—for she spoke of servants. She told me the story of Mary Jervis; whose mistress, wife of Col. Cleather of the Engineers, is a friend of hers. After Mary had left her service, Mrs. C. met her in Marshall & Snelgrove's, very well drest, but as gentle and respectful as ever, and told her to call next day; for she was fond of Mary. Next morning early, a card was sent up—'The Marchioness of Westmeath': and Mrs. C.'s late housemaid entered. 'Why Mary, is this your card—are *you* Marchioness of Westmeath?' 'Yes Ma'am,' said Mary, simply: and she was.

Monday, 1 April . . . Today I had a great shock: the news that my friend, and teacher & master, Professor Maurice, is dead! He died this morning, here in London. How many, besides me, will miss his beautiful venerable face—his piercing eye and wonderfully sweet smile, his cordial shake of the hand, and the devout earnestness of his tremulous fatherly voice!

Friday, 5 April . . . I went up to Highgate, to the funeral of my most revered friend and teacher, Professor Maurice. About 1 p.m. I reached Swain's Lane, and there near the gates of 'Holly Village' found the men of the Working Men's College assembled, all in mourning: Tansley, and Thrower, and Newton—most of the hearty kindly working men whom one has known at the College so long—I shook hands and joined them, and presently up came Professor Seeley, with whom I had some talk about Maurice's last hours; and then Lowes Dickinson, Vernon Lushington, and others of the Council. The Dean of Westminster, with Lady Augusta and George Grove, passed us, driving up to the Cemetery: and then about 1.15 the funeral carriages appeared: the hearse, and some ten mourning coaches, in which were Edmund Maurice, the Miss Sterlings, Charles Kingsley, Llewellyn Davies, J. M. Ludlow, J. S. Brewer, and others of his oldest friends. Behind the last coach, we, the other friends, and members of the W.M. College, fell in and walked in fours: the eight pallbearers first, of whom I was one. . . . I came back with Charles Kingsley.

Saturday, 6 April . . . to Kensington, called on . . . the Ashursts, who were at home. We talked of Mazzini, who was a great friend of theirs: of his humble lodgings here in Brompton, of his teaching & befriending Italian organ boys, and

[2] Richard Henry or Hengist Horne (1803–84). He received a civil list pension in 1874.
[3] But the diary records, with honesty, that he did not reach the office until 11.45 the next morning; he was not as young as he used to be.

of the Italian . . . who (there being no one to remonstrate) has had his body dis-interred and is embalming it to keep it above ground. Mazzini, it seems, had the greatest horror of such a fate—and the Ashursts, and James Stansfeld M.P. their brother in law, are trying to prevent the desecration.

I walked homeward through Kensington Gardens & Hyde Park. Men were placing in situ the third of the four white marble groups at the corners of the Prince Consort's Monument: the Asia, a very fine and beautiful group[4]—whilst it is clean and new. In the Gardens I met George Hudson, son of the Railway King, who told me that his mother, poor soul, is living at 22 Hornton Street, Kensington.

So the Club by 6, and dined and read there till 8.15, and then to Her Majesty's at Drury Lane, & heard Fidelio. . . . Seeing it at least once a year, this must be about the twentieth time that I have seen Fidelio, which to me is always a kind of religious service and spiritual test: and the great prison scene was this year almost overpowering, coming so soon after the funeral of Maurice. Often and involuntarily, between me and the scene I seemed to see his venerable beautiful face, looking up at me with intenseness of fatherly cordiality, as he used to do and will do no more. . . .

Friday, 19 April . . . Walked in the Temple Gardens, and on by Queen Victoria Street into the City, to dine in Milk Street, at a large restaurant which announces itself to me by circular as having 'a staff of quiet and wellconducted *waitresses*' instead of waiters. A wholesome innovation, and we may as well see whether it is 'attended with good results', as it should be. It was nearly 6 when I got there, and folk dine early in the City; so the first room I entered was empty, and its waitresses, all alone, were sitting at a table, making up accounts & getting their tea: four decent looking young women, all drest alike in striped cotton gowns of 'fashionable' cut, and dainty aprons, and broidered capless hair. They civilly explained that I could still dine, in another room; and one of them rose and showed me the way to 'The Saloon', a large well-appointed room, in which were three more waitresses, drest in the same livery; all of them girls of twenty or so; and three men, dining or about to dine. One of the waitresses sat making up her reckoning; another came forward to wait on me; the third and prettiest was standing by one of the three diners, who bent over her, holding both her hands and saying to her such soft endearing insults as 'gentlemen' bestow on damsels who have grace but not position. The girl, accustomed perhaps to such treat-ment, received his caresses with passive simpering acquiescence; her com-panions took no notice; and neither he nor she was disturbed by the entrance of a stranger. The other two men, who were young, dined quietly, but afterwards went and sat by the waitresses and gently flirted with them awhile: the first man, who seemed about forty and looked like a dissipated dragoon, continued his attentions to all the three girls; kissing his hand to them, seizing their hands &

[4] By J. H. Foley.

their skirts, begging them to sit down by him. And after dinner, when the waitresses began to collect knives & forks & fold up tablecloths, he went and joined the group, and 'chaffed' them, making indecent allusions. They laughed and did not resent these; perhaps they did not understand them. I, however, made a demonstration of disgust, which silenced him: and with an audible 'Damn', he left the room, shaking hands with the girls, who evidently bore him no ill will.

Apparently, the City is not yet ripe for female waiters. . . .

At the end of April the diary contains a reference to 'our besotted housekeeper', Sarah Mitchell, and records a visit by Munby with the other principal tenant at 6 Fig Tree Court, Mr. Rees, to the Inner Temple Treasury, where they pleaded that she should be given one more chance (26 April). The Benchers, however, thought otherwise and dismissed her. 'Thus this unhappy woman, my housekeeper for 15 years, who was born and bred in this house and who has lived here rent free, is content in spite of many warnings to ruin her home and her prospects for the sake of getting drunk' (27 April).

The possible consequences of the incident did not dawn on Munby until a month later. Hannah then left her job; she had been unwell and had hurt her hand, and her mistress proved 'cruel and contrary, and wouldn't pay me because of my bad hand'. She called on Munby to tell him this news, before going to stay in Clerkenwell, where she had relatives and friends. 'But I sit down sad and sick at heart: oh, if she should really become ill! And when will this long tragedy be over, and I able to do justice to that divinely beautiful soul and to myself, without saddening the old age of others as dear as she is? The strain can hardly be borne much longer' (23 May).

A decorous week-end with Hannah at Southend followed, the Sunday being her thirty-ninth birthday. She was 'graceful and ladylike, reading Coleridge's Poems or the Psalms' (26 May).

Friday, 21 June.   Walked with Julie Bovet in St. James's Park from 5 till 7, and had a long talk with her about my dearest Hannah and what I ought to do concerning her. Julie was sensible and severe, yet kindly as usual; and to no one else can I talk freely on that subject. Yet she too has her ladylike prejudices: 'Hannah is a good creature,' she says, 'but to a man so &c as you are, the manners of a maid of all work must always be revolting.' . . .

Mlle. Bovet may still have had hopes; she had tried hard to divert Munby from his infatuation; it was now too late. He was soon on his way to Hannah's home at Shifnal, Shropshire, determined to 'do somewhat at last, towards bringing this long trial to an end' (27 June). When he returned, he found that at the Theodore Martins', 'the brilliant rooms, the music, the sumptuous elegant women lounging on sofas, brought out in fine contrast the humble simple homes and the hardworking folk of my Hannah and her kin' (2 July).

Munby had taken his final resolve. On 8 August he made the significant note: 'Went . . . to the Canterbury Office in Doctors' Commons, to ask about marriage licenses.' And by 11 August he was back at Clifton Holme, observing family prayers through the window from the garden—'my father, seated at the library table, reading aloud; my dear mother on her sofa, near; Fred and Carry in due prominence; the footman in his corner; and the five women servants, in Sunday cap & apron, seated a-row in the background.' A daunting prospect indeed for an eldest son who was summoning courage to announce that he wished to marry a maid of all work! No wonder he left it until the last possible moment, the night before his return to London, before he broached the appalling subject:

Monday, 26 August . . . Late at night, when the rest had gone to bed, I had a pathetic and terrible scene with my dear Father: for I had schooled myself at last, to tell him of my love for Hannah—begging him however not to tell my dearest Mother. What matters it that Hannah is pure, honourable, gracious and comely & intelligent, devoted to me now for 18 years? She is *a servant*: and the shame and horror of that fact, to me so simple, was to my honoured father so overwhelming, that I could not bear it; and comforted him, by crushing—not *her*, God forbid!—but my own hopes.

Three days later, Munby again met Julie Bovet, being once more grateful for 'her sympathy and interest, and her staid & judicious opinion'. On 3 September, he wrote 'a very long letter to my father, concerning Hannah'. What he said in the letter can only be conjectured; he must have avoided a promise not to marry, but may have assured his father he would be no more troubled with the matter. The immediate effect of the painful scene was to postpone the marriage for a few months. Meanwhile, Hannah was introduced to 6 Fig Tree Court.

Saturday, 14 September. I left Charing Cross by the tidal train for Paris: to begin an aimless wandering, which looks little pleasant for me, being alone, for it should have been my wedding tour. And she, my darling, who should have gone with me so, now only came to meet me at the station, as a servant, with my luggage. 'Do not kiss me' she whispered 'the folks are staring so!' Yes—and their staring is hard to bear. She went back, to live alone (such is her wish) in my house till I return, and clean it & take care of it: and to enable her to be there, *I* must go away. . . . May she be blest, and kept from evil tongues, while I am away.[5] . . .

Despite the assertion above, the trip was hardly 'an aimless wandering' —Munby's excursions were never aimless—and he covered pages with an account of the damage he found in Paris after the siege. Moving on to the scene of the French defeat at Sedan, he discovered the cottage in which Napoleon III had met Bismarck to discuss his surrender.

Sunday, 22 September: Sedan . . . took the train at 12.10 for Donchéry, barely 3 miles off. It is a small quiet town, very little injured. Said the old postman, who walked in with me, the whole place was crowded with Prussians: they slept on straw littered in the streets: not a mouse 'pas un souris' had room to pass! The church . . . was filled with wounded French, after the battle. You pass out of the town by a worn wooden bridge, with a long weir slanting across the Meuse: then the double line of poplars begins, and the road to Sédan winds gently up the side of the hill above the river. On the top of that hill was 'Fritz'[6] and his staff. . . . Halfway up, as the road ascends, you pass two neat little stone houses, built as one, standing at the top of a little slope of grass and potatoes, unhedged, above the road. Neat white curtains shade the windows of the upper house; a geranium is in the parlour casement. Inside, a neat young wife sits sewing; in plain white cap and blue cotton gown. She rises and smiles, as I knock, and says Yes, Monsieur, this is the place. . . . And she took me round the end of the cottage, and opened a low backdoor. Just within it, was a narrow rude stair, up which we climbed. It led to a very neat first floor bedroom—'the only one we have, Sir'—with redbrick floor and white bed & duvet, and everything proper. And through that, was *the* room. A very small and narrow parlour, with no furniture save a handsome oak wardrobe, a small round oak table, two plain cottage chairs, all wood. The floor, uncarpeted, waxed and polished wood: a religious picture over the fireplace, a few little cups on the mantle shelf. Nothing else in the room. Through the clean figured muslin blinds of the two windows, there is a pleasant view, across the road and the poplars, of . . . the shining Meuse below, and in the distance, the far-reaching forest of the Ardennes. 'I showed them up the stair and through our bedroom, Monsieur,' said Mme

[5] As Munby's train puffed out of Charing Cross, a red carpet was unrolled for the Prince and Princess of Wales. Hannah stayed to watch: 'i thought the Princess look'd pretty & pleasant but very delicate, but there was 5 or 6 little children, so no wonder. And they look'd delicate too, but the Prince was much stouter & bigger nor i expected to see after such an illness as he had lately. It did me good watching the crowd & to think o' the different grades o' people there is in the world, that even gentlemen had to bow & scrape to the royal family . . .' (Hannah's Diary).

[6] The Prussian Crown Prince Frederick, later Emperor Frederick III (1831–88), *Unser Fritz* to his troops.

Fournaise, 'the Emperor and Bismarck, that morning, the 2nd of September 1870: and here they sat in this room, on these two very chairs, at this little table. They sat here 3 quarters of an hour; and then M. Bismarck went away, and the Emperor was alone here for an hour or more. And then one of his Generals came, to see him; so I showed the General up, and when I knocked and opened this door, there was the Emperor sitting in that chair, leaning on the table, with his face between his hands. And then he got up, & went down with the General, and he walked up and down our potato-plot, and smoked; and then M. Bismarck came back, in his full uniform, with the Hussards de la Mort, and the Emperor drove away, over there to Bellevue. And when he left, he gave me these four napoléons: I would not spend them, not I! I had them framed, as you see.' For on the mantelshelf was a humble black frame, supporting the 4 gold coins, and a card below them, on which was written 'Donnés par S.M. Napoléon III à Mme Farnaise-Liban, le 2me 7bre 1870'.

This was the simple story; simply told by an unimpassioned woman with an honest face. 'People have offered me money for a chip of the table or a bit of paper from the walls,' she added; 'but I say No—this room shall be kept as it is, as long as *I* live.' . . .

Munby returned by train from Paris on Sunday, 29 September, looking out of the window for 'female signalmen':

. . . They are mostly the wives and daughters of workmen on the line: and, as everyone knows, they keep the smaller crossings, where country roads cross the line. From Boulogne or Calais to Paris, and again to the Belgian frontier, each woman wears the same livery; a low crowned hat of black tarpaulin, and a cloak of light blue cotton; a very effective dress when the wearer is young and comely and sunburnt, . . . and stands en militaire to salute the train, holding a furled scarlet flag. Today we must have passed 40 or 50 such women between Paris & Boulogne: some of them robust matrons, some brisk coquettish lasses, and some few elderly. Often before the train is out of sight, the signalwoman doffs her hat & cloak, and you can see her enter her cottage in the white cap & dark frock of ordinary life. . . .

The experiment of putting Hannah in charge of 6 Fig Tree Court had been successful; his rooms were cleaner and brighter than Munby had known them. Hannah had been advised by other workers in the Temple to 'try for the place' of housekeeper, but warned that 'the master is "a fussy old bachelor"' (29 September); meanwhile she was to live at Clerkenwell and come daily to the Temple. The master was eager to surrender his bachelor-status; yet found himself still bashful in talking of his hopes. He called, for instance, on his friend the Rev. J. E. Vaux, of the

Church Times: 'To him, as an experienced clergyman, I meant to confide the story of my Hannah, and meant to ask him to marry me. Yet—perhaps owing to his cheery jovial manner—I could not even approach the subject; and I came away, after 12, sad enough at having said nothing' (16 October).

Worried or not, Munby was always capable of being delighted by an unexpected discovery in his collector's field:

Friday, 18 October . . . Passing the shop of R. J. Bush, bookseller & publisher, Charing Cross, today, I saw in the window a one volume novel, prettily bound, and lettered 'The Rose of Avondale: E. M. Parker'. On it was a ticket, inscribed *'written by a Domestic Servant'*. Straightaway I went in. 'Yes,' said Mr. Bush, 'the author is really a female servant: she is a housemaid, and she is now in service at a gentleman's house at the western end of St James's Place, here in London. I went and saw her there in the housekeeper's room, and I found her in a housemaid's dress—as nice and modest a young woman of 23 or so as you need wish to see; just like any other servant in manner, only very quiet. Her name is Elizabeth Mary Parker; she comes from some village in Bucks, near Stowe, and her father keeps the village inn. She brought her M.S. to me, to ask my opinion: I told her it would cost so many pounds to print; she took time to think of it, and now she has brought it out at her own risk. I have sold 130 copies already, and the reviews speak highly of the book as being pure and gracefully written.' So said Mr. Bush: and for my part, I left his shop in a glow of satisfaction, which for a time overpowered the dull day and my own sadness . . . so far as I know, this is the first servant maid who has written a novel.

Saturday, 19 October . . . Went to Bush's and bought 'The Rose of Avondale'. Mr. Bush, continuing what he said yesterday, told me he felt sure the housemaid-authoress had had no help from any of her betters: as for her master and mistress, 'she begged me' said he 'not to let them know of the book, lest they should be displeased'. The M.S., he added, was written in a number of copybooks, of different sizes; in a good firm hand, like a man's. There were a few mistakes in spelling, & he corrected them; but wisely left the style and wording alone. When he went to see her, she made him a curtsy, and called him Sir, and behaved like any other modest servant . . .

On 21 October came 'the alarming news that our dear brother John is much worse and not likely to live'. John Forth Munby was 41, next to Munby in age: a solicitor in partnership with his father and a Captain in the local Volunteers. Munby went to Clifton Holme at once, to be told that 'Mr. Ball, the able & kindly surgeon', had found that 'congestion of the kidneys had supervened on a congested heart' (22 October). He and his brothers were constantly at John's bedside until he died on 27 October. The funeral was unusually impressive. This was a tribute not only to an esteemed York family but also to a popular young man.

The burial took place at the village of Osbaldwick, where Munby's brother Joe had been buried five years before, and where the Forth family (to which Mrs. Munby belonged) owned several tombs. For the mourners this meant a journey of two or three miles through the city and out into the countryside beyond.

Wednesday, 30 October ... Soon after 2 p.m., people from the town began to approach Clifton Holme: the hearse (without plumes) and coaches crept into the forecourt, & stood with various private carriages, waiting within the halfcircle of autumnal trees and shrubs; the brown or golden leaves of beech and ash and willow falling ever in the windy air. The 1st West Riding Rifles, 200 strong, marched in, with their officers; and with them, also in full uniform, came the officers of the Volunteer Artillery. The coffin (of oak) had been placed in the outer hall, with his shako and sword (he was a Captain) and belt laid on it: and in the forecourt, his own company, who were to form the firing party, presented arms as it was borne into the hearse. The remainder of the regiment, and also the City Police, stood in two lines, on either side of the carriage drive. At 2.30, we moved out into the village of Clifton: first the firing party, then the band, then the hearse, bearing his accoutrements and guarded by officers of the artillery and rifles, on foot; then 3 mourning coaches; then the volunteers and police, and then a long array of about 20 private carriages and cabs, containing Lord Mayor and Sheriff of York, clergy, and other acquaintance. I was not prepared for all this; but what impressed me still more, was the respect shown to the cortége. Every house for a mile or more had its blinds drawn; many shops in the chief streets of the town were closed; and all the way to the far end of York beyond the Castle, a dense crowd filled the streets. ...

Such is the power of a wellspent life—of a character singlehearted, earnest, genial, and full of hearty love and simple selfsacrificing zeal.

For three days after his brother's funeral, Munby wrote nothing in his diary; a reaction to emotion that he also showed on several other occasions. But his bereavement may have had the effect of rationalising his attitude to his father, by making it absolutely impossible to reopen the subject of Hannah with him. Having returned to London, he pursued the central problem with increasing urgency. He was anxious, in his isolation, to be told by a responsible friend that Hannah was a worthy object of his affections, and that it was his duty to marry her. He himself had no doubts; but he badly needed support.

Marriage

Tuesday, 5 November.   J. E. Vaux came to breakfast, and kindly took a paragraph about poor John, for the Church Times. Again I was halfminded—but not quite—to make him a confidant about Hannah.

Monday, 11 November.   In the Strand this afternoon, I met my dear old friend Robert Borland, just come up from his rectory in Devonshire. We dined together; I took him home with me to the Temple; and after tea, being sorely in need of such an aid, I told him the whole story of my darling Hannah. He with warm interest listened and suggested; and we sat till after 3 in the morning, considering what should be done, to reconcile truth and honour with necessity.

The worthy Borland was persuaded, not without difficulty, to have a talk with Hannah—'even *he*', wrote Munby, 'hesitated at first about meeting a common maidservant under such strange circumstances'. Hannah was equally reluctant; and Munby carefully 'posed' her for the interview.

Thursday, 14 November.   It would take long to reproduce in words the strange scene of this evening, when for the first time I did what I have so often dreamed of doing—brought my Hannah face to face with one of my own best friends.

She sat by the table in my room, cutting a book—Warton's English Poetry—for me: she wore her old blacksilk 'frock', made spruce and newlike: the strap & buckle on her right wrist was not hidden by her clean white cuff; round her neck was a little frill of white net; her wavy brown hair was massed behind her ears, and rippled round her smooth white forehead. 'This is my Hannah,' I said: it was all that one could say: and she rose, as the embarrassed Rector approached, and made him a kitchen curtsy, but with the grace and flowing freedom of a drawingroom. 'How do you do? I have heard much of you,' said my dear old friend; and she said 'How do you do, Sir?' taking his offered hand with modest meekness. 'I have told Mr. Borland all about you, dear,' said I after a moment's pause. 'Yes, Massa!' she answered, still blushing, but admirably calm and self-contained: and then, coming forward, and speaking with evident effort what she had thought beforehand, she said to Borland 'Perhaps you can feel for me, Sir; I have been a servant all my life, and I never thought to be shown to any one like this! Massa and me have been alone together, and I have served him and enjoyed it: but if I am to be shown, the charm is gone!' 'No no—don't say that,' I interrupted, laying my hand on her arm: 'Ah, but it *is*,' she repeated, and drew back, and sat down at my bidding, & began again hurriedly to cut the book; taking refuge in *that*.

Then came a little forced talk, and then I left her alone with Borland; and he talked with her of his views as to me and herself, and she (as he told me) gained courage and told him *her* views. 'He is a very nice gentleman, and *very* gentle,' she said [to Munby] afterwards, 'but he doesn't understand *me*; gentlefolks *can't* understand a servant's feelings!' 'Could I have done all this' she said again 'if I hadn't made up my mind to please you, and put on a deal of *nerve*? But I

314

trembled when you made me *sit down.*' 'I hate to be stuck up before gentlefolks, & in my Sunday frock—how much better *this* is!' was her comment next day, as she knelt on the floor, in cotton frock, and apron, & white cap.

Hannah's own diary adds to our knowledge of the Borland interview. Munby 'look'd white & worried' when he introduced them, she says. Borland did not talk to her 'exactly on religion', as she had expected: 'it was more about duty to ones parents, & trying to *persuade* me into *almost* giving M. up cause his parents was so much against his having me ... i couldn't of course tell him *what* a peculiar love ours had bin, but i said it was quite impossible not to go on loving one another, but that i never wanted it known—i wanted to be a help not a *hindrance* to M.' Hannah realised that Borland meant well, but felt that 'his advice & reasoning was little *good* to me, & i think he must o' thought so too, for he left off talking at the last almost abruptly. ...' After the interview, Munby was discovered in his bedroom 'gone fast asleep, & i'd to call him': a detail omitted from Munby's version.

Hannah having been sent back to Clerkenwell in a cab, Borland 'spoke much of her beauty, & grace, and native modesty and refinement'; or at least, Munby said he did. But neither as a parson, nor as a friend, could Borland encourage the idea of marriage.

Saturday, 16 November. Borland came to breakfast with me, and talked over the scene of Thursday night, repeating his advice to me *not* to do what I desire— namely, marry,—but to live apart, or at any rate to house my darling here as a servant only. Ungrateful, it seems to me, and selfish, this would be ...

Tuesday, 19 November ... to 2 Bryanston Street, and dined with Litchfield. Only his wife & her brother George Darwin. Her father's new book on the expression of emotion[7] was on the table; and Mrs. L. said that often, at home, he used to make her and his other children go out in the garden and look steadfastly at some object, such [as] a particular twig on a tree, to study their faces as they looked. But often, she added, when her father in his rides had stopped to notice the expression of some crying child's face, he found himself saying 'Poor little thing!' and losing his power of observation in his sympathy with the object observed ...

On the events of the next few days, Hannah's diary is more candid than Munby's. She tells us that on 23 November he showed her a marriage licence, made out in their names, and that she expressed the hope that neither of them would 'be sorry for it'. Her feelings at this point about the formal ties of marriage seem to have been less than enthusiastic; she had quite decided, however, that she could not stay with Munby at Fig Tree

[7] *The Expression of the Emotions in Man and Animals,* by Charles Darwin (1872).

Court unless they were married. On Tuesday, 26 November, she moved into the basement as his servant for the first time; and, feigning ignorance, questioned Mrs. Newton, the Temple laundress, about Munby: 'Mr. Munby was a good payer, & she seem'd to like him only said he was very fidgetty & old maidish. i knew that, but i was glad she spoke well of him. . . .'

The same day, however, the couple had a tremendous row. Soon after greeting her on arrival, Munby rang his bell. Hannah thought: 'well that is showing off certainly,' and went upstairs in a towering rage. She lost her temper completely when Munby—always alive to the 'security' aspect of their situation—rebuked her for not having called him 'Sir' within hearing of a lad who was clerk to his barrister neighbour Mr. Rees. If he 'tantalized me in that way again i would leave him whether we was married or not', Hannah told him indignantly. She added in her diary that 'my passion was only the effect of love'; but Munby had been seriously upset. The quarrel was not made up for several days.

Munby now took Hannah's younger sister Ellen into his confidence, and the marriage became a more practical proposition: he told her about the 'horrible scene', but does not otherwise allude to it in his diary.

Saturday, 30 November . . . by 2.30,[8] to the Temple, where I had appointed that Ellen Cullwick should meet me. Ellen was at first a scullion; but now at 33, is a skilled and trusted nurse, earning £20 or £25 a year . . . of a far commoner type than Hannah, but much more tractable. . . . Hannah retired to the kitchen, whilst I had a serious earnest conversation with her sister, for more than two hours; going through the whole story, up to the horrible scene of Tuesday last. A good religious maiden she is, and it was a relief to tell her all; though we could settle nothing, as yet. . . .

Saturday, 21 December . . . Coming home at 2.30, I went down into the kitchen, and there I found my Hannah, 'in her dirt', looking like a chimneysweep. . . . 'I'm blacking myself, Massa,' said she, 'to do the stairs.' For it was part of the programme, that she should scour the stairs 'in her dirt', so as to look as unattractive as might be, in that public employment: and though she had cleaned the kettle, and scoured the stone floor of the kitchen, which was still wet, yet all this, and more, had not made her black enough. And still, she looked noble, even in rags and dirt, and in a kitchen. 'Where shall I find a clean place to kiss you, dear?' said her master: 'Nowhere, I think!' said the sooty maid, and yet turned, and showed a ruddy spot on her black cheek, which perhaps she had kept on purpose. Not long after, upstairs in my room, I heard the clank of her pail, and the sound of the scrubbing brush on the ancient stairs; and would have gone out to see—but my tenant Thornbury was in his chamber . . .

[8] After a morning's work at the office.

Half an hour later, there was a tap at my door; and enter a tall and graceful young woman, with soft brown hair massed around her white forehead, her bright and handsome face flushed rose with recent exertion. Nothing but her clean white apron, and the simple make of her neat green gown, showed that she was a servant—for she wore no cap. Could this be the tattered grimy drudge whom I had seen blacking her face in the kitchen? The very same, Sir! and she was come up to join her sister Ellen, whom I had sent for, and with whom I was having a talk about all these things. Ellen modestly chose a distant chair by a window. . . . Comely & rosy is her honest face; but it lacks the highbred air and the brightness of her sister's. She too is a servant; and she says 'Let *me* do it, Sir' or 'Let me help you, Sir', instead of expecting to be waited on: she represents the nobler women of simpler times and countries than ours. Hannah goes down to the kitchen again, to prepare tea for herself and her sister: and I say at parting 'and Ellen, whenever it *can* be, you must be her bridesmaid.' 'Thank you, Sir,' says Ellen the nurse, and meekly takes my offered kiss.

The Munby family Christmas of 1872 was a subdued festival, owing partly to the death of brother John, and partly to the financial anxieties of 'the father', who complained incessantly about his expenses.

Hannah had been officially installed as housekeeper in Fig Tree Court, and Munby remained at Clifton Holme into the new year.

1 January, 1873: York . . . In my kitchen at the Temple, my servant Hannah cleans and scrubs alone, and waits for me: she, most noble and devoted of women, who has loved and served me faithfully and purely for nearly nineteen years, and is still, in the world's eyes, only my hired maid of all work, and is treated as such by every one but me—nay, and by me also; for does she not wait on me and clean my boots and sleep on a servant's bed in the kitchen? Too late, now, to make a lady of *her*, in spite of her sweet highbred face and manners: but not too late to do her justice somehow.

'Not too late to do her justice. . . .' The thought must have been continually present in Munby's mind during his leave-taking from York on 4 January ('much distressed by the perpetual selftormenting of my father, and by the anxiety of my dear mother on his account'); and during a two-day visit to Turvey, Bedfordshire, where his brother George was Rector. But he could tell none of them his secret.

Monday, 6 January . . . I left Turvey Rectory at 8.20 a.m. and drove along the pleasant country road to the station. To Bedford by train, by 9, and thence to London by 10.30—one hour late.

'Is the servant upstairs?' I say to the man who carries home my luggage. 'Yes Sir,' says he: and a minute afterwards, the servant, bare armed as she is and wearing her large white cap and apron and her cotton frock, is clasped in her master's arms. She has decked the room with holly and winter flowers, and has made ready a breakfast: and says she is well and happy. . . .

Tuesday, 7 January . . . the United University Club at 5.30, and dined there, and read there till ten, and then home. Hannah had already gone down to her kitchen to bed, leaving a note for 'Massa'.

Wednesday, 8 January. Went to Gloucester Street Pimlico, to see my invalid colleague Digby Green. He was writing a note in his cosy sanctum, and a smartly drest young woman was sitting before him on the edge of a chair. She rose, seeing me, and retired with the note. 'Excuse me—she is *only a servant'* said D.G; 'she has been sent to bring me these grapes and this jar of—have some?' '*Only a servant*'? I went home at seven to dinner, and was received by one who also is only a servant.

The diary entries for the succeeding days are sparse. On Sunday, 12 January, appears a note: 'to Clerkenwell church.' Tuesday, 14 January, was a 'fair grey day, with sungleams'; Munby's recorded office hours on this day were peculiar, 11.45 to 6.0, but the need to work late is explained by the concluding words of the entry: 'To Clerkenwell by 9 a.m.' The rest of the space allotted to 14 January in the diary was left blank.

The marriage register of the parish church of St. James, Clerkenwell, is more informative. It records that in the church on 14 January, 1873, Arthur Joseph Munby, a barrister, was married by licence to Hannah Cullwick 'of this parish'. The 'rank or profession' of the bride is omitted; but there are Munby-ish descriptions of the fathers of the couple, Joseph Munby appearing as an 'Esquire' and Charles Cullwick as a 'Husband-man'.

Munby and Hannah were not married by the vicar, Robert Maguire—a Protestant pamphleteer, who would hardly have been to Munby's taste—but by the curate, the Rev. John Henry Rose. The witnesses were Martha Ellen Cullwick (the sister who had been asked to be bridesmaid); Mary Ann Cullwick (another sister, a shopgirl known as Polly); and Elizabeth Morris (a cousin who was a lady's maid).

The wedding invitations were confined to Hannah's relatives and friends; a small gathering, in this large eighteenth-century church which could hold 1500 people.

Munby was 44 and Hannah 39 when they were married. They were both too old to be shaken out of habit and routine. On the wedding day Munby insisted on her calling him 'Arthur': Hannah did so once, but never again—he was to be 'Massa' to the end, though she sometimes allowed herself an affectionate diminutive, 'Moussiri'.

The next day, Munby took his Latin class at the Working Women's College as usual. It was the first night of term; they were doing the *Aeneid*. On Thursday, the 16th, he went to his club from the office, then dined with his Pearson cousins in Bayswater. Outwardly, his strenuous bachelor social life continued, though a shrewd observer might have noted that he tried to get home a little earlier; inwardly, everything was changed. Henceforth Munby was not nearly so eager to write long diary descriptions of literary parties or public events. He had a source of endless inspiration at home; in the tragi-comedy of a secret marriage unknown to his family— and revealed only to Robert Borland, Henry James, and later Vernon Lushington, among his personal friends.

The facts of his Clerkenwell marriage are not stated by Munby in the diary; to all appearances he was turned into a married man gently, silently, as by a conjuring trick. Only after three days does an oblique reference appear:

Friday, 17 January . . . To shops in Regent Street . . . and in a milliner's gorgeous window, saw certain dresses at which a crowd of envious women were gazing; bridal dresses, not in themselves beautiful, but costly and cumbrous: whereat I smiled sardonically, remembering the simple servant's 'frock' in which my Hannah was married. 'What a deal it must cost gentlefolks to get married, Massa!' said she, sitting by me this evening in her white cap & apron, and eating her supper off her knees (her own way) whilst I dined on her providings, at seven o'clock.

Thirty years later, Munby placed in an envelope no less than thirty-six sonnets he had written to Hannah, most of them copied in her handwriting. They include the following:

> How well I recollect our Wedding Day!
>   She did her black work with a beating heart;
>   Then wash'd herself, and own'd a servant's part
> Waiting on me, and then she went away
> Down to the kitchen bedroom, where she lay
>   Among the pots, alone and quite apart;
>   There doff'd her servile dress, and with meek art
> For once did make herself a little gay:
>   Her long dark cloak: a red stuff gown quite new;
>   Her black straw bonnet with white cap: Oh no,
> No gloves, no flowers! 'Massa, shall I do?'
>   She cries; 'I have no looking glass, you know!
> 'Now, I am off! And mind you, all my life
> 'I shall be servant still to you, as well as wife.'

Marriage

Saturday, 18 January ... At 2 p.m. I took Hannah from London Bridge to Dorking and Holmwood; for it had been a brilliant morning, and we were to sleep at Ockley. But leaving Holmwood station about 3.15, the sky was clouded and wind and rain approaching: so we simply walked by the field roads, under the lee of the fair brown woods, round to the pretty hamlet and picturesque church of Holmwood, and then the 3 miles back to Dorking, across the Common, in driving rain. We had good fare and warmth at the White Horse, & Hannah played her part very fairly, by dint of natural sweetness. But now that she was drest in black silk, her shapely hands looked somewhat large and laborious, and her dear complexion somewhat coarse: whereas her face looks ladylike and her hands delicate, when she is in her own servant's dress. C'est sélon. We returned to London, to Charing Cross, by 8.

Sunday, 19 January ... In all day, among my books. In the forenoon, Tarrant the armourer-sergeant came to the door, and saluting me, said 'Oh if you please Sir I came to ask if your servant may do some chops for Capt. Batten.' My servant? He meant my wife. And soon after one o'clock, I went down to the kitchen, and found her busy doing them ... singing at her work, for joy, while smoothfaced ladies, coming from church, swept across the courtyard above her. 'I'm *cook* today, Massa!' said she, smiling; 'and I enjoy it. And Tarrant's going to give me a shilling for doing it' ...

... I went to Lincoln's Inn, and dined in Hall ... home by 8, and found my Hannah ... on her knees relighting the parlour fire; wearing her cap & apron with her black silk 'frock'; and her sleeves down in token that it was Sunday evening: for a servant bares her arms for work and hides them at times of leisure, whilst a lady covers hers in the morning time, and bares them at evening, for show. In due course Hannah had her supper; but insisted on going down to the kitchen & eating it there; and returned almost directly. She is so used to getting her meals anyhow and feeding on broken victuals, that I can hardly persuade her to eat leisurely and sit down by me: even now, she acts on the pathetic assumption that only my leavings are for *her*! She read to me a few chapters of Thomas à Kempis, and the Psalms for the day; and so to bed ...

Sunday, 26 January.   For reasons of prudence as well as of courtesy, I asked three men to breakfast with me today: my neighbours Josiah Rees and Capt. Batten of the 8th. Foot, and Colonel Pearson. Of course I consulted my Hannah first; and she highly approved: 'I can wait on them quite nicely,' said she who ought to have presided and been waited upon. But when I say 'How I wish you could sit with us at the table!' she answers ironically 'Oh yes, I fancy I see myself sitting down to breakfast with four gentlemen and pouring out tea for them—oh Massa, how *can* you be so silly!' Such is her view, who used to look on a parlour-maid's place as something too smart and fine for her. And so she brought the breakfast up, and set out the dishes, and cleared them away; silently and meekly;

320

unnoticed, like any common servant, and drest like a servant in cotton frock and apron: but she did not stay in the room to wait; the other was trying enough, but that would have been intolerable. That is one thing my darling wife did for me. Not quite unnoticed, however. 'What a very nice person your servant seems to be!' said Capt. Batten. I slipped down afterwards to the kitchen, where she was washing up, and kissed & thanked her. 'You are very welcome!' said this strange sweet spouse.

. . . to Warwick St., Eccleston Square, and sat with Walter Severn & his clever children & his sweet dainty wife. . . . Walter and I went by rail to Herne Hill, and by 6 arrived at his brother Arthur's; a large substantial old fashioned house among gardens and cedars; the house in which Ruskin was born. For Arthur's wife, Joan Agnew, is Ruskin's cousin; and a pleasant genial lassie she is. The house is full of Turners and other beautiful things, gifts of Ruskin's; and we spent a pleasant evening in talk, till 9, when Walter returned with me to town and went to the Cosmopolitan, and I home by ten, to my darling, whom I found in a clean white cap, with tea ready for her & me.

The sleeping arrangements of Munby and Hannah in Fig Tree Court (a good biblical name for the scene of Munby's great experiment) were unusually complicated for a newly married pair. Munby was the principal tenant at number 6, a house consisting of two floors and a semi-basement. He held four rooms comprising the whole of the first floor, subletting one room to Mr. Thornbury, and had a controlling share in the basement kitchen; but in between, on the ground floor, were chambers let to Josiah Rees, 'revising barrister'; who may have sublet[9] part of them to Captain Batten, of the 8th Foot. All this introduced an element of hazard, especially when Rees spent the night in his chambers, which fortunately was not his regular practice.

In the weeks before the marriage, Hannah had slept in the basement, like other Temple servants. Munby, not unnaturally, now wanted her to sleep upstairs. This she usually did; but she was liable to fits of diffidence or caution, which reinforced her instinctive servant's tendency to revert to the truckle-bed downstairs. But she seems to have used Munby's sitting-room quite freely in the evenings and at weekends.

They were happy, despite the difficulties—perhaps partly because of them. But for the next four and a half years, during their life together in the Temple, Hannah's wedding ring was not to be often in evidence.

Saturday, 1 February.   In the morning, came a man to measure the bedroom for new furniture.[1] Hannah, drest as usual in clean cotton frock and white cap

---

[9] The Inner Temple records do not indicate sub-tenancies.   [1] A larger bed?

& apron, lets him in, and stands by to advise: for I had said 'Hannah, you had better stay' and she replies 'Yes Sir'. A harmless ruse! . . .

Monday, 3 February. Home at 6.15 to dinner, and sat with Hannah till 9, and then dressed. 'How I wish *you* could be drest up too, and come with me!' '*Me*! What nonsense, Massa—I wouldn't be stuck up so, for worlds!' answers she, who has long since chosen the better part, fireside love and homely duty. I went in the snow & sludge to Mortimer Street, to a conversazione of the new Anglo Oriental Society. . . . I walked home by twelve, & went in to see Rees; who made to me an astounding proposal: namely, that I would allow 'my servant' to serve my neighbour Capt. Batten too! This morning, reading to me in Genesis the story of Noah, Hannah stopped and exclaimed 'Dear me, what a mess the earth must have been in when the Flood was over!'

Tuesday, 4 February . . . to St. Luke's Road Westbourne Park, in the wild Bayswater desert, to dine with Tyndall. . . .
   Home by twelve . . . Hannah, gone to bed, had left me a loving note . . . signed 'your affectionate servant and wife, Hannah.' 'I hardly like to write *that* word' added the sweet letter 'only you told me to.' Alas!

Sunday, 9 February . . . 'How well Hannah looks!'—said armourer-sergeant Tarrant yesterday, making his compliments to her at the kitchen door: 'I declare she looks ten years younger than when she came to live here.' 'Yes' answered dame Newton the laundress, 'we shall be seeing her have a beau, soon!' Hannah, standing by, simply says, 'Oh, never fear!' . . .

Tuesday, 18 February 'Capt. Batten came up last night when you was out,' said my sweet wife this morning, after her first kiss; 'and I know he was fidgetting about *me*.' How so, dear? 'Well, he wants you to let me light his bedroom fire of a morning and clean his boots. . . .' 'Oh, I shouldn't mind going into his bedroom when he was in bed, a bit—you know I used often to have to do it for gentlemen when I was underhousemaid, and quite a girl, so I might well do it now I'm a married woman! And I should like very well to clean his boots; you know I clean *yourn* every day; and I said to Tarrant "If you put 'em out I'll clean 'em with pleasure, along with mine".'
   What shall one think of the pure and lofty humility that is ready to do such things for her husband's acquaintances, and had rather do them than be openly acknowledged as her husband's wife?[2] . . .

Saturday, 22 February. In the afternoon I went to the Burlington Fine Arts Club to see the collection of George Mason's[3] works. . . . Mason's three great

---

[2] A somewhat disingenuous remark, considering that Munby was then only too anxious to keep the marriage a secret from most of the world; but it is hardly surprising that his thinking on the subject was confused.
[3] George Heming Mason (1818–72); A.R.A., 1869.

pictures were there—the Girls Dancing by the Sea, the Evening Hymn, and the Harvest Home; and it was a blessing to see them again: but besides these, there were majestic Roman peasant women, driving oxen, & the like; and above all, there were scores of pictures of English rural life, in North Staffordshire & elsewhere; fields and ponds and woods & wolds, country girls like my Hannah, in hoodbonnets & cotton frocks like hers; village children, horses, cattle, geese: and sweet sunshine of all hours, and exquisite grace and insight. Here, rendered in loveliest colour, were the common things and ways that I have beheld with such dreamlike delight, in real life, all over rural England. What pleasure to look on such pictures! If only She had been with me. . . .

I came home at 6.30 to dinner. In the evening, Hannah (in white cap and apron and green frock) read to me . . . the longer we live together, the more I wish 'to take her away from her slaving', and the more I regret that with all her intelligence, she does not share such a wish.

Friday, 28 February . . . at seven I walked with Hannah to Farringdon Street station, to meet her cousin Elizabeth Morris, whom I had commissioned to make for Hannah the only bonnet at all 'fashionable' which she has ever had. The good ladysmaid duly arrived with her bundle; and after shaking hands with her, I despatched the cousins to Clerkenwell . . .

Thursday, 4 March . . . Sat with him[4] till 10.30, and then home; and found Hannah (who had been entertaining her sister Ellen) gone to bed—in the kitchen, in spite of her promise this morning that she would continue to sleep upstairs. So hard it seems to make this sweet strange servant understand that she is my wife.

Wednesday, 12 March . . . Dined & sat an hour with Hannah: then at 8 to my Latin class, the last time. For the term is ended, and the class so reduced and so uncertain that I have determined to close it. The three remaining students . . . were very sorry, they said, and would gladly resume their Virgil with me hereafter. So we shook hands all round, and I left the Working Women's College, and walked home by ten to Hannah.

Munby tried to get out of town whenever possible at the week-ends; he was as familiar with mid-Victorian Gillingham and Chislehurst and Edgware, as he was with his favourite Surrey countryside. Delight in these long exploratory walks did not vanish with marriage, and he persistently urged Hannah to accompany him—mostly without success at first, her usual plea being that she was too busy housekeeping and cleaning. 'So I left for the country . . . with the feeling (as always now) that I am leaving

---

[4] Robert Borland, who was ill in Manchester Street.

my best behind,' wrote Munby on 15 March; and again, a week later: 'I wished that Hannah had been willing to come with me, instead of plodding through her Saturday errands in town.' And at those fashionable gatherings that Munby attended at Aubrey House and elsewhere his thoughts strayed continually to the unacceptable Mrs. Munby in the Temple. He was thankful to 'live in this quiet place, and have my chosen treasure here', he noted on 24 March: 'After dinner, we talked for hours, she sitting between my knees, of the long fellowship of nineteen years.'

Thursday, 27 March . . . After dinner, I with some difficulty persuaded Hannah to let me take her to the Albert Hall to hear the 'Creation'—which she had never heard or heard of. So, when she had cleared away, I helping her, she put on her new bonnet, her best things, her gloves—for now she wears gloves at times—and we went by rail to South Kensington. She enjoyed the music, enjoyed the photographs that hang round the great gallery: tender and charming she looked, and I contrived that the illuminati around should not notice her ignorance of the wellknown airs. When we came out, she whispered 'What a deal of money it must take to pay all them sing-gers!' Shropshire fashion. We got home by eleven.

Friday, 28 March . . . spent a long evening with my Hannah; part of the time, combating her strange fancies about herself: as, that she is 'not good enough' for one who is not worthy of *her*. Oh the 'divine humility of Love'! But it is my fault of other years, hard to be amended now, that this sweet soul has been brought so low in her own eyes. *That* was not what I meant, by those strange trials.

Thursday, 3 April . . . Home to Hannah . . . sitting in her red frock & white apron and neat cap, sewing; with the cat asleep on the hearthrug, and the kettle singing, and the old poets and other worthies looking down on her from the shelves around, and the evening sun shining in on the linnet in its cage and the myrtles & primroses growing in the window. I sat down and looked thankfully on this sweet homelike picture, and on her the central figure. . . . She told how she went to the Treasury yesterday & paid my rent, 'and the gentlemen never noticed me—and I said "Sir" to them, of course;' and how today, the tax-gatherer said 'You live in the kitchen, don't you?' and she—my wife—said 'Yes, Sir.' Not always! . . .

Saturday, 5 April. To the Haymarket Stores, & home by 3 p.m., & found Hannah getting ready. She had had a busy morning: 'I've cleared away' said she 'and made the bed, & dusted, & cleaned the rooms, & washed up, and fed the bird' and much more 'and I've cleaned the kettle, and cleaned two pairs of boots, and I've scoured the stairs on my knees:' and they were still wet with her scrubbing, when she came down them, drest in her new bonnet & best clothes, and looking like a lady. She and I went down the river together, to give her fresh air without fatigue, and walked awhile in the Park at Greenwich, and came back by the tramway, through the dreary faded suburbs . . .

Sunday, 6 April.   After prayers and reading of the Bible, Hannah went about her household work, upstairs and down: she brought up full cans of water, she dug coals and filled the heavy scuttle & carried it up from the cellar, not allowing me to help her. Rees returned from Circuit last night, and I sat with him awhile, talking over Lord Selborne's Bill.[5] This morning he met her on the kitchen stairs: she drest in her Sunday 'frock' of green stuff, & her clean white apron and large picturesque white cap. 'I like him—he is a kind gentleman,' said my Hannah: 'he said to me "Well, Mrs Cullick, how well you look!" and I thanked him and said "Yes Sir, but I've had a touch o' the rheumatics since you was away".' And so she had her dinner in the kitchen, refusing absolutely to have it upstairs: and helped me to begin a catalogue of my library; sitting by me with sweet eager face and saying 'It's nice—I can help you, and learn something at the same time.' Yes, indeed! And she tried on her new dress; grey and black, made in fashionable wise by a milliner (for once) to go out with me in; came gracefully into the room in it, saying 'Now I must try and think that I'm a lady!' But she took it off, and put on her humbler gown to go to the Temple Church in this afternoon, & from thence to her Clerkenwell friends to spend the evening . . .

My neighbour Captain Batten came up the other morning, with a posy of violets which he had kindly brought me from Dorsetshire; and tonight he was at the U.U. Club, & walked home with me. I did not ask him in, knowing that she whom he had seen as a servant was sitting quietly by the tea table in the parlour: but notwithstanding, I found that she had purposely retired into the back room. 'Oh, why didn't you ask him up?' said this meek darling, 'he would never have known!' 'What, dear—turn my wife out for the sake of an acquaintance?'

Monday, 7 April . . . Home to dinner at 6.15, and heard from Hannah the simple story of her day. The ancient kitchen of this house, in which she is supposed to live (and did live, before her marriage) is so damp now, that I wrote to the surveyor about it. The surveyor came; 'he is quite a gentleman, and he never noticed me,' said Hannah: never noticed what she was, because she wore a cotton frock and a cap, & had bare arms, and said 'Sir' to him: oh, the disguise is complete then. And this morning came the foreman, and she went down with him before I was aware. 'Hannah!' I called over the banisters, making believe to speak as a master. 'Yes Sir!' my sweet wife replied, with ready tact. 'Is Robert there?' 'Yes Sir,' she said again; and while I talked with him, she went

---

[5] For the reform of the judicature.

down to the kitchen to await him there. Later, two labourers came, and took up some flags in the kitchen floor. And what did *you* do? I enquired. 'Oh, I was with them, at work; I raked up the ashes with my hands, and I knelt on the hearth and cleaned the kettle!' And now this evening, what a contrast to that drudge was the sweet and noble woman who lay back in my easy chair, her dark uncovered hair rippling round her handsome mobile face, while in musical intelligent tones she read to me The Lovers of Gudrun![6] Yet even so, her old life was not forgotten: for when I had helped her at dinner, she said 'This is the first time I ever remember eating the wing of a fowl.' What? said I—then what parts *have* you eaten? 'Only the bones,' said my meek wife: 'we never expect to get anything else'—we common servants!

Munby and Hannah had looked forward to staying at the King's Arms, Ockley, over Easter, for 'our honeymoon'.

Good Friday, 11 April: Ockley ... When I drew the white curtains from our leaded lattice, and showed a dull grey morning with the sun steeped in wet cloud, Hannah said 'Ah, did you never notice that it's *always* dull on Good Friday morning, and generally bright on Easter Sunday morning? *I* have noticed it every year, and it's well known.' So, yesterday in the train, when she was eagerly noticing every trait of Spring & the Country, as we went along, suddenly she cried with happy face 'Oh, luck, luck! the lambs!' They were the first lambs she had seen this year, and she *saw their faces first*. That is good luck ...

Saturday, 12 April: Ockley ... 'How nice it is to be like a lady!' said my darling this morning, apropos of her leisurely toilet, her cold bath, her clean un-soiled hands, her general sense of ease and gracefulness. Yet she was careful to remark that she is as ready as ever to clean grates, or scour stairs. ...

Easter Sunday, 13 April: Ockley ... One thing to be noted in the Dorking country, is the great number of smockfrocks. Sir F. Palgrave, in 1837, spoke of the smockfrock as a thing all but extinct: yet in 1873, here at Ockley, men of all ages wear them, and lads, and little boys: brown or purple smocks, worn even on Sunday and at church, worn with corduroys and leggings. Another thing, is the wood fires. Besides the scent of flowers and the fresh air coming through the latticed window, the parlour in a morning is piquant with resinous odour of billets, cut up under the orchard behind the house, and laid on the fire with the bark on. We have a store on the red brick hearth, and burn scarce anything else. 'You must ring for Harriet, dear, to bring some more wood,' say I last

[6] A version of an Icelandic Saga, from William Morris's *The Earthly Paradise*. Munby had also been reading Morris's *Love is Enough* (1872) and quoted the title with feeling.

night, going out awhile. 'Ring for Harriet, Massa?' says my darling, looking up with a meaning smile: '*me* ring?' Me, a servant all my life, used to be rung for by others—am I now to have the honour of ringing for somebody else?

Ah yes, indeed! And to see her going to bed, afterwards, gliding gracefully out of the room, candle in hand, and smiling a sweet 'Goodnight, Mrs Wickens!' to the stout redfaced landlady, who looks up respectfully, and answers 'Goodnight, Ma'am,' with the deference of one who sees before her a *real* lady, this time.

Oh, Mrs Wickens! Do you know that my neighbour wants to hire this tall gracious lady, to clean his boots? . . .

Hannah's religious education had been supervised by Munby almost from the time of their first meeting; indeed, it was he who had arranged her confirmation. Their married life at Fig Tree Court was now regulated by morning and evening prayer, while Hannah assumed the task of reading the entire Bible aloud to her husband in daily instalments, a feat which was to take two years to accomplish.

At Ockley this Easter, they went to church on Good Friday, and again on Easter Sunday: 'the first Communion that I had made with Hannah since our marriage' (13 April). On Easter Monday they returned to town, but separated at London Bridge station—to avoid being seen approaching Fig Tree Court together, bearing the spoils of their holiday.

Easter Monday, 14 April . . . Hannah went home in a cab, taking with her a rushbasket full of Ockley eggs, laid soft in Ockley moss and lichen; and her great basket of primroses & violets, and her splendid posy of daffodils, and our luggage; all which she carried indoors, unaided and unnoticed.

I went on by train to Charing Cross.[7] Home by the Embankment at 5: and found there, not the elegant lady of this morning, but a servant, drest in a homely cotton frock and coarse apron and large white cap, and barearmed and hardworking.

'Mrs Wickens nor Harriet wouldn't say Ma'am to me *now*, Massa!' says she. . . . She has been sweeping and dusting all day, doing the work of four days: has found the cat & the bird delighted to see her again, and has filled the room with her flowers, arranged in bowls and baskets and pots, in the window, on the piano & the table—everywhere.

'How much nicer it is' says she 'to get your dinner and my own, than to sit still and see it brought, and be waited on!' And after dinner, she reads 'Our Village'[8] to me, a reminiscence of our happy visit to Ockley.

---

[7] To go to his office, surprisingly; but the Bank Holiday Act of 1871 was not yet fully operative in the modern sense.

[8] By Mary Russell Mitford.

Monday, 21 April . . . After dinner, I went to the Working Men's College in Great Ormond Street, to the general meeting, held in the new round room, which was densely crowded with students. T. Hughes presided, and he & Litchfield spoke first, and then R. W. Emerson[9] the American writer said a few commonplace words. A tall gaunt man, he is, with a hatchet face, a large nose, heavy eyebrows, shrewd mobile mouth; a head well developed behind, & covered with thin piebald hair. Such is he whose book on the soul[1] exercised me twenty years ago.

This morning, my Hannah had to get up again at 6, to my annoyance, to let the workmen into the kitchen . . . when I got home to dinner, I found her in her green best 'frock' and clean apron, and wearing a wonderful mobcap, with a border of antique lace and a violet ribbon: just such a cap as was worn by country girls about 1820, and is now coming into fashion again, for ladies. But she did not make it from the fashion books: she made it, today, from a picture I had shown her in Bloomfield's 'Wild Flowers', of a maidservant at church . . . looking charming in that picturesque cap, she rose, made an arch curtsy, and said laughingly 'In our courting days, Sir, you used to be more punctual!' . . .

Wednesday, 23 April . . . After dinner and a quiet fireside talk, I dressed to go to the P. A. Taylors': and through the doorway watched my wife as she sat at her supper—bare-armed, and in cap & apron and cotton frock; for she had not 'cleaned herself'. It is hard to make her eat with me; to persuade her that she must not keep the worst for herself and live on broken meats. The other day I made her eat a sweetbread: it was the first time she had ever done so. 'How nice it is! But it's too grand for *us*'—for servants. And then, in my evening dress, with her kitchen frock, her servant's cap, pressed close to me, how much more noble she seemed than those whom I was going to meet: worthier of jewels and finery, and yet happy in the thought that she knows nothing of either, and is free from such restraints. 'How I wish I could show you there!' 'I'm sure *I* don't,' says she, laughing: 'I should *hate* to be shown!'

It was a large & pleasant party, at Aubrey House. Among others, I had some talk with Miss Lydia Becker,[2] who, I find, thinks as I do about female labour, and respects the Lancashire pit girls and their work. Home by twelve.

Friday, 2 May. Hannah again jumped out of bed at 6 a.m., unbeknown to me, and ran downstairs to let the workmen in. And then she told me a thing that

---

[9] Ralph Waldo Emerson (1803–82), philosopher and poet.

[1] Probably the essay 'Nature' of 1836.

[2] Lydia Ernestine Becker (1827–90), the suffragist and editor of the *Women's Suffrage Journal*. Munby had written a letter to the *Manchester Guardian*, in support of the Wigan pit girls, as recently as 18 April. He firmly defended their wearing of trousers, and concluded that 'things have come to a pretty pass, when so-called Liberals seek to prevent one half of the human race from earning their bread in any honest way they choose'. (MS. in Yale University Library.)

strangely illustrates the difference which habit and use may make, in characters essentially alike. Yesterday, she said, the workmen were talking 'free' to her; one said 'I wonder you're not afraid to sleep down here, all alone'; and she 'Why should I? What have I to be afraid of?' and he 'Oh, some one might fetch you away!' and she 'Oh, I'm big enough and strong enough; it would take a strong one, to fetch *me* away!' And when was all this? Oh, said she in a shamefast [*sic*] whisper, 'while I was cleaning: *I cleaned the closet, before them all!*' Here is a woman graceful in person and manner, as a lady; pure, modest, naturally refined and sweet; shrinking from moral evil and moral foulness; knowing also that marriage has made her a lady, and fresh from her ladylike experiences at Easter; yet, because she was bred a servant and is used to it, she goes among rough men as an equal, and in their presence undertakes the most disgusting labour. True, she knows that in her husband's eyes, *any* labour, done by her, is noble and is sanctified. . . .

Monday, 5 May . . . Mr. Thornbury, my tenant, calls today: finds my Hannah, in her kitchendress, standing at the washtub; condescends to ask how she is; makes a sign to her to pick up his letters from the floor; 'so I said, "I'm very well, thank you Sir," and I knelt down and picked them up for him.' All which she duly tells me afterwards, seated in the easy chair, dainty in black silk & drawingroom cap, her fair head leaning back in repose, her sweet mouth smiling at the contrast: for, is she not a servant during the day, and a lady in the evening? and fulfils either part so well, that for the time she seems incapable of the other.

Wednesday, 7 May.   To shops in Regent Street & elsewhere, buying glass for Hannah's flowers, and china for her and myself: and home to dinner at seven. Miss Mitford's Our Village gives me opportunities of explaining many long words, bits of French, and proper names, to its fair reader. 'Anomaly', for instance. 'What is an *anomaly*?' she asks. Well—something out of the usual course; something you wouldn't expect, or that seems out of place. 'Ah' says she, 'then *I'm* an anomaly, sitting here in this room, and reading to you!' Blessed anomaly!

Today the workmen have finished the kitchen. I went down to see it, now clean and dry and cheerful, its damp flags replaced by a new boarden floor. And there were the flower boxes which the workmen have made for Hannah; all for nothing, and just to please her. It seems that she has taught all the folk about her to call her simply 'Hannah', just as she was called in service. 'I hope Hannah will be comfortable in her kitchen now; when does she get into it?' says my neighbour the Revising Barrister to me this evening. He little knows that I know of his 'goings on': how, the other day, he attempted to fling his arm round her waist and kiss her bonny face, and was only prevented by her wifely in-dignation and her strong right arm . . .

This operatic marriage fulfilled a poet's dream. Munby revelled in its implications. He had long understood that his most ambitious poem would have to be acted out in real life; and now, in justice to Hannah (and himself), he gladly assumed the task of describing their romantic union in pre-Raphaelite detail, with a full selection of Hannah's sayings and doings. He went further; he dramatised many of the situations with agonising sensitivity. The ménage at 6 Fig Tree Court was like an invention in the *Bab Ballads*; but it happened to be true, and it held as much pathos as comedy.

Each day increased Munby's sentimental fondness for his wife. On 8 May, a caller actually lifted his hat to her, while she was wearing her black silk dress, and said to someone: 'I didn't see the servant, I saw a tall fine looking *lady*!' 'Now that I've been taken for a *lady*, I couldn't possibly clean your boots!' Hannah pointed out.

The next day was Munby's turn to be witty. 'If you please Sir, the kitchen & cellar have got so dirty with the workmen's boots, I must have a charwoman to clean them!' said Hannah. 'Then get *Hannah*; she's the very best charwoman I know,' replied Munby, who added: 'These little comedies delight me, for they bring out my darling's graceful archness, and show that she is happy. "I get happier every day, Massa," said she the other night' (9 May). And now that the weather was warmer, she was more willing to go out of town at week-ends.

Sunday, 11 May: Southend . . . The chambermaid at the Ship Hotel is a gentle and comely young woman, with delicate features and superior ways: and the sanction of a married bed did not lessen her pretty bashfulness, when she brought in the hot water, and brought in the bath and the can, and arranged them; and answered a few questions, modestly keeping her eyes on the ground. When she had gone, 'I think she is not used to it,' said my lady Hannah, 'she seems so confused. *I* used to have to light the fires, even in the gentlemen's rooms, while they were in bed, when I was under housemaid; I used to walk straight in, and kneel down, and do the grate, and I thought nothing of it, though I was so young. That was because I was *ordered* to do it, and it was my *work*. But afterwards, when I had to wait at table, I felt so awkward and confused, and thought every one was looking at me. Still, now I'm older, I can wait at table very well, if you have any one to dinner.' So spake my lady, reposing at ease in her chamber . . .

Wednesday, 21 May . . . Dined about 6, and sat with Hannah till after 8; then dressed, and by rail to Notting Hill, to the last of the Wednesday parties at Aubrey House: the last, for ever. P. A. Taylor is going to sell this charming rus in urbe; ample widespreading old country house, with timbered lawns, and

330

acres of garden: all doomed, apparently.[3] The large rooms were filled with a crowd of people, famous or otherwise: blind Fawcett, holding forth in his corner, with a face that would be pathetic if he were not so selfasserting: hawklike cynical James Stansfeld, gliding coldly about, demure and silent; MacCallum, fresh from the East; and many more. Half my acquaintance seemed to be there. I left at 11.30, & home by rail: and after kissing Hannah, went in, as I had promised, to an uproarious party given by my neighbour Capt. Batten! A room walled in with rifles and bayonets; trumpets & flags over the fire place, big drums hung from the ceiling: the Recorder of Cambridge singing comic songs; the Revising Barrister playing the tambourine; officers of the 8th Foot, and other youngsters, making enormous noise, with voice & piano and drums . . .

Thursday, 29 May. To the Club, where James[4] met me at 5.30, and we walked to Fleet Street and dined at The London. I had arranged with Hannah that she should spend the evening with her Clerkenwell friends, in order that I might have a tête à tête with James, and tell him our story—the rest of it. As she was busy watering and trimming her window plants this morning, all in her servant's dress, I said 'I shall say to Mr. James, This is our Hannah's garden.' 'Ah' said she 'then he will say, "I suppose they are as rustic looking as she is"!' 'Tell her,' said James tonight, apropos of this, 'that when I saw that picture of her, I thought she was a duchess.' We came in from dinner at 7.30; found coffee ready, and everywhere the traces of a loving woman's thoughtful care: James lighted a cigar and took the easy chair, and by the twilight and the firelight I took up the story at the point where I left off when I sought his counsel in January 1872, and told him all: except the details of her past drudgery and humiliation as a charwoman, which to him might have seemed to mar the pure ideal of a rustic sweetheart. He listened intently, this wise friend of my youth, for nearly two hours: and said at last, 'You have done right, and you have given me enough to think of for a long time to come.' And then, while dressing, I told him of her ways: of her favourite saying, 'God made me for you!' and how she shook her head at the slaughter in Deuteronomy, and said 'That was not very nice of you, Mr. Moses!' At last, about ten, James drove with me to Chandos Street Cavendish Square; and we walked up & down there, still talking of Hannah, before we parted and I went in to Miss Warren's concert-party . . .

Whitsunday, 1 June . . . I found my darling, drest in her black silk 'frock' and a clean white apron, and without a cap, sitting in the armchair, finishing a long letter to her sister, Ellen the nurse. I asked leave to read it, and found that it was full of happiness, and praises of her husband: what a good husband she had got, and what a happy home. Sweet, loving soul, the praise is hers. She is indeed the wife of a man much above her in rank & education; she lives with him as an

---

[3] Aubrey House miraculously survived two world wars and other dangers.
[4] Henry James, of Cheltenham, had become a prosperous military coach.

equal and a beloved one, has no longer a mistress, but has her freedom, and has companionship, & culture at home with him, and is clothed and honoured as a lady whenever he can take her abroad: but here, among the neighbours, she is still only a servant; she still wears her kitchendress . . . and all who see her believe that she is her husband's hired servant and his drudge. For his sake, and for the sake of her own love and humility, she foregoes not only the name and place of a lady, which she thinks herself unfit for, but even her own due and cherished name of wife. What woman except Hannah would be capable of such lofty selfsacrifice? A lady-wife would scorn the menial work, the humble aspect and behaviour, which is natural to Hannah: an ordinary servant would look on marriage with a gentleman as the means of escape from toil, of obtaining fine clothes, of airing her new honours as a 'lady'.

I went down tonight to see Rees about some matter: and presently he began talking about Hannah. 'Where is your servant now?' said he. 'She's upstairs,' said I carelessly, 'packing my portmanteau: I'm going away tomorrow[5] for a week.' And again: 'I'm glad you set your face against having Tarrant and his wife, now,' said the Reviser; 'it's much better to have Hannah living in the kitchen; and she seems so anxious to make things clean and respectable.' 'Yes, she's very willing, and an excellent servant,' says Hannah's master, gravely.

Monday, 9 June . . . I went at 5 p.m. to Kensington, to one of Mrs Ashurst's afternoon levées; where was Mrs Stansfeld, Mlle Bovet, and a few others. I walked back through Kensington Gardens and the Ride, escorting the wise Julie; who informed me that I was 'a most worldly man', and that my love for a common servant like Hannah was perfectly ridiculous.[6] Said she, 'I might as well fall in love with a man-cook!' forgetting that in Hannah's eyes, a mancook is (or was) a superior being . . .

Friday, 13 June . . . home to dinner at 6.30. A new surprise: our bedroom . . . had been made fair, with white curtains, and green ribands, & new blinds: all put up today by our busy Hannah, who said smiling, when she was kissed for it, 'It does not cost much to give a deal of pleasure!' Well, surely folks will guess that something more than a hired servant is here: nothing but Love could have turned these dusky purlieus into a sweet and sunny home.

Hannah did not sit down by me today as usual; for she was busy in her kitchen; she went up & downstairs, in her servant's dress, and answered the bell (which I rang at her request) and took care to be seen . . . by Mrs. Newton, carrying trays up to the parlour; and then she cleared away, and descended again, because she would, and had her supper all alone in the kitchen; and then she 'washed up' at the sink there, and sang; I heard her voice floating up from the cellars; because she was happy? 'Yes!' said she: 'and I sang while I was cleaning the knives.' For she came up afterwards, and entered the room, with

---

[5] To Clifton Holme.   [6] Julie Bovet did not know they were married.

the large lamp in both her hands: 'Now I'm the servant, carrying the lamp!' she said, with childlike vivacity and with pathetic truth. And she brought in a sheet of white muslin, bought to make blinds of, and sailed round the room, her tall figure wrapt in it as in a ball-dress, and her servile clothes all hid by it, and her sweet face glowing in the midst of fantastic white headdresses made of its folds. 'What would they say of me downstairs' says she 'if they was to see me *now?*'

Monday, 16 June . . . Home to dinner at seven, and sat quietly with my darling till after 9; she, in her Swiss cap, leaning back in the armchair and watching with frequent words of delight the beauty of our three parlour windows in the sunset: the plants and ferns, the white gauze curtains and green blinds, the linnet in its cage, the cat, with scarlet ribbon round its neck, sunning itself among the flowers on the central sill. All this is her work. . . .

Wednesday, 18 June . . . Saw the Shah of Persia[7] arrive at Charing Cross, at 6.30 p.m. Sitting upright in an open carriage, a diamond aigrette on his tall black cap, he seemed to take no notice of the crowd and the cheering. But the Persians of his suite were all animated and curious; they bowed, and salaamed, and looked eagerly up at a Persian inscription hung across the street. I was struck by the sameness of their faces; all regular, intelligent, and alike. The vast crowd of spectators was most orderly and goodhumoured, and cheered this un-known Asiatic with a simple and pathetic enthusiasm. . . .

During the next few weeks, Mr. and Mrs. Munby spent a night together at Shepperton, and also a long week-end in the Isle of Wight, which Hannah had never visited and liked very much. After their return, Mr. Thornbury, the tenant, asked Hannah where Mr. Munby had been. Hannah said she believed he had been to the Isle of Wight: '"Ah" says he "it's a beautiful place!" and I said "Yes, Sir, I've heard as it's very pretty."' (5 July).

Friday, 11 July.   This morning at breakfast, Hannah by chance let fall a knife. 'There!' said she at once 'I shall see a strange man here today.' For she is ever full of picturesque rustic folklore; never omits to turn her tea cup three times round and study the dregs; and gives to every little domestic accident its proper symbolic meaning; having herself just that imaginative half-belief in such symbolism, which is so attractive, because it does not lessen your respect for her understanding.

When I came home to dinner at 6, Hannah, instead of being upstairs as usual, was in the kitchen. She ran up from the kitchen to meet me at the door, whisper-ing 'Massa, *Mr. Moore*[8] is upstairs! Hasn't it come true?' For she had never seen

---

[7] Nasiruddin (Nasr-ed-Din) Shah, the first shah of Persia to visit Europe.
[8] The Rev. F. J. Moore.

him before, and I had not expected him. 'Never you mind', she continued: 'the dinner is ready, and you just ring for me and take no notice of me, and I'll wait!' She was 'cleaned', and in her servant's evening dress; her longsleeved frock of green stuff, with white collar and brooch, her clean white apron & large white cap. Thus drest, she had opened the door to the strange man who, seeing a woman in servant garb, 'answering' the door and behaving to him with simple respect, had taken her position for granted and gone in without much looking at her. 'It's all right, he hardly noticed me!' said this sweet wife, so strangely wanting in love of admiration. I went up, and found the Vicar of Bottesford, just returned from his ramble in Belgium.

Making the best of the situation, I asked him to join me at dinner, and rang the bell. Instead of presenting our guest to my gentle graceful wife, and bidding him take the honour of a place by her at table, I had to treat her as one who served, and whom he would not care to notice. My wife came up from her kitchen to answer the bell; she entered the room in her kitchen dress, carrying a tray, looking demure & respectful; and the visitor never checked his talk nor looked at her. She set the dinner, waited silently on her husband and his friend, said 'Sir' when she was spoken to, which was but seldom; and only one of the two took any note of her graceful gliding ways and her noiseless neathanded and effective service. When dinner was over, and she had cleared away, she stood in the doorway and said 'Shall I make any coffee now, Sir?' 'If you please', said her husband: and she made it and brought it upstairs. And then, I made an excuse to the unobservant Vicar, and went down to the kitchen, full of sadness and self-reproach. She was there, standing at the sink, under the window, washing up our dinner things. And straightway, she left her work, and ran smiling and flung her wet arms around her husband, crying 'Well, Massa, what fun!' '*Fun!*' to see my wife waiting at table like a servant? 'Oh nonsense!' said this lively creature, who had seemed so demure in the parlour: 'You know it's quite natural to *me*, and I know how to wait: didn't I do it well?' 'Yes you did—but I felt as if I must tell you to sit down with us, and say "she is my wife".' 'It's a good job you didn't, then,' said our Hannah: 'the idea! you shanna let everybody know our secrets!' She brought a chair for her husband by the kitchen fire, and laid herself down on his breast, in the old delightful way; and thus they sat together for ten minutes or so, till she said 'You must go upstairs now, or you may have suspicion aroused.' 'Yes, and how long will he stay? To think that you are banished to the kitchen, and I dare not have my own wife to sit in her own parlour!' 'What of that?' said the wife, with one more kiss: 'it's warm and nice down here, and I've plenty of work; I want to wash and iron a bit, and I've several things to do for you. Besides, you can ring for me,' she added . . .

But he did not ring: after a time, she came upstairs of her own accord, and knocked humbly, and stood in the doorway and said 'If you please Sir, I should like to go out for the errands, before the shops shut.' 'Very well', said he, noticing (but his friend did not) that this time, she had on her old bonnet and her cloak.

At length, after 9 p.m., the goodnatured unobservant Vicar went away; and when he had gone, his hostess and servant came upstairs and resumed her rights. When she was waiting at table, she had heard his travel-talk & noticed his bad French; which now she criticized, lying back in the armchair, and amusing herself in the twilight by repeating in French and in German the numerals, the names of the months and days, and other words, which she had picked up years ago from her master the French cook and her German fellowservant.

Ten o'clock came and passed; and I wished my darling goodnight, & went to the Theodore Martins'. There I found grand music, and a gorgeous assemblage; men wearing stars and orders; a Bishop in purple coat and silver buckles; Sir Frederic Pollock, Sir Rutherford Alcock, Sir Arthur Helps with his bristling white hair and 'peart' white face, so like Mazzini, only not grave and sad, as *his* face was. I took Sir Arthur's daughter down to supper; a plain and quiet girl. No woman there had a face or figure to match my kitchen maid's: but one, Mrs W. H. Brookfield, reminded me of her—for she wore a mobcap.

I walked home by 2 a.m.

On 15 July, after leaving his office at 4.30, Munby 'wasted nigh three hours in making calls', in Regent's Park and Hampstead: 'All were out.' His invisible marriage allowed him to continue, at the age of 45, to play the rôle of an accomplished bachelor. Presumably he enjoyed it; he was always spurred on by curiosity, his restlessness being especially evident during the summer months in London. Having spent another week-end at Ockley with Hannah (19–21 July), he travelled all the way back to Gomshall by himself, two days later, to see the spot where the Bishop of Winchester (formerly of Oxford), Samuel Wilberforce, had just been killed in a fall from his horse. His view of this capable but contentious prelate had mellowed considerably since 1860, when he had thought his appearance 'not prepossessing'.

Wednesday, 23 July.   At 4.25 p.m. I went by train from Charing Cross to Dorking & Gomshall . . . Hannah laughingly refused to come. . . . From Gomshall station I walked back along the road through Abinger Hammer, and past the Hall, and up a deep shady lane to a lofty bit of common, rough with gorse. This is Evershed's Rough: and on the further and lower side of it, in a lovely spot opposite a thatched barn and sheepfold, I found the cross in the turf, and the smooth and trivial hollow where the Bishop fell.[9] Some 3 weeks ago, I was in the room with him, taking part in a discussion: I noted his dress and manner, his quaint cloak & staff, his episcopal ring on the forefinger, and above all, the charm of his talk and the mobile sweetness of his expressive manywrinkled face. One moment, and presto! this master spirit is—where? . . .

[9] The place is now marked by a granite cross.

Friday, 25 July . . . home to dinner by seven. 'Ring for me when you're ready, Massa' said my darling, who was at work downstairs: and she came up and sat by me in the easy chair, and picked currants for her future jellies, and talked in her sweet bright way. And then she went down and had her supper in the kitchen, as she loves; and came up again and arranged the window plants, and read to me, finishing Mrs Godolphin.[1] Last night, she insisted on sleeping alone, in the servant's bed in the kitchen, to air it. Tonight, when she had returned to me & I went my rounds, I found my sweet wife's scouring apron hanging to the kitchen fire to dry. . . . 'Tis a coarse brown woollen apron, striped with red and yellow . . . which I gave her years ago. . . . To strangers, a degrading and repulsive garment; to me, attractive and noble & sacred. . . .

In the midst of this strange but idyllic existence, comes a reminder of the underlying strain it entailed, and a portent for the future. On 5 August, Munby returned home at 6.30 'and found my darling Hannah strangely hysterical and unwell, so that I spent the evening in nursing her and putting her to bed. Among other burdens, this of a possible illness is ever upon me.'

The next day Hannah had recovered, and on 7 August Munby took her out of town—the weather was extremely hot—to stay the night at the Burford Bridge Hotel, near Dorking. Having cleaned the stairs at Fig Tree Court 'in her dirt' only a few hours before, she was to be seen 'in a drawingroom of the hotel, reading the Midsummer Night's Dream!' (an appropriate choice). Munby adds: 'Those clouds of dirt and affected coarseness are very necessary, if the light is to be hid.' Perhaps—but this was not Munby's original motive in preaching lowliness to Hannah; and it was now difficult for Hannah, having religiously demeaned herself for twenty years, to know whether she was supposed to be still a 'rude mechanical' or a bettermost lady of Titania's court.

Munby could no longer easily decide whether he wanted Hannah's hands to be rough and cracked, or smooth and soft. It was almost impossible to have it both ways, before the days of detergents and cheap hand-lotion. Determined to sponsor his wife as an intermittent lady, he busied himself in buying gloves for her, and a parasol—'I always forget that I've got it!' Hannah said (1 August)—and even a fan, which she greeted with alarm but suffered to dangle from her wrist.

Munby tried to make Fig Tree Court into a real home for his wife, and daringly allowed Hannah to invite her shopgirl sister, Polly, to stay with them in his spare-room for a week, 'trusting that Hannah's admirable

---

[1] John Evelyn's Life, published in 1847. The diarist was a man after Munby's heart, and the nearness of Evelyn's Wotton had helped to attract him to the Ockley neighbourhood.

sense and readiness of wit may manage as cleverly for Polly's peace & reputation as for her own they do' (9 August). It was an improving visit, which shocked no one. Munby took the sisters to the South Kensington Museum; they went by themselves to see Doré's pictures in Bond Street.

Thursday, 14 August . . . home to dinner with Hannah. Sister Polly was gone to see Sister Ellen[2] . . . but Hannah had stayed at home and 'had the sweep'; whereby she had become almost as black as he was, a-working with and after him. . . . Sister Polly came before ten; and sat with her bright complex hair and her elegant grey dress, by the table, trimming Hannah's Sunday gown, while Hannah, still in her servant's cap & apron & frock, and bare armed, read Heber's[3] Palestine aloud. Superior welldrest Mary had never heard of Heber or his poem. And afterwards, at Hannah's desire, I played and sang to the piano awhile, and they two, poor untaught Graces of the piano playing sex, sat by and listened, knowing no note of music, pathetically wishing that they did.

Saturday, 16 August.   This morning at Whitehall, a messenger came to my room with a telegram . . . & a note; & said that someone was waiting in the hall. I went down; and whom should I find among the messengers in the hall, but my own beloved wife! She was seated on the footmen's bench by the door, where humble folk wait; she was drest as a servant, in her lilac cotton frock and clean coarse apron; her old strawbonnet on, and her bare hands and arms visible beneath her old grey cloak. As I approached, she rose, looking demure and humble, as she used to do when she sat thus in gentlefolks' halls waiting to guard her mistress; she rose and stood before me, and made a rustic curtsy to her husband. He, longing to kiss her, said a few hurried words, as it were a message; and with another curtsy, she withdrew, saying 'Very well, Sir.'

When I got home, about 4 p.m., there she was, in the same dress, her sweet rosy face and arms new-washed, a-combing out her soft brown hair. 'Did you notice my curtsying to you, Massa?' she said, as soon as he let her speak. And she added, 'You saw what a figure I looked, just a rough servant? Well, would you believe it, a smart well-drest young man followed me ever so far as I came back, and at last he said "Oh you naughty girl!" and "Would you like a glass of ale?" But I turned round, and said to him "I beg your pardon, what did you say?" and when he saw my look, he went away.' . . .

Sunday, 17 August.   Brilliant day. This morning, after Hannah had 'done' the rooms, and when we were talking over our journey[4] and preparing for a late breakfast, I suggested that for certain reasons we should prudently ask neighbour Rees, the Revising Barrister, to breakfast. Hannah eagerly agreed; &

---

[2] The nurse at Putney.
[3] Reginald Heber (1783–1826), the hymn-writer; later Bishop of Calcutta.
[4] They were going to France together for ten days.

straightway went down, in cap & apron & bare armed, as she was, and gave a single knock at our neighbour's door. 'If you please, Sir,' I heard her say, 'my master sends his compliments, and would you breakfast with him?' Neighbour Rees comes up; and, to the casual eye, the loving and vivacious wife sinks at once into a mere servant. 'Hannah, are you there? take away, please.' 'Yes, Sir,' says his wife, coming out of a back room with her tray; and she clears away the breakfast things, a neat and silent waitingmaid, while neighbour Rees continues his talk & his pipe, with his back to her, and never rises nor regards her. Hard; yet sweet and noble, and done with a just purpose . . .

. . . The note she brought with the telegram yesterday was . . . to prepare me for seeing her. 'Dearest' it said 'I shall bring this myself, so as you may have it at once; and I shall come as a servant, but I shanna say *whose* servant I am.' As I write, she is trying on her new pair of kid gloves; *not* old ones of mine, but 'bought o' purpose', for once. They are 8's—the largest women's size . . .

Monday, 18 August.　　This morning at 9, Hannah, in her working dress, went out to fetch Roberts the foreman, apropos of whitewashing. 'Where is your master going?' says Roberts, as he and she walk back together. 'Oh' says Hannah carelessly 'he's going to France or somewhere, I believe': and she opens the door and says 'Mr. Roberts, Sir!' to her husband, and then retires. Presently she is called in: What time do you think you can be ready for the men, Hannah? 'About the 2nd or 3rd of September, Sir,' says she; and then, standing there in her cap & apron and shortsleeved frock, she speaks to Roberts, as a mature and trusted servant might speak, about the work.

After I was gone, she had a talk downstairs with 'the other laundress'—the blooming widow; who asked her (and she readily agreed) to clean Mr. Rees's room tomorrow. The blooming widow has a sweetheart: 'and what a pity' she says to my Hannah 'that a fine looking young woman like *you* doesn't never think of getting married!' 'Oh' replies the wife, speaking à la mode du pays, 'I never *did* think nothing o' them things, in my life!' . . . After dinner, Hannah tried on, in all sorts of charming surprises, the rustic felt hat I had bought for her tour; and sat down to the piano, still in her servant's dress, and puzzled out Home sweet Home; and went to and fro, singing scraps of hymns, in a low and tender voice.

Early the next morning, 19 August, Munby lay at ease in bed, listening first to Hannah cleaning the grate next door, and then to the distant crunch of coal being dug out of the cellar. 'Ah, what a wife—what rough robust energy in labours like these, what grace and unspeakable tenderness in all else!' he ruminated, until his conscience suddenly pricked him: 'Why not get up and help her?' But this alarm was soon over. 'Wait till tomorrow, when (please God) she has ceased for a while to be a servant, and is leaning on her husband's arm, making her first acquaintance with a foreign land; wearing this graceful hooded cloak which I buy for her today, and this ravissant hat of black felt, trimmed by herself with feather and with veil.' One visualises a period drawing by Cattermole, with Munby as the attendant cavalier.

At 10.30 on the morning of Wednesday, 20 August, Munby drove away in a cab with a portmanteau, saying firmly 'Goodbye Hannah'; and Hannah let it be widely known that she had been given ten days' holiday. At 4.30 in the afternoon 'a tall and elegant lady in travelling dress' met Munby at the Charing Cross station, and 'we walked together to the tidal train, in which I had already arranged her seat and her luggage: the very portmanteau which my servant Hannah carried to my cab this morning.'

Munby wrote a special account of their adventures abroad in a separate notebook. Filled with praise for Hannah's graceful performance, it includes a sentence reflecting the confusion in which he found himself on the lady-and-servant question: 'her hands are getting better—or worse—with leisure . . .'

There were heavy seas in the Channel that August. Munby and Hannah were obliged to spend the night at Folkestone, and did not land at Boulogne until the 21st. They then went, among other places, to Rouen, Honfleur, Lisieux, Caen, Falaise, Trouville and Étretat. Hannah noticed everything, appreciated the churches, and was quick to make comparisons with English scenery and people. Munby bought her several presents, including a servant's cap for 2 fr. 50 and a vitré shawl for the equivalent of five shillings (thus once more backing it both ways). Admiring her elegance at Trouville on 27 August, he wrote: 'It takes both these phases of circumstance, to bring out all the various beauty and force that is in her: and if I regret the kitchen half of her existence, it is not because I undervalue its charms.'

At Étretat, on the 28th, Hannah 'danced about the room like a girl, imitating the sprightly air and actions of French chambermaids. "You will find me a very noisy servant when we get home, Massa," says she; "I shall be running about and crying 'Oh oui Monsieur!' and 'tout de suite' all day long!"'

She was generally content to be idle, but at Caen 'she surreptitiously made our bed, to save the femme de chambre trouble'. Munby is at pains to stress that they occupied a double-bed; he noted a French preference for sleeping apart, and found that nearly all the chambermaids assumed they wanted two beds.

They had another unpleasant crossing on the return journey, by night, from Boulogne to Folkestone in the *Princess Clementine*, a second-class cargo boat. Munby was put into the men's cabin; Hannah into the ladies'. After the train journey, the usual parting followed; 'Cinderella had returned from the ball', wrote Munby. Her showing as a lady had pleased him. 'And, whatever the reason, she was free too from those strange moods of depression and "naughtiness" which affect her sometimes at home, and which perplex and sadden me so because she will not give me the clue to them nor let me comfort her . . . I have loved her for twenty years as a servant; and this year, now that I am her husband, I learn to love her as a lady too.'

Saturday, 30 August . . . Arrived at Folkestone from Boulogne, 5 a.m., and at Charing Cross, 9.46. Hannah returns to the Temple—I home in the afternoon, and find her metamorphosed from an elegant lady into a rough maidservant. With her till 5 p.m., then to King's Cross and by train to Yorkshire. Reach Clifton Holme before eleven: find my dear parents well, and Carry and Edward with them.

This return to York for his family holiday sounds precipitate. One wonders how much, if anything, Munby told his parents about the trip to Normandy; he salved his conscience by setting out immediately with his father for a tour of the Lake District. Hannah, left alone, embarked on the most rewarding of her spasmodic diaries. Reading aloud to Munby had strengthened her vocabulary.

Hannah's Diary: Saturday, 30 August, 1873 . . . I am just return'd home after ten days tour in France with my darling Massa & husband—We started from Boulogne at two o'clock this morning after lying in our berths nearly an hour. i kept well *to* Boulogne, & it was my first sea voyage too, except crossing the Solent for the Isle o' Wight with M. this year, & *this* Journey was rough, but I kept well a long time—*going up & down* with the waves in imagination & not opening my eyes, but I could hear all going on, & that my husband was very bad—i ask'd after him several times from the steward & sent messages—at last I was a little bit ill . . . and I went to sleep, for when I woke I was so pleas'd to see it was daylight & I felt better, & my first thought was to go & see Massa, so i jumped out . . . & run along the floor, tottering a little, & I found M. still sick & hoarse with retching—I wiped his face, & said i thought we were in harbour—he call'd me his child, & said how ill he'd bin & told me to go & lie down again, & so i was glad to do, for I felt sleepy & knock'd up, but soon after the man said we must land, & i got up again & fasten'd my clothes & pick'd my things up to go ashore—Massa came for me, & when we landed it was a fine calm Morning. . . . This ten days has been quite new to me of course, crossing from Folkstone to Boulogne—from Boulogne to Rouen—there we saw the ancient buildings statue of Jean d'Arc—and the beautiful churches. And at the Hotel d Albion where we stopp'd was a most amusing little maid—bowing & scraping in the most lively Attitude, & most civil to Monsieur & Madame—When i left she help'd me on with my cloak & as well as i could [i] said 'Nous revenez' & then 'How funny that you & i cannot understand one another' me meaning both being servants—but she only laugh'd & said 'Oui Madame'. We had a long sail from Rouen to Honfleur in the boat, but a very pleasant one, along the River Seine, & most days we have had long journeys, by rail & road or water, & seen a great deal in the time . . . and everywhere i was treated most respectfully—just as if i was a real lady—And Massa says i behaved nicely & look'd like a lady too. He bought me a felt hat & plume of cocks feathers to wear, & a veil, & a new brooch to pin my shawl with, & a new waterproof cloak, but i generally wore my blue skirt & jacket over my grey frock, with frill round my neck, & white cuffs, & grey kid gloves, & carrying my striped sunshade—all so different to anything i had got used to, that one day in the train I got almost illtemper'd at being so muffled up, & i felt i'd much liefer feel my hands free as they used to be—but M. made me put the gloves on again, & i thought it was hard to be forced to wear gloves—even harder than it was to leave em off altogether before i was married, as i did for over 16 year i think. When i started, i wore my old black bonnet to Folkstone, & changed it there, & the same back again, & put my plaid shawl over my skirt so i wasn't noticed coming into the Temple nor going out. . . . And here i am again—very glad to get back, & i've doff'd all my best clothes & put my own on again—my dirty cotton frock & apron & my cap—taken the top dust off the things & lighted the fire—fetch'd in some bread & butter, & got my dinner—then i rested till M. came in, & we unpack'd our bags & things & then pack'd the large portmanteau for M. to start home with—he was gone by $\frac{1}{2}$ past 5 after wishing me a hearty good bye & hoping i should not be dull—i said i shouldn't & didn't mean to be, but i think it's not possible to be any other—quite alone in this very quiet place, & not a soul to speak to confidentially—for i'm obliged to look at my words lest i sh^d say anything to Mrs Newton or anyone to betray myself. . . .

Sunday, 31 August . . . Mr Rees came in between ten & eleven—he saw the black door was open & came up stairs—i went to the door—he said 'You're come back Hannah' i said 'Yes sir'—so he told me how he was sleeping away at his Mother's for the present, & that i may keep the outer door shut as much as i liked. & then he went down again saying 'good morning' & i said 'good morning sir', and i saw no one else here the rest o' the day . . .

Monday, 1 September.   First thing i went to the Surveyors Office . . . after i'd said goodmorning sir, & if there was any answer to Mr. Munby's letter from the surveyor about the work—The foreman said he didn't think there was any need of an answer if Roberts had promised to see about it . . . so i wrote & told M.

what i knew & also how i miss'd the politeness i'd bin used to in France—the englishmen seem almost *rude* in their bluntness, & certainly civility & politeness is much the pleasantest—only i think everyone knows that the English don't *mean* to be rude, & it wouldn't be right to say the French only put on or *learn* their civility & do not really mean it. . . .

Friday, 5 September.   I was up & dress'd by six o'clock this morning to let the men in . . . i took the bedroom carpets, door mats & rugs, & the paper from under the big carpet to sweep in the court—i soon got dirty of course arms & face & all & i could feel the dust on my neck—Nothing new to me cause i've done the same thing so often before, but in the Temple i'm sure a working woman is look'd on as been particularly low—first cause they are nearly all very poor & drudging like, & being among so many single gentlemen hardly a respectable young woman would be expected to live here, but i *have* seen a many younger looking than me in the Temple. . . .

Wednesday, 10 September . . . One o' these men come down to me in the kitchen yesterday & ask'd me very abruptly if the master had left any beer money for them—i said 'No not especially—only i know he's not a bad one for that sort o' thing, and no doubt he'll leave it to me to give as i think proper.' He said 'Well, I hope you wont forget us' i said 'Why you've scarce begun work yet' & he went up stairs again, & i thought 'i shall see you more civil before i give you anything.' And i was at work with them most o' the day today—answering 'em civilly but dignified, & towards the evening they both was quite civil to me, & the one as didn't ask for the money i give a shilling to, to share, & he touch'd his hair & said 'Thank you Mum' . . .

Thursday, 11 September . . . this morning just before twelve when i was splash'd with dirt & was scouring near the door of M's room another working man was up there & as i was on my knees he tapp'd me on the shoulder & said 'i *should* like to come & have tea with you o' Sunday'—i said 'i'm seldom in Sundays'—he said 'Well you're not engaged, are you? Could i go out with?' i said i'm much obliged to you all the same but i want no company . . . i like to be free with all the workmen & civil of course, but some how i hate them to pretend making love to me—it annoys me, & then i can look so straight & tho' i look such a drudge & am ten times blacker than they are i feel as if they've no *right* to speak to me on that subject.

On the same day that Hannah fended off the attentions of the workman, her husband, released from attendance on 'the father', was enjoying himself at Wigan, his traditional hunting-ground.

Thursday, 11 September: Wigan.   At 5.30 a.m. I was awoke by the tramp of the factory girls. My window at the Royal Hotel looks upon the market place: I got up, and saw the broad street busy with women and girls, all in clogshoon and most of them with shawls over their heads, all tramping to work in groups of two & three, and talking broad Lancashire audibly. Hundreds of them; and hardly any men. The sun had not risen; it was dawn, and great rosy clouds were in the west. I went to bed again; . . . About ten, I went through the market place, and down Clarence Yard to the humble abode of Mrs Little, photographer, & cab-owner's wife. I enquired for Ellen Grounds. 'Hes yon wench coom?' 'Yea, hoo hes,' said Mrs Little; and she and her grown up daughter wore a puzzled smile, as if they were about to show me some strange creature. A moment afterwards, Ellen herself came out of the kitchen; and she was in her pit clothes, as she had promised. 'Well, Ellen, yo've coom!' 'Yah, Ah's coom, Sir!' said the collier-lass, who looked vastly better, and also bigger, in her working dress, than she did last night in woman's clothes. She wore her wadded bonnet, the front part tied tight over the forehead, and the hood encircling her head like an aureole; her loose bluepatched cotton bedgown made her full bust and broad shoulders look larger still; below it, came her striped skirt, gathered up round the hips; and under that, her breeches—the pair she showed me last night—and her ironshod clogshoon. She had forgotten to bring her top coat; and first she tried on a coat belonging to Mrs Little's son, a big lad; but it was too small for her; so she tried a rough coat, like her own, of *Mr.* Little's; and it fitted her well. Then she was furnished with a spade, to represent her great pit shovel. She shouldered the spade in workmanlike fashion, buttoned her coat, and stood readily and well, as I posed her; and she was taken, first in that guise, and then without the coat; I standing beside her, to show how nearly she approached me in size.[5] Indeed, the bigness of this bonny Ellen struck me more than ever: she seemed to fill the lobby and the portrait shed with her presence; she was as big as Mrs Little & her daughter together; . . . and she strode about the room in her sounding clogs, and laughed and chatted with the two women in a kindly and respectful way, but with the air of a strong man speaking to feeble folk. . . . She did everything just as she was told; and enlivened the proceedings by jests at her own expense, and hearty goodhumoured talk . . .

The next day Munby, in his rôle of inspector, undertook an extensive tour in search of local colliery-women; but, half-way through, he found himself suddenly home-sick for Hannah. He sent her a telegram, and impulsively hurried back to Fig Tree Court, interrupting his holiday.

Saturday, 13 September.   I awoke from sleeping, for the first time in my life, in a servant's bedroom in a kitchen—a cellar. In the low dark room was nothing but the bed, with a patched quilt on it made by Hannah out of her long series of cotton frocks, and two servant's boxes, and an old chair, and an old washhandstand without basin or ewer. For my lowly wife retains her old habits; she has no looking-glass, no jug or basin; she washes herself at the sink, and has not seen

5 See Plate 14, also Plates 12 and 13.

her own face for days; except yesterday, when she looked at herself upstairs, and found that 'I had a black streak across my nose, and my whole face was more or less dusty.' And with that face, and with hands and arms blacker still, she had just been out, in her coarse working clothes, and had her dinner for sixpence, along with labouring men, at a cookshop in Fetter Lane. And this is she who, only a fortnight ago, was taking her meals with me, as a lady, in a fashionable hotel at Trouville. What other woman would be capable of such sublime impartiality?

I too washed at the sink, perforce; but my darling, who was shocked (forsooth) that I should have to come down to her level in this, had provided me a basin and hot water, and my own bath. She took care, too, that I should see her clean my boots; and she set out a parlour breakfast on the kitchen table, opposite to a bright fire and a cleanly hearth. As usual, she would not sit down with me to eat, but sat & read a chapter; drest now in her own dress as an English servant, and looking charming in her large cap & lilac frock, and bare arms, and clean 'harden' apron; with a background of shelves, neatly ranged with dishes of her own washing, and a strip or two of matting on the new boarden floor, fresh-scoured by herself. 'My darling, how sweet this is, to be sitting thus in my own kitchen, with you! Do you know that you are my own wife, and that we never can be parted now, for ever?' And before the words are done, she is out of her chair and down on her knees before him, and her head is on his breast and her bare working arms are round him.

But there is not much time for petting: the workmen with whom she has wrought upstairs are gone, and now she has to 'clean after' them, and to scour the floors again. We go upstairs and above ground, to the parlour, now all in confusion; she in her hoodbonnet and striped scouring apron, and her dirty cotton frock. Whilst her skin is yet clean, she kisses him, and lifts him up with her arms into the air, to show her old strength; and she kneels down with her pail, and scrubs the floor, and soon her face and arms are as black as a collier-girl's, or blacker. 'Fancy any *lady* coming down to have to do *this* work!' she says: yet between her scrubbing she talks well & brightly; quoting Shakespeare aptly, asking me questions out of Enfield's History of Philosophy, which she has been reading.

And so at 4 p.m. we kissed again & parted; and I to Yorkshire, and reached Clifton Holme by eleven.

Hannah's Diary: Sunday, 14 September.　　Altho' Massa has bin & gone away again so sudden i've not felt dull to day, nor last night either—Mr Rees (the gentleman on the ground floor) coming in while M. was saying good bye, & Massa of course not wanting to be seen especially in the kitchen, it started both of us, & M. was off to get dinner before going to King's Cross, & i up Fetter Lane in the rain to get my errands in, & so when i come back to my tea in the kitchen i was at home again, & all was again as afore M. came, only i felt *happier*

—how could i help it, after having such a proof of his love—to come from impulse 2 hundred miles just to see me—after i had written to him what i didn't think was anything especially nice, but *he* liked it, & in the afternoon couldn't help starting from Wigan, to me, instead of going to his other home—all for *love*, and i was as much pleas'd as i was surprised when i got the telegram soon after six to say he would be here from ten to 11. i'd begun to feel very tired, but all that was gone, & i made haste & made his bedroom quite ready & air'd things— went out afore i wash'd me for things for his tea, & then i clean'd the kitchen round on my hands & knees & made a nice bright fire & teathings laid & all, for my dear Lord & Master—and it seem'd so much nicer & more homely & cozy somehow, getting the *kitchen* ready for *him*—Should i have felt *such* pleasure for a common working man—i *might* if i had found a working man as could love as purely & be as Massa is (i mean in everything but his learning) & honour him as much, but that's the difficulty i doubt, the finding such a one—and so when i was young & did meet with Massa (whose face i'd seen in the fire)[6] i made my mind up that it was best & safest to be a slave to a *gentleman*, nor wife & equal to any vulgar man—still with the wish & determination to be independent by working in service and without the slightest hope o' been rais'd in rank either in place or by being married—And so at last—After all these nearly twenty years, by Gods help & Massa's true heart & fervent love to me, (more than ever i could dare to hope for from anyone but him, & i always trusted Massa) i am as i am— a servant still, & a very low one, in the eyes o' the world—i can work at ease—i can go out & come in when i please, & i can look as degraded as ever i like without caring how much i'm despised, in the Temple, or in Fetter Lane, or in the streets—and with all that i have the inward comfort o' knowing that i am loved & honoured & admired by, & that i am united in heart & soul as well as married at Church to the truest, best, & handsomest man in my eyes that ever was born— No man i ever see, or ever saw, is so lovely. And M. is pleas'd with me, & after all this there can be no doubt of our being made for each other—And so May God bless us together, & give us both wisdom to live happily always, & health & strength to do the work afore us, & grace that we may never forget who is the giver of all our comforts, & to praise Him more & more.

But Massa would not sleep in his own room, but down stairs in the kitchen bedroom with me—& we talk'd together till two o'clock. And in the morning he noticed how rough my knees are—they feel like a nutmeg grater, so different to his, & M. was so pleas'd to feel 'em, cause he said 'it was such a true sign of being a servant.'

i went to S. James' Church[7] this evening & enjoy'd the service very much— such nice quiet singing—and i saw the clergyman who married us, & thought he look'd at me.

Munby's Diary: Monday, 15 September: York . . . To York to meet Mrs Ellis and her two daughters, who came from Whitby, elegant, sprightly, and with

---

[6] See pp. 14–15.   [7] Clerkenwell.

heaps of luggage. They came to Clifton to luncheon, and we to the train with them again at 3.40. As I handed Georgie Ellis, with her lemon kid gloves and costly sealskin jacket and infinite apparatus of ladyhood, into a first class carriage, I thought of that contrasted but far more beautiful She, who has become my wife instead of this one, who (they say) might have been my wife. Does this one, then, understand and realize a twenty years' passion like my sweet blackfaced Hannah, whose knees (as I found on Friday) are, even yet, rough and hard with years of scouring? . . .

Monday, 22 September . . . Reached the Temple before 4 a.m., and found my dear wife in the back room[8]: for, servantlike, after sleeping in the kitchen during my absence, she has gone the round of the beds, to air them. When I awoke at 9.30 or so, she had long been up and had got all ready: and how charming she looked, with her face full of love and smiles. She looks not at all like a lady, now: her bright face is rosy and full of health, thank God, after her three weeks' work. . . . The furniture is polished and shining; the pictures and their frames are lustrous and clear; the books and their many shelves have been dusted, and arranged with intelligent care; the curtains, white or crimson, hang crisp and newly washed. . . . But no mere housemaid she, though many take her even for a maid of all work still. And this has its inconveniences, now that surveyors & workmen are about the house. These are for ever paying attentions to 'the servant', to 'Mr. Munby's Hannah'. . . . One man . . . exclaimed 'You do more work than a dozen of *the other Temple women* put together!' Two others have asked permission to 'keep company' with her: and to one, a carpenter, she with her kitchen simplicity of manners gave leave to measure the girth of her right arm. It was (as it was ten years ago) $13\frac{1}{2}$ inches round the muscle: and the man's admiration was great; 'upon my word' said he 'you've a bigger muscle than any woman I ever saw in my life—and bigger than my own!' . . . The same, after remarking to Hannah that her master seemed a nice gentleman, enquired if she thought I had ever been married? 'What a question to ask *me*!' said my ready-witted wife. Even Mr. Roberts the foreman, whom she addresses respectfully as 'Sir', is attracted by her, surly and elderly as he is: 'Now, Mr. Roberts', cried she one day, looking down on the gruff little man from her goodhumoured height, and showing her arm, 'you know I could screw you up in less than no time!' And next day, somehow, Mr. Roberts came down to her kitchen, and sat half an hour, talking of his wealth. Another day this week, coming home at 5 p.m., I luckily went upstairs instead of down, and called 'Hannah!' over the banisters. '*Yes Sir*!' answered my wife from below, to my surprise: and running up in her working dress, she laughingly explained that 'her sweetheart' was in the kitchen,

---

[8] *Hannah's Diary*: '. . . put tea ready for M. after lighting the fire—left his shoes & night shirt airing—i wash'd all over & went to bed intending to get up to see after the fire, but i never woke till i heard M. open the bottom door & come up stairs. The Man brought the luggage up, & when he was gone Massa came to me in the back room & i welcomed him in my way tho' i was very sleepy, & he said he was pleas'd to get back to his own drudge Hannah.'

shelling beans for her. 'Which will never do,' said her husband; 'it is not fair to him': and her good sense agreed at once. . . . Every day this week (Monday to Thursday; 22 to 25 September) 'the master' has come in early, and dined at home, and enjoyed the loving companionship of his wife, who has read to him parts of The Earthly Paradise, and of The Village on the Cliff, whose scenes are laid in the places she has just been visiting with him. But never have I been able to persuade her to dine (or rather sup) with me. 'No' she says every day 'I had much rather have it in the kitchen, after you!' and malgré moi, she carries each course downstairs and finishes it in her kitchen, saying as she leaves the parlour 'You'll *ring for me* when you're done!'

Thursday, 2 October . . . meeting Rees at the door, whom I had not seen for long, I thought it well to ask him upstairs. He came, and sat some time; I wondering when he would go, and thinking of Hannah in the kitchen. At last he said 'I wish you would ask your servant about that 1/6 I owe you'—'Very well, I said, I will ring for her.' Ring for my wife, and in a strange man's presence! There came a tap at the door; the door opened and Hannah, in cap and apron, entered, and said 'Yes, Sir?' 'Oh', said Rees, 'do you remember whether I paid that 1/6?' 'No Sir' she answered demurely 'I give you the parcel, but you didn't pay me.' 'Very well—thank you'—and the gentle wife retires, backward: for, says she, 'I have always been used to go out of a room backward, before gentle folks!'[9] She had not come from the kitchen, but from the back room, to which she had retired when she heard her husband & his acquaintance approaching. When Rees had gone, she came in and had tea beside me, and I made it up to her for that humiliation. But she did not feel humiliated; she only laughed, and said 'If all that was wrote in a play and acted, folks'd say it couldn't be true!' No doubt: but to me it is rather tragedy than comedy. . . .

Saturday, 4 October . . . Today I meant to take Hannah to spend Sunday at Medmenham. But it was dull and threatening, so we did not go; and, I came home, and stayed with her all the afternoon & evening. I watched her . . . first sewing blankets, then ironing linen at the table; and thought, as she bent to and fro and moved her bare shapely arms to the work, that ironing is an occupation more graceful even than harp-playing, though the one is all curves & the other all angles.

A mild revival of stage-coaching now gave Munby the excuse he always sought for getting out of town whenever possible. On Monday, 6 October, he rode down to Leatherhead, where he stayed the night at the Swan. 'The fourhorse coach left the White Horse Cellar in Piccadilly at 3.15— guard blowing his horn, every one turning round to look at us. The

[9] *Hannah's Diary*: '. . . And so i back'd out o' the room to go down to the kitchen, my dear husband looking at me in a masterly way & saying "i shall ring again for you presently". . . .'

realities of one generation come to be the mere toys of the next: fancy all the traffic of London, by land, depending on these playthings!'

Having walked with him from Surbiton to Chessington on the Sunday, Hannah understandably refused the coaching jaunt; she made up for it by going to see Adelaide Ristori (1822–1906), the Italian tragic actress, three times in the course of the week. Munby escorted her to *Elisabetta Reina d'Inghilterra* on the Wednesday: 'The play is a sort of cento of Elizabeth's troubles: but Ristori's acting was so fine that even in Italian its power was deeply felt by my English country lass and by me' (8 October). The next day Hannah saw her in *Marie Antoinette*. By then Munby had travelled in a front seat of another coach to Rochester, whence he visited his ailing friend Cuyler Anderson at Gillingham—before spending Thursday night at the Sun in Chatham.

Such restlessness may have been an early example of the commuter instinct, but it does indicate a large tolerance at the Ecclesiastical Commission. Munby was, however, trusted and valued there—and during his outings he would often transact a little official business: an interview with a parson, perhaps, or the inspection of a church.

Monday, 13 October.   My old friend Vernon Lushington Q.C. and his wife have been living all the summer in that little house, Wheeler's Farm,[1] at Pyrford, and have more than once asked me to go there. They asked me to go today; and after talking it over with Hannah, I resolved to go; and went at 4.5 p.m. to Woking. From the station I walked, the old sacred way: past Oldlands Farm, along White Rose Lane, by Hoebridge Farm, and over Breakheart Field, and through Deadman's Copse in the dusk, and down the dark avenue to the village, and then straight into the churchyard first of all.

When you go back to a place where you have enjoyed the most exquisite imaginative delights and have gone through the keenest mental agony, how strange it seems that the lovely still life of the spot should show no traces of what has happened there. You bring such traces with you, and make the old haunts sad with them: but the old haunts themselves are very quiet and indifferent; you and your past are nothing now to them. Which is well; for it helps you to bear the change. I went first to old Mrs. Collier's charming cottage, and had some talk with her about the Carters; and then to *the* house. The green lane, the palings, the little garden, the whitegabled house, were just the same; but up in my bedroom window was a light, and a maid sat there sewing.

I went in; tall elegant Mrs. Lushington was in the house-place, now turned into a diningroom; and my room has become a handsome little drawingroom.

---

[1] Munby had probably introduced Lushington to Wheeler's Farm, the scene of his innocent but devastating romance with Sarah Carter.

Pictures & mirrors, Japanese fans & cabinets, tasteful costly trifles of all sorts, have wholly changed the two humble rooms in which those sweet romantic souls used to lead their lowly life: and this was well for me. . . . Vernon and I sat up till 1 a.m., talking of books, and of Comte. As of old, the moon was shining on the Abbey, and the water was tumbling at the weir.

Tuesday, 14 October.   I came down at 7.30; for Vernon & his wife had to go through my room to get downstairs. It was a lovely brilliant autumn morning; V. and I left on foot at 8, and Mrs. L. came to the garden gate with us, just as sweet Sarah or her mother used to do. We walked over the heath, a lovely walk, and silent and quiet; and so to town at 9.

Very pleasant and friendly and nice; but the spiritual glow and freshness of Pyrford have gone for ever with those old days.

I went home at 4; but my dear wife, in her servant's dress, came forward demurely as I opened the door, and said aloud 'The carpenter is in the back-room, Sir!' However, we got rid of him . . .

Monday, 20 October . . . spent the evening quietly with Hannah . . . she wrote her diary: and told me how 'Mr. Thornbury', my acquaintance & tenant here, had actually noticed her in the street: 'he nodded to me, and I made him a little curtsy', says she. . . . And again, she tells me that one day he came into the room when she was dusting, and asked leave to write at my table. Says she, 'I said "Yes, Sir," and I was going away; but Mr. Thornbury said "Don't leave the room—I rather like to see you about"; so I went on dusting a bit, but I soon slipped out, for I felt awkward being there like that.' Awkward! a rare scene, truly: here is a mere stranger, who comes into my wife's parlour while she is there, sits down to write, and coolly desires her not to leave the room, for he rather likes to see her about! . . .

Friday, 24 October . . . Hannah had expressed a wish to see 'Arkwright's wife' at the Globe Theatre; because, as she said, it was a working woman's play: and I had said I should follow her, if she went. She was gone; and had left me a note in rhyme, signed 'Your own Servant and loving Wife': and had made all things ready for me, before going. I went into her room: there was her servant's cap, and the coarse apron she wears to work in, and her mother's sampler and her own framed on the wall, and the homely patchwork quilt of the little bed she sleeps in when alone. No scented boudoir could be so dear to me. At the theatre, I found her in the gallery; for it never occurs to her to go anywhere else. Be-tween two decent working men, there she sat, leaning forward, her bare hands clasped upon her large white apron: her milkwoman's bonnet, falling back, showing her brown rippling hair, and that noble expressive profile which has charmed me for twenty years. She was no languid or selfconscious listener; she was intent on the scene, her whole face was alive with emotion, and every now and then, in rustic wise, she dashed away her tears with the back of her hand. I sat near, watching her unobserved; till she saw me with a start and a smile, and I made my way to her side, and sat with her hand in mine till the play was over. It is a poorish melodrama; but there were factory girls in it, and charity girls like Hannah, and a touch of Lancashire dialect; and Miss Helen Barry, who played the peasant wife, is a fine tall lass, and in her mob cap & kirtle looked not unlike my own wife.

We came home by ten; and after tea, Hannah finished reading to me The Village on the Cliff. Certainly she is very like Reine, in person and in character; and it is strange, that I used to talk (vaguely, of course) about Hannah, to Miss Thackeray, at the time when she was writing the story.

Sunday, 2 November . . . On Tuesday I weakly promised to take fair Charlotte Hill[2] to morning service at the Temple Church today; and did so accordingly, with no very good will, for the sight of those fashionable loungers crowding the historic church never fails to annoy me. And Charlotte, entering on my arm, was placed by the vergers in those very 'ladies' seats' from which my dear wife, who had gone there alone & in ignorance, was once turned out, because she was known to be only a servant. But she, this singular darling, took up with keen interest the visit of 'the young lady' to our home, though she knew—or indeed *because* she knew—that it would banish her to the kitchen, where she would have 'no fear of being seen'. She was not seen. Her handiwork, a neat little luncheon, was on the table when we came in; and all around were the signs of her taste and gentle skill in adornment: but she, the mistress of the place, could not appear before this chit of a girl, for whom her husband cared nothing. I went downstairs, and found my Hannah in her servant's dress, washing up at the sink. 'Well?' said she in high spirits, 'and how do you get on with the young lady? I shall get a sight of her from this kitchen, as you go out!' And so she did: this strange incomparable wife had to peep through the area-window at her husband's guest, whom she must not meet. It is too much: but 'No' she said afterwards 'I like getting luncheon for your friends in this way: right or wrong, *I like it!*' . . .

Two days later, the scene was more conventionally domestic. While Hannah sat reading aloud from *Clarissa* in the evening, there came an unexpected knock on the door of Munby's sitting-room. As usual, she got up and hid in the adjoining bedroom until her husband could identify the visitor. This time the caller was their confidant George Borland, who understood the whole situation and whom Hannah accepted as a friend. 'How do you do, Sir?' she said, emerging from the back room and making her curtsy; to which Borland responded by taking her hand 'with as much gallantry as if she were a lady born'. Hannah was then able to busy herself

---

[2] Daughter of 'Mrs. Hill of Ferrybridge', a Yorkshire acquaintance.

preparing tea, after which she sat sewing and listening. At eleven o'clock she retired. Munby and Borland 'sit up till one, talking, and chiefly of her. He wonders so that she likes to seem a servant still, and does not like to be a lady' (4 November).

But did either of these old bachelor cronies face the facts? For, if Hannah *had* insisted on becoming a lady-wife, Munby could not possibly have continued to live in the Temple during his parents' lifetime: the risk of the news reaching Clifton Holme would have been far too great. Hannah's reaction—at this period—was not only instinctive but also realistic.

Thursday, 6 November . . . I came home before ten, and found my darling already abed. I had stayed away in order that she might have some of her friends to visit her; cousin Elizabeth, the quiet lady's maid, Mistress Dunn, Hannah's old fellowservant, and Mary, a housemaid, whom Hannah describes as a sweet & patient girl with good working hands. For these three women she prepared cakes and tea; she showed them the pictures, the books, the flowers, the bird, the cat with a blue ribbon round its neck—all her own pretty arrangements of the ancient parlour; herself radiant in her black silk 'frock', and without her cap and apron. Four respectable female servants, enjoying themselves alone, in a barrister's chambers in the Temple; and one of them the barrister's wife. She showed them the kitchen, too, in which she does her rough work: but also she showed them photographs, read to them, and 'Here' she said at tea 'is a sonnet that my husband has just written to me'; and she read it to housemaid Mary and the rest, who thought it 'very pretty'. 'They all thought me looking so well,' says Hannah; 'and admired the house and everything; and Mrs. Dunn wondered that I could be so happy with—with *you*!'

Tuesday, 11 November . . . at 8, Hannah 'cleaned herself', and went with me in a hansom to the Quebec Institute in Seymour Street: for the papers announced that Mrs. Stirling would recite there certain poems, one of which was my Whaler Fleet.[3] It was the first time I have heard anything of mine read in public; and what I heard seemed to affect me precisely as if it had been written by somebody else. Mrs. S. read it with so much of dramatic action and style, that the rhythm of the verse was almost lost. The audience, which was numerous, applauded everything. As for Hannah, she knew her husband's verses, & enjoyed all she heard, and showed it freely. She cannot conceal her emotions, dear soul . . .

[3] See Appendix of Munby's poems. Mrs. Mary Ann (Fanny) Stirling, afterwards Lady Gregory (1815–95), played Cordelia to Macready's Lear, 1845, and Peg Woffington in *Masks and Faces*, 1852.

Marriage

Wednesday, 19 November . . . After dinner, I sat looking over the work for my Latin class; Hannah sitting at my knee, with Freund's Dictionary on her lap. 'I wish *you* could come to my class,' said I: 'Oh, I could never learn to be a scholar!' she answered, sadly; 'but I do wish you to teach me *French*.' She looked out the words, however, for me . . .

Saturday, 22 November . . . to the Working Women's college, at 8; for I had been asked to preside at a discussion on 'Faithful work in Common Duties'. If they could have known what a bright exemplar of this I had left at home! Some twenty people were present, all women, and mostly young; shopgirls and the like.

I spoke out plainly on the subject of servants' work and servants' hands; and several of the girls spoke, most of them agreeing that folk should not be ashamed of common work, but all in favour of soft white hands. . . .

Monday, 24 November . . . Hannah had already been, this morning, to see her sick friend[4] & take her something of her own making; & had tried in vain to buy material for making jelly for her. But after dinner, she went, unknown to me, to the Temple Kitchen and begged some jelly there; and she and I drove to Clerkenwell together, to take it. She went into the sickroom, talked to the patient & tended her, and spoke aptly and gently to the humble folks about . . . and then she would have me make myself known to Mrs. Smith and pray with her. 'This is Mr. Munby—my husband—will you shake hands with him?' said this dear soul, tearfully: and then we knelt down, and I prayed aloud . . .

I took the dying woman's hand—a large strong hand, even at 90—and Hannah walked home with me, and went to bed, overcome with halfhysterical excitement.

Tuesday, 2 December . . . home by the Embankment by 6, to dine: but found my Hannah suffering from pain in her back, and unable to do anything. The fear that she might be ill has always been to me a living and present horror: but only since my marriage have I realized this sweet but terrible burden, the being utterly *alone* with one who is dearest, and being unable to consult friends or have ready female aid, if she should have to suffer. I got her some tea and sat with her till 7.30, when she seemed better: then went for medicine to a chemist's, got some dinner, and home to her again, and nursed her and got her to bed.

Wednesday, 3 December.   Hannah, after I had rubbed her night & morning, was better, and went about cheerfully as usual, to my great relief . . .

Saturday, 6 December.   I left my Hannah, after breakfast, in her cotton frock, & cap, and apron, a bare-armed servant lass: but at 1.30, she met me at the

---

[4] Mrs. Smith of Clerkenwell, who had been Hannah's friend and protectress in London for twenty years. She died a few days later, aged 89.

Victoria Station, drest anew from top to toe, and looking not merely ladylike, but dignified and charming, as ever. I meant to take her to Eastbourne; but the cold wind decided us in favour of Dorking: which we reached about 3, and walked up to the White Horse, where they gave us a snug parlour and bedroom ensuite. . . .

Sunday, 7 December: Dorking.   After breakfast, Hannah and I were alone together in our pretty parlour at the White Horse, and she read to me: for a certain malaise kept us indoors, and prevented us from walking to Ranmore Church. . . . The Parish church of Dorking is being rebuilt, all save the chancel. . . . At 3, we went to service at the Public Hall, which is used as a pis aller by the Vicar and his Curates . . .

After service we had a walk . . .

Hannah lay down till near seven, and then we had tea and she read to me, the psalms and Hannah More. In the fields, she had shown her country girl's knowledge of birds and trees and plants, and her own delight in beauty: and now she unfolded all her sweet vivacity and childlike winsomeness, and all her womanly intelligence and sense. To see her as she sits opposite me now, dainty and beautiful, full of grace in countenance & movement, drest like a lady and with spotless shapely hands, and talking eagerly about Dr. Johnson and the rest of Mistress More's famous friends, a stranger would think it incredible that she ever was what she talks of being again tomorrow: for sitting here like a fine lady, she talks quite calmly of how she will fetch the sweep tomorrow, & will 'clean after' him, and will perhaps scour the stairs 'in her dirt'. . . .

Tuesday, 9 December . . . My Hannah, like Selene, has three aspects: the ladylike and etherial, as at Dorking on Sunday; the neat and homely—not too good For human nature's daily food[5]—as this evening; and the Hecatish or laborious. . . . In each she is equally charming to me; but though her sweet nature underlies them all, her manners and her talk are influenced by her dress and appearance, and are appropriate to it. Drest as a lady, her speech and attitudes and ways are all grace and dignity: drest as a drudge, she works with manlike vigour, rough, and black, and silent: drest, as tonight, like a servant after work is over, she uses kitchen ways & talk; eats her supper with her fingers' aid, wipes her mouth with the back of her hand. Says she, with a smile, 'You have such a deal to do, and yet you *will* go to them college meetings!' . . .

Wednesday, 10 December.   Dense fog all day. . . . Dined at Rouget's, and went to a Council Meeting at the Working Women's College; 25 members, men and women of various classes, present to discuss the question whether *men* shall not be admitted as students. Amos & the Mallesons strongly in favour of this: others, like myself, anxious to keep the College for women only. Result, nil, and general

[5] Wordsworth.

chaos. I had been anxious about Hannah all day, having had to leave her utterly alone so long, & knowing that she must go out . . . on errands in the fog. But at ten p.m., I found a bright warm room, and tea, and my bonny wife coming forward all rosy and cheerful. . . . She had been alone all day, but had not moped, oh no! '. . . so I haven't had a minute to read that article in the Athenaeum you told me of; but I will, now!'

She did; and we talked about the College.

Friday, 12 December . . . home by 6.30 to dinner, bringing the Christmas numbers of the Graphic and the Illustrated News, that my darling might please herself with the pictures. Her money for marketing ran short today: 'I was within two minds o' coming to you for some,' said she: 'and if I had, I should ha' come i' my working things, and brought a note; and I should ha' said "Will you please give that to Mr. Munby, and tell him his servant is waiting?"' This is the fourth day on which no sky nor daylight has been visible, and work has had to be done by gaslight. Hannah, busy in the house and strictly enjoined not to go out except on necessary errands, has not felt the loathsome atmosphere so much. . . .

Tuesday, 23 December . . . home at 4.30, with a porter to fetch my luggage. 'Is everything ready?' 'Yes, Sir,' said the servant who stood waiting. . . . And the porter took up the luggage and went away; and then that servant came into her master's arms; and his cab was kept waiting for a while. I have been troubled about leaving my Hannah this Christmas, and have had to feel more than ever her lowliness and loneliness; for now that the old dame of Clerkenwell is dead, she has not a house in London to go to, except a few kitchens where she herself once lived, and one or two poor dwellings of her old fellowservants. So I wrote to Sister Ellen, asking her to come here to Hannah; and she thankfully answers that she will, if her Missis give her leave; and I invited Sister Polly from Ipswich, offering to pay her fare. She too, after much difficulty with her masters, is able to accept with pathetic gratitude: . . . So she, and perhaps a friend of like estate, are to come by night train, arriving at Shoreditch at *4 a.m.*: and she is to walk hither at that strange hour, and pull a string which Hannah will attach to her own wrist and hang out of the bedroom window. Such is their plan; and Hannah is happy, and is preparing Christmas cheer; so I was able to leave her with less apprehension. I went by the 5.30 train: reached Clifton at eleven, and found there my dear parents, and Carry and Edward.

Thursday, 25 December. Christmas Day. I went with my father and sister to Clifton Church in the morning, and afterwards to Margaret's[6] house in the village. Then at 2.30, came the Christmas dinner: the dear parents presiding, Carry, Edward, and I; Margaret and her three children; Edward Pearson: but

[6] Widow of his brother John.

not my dear and lowly wife. We sat afterwards, giving presents to the children, and watching their play, and looking out on the lawn at sunset. . . .

Wednesday, 31 December.   Soon after 4 a.m. I reached the Temple. There was a good fire burning: tea made, my letters set out, the room looking bright and cleanly, and cheerful with Christmas holly. I go into the bedroom: there is her servant's cap, laid aside, and her apron, and there is her common cotton frock, in which she does her rough work, hanging up behind the door, along with her old strawbonnet. There are her mother's sampler, and her own, framed and hanging on the wainscot wall: and under the homely patchwork quilt, there is She, my bonny servant-wife. Her sweet rosy face is there, broad awake; watching for me, starting up to welcome me.

When I awake and dress, towards 10 a.m., the parlour fire is long since lighted, the room swept, the kitchen fire lighted too; the breakfast ready—*my* breakfast, for she has had her own. She, my Hannah, is moving about, busy and cheerful and bright; telling me of this and that, as I watch her through the doorway. . . . She is now busy to her heart's content; unpacking my dear mother's big hamper, showing forth its contents with critical eye—ham, and brawn, & brown-bread; she unpacks too the furniture I have brought, and determines to use its matting-cover as an approach to her kitchendoor; she clears away the débris, and tastefully adds my bayleaves and barberry leaves to her Christmas greenery. . . .

After dining at the Club, I went home at seven to this sweet wife: whom I found now in her evening dress of redbrown stuff, with long sleeves, and a black silk apron; and we spent the last evening of this eventful year together, not without a final prayer, as the midnight bells began to ring, in the moonlight.

For once Munby discards the note of gloom with which he habitually ends the year: husband and wife are left isolated in their hard-won, precarious happiness. But Hannah too has struggled to the final page of her own less formal diary.

Hannah's Diary: undated . . . M. went home for a week this Christmas, & i had my sister Polly up for a day or two—Mr. Thornbury came the morning after Christmas day . . . i was in my cotton frock & cap as usual, & Mr. T. came in this room as he sometimes does to read his letters, & all the while he seem'd in a particularly good humour & talk'd about several things, himself & Mr. Munby to me, & was in such good spirits, he told me, & i answer'd him civilly, calling him 'sir', & being quite respectful only talking freely too, for i felt in good spirits too, after spending the day yesterday with Ellen & the children in the nursery at Putney. Well, when he got up to go i was so surprised to hear him ask if i'd any misletoe, & he look'd all round for it. I said 'Oh no sir i never think o' that.' he said 'Oh but now is the time, & I sh^d *like* to kiss you under it.' I said thank you sir, your very kind, i dare not, & indeed i *wouldn't* allow it, & i walk'd round the table. He was very civil, & said 'Well, shake hands', so i did & he wish'd me a very good Christmas & a happy new year. I thank'd him & wish'd him the same, & he went away. I thought M. would be vex'd to hear it, but i told him—he was not vex'd, & said it show'd how Mr. T. never suspected i was anything but a servant, & i thought so too. Mr. T. has been exceedingly civil ever since to me.

9

YEARS OF CRISIS
1874–9

At the beginning of his diary for 1874, which like its predecessor amounted to approximately 75,000 words, Munby set down a number of events in the year which struck him in retrospect as significant. One was his father's seventieth birthday. Another he described as follows: '*12 March.* The small estate of *Naburn Lodge*, which has belonged to my family for more than a century, sold by my father for £13,600.' As the Naburn estate derived from Munby's maternal grandmother Elizabeth Woodhouse (Mrs. Forth), its disposal suggests a family arrangement to ease Joseph Munby's financial worries. The device seems to have succeeded; the complaints of 'the father' disappear from his son's diary for the short remainder of his life.

Another problem was resolved less satisfactorily. The Working Women's College, where Munby taught Latin, had split over the question of introducing mixed classes, and in 1874 divided into two separate institutions. The majority body remained at Queen Square and was henceforth to be known as 'The College for Men and Women'. Munby sided with the minority, who preferred to keep the classes exclusive to women: '*16 October.* The *College for Working Women*, of which I am one of the promoters, opened at 5 Fitzroy Street.' This proved to be a short-lived institution.

In the Temple, the conjugal charade continued. Hannah scrubbed on. She cleaned the windows. She cleaned the yard outside their house with pail and broom, looking as dirty as possible, to show that she was an honest servant, not afraid of work. This was a feat Munby particularly liked to watch, and which he later described in *Dorothy*:

> Then, she can scrub, and scour, and swill with the bucket and besom,
> Flinging her pailfuls afar mightily over the yard;
> Sweeping the water away with rapid and vigorous movement,
> Till on the clean wet flags never a footmark appears. . . .

The consequent state of Hannah's hands provided an excuse for her refusing to accompany Munby into the country at week-ends. '"They are quite *hard* again—feel—" she said on 10 January; "and they'll never come cleaner, till the winter's over. So it's no use me going with you as a lady now, Massa!"' One detects a note of triumph, which Munby may have missed. But Hannah had another reason for wishing to avoid country walks: an old lameness had lately grown worse.

Tuesday, 13 January, 1874.   Home to dinner by 6, and sat with Hannah till 8; and then my darling helped me to dress, with as much eagerness and vivacity as if she herself were going to this musical party which to me seems so tame and unattractive. But she laughs lightly at the idea of my even wishing I could take her with me—at the bare thought of seeing herself in evening dress and among 'gentlefolks'. . . .

They had about 80 people, in Hyde Park Square, and had one of the Toy Symphonies, and other music. A not unpleasant party: and the women's dresses are becoming decent—shoulders and arms covered, in the graceful Puritan way, or like Hannah and her fellows nowadays. . . .

During the day, I went in to hear the Tichborne case: a melancholy example of human ignorance: apparatus of judges and jury trying for months to find out what that bloated scoundrel who sat near me could tell them in a moment.

Saturday, 17 January . . . I went alone to Orpington in Kent, and found the house of Mr. G. Allen[1], who publishes Ruskin's Fors Clavigera. An intelligent workman, is G. Allen; knew my name, & very civilly detained me for an hour, showing me the new editions of R.'s works, & explaining R.'s odd but earnest ways of issuing his books. Allen's house is a superior villa, with $2\frac{1}{2}$ acres of garden ground aslope on a breezy open hillside: R. has evidently helped him to pay for it. . . .

Monday, 26 January.   I went to the Charing Cross Hospital about my darling's lameness: for she had said to me, 'No dear, I had rather not go as a lady *anywhere*—I had rather go as a working woman. And besides, then I can tell them how it happened, you know.' For it happened when she was cleaning out a brewing tub . . . years ago; and the tub fell on her foot. So the civil surgeon told me she could come tomorrow: I offering to pay for all. . . .

Today, Parliament is dissolved: Mr. Gladstone's coup d'état is complete: and all over England, the rabble of squires, lawyers, politicians, and democrats are let loose at each others' throats.[2] But Hannah and I hear them not.

[1] George Allen (1837–1907), originally a joiner by trade, had been Ruskin's pupil at the Working Men's College, and became a skilled engraver who illustrated *Modern Painters*. His publishing firm is now Allen and Unwin. Like Munby, Allen had married a housemaid named Hannah (the maid of Ruskin's mother).

[2] The Liberals lost the election, Gladstone being succeeded by Disraeli.

Wednesday, 28 January.   To the Charing Cross Hospital at 5. There, as we had arranged, Hannah met me: and with her, Sister Ellen, whom I had sent for, and homely Emma Smith.

Yesterday, Hannah went there alone, and in her cotton frock and white apron and old bonnet, as a servant; and when the doctor said there must be an operation, and asked who could come with her, she had answered 'I don't know of any one to bring with me, Sir; but perhaps the Master wouldn't mind coming!' But since then, 'the master' had seen the doctor and told him all: feeling that he could not bear to be absent, nor to be present and not treat her as a wife. So today, all was changed, and she came in her best clothing. She had suffered little by anticipation: but I had; and I could not help thinking what one would suffer if she were about to have a child.[3]

We all went into the doctor's room; and Hannah, cheerful and determined to be brave, lay recumbent in a chair and bared her foot; and one house surgeon pumped aether spray upon it, while the other (Mr. Leonard) prepared to operate. Hannah laid her head on her sister's breast; I stood between her and the sight, and held her hand, and kept my face to hers. She never screamed nor started: only, her noble beautiful face kept working with pain, and her dear lips moved against mine in half-convulsive kisses all the time. In five minutes or so it was over; and for awhile she lay on a sofa, looking faint and fair, and saying how strange it felt, after her foot was bandaged.

Then I went for a cab, and helped her into it with the other women; and followed them, when I had taken Mr. Leonard's directions: calling on the way to arrange that Mrs. Newton and her daughter Hetty shall come every day, to help and to attend to her. When I got home, my darling was lying in the easy chair, her bandaged foot resting on another, and the two women with her. Unselfish as ever, she was planning how to help in the housework still, how to make my coffee, my dry toast, and such like matters.

Presently, Sister Ellen had to go to her place of service, and Emma to her home: and at 8, I was obliged to go to my Latin class. . . . I put her to bed on my return. She was overflowing with love & tenderness: 'Oh, how glad I am it was not *your* foot!' she cried; 'and yet I should like it too, then I should nurse you.'

Monday, 2 February.   Home, with Mr. Leonard, at 5. After dressing Hannah's foot, he tested her lungs and heart, and to my great relief pronounced both sound and healthy. He spoke, as he well might, of her refined and delicate organization, so strangely co-existing with great physical strength, & so wonderfully hightoned and uninjured, after a life of rough hard labour. And he guessed her age at 33.[4] . . .

---

[3] Hannah had no children. Munby, as has been already noted, showed little sexual passion. Any conclusions would be entirely speculative, but later letters of Hannah's (see pp. 407–411) suggest that he was the reverse of an exacting husband in the physical sense.

[4] Hannah was forty.

Saturday, 7 February . . . at 8, went to the Working Women's College to hear my friend Ralston lecture on 'Our Fairy Tales, their meaning and origin'. The room was crowded, and the lecture as usual was able & original and lighted up by an apt humour which the women present (for nearly all were women) enjoyed heartily. Afterwards I walked away with Ralston . . . home at 10.30.

Tea was ready, & everything bright & cheerful; and my Hannah, saluting me, asked with a wonderful smile if Mr. Ralston's lecture was not a very nice one? I had been lamenting that she could not be there; and all the time, she *was* there: seated in the same row with myself, unknown to me. 'That young lady next you did stare at me, when she saw me look at you so,' said my darling; 'but I was determined you shouldn't see me, and so I slipped away behind you, at the end, and came home. Oh, and do you know, as I went there, a woman called me "*my lady!*" I asked her the way (she was out marketing) and she said "This way, my lady!"' The woman was right. Today, Hannah went (in a cab) to the Hospital, and the doctor reported her cured: so she ventured on foot to the lecture.

Hannah's French was improving, thanks to tuition from her husband and practice with Mr. Rees's clerk Gerald: 'Voulez vous danser ce soir avec une grande dame?' she asked Munby as he went out on 17 February. She was still averse to taking long country walks, saying 'When a woman gets married, she ought to have the inestimable benefit of staying at home!' But the couple were still deeply, devoutly, in love. Later in the month, at the parish church of Clerkenwell, where they had been married, 'we two went up behind the great pulpit to the altar rails, and knelt down there & prayed together; for there it was that we had knelt before'. And then Munby watched Hannah walking away to have tea with a Clerkenwell friend—'gliding up the shabby street among the tawdry Londoners: and she turned and turned, a-watching me. "We was like two sweethearts!" she said afterwards: and long may we be so'.

On Saturday, 28 February, Hannah consented to be taken to 'No. 17, the very best bedroom', at the Royal Hotel, Southend. She came down to the tea-room wearing that 'Vitré shawl' Munby was so proud of, 'over a rich black dress', and with 'dainty gloves on her poor hands'. She asked her husband: 'What do you think of your drudge, now?' But, inevitably, Monday morning brought the transformation scene.

Monday, 2 March. We breakfasted early at the Royal; & left Southend at 8.15. . . . My darling looked all the better and brighter for this short outing. 'I have been thanking God for my good husband,' said the sweet soul last night, just as she went to sleep in his arms: and how much more may he thank God for her!

We parted at Fenchurch Street: she walked leisurely home, and I by rail to

Charing Cross. . . . I went home at 6 to dinner: and found the Princess become a servant again. She was in her red stuff gown, her white apron, and large white cap. 'How different I look now!' she said: 'but you like me this way as well as the other.' No need to hide her sweet ruddy hands now: they suited her dress and her work. Last night, she was reclining on the sofa as a lady: this morning, obsequious waiters call her 'Ma'am', and the civil landlord takes his hat off to Madame. And by noon today, she is sweeping, & lighting fires, and going on errands in her old bonnet and white apron, and behaving humbly to friend Thornbury, who calls her 'Hannah'. . . .

Tuesday, 3 March . . . home at ten. Hannah . . . told me of her window-gardening (for the room is bright with her flowers) and how clerk Gerald, the gentle boy, had been helping her, and had said to her, as well he might, 'I couldn't stay here, but for you, Hannah—you are the life of the place, to me!' Clerk Gerald is but twelve years old, so I can feel kindly towards him for this. Also, Hannah and he had walked up Oxford Street together, today; and she had told him about her 'master'. 'What do you do while Mr. M. has his dinner?' said the boy. 'Oh, I wait on him, and go up and down: and once, I was frying some pancakes for him, and I ate one behind his back, and he never saw me!' 'But doesn't he turn round?' 'Oh no! gentlefolks never do—they don't notice you while you wait on 'em!' All which she demurely reported to me.

Saturday, 7 March . . . Returning before 2 p.m., I found Whitley at the door. We went upstairs: brooms and dustpans were about, doormats hung over the balusters. The parlour was all adust and in confusion; and on the hearth, in brilliant sunshine, crouched the dirtiest object of all—a woman. She wore a rustic hood bonnet; a lilac cotton frock, soiled, & pinned up over a Wigan pit-girl's skirt; thick boots, and a coarse striped lindsey apron. All around her were fire irons, blacking pots, and the like; and she, prone on her hands and knees, was earnestly scrubbing the fender. Her bare round arms were streaked and disfigured with soot and grime: but her face was soot all over—absolute blackness, so that not a feature could be distinguished.

And this was my Hannah: how unlike her aspect at Southend, this day week! 'My dear, let me introduce Mr. Whitley to you'—suppose her husband had said *that*! But he only said 'Don't let us disturb you'; and the black woman, speaking low and in a sweet voice, answered 'Never mind, Sir', and prepared to remove her offensive presence: gathering up some of her horrors, she crawled out of the room, without rising.

What a wife, to choose to be seen *thus* by her husband's friends! But as for Whitley, he walked straight to the window, and never once deigned to notice that humble creature on the floor. . . .

Tuesday, 10 March . . . home unexpectedly, in the dusk, about 6. I found the parlour fragrant with scent of oranges; and my Hannah, bare-armed and in her servant's dress, was busy making of marmalade, helped by Gerald the boy. 'We was just making some more marmalade, Sir,' says my wife, rising, as her rôle required: and the boy prepared to go. I felt it necessary to say severely 'What, are you making it *here*, and not in the kitchen?' and she answered 'Yes, Sir!' with a contrite air.

When we were alone, and had agreed that there was nothing like an evening together, I went out and dined at the Cock, while she 'put straight' and did her ironing (which I love to see, and came back in time), and then we had our wish, and Dr. Johnson.[5]

'This life seems to suit her exactly,' remarked George Borland, after a visit on Sunday, 8 March, during which Hannah, 'all smiles and blushes', played hostess to the only friend of Munby who knew them intimately as husband and wife. 'I don't mind *Mr. Borland*. . . . I'm not afraid of *him*, now!' she said.

Hannah seemed well and happy; and Munby's hopes were revived of making her a permanent 'lady'. He contemplated taking her with him to Venice and Rome, and an important decision was recorded on 20 and 21 March, when a working couple 'Mr. and Mrs. Skeats took up their abode in the kitchen; the latter, as servant (so far as is needed) to my wife'. They had come '"to live with me in the kitchen", as Hannah gives it out among the folks here: in reality, to relieve Hannah of some of the housework, to be at hand and help in need, and to take care of the house when we are away'.

It is hard to tell whether any of Munby's friends and neighbours, or the Temple servants, guessed his relationship with Hannah. In any event, it was not a bad thing that the couple should have allies on the premises who were in the know. But if Munby had hoped that a ladylike Hannah would be content to rule over the Skeats, he was rapidly disillusioned. Ever willing to please, she was soon scrubbing the yard and cleaning the kitchen windows, while Mrs. Skeats 'was doing much lighter work indoors'.

Wednesday, 25 March . . . I went to see Rees and condole with him on the loss of his mother, an old lady of 86. She was in the Mediterranean, he said, in 1798, and sat on Nelson's knee at Naples, before the battle of the Nile: and he said to her, 'Now, Mary, mind how you climb up; for you know I've only one arm'.

Tuesday, 7 April . . . Last night, in the inn at Ockley,[6] when Hannah . . . was reclining in the armchair and reading Boswell to me, Harriet the maid came in for orders, and respectfully said 'Goodnight, Ma'am.' 'Goodnight, Harriet,'

---

[5] Hannah was reading Boswell aloud in the evenings.
[6] Where they had been staying over Easter.

Hannah replied, inclining her comely head with a sweet smile and a gracious air, as if she had been used to dismiss her maid thus every night of her life. But afterwards, 'Ah' she said 'Harriet little thinks that I am only a servant, like herself! What fun! . . . to think that I can be *like this*, and yet be your servant at home, and no one know!'

Well: at 6 p.m. today, what had become of that elegant and tastefully drest lady of Ockley? The door was opened to me by a maidservant; a tall robust young woman . . . her muscular arms are bare, and round her wrist, instead of that scented bracelet, she wears the rude leather strap and buckle which for so many years she wore in service. . . .

And, coarse as she may be now, the rooms are full of evidence of her skill and taste: the ferns & flowers from Ockley are arranged in lovely order. After dinner and 'washing up', Hannah read to me some of Boswell: but she was tired with her day's work, and left off soon, and went to sleep in her chair while I wrote. She lay there, in her big cap & cotton frock, her bare arms folded in her coarse apron, looking, in mien and attitude, not at all like a lady, but like what she was: a lusty hardworking servant, asleep by the kitchen fire. But I gazed upon her with reverence as well as affection; for I saw before me a woman made thus by thirty years of noble and unselfish drudgery. When she awoke, she reminded me that in Shropshire, today is the lasses' 'heaving-day'; and so she took me in her arms and lifted me off my feet: which only a strong servantmaid could do.

When she had gone to bed, Ralston came in, and gave me an account of his interview last Thursday at Buckingham Palace with the Duchess of Edinburgh[7]: she conversed with him near half an hour, and he found her a pleasant, intelligent, unaffected girl.

Friday, 10 April.   To shops, and home to dinner at seven. 'I am always so much happier when you've come home!' cries my bonny bare-armed kitchen wife, laying her whitecapped head on my shoulder. And truly, to come out of those hideous roaring streets into her peaceful presence, and see her innocent rustic ways, her meek delight in the flowers and 'little fishes' she has so well arranged, is like coming into harbour after a storm. Yet she, as a thoughtful woman who has known much of poverty and hard work, feels as deeply as I do the sadness and misery of life: which accounts for her keen interest in Dr. Johnson. This evening, after reading to me what Boswell says of Rasselas, 'I must read that Rasselas!' she said: 'do you know, when I hear lovely music, I think to myself, "I should not hear this if I were dead," and then it seems as if life was worth having, for that and *love*.'

Monday, 13 April.   I went at 5.30 to Duchess Street Portland Place, No. 3, and called on Mrs. Stirling the actress, by appointment: for she has been reading my

---

[7] The only daughter of Tsar Alexander II of Russia, she had recently been married to Queen Victoria's second son.

verse at Dublin, Hull, and elsewhere, & has sent me such glowing accounts of the matter that I felt bound to go & thank her. I found her in a pleasant quiet little house, and she was extremely agreeable and conversational: but withal she has a certain hard and artificial manner that betrays the professional actress, and suggests a sad suspicion of narrow circumstances. Her beauty is gone, but she retains her bright look & air. . . .

Tuesday, 14 April . . . Sat with my Hannah, from 5 till after 7 p.m.; and while she had tea, I found with her help that her clothing and ornaments have cost, during the year 1873, somewhat less than *ten pounds*. No more: and most of this was paid for by herself, out of her wages. Her 'wages', £10 a year, are the interest on her own savings, which I give her as pocket money: and, as she could not bear to be without wages, we give it that familiar name. . . .

Thursday, 16 April . . . At 8, I dressed and went to the P. A. Taylors' new house in Ashley Place, to a meeting of the Pen and Pencil Society; Hannah having copied out my verses for me, and read them aloud. Messrs Austin Dobson and Edmund Gosse[8] read some good verse of their own: & the party was agreeable. But every one misses Aubrey House. . . .

Sunday, 19 April . . . This morning about ten, Edward Peacock[9] of Bottesford unexpectedly called on me, and asked for some breakfast. Hannah had swept & dusted the parlour, had had her own early breakfast, and was preparing mine. She was in her servant's dress, and her hands and face were somewhat dusty: but instead of being annoyed or ashamed that her husband's friend should see her thus, she brightened and grew joyous. 'What are you going to do, dear?' said I, going to her in the back room. 'Why, wait on you, of course!' she answered, with a kiss: 'I shall give you a steak and an omelette, and I'm going down to Mrs. Skeats to do them, and you'll ring for me to bring up the breakfast and wait— it'll be nice, you know!'

Meanwhile, the unconscious Peacock talked archaeology to me, till I rang the bell: then came footsteps on the stairs, and a respectful tap at the door, and enter the mistress of the house . . . carrying a tray of dishes. She was clean and neat now, in her Sunday servant's dress. . . . She set down the tray, arranged the dishes, gave hot plates to her husband and his guest, and moved quietly about, as a neathanded Phillis, behind their chairs. . . . One would have thought that, even as a servant, her unusual stature and her quiet and graceful ways would

[8] This was the occasion of the first meeting between Gosse and Dobson, whose subsequent long association, both in private and at the Board of Trade, lasted for 48 years and was commemorated in a famous caricature by Max Beerbohm. The Pen and Pencil Society closed down in December, 1874.

[9] Edward Peacock, F.S.A., was Lord of the Manor of Bottesford, near Brigg, in Lincolnshire. An antiquarian and philologist, he was also the author of several three-decker novels, including *John Markenfield* (Chapman and Hall, 1874).

have attracted attention; and from ladies, they certainly would; but such is the stupidity of men, that Peacock continued to talk to his distracted host, and never noticed nor looked at the tall neat servantmaid who respectfully changed his plate, or stood in the background, waiting. He talked of his new novel 'John Markenfield', while all the time, a romance such as few could dream of was being enacted before his eyes. 'You like rustic scenes—I have a scene of a servant girl and her master,' said he. 'It is hard to describe servants aright,' I said: 'the life of a kitchen is so different to that of our class!' 'Yes,' he answered, 'and unhappily they have not culture enough to describe it.' This was when the tall maidservant had just left the room, after clearing away our breakfast things in silence; and she had stooped in front of Peacock, as he sat in the easy chair, to remove the kettle and sweep the hearth; and then she had withdrawn, on tiptoe and walking backwards . . . with her hands full of dishes, and her countenance demure and respectful. But he noted not her countenance nor her movements: nor knew that she, without any culture at all, has described her own life effectively for nearly twenty years. 'When do you have your dinner?' I thought it best to say, as she retired. 'About one o'clock, Sir,' my wife answered. 'Then perhaps you had better do the bedroom.' 'Very well, Sir,' said she, quite gravely: and soon she reappeared with all her housemaid's gear, and slid as quiet as a mouse behind our backs into the bedroom, and drew the curtain behind her but did not shut the door: for I knew that she was secretly enjoying the conversation, though I could hear her vigorously emptying slops and lustily making the bed. Peacock, however, took no more notice of her presence there than if she had been a dog: he continued talking, in his clever rambling way; pouring out miscellaneous learning antiquarian and philosophical, talking Spinoza and Berkeley, reading Kingsley's poems aloud, reciting ballads of his own: and all this while, the lady of the house, to whom he should have been introduced, was doing housemaid's work in a servant's dress behind a curtain, as if unfit to be mentioned before him. At last she came out, with her bare arms and her face flushed with work; tall, silent, carrying her full pail, but out of sight; and stole one look of love at her husband, as she passed out of the room to go downstairs. . . .

. . . At last, after 3 p.m., I persuaded my guest to go out with me; and in Piccadilly we parted . . . home by nine, to tea. Now at last, the wife was free to talk with her husband as an equal. . . . 'What a strange gentleman he is—and how he did quote poetry, and make clever talk! I was listening to it all, when you thought I was only thumping the pillow and wiping the basins out. But as for him, he'll go mad, with his talk about not trusting our senses, and the things we see not being real! How do I know it's *you* that kiss me, or *you* I've loved these twenty years? Why, God gave us our senses, & if we can't trust them, what *can* we trust?' Such was the verdict of Hannah's plain common sense: so much notice had that lowly waiting maid of this morning taken of the clever gentleman who ignored her. Then she told me of the old folks downstairs. When Hannah, leaving her parlour to the unexpected stranger, had retreated to the kitchen as a servant, Mrs Skeats naturally wondered what she would do. 'Wait on them, of course!' was the ready answer. '"But won't it be very awkward for you?" "Not at all," I said; "in this dress, no one will notice me; the gentleman will think I'm Mr. Munby's servant; and I *am* the servant, you know," I said to her, quite straight.' So that was settled; and Mrs Skeats was too dull to wonder much. . . .

Monday, 20 April. On Saturday, at the Charing Cross station, I was 'struck all of a heap' by seeing in a new paper, the Pictorial World, a picture of Wigan wenches working at brow. What right had this artist to poach on my manor, to exhibit my heroines thus, and perhaps send people to see & spoil them, or to try & 'put them down?' No picture of these women has ever appeared before, that I know of, except one, in 1867, in an obscure penny paper called Bow Bells. . . .

Wednesday, 22 April. . . 'Mrs Skeats has been saying to me today' said she '"Wouldn't you like to be a lady?" says she; "you ought to be!" "Mrs Skeats," I said to her, quite straight, "Do you really think I could wish to be a lady, after being used to *work* all my life?" "Well, perhaps not," says she. And Rachel[1] said to me today "It must be very awkward for you; and you haven't got your rights" —meaning, as a gentleman's wife. But I said, "Why, it was my own wish to be like this, and it's most convenient! I *couldn't* be a lady here, nor anything like one; and I'd liefer live here, and work and do as I like, and behave as I'm used to, than live anywhere else and be set up and stared at. Besides" I said "I'm forced to be a sort of lady, when Mr M. & me go out together." You see, Massa' my darling added 'they canna understand it—*no one* can: they're all for finery, and being thought much of.' After dinner, she insisted on going out on errands; and over the ancient balustrade I watched her as she went forth into the street, clad in that old bonnet and cloak and a coarse soiled apron and a cotton frock. . . .

Monday, 4 May . . . At 5 p.m. I went home to my darling.[2] She was at work in the kitchen: I rang the bell (not knowing who was with her) and she came upstairs, in her servant's dress, wearing a clean frilled cap; rosy and bright and full of tender welcome, and enquiries after 'Mr. Borland', and delight in her flowers.

How had she spent the time? Well, she had been alone in the kitchen all yesterday, but not dull, oh no! and to church in the evening: and today, she had been 'cleaning after the sweep', Very well: but now, Cinderella dear, you must 'clean yourself', and go with me to the Opera, to hear Fidelio again. 'Must I?' her eyes brighten, and soon after 8, she is ready. She goes out in her long grey cloak and her old milking-bonnet, as if on errands: but in a quiet corner with me, her cloak is doffed & her bonnet crushed into her pocket: and then the

---

[1] Step-daughter of Mrs. Skeats.

[2] Munby had spent the weekend with Borland in Hampshire, discussing Hannah's 'beautiful double life of wife and servant, lady and laundress' (2 May).

stately kitchenmaid sails up the grand staircase of Drury Lane on my arm, wearing a rich silk dress and a soft white Vitré shawl, and simplex munditiis as to her beautiful hair. She moves with ease and modest self possession among the crowd of ladies, and looks at least as ladylike as any of them. . . .

Thursday, 7 May. Went to the Royal Academy, hoping to take Hannah there soon[3]: and home thence at 7.30, to dinner. Found my darling in her working dress, and in high spirits. . . .

. . . she and Mrs Skeats had been together today to the Haymarket Stores. Mrs S., a plain commonplace woman, was in her best; but Hannah, her handsome mistress, was drest as a servant; her cotton frock and bare arms showing beneath her old grey cloak. 'Well,' said Mrs S., 'I never did see, how all them ladies stared at you at the Stores! They must have took us for gentlemen's servants, or something.' 'Aye, and the men stared at me in the street and all,' said Hannah. 'And Mrs S. said' she continued '"I don't think any woman in the world'd do as you do, going about like this, as a servant, and you a gentleman's wife!" "Perhaps not," I said: and she said too, "I think, if you're a servant ever so, Mr. Munby's got a *catch* in you; for no *lady* could do all for him, as you do." And what do you think Mrs S. says, when I'm in the kitchen, and you ring the bell for me? She always says, quite seriously, "There's your master a-wanting you": and I say "Yes": but I mean to tell her, how in Shropshire we call our husbands *masters*. Ah,' my darling added, as she sat talking thus, in the easy chair, still in her working dress, but her face and her bare arms now rosy and clean, 'Ah, ours is a story that, a hundred years hence, no one would believe!' Not so: perchance they shall both know and believe it; and, if they honour her as she deserves, it is enough for me.

During the next few weeks, Munby described a further series of domestic adventures not differing essentially from the many already recorded. The emphasis was on neighbourly flirtation with Hannah: '"I must put an end to this!" said Hannah the other day, when she "answered" the door and took in a letter; "here's the postman has been squeezing my arm—and Mr. Rees feeling my muscle, too, and Mr. Thornbury wanting to kiss me!" And she laughed. . . .' (16 June.) The incorrigible Thornbury was, however, easily rebuffed.

Friday, 26 June . . . After dinner, I sat with Hannah till near ten: and she . . . went about as a servant, cleaning my boots, brushing my clothes, airing my linen, helping me to dress; and all the time, cheerful and pleased, pitying me for my hard fate in having to go out to a grand party just when she was going quietly to bed. 'And what will you do among all them grand folks, Massa?' said she:

---

[3] He did so on 29 July.

'you'll find a many fine ladies to talk to, I'll be bound—and I lay a halfpenny Miss Bovet'll be there!' Nevertheless, she went to bed, with kisses, without being jealous: and when I went up the grand staircase and through the lace curtains into the crowded drawing rooms at Kensington, Miss Bovet *was* there: she who once described Hannah to me as 'le malheur de votre vie,' and had her own reasons for doing so. She talked a while to me in French; enquiring impudently 'Comment se porte Madame?' . . .

Monday, 29 June.   Today Hannah was doomed to be a lady . . . and that in a wondrous way: for her late mistress[4] had asked her to tea, and I had promised to go & fetch her home from thence. So at 4 p.m., Hannah, in her best, and 'Miss Margaret', whose boots she used to clean, went together to see Doré's pictures in Bond Street, and thence to Gloucester Crescent, where I joined them at 6. The last time I entered that house, Hannah was servant there; the family were away, and she had been left as charwoman, and had just cleaned the whole house down on her hands and knees, unaided; and she was black, and rough, and drest as a maid of all work. Now, Grace the parlourmaid, with mute deference, showed me up into the drawing room, and there was my maid of all work, drest as a lady, seated blushing on a sofa, by the side of her mistress. She rose & blushed yet more, as 'Miss Margaret' introduced to her mother the husband of her mother's servant: but we were soon at ease, and I talked to the old lady (the widow of an Indian colonel) while Hannah with a child's delight was listening to the elder Miss Henderson's explanations of her Italian photographs. My sweet wife talked little; she felt strange and awkward, sitting as an equal, among those ladies whom she used to serve, in that drawing room which she never entered before except with a curtsey when they were present, or with her broom and pail when they were not. She was a little ashamed of her hands, too, though they looked very well; but her bashfulness and meek confusion did not lessen the grace of her behaviour. At last she got up, to pay a visit to her kitchen & her old fellow servant Emily, downstairs; and as she left the room, she said to Mrs Henderson, with all her old respect, 'May I take the tea things down, Ma'am? I could do it so easily!' 'Oh, no!' cried the ladies, in chorus: 'Then will you please to ring for me to come up again?' said she, and went. When she had gone, the three ladies, who had treated her with all kindness & consideration, and quite as an equal, expressed to me their admiration of my wife; and I said, what is far less than the truth, that she is the most beautiful character I ever knew among women. Presently she came back, entering the room in a modest diffident way; and then she put on her bonnet, and they parted from her warmly and affectionately; she on her side smiling & blushing and half curtsying as she shook hands, and saying 'Ma'am' to all. 'Goodbye, William!' she said to the page boy who

---

[4] Mrs. Henderson, of 20 Gloucester Crescent, Paddington. Her younger daughter Margaret had always admired Hannah, understood her story, and kept in touch with her after she left them.

opened the hall door for us: he for his part did not answer, being confounded by the reflection that he had just been sitting in the kitchen with this fine lady. And so my darling, ladylike and handsomely drest, walked arm in arm with her husband, down those steps which she used to clean on her hands and knees in sight of all men, and past that cellar kitchen where she dwelt, and along those street flags where she used to sweep & crawl and be called a 'dirty creature' by passersby. . . . Often have I wished for a chance of introducing that lowly drudge into Society as a lady; and now the chance had come, and on the very spot where she was lowest. As for her, her gentle soul was in a maze of wonder: 'Oh, to think of the contrast!' she exclaimed. She said, 'I never thought they would take me into the drawing room, and I asked them not; and when they told me to sit by the Missis, I said "Oh, I never can sit on the same sofa with you, Ma'am!" but I had to do it; only, I sat as far off her as I could, & I got up soon. Only fancy!' she added, 'fancy the Missis taking hold of *my* hand, and *patting* it too, when she said, "You must come again!"' And how did you get on in the kitchen, dear? 'Oh, nicely; the servants was looking up at *you* from the area, when you come, and Emily asked me how I liked being wi' the ladies upstairs; and I said, "Oh, pretty well, but I'd liefer be wi' you down here".' Then, as we walked along, Hannah proposed to go and see another old fellow servant of hers, Mary Dunn, in Kildare Terrace. She did so; and when I came home to her at 10.30, after dining at the Club, she said 'Well, I've had such a nice evening! I've been helping Mary Dunn. Her master was having a dinner party, and so I went errands for her, and washed up the dishes.' What, in your lady-dress? 'Oh yes! I tucked up my silk frock, & put an apron on. Ah well,' she added, 'it's been a nice day, just for once; but I wouldn't be in a drawing room always, for anything; I shall be glad to get back to my own cotton frock & cap, again.'

That entry is a sad mixture of success and failure. While rejoicing at Hannah's hour of triumph, 'on the very spot where she was lowest', Munby knew that the vision on Mrs. Henderson's sofa was only a mirage; that Hannah 'wouldn't be in a drawing room always, for anything'.

The realisation must have been the more poignant because he had largely decreed his own fate. Years afterwards, in 1895, collecting together a bundle of letters Hannah had written to him from 20 Gloucester Crescent, Munby confessed, with his occasional use of the third person, that 'he erred greatly, in trying his own purity and hers too much and too long; and in allowing her to call herself his "slave" and his "drudge", and to be so, as far as she could . . . she wished to think herself a slave for Love's sake; and he only worshipped her the more, for her lowliness and humility. Yet it was an error that has blighted both their lives, though it has not touched their love.'

In the summer of 1874, neither Munby nor Hannah dared to look far ahead. Soon Hannah was writing to Miss Knight, at that Margate lodging house, to tell her she was married 'and as happy as one can be, on this side the grave' (1 July). Sometimes she went into the country with her husband at the weekend; more often not. Exhausted after a long walk on 19 July, Munby, who had intended to come home, stayed the night at Croydon with his friend John Flower—'trusting that Hannah, with her calm good sense and her courage, would go quietly to bed'.

Monday, 20 July.   Left Croydon about 9, & reached the Temple about 9.30: and was shocked to find that my darling had sat up half the night for me, & had distressed herself at my absence; having no one to comfort her but the silly old dame downstairs, who said to her, 'Well, if anything has happened to Mr. M., shall you go into service again?' 'I'm sure I don't know,' said poor Hannah; & coming up from the kitchen, she asked 'Mr. Thornbury' if he thought any accident had happened to her master. I stayed with her till she was better, and came back to her in the afternoon, & left her happy & calm again. . . .

Hannah was not only learned in the lore of household omens and tea-leaf prophecies; she was also a student and interpreter of dreams. She herself dreamed, nearly always, of being in service. The dreams of the couple reflected the strains of their life together.

Thursday, 23 July.   This morning, before she got up to 'do' the rooms, Hannah told me a dream she had just had: 'I dreamt that you was stopping in a Margate lodging house,' she said, 'and I was the lodging house servant; and I was waiting on you, & found some ladies there; so I thought "I mustn't be familiar with him now", and so I called you "Sir".'
Soon afterwards, this dream (as she said) was interpreted: for she had to answer the door to a railway porter who brought a hamper; and hearing him talking to her in the lobby as a servant, I called 'Hannah!' from our room. 'Yes, Sir!' my darling answered, coming to the door, & saying 'If you please, Sir, the man is waiting to be paid.' While I talked with him, Hannah, in her cap & apron, & broom in hand, was sweeping the floor in the background; & then she went out with the porter, to get change. . . .

Saturday, 25 July.   Again, Hannah dreamt of being my servant: and I also, dreaming of having to find some excuse for her meek presence before certain ladies, said aloud in sleep 'My boots, Hannah, please!' The words woke her; she jumped up with a kiss, saying 'What a good job you said that, Massa!' and went off to do what I had dreamt of. . . .

Munby's relationship with Hannah may have been a subject of discussion in the Temple; yet her occasional appearances at her husband's

370

office in Whitehall Place can hardly have raised suspicion. She would arrive there as a messenger of the humblest kind. If Munby came straight to Whitehall from the country on a Monday morning, Hannah sometimes brought him his letters. She did so on this August bank holiday in 1874 (still a working day for some).

Monday, 3 August . . . to London by ten. About eleven, happening to approach one of the waiting rooms at Whitehall, I saw the lower part of a female figure projecting across the doorway of the open door. It was only a servant, evidently, and a rough one; for what I saw was a short lilac cotton skirt, a coarse white apron, and a pair of strong & big laced-boots. Surely, I thought, there is only *one* woman so drest who would come here! I went near, and it was she: my Hannah! She stood up: there was no one by, so she did not curtsy, but smiled freely; and, shutting the door, I clasped and kissed her. 'Don't shut the door, Massa!' she said, with a wise instinct; 'I'm only come to bring your letters, and to carry your bag home.' Darling! says he—and kisses her again: and then he parts from her as a master, lest any should see: and then (for *she* had never told him) he finds that 'that woman' had been kept waiting there for nearly half an hour: he being engaged, and no one caring to disturb him for the sake of a humblelooking creature who had announced herself as *his servant*. When I got home to dinner at 6, I found her . . . in her clean cap and apron; full of bright affection, full of gentle glee at her adventure of this morning. . . .

Thursday, 6 August . . . This morning and last night, Hannah and I had great consultation as to the results of her shopping. She had bought, to please me, a grand new lady-dress for travelling, and a veil, and gloves: and now, her mind was that all this costly trumpery was unfit for a servant like her, who was content with her station and its proper costume. 'Why' said she 'I dreamt last night that I was maid of all work at a butcher's; and I had pigs to feed, and cattle to litter and clean after, and oh, such a many black saucepans to clean!'

But chiefly she was distressed at having had to spend money on gloves and a veil. 'It's a shame of you, Massa,' she said, 'to make me wear a veil or gloves, *ever*; things I've never been used to in all my life!' 'Look at this hand!' my darling said again, very earnestly, holding out that strong and true right hand of hers, which has wrought for me and others, in rough work, for twenty years: 'Look at this hand, how broad and *spread* with work it is! Is that a hand to put a glove on? Why, I canna *bear* to wear gloves, they make my hands as foolish as a stuffed tabby!' . . . when she tries on that fine ladydress, to show me, she looks (for the present) like a servant drest up in her missis's clothes. 'Yes, Massa,' she says, 'it's so hard for me to look like a lady, on account of my hands!' But there's one comfort, dearest (I said) & that is that in my eyes you look best in your own maid of all work's dress. 'Ah yes!' she answers eagerly, 'and *I* like it best, of course; if only you wasn't obliged to be ashamed of me in it!' How sad it is—I

371

could only say—*you* love to be as you are, and *I* love you best as you are; & yet we must dress you up like this, whenever we go out together!

Soon afterwards, Mrs. Skeats elicited an important statement from Hannah. 'If Mr. M. was to retire & live in the country,' she asked her, 'should you be with him as a servant, like you are now?' 'I canna tell, Mrs Skeats,' said Hannah; 'but I know I should like to be just as I am now!' Transcribing this dialogue on 8 August, Munby must have known its meaning; for it put an end to all hope that his marriage might sometime— after the death of his parents—prove socially acceptable. Hannah's resistance to fine clothes, to gloves that 'baffled' her hands, had noticeably increased. Abandoning the idea of escorting her to Italy, Munby had fallen back on an invitation to the nearer and less exacting Ardennes. But the truth was beginning to emerge—Hannah had already seen enough of Europe. She was never to go abroad again.

Thursday, 20 August . . . Home before 5, and put it finally to my darling, whether she had liefer go with me on Saturday to Calais, & Brussels, & the Ardennes, or go to Ockley; and she chose Ockley. 'It would be so nice to be quiet there to- gether, Massa—out o' the world, like—and I should read to you, and you would read to me while I did your sewing, you know.' So I sat down & wrote; and then Hannah went out just as she was, in her white cap and apron, her lilac cotton frock, and with bare arms, and carried to the post, as a servant, the letter which announced that she is coming as a lady and must have a carriage to meet her. . . .

The straggling village of Ockley, centred on the long, straight Dorking to Horsham road, was reckoned 'unspoiled' by Munby's standards in 1874. A century later, the troops of smocked villagers have deserted the two churches and road traffic has greatly increased (even Munby noted it as occasionally heavy); aircraft are troublesome, but the railway remains happily distant, the old cottages still surround the green and its cricketers, while to the north Leith Hill continues to dominate a gentle landscape of fields and woods. The happiest days of Munby's marriage may have been those he and Hannah spent in the little inn at Ockley.

This August, it was a whole fortnight before the waggonette took them back to Ockley station. Their only embarrassment during the visit was caused by the well-meaning Rector's wife, who introduced herself to Hannah outside the parish church. Munby hurried, as he thought, to her rescue; but Hannah later told him: 'you came a little too suddenly—the lady would see there was a *something*'. Mrs. Dusautoy was undaunted; she left her card at the King's Arms—which meant, as Munby gravely informed his wife, that they must return the call at the Rectory.

Wednesday, 26 August . . . 'Oh Massa, what a trial!' she exclaimed: and again she said, 'Must my trial really be *today*?' But when this was settled, she prepared for the dread event with her usual calmness and good sense. 'Tell me what I am to do when I get into the room, Massa; only don't make me feel my own littleness too much. After all, I must just keep my selfpossession, and say as little as I can. But, must I *shake hands* with the lady, when I go in?' The Rectory is a large oldfashioned house, looking southward over the Weald. When we got there, the Rector's pony carriage was at the door; an excellent excuse for shortening our visit. We were shown into a dimly lighted drawing room; & Hannah had time to arrange herself on a sofa with her back to the window, so that her blushes and tremors might not be seen. She wore her pretty broad hat of black felt, with a violet veil wrapt around it; it made a picturesque background for her shining hair and sweet loving face; and she wore a dress of pale grey, with black ornaments; and grey gloves, which she was on no account to take off. And then Mrs Dusautoy came in, & Hannah rose and bowed with a timid grace and took the lady's offered hand, This is she (one might think) whom friend Rees accosts with a careless 'Hollo, Hannah!' as he meets her coming up the kitchen stairs with her pail! But, though her behaviour was charmingly naive and graceful, she was too much out of place (as she fancied) and too much in awe of the gentlefolks, to talk: and it was sad to think that all that quick intelligence, and bright humour, and cheerful and noble demeanour, which she shows with me, was now obscured, partly by her lack of experience, and partly by her humbling recollections of her own rough and abject life in service. She smiled, however, and answered Yes and No, and said a few words now & then in her softest tones; but I could see that they wondered at her silence. Mr. Dusautoy accompanied us to the garden gates; and soon afterwards, when I had gone into a cottage, and Hannah was standing, tall & gracefully posed, by the wicket, they drove past & bowed, and she bowed too.

But she had made one 'dreadful mistake', as she called it. 'Do you know, I said "Goodbye *Ma'am*," to Mrs Dusautoy. It came quite natural; it is so hard for me to speak to a lady, & *not* say "Ma'am" to her! And I said "Goodbye *Sir*", to Mr. Dusautoy; because I thought I ought to show him respect as a clergyman.'

'Ah well, Massa,' she added 'it's over, and I'm glad of it. Do you see that servantmaid shaking her mats again yon tree? *That's* my work; and I'd liefer be doing it than calling on Mrs Dusautoy. But' she concluded 'if *you* think I ought to call on gentlefolks, I must try and bear it as well as I can!' . . .

Those last remarks formed Hannah's theme for the rest of the holiday. When Munby went out for a long walk, she would have dined on bread and meat and a glass of beer, 'if I had not shown her that she ought to dine like a lady, for my sake'—a sad admission. A carriage drive to Ewhurst pleased her; but Hannah's nagging conscience allowed no lasting acceptance of her elevation.

Sunday, 30 August . . . After tea, Hannah, sitting at ease in her lady dress, with all things cheerful and bright around her, and preparing to read aloud, again remarked that her hands—her large, but sweet and shapely hands—were now quite clean. 'Only fancy, Massa—your hands are always clean, and mine have been black for thirty years! but I can do a many things that you can't: scrubbing, cleaning grates, blacking boots! Oh,' she said, looking round, 'I couldn't bear always to lead such a life as I've led this week; if I was to sit like this and be waited on always, I should think I had got my heaven on earth, and couldn't hope for one hereafter!' . . .

The holiday, nevertheless, passed happily—with picnics, the gathering of mushrooms, the reading of Jane Austen, and a day excursion to Brighton. A Dorking photographer 'evidently charmed with his subject' made some pictures of Hannah 'à la Gainsborough, in her hat'.[5] After a whole fortnight in the guise of a lady, even Hannah found it difficult to resume her life as a servant. Munby himself no longer pretended to find merit in the change. 'It seemed at first utterly sad,' he wrote, 'that all that sweet blossoming of ladyhood in her should be repressed once more, and she reduced to be a drudge again.'

The most memorable event of the autumn was Hannah's enrolment at the newly founded College for Working Women, where she joined the French class.

Friday, 16 October. Home at 5 p.m., and dined; and persuaded Hannah to go to the opening meeting of our College for Working Women, at 5 Fitzroy Street, at 8 o'clock. I, sitting among the Committee, beheld among a crowd of plain faces & tawdry London dresses that tall lithe figure in the grey cloak, and watched the glow of emotion brightening and softening on that sweet healthful country face, as she sat there and listened to the simple earnest prophetlike utterance of George Macdonald the poet. 'The ladies did stare at me as I come in!' she said, after; 'perhaps they thought a Sister was coming among em!' When all was over, and I had talked with the Litchfields & Tansleys and with Macdonald and with T. Hughes, I came home by 10.45, and found Hannah returned and waiting tea for me . . . she was 'liven'd up' by all she had heard.

Wednesday, 21 October . . . She was in high spirits at the thought of going tonight to the Working Women's College, to join the French class. 'You'll see

[5] See Plates 18 and 24.

20. Zazel, an English girl acrobat of eighteen
22. Azella, a French colonial girl acrobat who appeared at the Holborn Empire Theatre, 1868–9

21. Zazel, on her first appearance at Westminster Aquarium, 1877
23. A milkwoman from Sims's Dairy, Jermyn Street, London, aged about 27: 4 June, 1864

24. Hannah at Dorking, 1874

I shall learn French quite well!' she said; 'and I shall behave quite respectful too, and as a servant should.' And what shall you put yourself in the book, dear? 'I shall put "Hannah Cullwick, Servant, aged 41"; and the master will say "Dear me, I wonder you can do French so well, after being 30 years in service!" and' she continued, prolonging the joke, 'if Mrs Tansley asks me who I am, I shall say "Ma'am, I am the wife of Mr. M., who teaches here"; and then she'll say, "Why, I think the woman's mad!"' So, at 4.30, I left this dear soul in her servant's dress, and went by the 5 p.m. train to Woking station, with Vernon Lushington, who had called and asked me to spend the night again in Eden—at Pyrford. The brief fierce gale and storm had cleared away, and he and I had a delightful walk together across the heath by moonlight, reaching Pyrford about 6.30; and Mrs Lushington, without her bonnet, came out to meet us in the lane. It is perhaps fortunate that attention to her, and the bright and cultivated talk of Vernon—and hers too—and the transformation which their wealth and taste has made in the cottage, help to veil the sad memories of 1867: but these things also distract one, and the full joy of Pyrford can only be had alone—or with a wife. We sat and talked, and dined about 8, and then coffee & talk again, and a turn in the garden under a brilliant cloudless moon, with the weir sounding full and soft as ever. And V. and I sat up till one, smoking in the kitchen, and talking of Positivism and of Wordsworth. The little drawing room, with its pretty furniture and costly and refined decorations of old china and pictures, is happily improved: but it is rather absurd to find four maidservants and a *footman*, in that little house where there was no servant at all, and where V. & his wife have to go to their bedroom through mine.[6]

Saturday, 5 December.   Went to 31 Onslow Square, & called on Mrs Theodore Martin, who was out; but in the square I met her husband, who talked with me some time about his Life of Prince Albert, of which the first volume is just out. He says the Queen leaves him quite free in the matter, but that he finds it a task of extreme delicacy, to avoid seeming to compromise or commit her, or other people still living, in dealing with the Prince's relations to politics. Also his letters are mostly in German, & their German style is not good; and many things are so secret that only Martin himself may see them & copy them. Altogether it is 'wearing his life out', he says. . . .

During the concluding months of 1874, Munby's diary had some unusual gaps, and the entries were sometimes perfunctory. For a few days in December he was 'unwell', being tended by Hannah 'with unfailing skill and unfaltering good temper and affection'. On 17 December, 'Hannah with all sweetness and skill helped me to arrange and pack up Christmas

---

[6] Munby paid another visit to Wheeler's Farm (or Priory Cottage, as it was once known) on 28 October, when his friend Mrs Collyer, an old lady who lived nearby, told him that his former beloved 'poor Sarah Carter has lately gone to America with a clergyman's family'.

presents for other folks, whom she never knew, who would despise her, and who will never send presents to her or to me'. Munby's departure to spend Christmas at Clifton Holme was depressing to them both. They 'prayed together, and kissed many a time at the door: and so with divided heart I left my darling—not alone, indeed, but with only the old folks of the kitchen to keep her company indoors'.

This was the last family Christmas at which Munby's father would place the Yule log on the fire on Christmas Eve, brew the punch 'in one of our antique china bowls' and ladle it 'with one of our George the Second silver ladles'. The weather was intensely cold; the Ings and the river were frozen and deep in snow. On Christmas Day, the party in the servants' hall rivalled that in the parlour—the manservant, the five maids, and the gardener and his wife were hosts to 'several others, outsiders'.

At Fig Tree Court, Thornbury abandoned his seasonal attempt to kiss Hannah.

Wednesday, 30 December: York . . . This morning I heard again from my darling, of her doings . . . how my tenant Thornbury came yesterday, and gave her—my Hannah—a Christmas box. 'I went up out of the kitchen to let Mr. T. in,' she says; 'and then I said, "I've took the liberty, Sir, to give the postman a shilling from you." "That's right," he says; and putting 3 shillings in my hand, he says "And there's a trifle for yourself"; and I said "Thank you, Sir,"' Doubtless he thought that she, being only a servant, meant to give him a hint that he should 'tip' her!

In January, 1875, Munby began to make entries in a miniature pocket diary, much smaller than any he had used before. He never resumed his day-to-day record on the previous scale, but he employed separate note-books for special subjects. There are two small volumes devoted to Hannah's doings in 1875–7, parts of which can be interpolated here.

Friday, 1 January, 1875. As I came home to dinner today, I heard folk talking on the stairs, within the outer door. It was the lamplighter and *Hannah*: he was talking to her freely, and as an equal; and she, in her servant's cap & cotton frock and apron, was above, leaning over the ancient balustrade, and freely answering him. When I appeared, they broke off at once, like two servants caught gossiping by their master; he slipped away, and Hannah retired indoors, without another word. 'Ah, Massa!' she laughingly said when the door was shut, 'you should have heard our talk . . . he's a very nice young man, I assure you! . . . But he said, "Don't you wish to get married?" "Not I!" I said; "I've seen too much of that, with father and poor mother!"'

376

Thursday, 14 January . . . Drest in ladylike silk, and with a camellia in her lustrous hair, she received her guests at tea—sister Ellen and cousin Elizabeth, who came to do honour to this anniversary[7]; and she & they received brooches, all of one pattern, as memorials. And when her 'master' came in to join them, she did not call him 'Sir' nor wait in silence, but ran boldly up to him, and kissed him before them all, and called him a 'dear old darling!'

Wednesday, 27 January . . . Sat with H. till 7: then she to her French class, & I to Bryanston Street by 7.30, & dined with Litchfield. F. J. A. Hort,[8] who is on the N.T. Revision Committee; and Miss Julia Wedgwood.[9] Much able talk on general subjects, and on poor Kingsley.[1] He and Maurice gone, one feels oneself to be in an alien world.

Thursday, 11 February.   Went by rail to 8 Southwell Gardens, to an afternoon tea at Miss Thackeray's. . . . Robert Browning was there, airy and sprightly and affecting commonplace fashion: he does not command or seem to seek the reverence due to a great poet. Miss T. was amiable & gushing as usual; Mrs Leslie Stephen had her strange child Laura at her knee.[2] . . .

Friday, 5 March . . . to my Latin class at 8, and home 10.15 to H., to tea. She had been scrubbing on her knees today in the afternoon; and in the evening, had read quite through the new volume of Tennyson—i.e. Maud and Enoch Arden. With the latter she was delighted; but of Maud, she said 'I canna make top nor tail of it, Massa!'

Wednesday, 10 and Thursday, 11 March.   My brother Frederick came suddenly to stay a night with me. But Hannah was not at all put out: 'I can sleep in the kitchen quite well, Massa,' said she; 'and I shall wait on your brother, of course. I shall *enjoy* it; and he'll never notice me! I'll make myself look so as he'd never think for a moment that you could care for *me*.' And when we came back from Hamlet,[3] I found that she had made his room ready and bright and tidy; and I found *her* asleep on a rude sofa bed in the kitchen. In the morning . . . I

---

[7] Of their wedding in 1873.

[8] Fenton John Anthony Hort (1828–92), scholar and divine, had been a Trinity contemporary of Munby.

[9] Julia Wedgwood (1833–1913), a bluestocking with 'a passion for righteousness', had had a fairly intense friendship with Browning after his wife's death. This was over now, and she figures often in Munby's diary.

[1] Charles Kingsley had died on 24 January, aged 55.

[2] Mrs. Stephen (formerly Minnie Thackeray) died suddenly in the autumn of this year. Her daughter Laura was mentally deficient. By his second wife, Julia Duckworth, Stephen became the father of Virginia Woolf.

[3] Irving's *Hamlet* at the Lyceum: 'better than Fechter's, and the best I have ever seen' (Diary, 10 March).

heard her knock at his door and say 'If you please Sir, I've brought your hot-water and boots.' He left at 11 a.m., after walking to Westminster with me. She told me afterwards, that when he came back for his luggage, he met her on the stairs . . . 'and oh, I *did* look a poor hardworking drudge, with my dirty cap and frock and coarse apron, and arms and face blacked o' purpose! But that was how I *wish'd* to look, before *him*, you know. He put a shilling in my black hand, and I said 'Thank you, Sir'. And he ask'd me to carry his luggage to the cab, and I did. . . . And as I followed your brother, I wondered if *his* wife'd do as much for *you*, when you go to see her! . . .'

Thursday, 25 March: Ockley . . . Hannah now sat gracefully reclining in an easy chair; drest in black silk and lace, with a pretty ruff round her long throat, and her bright crêpè brown hair neatly drest, and a wedding ring and 'keeper' on her clean and shapely hand: she sat listening with condescending grace to the land-lady's domestic story. . . . And then Mrs Wickens spoke of the village news, and about the new Incumbent of Oakwood Chapel, Mr. Evelyn, a brother of Evelyn of Wotton. A nice gentleman, she said he was; but it was a sad thing, the family won't notice him: 'For you see, Ma'am,' said Mrs Wickens, turning to Hannah, 'he married *a servant*; and so *of course* the gentlefolks couldn't notice him!' Such a home thrust as this might have been too much for an ordinary woman: but Hannah neither reddened nor started nor in anywise betrayed herself; she only leaned forward, as with interest in the tale, and said with a wave of her hand 'Oh, no, of course not—what a sad thing!'

I, the sole spectator of this comedy, looked at her with half-incredulous admiration: can it be, that this handsome and dignified lady is really *not* a lady, but is acting a part, and one she never learnt? Can she really be only Hannah, the maid-of-all-work who cleaned my boots this morning? What a shame, then, that she should ever go back to such work! And yet, the wonder is, that she prefers *that* condition of life to this.

Saturday, 27 March: Ockley . . . I called alone on the Rector, and told him in confidence that Hannah was not a lady born: I did not venture to confess that she is a servant. He seemed surprised; and said emphatically 'I should never have known it.' 'I'm so glad you've told him, Massa!' said Hannah. . . .

Saturday, 15 May. After cleaning and packing, H. went off at 11.30 with brother Dick, by excursion train to Shropshire: so when I returned at 2, the Light of the house was gone, but had set all in order for me. I left King's Cross at 3 p.m.: the country en route all green & lovely & steeped in sunshine. . . . Reached Clifton Holme by 11, & found my father mother & Carry well.

Wednesday, 26 May . . . to my class at 8, teaching Latin in one room while H. was learning French in another. She & I drove thence together, and she home

378

and I to the P. A. Taylors' last party. H. Fawcett, Mrs Anderson, Moncure Conway, Austin Dobson, Gosse. . . .

Thursday, 3 June.   I came home at 7.45 to dinner, and George[4] arrived unexpectedly just afterwards, so of course he dined with me. Hannah was in the room when he came; drest as a servant, in cap and white apron, and arranging the table. She understood the situation at once, & silently laid another napkin, without being told to do so. She took it as a matter of course, when he sat down in the chair she would have occupied if I had been alone: she resumed her servant's manner, and stood behind my chair and waited on us with alacrity and ease. . . . George spoke to her occasionally as to a servant, but never noticed her or looked at her. When he had gone, 'I looked at him' she said 'and thought, "Ah, Sir, I wonder what you'd say if you knew this is Hannah!"'[5] . . .

Tuesday, 6 July.   Dined at the Club, & at 8.30 to Covent Garden, & found H. seated as a lady in an amphitheatre stall, intensely enjoying *Lohengrin*, the libretto of which she had read over to me. The third Act is specially beautiful. We got home at 12.30.

Thursday, 22 July . . . I home at 7 to dinner; and found H., as I had left her after breakfast, in cap and coarse holland apron, clean lilac cotton frock, bare arms, & her leather strap on her wrist. Thus drest, she had waited on T.,[6] had been out on errands, & the grocer's man had condescended to talk to her: thus drest, she sat in her armchair, after 'washing up', and read to me Stebbing's Life of Dante, which she thought 'most interesting'. . . .

While Hannah could speak some French and read aloud intelligently from the books in Munby's library,[7] her interest in continental travel— and in the ladylike deportment it demanded of her—had not advanced. On 3 August, Munby regretfully recorded that he had 'consented' to take his young cousin Henry Pearson to Italy: 'poor fellow, a sorry substitute for H., & in spite of his good nature a strange comrade on such a pilgrimage.' When he left the Temple on 14 August, 'Hannah talked cheerfully of the happy days she will have with Sister Ellen, at work here in her own way. But I would that she were with me in my way.'

It would have been better for Henry Pearson if Hannah had gone, as the journey proved disastrous. Henry was taken ill at Bellinzona, apparently from sunstroke. The heat was so intense that, 'even with puggaree &

---

[4] Munby's brother, the Rector of Turvey.
[5] George was amazed to learn more than thirty years later, after Hannah's death, that she had been his sister-in-law (see p. 435).
[6] Thornbury.
[7] She had just completed a catalogue showing a total of 1,372 volumes.

umbrella', Munby 'could only creep along the shady side of the old arcaded streets' in search of a chemist and a doctor. When Henry did not improve, his parents were summoned. Their arrival released Munby for 'an exquisite visit of 5 days' in Venice and for expeditions to Bologna, Ravenna—where he saw the tomb of Dante ('Knelt, of course')—and Turin. He returned to London to find Hannah well, and his chambers newly painted, papered and whitewashed; but on 21 September had to note: 'Poor Henry Pearson died at Bellinzona on the 16th.'

Friday, 22 October . . . Home 10.30 to H., who had been to the Working Women's College, and had for the first time attended the English Literature class. She was in high spirits, and had much to tell me about the Puritans and Charles II; and told it all in her own childlike rustic way, with all the eagerness of a schoolgirl. 'And when he said that every good poet has a high standard of virtue, I thought of *you*, Massa!' Who could resist *that*?

Friday, 29 October. Went to Gloucester Crescent, 5.30 p.m., & called on Mrs Henderson, H's old mistress. H. would not go with me: 'No, Massa,' said she: 'I don't like to go to the front door—the servants'd think me *proud*; and if I go down the area, I don't know as they want me!' Again: 'If I dress smart, they'll envy me; and if I dress plain, they'll say I'm shabby.' 'But,' said Miss Henderson when I told her this, 'Hannah always looks nice and ladylike'—'Pray tell her she *must* come.'[8] . . .

Wednesday, 1 December . . . At 5 p.m., Mr & Mrs Wilson & Josiah Rees came to afternoon tea: and after tea, Mrs W. sang to my piano, & I also sang. Mean while H., who had arranged all with neatness & good taste, was at work unseen, in a back room; & actually listened at the keyhole, to the music of her own guests! 'Oh no, Massa,' she said afterwards, 'I wouldn't sitdown with 'em for anything: but' laughing 'you might ha' said to them, "If you want to see my wife, you've only to look in the back room!"' . . .

Thursday, 2 December. Heard this morning from Fred, of my dear father's illness. . . . Home at 6 to dinner: and all the evening, my darling exerted herself to comfort and to cheer me. Last night at 8, we both went to the Advent service at the Temple church: I to my seat, on the I.T.[9] side, she to the M.T.[1] side. 'And I fell in love with you again' said she, 'looking at you across the church. "There he is," I thought, "that I used to look at like this, twenty years ago!"' And I too with her.

---

[8] She went on 22 November and was entertained first upstairs, then downstairs.
[9] Inner Temple.   [1] Middle Temple.

Friday, 3 December.   'If you find the fire in, when you come to light it in a morning, you're sure to hear of an illness: and you know, I found this fire in, on Tuesday morning.' 'If you chance to say your words backwards, you'll see a stranger that day: & you know I said "bread my toast" today; and I saw Roberts!' per H. . . .

Munby soon went to York, and for the remainder of the year filled the diary with a harrowing long-drawn description of his father's last illness. As early as 5 December, Joseph Munby was speaking 'of trust in God and how it is not hard to die', but during the next fortnight his condition fluctuated—'much better', 'worse again', 'very precarious', 'decidedly better', 'not quite so well'. His family accepted the ordeal with Victorian piety. Munby's brother George, the Rector of Turvey, returned thanks in the sickroom after one temporary improvement, and later celebrated the Communion: 'The father no worse for this exertion.'

Monday, 20 December: York . . . at their evening visit, 9 p.m. the doctors said there was no more hope. My poor mother sat or lay in the morning room, painfully anxious, crossing the corridor every now & then to visit the sick room. Carry and I also sat there with the nurses. My dear father knew us all, and said to me 'my darling Arthur!' more than once. About 11.30, Mr. Ball said he was sinking rapidly. The maid & nurse held him up in bed: he breathed hard and short, but had no pain: he was too feeble to speak much, but he followed audibly the prayers and psalms from the Visitation Service, which Fred and I read by turns, and he joined in the Lord's Prayer: finally, Fred read the hymn 'Just as I am', and my dear father repeated the words in it 'Oh Lamb of God, I come', and then without a struggle his breathing ceased, and his devout and manly spirit passed away. My dear mother sat in silent agony by the bed, in my arms; and then we carried her away. I returned, to be with him alone, and kissed him thrice.

Joseph Munby died of congestion of the lungs shortly after midnight on the morning of 21 December, and was buried on the 23rd. 'The funeral was one of the largest which has occurred in this city for some years past,' said the *York Herald*, 'the *cortège* consisting of sixty-eight carriages, the representatives of most of the public bodies, institutions, and societies of York, and was witnessed by many hundreds of the citizens.' The tribute was well deserved, for Joseph Munby was not only highly respected as a solicitor and clerk to the city magistrates, but honoured for his close association with virtually every charitable institution in York; he had also played a considerable part in its musical life.

His eldest son was the chief mourner—a dignified 'bachelor', for 'Mr. Arthur has never married' (yet a letter from Hannah came nearly every day). He followed the hearse in the first coach with his sister and 'Mrs. J. Forth Munby and daughter'. Six other coaches conveyed the family and close friends, and next came the carriages of the Lord Mayor and the City Police, 'Mr. Munby's private carriage, with drawn blinds', a carriage containing 'Mr. Munby's office clerks'—a good subject for 'Phiz'—and then many more carriages. The procession made its way slowly through silent streets to Osbaldwick, where the little church was 'far more than full'. 'The setting sun shone, as we laid our honoured father to rest, in the vault where Joe lies, under a white cross.'

Munby rose to his duty with a courage we can admire because we realise the sensibility underlying it. He had acquired by long practice a convincing self-control on social occasions. On Christmas Day, he wrote, 'at 9 p.m. I took my father's place, & read a sermon to the household'. His mother 'put on her widow's cap, and cried: before I entered the room to see her in it, I thought of her for the last time as she was, without it, and with *him*'.

Monday, 27 December . . . Fred and Edward came to Clifton; and in the afternoon, they, with George & myself, drove to Osbaldwick, to see the grave once more together. We stood together in the twilight, four sons, around our father's and brother's grave; George prayed aloud, extempore; then all joined in the Lord's Prayer: then I pronounced the blessing; and we kissed one another, and walked together home.

The Victorian way of death, so exacting in its discipline, had the advantage of providing emotional outlets. An eldest son was kept busy. After his return to London, Munby superintended the printing of a memorial card, and of a booklet in memory of his father compiled from the Yorkshire newspapers, containing also 'the sketch of his last hours which George and I drew up'. 'When midnight struck' on 31 December, he 'went and said a prayer for H. by her bedside. So ends a year in which I have had the infinite delight of seeing Italy; but in which I have suffered the greatest loss and keenest sorrow that I have ever known yet. Beloved father!'

It is noticeable that in the pocket diary for January, 1876, Hannah appears as 'my faithful servant'; she is not mentioned as a wife. Such phases of apparent indifference are not uncommon with Munby; they may be partly explicable as indicating a guilt-complex stimulated by imminent thoughts of the parental home (the diary might also have fallen into the wrong hands). When he reports Hannah's conversation in this mood, she is made to call him 'Master' not 'Massa', while diary details about her are restricted to anecdotes that could apply to any ordinary servant. It is as if he felt his parents looking over his shoulder.

Munby spent the next few months supervising and distributing his father's memorial cards and booklets. He sent his mother a mounted copy of the card framed in black wood. He ordered a memorial brass for Clifton Church; and for his mother an enlarged photograph of his father, re-touched by an obliging female artist. With his brother Fred, he acted as executor of the will, proved in April. Joseph Munby left £32,800, in trust for his wife for life, and after her death to be divided equally between each of his five surviving children and the widow and children of his deceased son John. Thus the eldest son did not immediately benefit.

On 7 March, Munby watched the Queen and Princess Beatrice driving to open the London Hospital: 'The Queen was badly drest, and looked red and blowzed & commonplace; and not amiable either.' A few days later in the Green Park he 'met Mr. Disraeli, on foot, looking worn and gaunt' (15 March). Considering himself to be in mourning for his father, Munby went to no parties for several months, but confined himself to his usual country excursions, and to meetings with cronies such as Borland and Ralston.

By the end of May, Munby again felt able to indicate circumspectly in the diary that he and his 'faithful servant' had a special relationship. He travelled to Shropshire to meet some of his wife's relations.

Saturday, 20 May, 1876 ... Reached *Newport, Salop*, at 7.15. Hannah was waiting, & we walked through Newport together; she showing me the house where she once was nursemaid. A pleasant quiet little redbrick town, with a few gabled halftimbered houses left. ... Charming woods & lanes beyond, and by these in a glowing evening across fields to Cousin Gosling's 9 acre farm. Cordial reception by grave Thomas & sprightly Ellen & old father Morris, in a small antique kitchen with redbrick floor. Tea in state in little parlour, & talk after-wards in kitchen, and to bed in snug little room looking over the buttercup meadows.

One of the tragedies of this strange marriage was that Munby, the fastidious man of society, always found himself thoroughly at home in the abodes of the poor; while Hannah, with her veil and gloves, made only a fainthearted 'lady' in the haunts of the well-to-do. If Munby could have abdicated his gentility—impossible thought—he might have lived happily ever afterwards in a workman's cottage with Hannah. Indeed, in the long run he did contrive to do just this—but only for short periods at a time. Unfortunately, the compromise was not reached until after a shattering break in the marriage.

From Newport, Munby and Hannah moved on to spend two days with her brother Jim, a carpenter, at Wombridge, about six miles away, on the road to Hadley and Wellington. It was a neighbourhood they both eventually came to know well.

At Fig Tree Court, Hannah's sister Ellen was taken into Munby's service, in place of the Skeats.

Wednesday, 26 July . . . To shops, and dined at the Club, and home 8.45, unwell.[2] Hannah and Ellen had three of their cousins to tea with them: Elizabeth, Ann, & Maria Morris: all of them servants, and respectable trusty young women. So that five female servants at once were at ease in my bachelor house today.

Thursday, 3 August. Today, I had to send my boy to the Temple, for my medicine. When he returned—Did you go to the kitchen? 'Yes Sir.' And whom did you see? 'I saw that tall servant, Sir,' meaning Hannah. Had she her bonnet on? 'No Sir, she had a big cap on, and a cotton frock.' So she was at 7.30, when I came home after a hot bath at the Club. My dinner over, she would have taken down the remains for her own supper in the kitchen. 'Eat them here,' said her master; 'for once, you need not be a servant.' 'Am I not *always* a servant?' she replied smiling.

The modest visit to Shropshire in May was followed by a longer journey in August, when Mr. and Mrs. Munby stayed at the best hotels:

Saturday, 19 August. Left Euston Square at 3 p.m., and by Stafford & Newport to *Shrewsbury*: arrived 8.20, and to the Raven Hotel.

This morning, Hannah cleaned boots and blacked the grate and carried coals and water as usual, wearing her rough servant's dress. This evening, she sailed into the ladies' coffeeroom at Shrewsbury, drest and adorned as a lady, self-possest and elegant and comely as if she were to the manner born; and she knew how to behave with condescending grace to the obsequious chambermaid who showed her to her room. Her hands, too, had grown clean and almost white.

From Shrewsbury they went south to spend several days at Church Stretton, where they climbed the Long Mynd and Caer Caradoc. Two

---

[2] The word 'unwell' appears with some frequency in the diary at this period; the cause is never stated.

nights at The Feathers in Ludlow followed; in the castle they enjoyed 'the view from the keep & the recollections of Comus, and sitting long in the deep embrasure of the guardroom window which overlooks the river & the meads, while H. read *Sir Charles Grandison*[3] aloud, in her apt enthusiastic way'. Then to New Radnor—whence Munby, restless as usual, took the coach to Aberystwyth, leaving Hannah alone for a night at the Eagle Inn. The final stops were at The Royal in Ross-on-Wye and The Beaufort Arms at Monmouth. By then Hannah had had enough of being a lady.

Saturday, 2 September . . . Hannah bought eggs, butter, fruit, which, with ferns from Goodrich, filled her large new marketbasket.
    At 12.15, we left Monmouth by rail, and so to Ross, and Gloucester, and Swindon & Didcot. 'Thank goodness, Massa, we're going home!' said H.; and in the train, when we were alone, she changed her dress from lady to servant: rejoicing to leave off gloves, and looking forward to her kitchen. . . .

Tuesday, 5 September . . . Hannah, in her new peasant's bonnet & lilac cotton frock, bought by herself at Church Stretton 'for her servant', got up early again, blacked the grate, cleaned my boots, fetched water, waited at breakfast: all which she much prefers to her recent lady-life. 'The idea o' *me* being a lady and called "Ma'am"!' she said, showing her soiled hands.

Munby was no less fond of Hannah the servant than of Hannah the potential lady. After leaving on 16 September to visit his mother at Scarborough, he made an affectionate drawing of Hannah from memory, showing her standing beside his cab in Middle Temple Lane, pointing the way for a stranger. Hannah remained devoted to Massa, but there was an underlying bitterness in her rejection of the rôle of the ladywife which was sometimes disquieting to Munby.

Thursday, 5 October . . . Hannah says that my new grate makes her hands blacker than ever; since she has to clean the cakes of soot off the glazed tiles every morning. 'But I'd liefer have my hands black nor clean,' she said; 'and I'd liefer go to bed tired wi' scrubbing, nor wi' climbing great hills, or staircases of hotels. I *will* be your servant to my life's end', she added, 'and I hope you'll never take me out again as a lady. It makes me miserable; I feel so useless & idle!' . . .

The flaw in the marriage developed slowly in the course of 1877; and here the diary entry of 19 December, 1876, is significant: '. . . sat some time with Rees, who is to be married on Thursday at Teignmouth, and arranged with him that I should have the refusal of his chambers.'

[3] Samuel Richardson's novel.

Munby's decision to rent Josiah Rees's ground-floor rooms in addition to his own, and thus to control the whole of 6 Fig Tree Court, precipitated a crisis by giving the ever-willing Hannah an excuse to take on more work than even she could manage.

Thursday, 4 January, 1877 . . . Hannah told me that she had crawled under my bed to the farther side, and with her fingers had stopped up all mouse-holes in the ancient wainscot, with soap. ''Cause mice winna eat through soap,' she explained. . . .

Tuesday, 16 January . . . As from yesterday, I take from Rees the groundfloor of this house: and Hannah is promoted to be 'laundress' pro tem., vice Mrs Newton. 'I was on the stairs with my pail, & I met Mrs N.,' said H.; 'and she says, "Well, Hannah, I suppose you & Ellen'll be able to do *these* chambers too?" "Oh yes!" I says.'

Tuesday, 23 January.　　Today, Hannah entered in earnest upon her new duties as laundress of the ground floor, or rather as charwoman: for her first great work is to clean out the filthy rooms. . . . I came home soon after 5 today, and found her at work in Rees's bedroom . . . she was pleased that I was watching her, and she was in a didactic mood. After she had scrubbed a square yard or two, 'Now, Massa,' she said, looking up archly, 'if you was me, which bit would you scrub next?' 'I think I should go lengthwise down the boards,' said Massa, gravely. 'Right!' said the servant: 'but you could *never* scrub like me!' . . .

Monday, 29 January.　　Fred returned from Turvey, & went to my house, where Hannah waited on him. 'A most attentive and devoted servant,' said he; 'and before I left, she insisted on cleaning my boots, because they were foul with Bedfordshire mud.' . . . Home . . . by 11, and found the spare room clean & bright and ready for Fred to sleep in.

Tuesday, 30 January . . . This morning, after lighting the fire & sweeping, she knocked at my brother's door. 'Eight o'clock, Sir, if you please; and I've brought your hot water and boots,' I heard her say: for she had just cleaned his boots again. At 9 o'clock, opening my door, I saw my brother seated in an armchair by the parlour fire, reading his letters; and at his feet, on the hearth, Hannah was kneeling in silence, toasting bread. Her arms were bare; she wore her blue cotton frock and big apron, and her own large frilled cap of white net; the same that she always wore in service. 'Mr. Frederick' did not notice her or speak to her; but Massa did. 'Good morning, Hannah!' said he, after greeting his brother. 'Good morning, Sir!' answered his wife, rising from her knees, in her servant's dress, and putting a final touch to the neat breakfast equipage which she had arranged for him.

Hannah directs a stranger in Middle Temple Lane. (Diary, 16 September 1876)

The two men sat down—for family prayers were suspended on this occasion—and Hannah waited on them, of her own accord & in her own way. . . .

Wednesday, 31 January.   Hannah waited as yesterday: Fred struck by her devotedness. He left for Yorkshire 2.30 p.m. 'Shall I carry your luggage, Sir?' says H. 'Yes, you may take that'—Takes large bag, &c—Gives her 2/6. . . .

Wednesday, 7 February . . . Contrary to my orders (for I desired her to rest, & not work so hard) Hannah cleaned out the clerk's room downstairs today: cleaned the ceiling and the wainscot walls, scrubbed the floor on her hands & knees, and then went out and spent ½ an hour in the street, in the rain, cleaning the great window, swilling it with pail and broom. 'You can do it better in the rain,' said she.

Thursday, 8 February.   Home at 6 to dinner. . . . And at 6, a stranger, *Mr. Henry Conynghame* of John's, a bright young man of 30, came. Hannah showed him in, and he arranged to take the ground floor, for himself, a Mr. Asquith[4] of Balliol, and an Hon. Mark Napier of Trinity. Was charmed with my room—all Hannah's work, as I told him.

Friday, 9 February . . . Mr. Conynghame called again, shown up by Hannah who was in the kitchen. He had been here during the day, giving her directions. He now proposed to me to take her as his laundress, saying 'Your servant is an excellent woman, and has capital ideas of cleaning—she is very different from the common Temple women.' I evaded this by saying that she *or her sister* should do the work: knowing however that Hannah is charmed with the prospect, & will insist on doing the cleaning.

As Roy Jenkins commented in his biography *Asquith*, the future prime minister's appearance at 6 Fig Tree Court marked the beginning of 'seven extremely lean years' for him. He and his companions had all been pupils in the distinguished chambers of Charles Bowen (later Lord Bowen), and were thought to be highly promising. But there was no aura of legal success at Munby's house—'no one in the chambers', to quote Mr. Jenkins, 'from whom work might filter down to him'. And so Asquith was temporarily driven to correcting examination papers, lecturing to other lawyers, and writing for the *Spectator*.

Of the three new arrivals who now came under Hannah's care, Mark Napier seems to have been her favourite (he later took over the sub-tenancy). Asquith 'looks so straight, & makes you keep your distance,' Hannah told Munby on one occasion; whereas 'the Honble Mark . . . said

4 Herbert Henry Asquith, later first Earl of Oxford and Asquith (1852–1928).

"I'm very glad to see you, Hannah!"' (5 October). In a letter to Munby at Scarborough, Hannah detected some more hopeful signs in Asquith, but she did not find his manner encouraging. 'Hannah writes, with black hands, that she has just been waiting on one of her 5 masters, Mr. Asquith. "He calls 'Hannah!' in such a tone!" says she: "and when I took the coals in just now, I *was* so black—hands & arms & face & all—and my striped apron on. He seems to show some respect for me, though I do look so dirty: perhaps that's why he respects me!"' (18 October).

If the young barristers had realised that their erudite literary landlord was the husband of their servant—and if Munby had known that one of his tenants was destined to become prime minister—the situation would, no doubt, have been more intriguing for all concerned. As it was, one can see that Hannah wore herself out during 1877, by doing far more than her share of the work for the whole house. Having cleaned the ground-floor the whole of one Sunday, she still had enough spirit to amaze Munby 'by appearing in Rees's volunteer uniform—a fine handsome young *man!*' (12 February).

Wednesday, 14 February.   To the Club, and at a writing table there, found myself sitting vis-à-vis to Mr. Gladstone: old, eager, hurriedly writing: pen in mouth. Home to dinner 6.30. Hannah had been downstairs, waiting on Cunynghame; dusting & putting up pictures for him. . . .

Wednesday, 21 March . . . Hannah, kneeling on the hearth & washing her master's feet, said 'Massa, your friends'd cut you fast enough, if they was to know you had married a servant!' But would *they* do as much for him? 'I consider' she said again, 'that my soul's as much value as yourn; but our *degrees* are very different: my work is very low, but then it's work as others wouldn't like to do. . . .'

Friday, 20 April.   To the Aquarium at 5, & again saw "Zazel"[5] and again astonished (as every one was) at the courage and coolness and skill of this girl of 18: who, drest as an acrobat, walked the tightrope without a pole, lay down on it & rose again on one leg, & the like: Then swung herself about on the trapèze like a monkey, and sat on it like a strong man, with big arms folded, and sitting thus, flung her body round and round it, holding it by the hollow of her knees: then leaped 60 feet down, head fore most: Then let herself down, feet first, into a cannon, and was literally fired thence into the air, falling flat on a net: and 15 minutes afterwards, was seen in neat woman's clothing, walking quietly home with her sister, as modest and demure as any schoolgirl. . . .

[5] See Plates 20 and 21.

Tuesday, 15 May.   To Onslow Square, & called on Mrs Theodore Martin. Met her in the square, & went home with her and had a very pleasant half hour's tête à tête. She advised me to marry, and spoke eloquently, in her graceful way, of the pleasures of female companionship, and of love and emotion which is independent of time and age. I assented warmly, for reasons which she could not know. . . .

The couple spent a happy Whitsun at Ockley. Hannah's brother-in-law 'Mr. Frederick' stayed again at Fig Tree Court and tipped her another half-crown, for which she curtsied respectfully (30 May). On 23 June, Munby went to Turvey to spend the week-end with his brother George:

Saturday, 23 June.   'I'll come and meet you o' Monday morning, Massa, & bring back your luggage, & the flowers you'll bring.' 'And shall you come just as you are—in cotton frock and apron?' She sprang forward, and kissed him fervently: 'Yes' she cried—'Just as I am, without one plea, Excepting that thou lovest me!' . . .

Monday, 25 June.   Left *Turvey* 8.20 a.m.; a charming walk through the bright village and the wooded park to the station. At Piccadilly Circus, at 11, Hannah was waiting; in straw bonnet & cloak & cotton frock & apron, & bare armed. She took my flowers, & bag, & things; & handed me letters—one from herself, telling how she had been cleaning, & sweeping carpets in the court, & how she enjoyed it. And so she walked away, graceful, unlike any one else. . . .

There is no hint that Munby contemplated a continental holiday with Hannah this year; he had given up that idea as illusory. In August she went to her brother's cottage at Wombridge, while Munby travelled to Switzerland with Ralston (who injured himself climbing the Eiger). Mr. and Mrs. Munby did not see each other again until the beginning of October, after Hannah had 'been living the life of a Shropshire peasant woman for nearly 8 weeks'. One senses that Hannah returned to London somewhat reluctantly, and that her relationship with her husband now suffered a subtle but significant change. Munby's innate bachelorhood, temporarily muted by marriage, re-asserted itself as he decided, reluctantly but finally, that Hannah would never make a conventional wife. Still loving her, he braced himself to act independently of her.

Nevertheless, Hannah's abrupt return to Shropshire, on doctor's orders, after only three weeks in London, comes as a surprise. No explanation is given in the diary of her 'illness', which almost certainly involved an hysterical outburst and a painful scene. One might conjecture that it was caused partly by overwork—for she had again thrown herself furiously into her cleaning; partly by emotional frustration; partly perhaps by the onset of the 'change of life'.

Thursday, 25 October.   To shops, and home at 6 to dinner. Hannah in bed: went to 85 Harley Street at 8 p.m. to Dr. Julius Pollock (a son of the Chief Baron) who came home with me and saw her, and stayed till 11 p.m., most courteous and patient and kind. He advised me to send her into the country at once.

Saturday, 27 October.   Hannah, in her servant's dress . . . did her usual morning's work in the parlour: lighted the fire, cleaned the grate, laid the breakfast table, prepared my breakfast: and as usual too, read to me the Psalms for the day; which (as usual too) were singularly appropriate.[6] At 12 o'clock, she started for Shropshire. I went by train to *Woking*, arriving there 3.20. Walked by the mossy old barn, along White Rose Lane, under the sandstone cliff where the martins build, to Hoebridge Farm; and thence up the shady lane out on to the high terrace of Breakheart Field: glorious view over the vale—a sea of golden leafage & ruddy farms: on the high land, golden elms glowing in sunset against deep purple rain cloud. So to *Pyrford* by 5; called at Mr. Cole's farm, and talked with him of the house: and across the meads after dark to *Ripley* and the Talbot, before 7.

These sentences are among the most significant in the whole diary. They not only mark Hannah's departure from Fig Tree Court—and she hardly ever came back except for an occasional brisk bout of spring-cleaning; they are also linked in Munby's mind with the prospect of a new country life opening for him at Pyrford. The wealthy Vernon Lushingtons (already having a place called Pyports at Cobham, and being about to occupy a house in Kensington Square) had left Wheeler's Farm empty, and were hoping that Munby would take over their sub-tenancy from Farmer Cole. This time, after some hesitation, Munby did rent the house, which was to become his principal home until his death.

In 1877, he probably hoped that, one day, Hannah would live at Wheeler's Farm with him (long afterwards, when it was too late, he certainly expressed this wish). But one of his main motives in acquiring the Pyrford house may have been to put an end to the extraordinary Box-and-Cox situation in the Temple, which, after four and a half years, no longer seemed romantic or exciting, as it had formerly done. The last thing Munby wanted was to introduce the 'disguised wife' theme into the

[6] E.g. Psalm 120: 'When I was in trouble I called upon the Lord: and he heard me.' Psalm 121: 'I will lift up mine eyes unto the hills: from whence cometh my help.'

peaceful atmosphere of his dream cottage. Besides, the whole concept of Pyrford, with its bitter-sweet memories of Sarah Carter, was in a way hostile to Hannah.

For the time being, Munby wrote occasional letters to his wife and awaited events. He discussed her welfare with Borland, and with Margaret Henderson (the daughter of her former employer). Hannah soon announced that she was selling fish at her brother's stall in Oakengates market (9 November). Munby reported this to Borland, adding in the diary 'I too honour her for this'. Meanwhile, sister Ellen took Hannah's place at Fig Tree Court, 'handy and willing, and looking just nice enough to make one miss Hannah the more'. A third sister, Lizzie—she who usually managed the fishstall—also paid them a visit. But it was at best an uncertain end to the year; and as Munby watched the workmen taking down Temple Bar in the days before Christmas, he might have found a touch of symbolism in their proceedings.

For most of 1878, he was engaged in occupying and furnishing his new home. 'Paid Mr. Cole, and with him to *Wheeler's Farm*; and for the first time in my life, gathered flowers (they were daffodils) in my own garden' (24 March). He was not really happy about it. On 4 May, in Guildford, 'I bought things for Pyrford: with no joy or hope, however, but rather with an infinite desire to be away from all such incidents of this pilgrimage'. He had then just paid a visit to Hannah at Wombridge, 'where "the woman as stands at the fishstall" moved cheerily about, in her large white apron, and her bonny face glowing in a lilac hood bonnet, to make the kitchen tidy & to get my tea ready'. Their reunion did not result in Hannah's coming to Pyrford; and by 12 May, Munby was writing of his old friend Mrs. Collyer being 'installed in my kitchen; and Wm Hopkins, a pleasant man, who is to be gardener'. He slept there for the first time on 18 May.

It was daring of Munby to commit himself to maintaining separate households in town and country, and he also had to provide a small allowance for Hannah; but the scrupulous accounts of expenses now appearing at the end of each diary show that he could buy a hair-cut for sixpence, two ounces of tobacco for tenpence, and a return ticket from Waterloo to Woking for 3s. 8d. In that economic climate, Munby flourished on his salary with the help of one or two private investments.

He was careful, but not mean. His accounts record innumerable small presents to children and working women. No one at Pyrford had any idea, during his lifetime, that Munby was married. Young Mr. Cole (the son of the farmer from whom Munby leased Wheeler's Farm) remembered him as he was in the seventies:

... When I first knew him he was a tall, handsome-looking man, with a carefully-trimmed beard and moustache, and with a most kind expression in his eyes. . . . Mr. Munby frequently spoke sympathetically about people who had to work for their living, and when walking along the lanes he would, if he saw a working-girl, stop and speak words of good cheer to her.

He was really a most charming man, and his one idea seemed to be to make people happy.[7]

In 1878, H. F. Turle, newly appointed editor of *Notes and Queries*, approached Munby, who was already an occasional contributor, with a request that he should review books. He began boldly with 'Keats's Love letters'. Munby now also became a friend and contributor of Norman MacColl, editor of the *Athenaeum*—both these worthy periodicals being owned by Sir Charles Dilke. Only a few diary entries are needed to represent this year:

Tuesday, 19 February.   To Orpington by train, by 5. Walked thence to *Down*, 4 miles of rather dull country roads, rising at last up a pretty hollow to the high Kentish downs. The village, commonplace, but a good old church. Mr Darwin's is a substantial oldfashioned villa, remote & rural. In the drawingroom, Litchfield on a sofa, his wife, her mother Mrs Darwin, a comely quiet woman, Frank D.; and at dinner I was introduced to Mr. D. himself[8]; a fine vigorous man of 65 or so. He, like the rest, talked affably & simply on general subjects. At 9.30, drove back to O., and to town by 11.

Wednesday, 1 May.   Went to Putney by train at 6.10 p.m., to dine with John Brett at his new house there, designed by himself. It is a bungalow, all on one floor; no staircase, no chimneys nor fireplaces, no bells. The whole house warmed by hot air; a large central room, with smaller rooms all round it; a flat terraced roof, where is his observatory; with a view of trees and gardens around. In the kitchen he showed me his two Cornish servant maids: robust rustic lasses . . . the parlour maid, whose name is *Charity*, . . . waited outside the door during dinner; and her master clapped his hands for her as for an eastern slave. . . .

Wednesday, 29 May.   At 4 p.m., to the General Meeting of the U.U. Club.[9] Subscription raised from 7 guineas to 8. Mr. Gladstone was there, and spoke warmly in favour of admitting the new 'unattached' students of Oxford &

---

[7] *Daily Mirror*, 4 July, 1910.
[8] Charles Darwin (1809–82). Munby was aware that this entry was hardly worthy of an important occasion. On 21 February he added: 'Note, that last Tuesday I was (as I have said) introduced to Mr. Darwin' 'Frank D.', Darwin's son, became Sir Francis Darwin, F.R.S.
[9] United University Club.

Cambridge as members. It was interesting to watch, from so near, his eager mobile face, noble in feature & earnest in expression, and his easy apt flow of words. . . .

Monday, 1 July . . . An organ on wheels was playing by the Cock, a man grinding it, & with him one of the many Italian lasses in costume, who are now in London. She was a girl of 17, from Naples, she said: with fair hair & complexion, and a most sweet & innocent face. In her boddice & braces, & coarse red kirtle, & white couvrechef, she moved about with a simple joyousness that was charming to see: she went humbly into the shops to beg, & then danced across the street, among the cart wheels, and held out her brown hand to any well drest folk. When the tune ceased, she put herself in the shafts, & dragged the cart away; but turned round as she did so, and smiled a childlike smile at me—for I had given her a penny.

Tuesday, 16 July . . . At 5 p.m., at Whitehall, saw Lord Beaconsfield drive past, returning from the Berlin Congress. He sat in an open barouche, and was vociferously cheered by thousands of people, who filled the streets. Thus the Great Panjandrum attains his highest: soon, probably, to have his works undone or at least vilified.[1] . . .

Having acquired Wheeler's Farm, it became Munby's chief joy to relish his property and show it to appreciative friends. Ralston and Borland were soon invited. 'Passing along the quiet lane, in sight of the Abbey & the vale, to my secluded farm, B. said, as I say to myself daily, that the loveliness & secrecy of the place make it seem like a vision, too charming to be real' (29 August). In September he paid another brief visit to Hannah—it was clearly not a success—and he then spent several weeks in Yorkshire with his mother, who was becoming increasingly frail.

For the rest of the year, whenever he could, whatever the weather, he went to Pyrford: 'Outside, driving rain on the verandah & across the lawn; leaves falling, bushes swaying: but it was the Country; and indoors, bright fire, cuckoo clock ticking, & the cheerful old dame hard by' (10 November). This was no time to linger at Fig Tree Court, when she, who lately had been 'the light of the house', was sequestered in something like disgrace. He was glad, then, to reach 'dear Wheeler's Farm' on New Year's Eve, after a subdued Christmas at York. 'So, among many blessings, ends an anxious unhappy year.'

Just how far his marriage had deteriorated by the end of 1878 is shown by the draft of an unpublished poem dated 27 December, written on a

[1] Disraeli had forced the congress on Russia at the end of the Russo-Turkish war. He was made K.G. on 22 July, and resigned after being defeated at the general election of 1880.

sheet of paper found in one of the notebooks devoted to Hannah. Munby
begins by asking the question

> Was there once, my heart, a woman:
>   Whom I loved when I was young;
> Whom so ardently I worshipp'd,
>   And so tenderly I sung. . . .

to which he answers Yes in the course of six more stanzas, and then continues:

> What, was *that* the glad beginning,
>   And the ending such as *this*?
> Loathsome words, & shameful spewing,
>   From the lips I used to kiss?—
>
> Do not tell that hideous story—
>   Do not rouse that piercing pain!
> Love would chafe himself to madness
>   If he dwelt on it again. . . .

Munby's collection *Vestigia Retrorsum* (1891) contains a more polished
expression of his disillusionment in the sonnet 'Varium et Mutabile':

> She whom I loved, who loves me now no more,
>   Hath two conflicting natures in her soul:
>   And one of these she gave me; gave it whole,
> And with an innocent emphasis did pour
> That self of hers, full-brimm'd and running o'er,
>   Into the heart I offer'd her—a bowl
>   Homely perhaps, yet neither slight nor foul,
> And apt to hold the treasure that it bore.
>
> But then, her other self arose and cried
>   Against my gift, against her plenitude
>   Of sweet acceptance; and in alter'd mood
> Sudden she flung that lifted bowl aside:
>   So, all the love therein, both hers and mine,
>   Lies on the sand, blood-red like wasted wine.

Anyone reading the diary only at each year's end, and finding Munby
at his most introspective and self-pitying, might conclude that he suffered
from overwhelming melancholy. It would be a misleading impression of
one whose energy and wide-ranging curiosity ensured him, at least intermittently, much enjoyment of life. But if 1878 was anxious and unhappy

395

for Munby, its successor demanded still more serious adjectives: the death of his mother, accompanied by the continuing estrangement from Hannah, made 1879 his worst year.

There was, it is true, one triumph. In January, 1879, Munby was elected a Fellow of the Society of Antiquaries, on the proposal of the Treasurer, Charles Spencer Perceval. His seconder was Edward Peacock of Bottesford—a service Munby may have had in mind for him throughout that excruciating breakfast, five years earlier.[2] Munby's supporters included Lord Houghton, John Evans the numismatist, Alexander Macmillan and F. W. Burton.

Although he spent as much time as he could at Pyrford, and soon bought a season ticket, his London social life remained busy enough. Thackeray's daughter, Mrs. Ritchie, told him how 'once as a child she spent 10/- on the bears at the Zoo', and her father had been gravely displeased; 'he said "Never mind—we'll all go without butter for a week"; and they did' (14 January). At St. James's Hall, William Rossetti 'gave me a very sad account of his brother Dante' (5 March); and at the Westlakes', Lewis Morris[3] 'begins to seem just a little spoilt by his success as a poet' (6 March).

Munby remained constantly in touch with R. D. Blackmore, and during this year of trial saw more of him than usual, for he was reading the proofs of Blackmore's novel *Mary Anerley*—a title derived from one of Munby's own poems. He appears not to have confided the secret of his marriage to Blackmore, who looked upon Munby's glorification of women servants as a 'crotchet'; but Blackmore was one of those whose company in times of stress was to be valued for its own sake. 'His gentle and placid character gives one always a sense of confidence and repose.'

What was going on between Munby and Hannah in 1879? When Munby 'passed by Ockley, & Leith Hill', on 22 March, 'the fair hills & woods were as sad as my own recollections'. They still wrote to each other, the diary shows, about once a fortnight. The letters have not survived; but there are some clues to their contents. On 1 May, Munby received a letter from Hannah, to which he replied by return of post. On the same day he went 'to Harley Street at noon, but did not see Dr. Pollock' (the doctor who had advised him to rusticate Hannah). On 2 May he wrote to Dr. Pollock, and on 7 May he returned 'to Harley Street, & spent an hour with Dr. Pollock'. From Saturday, 10 May, until Tuesday, 13 May, the diary is blank—often a sign that something unusual is afoot. He was disgruntled on 14 May,

---

[2] See 19 April, 1874.
[3] Lewis Morris (1833-1907), poet and Welsh educationist; knighted, 1895.

after 'Messrs Maskelyne & Cooke's very childish & stupid "entertainment", which George wished to see'. On the same day he wrote again to Dr. Pollock, receiving a reply from him on the 17th.

Hannah's chief wish was to be her husband's servant—preferably his *only* servant. She viewed his employment of others with real sorrow (her sister Ellen being a possible exception). One may conjecture that she had asked to be allowed to return to Fig Tree Court; that Munby had fortified himself with an adverse opinion from Dr. Pollock; and that on 10 May he went up to Wombridge to break the news to Hannah and talk over her future.

He could not bring himself to describe that week-end in the diary. For Hannah's future appeared lonely. To install her again in the Temple would have meant giving a larger emphasis to his London pied-à-terre than Munby now intended; and anyway she was better off in the country. He himself had always wanted to escape from the city and take Hannah with him; but it would not do to have her at Pyrford except upon equal terms, able and willing to call at the vicarage—something obviously impossible. And so the months dragged by with growing and mutual resentment, particularly on Hannah's side.

The sudden death of his mother imposed a deeper sadness. Munby 'bade farewell to my darling Mother' at Clifton Holme on 16 April, and later noted that it was 'a *last* farewell: after a thousand embraces, I turned back and kissed her again. It was a presentiment.'

Wednesday, 2 July. Yesterday, Tuesday July 1, 1879, at 25 minutes to 10 a.m., my darling Mother died: sitting up in bed, taking her cup of milk, she lay back, looked around at those with her—my sister, my Aunt Ann, and Fanny Sever the maid—and without a word or a struggle or a sigh, passed away; and left us desolate, yet not comfortless.

Munby outlined these sentences in ink; henceforth he did the same with every successive diary entry of 1 July, 'Darling Mother's death day'. The account of the funeral and its preparations is affecting, emotional, but what Munby really felt was well expressed a fortnight later, on 19 July, when he had returned to Pyrford: 'Sat under the verandah & read Virgil: flowers all around, & the Abbey, & the sounding weir, & songs of birds; but I would have given them all, for one more kiss of dear Mother.'

Earlier, on 6 July, he had written a letter to Mrs. R. B. Litchfield, his old friend's wife and Darwin's daughter, part of which deserves to be quoted:

... My mother belonged to a type of woman and of lady that is very oldfashioned now. Even her accomplishments, such as flower-painting and the harp, recal the ladies of Miss Austen's day. She cared little for general subjects; nothing at all for politics: as for religion, she took all its details for granted, in her pious gentle way, and believed as devoutly in my father as he believed in God ('Almighty God', his favourite phrase was) and in Christ. Perhaps it was his tender and exquisite devotion to her that first drew out that of her children. She was his first love, & he was hers: and all his life, for near fifty years of wedlock, he showed his love, not only in all greater matters, but in a thousand little fantasies of affection and courtesy, which we only knew of by degrees or by accident. Even her name —Caroline—he continued to emphasize in all things: he used the letters of it as symbols, in arranging his library and his music: he planted the village street with a line of trees—Chestnut, Elm, and Maple, alternately, which now, in full leaf, represent her initials[4] over & over again.

And she was 'worthy for whom he should do this': not only for the fair delicate face, and golden-auburn hair, and dainty figure, which I can remember at their best; and not only for her sound judgement and fine taste, and her excellent gentleness of spirit; but chiefly, I think, for her singular *power of loving*. Her whole being dwelt always in the region of the affections: her husband first, and all her children next; so equally, that each of us might almost feel as if he were her only child. And though she was firm and judicious as a mother, her love was so tremulous and tender, and her health so delicate always, that each of us felt it might even kill her, if he went into the army or navy, for instance, or went away very far or for very long. To the last, my partings from her after every visit at home were almost heartbreaking, though she knew I should return in a few months.

After my father's death had shaken and saddened her—though she showed presence of mind and strength of character, even then—she seemed to become to us all a thing too precious and sacred to be let go out of the world at all. She used to look at me with a sweet wistful smile, as if she wondered what her great sorrow meant. And my delight was to sit and look at her as she sat; to sit at her feet sometimes, and retrace her whole career: for I could remember all, from the charming vivacity of her youth to the serene beauty of her old age. And now, all that we dreaded for her is over; or rather, it has not come and will not come. 'She walked with God; and she was not: for God took her.' ...[5]

An affectionate portrait; yet it makes clear that the sensitive eldest son of these devoutly sentimental parents grew up under great pressure, and was severely tested. Munby inherited his full share of kindliness and principle. His love for a tremulous delicate mother had broadened into a chivalrous concern for women in general, especially for those in need or subjection; it had not helped him to achieve a normal sexual relationship

[4] Caroline Eleanor Munby.   [5] Dr. A. N. L. Munby's collection.

398

with a woman of his own class. A subconscious longing for something tougher and rougher led to some of the strange encounters of his life—and ultimately to the tragic dilemma in which Munby found himself in 1879.

The loss of his mother brought him no closer to Hannah. He had never been able to tell her about his marriage, and the mechanism of conscience and social duty now operated to induce an even closer concealment of that indiscretion.

During August Munby was busy sorting family papers at Clifton Holme; he then travelled in Northumberland and the Lake District. On 2 September ('Darling Mother's Birthday'), he was at Patterdale with William Allingham, and the next morning they walked to Aira Force: 'Much interesting talk with him, about his own poetry, and Tennyson & Browning, and Carlyle, whom he is on his way to visit at Dumfries.' An entry among 'Occasional Memoranda' at the end of the diary held more personal significance:

Wednesday, 3 September . . . At the Ulleswater Hotel today, I had a strange example of the influence of class and habit on the feeling of modesty in a woman. Going up to my room after breakfast, I passed the open door of another bedroom, in which a house maid was doing her work. I went in, and spoke to her about some washing, without observing what she was doing. She was a stout lusty country lass, with a rosy honest face, and with large coarse arms and hands: bare thick red arms, rough in texture, and all one tint of pure healthy vermilion, from the shoulder to the finger tips. A most wholesome and blooming rustic maid, and just in the bloom of eighteen—the very hour of virgin bashfulness. What was she doing? Cleaning out a chamberpot! And when I entered, she did not drop it, or hide it, or look confused, or blush: on the contrary; she stood still, looking at me with frank blue eyes, answering my questions, telling me (in good broad Cumbrian) how things could be washed; and all the time, she continued holding the vessel in one hand, and dabbling in its contents, mechanically, with the other. And, as she ceased speaking, she calmly emptied it, and replaced it under the bed.

Consider the difference which this implies, between her mental condition and that of a young lady, even of the humblest order. . . .

It is an elementary but telling observation. The full implications of Munby's pervading studies of sex and class distinctions, in his diaries and notebooks, were larger than he realised or cared to contemplate. This admirer of working women was a pioneer sociologist no less inspired than the amateur collectors of folk-song.

The death of his mother made Munby relatively well-to-do. She herself died intestate leaving less than £3,000,[6] but her husband's estate could now be divided among her children, who also benefited from the distribution of a trust fund established by their grandmother, Mrs. Forth.[7]

Perhaps it was the prospect of increased affluence that induced Munby to give a supper at Pyrford in January for '12 old folks', yet he ended the year on a note of deep depression:

Wheeler's Farm, Pyrford, Surrey: (31 December 1879, 11 p.m.)
The loss of my beloved Father in 1875 was followed this year by the greatest bereavement that any man can ever suffer: the death of my own darling and infinitely precious Mother. This year too my unutterable private sorrow came to a head, and gave me work enough to keep my wits together under it. And Clifton Holme, the charming home of us all for thirty years, may perhaps not be ours much longer.

Therefore I here end the making of a regular diary, such as I have kept since 1859: meaning only, God willing, to note down at intervals matters—as to the aspects of Nature, or as to women's outdoor work,—which seem worth recording. Thus sadly ends a gloomy miserable year.

A.J.M.

[6] Somerset House.
[7] Munby Family Papers, Acc. 54: 57 (York City Library). The final release by A. J. Munby, the last surviving trustee of the Forth trust, is dated 27 May, 1885.

10

A COTTAGE IN SHROPSHIRE

1880–9

One might have expected, despite the firm statement at the end of 1879, that the diary would go steadily on. And so it did—though for the time being only as a formal trickle of events and engagements rarely deserving quotation. Munby's social observations were sometimes written in separate notebooks:

Monday, 1 March 1880.　In Portland Street, about 10.30 a.m., I saw a bare-armed servant girl on her knees in the street. . . . As I passed her, she happened to look up; and I saw that she wore *spectacles*. The first time I ever saw a girl of her class and calling doing so.

Thursday, 10 March, 1881 . . . In Trafalgar Square, 5.30 p.m., saw a strong rosy comely milkwench striding along towards her cans, carelessly eating an apple in her ruddy hand. She passed behind a policeman on duty, a tall fine young man; and lightly touched him in the small of the back with her finger, as she went. He turned, grave & scornful, & looked at her: to be touched by a rough milk lass, in short frock and shabby plaid shawl! . . .

The diaries of 1880 and 1881 contain no mention of Hannah. The couple probably corresponded, but, as Munby had abandoned his record of letters received and sent, we can have no certain knowledge. From later diary references, it appears that Hannah did not remain at Wombridge all this time. She seems to have taken jobs as a servant in various places.

Munby was kept occupied by the melancholy duties involved in the break-up of his old family home. At Harker's Hotel, York, on 9 June, 1880, 'our dear Clifton Holme was sold by auction for £8000 to a Mr. Sydenham Walker'. This announcement received the emphasis of a black ink border. On 12 June, Munby said farewell 'to every spot & room in our sweet and beloved home . . . bade goodbye to all, and for ever'; and in August the contents of the house 'were dispersed among ourselves'.[1] One positive result of these sad events was the appearance in 1881 of a

---

[1] Clifton Holme, re-named St. Hilda's Garth, is now used as a local authority children's home (1970).

cyclo-styled booklet, *A Few Records of the Name and Family of Munby . . .* 'compiled by Arthur Joseph Munby, M.A., F.S.A., of Lincoln's Inn, Barrister at Law'.

The 'infinite blessing of Pyrford & its country quiet' helped him to get through the year. During the summer he diverted himself mildly with 'pretty Miss Taylor, the village schoolmistress', to whom he lent books. On 13 November, 1880, after he had found her 'all alone in her little room, at tea, with a book about Heroes', she became 'Miss Taylor, our pretty modest schoolmistress, aged 19'. She last appears in the diary on 9 May, 1881, when Munby saw her 'returning from her early walk with her new sweetheart. Thought I didn't know it, poor dear!'

He must have found solace in the composition of his long poem in elegiac verse, *Dorothy: A Country Story*,[2] begun early in 1879 and published anonymously by Kegan Paul in November, 1880. Among the curiosities of Victorian literature, *Dorothy* deserves the benefit of a second look. Why was it anonymous, unlike Munby's previous books? Possibly because he felt it touched too closely on personal sanctities. No one but Munby could have written it. He fully understood his subject—the girl farm-worker—and he had the gift of painting, with affectionate precision, small landscapes and genre pictures of country life. In the tradition of Victorian melodrama, the plot is full of absurdities, which do not lessen *Dorothy's* appeal as a period piece. And Munby's vigorous theme—that a woman should be allowed to do the roughest labour 'if she has heart for the work'—has still not lost its controversial aspect for trade unionists.

Munby contrived to introduce many cherished ideas into the poem. Dorothy's hard but honest hands play a vital part in repelling snobbish or flirtatious aristocrats. Beautiful 'Dolly' herself is obviously based on Hannah, though the poet claimed that his Pyrford housekeeper, Ann Collyer, was a 'part original'. Munby's boldest stroke was to make her the illegitimate daughter of Colonel St. Quentin, M.P., sponsor of a *Bill to Regulate Female Employment*. Observing how well Dolly had worked on the farm, the Colonel gave her five hundred pounds when she married the gamekeeper; and it was hoped he would now abandon his Bill:

> Leaving to *doctrinaire* dames the impertinent crazy endeavour
> Thus to give women restraints none would impose upon men.

In a preface to *Dorothy*, Munby said that he himself had 'known or seen at least six English girls who could plough and did plough', like his heroine.

[2] Two passages from *Dorothy* are given in the Appendix.

The poem was dedicated 'To my singular good friend and antient comrade Richard Doddridge Blackmore, M.A., author of "Lorna Doone".' Certain editions of *Lorna Doone*, though not the first, were dedicated to Munby.

The Pyrford countryside provided the setting for *Dorothy*, and Munby commemorated Wheeler's Farm in a prefatory sonnet:

> In England, by the quiet streams of Yore,
>> Is that lone house they live in and they love:
>> An upland shaw defends it from above,
> With hazels and with hawthorn-clumps, the store
> And brooding-place of birds; and evermore
>> Across the meads, the various milk and gold
>> Of buttercups and daisies, they behold
> The woods and hills, the ruins high and hoar,
>> And that old church, to some at least still dear,
>> Where the meek dead are garner'd year by year
> From love and work, from sorrow and from joy.
> Ah, what sweet memories may their souls employ,
>> While in a summer eve they sit and hear
>> The distant dying waters, falling at the weir!

The public's reaction to *Dorothy* was disappointing until, about eight months after its publication, the following letter reached the publisher:

19 Warwick Crescent, W.
July 15, '81

Dear Mr. Kegan Paul,

I want your goodnatured intervention in a little matter. You must know, I received, perhaps many months ago, a little book—*Dorothy, a Country Story*. By whatever the chance, it escaped my notice altogether until a few days ago when I withdrew it, by accident, from a pile on the table—and, finding the leaves cut, dipped into the middle: a minute's reading sent me back to—not the Preface, but line the first—whence I proceeded to the last with a surprise of delight as rare as it was thorough. Then, enquiring about the mysterious adventurers with the paper-knife, I found to my confusion that my Sister had anticipated all my experience, and that my Son,—short as his stay with me was, had pronounced the poem to be, over and above the literary charm, 'a perfect picture-gallery'. 'It was impossible' my sister thought 'that I could be unaware of their praises'— but, all the same, unaware I certainly was: and that everybody else should remain so, seemed such a wrong that I at once carried the book to our friend Mrs. Orr, and yesterday finished a reading which, in its effects, justified all my expectations of success. Now,—the book was consigned to me 'with the compliments of the Author', as the printed form ran: and I cannot help begging you to say for me to that Author that it is literally years since I have admired and enjoyed a poem *so much*—and I am carefully sober in professing no more. I have never seen the minutest notice in the periodicals,—of course I make no sort of guess at who the Author may be: but from some signal exquisiteness of observation, I almost fancy the fine hand must be *feminine*: if I mistake, my blunder is one tribute the more to a consummate male craftsman.

There,—I have somewhat discharged my mind, despite the hot weather, which might incline 'expressive silence to muse the praise' which I have put down αμωσγέπως.[3] Will you help it along? and believe me

Ever truly yours
ROBERT BROWNING[4]

Kegan Paul forwarded the letter to the anonymous author, who noted on 19 July: 'Letter from Robert Browning, about "Dorothy".' Browning's praise came as a pleasant surprise to Munby, who speedily revised his current estimate of him as man and perhaps as poet (for in the diary he had strongly condemned one of Browning's later productions). He saw the light in time to be present at the inaugural meeting of the Browning Society on 28 October 1881, with Furnivall in the chair. Soon he was engaged in reciting Browning's verses to his fellow members.

With his zest for French quotations, Munby might have commented 'C'est toujours l'inattendu qui arrive'. Tempting as it is to be cynical about Munby's change of heart, it is more to the point to record his gratitude, and his continuing affection for Browning in the latter's closing years. Naturally he thanked him warmly, and they met and corresponded. Kegan Paul used the Browning letter to good effect in procuring publicity for *Dorothy*—including a puff in the *Academy* ('Many as have been the testimonies to the worth of his *Dorothy*, none has gratified the author like this from Mr. Browning. . . .')—and in persuading Roberts Brothers of Boston to publish the poem in America. Henceforth, the secret of Munby's authorship was not strictly kept.

Browning's sincerity is beyond question:

Wednesday, 22 February, 1882 . . . by 7.30, to F. J. Furnivall's, St. George's Square, Primrose Hill, and took part in reading Browning's *Strafford* aloud. Mrs. Sutherland Orr, Sir F. Leighton's sister, a great friend of Browning's, spoke of his 'immense admiration' of *Dorothy*. . . .

---

[3] 'In some way or other.'

[4] Huntington Library. The text is that in *New Letters of Robert Browning*, ed. W. C. DeVane and K. L. Knickerbocker (Murray, 1951). The editors have usefully annotated the letter.

Friday, 24 March, 1882 . . . To 40 Queen's Gate Gardens, Kensington, by invitation of Browning, to see his son's new pictures: 2 noble lifesize figures of Ardennes peasant girls, with brown arms & coarse hands. R.B. & his sister most cordial & friendly; talk for an hour, his bright face gazing at me, his hand on my arm. Told me of their beautiful & charming housemaid and cook: the latter came in, a tall comely girl & a modest. 'Why, it's my cook!' said R.B., & pressed *her* arm. . . .

Their acquaintance was cordial but did not become intimate. Browning supported Munby as a candidate for the Athenaeum Club, proposed by Theodore Martin, seconded by F. W. Burton, and on 14 February, 1882, he wrote to him: 'I congratulate the club, and especially myself and friends on your election yesterday.' Munby sent Browning a copy of the American edition of *Dorothy*—'which I read through once again', Browning replied on 12 June, 1882, 'as if I might get still some new good out of a new printing'; and he went on to mention the pictures by his son Pen 'which had the good fortune to please you. "The seated figure" had no such luck at the Academy, but was found "too uninteresting" . . . and "coarse" besides, so your approval is consolatory as well as pleasant.'[5]

It is doubtful whether Munby benefited financially from the 'unremitting kindness' (as Tupper put it) of his American publishers; but his book was re-set, and much better produced than by Kegan Paul; and it was widely reviewed. He wrote to Roberts Brothers in Boston on 5 April, 1882:

. . . I have read these reviews which you have been good enough to send me with much interest and with great pleasure: not merely because of the praise they give to my book, but because it is so pleasant to find that subjects and scenes taken from this old England are welcomed so warmly on your side, and that justice is done to the views about hard work, which I have tried to advocate. . . .

. . . 'Dorothy' is the fruit of long experience and observation: I have by me, in MS. diaries and notebooks, accounts of 'walks & talks' with scores of such girls, in England and elsewhere: servantgirls, farm-girls, fishergirls, colliergirls, & so on.

Some day I may publish some of these—*piéces justificatives*, as the phrase is: and after the reception Dorothy has had with you, I am not sure that your side of the water would not suit them best.[6] . . .

[5] The quotations from these Browning letters are in Maggs' Catalogue, No. 262, December, 1910, which lists four letters sold at Sotheby's by Munby's executors, 6 July, 1910. The same catalogue offers 29 letters to Munby from Blackmore.

[6] MS. in Royal Cortissoz collection, Yale Collection of American Literature, Yale University Library. Roberts's book went into a second edition, and there was also a ten-cent edition in Munro's Seaside Library.

The *Dorothy* episode throws light on Browning as well as on Munby; for they had common characteristics. Both poets could show warm affection to other men; both enjoyed cultivated female society (they possessed several mutual women acquaintances, and Munby had followed Browning as a friend of the high-minded Julia Wedgwood). Both poets, again, turned an admiring eye on the muscular peasant woman: this liking being part of an inescapable need to be dominated, in one way or another, by the opposite sex. Browning's interest in lower-class women never became the obsession it was to Munby—yet peasant girls held a notorious attraction for his only son, the problem child, Pen. Thus Munby's thin volume had appropriate qualities singling it out from the pile of books on Browning's table.

Munby later met Browning occasionally, at the Athenaeum or at parties. 'Talk with Robert Browning, at the Theodore Martins'. He as usual most warm and kind in praise of my Dorothy to me and others' (15 January, 1885); and, looking ahead a few years, we come to the valediction:

Tuesday, 31 December, 1889 . . . By the Embankment to Westminster Abbey by 11.30 a.m. to *Robert Browning's funeral.* His kindness to me, and his bright genial talk and presence, I can never forget. . . .

In 1882, Munby advanced his acquaintance with another older poet, whom he had first met at Rossetti's in 1866. The diary of 2 February, 1882, records: 'Talk with Mr. Asquith my tenant. To Chelsea by rail, and dined at 8 at Old Swan House with the Wickham Flowers. Much talk with Wm Bell Scott, on poetry. . . .'

For the next few years, until W. B. Scott's death in 1890, the two men kept close contact. Being not only a poet but also a painter, Scott was well qualified to revive mutual memories of the pre-Raphaelite circle which were stirred by Rossetti's death in April, 1882. Scott himself, now in his seventies, made a charming host and had many friends among writers and artists. He was soon inviting Munby to dinner 'because Andrew Lang whose name at least you may know, has volunteered to come and dine with us, and I think you would like him' (25 April, 1882); while on another occasion 'we only expect Tadema and his dear wife Laura, and Hueffer[7] with his wife' (17 November, 1883).

Scott's friendliness was not entirely disinterested. Being aware of Munby's wide literary acquaintance, he asked him to tell E. C. Stedman,

[7] Francis Hueffer, *The Times* music critic; father of Ford Madox Ford, the novelist.

25. Wheeler's Farm, Pyrford, Surrey: Munby's home from 1878 and where he died in 1910
26. Hannah's semi-detached cottage (left half) at Wyke Place, Shifnal, Shropshire, where she lived from 1903 until her death in 1909. Photographed in 1971 with the recent porch

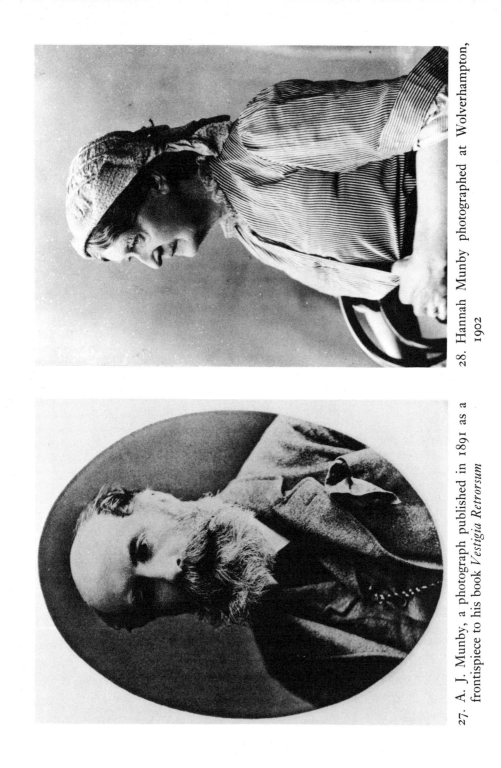

28. Hannah Munby photographed at Wolverhampton, 1902

27. A. J. Munby, a photograph published in 1891 as a frontispiece to his book *Vestigia Retrorsum*

the American critic, about his latest book, 'and so give me a lift towards the celebrity your Dorothy is now enjoying' (10 May, 1882).

After four years of silence, Hannah re-appears with a characteristically vivid and perceptive letter. The curtain rises on the village of Bearley, close to Stratford-upon-Avon, where she is staying to be near her maternal grandmother, 'Granny Gibbs'.

(Bearley: 1 June, 1882)

... One thing dear, I feel *happy*, & that's what I haven't done for many a day, I was a singing this morning quite merrily, & I go to bed & get up again with a lighter heart nor I have had for a good while. You didn't say anything to make me *permanently* happy ... but I enjoy'd your visit—you was very nice & as sweetmouth'd as ever, for kissing, & I enjoy'd working for you & waiting on you —so perhaps you'll wonder what's made me happier—It's this darling—I see that you love me as much as ever your nature will let you, & I also see that you enjoy being alone as a bachelor, & haveing no inclination like other men for a wife it's decidedly better that you shouldn't be bother'd with one about you, & so my mind is more settled & it would be weak & foolish of me to fret for what we have as it were done on purpose, tho' *I* was quite innocent as to the consequences of such a long engagement, but I must say I used to wonder how ever it would end, & I used to feel every year that the rod was soaking the longer for my own back—so it has proved, 'tho I didn't expect this sort of suffering—to be *alone* in the world—that is of all things the worst thing that a *woman* can have to endure I am sure, still dear, I do not complain, & indeed you will not let me—so I will not seem to—Time passes wonderfully quick with me so quick that I hardly reckon it, therefore don't you be anxious about me, nor trouble for me. ... I send you my love & best wishes darling, hoping nothing I've said will vex you, for I'm sure I don't want to do that—I wish you all good & may God bless you as well as myself—

Your loving HANNAH

(Bearley: 9 June, 1882)

My own darling Moussiri

Your letter *is* a nice one, & I feel so glad as you feel so much the better & happier for your visit to me—I am *decidedly* better & happier, & when I want to indulge a bit in love, I think over again the few minutes we had a *kissing*, in the train to Warwick that last day—I enjoy'd it so much, & shall never forget it I hope—It was a feeling I very seldom give way to all the years I have known you, but it's delightful & no sin either now we are married, but for all that it has always seem'd to me an indulgence that women shan't give way to, but I felt it was my last minutes with you, & I don't think you'll mind me telling you no more nor I mind what you have told me in yourn, & it pleases me to think you can enjoy the sight of me, if it's ever so little. God made the woman for the man, & it's a *good* thing to care only for one, as I care only for you . . . but then, when I'm away from you, I don't feel at home with *any one* else—I would liefer be alone or in bed, still I hope something will turn up for the winter—I s^{hd} like to be in a little kitchen, & do for some gentleman, or an old lady what canna do her own housekeeping, but old lady's are sometimes very fidgetty . . .

. . . I doubt I shall hardly do justice to your letter my darling—but I'll write & tell you all while I am here if all's well, but I don't wish *you* to write me so much again—I don't like burning your letters & I don't like to *keep* them either —short & sweet is what I like from you, but I know you like to hear all you can from me about the folks I meet with. . . .

In tune with Hannah's diagnosis of a reversion to bachelorhood, Munby at Pyrford was soon remarking on the 'ineffable charm of being *alone* in this sweet cottage' (18 July, 1882); and by 26 November his marital problems seemed no nearer solution: he then quoted from one of Hannah's letters, 'I know I am only your servant, but that was all I wanted to be!' and added the comment 'Sweet, hapless soul!'

At the end of 1882, Munby announced that in future 'the dull sad days may go unrecorded', but he duly acquired another diary, 'The Gentleman's Pocket Daily Companion', and on 1 January, 1883, he noted that half a dozen masked mummers had sung 'God rest ye' outside his house. Any financial anxieties had now been alleviated; by 1884 the firm of Munby and Scott, who handled his family affairs, were crediting him with an additional income of about four hundred pounds annually; but in the same year he had to dismiss two housekeepers, at the Temple and at Pyrford, for drunkenness. The Pyrford replacement Mary Willsher, 'spinster, aged 53', proved so successful, however, that Munby was able to invite Lowes Dickinson, Ralston, Vernon Lushington and Austin Dobson to stay with him between May and September.

6 August, 1884: London . . . Dining Room, Health Exhibition: 40 young women waitresses, each in livery of black frock, large white apron and bib, large white cap, corkscrew hung from the waist. Each girl was *numbered*: a large cardboard ticket of oval shape fixed on the centre of her breast. My waitress was *No. 30*; a comely respectable girl, Elizabeth Gill by name, a servant out of place. 'I heard of this, Sir, & was glad to get it,' said she. The words 'No. of attendant' were printed on my bill, and she wrote '30' after them.

13 September, 1884. Lympstone, on the Exe. Talk there with sailors & women, who say no women now go out to get bait, wading and wearing trousers, as I saw them do in 1860: only one or two of the older women still do so. Old sailor spoke of this change with great contempt. 'I mind' said he 'when I was married, first thing I did was to get my wife a new pair o' breeches, and a jacket, to go out baiting in.' And what do the girls do now? 'Sits on a sofa and reads novels'! said he.

28 February, 1885: Pyrford . . . My housekeeper Mary Willsher says that Agnes my housemaid, aged 17, is 'always whistling and singing' when I am away. 'I think *all* girls whistle, now, Sir,' says M.W.

Hannah was still at Bearley throughout 1885. Some revealing letters show that she found difficulty in reconciling herself to the situation. 'I love you more deeply nor ever you can think,' she wrote on 26 October, '& what vexes me most is, that what I have labour'd for most in my life—to be just all in all, or factotum to you, I have lost—the best of my years are gone, & I am nothing, nor nobody. . . .' Munby pasted an extract from this letter on to a piece of cardboard, and added the comment: 'A sad story: but thank God, her strength of character was shown in this: that by His help she overcame, and recovered her position.' But Hannah was a volatile, unpredictable correspondent; a few weeks earlier (6 October) she had been writing engagingly about the easy life enjoyed by her young cousin Jane Gibbs in service at Harborne:

. . . My word, her Missis *is* good & indulgent to her—fancy her giving Jane one of her old dresses—a satin stripe as good as new, & when Jane had made it up again after turning it,—in the same style it was in before & then going in to show her Missis how she herself look'd in it, & one o' them big birdcages stuck under it behind, as they call them big wire bustles—I never lived with any Missis as one could speak to, much less show a fine dress to. . . . What a change there is in service now to what there was when I was in it. . . .

(Bearley: 31 December, 1885)
. . . I think this place too far from you, but I think this is the liveliest country place I ever was at. I like this new sonnet my darling—it very near ends in '*wife*' as well as them others. For my *own* sake dear I want no child—I am *quite* satisfied—children are joys & troubles together, like a wife is to a man, for *he* no more nor other folks can have *all* pleasant in this life, but if you love me at all in that way my own dearest, I am sorry as *you* have no *joy* that way—for myself I *never* think about it, & very seldom about *you*—it's so wonderful that I am so very happy & contented, feeling myself a nothing nor nobody. . . .

(Bearley: 12 January, 1886)
. . . I am exceedingly happy over my own trouble now, & am thankful I have gone through it all, and my dearest these troubles are good for everybody—and

gentlefolks that have been rich or *are* rich have lessons to learn for their good in the end. . . .

Our supper was on the *Tuesday*. . . . I got it all ready myself. . . . I ask'd 'em all to seat themselves on the chairs I'd put, & *borrow'd*—Granny on my left hand . . . I stood up to carve, & I see Ned was going to drink so I said 'One Minute—I'm going to ask you all to drink a health & I said—holding my glass up Here's to him I love the *best*—likewise to you Granny & all the rest—Tho' he's not here to take my part—I'll drink his health with all my heart,' & they said that's Mr. Munby! hear, hear—& so they & I drank, & then I help'd 'em all to roast beef gravy & tato's, & they all had stew'd rabbit after—Plum pudding hot & cold mince pie—apple pie jam tart & blanc mange. We didn't hurry over it. . . .

(Bearley: 24 February, 1886)

. . . I am *not* changed dear, to what I always was, in principle nor religion. . . . I feel to you the same as ever—I think that *desire*, as you mention'd, only comes to a woman as she chooses to induldge in it, & when I found how you was my darling I never thought of it, & so I may say I never have it, on your account, & I feel sure no other could make me feel it. . . .

Munby now paid regular visits to Hannah, and in the autumn of 1885 she came up to London. He took her to the Exhibition of Inventions at South Kensington, and recorded her 'boundless delight at the Gardens lit with coloured lamps, and illuminated fountains'. In March, 1886, she was, however, shocked to learn, after the event, that he had been operated on for piles, and most disappointed that she had been unable to nurse him. All her old bitterness welled up in one of the saddest letters she ever wrote:

(Bearley: 12 March, 1886)

. . . I told you in my last that I thought nothing as ever may happen could make me unhappy, but I see I am not sure o' that, for directly I'm not sure how you are I can be as restless as ever I was. And it must be always so while we're apart I reckon. . . . And to think as you've been through all that in this last fortnight, and had me so much on your mind as you even shouted out how you *had* loved me! Over & over again, and the doctors *might have heard you*. I am too much knock'd back, to say anything about all this my darling, but I am very glad to hear you're better again—There must have been much to be done with you & for you that's only fit for a wife to do, but then you didn't want the gentlemen to *know*—so I'll say no more—but you *did* know that it would have been nothing but a journey of love & satisfaction for me . . . be *quiet at home* till you're quite well—the walk to your work will be enough to begin with. Oh the miserable & false step you took when you separated me from you, by the doctor's orders—And this shows it more & more, without saying a word of all *my* loneliness &

humiliation, & grief of mind & spirit all these years. . . . I *must* say that if men & women *wait* for perfection in each other to live together, they'll have to wait till nearly their dying day, for as soon as they're made perfect in God's sight He takes them to himself. It *is* in this life we want companionship—to bear one another's burden, in the next life we shall not require that help—I could wish that you & me was already at rest. . . . I feel *sad* & down hearted just now but it'll wear off with time. . . .

(Bearley: 5 December, 1886)

. . . The reason I ax'd you not to be in a hurry over sending to me, *is*, cause I know you have such a *many*, ladies, & gentlemen & others to write to, besides your poetry making & writing, & your business as well, o' days, so it's nice for you to know that I *shan't* be worried if I didn't hear from you very soon—so as I think *that* needn't o' put you out at all, nor me telling you about Jane's vulgar way which you saw for yourself a bit when you was here—& by the way—she has got a place to go to next *Thursday*, at Pinley House, by Coventry.[8] . . . And again My Massa, why s^hd you be put out cause I had the lumbago & them sweats & languid feelings—I shall not like telling you if anything's the matter if it puts you out o' sorts, as you say—I know you'll say it's love & all that, but I know how *soon* you *wince*, & are really put out if all doesn't go to your liking, & if you was a married man with a family & delicate wife & kep a lot a servants you'd often ha' things to vex I can tell you . . .

Jane has slept with me . . . I find it cold in bed when Jane sits up *all* night, as she often does—And I think how nice it'd be if I'd a husband to sleep with me *always* . . . .

The couple had at last begun to recapture the affection of earlier days, and on 17 December Hannah, suddenly become Quakerish, wrote: 'Oh, my darling—how happy I am wi thinking about *thee*! How different to the common sort o' lovers—And how true thee bist. . . .' In the following summer she stayed at Fig Tree Court while Munby was abroad, and gave the place a thorough cleaning in her best style.

Friday, 28 January, 1887 . . . 5 p.m., to 56 George Street Portman Square, & sat an hour with Miss Julia Wedgwood. Dine Athenaeum. Lord Salisbury (Prime Minister) next to me, and my old acquaintance Henry Mathews, Home Sec^y, opposite. . . .

Friday, 25 March . . . *Boardwomen*. Today about 10 a.m., I saw, for the first time anywhere, women carrying advertisement boards in the street. Ten women,

---

[8] A letter enquiring whether Jane Gibbs was free to become a parlourmaid at Pinley House was enclosed. The only questions asked were 'Are you strong? & do you wear a fringe?' The answers given—apparently the right ones—were Yes and No, respectively.

some of them young, all in a livery dress, warm grey shawls and plain black straw bonnets, walking in single file, with some men also, up Northumberland Avenue; each woman carrying a large board on her back and another in front. On the boards, which were red, a 'poster' about a new paper called Men & Women. No one molested the women, & they were quiet & demure.

Munby received several entertaining letters from W. B. Scott towards the end of Scott's life; but his notions of gentlemanly behaviour compelled him to disapprove of what he considered unnecessary 'revelations' about Rossetti's personal habits. He found some of these in W. B. Scott's posthumous autobiography, as might have been predicted from Scott's letter of 31 March, 1887:

... Perhaps you know that everything printed about the dear old pagan D.G.R. passes through the hands of W.M.R. and gets emasculated if anything crops up about his private history. I remonstrated with William about this on the ground that he made his brother an infinitely less interesting man than he really was. He did not approve of my point of view; could not, I fancy, quite see it. ...[9]

The diary of 1887–8 shows Munby and Austin Dobson becoming increasingly friendly, with Dobson frequently asking him to read and criticise his verses. Older friends were not neglected: 'To R. D. Blackmore, and sat with him. His wife Lucy, whom he deeply loved, died on the 1st' (6 February, 1888). The unexpected death of Matthew Arnold was 'a great and grievous loss'. Munby had had little enough to say about Arnold in the diary, but now recalled: 'the last time I met him was at Pyports'—the Vernon Lushingtons' country house—'when I took his wife in to dinner, and had much talk with him, & hearing of him, after dinner' (15 April, 1888). A fortnight later, Lushington introduced him to a writer of the younger generation:

Monday, 30 April, 1888 ... To Kensington Square by rail, dine Vernon Lushington. Music by the 3 girls. Thomas Hardy, novelist, there: small, brownbearded, kindly, shrewd.

More important than literary gossip was a visit Munby and Hannah paid to Hadley, Shropshire, on 3 April, when he took a cottage for his wife, in which they could hope to rebuild their marriage after the ten

---

[9] When Munby sent Scott a drawing, Scott replied: 'The sketch is admirable—I did not know you were like myself both artist and poet' (24 July, 1887). Quotations from Scott's letters to Munby are from the MSS. in the University of Chicago Library.

troubled years. Hannah moved in on 4 May, and Munby wrote: 'May it be blest to her, and to me' (9 May). On 19 May, he stayed there with Hannah for the first time.

The workman's cottage did prove a blessing to them both. On 1 January, 1890, Munby was able to write: 'My darling Hannah . . . is better there and happy.' Though the world of society knew only of his residences at Fig Tree Court and Pyrford, it was Hadley that became his spiritual home. (The area, with its old slag heaps, industrial canals, and shoddy factories, shows marked deterioration eighty years later.)

The autumn of 1888 involved Munby in two disturbing incidents. In the first, while walking back to the Hadley cottage after calling on the Vicar of Wombridge, he was accosted by seven collier lads. The leader 'rudely demanded my name, which of course I refused to give. "Then," said he, "you are Jack the Ripper; and you'll come along wi' us to the police . . ."'. After some parleying, and having taken refuge in the cottage of a friendly pitman, Munby was preserved to write a letter signed AN ELDERLY GENTLEMAN which appeared in *The Times* of 15 October, headed 'The Whitechapel Murders'.[1]

It might have been expected that Munby's casual habits of chatting to colliery women would have led him into trouble with their male colleagues; but it is a measure of the hysteria generated by the Whitechapel crimes that he should have been suspected of being Jack the Ripper. A more unlikely choice could hardly have been imagined; similar false accusations were, however, then being levelled at solitary strangers all over England.

The second episode was more distressing but more predictable. It involved his old friend William Ralston, who had become increasingly unbalanced since he had left his job at the British Museum in 1875. It seems possible that Ralston's brilliant gifts as a public reciter, which led to his being favoured in court circles, overtaxed a nervous constitution barely able to support his prolific exertions in the cause of Russian literature.

Friday, 9 November . . . Dine Athenaeum, 6, and Ralston joined me there, most excited and insane—painful scene with him. . . . Drove with R. to his rooms; to the Middlesex Hospital & got him a male nurse. . . .

During the ensuing weeks, Munby paid visits on Ralston's behalf to the Lunacy Commission and to Bow Street. On 1 March, 1889, he went to

---

[1] Yale University Library has an MS. draft of the letter.

Alfred Place 'and sat 2 hours with my poor friend Ralston, discussing his literary & other troubles'. There was, however, no cause to expect the announcement of Ralston's death which he read, at Bormio, Italy, in the *Morning Post* of 12 August: 'a great shock to me'. Ralston had been found dead in bed, having left all his money, £3,000, to a young woman to whom he had become engaged, and whom Munby now had to console. It was a sad end for a man approaching genius, whose pioneering appreciation of Russian literature is still insufficiently recognised.

In 1889 Munby retired from the Ecclesiastical Commission, a prospect he will have had in view when acquiring Hannah's cottage at Hadley:

Friday, 28 June, 1889 ... Final handshaking at Whitehall, with Earl Stanhope and Sir J. R. Mowbray. 'Very sorry to lose you'—'Such a valuable officer'—'Suppose you will now take wholly to literature', &c. Very civil and courteous. To the Temple in cab, with my effects. ...

Saturday, 29 June ... To Whitehall for the last time, under the trees of the Embankment. Kindly farewells from my colleagues; men coming to my room all the morning, to say friendly words.

So, after a prayer alone, to the U.U. Club. ...

Sunday, 30 June.   As from this day, I retire from Whitehall, after 29½ years. The Lords of the Treasury allow me 5 extra years, for special services; so the retiring pension is £340 p.a.

Thus the passing of the Eighties left Munby with leisure; an adequate income; a new marital home to alternate with his bachelor town and country residences. As a diarist he was now subdued, but remained, whenever he cared to exert himself, an observant social historian:

26 September, 1889.   3 p.m. today, in Bloomsbury Square, passed a street-piano on a handcart, and a lady turning the handle. Thickly veiled, but thoroughly ladylike in dress & air and manner. Placard on instrument, 'I am a lady by birth, but have lost all my property through no fault of my own.' 'Thank you very much', she said in soft ladylike voice.

11

THE END OF THE STORY

1890-1910

Munby's retirement showed positive results with the publication, by Reeves and Turner in 1891, of two books that had been in his mind for many years. The first was a collection of his poems, some of them in dialect, called *Vulgar Verses*, which included a series of character sketches based on his encounters with working women. Mindful of the success of *Dorothy*, he published this book under the pseudonym 'Jones Brown'. These lively verses reflect the vigour of the lower-class life of the time.

The second book was *Faithful Servants*, Munby's assembly of nearly 700 churchyard epitaphs on servants, which had long occupied him on his excursions up and down the country, and was a proper task for an anti-quarian contributor to *Notes and Queries*. He was helped by an earlier book of epitaphs, but discovered and copied most of the collection himself.

In the same year, 1891, a new collection of Munby's more serious verse, *Vestigia Retrorsum*, was published in the Rosslyn series of poets, with a frontispiece photograph (Plate 27) showing the venerable poet full-bearded and almost bald. Some excerpts from this volume appear in the Appendix.

Almost from habit, Munby still voyaged through London literary society and charted its gossip. Lewis Morris had, he felt, 'some claim to the Laureateship, when vacant, Wm Morris & Swinburne being im-possible. Edwin Arnold and Alfred Austin are said to be touting for it. But Christina Rossetti is *my* candidate. . . . A most unsatisfactory time of cliques and small writers' (3 March). He visited W. M. Rossetti at his new home in St. Edmund's Terrace, Primrose Hill: 'W.M.R. pleasant as in our old days, his wife most kindly; her father, Ford Madox Brown, also there, and Christina R., looking charming with her white hair and her beautiful complexion' (22 April).

If Munby's absences and reticences made him something of an enigma in Pyrford, there was another local resident, of much greater fame, who had become a public notoriety since the ambiguous but damaging scandal in which he had been involved in 1886. Sir Charles Dilke's dubious record cannot be compared with Munby's one idealistic faux pas, but these bearded men with uneasy melancholy eyes look, from their photographs, rather alike.

Wednesday, 23 September, 1891.   I called on Sir Charles[1] & Lady Dilke; John Westlake Q.C. having asked me to do so. About 5 years ago, just after his fiasco, he Sir C. W. D. built a bungalow in the firwoods of Pyrford Rough; the very place which was one of my favourite haunts. There, he and Lady D. come at times and live alone together for awhile. 'It is a place where we *work*,' he said today. He & Lady D. were both at home, and were most civil and friendly: knew my name, & some of my friends. . . .

Friday, 25 September.   This afternoon, Sir Charles Dilke returned my call of day before yesterday. I showed him some books and pictures, and then he walked up and down the garden with me, talking of various common friends— Whitley Stokes, for one—and of this neighbourhood, and of Italy, and of Provence, where he has a house between Toulon and Hyères, & the Provençal language and revival. A fine man, with a strong face and keen eyes: now and then a lofty manner, as who should say 'I am Sir C.W.D., Baronet and Privy Councillor, and once member of Government and mean to be again': but for the most part, affable and friendly, and full of clever talk and agreeable omniscience. . . .

The Dilkes occasionally entertained Munby at their house in Sloane Street. Lady Dilke he found 'frank and impulsive' (25 March, 1892). She told him about her Arab horse, 'brought hither by Grace and firman of the Sultan, in charge of a Turkish soldier'. When the soldier parted from the horse, he kissed it on both cheeks and made the sign of the cross on its forehead and down its nose, said Lady Dilke (25 September, 1892).

Tuesday, 27 September, 1892.   Lady Dilke brought her Arab to see me, as she had offered to do, and I went out and talked with her in the lane. An entire horse, of course; cinnamon bay, black flowing mane & tail; small, exquisitely made, full of spirit, & of an almost human sympathy. I kissed him on both cheeks, as Lady D. suggested, and made the sign of the Cross on his face; and he was evidently pleased and soothed by these attentions, which no English stallion would have understood or allowed.

Munby's later diaries are often sketchy, but he supplemented them in separate notebooks by lengthy accounts of his Shropshire visits to Hannah. He records Hannah's description of a call she received from a neighbouring vicar Mr. Gowan whose church she had attended:

[1] Sir Charles Wentworth Dilke, Bt. (1843–1911), M.P. for Chelsea, 1868–86; entered cabinet, 1882; his success ended by the divorce court proceedings of 1885–6.

Tuesday, 25 August, 1891 . . . I showed him in here, an' sat him down i' your chair; and I stood up afore him for a bit, an' then I sat down in the other chair. "Well", he says, "I've found you at last! I've been wantin to find out who you was . . ." 'That was how Mr. Gowan begun, Massa,' said Hannah; 'an' then, I told him first off as you was a gentleman, an' me nothing but a servant all my life. "He picked me up in London, Sir", I says, "when I was in service; an' he never married me for to raise me to be a lady, for I never wished it, nor I wouldna be one if I could; I like to do my own work, an' work for *him*; an' *he* likes me to be like a servant always, an' so do I like it too; an' I know as no one can do for him like *I* can!"'

'You said all that to Mr. Gowan, dear?' says her husband, turning up her face to his, and kissing her.

'Aye, Massa, I did!' says she, with a smile on her lips and in her clear blue eyes; 'you see, Mr. Gowan looked that happy an' nice, an' spake so free, an' I know'd he was a Christian man, an' a right man for the poor; so I wasn't ashamed to tell him all about myself; it did me good to tell him. . . . I told him what a lot o' books you've got, an' as I used to dust 'em all when I lived wi' you, an' read bits of 'em. An' I says to him, "My husband brings a lot o' books here, Sir, whenever he comes, an' always has a book stuck up afore him. I says to him, Whatever is the good of all them books? But it's better to read books, nor to go mochin an' traipsin about". Eh, Mr Gowan did laugh, to hear my plain country talk! But he's a real gentleman; never axed no questions as he shouldn't ought to. "It's a pity you live alone", he says. "Well Sir", I says, "it's rather a sad story, is ourn"; an' I tell'd him some of it. I said as the doctors said I mustn't be in London; an' as you come to stop wi' me about every three months. "Ah", he says, "then both your lives is blighted!" "Yes Sir", I says; "an' yet, not altogether; cause we're very happy when we're here alone by ourselves. But him 'an me *has* to be alone; I never feel right, nor him neither, if any one comes betwixt us; an' besides, he can do wi' *my* folks, but I couldna do wi' *his*, ony to wait on 'em." "An' how long have you been married?" Mr. Gowan says. "Seventeen year, Sir," I says; "but I've knowed him five an' thirty year, an' more. You see, Sir," I says, "he's the ony sweetheart as I ever had; an' I know as he loves me dearly."' 'That's right, dear, to tell him that,' said her husband; 'but did you tell him as you love me?' 'No, Massa, not to say it exactly; but of course I let him see as I *do* love you very much. Oh, an' I told him as I've been to a many places wi' you, since we was married: Ockley, an' Wales, an' th' Isle of Wight, and in France an' Normandy an' that, you know. "But", I said, "Sir, I didna care much about it, wi' me not being a lady, an' knowin nothink about them places; an' besides," I says, "I'm such a one for stoppin at home." An' I told him as you keep wantin me to have a servant, here; but "Sir", I says, "what should *I* do wi' a servant—me, as is a servant myself! An' there inna work enough for two, ony when he's here", I says. Then Mr. Gowan axed what for I come to live here; an' I told him it was along o' my

417

brother Jim, as is a wheelwright at Wombridge, an' I've got other kin at Shiffnall.

So he stopped about half an hour; an' when he got up to go, he offered to shake hands wi' me, an' I did shake hands wi' him. . . .

Thursday, 27 August . . . I got up about 8. Yesterday morning, I had my bath all alone, as usual. This morning, Hannah said 'You mun let me soap you all over, Massa; it's good to get the sweat off; I always soap myself.' And, as I stood in the bath, she did this for me, with vigour and address; rubbing me down afterwards with equal skill.

She stood there, tall as myself nearly; drest humbly in blue cotton frock and large white cap and coarse white apron; her loving face and her bare strong arms glowing red with the work: an obvious servant, yet an obvious wife; for none but a wife might do such a thing . . . The cottage stair descends straight into the kitchen; and when I came down, today as every day, Hannah in that same dress was preparing my breakfast at the kitchen fire. She came into the parlour to prayers, as usual; and knelt down by me, my arm around her and her cheek against mine; and then she brought in the breakfast. . . .

. . . at bedtime, she went upstairs to have her bath. For she had said this morning, 'I shall use this water again tonight, to wash myself all over; ony I mun spit in it first, else we shall quarrel': it being well known in Salop, that if two wash in the same water, they will fall out, unless that rite be observed.

When she was ready, I joined her, and did for her what she had done for me in the morning. To me, it is nothing carnal or voluptuous, but a thing of infinite sacredness, the sight of the fair pure body: still plump and firm and strong, the healthy skin soft and pink-white everywhere, except on her face and neck and her robust round arms and roughened hands. And even all these were softened and made more delicate by the bath. I saw her safe into bed, and came down again to write.

These notebooks chronicle the incidents of Hannah's daily life—the garden pears she sells at the door; her walks and excursions, her stick-gathering and gleaning; Oakengates market, where she stands at her brother's fish stall in her grey cloak ('a shawl's bad to serve fish in: it flaps again your arms'); her savings of over £500, administered by her husband. Hannah's return to a peasant's existence had brought back her elemental rustic skills. The notebooks are a rich repository of Shropshire folk-lore, superstition and dialect. The 1891 notebook concludes with a glossary of 'Some of Hannah's words in this volume':

> *Bur*, sb. = the sweetbread of a calf.
> *Gain*, adj. = handy or convenient.
> *Grig*, sb. = ling, furze.

Jannock, adj. = straightforward & right.
Lenty, adj. = dull and lazy.
Magging, part. = gossiping idly.
Mawkin, sb. = a scarecrow.
Mochin', part. = talebearing, idling.
Mosy, adj. = rotten, or 'woolly', of a pear, but *not* of an apple.
Recklin', sb. = the smallest pig of a litter.
Rodney, sb. = a loafer, an idler.
Traipsin', part. = sauntering idly.

One wonders what Munby's brothers thought of his quarterly visits to 'Hadley, Wellington, Salop'—the sole address on letters he wrote from Hannah's cottage. Were they utterly incurious, or had they decided it was futile to probe Arthur's obduracies? Anyway, they do not seem to have guessed his secret; wherever he was, he went on writing, happy in his release from Whitehall. In 1892 we find him sending a series of letters to George Bentley about contributions for *Temple Bar*.[2] Henceforth his chief anxiety was the state of Hannah's health during his absences. He even doubted whether he should accept an invitation to visit Switzerland because he had heard rumours of an outbreak of influenza in Shropshire. Hannah reassured him:

. . . *I* am not afeard of it, so my darling, you could go to Fleurier, & come to me after, quite well—if you'd like to go—I canna counsel thee over the matter, for thou knowest thy own mind best, & the way thou art fix'd over thy friends, & as it's gone on *so* long & they know not of thy disgracing thyself so, wi' having a servant for thy slave & wife, why, it can as easily go on to the close & they need *never* know—I feel quite sure I shall die afore thee & then thou canst let the secret die too. But while I live I shall have the same pleasure in workin' for thee as ever I had, & my love for thee will be the same . . . (12 January, 1892).

In 1892 Munby's admiration for Tennyson reached its climax. All his life he had longed to meet him, but he never did, and it must have been a sense of foreboding mixed with homage that brought him to Tennyson's Lane, Blackdown, on 6 August, 1892: 'This is Tennyson's 83rd birthday, and he is here, at Aldworth; but I had no call to intrude. . . .'

However, on 5 September, Lowes Dickinson, while staying at Pyrford, spoke of a visit he had paid to Tennyson, and said he was 'a beautiful wreck. . . . He tells me that T. knows my Dorothy, and was pleased with my wish to do him homage on his birthday'. On the same occasion,

---

[2] University of Illinois Library, Urbana.

Dickinson 'looked earnestly at the photograph of Hannah that hangs in my dining room, and said "What a noble and beautiful face! Who is it?" "It is the face of the only woman I have ever really loved"'.

When Tennyson died on 6 October, Munby commented: 'His death is like the beginning of the end, to me; so strong, and so personal & intimate, has been his influence, for more than forty years.' Of course he attended the funeral:

Wednesday, 12 October ... I got to the Abbey at 11.40: a crowd outside, & people pouring in at the South door, without tickets ... At 12.30, procession came in; coffin draped with Union Jack, & wreaths. Volunteers, and boys of Gordon Home, lined the nave on both sides. The whole service transcendently solemn & beautiful, and most of all, the lowering of the coffin into the grave. The music lovely, & especially Dr Bridge's setting of Over the Bar ... as we left at 1.30, we passed through a lane in the vast crowd of humble and sympathizing folk outside, who were eagerly buying for a penny his likeness and Over the Bar. The crowds were much larger than at Browning's funeral.

The diaries tend to be dominated henceforth by the theme of Munby's separation from Hannah. Regularly, at Hadley, three or four times a year, Hannah would put away the silver and shut up the little parlour which was opened only for her husband; she tidied away the hair-brushes, washbasin and other luxuries of their bedroom. The couple then settled down to a mutual longing for 'the next time'. At the first sign from Hannah of illness or accident, Munby would send telegrams and restlessly prepare for a journey. No wonder he contemplated, again and again, the absurd predicament that compelled him to maintain a comfortable home at Pyrford (staffed by two servants) in which his wife could have no part. But always the answer was the same: Hannah refused to live under what she considered false pretences, she would not be a lady; conversely, she was too rough and too humble to play the conventional housekeeper. 'If my darling were but here!' cried Munby (19 April, 1893), 'And yet, she cannot be: her rough hands, her servant's dress and work, her country dialect—things all dear to me as a part of herself—make this impossible.' 'Surely, *some* way will open, soon!' he exclaims (10 January, 1894). It never did; and later he was only comforted by the firm advice of his old friend Vernon Lushington, the judge, not to bring Hannah to Pyrford.

Munby's poetic inspiration was similarly dominated by the marriage problem. In 1893, Reeves and Turner published a long poem, *Susan*, telling the story of the romance without much disguise; the poem impressed Edmund Gosse, who compared it to Drayton and Daniel, but a reviewer in the *Athenaeum* annoyed Munby by affirming 'that no such woman as Hannah is possible'. *Ann Morgan's Love* (1896) was another variation on the theme: R. H. Hutton in the *Spectator* summed it up as 'poetry with no high flights of expression, but only the simple utterance of a genuine but noble mind'. Hutton did, however, have something to say about 'the topsy-turvy fastidiousness which seems to be positively repelled by the least preference for what may be called *conventional* refinement'. Another verse manuscript of this period remained unpublished; this was *Leonard and Elizabeth*, the story of a beautiful colliery girl whose face is terribly mutilated in an explosion at the pit face[3]—a reversion to Harriet Langdon and the old preoccupation with disfigurement.

Hannah could occasionally relent, even at sixty. In September, 1893, they stayed a weekend at the Marine Hotel, Barmouth, 'had a spacious bedroom, No. 12, looking on the sea, and Hannah came down with me to tea as a lady, looking noble and behaving with unaffected grace and dignity'. On the Sunday evening, however, she was 'unwilling to face the ladies downstairs', and Munby played the piano to her in the drawing-room during the table d'hôte. Back at Hadley a few days later, 'she sang at her work, for she was now a servant again'.

Year succeeds year, and now the strongest impression is of the sadness of the regular partings. Hannah is either waving goodbye from the cottage door or welcoming Munby at the little railway station, where he arrives looking like Johnny Town-Mouse: what happens in the interval seems increasingly unimportant, even if Sir Charles Dilke asserts 'the Labour members will *not* increase' (4 October, 1893); and sometimes Buttercup Farm (Munby's nickname for Wheeler's Farm, because of the buttercups in the meadows) lost its attraction, though it was pleasant to have Austin Dobson down for the week-end, 'always genial and kindly and full of information on his own subjects: apt, like other men, to talk chiefly of his own doings, but withal an excellent fellow' (18 June, 1894).

By 1894, Munby had forgotten that he had ever criticised Ruskin, and still tried to keep unspoiled his memories of Rossetti. He wrote to his friend W. J. Linton, the engraver, estranged husband of Eliza Lynn Linton, on 7 March, 1894:

. . . I am very glad that you speak so warmly of Ruskin, and I more than agree with all you say. To me, and to the men of my generation, & especially to those

---

[3] The MS., 108 leaves, quarto, was acquired by Dr. A. N. L. Munby in 1970. Internal evidence dates it to 1893–6.

who have known him personally, as I have, Ruskin must always be an object of the deepest respect and love. I feel that I owe to him more than I can tell, not only in Art, but in Religion, in Politics and Ethics, in the imaginative enjoyment of natural beauty. Alas, his brain has been too much for him: he worked it so intensely in youth and earlier manhood, that now it is all awry. Sometimes, I am told, he wakes up and talks, but only on ordinary subjects; and then, his mind collapses, and he sits 'like a greatgrandfather of 90' unconscious of all around him. My friend Litchfield, whom he has known since 1853, was not at all sure that Ruskin knew who he was, though Mrs Arthur Severn thought he *did* know; and when his great friend Dr Acland came to Brantwood, Ruskin (as I hear) stared at him, unconscious; then suddenly embraced him, saying 'I know you—but I don't know who you are!'

Is that not sad and touching?.[4]. . .

Rheumatism became a pre-occupation; both Munby and Hannah took brine baths at Stafford. Then there were days when Hannah would be emotionally overwrought, and there might be scenes with a girl whom Munby had engaged to help her. But usually she was happy when Munby was there, capable of making a little verse while she was cleaning the grate:

> Of all the servants I possess
> My Hannah is the best,
> And with her peasant's bonnet on,
> No lady's better drest.

'She came into the parlour, and repeated it to me, laughing and blushing at her feat' (18 June, 1895). Hannah often copied out Munby's verses, and her own literary ingenuity was exhibited in postcards to her husband. Some were written in a mixture of French and English; one or two were written backwards: codes they adopted to defeat rustic inquisitiveness.

Early in 1897, Munby began to arrange his and Hannah's papers, photographs and notebooks: an activity that was to continue for a decade. In June of the same year he was operated on, at a London nursing-home, for chronic glaucoma of the right eye. He had already complained in a letter to W. J. Linton of having to use 'not only spectacles, but a magnifying glass also', to read some books Linton had sent him.[5]

The diary still holds its surprises—as in March, 1898, when Munby was living at Fig Tree Court in the care of his London housekeeper Mrs. Denny:

Saturday, 26 March, 1898.   Wet miserable day. Indoors till 3.30. About noon, a single knock at my outer door. 'Some one to see you, Sir,' said Mrs. Denny.

---

[4] Yale University Library.   [5] 27 May, 1896: Yale University Library.

Enter a tall fine woman, plainly drest but dignified; a bright smile on her hand-some face. To my amazement, it was my own Hannah! She was in my arms in a moment; as of old, I sat long on her strong knees, in the old arm chair, while she told her tale. She had come up from Salop by a cheap train: left at 5.30 a.m. today, & is going back at midnight. 'I come sudden; I shouldna ha' coom, ony I know'd you was here.' She looked radiant: a splendid woman, full of rustic health & vigour, & one of Nature's ladies. . . . 'How smart your rooms is! An' yo've got a new carpet—what a shame! It must ha' cost you a deal o' money!' She adjusted the flowers, and went down on her knees and swept the hearth with her hands, having no brush.

After 2 hours of delightful talk & petting, she went down to the kitchen where she used to live. 'It's a good job as I catch'd the Master in!' she said to Mrs D. Then she to Sister Ellen. At 11.15 p.m. I met her at the station, & saw my darling off at 12.20.

Funerals were a recurring obligation; one of the most affecting being that of his old friend Helen Faucit (Lady Martin) in November, 1898. In a letter to Munby, Sir Theodore Martin mentioned a 'burst of sunshine' as the coffin was lowered into the grave: 'It seemed to tell me she was happy, & not to mourn.'[6]

At the close of 1898, Munby's diaries were yet again—this time finally—brought to a conclusion: '*Mem.* This volume ends the series of my Diaries; which have been kept by me consecutively for forty years: i.e. since the year 1859, inclusive. At 70, il faut finir. A.J.M.' He continued to make intermittent notebook entries about Hannah, and they offer an interesting picture of life in an obscure Shropshire village. However, in the last month of 1898, we find a passage that illumines the marriage relationship. It is written in the third person:

Saturday, 3 December, 1898.   In the little brickfloored parlour, today, the hus-band sat writing letters & other things, at his desk; and through the open door he could see his wife, who was cleaning brass candlesticks in her kitchen. When she had done this work, she took her pail, and went down on her hands and knees, and scoured the kitchen floor as she had already scoured the parlour floor. But presently she got up, and came into the parlour, with her hands full of coals. She flung the coals on her husband's fire, arranging them among the red hot embers with fingers which did not mind the heat . . . When all was clean (except herself) she arose, and passed behind her husband, kissing his forehead as she did so, towards the door. But, as she looked down at the table, and saw his writing, one of her strange pathetic fits of jealousy came on.

[6] 29 November, 1898. This and several other letters from Martin to Munby are in Yale University Library (Osborn Collection).

She stopped. 'Massa'. she said, 'if I know'd as many folks as you do, an' kep on writin to 'em every day, like you do, how would you like it?' 'Not at all, dear!' said he; but, as he looked up and saw how sad and earnest her face was, he added 'My darling, you know I always tell you about my letters and things, except them business ones, as you canna understand.' 'Oo aye!' she replied, in a melancholy tone; 'but that's not it!' And instead of retiring, she crossed the room, and sat down in a chair facing him, beyond his table. A strange grotesque figure she was, seated thus before him. Her coarse sacking apron, soiled and wet with scouring; her bare strong ruddy arms, blackened and splashed with sludge from the kitchen floor, and her rough black hands, stretched out and grasping her knees . . . all this made her seem unfit to sit down even in so humble a parlour as her husband's.

But her face is still beautiful, in feature and in expression; & to her husband she was as loveable in this guise—which after all, is her *own* guise—as in any other, and was the more pathetic for her roughness. She sat thus awhile in silence, looking earnestly at him with her clear blue eyes; and then, leaning forward, she said 'Massa! I am your slave—' 'You are my *wife*, you dirty darling!' said he, interrupting her. 'Aye, aye, Ah know that! But I are your slave an' all. It was me as suggested it, an' I've never bin sorry for it—never! . . . But,' she added with a sigh, 'it *is* hard to be a slave to a littery person like you, as keeps on writin books an' letters an' things, all day long!'

Before he could reply with becoming gravity to this complaint, she began again; leaning forward with her elbows on her knees, and looking at him more keenly than ever: 'Massa,' she said, 'don't I do more work for you, nor all your other servants put together?' 'Yes, dear!' he warmly replied, 'and you do it better, too. Don't you remember what Mr. Ruskin said, that the best of all service is *unpaid* service, 'cause it's done *for love?*'

'Aye, Ah remember,' she said, 'an' it's true. But', she went on, mournfully gazing, 'it *do* wherrit me over them other women—traipsin an' dollopin wi' nothing to do, when you're not theer; an' doing *my* work—me, as always hoped to be your *only* servant when we was married, an' now you've got them other three an' all!'

This is her standing grievance, her one accusation against her husband: that he cannot & will not allow his wife to be his *only* servant . . .

In the early months of 1900, and also of 1901, Munby was not well enough to leave Pyrford; yet by the close of 1901 he had ready a new book of *Poems: Chiefly Lyric and Elegiac*, published by Kegan Paul with a dedication 'To my friend of forty years Austin Dobson'. 'We are very glad,' wrote C. L. Graves in the *Spectator*, where several of the poems had first appeared, 'to welcome another volume of verse from the pen of Mr. Munby, a writer whose work is marked by an elevation of thought and purity of style never so noticeable as when he is handling the humblest themes.' Munby could certainly be relied on to pursue humble themes, but the volume as a whole has the attraction of variety and contains some of his best short poems. It includes a deeply felt tribute to R. D. Blackmore, who had died on 20 January, 1900 (a sonnet prefixed to some later editions of *Lorna Doone*):

> A strong, calm, steadfast, single-hearted soul,
>> Sincere as Truth, and tender like a maid,
>> He lived as one whom nothing could persuade
> From reticence and manly self-control.
> Insight, and humour, and the rhythmic roll
>> Of antique lore, his fertile fancies sway'd,
>> And with their various eloquence array'd
> His sterling English, pure and clean and whole.
>
> Fair Nature mourns him now, as well she may
>> So apt a pupil and so close a friend;
> But what of us, who through his lifelong day
>> Knew him at home, and loved him to the end?
> One thing we know: that Love's transcendent name
> Is link'd with his, and with his honour'd fame.

A longer memorial poem, to Queen Victoria, has its moments of lapidary truth and prophetic insight, but might have been even better if Munby had followed his own previous inclination, as expressed to Austin Dobson, instead of being overawed when it came to the test:

... To my thinking, the finest & most poetic thing that can be said about the Queen, is a thing that cannot be said during her life. It is, that her virtues and powers are *not* those of a great woman, like Elizabeth or Catharine II or Maria Theresa, but are the virtues and powers of an ordinary woman: things that any person, however humble, can appreciate and imitate. To have had such virtues and powers exhibited uniformly and always, in the very highest station, is an example inestimably precious to the whole world. And I hope that some one will say this, & say it in verse, when the right times comes.[7] ...

Munby was now spending many of his Christmases with Hannah, something he had not done for years, and which may have involved him in making excuses to his brother George. At the end of 1902 he extended his Christmas stay to ten weeks. Under the date, June and July, 1903, in one of the notebooks, there is an unusual glimpse of Hannah as a discreet secretary. Munby had asked her to send Fanny Burney's biography of her father to Austin Dobson:

[7] Letter to Austin Dobson, 4 July, 1897 (Mr. Kenneth Dobson's collection).

... The result of Hannah's search shows her resolve to appear always as my *servant*. 'I hunted every book over an' it's *not* here,' she wrote; 'so I wrote Mr. Dobson a post card afore 12 & posted it. I said "Sir, I have had orders from Mr. M. to send you the Life of Dr Burney in 3 volumes. I have look'd well over all the books here & canna find it amongst 'em. I will write & tell the Master so. I am Sir yours obediently H." '

In July, 1903, Hannah decided to leave Hadley and go to live at Shifnal, a few miles away, in a cottage recently acquired by her brother Jim. The rent was half-a-crown a week. The cottage stood in Wyke Place (Plate 26), a yard near the Red Lion Inn (since closed), where Hannah had been a pot girl as a child. This yard had a pair of brick-tiled cottages at the far end; beyond them were gardens, and then the fields and woods. It was an even smaller cottage than the one at Hadley, for it consisted only of a single kitchen into which the front door opened at ground level (no door-step to clean) with a scullery beyond; upstairs were two small bedrooms, one without a fireplace.

Moving into her new home on 7 September, 1903, she liked it immediately. It seemed a more convenient place for an old woman of seventy who still did everything herself. And she enjoyed hearing the church bells ringing as they had done when she was a child.

Munby visited the new cottage a month later. He approved the folding doors which shut off the yard from the noise and turmoil of Shifnal; he admired the freshly painted green front-door and the two mullioned windows, one above the other. Hannah had made the kitchen into a parlour for him, retreating herself into the scullery. There were her few bits of old furniture, the grandfather clock and the brass warming-pan. On the walls hung coloured plates from the Christmas numbers of the *Illustrated London News*, given her by Munby; her sampler; the flower pictures she had dried and arranged. Over the mantelpiece were photographs of Munby, and of Hannah as a 'lady'. On the window sill stood her plants: geranium, myrtle and balsam. Munby was pleased with what he saw, and relieved to think that Hannah could live more comfortably there; he prudently made his way to the Shifnal Cottage Hospital, and arranged to pay a regular subscription for her.

Did Hannah realise what he had suffered by marrying her? Possibly not, thought Munby in one of his moods of self-pity.

December, 1903 ... One day in this month, I had a letter from an old friend, a lady, who expressed her regret that I 'have never married'. I read this to Hannah.

She laughed gaily, and clapped her hands like a girl, and cried 'Eh, what fun! What a romance! They'll never know as you've married a wench like me!' She has always enjoyed the romantic side of her love and mine. Her unselfishness delights in thinking that by marrying her I have suffered no degradation among my own friends and kindred; and she does *not* feel the painful reticence which her living method has imposed on me. For there is *no* reticence on her side. All her kinsfolk and neighbours know that she is my wife as well as my servant; and her cottage is the only place in which I can live freely and openly with her as man and wife, without calumny, and without disgrace to her or to myself.

Munby was at the cottage again towards the end of May, 1904, to celebrate the fiftieth anniversary of their meeting, and he stayed until 8 June:

. . . As I left the yard, I turned round, for a last look at her: she was just stooping into the coalshed, to dig and carry her two bucketfuls of coal. Nothing could be better, as a picture to dwell on: for this fair and devoted woman is only a peasant, a country servant, a labourer who has dug and carried coals since she was 8 years old: and yet she is *my wife*; and her love is a nobler thing by far, than the love of an equal could be. . . . 'Do you want her, Sir? Shall I fetch her?' said Mary Townsend, who from her door had seen me turn round. 'Oh no, thank you: I have her with me—Goodbye!'. . . .

Hannah composed some verses 'on the eve of our Jubilee':

> Fifty years ago, tonight—
>   I little thought to see
> The morrows pure delight
>   My master brought to me
>
> And since that morrow came
>   He's loved me more an' more
> And I have done the same
>   To him I do adore.

These verses were signed 'Hannah Munby Wife & Servant'. As an afterthought, she added the following:

> Tis fifty year since we met
>   And we are happy yet
> Joggin' on through life
>   Without quarrel or strife.

427

Our Jubilee.

25th May
1904

Fifty years ago, to night –
I little thought to see
The morrows pure delight
    My master brought to me

And since that morrow came
    He's loved me more an' more
And I have done the same
    To him I do adore.

Hannah Munby
Wife &
Servant

'Tis fifty years since we met
    And we are happy yet
Jogging on through this life
    Without quarrel or strife.

After copying the first two stanzas into his notebook, Munby wrote: 'with them, I close this record of her obscure and laborious, but imperial life: a record which I have kept partly for my own pleasure, but chiefly in honour of her. For surely, someday, somewhere, some one or other will see as I do now, the beauty and the nobleness of such a character and such a love as hers.' He added the word 'Finis' and the date: 'Pyrford, 19 June, 1904.'

Here was another serious attempt at finality; and Munby's seniority was again emphasised on 16 July, 1904, when he was present at the laying of the foundation-stone, by the Prince of Wales, of the new buildings of the Working Men's College in Crowndale Road, Camden Town. E. M. Forster and G. P. Gooch were with him on this occasion, as was Mrs. R. B. Litchfield[8]—now a widow, for Munby's old friend had died in 1903. It was Munby's last appearance at the College.

Some lines by Munby in the *Spectator* of 18 February, 1905, 'In Eternum, Domine', refer to his marriage. They include the stanza:

> One may go first, and one remain
> To hail a second call;
> But nothing now can make us twain,
> Whatever may befall.

In March, 1905, when Hannah was ill with bronchitis, Munby had to stay at the Jerningham Arms. But she recovered, and was soon well enough to answer her husband's question, 'Do you know what mésalliance means, dear?'—'Yes, Massa—you and me!'

Munby had outlived many of his contemporary friends, but those that remained had not forgotten him, and in two affectionate letters of 1905–6 written in a straggling hand, Lowes Dickinson discussed with him his son Goldsworthy Lowes Dickinson's *A Modern Symposium*, showing pride in its success. He ended the second letter: 'God bless you old friend! I enjoyed a visit and long talk with Vernon Lushington last week—much of it about you.'[9]

A typical farewell statement of faith from Hannah occurs in a notebook entry of Munby's dated 14 May, 1906:

... 'I say, Massa,' she exclaimed, '*what* a good job, as I arena a lady! One thing, I should hate to be stuck up, an' dress fine, an' keep that nesh an' prim,

---

[8] *Working Men's College Journal*, Vol. VIII, 1903–4.
[9] 8 April, 1906. The letters are in the archives of the Working Men's College.

an' talk affected, like ladies do by what I've heerd, an' sit on sofas, an' have soft hands, 'an have company, an' all such as that. Eh, I wouldna be a lady, not for a thousand pound! But now, I can sweep an' scour, an' clean your boots, an' clean grates, an' get coals in, an' all the jobs as I've always bin used to in service, an' I can talk my own plain talk, an' I can do everything for you —aye, an' I can read out to yo as well as any lady could!' And she threw her arms round him & kissed him. . .

Scattered jottings of 1906–8 show Hannah still picking up sticks in the fields and collecting the potatoes, turnips and coals that fell into the roads from passing carts. The couple spent the Christmas of 1907 together at Shifnal; and there are records of Munby's covering, in a shaky hand, the months of October and November, 1907. In January, 1908, he placed inside an envelope the 'Keys of the 3 Deed boxes mentioned in my will', and wrote on the back that they were not to be opened before 'the 1st of January 1950'. His handwriting here is almost as clear and legible as it had been forty years earlier; and the same can be said of a letter to Austin Dobson dated from 'Shifnal, Salop', 17 September, 1908, and containing an appreciation of Edmund Gosse's recently published *Father and Son* which demonstrates that, at eighty, Munby's critical faculties were un-impaired. This was one of the last letters Munby wrote in Hannah's parlour, with the sampler on the wall and the plants on the window sill.

. . . I have read it straight through, and with great interest: for the psychology of childhood and youth is an attractive subject, and this book states it clearly & simply, and with all due regard to a proper filial feeling. Indeed, the writer does full justice to his father, and but scanty justice to himself.

Any one who has a sense of the ludicrous, and who hates John Calvin and all his works (especially the murder of Servetus) as much as I do, will probably read the book as a clever and amusing satire on certain grotesque forms of Protestantism: and I have read it in that way. But I have also read it seriously: for its story is a terrible example of erroneous judgement and mistaken piety. It is a pathetic figure indeed, that of a devout father, striving earnestly and for twenty years to keep his one child within the narrow limits of what he believes to be the only true religion, and then finding that after all, he has only driven his son further and further beyond those limits, and perhaps out of religion altogether. On the other hand, it is very creditable to the son, that he was not driven out of all morality too, by such a monstrous education. The son has done a public service, by issuing such a book: and to write it all, must have been no easy or pleasant task. One observes, also, a thin but sufficient glaze of genial humour, which lights up certain parts of the story, and is visible to the carnal eye, though *not* to the eye (if he has one) of the Plymouth Brother. But the pity of it all is, that the very people who need such a book most, namely the 'Evangelical' Protestants, are just those who will not profit by it. They will either refuse to read the story at all, or they will read it and denounce the author as a worldling and a backslider.[1]. . .

According to Mrs Osborne, wife of the Vicar of Pyrford, Munby was 'an invalid' from the time of their arrival at the Vicarage in 1907: 'he never went out except in a hired carriage, as he was too feeble to walk.' However, Munby twice called at the vicarage, and Mrs. Osborne and her husband visited him frequently. 'We always found him sitting in a chair. As he was almost blind, we used to read the newspapers to him, and he took the keenest possible interest in everything. He loved to talk of the old times, but he never mentioned that he was married. . . . Besides being a most charming man to speak with, he had a very generous heart, and every Christmas he distributed gifts in money and kind to poor people.'[2] His intellect certainly remained bright. As late as April and June, 1909, he engaged in a vigorous correspondence in the *Working Men's College Journal* on the effects of the Workmen's Compensation Acts.

Hannah was destined to 'go first'. There is no information about her last days beyond the official wording of her death certificate, which states that Hannah Munby died at Wyke Place, Shifnal, on 9 July, 1909, aged 76, from 'Failure of Heart action' and 'Senile Decay'. Her niece Emily Gibbs was with her when she died. Munby had obviously been unable to get to her. She was buried in Shifnal churchyard, where in due course an inscription on a stone kerb commemorated 'Hannah for 36 years the beloved wife and servant of Arthur Joseph Munby'.[3]

Munby survived Hannah by only six months, but he was able to see his last gathering of verse, *Relicta*, published by Bertram Dobell.[4] The prefatory note is dated from 6 Fig Tree Court, Inner Temple, October, 1909, and the book is 'Dedicated to the gracious and beloved memory of HER whose hand copied out and whose lifelong affection suggested all that is

---

[1] MS. in Mr. Christopher Dobson's collection.

[2] *Daily Mirror*, 4 July, 1910.

[3] *Morning Leader*, 4 July, 1910.

[4] Bertram Dobell took over the 'remainder' of several publications by Munby, and (up to 1940 at least) had copies of *Relicta* and others for sale at 1s. 6d. Munby's correspondence with him, in Mr. R. J. Dobell's collection, shows that he had every confidence in his last publisher. Munby paid the printer's bill for *Relicta* (£21 18s. od.) and refused to accept a royalty.

best in this book'. On the verso of the title-page appears the following quatrain by Munby:

> There was a morning when I follow'd Fame:
> There was a noonday when I caught her eye:
> There is an evening when I hold my name
> Calmly aloof from all her hue and cry.

Munby's lament for the motor-car in 'London Town' is included in the Appendix of his poems; it is too searching and prophetic to be ignored. But taking this final volume as a whole, one has the feeling he was no longer concerned to be cautious, or to disguise the truth of the old love story retold in one after another of the poems. There is even a poem 'Hannah' containing the line: 'But the best of all my servants is my faithful servantwife.' Many of the poems are moving; none more so than the last, 'Death and Life':

> This is the room in which my darling died:
> A cottage bedroom with a sloping roof,
> Simple, and old, and quiet; looking out
> Over green gardens, on the woods and hills
> Beyond that village where her life began
> And where it ended. Nothing on the earth
> Is nearer heaven than a home like this,
> When two twin souls inhabit it, and live
> In love and peace, together and alone.
>
> And still we are together and alone:
> Not in the lovely churchyard, where indeed
> Her fair and lissome body and sweet face
> Lie waiting for the husband of her youth;
> Nor in that cottage home; nor here—so far
> From all she loved and cared for, and so full
> Of petty interests, that exasperate
> The soul of sorrow; no indeed, not here!
> But in a region only known to those
> Whose lives have climb'd up towards it, and who now,
> Now in their hour of need, have leave to meet
> And commune there, unfetter'd by the bonds
> Of flesh and blood, of distance, and of Time.

There was no need for Munby to prolong the double struggle of living and concealing. In November, 1909, his brother George visited him at Pyrford, and was told the whole story of his marriage.[5]

---

[5] See p. 435.

He fell ill with pneumonia four days before he died at Wheeler's Farm on 29 January, 1910. John Cole, the farmer, of Church Hill—whose father had been his first landlord—was with him when he died. As he shut the front-door behind him, Mr. Cole may have glanced at an inscription Munby had caused to be placed over the lintel: ILLA PLACET TELLUS IN QUA RES PARVA BEATUM ME FACIT.[6]

[6] 'That piece of earth pleases me in which a small possession makes me happy' (Martial). Munby had stipulated in his will that he should be buried 'in that place where I may happen to die', and he was buried in Pyrford churchyard on 3 February. The service was taken by his nephew Henry; afterwards his brother Fred, the solicitor, read his will to the assembled members of the family. A brass memorial was later erected in the church to the memory of 'Arthur Joseph Munby M.A., F.S.A., of Trinity Coll. Cambridge & of Lincoln's Inn, Barrister at Law, eldest son of Joseph Munby of Clifton Holme in the Wapentake of Bulmer. . . .'

433

THE WILL AND THE DEED-BOXES

For several months after his death the contents of Munby's will remained a secret to all but his family. It was an awkward time for them, because they knew that, in the social climate of 1910, the will would prove highly tempting to journalists.

They hoped, in vain, that, somehow or other, they might be spared the embarrassment of the revelation of Uncle Arthur's domestic affairs which the will contained. How much better, they felt, if the public could be satisfied with the admirable obituary notice that Mr. Austin Dobson had written for *The Times*.[1]

The notice declared that Munby's poetry was 'characterized by its variety, its technical skill, its scholarship, its excellent English, and its exquisite appreciation and observation of Nature and rural life'. It mentioned that 'on the question of woman's rights and duties Mr Munby had pronounced opinions, and he was never tired of enforcing them in his books'. *The Times* continued:

... Known to a few, he never received the recognition he deserved. This was partly owing to the singular modesty and reticence of his nature, and partly to his absolute disdain of *réclame*. ... Mr Munby's individuality was one of singular amenity and charm. He had read and remembered much. In a long life he had known many notabilities in art and letters; and if his Diaries should ever be published they cannot fail to be interesting, while they are sure not to sin against good taste. Those who ... were privileged to enjoy his conversation will not easily forget his unfailing courtesy, his retentive memory, and his inexhaustible store of recollections.

There is no reason to imagine that Dobson suspected that his old friend was not a bachelor.

Soon after the appearance of *The Times* obituary, Munby's brother George sent the following letter in a mourning envelope to his daughter Mrs. Cockin:

Hitchin
My dearest Florence,   Feb. 7th 1910.

Dear Mother has told you about Uncle Arthur's death, and our going to Pyrford on Thursday. I send you an account of him, from last Saturday's

[1] 5 February, 1910.

'Times', which is very well,—gracefully and truly,—told, by his old friend—to whom he dedicated his book of Poems, published in 1901—Austin Dobson. No one could have done it better, and it is entirely accurate. Austin Dobson wrote to Mother at Pyrford, and told her he had written it at the request of the Editor. I am not sure whether you know that, last autumn, Uncle Arthur published another book of Poems, called 'Relicta', which [means] 'things which are left, or remain.'

You perhaps remember that, when you were here, in November, I went to Pyrford, for a few hours, and was very sad when I came back. You, very nicely, asked me no questions; but, most likely, I told you that I would let you know, some day, what had happened. What happened, was this. His new book is dedicated 'to the gracious and beloved memory of her whose life-long devotion suggested' it all. He spoke to me about the book, and I naturally asked him who this was. He then told me that he wished me to know that, for years, he had been *married*, and that he never loved any one but her who had thus been his wife: and then he told me all the story. Not only his last book, but almost *all* his books,—'Ann Morgan's Love', 'Susan', the 'Poems' dedicated to Austin Dobson, and others, contain descriptions—most of them exceedingly beautifully told, but all, harping upon the same string—which is the love of an *educated man* for a *peasantwoman*. Every body always thought that these were his poetic creations—the ideal conceptions of a poet's mind. Now it comes out that they are all absolute fact. Perhaps the simplest of them is 'Dichter und Bauerin'[2] in Relicta, that is 'Poet and Peasant maiden', p. 36. His 'Bauerin' was Hannah Culwick [*sic*], whom he married in 1873. She was born in 1833, and died last year, 1909: so she was at last quite an old woman. I do not think that any of his friends, except three,—these are Borland, Vernon Lushington, the Judge, and James of Cheltenham—who is now dead—had the least idea that he was married, and it is wonderful to think of the fact being kept secret so long. However, they were honourably married in Clerkenwell Church, and Uncle Fred read his Will to the Nephews who were present at the funeral, which told all the story of his love for her and hers for him. I forget whether you have any of his books: but, if you have, you will have, pretty well, all the story of his love and hers, told in them, under, of course, imaginary names. I tell you all this, because, by this time, I expect, all the nephews and nieces know about it. But it is my earnest hope that the newspapers will not get hold of it. Please therefore, in talking about him, speak of him, in the way that Austin Dobson does, in which way he well deserves to be spoken of; and, as to his marriage, it will be wise to be silent, at all events for many days to come.

Ever your affectionate father
G.F.W.M.[3]

[2] See Appendix.
[3] Dr. A. N. L. Munby's collection.

Epilogue: The Will and the Deed-boxes

Mrs. R. B. Litchfield contributed a warmly appreciative memoir of Munby to the *Working Men's College Journal* of March, 1910. On one significant point she may satisfy inquisitive readers:

... He had strong views on women's rights and duties; and from his poems it would almost seem that he thought a woman whose hands were not hardened by toil was scarcely worthy of the reverence due to womanhood. His personal attitude to a woman such as myself, whose hands are not roughened by work, was in curious contrast to these views. His courtesy had all the ceremony and chivalrous delicacy of feeling which are now associated with a by-gone age....

So far, so good. No member of the Munby family could possibly have objected to these tributes to Uncle Arthur; but, with the publication of his will in July, the public attitude towards Munby entered a new and larger dimension—a world of folk-lore appropriate to heroic romance. Munby had signed his will on 24 March, 1900, and added a codicil in 1905. He had discussed the document with Hannah, and it had been drafted on the assumption that she would survive him; but Munby was determined to use this opportunity of making a personal statement, and he did not alter the will after her death.

Probate was granted on 30 June, 1910, Munby's estate being valued at something over £25,000; the will then became public property. After twenty lines of preliminaries, Munby went straight to the heart of the matter:

... And whereas Hannah Cullwick servant born at Shiffnall in the county of Salop and bred at the Charity School of Aston Brook by Shiffnall has for forty five years and upwards been beloved by me with a pure and honourable love and not otherwise and she the said Hannah has during all that time been as faithful and loving and devoted to me as ever woman was to man And whereas after vainly trying to explain this state of things to my father I married the said Hannah (she being then in my service) publicly in presence of all her kindred who could be got together at the parish church of Clerkenwell in the county of Middlesex on the fourteenth day of January 1873 And whereas there has been no issue of the said marriage And whereas notwithstanding her said marriage the said Hannah has always refused and still refuses to have the position which as my wife she might and could have had and has always insisted and still insists on being my servant as well as my wife her one grievance being that she cannot be my only servant And whereas owing chiefly to this noble and unselfish resolve of hers I have never been able to make known my said marriage to my family or to the world at large and the same has been and is known only to her kin and friends and to three of my most intimate college friends of whom

436

the said Robert Spencer Borland is the only one who knows the circumstances of the case and who knows the said Hannah personally And whereas the said Hannah is now and for some years has been living among her own people at my expense and under my name and as my acknowledged wife in a dwelling chosen by herself and provided by me at the village of Hadley in the said county of Salop in which dwelling I am in the habit of spending as much of every year as is possible along with her And whereas . . .

Announcing his desire to provide comfortably for his 'most dear and beloved wife and servant . . . in that state of life wherein she was born and which she prefers to any other', Munby went on formally to leave to Hannah all her own savings, amounting to five hundred pounds or more, which she had entrusted to him for investment; all the furniture and household effects in her cottage; and an annuity of seventy pounds. The remainder of the long will was devoted to a scrupulous partitioning of his resources and family possessions between his brothers and sister, his nephews and nieces. Munby also bequeathed his collection of specified books to Trinity College, Cambridge, and the deed-boxes with their contents to the British Museum (or by reversion to Trinity College—which was where they actually went). His annuity for Hannah was paid to her niece Emily Gibbs until her death in 1920.

Publication of the will was the signal for an outburst in Fleet Street. All that had been dreaded by George Munby—and more—came to pass at the beginning of July, 1910; and the impact on the Munby family can have been no less than it would have been for Galsworthy's Forsytes.

'Wife Who Would be a Servant'—'Romance Revealed in Barrister's Will'—the story was featured in every paper, but nowhere to greater effect than in the *Daily Mirror* of 4 July. Here the story was unfolded beneath a five-fold heading: 'ROMANCE OF BARRISTER'S MARRIAGE—Further Light on Remarkable Will Disclosure—WIFE AND SERVANT—Verses Upholding His Choice Against World's Criticism—COTTAGES IN COUNTRY—Brother of Mrs. Munby Describes Their Life Together.' Next came 'BROTHER'S STORY', an interview with Jim Cullwick by 'Our Special Correspondent, Wellington (Salop), Sunday'. It gave a very fair account of the marriage from the Cullwick angle. A summary of the will was followed by 'ALWAYS THOUGHT A BACHELOR' from 'Our Special Correspondent, Byfleet (Surrey), Sunday': an interesting piece, embodying Pyrford recollections of Munby which have already been quoted. A note on Munby as the laureate of the maidservant concluded this lavish 'coverage' running to four columns.

A photograph in the paper of the Cullwick sisters is a reminder that one of them had bettered herself to the extent of becoming a shopkeeper at Gippeswich. Another sister, said the *Daily Mirror*, 'was married to an East London registrar'. In one of his later notebooks, Munby maintained that a second cousin of Hannah's, 'now dead, was a member of the Bar', and that three others were clergymen; he also claimed two peers, Lord Truro and Lord Penzance, as distant cousins of hers (16 June, 1899). These assertions probably dated from the days when Munby seriously hoped to make a valid lady of his wife; they might not have borne strict examination.

That Munby's marriage made an impression on the British public is indicated by the occasional garbled re-telling of his romance in popular papers during the next forty years. Surprisingly, he had not been forgotten by the Press when the time came for the opening of his deed-boxes in 1950. Hannah's relatives had asked the authorities at Trinity College if they could be present; they were told that the opening was private; but Dr. A. N. L. Munby represented the testator's family. Journalists prowled round the Wren Library on 14 January, which by coincidence was Munby's wedding day; the way up the staircase was closed. The Librarian (Mr. H. M. Adams) and several members of the Trinity council waited some time for the Master, Dr. G. M. Trevelyan, to perform the ceremony. There was a discussion as to how late the Master had to be before anyone incurred his displeasure by reminding him. But at last he arrived; and he opened all three boxes. The statement drafted by the Master for the Press was not designed to encourage sensational expectations:

The three boxes of A. J. Munby (*ob.* 1910) were opened today (Jan. 14) by the College authorities, in the presence of a representative of the Munby family. They contain diaries and poems by Mr. Munby, and letters to him by his wife. Also photographs and studies of working women of the later Nineteenth century, in whose conditions of life Mr. Munby took a sociological interest.

Seeing a newspaper report of the opening, Hannah's great-niece Ada Perks wrote at once to Dr. A. N. L. Munby to say she 'felt very sorry' for him, 'as I expect you, like me, had always heard so much of the boxes for the last 40 years. . . . What a surprise for you nothing of value or any relics for the college.' She added her recollections of her great-uncle: 'Mr Munby was always very kind & considerate to us. . . . So tall & with lovely white whiskers. . . .'

Dr. Munby was asked to report on the contents of the boxes. He emphasised the great social and literary value of the diaries and suggested that an American scholar, already in correspondence with him about his great-uncle's papers, should be approached to edit them. This was the late Professor Waldo Hilary Dunn, whose biography of R. D. Blackmore had given him an interest in the subject. Professor Dunn accepted Trinity College's invitation to work on the material, which was reserved for his use; but he was already of an advanced age and died before commencing the task.

Thus it happened that, nearly twenty years later, the present writer found it was his privilege to tell the story of an epic Victorian adventure. Henceforth Munby will, it is hoped, be remembered as a chivalrous, quixotic idealist, who in partly thwarting the *apartheid* of class and sex, anticipated a century of progress; and Hannah and 'Massa' be remembered for the faithfulness of their love.

In a book on those Edwardians among whom Munby ended his long life, J. B. Priestley has written: 'What catches and holds the imagination of the English is not successful achievement in the ordinary sense. What they cherish, even though most of them would immediately deny it, is any action, though it may be accounted a failure, that appears when it is recorded to be epic, that takes on a poetic quality, that haunts the mind like a myth.' Such an action was the marriage of Arthur Munby to Hannah Cullwick at Clerkenwell parish church, 14 January, 1873.

APPENDIX: SOME POEMS BY A. J. MUNBY

BIBLIOGRAPHY

APPENDIX: SOME POEMS BY A. J. MUNBY

Munby's poetry is represented in several old-established anthologies, notably (in America) E. C. Stedman's *A Victorian Anthology*, and (in England) Alfred H. Miles's *The Poets and the Poetry of the Century*, published during the nineties. In the latter, however, he is introduced as an afterthought, and he has not been given fair treatment in relevant anthologies that have appeared since his death. Reviews published during his life-time were usually friendly, though P. B. Marston in the *Atlantic Monthly*, April, 1882, was frankly sceptical of *Dorothy*. One of the few critics to mention Munby since 1910 has been George Saintsbury, who included him among 'Lesser Poets of the Middle and Later Nineteenth Century' in *The Cambridge History of English Literature*, Vol. XIII (1922). After praising Arnold, Patmore, Allingham, and Macdonald, Saintsbury mentioned a few other poets, such as Massey and Woolner, but added 'none of these excite either personal enthusiasm or a sense of historical importance in some minds.' He continued in a footnote: 'Some would rank above them all an eccentric poet of rather wasted talent, Arthur Joseph Munby, who wrote verse at intervals from the time of his leaving Trinity College, Cambridge, in 1851, till his death, all but sixty years later. Nor would this estimate lack arguments to support it.' Oliver Elton also has a word of praise for Munby in Vol. II of *A Survey of English Literature: 1830–1880*. (1932).

Some of his best work in the shorter forms has already been quoted in the text. Without making extravagant claims on Munby's behalf, it may be that the qualities mentioned by Austin Dobson in his obituary—variety, technical skill, scholarship, excellent English, and 'exquisite appreciation and observation of Nature and rural life'—may still be allowed to commend him as a neglected minor poet.

THE WHALER FLEET

Full merrily sail'd our whaler fleet
  When the wind blew out to sea;
And many a one came forth to greet
  Each good ship's company.

For there was the Dove and the Good Intent
  (How the wind blew out to sea!)
And the Polly o'Sleights with her bran-new sails;
  But the Mary Jane for me!

Oh, Captain Thwaites of the Mary Jane,
  When the wind blew out to sea,
Full many a time his ship had sail'd,
  Full many a time had he.

He has Jack of Grosmont and Tom o' the staith,
 (How the wind blew out to sea!)
And Handsome Jim from Hayburn Wyke;
 But 'twas Robin Hood Will for me.

My Willy he kiss'd me before them all,
 When the wind blew out to sea;
My Willy he stood the last on deck
 A-waving his cap to me.

So off they sail'd out over the main,
 While the wind blew out to sea;
Till the ice was all under their beamed bows,
 And the ice drove under their lee.

The months they went and the months they came,
 And the wind blew hard at sea;
And many a time in the stormy nights
 My mammy she wept with me.

But when the harvest moon came round,
 And the wind blew in from sea,
'Twas merrily came our whaler fleet
 All home from the north country.

The folk they call'd and the folk they ran,
 And the wind blew in from sea;
From the thick of the town to the lighthouse tower,
 'Twas throng as throng could be.

I saw them atop of the old church stairs,
 When the wind blew in from sea;
And the waves danced under their beamed bows,
 And the foam flew under their lee.

I saw them at foot of the old church stairs,
 When the wind blew in from sea;
And the foremost ship of our whaler fleet
 Was rounding the lighthouse quay.

Oh, there's the Dove and the Good Intent,
 (Still the wind blows in from sea),
And the red red sails of the Polly o'Sleights–
 Her men are plain to see.

Now every one hath pass'd the bar,
    And the wind blows in from sea;
And every one in harbour lies,
    Right up against the quay.

But where, oh where, is the Mary Jane,
    Now the wind blows in from sea?
There's many a lad hath clipt his lass,
    And when doth my lad clip me?

Oh, tell me where is the Mary Jane,
    For the wind blows in from sea?
'The Mary Jane went down by her head
    With all her company!'

Now take me home to my mammy so dear,
    Though the wind blows in from sea;
There's never a billow rolls over my lad,
    But I wish it roll'd over me!

And take me home, for I care not now
    If the wind blows in from sea:
My Willy he lies in the deeps of the dead,
    But his heart lives on in me.

Verses New and Old (1865)

QUESTION AND ANSWER

Are there no lilies on Havering pond,
    Under the elm-tree boughs?
        Many a one!
Are there no maidens fair and fond
    Left in the manor-house?
        Never a one.

Are there no tufts of London-pride
    Under John Watson's wall?
        Many a one!
Hath he no sons still by his side,
    To answer the old man's call?
        Never a one.

Are there no cattle on Fielden farm,
    No doves in the dove-cote, still?
        Many a one!
And how many friends sit snug and warm
    Round the ingle of Farmer Will?
        Never a one.

445

Are there no people in Havering church,
   At matins and evening prayer?
      Many a one!
And the parson who planted that silver birch,
   Are he and his house still there?
      Never a one.

Do the tall flags yet rustle and wave
   In the water above the mill?
      Many a one!
And the flowers that grew upon Laura's grave,
   Doth any one tend them still?
      Never a one.

                    Verses New and Old (1865)

TWO EXTRACTS FROM *DOROTHY* (1880)

Ah, what a joy for her, at early morn, in the springtime,
   Driving from hedge to hedge furrows as straight as a line!
Seeing the crisp brown earth, like waves at the bow of a vessel,
   Rise, curl over, and fall, under the thrust of the share;
Orderly falling and still, its edges all creamy and crumbling,
   But, on the sloping side, polish'd and purple as steel;
Till all the field, she thought, looked bright as the bars of that gridiron
   In the great window at church, over the gentlefolks' pew:
And evermore, as she strode, she has cheerful companions behind her;
   Rooks and the smaller birds, following after her plough;
And, ere the ridges were done, there was gossamer woven above them,
   Gossamer dewy and white, shining like foam on the sea.
Well may she joy in such things, in the freedom of outdoor labour—
   Freeborn lass that she is, fetter'd by Duty alone:
Well may she do—being young, and healthy and hearty and fearless—
   Things that a town-bred girl dared not adventure at all.

'Twas but a poor little room; a farm-servant's loft in a garret;
   One small window and door; never a chimney at all:
One little stool by the bed, and a remnant of cast-away carpet:
   But on the floor, by the wall, carefully dusted and bright,
Stood the green-painted box, our Dorothy's closet and wardrobe,
   Holding her treasures, her all—all that she own'd in the world!
Linen and hosen were there, coarse linen and home-knitted hosen;
   Handerchiefs bought at the fair, aprons and smocks not a few;
Kirtles for warmth when afield, and frocks for winter and summer,
   Blue-spotted, lilac, grey; cotton and woollen and serge;

446

All her simple attire, save the clothes she felt most like herself in—
   Rough coarse workaday clothes, fit for a labourer's wear.
There was her Sunday array—the boots, and the shawl, and the bonnet,
   Solemnly folded apart, not to be lightly assumed:
There was her jewelry too; 'twas a brooch (she had worn it this evening)
   Made of a cairngorm stone—really too splendid for her!
Which on a Martlemas Day Mr. Robert had brought for a fairing:
   Little she thought, just then, how she would value it now!
As for her sewing gear, her housewife, her big brass thimble,
   Knitting and suchlike work, such as her fingers could do,
That was away downstairs, in a dresser-drawer in the kitchen,
   Ready for use of a night, when she was tidied and clean.
Item, up there in the chest were her books; *The Dairyman's Daughter*:
   Ballads: *The Olney Hymns*: Bible and Prayer-book, of course:
That was her library; these were the limits of Dorothy's reading;
   Wholesome, but scanty indeed: was it then all that she knew?
Nay, for like other good girls, she had profited much by her schooling
   Under the mighty three—Nature, and Labour, and Life:
Mightier they than books; if books could have only come after,
   Thoughts of instructed minds filtering down into hers.
That was impossible now; what she had been, she was, and she would be;
   Only a farm-serving lass—only a peasant, I fear.

————

OUT OF HEART

Out of heart, because the times are moving
   Faster than our settled pace can move:
Out of heart, because the art of loving
   Is not perfect as the power to love.

Out of heart, because the folk of station
   Are not earnest, are of shallow mind;
And, for reverence and imagination,
   Those less lofty are but fools and blind.

Out of heart, because the new days o'er us,
   Brilliant doubtless, but severely cold,
Never, never, shall again restore us
   What they take in beauty from the old.

Out of heart, because we are not learning
   Freedom's noblest lesson and her last—
How to rear the fruits of free discerning
   In the stately gardens of the Past.

Out of heart, because no human guiding
    Fits mankind for triumphs that endure;
Wisdom self-controll'd and self-abiding,
    Purest aims and methods also pure.

Out of heart, because belief is failing,
    Old creeds dead and new ones fond or foul;
Little left to cheer the weak and ailing;
    Little left to stay the manly soul.

Out of heart, because ourselves are erring,
    Always feebler than the good we know;
Much within us still alive and stirring,
    Which might well have perish'd long ago.

Yes, indeed, for many an ample reason
    We who live such lives and must depart,
After living thus so short a season,
    Well may falter, well be out of heart.

But of one thing Time has not bereft us,
    One thing is; and, be it weak or strong,
Hold by that, if nothing else is left us:
    That, the living sense of Right and Wrong.

Vestigia Retrorsum (1891)

AT THE WINDOW

She is standing in the parlour, leaning on her carpet broom;
She has done her daily sweeping, and has dusted all the room;
She is looking out of window: is she gazing at the view?
No, indeed—she only wonders if her fortune will come true.

For this morning in the kitchen she has turn'd her teacup thrice,
And the things she saw within it were so novel and so nice!
There were kisses, and a letter, and a sweetheart, and a friend,
All arranged within that teacup, in a most engaging blend.

Sure, the sweetheart is *her* sweetheart; and the kisses must be his;
And the letter, he have wrote it for to tell her where he is;
And the friend—why, that's his sister, Captain Thompson's Mary Ann,
Which was married last September, to the undertaker's man!

448

Ah, she sees it all, in vision: Jack is coming home from sea,
And he's wrote for her to go to him, at Mary Ann's, to tea;
And the kisses—she will have them, every one of 'em, no doubt,
On the very next o' Sundays, which it is her Sunday out!

So she stands, our pensive Polly, with her dustpan, and her fears,
And her hopes—but, Goodness gracious! What's them footsteps as she hears?
Oh, for certain, it's the Missis—and she's bustling down to prayers,
And I arena' clean'd and tidied—is there time to run upstairs?

Yes, there's time; and she has done it! Enter Polly, if you look,
In a tidy cap and apron, walking after Mrs Cook:
With her eyes demurely downcast, as she sinks upon her knees,
And remembers there her sweetheart, just a-coming o'er the seas.

Poems (1901)

LONDON TOWN

Oh how I wish it were day! There is nothing so dull as the darkness
    When with the light of the sun everything pleasant has gone:
Everything—colour and form, and the pomp of clouds in the heavens,
    And on the earth around, voices and movement and life.
Here, we are under a shroud, like that which envelopes a dead man,
    Lying unconscious and cold, waiting to go to his grave;
Seeing no more of the world he has left, or the people within it,
    Than through our darken'd panes we can behold of it now.
Yet I had rather be here, in the quiet and peace of the country,
    Silent and sad as it is, than in the terrible town:
Terrible, not for its crimes, nor the selfish stress of its efforts,
    Nor for its noisy crowds, hurrying ever along,
Each with a hard grim face, indifferent quite to the others,
    Thinking of money alone, anxious and eager for gain—
Not for such spectres as these, for we know them of old, they are evils
    Bred in the nature of towns, everywhere always at hand—
But for a new strange thing, a real and scandalous danger,
    Which in these difficult days meets us wherever we go:
Danger, the latest gift that civilisation has brought us,
    Danger to life and limb, threatening death to us all.
Hark! to the hideous roar of the ugly implacable monsters
    Forging in frantic speed, each with the other at war;
Howling and growling and hoarse, in the riot of insolent triumph,
    Deaf to authority's voice, reckless of order and law.
Here then at last is a force that none have the courage to cope with,
    None have the wit to suppress, none even dare to control:
Foul as a lava stream, shot straight from its hidden Inferno,
    Making the fair broad streets seem like a vision of hell.

449

Aye, and we too are doom'd, though we live remote in the country,
    If but a road be near, still to encounter the foe;
Still to endure its stench, its cruel and culpable presence,
    Killing all beauty and grace, crushing the charm out of life;
Making us bitterly feel that our impotent civilisation
    Cannot contrive to be free, cannot be noble and calm.

Relicta (1909)

DICHTER UND BAUERIN

My soul is full of love for her,
    Whatever she may be:
And well I know, her pulses stir
    Only with love for me.

All, all are mine! And every beat
    In that true heart of hers
Recalls our far-off days and sweet—
    Young Love's interpreters.

She, bred to labour with her hands,
    And train'd by that alone:
Obeying other folks' commands
    Although she was my own:

While I in fields of larger growth
    And wider culture stray'd,
Yet ne'er forgot my plighted troth
    To that untutor'd maid.

Ah me, those waiting years were long!
    Yet they were fond and free;
She knew I would not do her wrong:
    For love is purity.

At last, at last, the wedding came,
    And her few friends were there:
But, though she bore to take my name,
    My place she would not share.

Still she preferr'd her own degree;
    For thus, throughout her life,
She could be all in all to me:
    My servant, and my wife.

450

Shall I then love her less, for this?
    Or shall I feel ashamed
To stand beside her as she is—
    Obscure, and never named

Save in those dwellings of the poor
    Whereof her home is one—
A cottage with an open door,
    Not closed till day is done?

No! For beside that cottage fire,
    Where we together live,
A nobler spirit dwells and higher,
    Than rank or wealth can give.

Relicta (1909)

BIBLIOGRAPHY

1. A. J. MUNBY (MSS.)

The Munby Papers at Trinity College, Cambridge, comprise the complete set of diaries from 1859 to 1898; numerous additional notebooks, with descriptions of special expeditions, and accounts of Hannah's life; several sketchbooks containing ink and pencil studies of working women; and many MS. poems, published and unpublished. There is a large collection of photographs of working women, mostly British but including foreign examples and many photographs of Hannah covering a period of fifty years. Papers of Hannah's preserved by Munby include several fragments of autobiography and passages from an intermittent diary (these dating mostly from before or just after her marriage); and packets of letters, carefully arranged and annotated, belonging largely to the last thirty years of her life. Dr. A. N. L. Munby has a private collection including letters, photographs and newspaper cuttings.

There are letters and MSS. of Munby's at the Working Men's College and the University of London Library; at Yale University library and the University of Illinois Library; while the Osborn Collection, Yale University, has letters written to him by Sir Theodore Martin and Chicago University Library by William Bell Scott. Mr. R. J. Dobell has a considerable collection of letters from Munby to Bertram Dobell, and Mr. Christopher Dobson and Mr. Kenneth Dobson have letters of his to Austin Dobson. The British Museum has the MS of *Ann Morgan's Love*, and Dr. A. N. L. Munby the MS of the unpublished poem *Leonard and Elizabeth*. There is a large collection of Munby Family Papers in York City Library, mainly relating to the period 1790–1840.

2. A. J. MUNBY (Works)

Benoni. Poems by Arthur J. Munby, B.A. (John Ollivier, 1852).

Centenary Poems; selected from the Competitive Verses written for the Burns Festival, at the Crystal Palace, Jan. 25, 1859 (1860). Contains a poem by Munby.

Verses New and Old. By Arthur Munby. (Bell and Daldy, 1865.)

A Memorial of Joseph Munby, of Clifton Holme, near York (1875.) Booklet with prefatory note signed A.J.M. Privately printed.

Auld Lang Syne: Selections from the Papers of the 'Pen and Pencil Club' (1877). Contains two poems by Munby. Privately printed.

Dorothy: A Country Story. In Elegiac Verse. With a Preface. (Kegan Paul, 1880). Published anonymously. See also the edition published in Boston by Roberts Brothers, 1882, where the text is re-set and the Preface transposed and printed as an Appendix.

Bibliography

A Few Records of the Name and Family of Munby and of some other allied Families. Compiled by Arthur Joseph Munby, M.A., F.S.A., of Lincoln's Inn, Barrister at Law (1881.) Cyclostyled booklet for private circulation.

Vulgar Verses. By Jones Brown. (Reeves and Turner, 1891.)

Vestigia Retrorsum. Poems by Arthur J. Munby. (Eden, Remington, 1891). With a frontispiece photograph of the author. By 1899 the publication had been taken over by John Macqueen.

Faithful Servants: Being Epitaphs and Obituaries recording their Names and Services. Edited and in part collected by Arthur J. Munby, M.A., F.S.A., of Lincoln's Inn, Barrister at Law. (Reeves and Turner 1891.)

Susan: A Poem of Degrees. By the Author of 'Dorothy: A Country Story in Elegiac Verse', 'Vulgar Verses,' Etc. (Reeves and Turner, 1893.)

Ann Morgan's Love: A Pedestrian Poem. By Arthur Munby. (Reeves and Turner, 1896.)

Poems Chiefly Lyric and Elegiac. By Arthur Munby. (Kegan Paul, 1901.)

Relicta. Verses by Arthur Munby. (Bertram Dobell, 1909.)

3. A. J. MUNBY (Miscellaneous)

Woolman's Exeter and Plymouth Gazette, 3 July, 1852: review of *Benoni,* unsigned but by R. D. Blackmore. *Atlantic Monthly,* April, 1882: 'A Realistic Poet', review of *Dorothy* by P. B. Marston. *Working Men's College Journal,* June and July, 1890 (Munby's article on the Roman villa at Birdlip, Glos). Ibid. March, 1903; July, 1905; April and June, 1909; March, 1910 (obituary); etc. *Gentleman's Magazine,* January, 1892, and November, 1904 (criticism). *Spectator,* 7 March, 1896: review of *Ann Morgan's Love,* unsigned but by R. H. Hutton. Ibid., 9 November, 1901: review of *Poems,* unsigned but by C. L. Graves. *The Times,* 5 February, 1910 (obituary). *D.N.B.:* A. J. Munby, by Austin Dobson. See also Appendix, and references in the text *passim.*

4. GENERAL

BALL, W. W. R., and VENN, J. A. *Admissions to Trinity College, Cambridge.* Vol. IV, 1801–1850. (1911.)

BEST, Geoffrey. *Temporal Pillars.* (1964.)

BIRKENHEAD, Sheila Countess of. *Against Oblivion: The Life of Joseph Severn.* (1943); *Illustrious Friends: The Story of Joseph Severn and his son Arthur.* (1965.)

BOUCHERETT, Jessie, and BLACKBURN, Helen. *The Condition of Working Women.* (1896).

CADBURY, Edward, MATHESON, M. Cécile, and SHANN, George. *Women's Work and Wages.* (1906.)

CARTER, Harry. *Wolvercote Mill.* (1957.)

453

CURLE, Richard (Ed.). *Robert Browning and Julia Wedgwood*. (1937.)

DEVANE, William Clyde, and KNICKERBOCKER, Kenneth Leslie (Ed.). *New Letters of Robert Browning*. (1951.)

DOBSON, Alban. *Austin Dobson: Some Notes*. (1928.)

DOUGHTY, Oswald. *A Victorian Romantic: Dante Gabriel Rossetti*. (1949.)

DUNN, Waldo Hilary. *R. D. Blackmore*. (1956).

E. J. (Ed.). *The Life and Letters of Sydney Dobell*. 2 vols. (1878.)

FURNIVALL, Frederick James. *A Volume of Personal Record*. (1911.)

GLEICHEN, Lord Edward. *London's Open-air Statuary*. (1928.)

GRYLLS, Rosalie Glynn. *Portrait of Rossetti*. (1964.)

HARRISON, J. F. C. *A History of the Working Men's College 1854-1954*. (1954.)

INGELOW, Jean. *Some Recollections of Jean Ingelow and her early Friends*. Anon. (1901.)

JENKINS, Roy. *Asquith*. (1964.)

LAYARD, G. S. *Mrs. Lynn Linton*. (1901.)

LITCHFIELD, H. E. (Mrs.) *Richard Buckley Litchfield: A Memoir Written for his Friends by his Wife*. (1910.)

MAGNUS, Philip. *King Edward the Seventh*. (1964.)

MANDER, Raymond, and MITCHENSON, Joe. *The Theatres of London*. (1963.)

MAURICE, Frederick (Ed.). *The Life of Frederick Denison Maurice*. 2 vols. (1884.)

MILLER, Betty. *Robert Browning: A Portrait*. (1952.)

MINTO, W. (Ed.) *Autobiographical Notes of the Life of William Bell Scott*. 2 vols. (1892.)

MORGAN, Charles. *The House of Macmillan (1843-1943)*. (1943.)

NEFF, W. F. *Victorian Working Women*. (1929.)

NORTON, Graham. *Victorian London*. (1969.)

NOWELL-SMITH, Simon (Ed.) *Letters to Macmillan*. (1967.)

RAINE, Angelo. *History of St. Peter's School: York*. (1926.)

ROSSETTI, Dante Gabriel. *Letters*, ed. Oswald Doughty and John Robert Wahl. vols. I–III. (1965-7.)

RUSKIN, John. *Works*, ed. E. T. Cook and Alexander Wedderburn. 39 volumes. (1903-12.)

SYKES, Christopher. *Four Studies in Loyalty*. (1946).

TREVELYAN, G. M. *Trinity College*. (1943.)

VENN, J. A. (Compiler). *Alumni Cantabrigienses*. (1940.)

WINSTANLEY, D. A. *Early Victorian Cambridge*. (1940.)

YOUNG, G. M. *Victorian England: Portrait of an Age*. (1953, 2nd edition.)

INDEX

455

Index

457

Index

Hannah, 182; Garibaldi's visit to London, 186–189; discovers Wheeler's Farm, Pyrford, 190; observes Dickens, 191; liking for milkwomen, 196; describes London outcasts, 198–200; in Britanny, 200; riding accident, 202; observes Tennyson, 208; publishes *Verses New and Old*, 212; death of Mary Newton, 216; the two Miss Thackerays, 218; Lord Houghton, 219; the Mines Committee, 220; Sarah Carter and Julie Bovet, 228; admiration for Helen Faucit, 230; meets Mazzini, 231; London under snow, 235; Hannah at Margate, 240; parting from 'sweet Sarah', 244; acrobats, 252; girl climbers at Brail Head, 255; secret return to Pyrford, 258; meets Austin Dobson, 276; Women's suffrage, 281; tête-à-tête with Swinburne, 282; Rossetti and Mrs. Brookfield, 285; 'the Inspector' at Wigan, 290; to South Wales, 291; Blackmore's *Lorna Doone*, 295; Froude and Kingsley, 301; death of F. D. Maurice, 306; tells his father about Hannah, 309; visits Sedan, 310; death of his brother John, 312; marries Hannah secretly at Clerkenwell, 318; their life together at Fig Tree Court, 320 *et seq.*; to France with Hannah, 339; Hannah's wish to remain a servant, 369; Munby's 'great error', 369; death of his father, 381; the young Asquith, 388; separation from Hannah, 391; rents Wheeler's Farm, Pyrford, 391; death of his mother, 397; sale of Clifton Holme, 401; his *Dorothy* praised by Browning, 403; Browning and Munby, 406; reconciliation with Hannah, 407; takes cottage for her at Hadley, Salop, 412; publishes *Vestigia Retrorsum*, 415; death of Tennyson, 420; Hannah moves to Shifnal, 426; 'Our Jubilee', 427; death of Hannah, 431; his own death, 433; *Times* obituary, 434; publication of will, and newspaper publicity, 437; opening of his deed-boxes, 438
Munby, Caroline, 86
Munby, Caroline Eleanor, *née* Forth (mother), 7, 126, 247, 397, 398
Munby, Frederick James, 29, 35, 36, 75, 380, 382, 386
Munby, George Frederick Woodhouse, 7, 42, 113, 283, 317, 377, 379, 380, 386, 390, 432, 434
Munby, Mrs. (Hannah), see Cullwick
Munby, John Forth, 7, 312
Munby, Joseph (father), 7, 8, 11, 34, 35, 137, 203, 275, 309, 380–2, 436
Munby, Joseph (grandfather), 7
Munby, Joseph Edwin, 36, 93, 95, 245
Munby and Scott, 8
Munro, Alexander, 30, 165
Munro, Hugh Andrew Johnstone, 270
Murchison, Sir Roderick Impey, 94, 283
Myers, Frederick William Henry, 17, 95

Napoleon, III, Emperor of France, 32, 92, 310–11
National Society for Aid to the Sick and Wounded, 290
Neate, Charles, 225, 226
Negretti and Zambra, 268
Newell, Mary, 110
Newspaper girl, 53
Newport, Mon., 42
Norman-Neruda, Mme, 277
Norwood, 31
Notes and Queries, 393

O'Cagnay, Kate, 107, 178
Ockley, Surrey, 298, 320, 326, 327, 335, 336, 362, 372
Organ grinders, 394
Origin of Species, 63
Ormsby, John, 23, 28, 62, 126, 127, 173, 297, 304
Orr, Mrs. Sutherland, 404
Outcasts, London, 198–200
Overland Route, The (by Tom Taylor), 54
Oxford English Dictionary, 123
Oxford Music Hall, 119
Oxford v. Cambridge boat race, 57

Palmerston, Viscount Henry John Temple, 25, 211
Parker, Ann, 228
Parker, Elizabeth Mary, 312
Parkes, Bessie, 226
Parkes, Catherine, 113, 114
Patti, Adelina, 96, 165
Peacock, Edward, F.S.A., 364, 396
Pen and Pencil Society (or Club), 217, 245, 276, 364
Perceval, Charles Spencer, 396
Persia, Shah of, 333
Phillpotts, Henry (Bishop), 172
Philological Society, 123
Pollington, Lord, 94
Pollock, Sir William Frederick, 126, 335
Porters, female, 37
Postwoman, 108
Prostitutes, 22, 24, 28, 30, 35, 40, 41, 50, 69, 84, 130, 214
Pyrford (and Wheeler's Farm), 159, 190, 210, 228, 232, 239, 243, 244, 258, 294, 348, 375, 391, 392, 400, 402, 403, 408, 409, 416, 420, 431, 433, 435
Railways, London, 145, 174, 175, 194, 284
Ralston, William, 10, 13, 24, 36, 46, 58, 83, 91, 112, 113, 119, 124, 127, 128, 140, 147, 159, 160, 163, 221, 298, 305, 360, 363, 390, 394, 406, 413
Rawlinson, Sir Henry, 25
Red House, Battersea, 29
Red Lion Square, 12
Reed, Mrs. German, 227
Rees, Josiah, 321, 362, 380, 385–6
Rees, L. E. Ruutz, 27